D1222400

THE LOEB CLASSICAL LIBRARY

FOUNDED BY JAMES LOEB, LL.D.

EDITED BY

G. P. GOOLD, PH.D.

PLUTARCH'S
MORALIA
XIII

PART I

PLUTARCH'S
MORALIA

IN SEVENTEEN VOLUMES

XIII

PART I

999 c—1032 f

WITH AN ENGLISH TRANSLATION BY
HAROLD CHERNISS
THE INSTITUTE FOR ADVANCED STUDY, PRINCETON, N.J.

CAMBRIDGE, MASSACHUSETTS
HARVARD UNIVERSITY PRESS
LONDON
WILLIAM HEINEMANN LTD
MCMLXXVI

American
ISBN 0-674-99470-1

British
ISBN 0 434 99427 8

Printed in Great Britain

PA
4368
.A2
1962
v.13
pt I

CONTENTS OF VOLUME XIII
(PART I)

PREFACE

THE following are the manuscripts used for the edition of the six essays in this volume and the sigla that refer to them :

A = Parisinus Graecus 1671 (Bibliothèque Nationale, Paris)—A.D. 1296.

B = Parisinus Graecus 1675 (Bibliothèque Nationale, Paris)—15th century.

E = Parisinus Graecus 1672 (Bibliothèque Nationale, Paris)—written shortly after A.D. 1302.

F = Parisinus Graecus 1957 (Bibliothèque Nationale, Paris)—written at the end of the 11th century.

J = Ambrosianus 881 - C 195 inf. (Biblioteca Ambrosiana, Milan)—13th century.

X = Marcianus Graecus 250 (Biblioteca Nazionale di S. Marco, Venice)—the first part (containing the *De Stoicorum Repugnantiis*) written in the 11th century, the second part (containing the *Platonicae Quaestiones*) written in the 14th century.

d = Laurentianus 56, 2 (Biblioteca Laurenziana, Florence)—15th century.

e = Laurentianus 70, 5 (Biblioteca Laurenziana, Florence)—14th century.

f = Laurent. Ashburnham. 1441 (not 1444 as in Hubert-Drexler, *Moralia* vi/1, pp. xvi and xx) (Biblioteca Laurenziana, Florence)—16th century.

g = Vaticanus Palatinus 170 (Bibliotheca Apostolica Vaticana, Rome)—15th century.

m = Parisinus Graecus 1042 (Bibliothèque Nationale, Paris)—16th century.

n = Vaticanus Graecus 1676 (Bibliotheca Apostolica Vaticana, Rome)—14th century (*cf. Codices Vaticani Graeci* : Codices 1485-1683 rec. C. Giannelli [1950], pp. 441-443).

r = Leiden B.P.G. 59 (Bibliotheek der Rijksuniversiteit, Leiden)—16th century (see p. 150, n. *b* in the Introduction to the *De An. Proc. in Timaeo*).

t = Urbino-Vaticanus Graecus 100 (Bibliotheca Apostolica Vaticana, Rome)—A.D. 1402.

u = Urbino-Vaticanus Graecus 99 (Bibliotheca Apostolica Vaticana, Rome)—15th century.

v = Vindobonensis Philos. Graec. 46 (Nationalbibliothek, Vienna)—15th century.

z = Vindobonensis Suppl. Graec. 23 (Nationalbibliothek, Vienna)—15th century.

α = Ambrosianus 859 - C 126 inf. (Biblioteca Ambrosiana, Milan)—finished in A.D. 1295 (*cf.* A. Turyn, *Dated Greek Manuscripts of the Thirteenth and Fourteenth Centuries in the Libraries of Italy* [University of Illinois Press, 1972] i, pp. 81-87).

β = Vaticanus Graecus 1013 (Bibliotheca Apostolica Vaticana, Rome)—14th century.

γ = Vaticanus Graecus 139 (Bibliotheca Apostolica Vaticana, Rome)—written shortly after A.D. 1296.

δ = Vaticanus Reginensis (Codices Graeci Reginae Suecorum) 80 (Bibliotheca Apostolica Vaticana, Rome)—15th century.

PREFACE

ε = Codex Matritensis Griego 4690 (Biblioteca Nacional, Madrid)—14th century.

Bonon. = Codex Graecus Bononiensis Bibliothecae Universitatis 3635 (Biblioteca Universitaria, Bologna)—14th century.

C.C.C. 99 = Codex Oxoniensis Collegii Corporis Christi 99 (Corpus Christi College, Oxford)—15th century.

Escor. 72 = Codex Griego Σ-I-12 de El Escorial (Real Biblioteca de El Escorial)—15th and 16th centuries (ff. 75^r-87^r, which contain the *De An. Proc. in Timaeo*, were written in the 16th century).

Escor. T-11-5 = Codex Griego T.11.5 de El Escorial (Real Biblioteca de El Escorial)—16th century.

Laurent. C. S. 180 = Laurentianus, Conventi Soppressi 180 (Biblioteca Laurenziana, Florence)—15th century.

Tolet. 51, 5 = Toletanus 51, 5 (Librería del Cabildo Toledano, Toledo)—15th century.

Voss. 16 = Codex Graecus Vossianus Misc. 16 (I) = Vossianus P 223 (Bibliotheek der Rijksuniversiteit, Leiden)—15th century.

In such matters as accent, breathing, crasis, elision and spelling I have followed without regard to the manuscripts the usage explained in the Introduction to the *De Facie* (*L.C.L. Moralia* xii, pp. 27-28).

The readings of the Aldine edition I have taken from a copy that is now in the library of The Institute for Advanced Study (Princeton, New Jersey) and that has on the title-page the inscription in ink, —: Donati Jannoctii :—Ex Bibliotheca Jo. Huralti Borstallerii : Jannoctii dono ; and from the margins of this copy I have cited the corrections or conjectures which in a note at the end of the volume (pp. 1010 f.) *a* written in the same ink as the inscription on the title-page are ascribed to Leonicus and Donatus Polus.

For the editions and other works to which there is frequent reference in the *apparatus criticus* and notes the following abbreviations or short titles are used :

Amyot = *Les œuvres morales et philosophiques de Plutarque*, translatées de Grec en François par Messire Jacques Amyot, . . . corrigées et augmentées en ceste presente édition en plusieurs passages suivant son exemplaire, Paris, Claude Morel, 1618.*b*

Andresen, *Logos und Nomos* = Carl Andresen, *Logos und Nomos : Die Polemik des Kelsos wider das Christentum*, Berlin, 1935.

Armstrong, *Later Greek . . . Philosophy* = *The Cambridge History of Later Greek and Early Medieval Philosophy*, edited by A. H. Armstrong, Cambridge, 1967.

Babut, *Plutarque de la Vertu Éthique* = *Plutarque de la Vertu Éthique : Introduction, texte, traduction et commentaire* par Daniel Babut, Paris, 1969 (Bibliothèque de la Faculté des Lettres de Lyon XV).

---

a It is the same note as that quoted by R. Aulotte (*Amyot et Plutarque* [Genève, 1965], p. 180) from the end (p. 877) of the Basiliensis in the Bibliothèque Nationale (J. 693), the title-page of which, he says, bears the inscription *Donato Giannotti.*

b This definitive edition has been compared with the first edition, *Les œuvres morales et meslées de Plutarque . . .*, Paris, Michel de Vascosin, 1572, and with *Œuvres Morales et Mêlées de Plutarque* traduites du Grec par Jacques Amyot avec des Notes et Observations de MM. Brotier et Vaulvilliers, Paris, Cussac, 1784–1787 = Tomes XIII–XXII of *Œuvres de Plutarque . . .*, 25 vols., 1783–1805.

PREFACE

Babut, *Plutarque et le Stoïcisme* = Daniel Babut, *Plutarque et le Stoïcisme*, Paris, 1969 (Publications de l'Université de Lyon).

Basiliensis = *Plutarchi Chaeronei Moralia Opuscula . . .*, Basiliae ex Officina Frobeniana per H. Frobenium et N. Episcopium, 1542.

Benseler, *De Hiatu* = G. E. Benseler, *De Hiatu in Scriptoribus Graecis*, Pars I : *De Hiatu in Oratoribus Atticis et Historicis Graecis Libri Duo*, Fribergae, 1841.

Bernardakis = *Plutarchi Chaeronensis Moralia* recognovit Gregorius N. Bernardakis, Lipsiae, 1888–1896 (Bibliotheca Teubneriana).

Bidez-Cumont, *Les Mages Hellénisés* = Joseph Bidez et Franz Cumont, *Les Mages Hellénisés*, 2 volumes, Paris, 1938.

Bolkestein, *Adversaria* = Hendrik Bolkestein, *Adversaria Critica et Exegetica ad Plutarchi Quaestionum Convivalium Librum Primum et Secundum*, Amstelodami, 1946.

Bonhöffer, *Epictet und die Stoa* = Adolf Bonhöffer, *Epictet und die Stoa : Untersuchungen zur stoischen Philosophie*, Stuttgart, 1890.

Bonhöffer, *Die Ethik . . .* = Adolf Bonhöffer, *Die Ethik des Stoikers Epictet*, Stuttgart, 1894.

Bréhier, *Chrysippe* = Émile Bréhier, *Chrysippe et l'ancien stoïcisme*, Paris, 1951 (nouvelle édition revue).

Bréhier, *Théorie des Incorporels* = Émile Bréhier, *La Théorie des Incorporels dans l'ancien Stoïcisme*, Paris, 1928 (deuxième édition). This was originally published in 1908 as a " Thèse pour le doctorat." It was reprinted in 1962.

Burkert, *Weisheit und Wissenschaft* = Walter Burkert, *Weisheit und Wissenschaft : Studien zu Pythagoras*,

Philolaos und Platon, Nürnberg, 1962 (Erlanger Beiträge zur Sprach- und Kunstwissenschaft X). There is an English edition, " translated with revisions," *Lore and Science in Ancient Pythagoreanism* (Harvard University Press, 1972) ; but this appeared too late to permit the use of it instead of the German original.

Cherniss, *Aristotle's Criticism of Plato* . . . =Harold Cherniss, *Aristotle's Criticism of Plato and the Academy*, Vol. I, Baltimore, 1944.

Cherniss, *Crit. Presoc. Phil.* =Harold Cherniss, *Aristotle's Criticism of Presocratic Philosophy*, Baltimore, 1935.

Cherniss, *The Riddle* =Harold Cherniss, *The Riddle of the Early Academy*, Berkeley/Los Angeles, 1945.

Cornford, *Plato's Cosmology* = *Plato's Cosmology : The Timaeus of Plato* translated with a running commentary by Francis Macdonald Cornford, London/New York, 1937.

Diels-Kranz, *Frag. Vorsok.*[6] = *Die Fragmente der Vorsokratiker*, Griechisch und Deutsch von Hermann Diels, 6. verbesserte Auflage hrsg. von Walther Kranz, 3 volumes, Berlin, 1951–1952 (later " editions " are unaltered reprints of this).

Döring, *Megariker* = *Die Megariker, Kommentierte Sammlung der Testimonien* . . . vorgelegt von Klaus Döring, Amsterdam, 1972 (Studien zur antiken Philosophie 2).

Dübner = *Plutarchi Chaeronensis Scripta Moralia.* Graece et Latine ed. Fr. Dübner, Paris, 1841.

Dyroff, *Die Ethik der alten Stoa* =Adolf Dyroff, *Die Ethik der alten Stoa*, Berlin, 1897 (Berliner Studien für classische Philologie u. Archaeologie, N.F. 2ter Band).

PREFACE

Dyroff, *Programm Würzburg*, 1896 = Adolf Dyroff, *Ueber die Anlage der stoischen Bücherkataloge*, Programm des K. Neuen Gymnasiums zu Würzburg für das Studienjahr 1895/96, Würzburg, 1896.

Elorduy, *Sozialphilosophie* = Eleuterio Elorduy, *Die Sozialphilosophie der Stoa*, Gräfenhainichen, 1936 (= *Philologus*, Supplementband XXVIII, 3).

Emperius, *Op. Philol.* = *Adolphi Emperii Opuscula Philologica et Historica Amicorum Studio Collecta* edidit F. G. Schneidewin, Göttingen, 1847.

Festa, *Stoici Antichi* = *I Frammenti degli Stoici Antichi* ordinati, tradotti e annotati da Nicola Festa, Vol. I e Vol. II, Bari, 1932–1935.

Giesen, *De Plutarchi . . . Disputationibus* = Carolus Giesen, *De Plutarchi contra Stoicos Disputationibus*, Monasterii Guestfalorum, 1889 (Diss. Münster).

Goldschmidt, *Le système stoïcien* = Victor Goldschmidt, *Le système stoïcien et l'idée de temps*, Paris, 1953 (Seconde édition revue et augmentée, Paris, 1969).

Gould, *The Philosophy of Chrysippus* = Josiah B. Gould, *The Philosophy of Chrysippus*, Leiden, 1970 (Philosophia Antiqua XVII).

Grilli, *Il problema della vita contemplativa* = Alberto Grilli, *Il problema della vita contemplativa nel mondo Greco-Romano*, Milan/Rome, 1953 (Università di Milano, Facoltà di Lettere e Filosofia, Serie prima : Filologia e Letterature Classiche).

Grumach, *Physis und Agathon* = Ernst Grumach, *Physis und Agathon in der alten Stoa*, Berlin, 1932 (Problemata 6).

H. C. = the present editor.

PREFACE

Hahn, " De Plutarchi Moralium Codicibus " = Victor Hahn, " De Plutarchi Moralium Codicibus Quaestiones Selectae," *Académie Polonaise : Rozprawy Akademii Umiejetności*, Wydzial Filologiczny, Serya ii, Tom xxvi (1906), pp. 43-128.

Hartman, *De Avondzon des Heidendoms* =J. J. Hartman, *De Avondzon des Heidendoms : Het Leven en Werken van den Wijze van Chaeronea*, 2 volumes, Leiden, 1910.

Hartman, *De Plutarcho* =J. J. Hartman, *De Plutarcho Scriptore et Philosopho*, Lugduni-Batavorum, 1916.

Heath, *Aristarchus of Samos* =Sir Thomas Heath, *Aristarchus of Samos, The Ancient Copernicus*, Oxford, 1913.

Heath, *History* =Sir Thomas Heath, *A History of Greek Mathematics*, 2 volumes, Oxford, 1921.

Heath, *Manual* =Sir Thomas L. Heath, *A Manual of Greek Mathematics*, Oxford, 1931.

Helmer, *De An. Proc.* =Joseph Helmer, *Zu Plutarchs " De animae procreatione in Timaeo ": Ein Beitrag zum Verständnis des Platon-Deuters Plutarch*, Würzburg, 1937 (Diss. München).

Hirzel, *Untersuchungen* =Rudolf Hirzel, *Untersuchungen zu Cicero's philosophischen Schriften*, 3 volumes, Leipzig, 1877–1883.

Holtorf, *Plutarchi Chaeronensis studia . . .* =Herbertus Holtorf, *Plutarchi Chaeronensis studia in Platone explicando posita*, Stralesundiae, 1913 (Diss. Greifswald).

Hubert-Drexler, *Moralia* vi/1 =*Plutarchi Moralia* Vol. VI Fasc. 1 recensuit et emendavit C. Hubert†, additamentum ad editionem correctiorem collegit H. Drexler, Lipsiae, 1959 (Bibliotheca Teubneriana).

Hutten = *Plutarchi Chaeronensis quae supersunt omnia* . . . opera Joannis Georgi Hutten, Tubingae, 1791–1804.

Jagu, *Zénon* = Amand Jagu, *Zénon de Cittium : Son Rôle dans l'établissement de la Morale stoïcienne*, Paris, 1946.

Joly, *Le thème* . . . *des genres de vie* = Robert Joly, *Le Thème Philosophique des Genres de Vie dans l'Antiquité Classique*, Bruxelles, 1956 (Académie Royale de Belgique, Mémoires de la Classe des Lettres, Tome XXIX, fasc. 3).

Jones, *Platonism of Plutarch* = Roger Miller Jones, *The Platonism of Plutarch*, Menasha (Wisconsin), 1916 (Diss. Chicago). References are to this edition, in which the pagination differs somewhat from that of the edition of 1915.

Kaltwasser = *Plutarchs moralische Abhandlungen* aus dem Griechischen übersetzt von Joh. Fried. Sal. Kaltwasser, Frankfurt am Main, 1783–1800 = *Plutarchs moralisch-philosophische Werke* übersetzt von J. F. S. Kaltwasser, Vienna/Prague, 1796 ff.

Kilb, *Ethische Grundbegriffe* = Georg Kilb, *Ethische Grundbegriffe der alten Stoa und ihre Uebertragung durch Cicero im dritten Buch de finibus bonorum et malorum*, Freiburg im Breisgau, 1939 (Diss. Freiburg i.Br.).

Kolfhaus, *Plutarchi De Comm. Not.* = Otto Kolfhaus, *Plutarchi De Communibus Notitiis Librum Genuinum esse demonstratur*, Marpurgi Cattorum, 1907 (Diss. Marburg).

Krämer, *Arete* = Hans Joachim Krämer, *Arete bei*

PREFACE

*Platon und Aristoteles : Zum Wesen und zur Ge-
schichte der platonischen Ontologie*, Heidelberg,
1959 (Abhandlungen der Heidelberger Akademie der Wissenschaften, Phil.-Hist. Kl.,
1959, 6).

Krämer, *Geistmetaphysik* =Hans Joachim Krämer,
*Der Ursprung der Geistmetaphysik : Untersuch-
ungen zur Geschichte des Platonismus zwischen
Platon und Plotin*, Amsterdam, 1964.

Krämer, *Platonismus* =Hans Joachim Krämer, *Platonismus und hellenistische Philosophie*, Berlin/New
York, 1971.

L.C.L. =The Loeb Classical Library.

Latzarus, *Idées Religieuses* =Bernard Latzarus, *Les
Idées Religieuses de Plutarque*, Paris, 1920.

Madvig, *Adversaria Critica* =Jo. Nic. Madvigii *Adversaria Critica ad Scriptores Graecos et Latinos*, 3
volumes, Hauniae, 1871–1884 (Vol. I : *Ad Scriptores Graecos*).

Mates, *Stoic Logic* =Benson Mates, *Stoic Logic*, Ber-
keley/Los Angeles, 1953.

Maurommates = Πλουτάρχου περὶ τῆς ἐν Τιμαίῳ ψυχογονίας, ἐκδόντος καὶ εἰς τὴν ἀρχαίαν συνέχειαν ἀποκαταστήσαντος Ἀνδρέου Δ. Μαυρομμάτου Κορκυραίου, Athens, 1848.

Merlan, *Platonism to Neoplatonism* =Philip Merlan,
From Platonism to Neoplatonism, second edition,
revised, The Hague, 1960. The later " editions " are merely reprints of this ; the first
edition was published in 1953.

Moutsopoulos, *La Musique . . . de Platon* =Evanghélos
Moutsopoulos, *La Musique dans l'Œuvre de
Platon*, Paris, 1959.

B. Müller (1870) =Berthold Müller, " Eine Blätter-
xvi

PREFACE

vertauschung bei Plutarch," *Hermes* iv (1870), pp. 390-403.

B. Müller (1871) =Berthold Müller, " Zu Plutarch περὶ ψυχογονίας," *Hermes* v (1871), p. 154.

B. Müller (1873) =Berthold Müller, *Plutarch über die Seelenschöpfung im Timaeus*, Gymnasium zu St. Elisabet, Bericht über das Schuljahr 1872–1873, Breslau, 1873.

Nogarola =*Platonicae Plutarchi Cheronei Quaestiones.* Ludovicus Nogarola Comes Veronensis vertebat, Venetiis apud Vincentium Valgrisium, 1552.

Pearson, *Fragments* =A. C. Pearson, *The Fragments of Zeno and Cleanthes with Introduction and Explanatory Notes*, London, 1891.

Pohlenz, *Moralia* i =*Plutarchi Moralia*, Vol. I recensuerunt et emendaverunt W. R. Paton† et I. Wegehaupt†. Praefationem scr. M. Pohlenz, Lipsiae, 1925 (Bibliotheca Teubneriana).

Pohlenz, *Moralia* vi/2 =*Plutarchi Moralia*, Vol. VI, Fasc. 2 recensuit et emendavit M. Pohlenz, Lipsiae, 1952 (Bibliotheca Teubneriana).

Pohlenz-Westman, *Moralia* vi/2 =*Plutarchi Moralia*, Vol. VI, Fasc. 2 recensuit et emendavit M. Pohlenz. Editio altera quam curavit addendisque instruxit R. Westman, Lipsiae, 1959 (Bibliotheca Teubneriana).

Pohlenz, *Grundfragen* =Max Pohlenz, *Grundfragen der stoischen Philosophie*, Göttingen, 1940 (Abhandlungen der Gesellschaft der Wissenschaften zu Göttingen, Phil.-Hist. Kl., Dritte Folge Nr. 26).

Pohlenz, *Stoa* =Max Pohlenz, *Die Stoa : Geschichte einer geistigen Bewegung*, 2 volumes, Göttingen, 1948–1949 (ii =2. Band : *Erläuterungen*, 4. Auflage, Zitatkorrekturen, bibliographische Nach-

PREFACE

träge und ein Stellenregister von H.-Th. Johann, 1972).

Pohlenz, *Zenon und Chrysipp* = M. Pohlenz, *Zenon und Chrysipp*, Göttingen, 1938 (Nachrichten von der Gesellschaft der Wissenschaften zu Göttingen, Phil.-Hist. Kl., Fachgruppe I, Neue Folge: Band II, Nr. 9) = Max Pohlenz, *Kleine Schriften* i, pp. 1-38.

Problems in Stoicism = *Problems in Stoicism* edited by A. A. Long, London, 1971.

R.-E. = *Paulys Realencyclopädie der classischen Altertumswissenschaft* . . ., Stuttgart, 1894–1972.

Rasmus, *Prog.* 1872 = Eduardus Rasmus, *De Plutarchi Libro qui inscribitur De Communibus Notitiis Commentatio*, Programm des Friedrichs-Gymnasiums zu Frankfurt a.O. für das Schuljahr 1871–1872, Frankfurt a.O., 1872.

Rasmus, *Prog.* 1880 = Eduardus Rasmus, *In Plutarchi librum qui inscribitur De Stoicorum Repugnantiis Coniecturae*, Jahres-Bericht über das vereinigte alt- und neustädtische Gymnasium zu Brandenburg von Ostern 1879 bis Ostern 1880, Brandenburg a.d.H., 1880.

Reiske = *Plutarchi Chaeronensis, Quae Supersunt, Omnia*, Graece et Latine . . . Io. Iacobus Reiske, Lipsiae, 1774–1782 (Vols. VI-X [1777–1778]: *Opera Moralia et Philosophica*).

Rieth, *Grundbegriffe* = Otto Rieth, *Grundbegriffe der stoischen Ethik : Eine traditionsgeschichtliche Untersuchung*, Berlin, 1933 (Problemata 9).

Robin, *Pyrrhon* = Léon Robin, *Pyrrhon et le Scepticisme Grec*, Paris, 1944.

S.V.F. = *Stoicorum Veterum Fragmenta* collegit Ioannes ab Arnim, 3 volumes, Lipsiae, 1903–1905.

Sambursky, *Physics of the Stoics* = S. Sambursky, *Physics of the Stoics*, London, 1959.

Schäfer, *Ein frühmittelstoisches System* = Maximilian Schäfer, *Ein frühmittelstoisches System der Ethik bei Cicero*, Munich, 1934.

Schmekel, *Philosophie der mittleren Stoa* = A. Schmekel, *Die Philosophie der mittleren Stoa in ihrem geschichtlichen Zusammenhange dargestellt*, Berlin, 1892.

Schroeter, *Plutarchs Stellung zur Skepsis* = Johannes Schroeter, *Plutarchs Stellung zur Skepsis*, Greifswald, 1911 (Diss. Königsberg).

Stephanus = *Plutarchi Chaeronensis quae extant opera cum Latina interpretatione* . . . excudebat Henr. Stephanus, Geneva, 1572.

Taylor, *Commentary on Plato's Timaeus* = A. E. Taylor, *A Commentary on Plato's Timaeus*, Oxford, 1928.

Thévenaz, *L'Âme du Monde* = Pierre Thévenaz, *L'Âme du Monde, le Devenir et la Matière chez Plutarque avec une traduction du traité " De la Genèse de l'Ame dans le Timée"* (*1ʳᵉ partie*), Paris, 1938.

Treu, *Lampriascatalog* = Max Treu, *Der sogenannte Lampriascatalog der Plutarchschriften*, Waldenburg in Schlesien, 1873.

Treu, *Ueberlieferung* i, ii, and iii = Max Treu, *Zur Geschichte der Ueberlieferung von Plutarchs Moralia* i (Programm des Städtischen evangel. Gymnasiums zu Waldenburg in Schlesien 1877), ii (Programm des Städtischen Gymnasiums zu Ohlau 1881), iii (Programm des Königl. Friedrichs-Gymnasiums zu Breslau 1884).

Turnebus, *Plutarchi de procreatione* = *Plutarchi dialogus*

PREFACE

de procreatione in Timaeo Platonis Adriano Turnebo interprete, Parisiis, 1552.

Usener, *Epicurea* = *Epicurea* edidit Hermannus Usener, Lipsiae, 1887.

Valgiglio, *De Fato* =Ps.-Plutarco *De Fato* (περὶ εἱ-
μαρμένης) : *Introduzione testo commento traduzione*
di Ernesto Valgiglio, Rome, 1964.

van Straaten, *Panétius* =Modestus van Straaten,
*Panétius : sa vie, ses écrits et sa doctrine avec une
édition des fragments*, Amsterdam, 1946. The
third part of this book, the text of the fragments
(pp. 325-393), is replaced by *Panetii Rhodii Fragmenta* collegit tertioque edidit Modestus van
Straaten O.E.S.A., editio amplificata, Leiden,
1962 (Philosophia Antiqua V).

Verbeke, *Kleanthes* =G. Verbeke, *Kleanthes van Assos*,
Brussel, 1949 (Verhandelingen van de K. Vlaamse
Academie voor Wetenschappen, Letteren en
Schone Kunsten van België, Kl. der Letteren,
XI [1949], No. 9).

Volkmann, *Philosophie des Plutarch* =Richard Volkmann, *Leben, Schriften und Philosophie des Plutarch von Chaeronea*, Zweiter Teil : *Philosophie
des Plutarch von Chaeronea*, Berlin, 1869.

Wegehaupt, *Plutarchstudien* =Hans Wegehaupt, *Plutarchstudien in italienischen Bibliotheken*, Höhere
Staatsschule in Cuxhaven, Wissenschaftliche
Beilage zum Bericht über das Schuljahr 1905/
1906, Cuxhaven, 1906.

Wegehaupt, " *Corpus Planudeum* " =Hans Wegehaupt, " Die Entstehung des Corpus Planudeum
von Plutarchs Moralia," *Sitzungsberichte der K.
Preussischen Akademie der Wissenschaften*, 1909,
2. Halbband, pp. 1030-1046.

PREFACE

Weische, *Cicero und die Neue Akademie* = Alfons
   Weische, *Cicero und die Neue Akademie : Unter-*
   suchungen zur Entstehung und Geschichte des an-
   tiken Skeptizismus, Münster Westf., 1961 (Orbis
   Antiquus 18).

Weissenberger, *Die Sprache Plutarchs* i and ii = B.
   Weissenberger, *Die Sprache Plutarchs von Chae-*
   ronea und die pseudoplutarchischen Schriften I. Teil
   (Programm des K. hum. Gymnasiums Straubing
   für das Schuljahr 1894/1895), II. Teil (Programm
   des K. hum. Gymnasiums Straubing für das
   Schuljahr 1895/96), Straubing, 1895 and 1896.

Westman, *Plutarch gegen Kolotes* = Rolf Westman,
   Plutarch gegen Kolotes : Seine Schrift " Adversus
   Colotem " als philosophiegeschichtliche Quelle, Hel-
   singfors, 1955 (Acta Philosophica Fennica, Fasc.
   vii, 1955).

Witt, *Albinus* = R. E. Witt, *Albinus and the History of*
   Middle Platonism, Cambridge, 1937 (Transactions
   of the Cambridge Philological Society, Vol. vii).

Wyttenbach = *Plutarchi Chaeronensis Moralia, id est*
   Opera, exceptis Vitis, Reliqua . . . Daniel Wyttenbach, Oxonii, 1795–1830 (Wyttenbach, *Animad-*
   versiones = Vols. vi and vii ; *Index Graecitatis* =
   Vol. viii).

Xylander = *Plutarchi Chaeronensis omnium, quae ex-*
   stant, operum Tomus Secundus continens Moralia
   Gulielmo Xylandro interprete, Francofurti, 1599.
   At the end of this volume, separately paged,
   there are Xylander's annotations followed by
   those of Stephanus and then variant readings
   ascribed to Turnebus, Vulcobius, Bongarsius,
   and Petavius as well as those of the Aldine and
   the Basiliensis.

PREFACE

Zeller, *Phil. Griech.* = Eduard Zeller, *Die Philosophie der Griechen in ihrer geschichtlichen Entwicklung*, 3 parts in 6 volumes, Leipzig, 1920–1923 (last revised editions) : I/1 and 2, 6. Auflage hrsg. von Wilhelm Nestle ; II/1, 5. Auflage mit einem Anhang von Ernst Hoffmann ; II/2, 3. Auflage (4. Auflage = Obraldruck) ; III/1, 4. Auflage hrsg. von Eduard Wellmann ; III/2, 4. Auflage.

THE TRADITIONAL ORDER of the Books of
the *Moralia* as they appear since the edition of
Stephanus (1572), and their division into volumes
in this edition.

xxiii

THE TRADITIONAL ORDER

THE TRADITIONAL ORDER

THE TRADITIONAL ORDER

xxvi

PLATONIC QUESTIONS
(PLATONICAE QUAESTIONES)

INTRODUCTION

Of Plutarch's works which, to judge by the titles
listed in the *Catalogue of Lamprias*, were devoted
particularly to the interpretation of Plato [a] only two
are extant, the Περὶ τῆς ἐν Τιμαίῳ ψυχογονίας (65)
and the Πλατωνικὰ ζητήματα (136).

The term ζητήματα had come to be used in a quasi-
technical sense for problems or questions raised concerning the meaning first of expressions or verses in
the text of Homer and then of specific passages in
other texts or of particular statements or opinions
or incidents, problems which with the solutions suggested might be made available to interested readers
in the form that today would be called " collected
notes " but sometimes in that of a "symposium," [b]

---

[a] Nos. 65-68, 70, 136, and 221 ; *cf.* also on Academic
doctrine Nos. 64, 71 (=131 ?), 134, and especially No. 63.

[b] For the history of the term and genre, ζήτημα, *cf.*
A. Gudeman, *R.-E.* xiii/2 (1927), cols. 2511, 46–2529, 34
(cols. 2525, 18–2527, 13 on Plutarch) ; H. Dörrie, *Por-
phyrios'* " *Symmikta Zetemata* " (München, 1959), pp. 1-6 ;
K.-H. Tomberg, *Die Kaine Historia des Ptolemaios Chennos*
(Diss. Bonn, 1967), pp. 54-62 ; R. Pfeiffer, *History of
Classical Scholarship* (Oxford, 1968), pp. 69-71 and p. 263.
Dörrie (*op. cit.*, p. 2) says that in the technical vocabulary
of philosophers the word was almost entirely avoided.
Nevertheless, Plutarch cites works by Chrysippus entitled
ἠθικὰ ζητήματα and φυσικὰ ζητήματα (*De Stoic. Repug.* 1046
D and F and 1053 E-F, *De Comm. Not.* 1078 E and 1084 D) ;

a literary frame not inappropriate, since in intellectual circles questions like these were proposed for
discussion by the company after dinner.[a] Plutarch
himself in his *Symposiacs* [b] uses the term ζητήματα of
the questions or problems there propounded and
discussed,[c] of which several without their literary
embellishment could appropriately have been included in the *Platonic Questions*,[d] just as all the latter
could have been used as material for the *Symposiacs*.

The *Platonic Questions*, as we have them, are ten
separate ζητήματα,[e] each concerned with the meaning of a passage or apparently related passages in
the text of Plato [f] but unconnected with one another

---

a work entitled σύμμικτα ζητήματα is ascribed to Aristotle
(V. Rose, *Aristotelis Fragmenta* [1886], p. 17, # 168 ; *cf.*
P. Moraux, *Les Listes Anciennes des Ouvrages d'Aristote*
[Louvain, 1951], p. 117, n. 17 [on pp. 118-119] and pp. 280-
281) ; and Porphyry (*Vita Plotini*, chap. 15, 18-21) says
that Eubulus wrote and sent from Athens συγγράμματα ὑπέρ
τινων Πλατωνικῶν ζητημάτων.

[a] *Cf.* Plutarch, *Quaest. Conviv.* 614 A-E and 686 B-D ;
Aulus Gellius, vii, xiii, 1-12 and xviii, ii, 1-16 (especially
6-14).

[b] For the literary form and " historicity " of Plutarch's
Symposiacs cf. J. Martin, *Symposion* (Paderborn, 1931), pp.
167-184 ; H. Bolkestein, *Adversaria*, pp. 1-46 ; K. Ziegler,
R.-E. xxi, 1 (1951), cols. 886, 40-887, 55.

[c] *Cf. Quaest. Conviv.* 645 c, 660 D, 736 c, 737 D.

[d] Notably *Quaest. Conviv.* vii, 1 and 2 ; viii, 2 ; and ix, 5.

[e] That they are just ten may be only an accident ; but
ten is also the number of questions that Plutarch expressly
allocated to each book of the *Symposiacs* (*cf.* 612 E, 629 E,
660 D) save one, the ninth, which he begins with a special
apology for exceeding " the customary ten " (736 c).

[f] Question VIII (1006 B—1007 E), for example, begins
with *Timaeus* 42 D 4-5, considers the possible relation to
this of 40 B 8-c 2, and then returns to interpret 38 c 5-6 in

3

PLUTARCH'S MORALIA

by any transition and without any general introduction or conclusion to give the collection unity or to
suggest a reason for the sequence in which the questions are arranged.[a] Had the sequence been deter-
mined by the subject-matter, II and IV would not
have been separated from each other by III and VI
would not have been placed between V and VII;
and, if by the source of the passages treated, III
and IX, which deal with the *Republic*, would have
come together, as would II, IV, V, VII, and VIII,
all five of which deal with the *Timaeus*. The ten
ζητήματα may not all have been written at one time
and for a single work. It is at least as likely that at
some time Plutarch put together ten separate notes
on Platonic passages that he had written at different
times and had found no suitable occasion to incor-
porate into his other compositions.[b] If this is so,
any indication of the relative chronology of one of

---

relation to expressions in *Republic* 506 E—509 D and
Timaeus 37 B—39 B. By the remark at the end of VIII, 3
and the beginning of VIII, 4 Plutarch practically admits
that VIII is in fact two ζητήματα rather than one.

[a] *Cf.* what is said by Elias (*In Aristotelis Categorias*,
p. 114, 13-14) of the σύμμικτα ζητήματα ascribed to Aristotle
and by Athenaeus (v, 186 e = Usener, *Epicurea*, p. 115, 9-11)
of the *Symposium* of Epicurus.

[b] *Cf.* what he says of his *De Tranquillitate Animi* at the
beginning of that essay (464 F) : . . . ἀνελεξάμην περὶ
εὐθυμίας ἐκ τῶν ὑπομνημάτων ὧν ἐμαυτῷ πεποιημένος ἐτύγχανον.
Paccius had asked him also for something on the passages
of the *Timaeus* that require exegesis (464 E), and Plutarch
probably had in those " note-books " of which he speaks
such things as our ζητήματα or the material for them. One
can well imagine that *De Defectu Orac.* 421 E—431 A (chaps.
22-37) is the elaboration of such a ζήτημα concerning *Timaeus*
55 C 7—D 6 (*cf.* K. Ziegler, *R.-E* xxi/1 [1951], col. 834, 47-53).

the ten would not necessarily be pertinent to that of the others.

That Plutarch had not himself been the first to pose questions about these particular Platonic passages is clear from the fact that he commonly discusses or refers to answers other than those he finally gives as his own.[a] That he had himself discussed at least one of them earlier is made certain by the remark that his answer is τὸ πολλάκις ὑφ' ἡμῶν λεγόμενον (1003 a). This is the answer to IV, which is a complement of that of II [b] and together with it gives in brief the interpretation that Plutarch was later to set out in detail in the *De Animae Procreatione in Timaeo* but himself says here had frequently been stated earlier than IV.[c] There is no other indication even of the relative chronology of any of these ζητήματα unless the mistake in V, " each of which consists of thirty of the primary scalene triangles " (1003 d) be thought to prove V earlier than *De Defectu Orac.*, where in 428 a this is corrected ; but that would be a precarious inference, for the mistake in 1003 d is part of the interpretation of others to which Plutarch then gives his own as an alternative.

The text of this work, No. 136 in the Catalogue of

[a] In IV he gives only his own answer. The authors of the answers that he rejects are not identified more clearly than by some such expression as δόξει δ' αὐτόθεν (1001 d), ὡς ὑπονοοῦσιν ἔνιοι (1003 c), or οἱ . . . ἀποδιδόντες ἀγνοοῦσιν ὅτι . . . (1008 b-c).

[b] See also the end of VIII (1007 c-d) ; cf. *Quaest. Conviv.* 718 a and 719 a with H. Dörrie, *Philomathes . . . in Memory of Philip Merlan* (The Hague, 1971), pp. 40-42.

[c] So he begins *De An. Proc. in Timaeo* itself by saying that it is to bring together in a single work τὰ πολλάκις εἰρημένα καὶ γεγραμμένα σποράδην ἐν ἑτέροις ἕτερα. . . .

Lamprias and No. 38 in the Planudean order, is here
printed on the basis of X J g a A β γ E B ε n Voss. 16
Bonon. C 3635 and Escorial T-11-5, all of which I have
collated from photostats. Of these only X J g E B ε
and n contain the whole of the work ; and in E itself,
although the whole is written by a single hand, folio
606ʳ has above the first column, which begins with
the words τοῦ νοητοῦ μόνον ἐστὶν ὁ νοῦς (1002 D),
the superscription Λ Θ πλατωνικὰ ζητήματα ὧν οὐχ
εὑρέθη ἡ ἀρχή, through which in the same ink a line
has been drawn.[a] This same superscription occurs in
a A β Bonon. C 3635 Voss. 16 and Escorial T-11-5, in
all of which τοῦ νοητοῦ κ.τ.λ. (1002 D) are the first
words of the work preserved,[b] and also in γ, where
the first words, however, are τί δήποτε τὴν ψυχὴν
(1002 E), the beginning of QUESTION IV.[c]

[a] This was accurately described by Treu (*Ueberlieferung*
i, p. IX). *Cf.* Pohlenz, *Moralia* i, p. x, n. 3 (p. XI) ; Wegehaupt, *Philologus*, lxiv (1905), p. 396 ; Sandbach, *Class.
Quart.*, xxxv (1941), p. 110 ; Manton, *Class. Quart.*, xliii
(1949), p. 98.

[b] This is true also of δ = Vat.Reg.80 (*cf.* H. Stevenson,
*Bibliothecae Apostolicae Vaticanae . . . Codices Reginae
Suecorum et Pii PP.* II *Graeci* [Romae, 1888], p. 63 and
Hahn, " De Plutarchi Moralium Codicibus," p. 57) and of
Marcianus 259, in which latter, however, the text ends with
ἀλλὰ ἕτερον in 1008 A, where the first hand of n leaves off
(*cf.* Treu, *Lampriascatalog*, p. 23 and Hubert-Drexler,
Moralia vi/1, p. XIV). In Voss. 16 by an error in binding
the text of the work has been divided ; it appears on folios
2ʳ-10ᵛ and 26ʳ-28ᵛ.

[c] This is also the case with Laur. 80, 5 and Laur. 80, 22
(*cf.* Wegehaupt, *Plutarchstudien*, pp. 27-28 and " Corpus
Planudeum," p. 1034, n. 1), with Marcianus 248 (*cf.* Treu,
Lampriascatalog, p. 23 [where what is said of the beginning
in Parisinus 1671 = A, however, is a mistake]), with Tolet.
51, 5 (*cf.* Fletcher, *Class. Quart.*, xxi [1927], pp. 166-167

If γ was copied from A, as has been supposed,[a] the scribe of γ must purposely have omitted the end of QUESTION III (1002 D-E) which a and A preserve, to begin with QUESTION IV (τί δήποτε) and must also have disregarded either purposely or inadvertently the lacuna indicated in a and A between σωμάτων and ὁ σίδηρος in 1005 C. Otherwise γ differs from a and A (uncorrected and corrected) in only six places, none of which is decisive.[b] Only once does γ agree with a against A (1005 C [μέν τι : μέντοι -A, Esc.]). Four times it agrees with A against a (1003 A [ἦ : ἦ -a], 1005 A [οὐρανὸν : ? -a[1] ; ἦκον -a[2], n ; εἶκον -A, γ and all other mss.], 1007 A [ἔκγονος : ἔγγονος -A, γ], 1011 A [τὸν : τοῦ -a]) and twice with A[2] against A[1] and a (1003 E [πασῶν : παθῶν -a, A[1]], 1005 C [τρίψει : τῇ τρίψει -A[2], γ]). It appears, then, that the scribe of γ copied this work from A after A had been corrected.

Since β contains the end of QUESTION III (1002 D-E), which is not in γ, the source of β for this work cannot have been γ. Nor can it have been X, J, g, B, ε, n, or E.[c] All these contain the beginning of the work,

---

and p. 170, n. 6), and with Parisinus 2076 (ff. 132[v]-145[v]), which last was generously verified for me by M. Joseph Paramelle of the " Centre National de la Recherche Scientifique."

[a] Cf. B. Einarson and P. De Lacy, Class. Phil., xlvi (1951), p. 103, col. 1 and Valgiglio, De Fato, p. XLII.

[b] 1003 B (σπέρματος : σώματος -γ), 1006 D (λαμβάνοντας : λαμβάνοντος -γ, Esc.[1] ; λαμβάνοντα -a, A, E, B, ε, n), 1008 C (περὶ ὦτα : περὶ τὰ ὦτα -γ), 1008 D (λογιστικὸν : λογικὸν -a, A, β[1], E, B, ε), 1010 C (ἄλας : ἄλλας -γ, J). In the sixth (1006 A) γ has the negative οὐ which is erased in a and cancelled in A ; but this cancellation, a dot under the οὐ, might easily have been overlooked.

[c] B and g are presumably younger than β anyway, being

which β does not have and says has not been found ; but besides that in one passage or another after the point at which the text in β begins all of them lack words that were present in β even before correction,[a] as do α, A, and γ also.[b] In more than a dozen places where β originally agreed with α, A, E it has been changed so that it agrees instead with the reading of Bonon., which is frequently shared with X and n and occasionally with J or ϵ. In half a dozen of these places words not present in α, A, E, and γ have been added by β^2 either in the margin or superscript (1005 C-D, 1007 D [bis], 1010 C, 1010 D, and 1011 B). In 1010 C β^2 has added in the margin ten words that occur in X, ϵ, n, Bonon., Voss., and Escor., nine of which are omitted by J, g, α, A, γ, E, and B. In 1005 C-D, where J, g, and γ have $\sigma\omega\mu\acute{\alpha}\tau\omega\nu$. $\acute{o}$ $\sigma\acute{\iota}\delta\eta\rho\sigma$ and where a lacuna of varying length between $\sigma\omega\mu\acute{\alpha}\tau\omega\nu$ and $\acute{o}$ $\sigma\acute{\iota}\delta\eta\rho\sigma$ is indicated by α, A, E, B, and β^1, the five words $\acute{\iota}\lambda\nu\sigma\pi\tilde{\alpha}\nu$ $\sigma\check{\nu}\tau\omega$ $\acute{\upsilon}\pi\grave{o}$ $\tau\sigma\tilde{\upsilon}$ $\Pi\lambda\acute{\alpha}$-$\tau\omega\nu\sigma$ have been added in the margin by β^2. These five words with the last four deleted are in Bonon. ; otherwise they are preserved—but with $\epsilon\acute{\iota}\lambda\nu\sigma\pi\tilde{\alpha}\nu$ instead of $\acute{\iota}\lambda\nu\sigma\pi\tilde{\alpha}\nu$—only in X, ϵ, and n. Moreover, β

of the 15th century, whereas β is of the 14th ; n, which has generally been dated to the 15th century, is of the 14th according to C. Giannelli (*Codices Vaticani Graeci* [1950], pp. 442-443).

[a] This eliminates the possibility that β might have been copied from E before the lost beginning had been discovered and added to that MS.

[b] *e.g.* 1005 A ($\check{\alpha}\mu\alpha$ -omitted by n), 1006 A ($\sigma\check{\upsilon}$ -omitted by X, ϵ, n [erased in α and cancelled in A]), 1006 C ($\acute{\iota}\lambda\lambda\sigma\mu\acute{\epsilon}\nu\eta\nu$ ... $\acute{\alpha}\nu\epsilon\iota\lambda\sigma\nu\mu\acute{\epsilon}\nu\eta\nu$ -omitted by J, g), 1009 B ($\lambda\acute{o}\gamma\sigma\nu$ ... vac. ... $\kappa\alpha\grave{\iota}$ -α, A, γ, B), 1011 A ('$O\delta\upsilon\sigma\sigma\acute{\epsilon}\alpha$ ... vac. ... $\sigma\check{\upsilon}$ -X, α, A, γ, E, B, ϵ).

has uncorrected readings that differ from those of a, A, and E and agree with those of Bonon., shared sometimes by X, J, n, or ϵ as well (1006 D, 1007 C, 1009 A, 1009 B, 1010 B, 1010 D, and 1011 A [*bis*]) ; and in the last of these places β^1 agrees exactly with Bonon. alone ($\lambda\upsilon\gamma\hat{\omega}\nu\tau\alpha$ $\pi\rho\grave{o}s$ $\tau\grave{\eta}\nu$ $\tau\hat{\omega}\nu$ $\pi\rho o\beta\acute{\alpha}\tau\omega\nu$ $\sigma\upsilon\nu$ . . .). It is probable therefore that β was not just corrected by reference to Bonon. but was copied from the archetype of the latter.

Bonon. C 3635 not only has the end of QUESTION III, which is not in γ, and words that are not in β^1 but also preserves words that are missing from X, from J, and from a, A, γ, E, ϵ, and n.[a] Though very often in agreement with a and A against J and sometimes against X or both X and J, it agrees at times with X or J or both of them against a and A and occasionally disagrees with all four—X, J, a and A.[b]

---

[a] There are more than 35 places where Bonon. with a, A, and X preserves words lacking in J, among which see 1003 B ($\tau\hat{\omega}\nu$ $\delta\grave{e}$ $\kappa\upsilon\kappa\lambda\iota\kappa\hat{\omega}\nu$ . . . $\tau\hat{\omega}\nu$ $\epsilon\vartheta\vartheta\upsilon\gamma\rho\acute{\alpha}\mu\mu\omega\nu$), 1004 A ($\delta\tau\iota$ $\tauo\acute{\iota}\nu\upsilon\nu$ . . . $\tau\grave{o}$ $\epsilon\vartheta\vartheta\acute{\upsilon}\gamma\rho\alpha\mu\mu o\nu$), 1006 C ($\grave{\iota}\lambda\lambda o\mu\acute{e}\nu\eta\nu$ . . . $\grave{\alpha}\nu\epsilon\iota\lambda o\upsilon\mu\acute{e}\nu\eta\nu$). For words in Bonon. lacking in others see *e.g.* 1003 B ($\grave{\upsilon}\pi\grave{o}$ $\tau\hat{\eta}s$ $\psi\upsilon\chi\hat{\eta}s$ omitted by X), 1005 B ($\tau\grave{o}$ δ' $\mathring{\eta}\lambda\epsilon\kappa\tau\rho o\nu$ . . . $\tau\grave{o}\nu$ $\sigma\acute{\iota}\delta\eta\rho o\nu$ omitted by ϵ), 1005 C-D ($\grave{\iota}\lambda\upsilon\sigma\pi\hat{\alpha}\nu$ . . . $\Pi\lambda\acute{\alpha}\tau\omega\nu os$ omitted by J, g, γ, a, A, E, B, β^1), 1007 D ($\mu\grave{e}\nu$ omitted by all except Bonon., Voss., Escor., β^2 ; and $\grave{e}\sigma\tau\iota$ omitted by a, A, β^1, γ, E, B, ϵ, n), 1009 B ($\mu\epsilon\rho\hat{\omega}\nu$ $\mu\eta\delta\grave{e}\nu$ $\check{\alpha}\mu\alpha$ omitted by a, A, γ, B), 1010 C ($\kappa\rho\acute{\alpha}\tau\iota\sigma\tauo\nu$ . . . $\epsilon\tilde{\iota}\nu\alpha\iota$ omitted by J, g, a, A, γ, E, B), 1011 A ($\lambda\upsilon\gamma\hat{\omega}\nu\tau\alpha$ . . . $\sigma\upsilon\nu$ omitted by X, a, A, γ, E, B, ϵ), 1011 B ($\nu\grave{\eta}$ $\Delta\acute{\iota}\alpha$ omitted by J, g, a, A, β^1, γ, E, B).

[b] Examples of this last case are 1011 A in the preceding note, 1010 B ($\delta\iota\acute{\alpha}\lambda\epsilon\kappa\tau os$: $\delta\iota\acute{\alpha}\lambda o\gamma os$ -Bonon.), 1010 D ($\mu\grave{\eta}$ omitted by X, J, a, A) ; of agreement with X against a and A 1005 C-D, 1009 B, 1010 C, and 1011 B in the preceding note and 1006 C ($\tau\epsilon\tau\alpha\mu\acute{e}\nu o\nu$) and 1009 A ($\tau\hat{\omega}$) ; of agreement with J against a and A 1002 D ($\check{\alpha}\lambda\lambda\alpha$ $\check{\alpha}\lambda\lambda o\iota s$), 1004 B ($\mu\grave{e}\nu$ omitted by X, a, A), 1009 E ($\kappa\alpha\vartheta'$ $\alpha\check{\upsilon}\tau\grave{\alpha}$) ; of agreement with X and J

It must have been copied from a ms. which, though
mutilated at the beginning of the work in the same
way as *a*, had a text in some cases nearer to that of
X and in a few nearer to that of J than to that of *a*.

The text of Voss. 16, though for the most part
identical with that of Bonon., differs from it in seventeen places.[a] In six of these differences, moreover,
Voss. agrees with J[1] and in three others with n [b];
and this suggests that Voss. was copied not from
Bonon. itself but possibly from the latter's archetype
or a ms. very much like it.

The same is true of Escor. T-11-5, which agrees
with Voss. against Bonon. eight times and with
Bonon. against Voss. seven times but disagrees with
both Bonon. and Voss. in 31 cases,[c] in two of which

---

against *a* and A 1006 D (λαμβάνοντας), 1007 D (ἐστι omitted
by *a*, A), 1008 D (λογιστικόν), 1011 A (τὰς omitted by *a*, A).

[a] This is assuming that in 1005 C-D (where Hubert's
apparatus is doubly in error) the line through οὕτως ὑπὸ
τοῦ Πλάτωνος was drawn by the first hand of Bonon. Otherwise the differences would be eighteen.

[b] 1004 A (εὐθύγραμμοι: εὐθύγραμμον -J, g, Voss.); 1004 A
(συναρμοττομένοις: συναρμοττόμενος -J, g, Voss.[1]); 1005 A
(ἀφιεμένῳ: ἐφιεμένῳ -J[1], g, Voss., Escor.); 1005 C (τῷ: τὸ -J,
g, Voss.); 1005 E-F (πληθύοντες: πληθύνοντες -J, g, Voss.,
Escor.); 1011 B (θεωρικὰ: θεωρητικὰ -J, g, Voss., Escor.);
1010 C (Εὔηνος: εὔωνος -n, Voss.); 1011 A (παρὰ τοῖς: παρ'
οἷς -n, Voss.); 1011 A (τῶν προβάτων συν . . .: συν omitted
by n and Voss.). The last is one of the two passages adduced
by Pohlenz and Hubert (Hubert-Drexler, *Moralia* vi, 1,
p. XIV); in the other, 1003 A, though Voss. disagrees with
Bonon. and others (συνυπῆρχον), its reading, συνυπάρχον, is
not that of J[1] as it is there said to be.

[c] Perhaps a dozen of these are errors of the scribe of
Escor. himself, one of which is interesting as a warning,
however, for it can be only by a coincidence that in 1004 A
Escor. omits seven words that are omitted by J and g but
are preserved by all other mss.

PLATONIC QUESTIONS

it agrees with others in the correct reading.[a] In
1011 A Escor. like Voss. and n omits the prefix συν
preserved by Bonon. and β alone but alone has λέγοντα instead of the λυγῶντα of these four MSS., and
in 1003 A it alone has συνυπάρχουσιν instead of the
συνυπάρχον of Voss. and the correct συνυπῆρχον of
Bonon. Moreover, it alone has καὶ ἰλυσπᾶν in 1005 c,
παραλιπόντα μηθὲν καὶ in 1009 B where Bonon. and
Voss. have μερῶν μηθὲν ἅμα καὶ, and in 1010 D ὁρῶ . . .
vac. 30 . . . ἀλλ' ὥσπερ ὁμοῦ instead of their ὁρῶ
μέλλων νῦν ὁμοῦ τι.

In that part of E that fills folios 606r-610r (τοῦ
νοητοῦ μόνον [1002 D]—to the end) and was copied
before the beginning of the work had been found
E never agrees with α against A. It agrees with
A, α² and others against α¹ thrice,[b] with A against α
eight times,[c] and with A² against α and A¹ twice [d] ;
but once it agrees with α¹ and A¹ against α and A as
corrected,[e] and eight times it disagrees with both
α and A. One of these differences is a matter of
word-order and is changed by E² (1003 B), one is
the omission by E and B of two words that appear in
all other MSS. (1010 A : καθ' αὐτό), and three concern

[a] 1004 B (ἐντάσει -E, B, n, Escor.), 1008 E (ὂν -Escor.
with all except n, Bonon., Voss.).

[b] 1002 E (δεῖ : δὴ -α¹, ε), 1009 D (τὸ πρῶτον omitted by α¹),
1009 F (τὸν λέγοντα : λέγον -α¹).

[c] In five of these cases E and A are wrong, though α is
right (1006 B [ὁ δὴ -α], 1007 A [ἔκγονος -α], 1007 F [πρότε-
ρον -α], 1008 C [τιμωρίας -α], 1009 E [καὶ -α]) ; in two E and
A are right and α wrong (1003 A [ἢ -E, A] and 1011 A
[τὸν -E, A]) ; and in one all are wrong (1005 A [ἧκον -α² ;
εἶκον -E, A]).

[d] 1003 E (πασῶν -E, A²) and 1005 c (τῇ τρίψει -E, A²).

[e] In 1006 A the οὐ after πρότερον that is absent from X, ε,
n and is erased in α and cancelled in A is present in E.

11

the form of a single word [a] ; but in two cases E with B has a word that is in no other MS.,[b] and in 1009 B there are in E three words, μερῶν μηθὲν ἅμα, that are absent from the lacuna in a, A, γ, and B and occur only in X, β, ε, n, Bonon., and Voss. The scribe of E might have found these three words in the MS. from which he later copied the beginning of the work and might then have entered them here in the lacuna that he had left ; but, if so, it is strange that the scribe of B, whether he copied the whole work from E or from the MS. whence E took the first part of it, omitted just these three words and preserved exactly the lacuna of a, A, and γ. It is more probable that the scribe of E copied the three words in question and all this second part of the work from a congener of a, which was also the source of A's corrections.[c]

In the first part of the work (999 c—1002 D), which the scribe of E added later, there are 53 cases in which E agrees with X against J ; and in fifteen of these E preserves a word or words missing from J (cf. 1000 A, c, and E ; 1001 c and D ; 1002 A). In only two cases does E agree with J against X ; and in another, where it agreed with X, it was changed so that E² agrees with J instead.[d] In eight cases

[a] 1004 B (ἐντάσει -E, B, n, Escor. ; ἐνστάσει -all other MSS.), 1004 C (κυκλοφορητικὴν : κυκλοφορικὴν -E, B, n), and 1005 A (συνεπιταχύνων : ἐπιταχύνων -E, B, Escor.).

[b] 1007 F (σελήνην : τὴν σελήνην -E, B) and 1009 A (μεσότητας : ὡς μεσότητας -E, B).

[c] Cf. Valgiglio, De Fato, p. xl and his references to Treu and Larsen, p. xxxix, n. 36.

[d] 999 D (πότερον -E, B, J, g ; πότερα -X, ε, n), 1001 B (τῇ ὕλῃ -E, B, J, g, ε, n ; τῇ ἕλῃ -X), 1001 c (γένους -E¹, X, ε, n ; γένος -E², J, g, B).

12

PLATONIC QUESTIONS

E with B in agreement has a reading different from that of X and J [a] ; and in still another E, agreeing with X and J, was changed by E[2] to disagree with both.[b] The first part of the work, then, must have been copied by E from a ms. the text of which was much nearer to that of X than to that of J.

In the first part of the work (999 c—1002 d) B disagrees with E and all other mss. seven times,[c] in agreement with J disagrees with E and all others once,[d] and in agreement with E[2] disagrees with E[1] thrice.[e] In the second part of the work B agrees once with E[2] and all other mss. against E[1] in the order of words (1003 a-b), disagrees with E eight times,[f] and once, though agreeing with E, has a " correction "

---

[a] 1000 F (ἢ : καὶ -E, B ; omitted by X, J, g, ε, n.). The other seven cases are 999 F, 1000 B, 1001 D (*bis*), 1002 A, 1002 B, 1002 D.

[b] 1002 A (ἐμφαινομένων -B, E[2] ; ἐκφαινομένων -X, J, g, E[1], ε, n).

[c] Twice in the order of words (999 E-F and 1001 B), thrice by wrongly omitting a word (1001 B [ἔοικεν], 1002 A [ἐν after ὥσπερ], and 1002 B [τῆς after ἔκ τε]), and twice in the form of a word (1000 A [διανομὴ : νομὴ -B] and 1000 D [νοητὸν : νοητὴν -B]).

[d] 1002 B (μικρότητα : μακρότητα -J, B).

[e] 1001 C (γένους -E[1], X, ε, n ; γένος -B, E[2], J, g), 1002 A (ἐκ δὲ : δὲ with three dots superscript -E ; δὲ omitted by B), and 1002 A (ἐμφαινομένων -B, E[2] ; ἐκφαινομένων -E[1] and all other mss.).

[f] 1004 B (καμπυλωτέρας : καμπυλοτέρας -B, ε), 1007 E (ἁρμονία : ἁρμονίαν -B), 1007 F (τὸν ἐν μὲν τοῖς : τὸν μὲν τοῖς -B ; τὸν μὲν ἐν τοῖς -J, g), 1008 C (ὀρέξει : ἕξει -B), 1008 C (τῷ λογισμῷ καὶ σύμμαχον : καὶ σύμμαχον τῷ λογισμῷ -B ; καὶ λογισμῷ σύμμαχον -n), 1008 D (ὑπάτη : ὑπάτην -B), 1008 F (ὁτὲ μέν τε μετὰ : ὁτὲ μὲν μετὰ -B ; ὁτὲ . . . vac. 5 . . . μετὰ -J ; ὁτὲ μετὰ -g), 1009 B (λόγου μερῶν μηθὲν ἅμα . . . vac. 13 . . . καὶ -E ; λόγου . . . vac. 34 . . . -B).

op

that points to a variant resembling the readings of J and g.[a] This last and the lacuna in 1009 B are the strongest indications that the second part of the work in B was copied neither from E nor from the source of E for this part; and, although no single passage decisively proves that B did not copy the whole work from E after E had been corrected,[b] it is at least equally possible that B copied it from the MS. whence E had taken the first part of it.

Of the extant MSS. containing the whole work the oldest is J (13th century),[c] for the part of X that contains it was written in the 14th century. It has been asserted that J is nearer than X to the Planudean text,[d] but the very opposite is true. In that part of the work which is preserved in a and A (1002 D ff.) J and X agree against a A E seven times and three more against a [e]; but, where J and X disagree, while J agrees with a A E against X twenty times, with a^1 A^1 E against X a^2 A^2 once, and with a^1 against X a^2 A E once,[f] X agrees with a A E against J 167 times and with a against J four

---

[a] 1003 B (διάφωνον -B; διαφέρειν -J; διαφέρον -g; διάφωνον -E and all other MSS.).

[b] For the controversy concerning the relation of B to E see Plutarch, Moralia (L.C.L.), xii (1957), pp. 26-27 and 31-32 (with B. Einarson, Class. Phil., liii [1958], p. 265, n. 3), ix (1961), p. 305, and xi (1965), p. 6; Pohlenz-Westman, Moralia vi/2 (1959), pp. 228-229.

[c] J^4 = the corrections made by Demetrius Ducas in preparing J as "copy for the printer of the Aldine edition" (cf. Treu, Ueberlieferung iii, pp. 22-26).

[d] Hubert-Drexler, Moralia vi/1, p. xII.

[e] In all cases I disregard differences of accent and breathing alone.

[f] Of these 22 cases two are omissions of words in X and two are omissions of words in J.

times more.[a] Since not only X but all other mss. preserve words that J omits, J cannot be the source of any other ms. for this work, not even of g.

The agreement of g with J is striking even in the omission of words that are present in all other mss.[b] and in the preservation of words that are missing from X[c]; but g agrees with X and others against J at least 38 times,[d] in two cases preserving words that are omitted by J alone.[e] The close agreement of g with J suggests, therefore, that both were copied from the same ms. and that this ms. itself exhibited most of the errors and omissions common to J and g. It may have been a copy or a twin of the archetype of X and may have contained some of the variants that X appears to have preserved from that

---

[a] Of these differences between X and J 35 are omissions of a word or words in J and three are omissions of a word or words in X. If these omissions were the fault of the scribes of J and X themselves, their originals may have shown less of a difference in relation to α A E, as is indicated by 1006 c, where X agrees with α A E in preserving sixteen words omitted by J and yet in these sixteen words differs from α A E three times.

[b] J and g agree against all other mss. more than 150 times, in 45 of which they omit words that all others have, e.g. 1000 E (καὶ δεόμενον and καὶ βεβαιοῦντος), 1003 B (τῶν δὲ κυκλικῶν . . . τὰς τῶν εὐθυγράμμων), and 1006 c (ἱλλομένην . . . ἀνειλουμένην).

[c] 1003 B (ὑπὸ τῆς ψυχῆς) and 1011 A (λυγῶν πρὸς τὴν τῶν προβάτων -omitted by X, E, B, and ε as well as by α, A, γ).

[d] There are also about 25 unique readings in g, some ten of which are omissions of a single word, probably the fault of the scribe of g himself.

[e] 1000 c (οὐ προσδέξεται . . . τὸ πλῆθος) and 1004 D (πλειόνων). The statement in Hubert-Drexler, *Moralia* vi/1, p. xiii, line 1 concerning νοούμεν(ον), " exhib. g," is erroneous.

archetype, *e.g.* 1005 F ($\overset{\ddot{\iota}}{\kappa\epsilon\nu o\upsilon\mu\acute{\epsilon}\nu as}$ -X[1]; $\kappa\iota\nu o\upsilon\mu\acute{\epsilon}\nu as$ -J; $\kappa\epsilon\nu o\upsilon\mu\acute{\epsilon}\nu as$ -g and all other MSS.), 1006 B ($\overset{\tau\epsilon}{\gamma a\rho}$ -X[1]; $\overset{\tau\epsilon\rho o\nu}{\tau\epsilon}$ -J, g; $\gamma\grave{a}\rho$ -all other MSS.), 1008 E ($\mathring{a}\nu\omega\tau\acute{a}\tau\omega$ -X[1]; $\mathring{a}\nu\acute{\omega}\tau\epsilon\rho o\nu$ -J, g; $\mathring{a}\nu\omega\tau\acute{a}\tau\omega$ -all other MSS.).

Both ϵ and the part of n written by the first hand [a] agree with X in preserving the many words omitted by J and g and almost never agree with J or g or J g alone against X,[b] and in the part of the work that is missing from the mutilated MSS. (*i.e.* before $\tau o\hat{\upsilon}$ $\nu o\eta\tau o\hat{\upsilon}$ in 1002 D) they agree in several significant readings with X, J, and g against E and B.[c] Thereafter, although they occasionally agree with a, A, E, and B against X, J, and g,[d] they preserve with X words that are missing from these MSS.[e] and never agree with Bonon., Voss., or Escor. against all others; but both of them also preserve words omitted by X,[f] and each of the two has words

[a] That is from the beginning of the work through $\mathring{a}\lambda\lambda\grave{a}$ $\overset{\ast}{\epsilon}\tau\epsilon\rho o\nu$ at the end of 1008 A = folios 1^{r}-6^{v} (see p. 6, n. *b supra*).

[b] The exceptions are 1001 C ($\mu a\theta\eta\mu a\tau\iota\kappa\acute{o}\nu$: $\mu a\theta\eta\tau\iota\kappa\acute{o}\nu$ -J, ϵ), 1001 D ($\delta\grave{\epsilon}$ $\tau o\hat{\iota}s$: $\delta\grave{\epsilon}$ $\tau\hat{\eta}s$ -J, g, n), 1005 D ($\tau\iota s$ -omitted by J, g, ϵ), 1005 F ($\mathring{\upsilon}\pi\epsilon\acute{\iota}\kappa o\nu\tau os$: $\mathring{\upsilon}\pi\acute{\eta}\kappa o\nu\tau os$ -J, ϵ, n), and 1006 B ($\tau\grave{o}\nu$: $\tau\grave{o}$ -J, g, ϵ).

[c] 1000 B ($\phi\iota\lambda o\sigma o\phi\acute{\iota}a$ -X, J, g, ϵ, n; $\sigma o\phi\acute{\iota}a$ -E, B), 1000 F ($\mathring{\eta}$ $\tau\hat{\eta}$: $\kappa a\grave{\iota}$ $\tau\hat{\eta}$ -E, B; $\tau\hat{\eta}$ -X, J, g, ϵ, n), 1001 D ($\mathring{a}\nu\iota\sigma a$ $\tau\mu\acute{\eta}\mu a\tau a$ ... $\overset{\ast}{\epsilon}\tau\epsilon\mu\epsilon$ -E, B; $\mathring{a}\nu\iota\sigma a$ $\tau\grave{a}$ $\tau\mu\acute{\eta}\mu a\tau a$ ... $\overset{\ast}{\epsilon}\tau\epsilon\mu\nu\epsilon$ -X, J, g, ϵ, n), 1002 B ($\theta\epsilon\acute{\iota}o\iota s$: $\theta\epsilon o\hat{\iota}s$ -X, J, g, ϵ, n; $\nu o\eta\tau o\hat{\iota}s$ -E, B).

[d] 1006 D ($\lambda a\mu\beta\acute{a}\nu o\nu\tau as$: $\lambda a\mu\beta\acute{a}\nu o\nu\tau a$ ϵ, n, a, A, E, B), 1007 D ($\overset{\ast}{\epsilon}\sigma\tau\iota$ -omitted by ϵ, n, a, A, β^{1}, γ, E, B), 1007 E ($o\mathring{\upsilon}$ $\phi a\acute{\upsilon}\lambda\omega\nu$: $o\mathring{\upsilon}\delta\grave{\epsilon}$ $\phi a\acute{\upsilon}\lambda\omega\nu$ -ϵ, n, a, A, β^{1}, γ, E, B, J^{2}).

[e] 1005 C-D ($\sigma\omega\mu\acute{a}\tau\omega\nu$ $\epsilon\mathring{\iota}\lambda\upsilon\sigma\pi\hat{a}\nu$ $o\overset{\ast}{\upsilon}\tau\omega s$ $\mathring{\upsilon}\pi\grave{o}$ $\tau o\hat{\upsilon}$ $\Pi\lambda\acute{a}\tau\omega\nu os$ $\acute{o}$ -X, ϵ, n; $\sigma\omega\mu\acute{a}\tau\omega\nu$ ... vac. ... $\acute{o}$ -a, A, E, B; $\sigma\omega\mu\acute{a}\tau\omega\nu$. $\acute{o}$ -J, g, γ).

[f] 1003 B ($\mathring{\upsilon}\pi\grave{o}$ $\tau\hat{\eta}s$ $\psi\upsilon\chi\hat{\eta}s$), 1007 F ($\kappa a\grave{\iota}$ -omitted by X alone).

PLATONIC QUESTIONS

that the other omits.[a] Neither ε nor this part of n,
then, could have been derived from any of the extant
MSS. ; and both are probably independent copies of
the archetype of X.

This is not the case, however, with folios 7ʳ-9ᵛ of n
(οἱ γὰρ ὡς κυρίαν [1008 A sub finem] to the end of the
work). The text of these folios, written in a hand
different from that of folios 1ʳ-6ᵛ, while agreeing
with ε and X in preserving words omitted by J and
g, by E and B, and by a, A, and γ,[b] also preserves
words omitted by ε and X [c] ; and in all these passages
n is in agreement with one or more of the group consisting of Bonon., Voss., and Escor., as it also is in
23 of the 24 cases in which—besides five readings
unique to it—it disagrees with ε. In eleven of these
23 cases, moreover, n is in agreement only with one
or more of this group (β¹ or β² included in some
cases). It was certainly from a MS. related to this
group, therefore, and possibly from the archetype
of Bonon. that this last part of the work in n was
taken.

[a] e.g. 1001 A sub finem (τοῦ τεκνώσαντος -omitted by n
alone), 1005 A (ἅμα -omitted by n alone), 1005 B (τὸ δ᾽ ἤ-
λεκτρον . . . συνεφέλκεται τὸν σίδηρον -omitted by ε alone),
1007 E (καὶ πρώτῳ -omitted by ε alone).

[b] 1009 B (λόγου μερῶν μηθὲν ἅμα καὶ -ε, n, X, β, Bonon.,
Voss. ; λόγου . . . vac. . . . καὶ -a, A, γ, B), 1010 A (καθ᾽ αὑτὸ
-omitted by E, B), 1010 C (κράτιστον . . . μέρος εἶναι -omitted
by J, g, a, A, γ, E, B, β¹), 1011 B (νὴ Δία -omitted by J, g,
a, A, γ, E, B, β¹).

[c] 1010 D (ἐκπώμασι μὴ -n, Bonon., Voss., Escor., β² ;
μὴ omitted by all other MSS.), 1011 A (Ὀδυσσέα λυγῶντα πρὸς
τὴν τῶν προβάτων . . . vac. . . . οὐ -n, Voss. ; Ὀδυσσέα . . .
vac. . . . οὐ -X, a, A, γ, E, B, ε).

17

ΠΛΑΤΩΝΙΚΑ ΖΗΤΗΜΑΤΑ[1]

ΖΗΤΗΜΑ Α΄

1. Τί δήποτε τὸν Σωκράτην ὁ θεὸς μαιοῦσθαι[2]
μὲν ἐκέλευσεν ἑτέρους, αὐτὸν δὲ γεννᾶν ἀπεκώ-
λυσεν, ὡς ἐν Θεαιτήτῳ λέγεται; Οὐ γὰρ εἰρω-
νευόμενός γε[3] καὶ παίζων προσεχρήσατ᾽ ἂν τῷ
D τοῦ[4] θεοῦ ὀνόματι. καὶ ἄλλως ἐν τῷ Θεαιτήτῳ
πολλὰ μεγάλαυχα καὶ σοβαρὰ Σωκράτει περι-
τέθεικεν, ὧν καὶ ταῦτ᾽ ἐστί· " πολλοὶ γὰρ δή,[5]
ὦ θαυμάσιε, πρός με οὕτω[6] διετέθησαν, ὥστ᾽
ἀτεχνῶς δάκνειν[7] ἐπειδάν τινα λῆρον αὐτῶν ἀφ-
αιρῶμαι· καὶ οὐκ οἴονταί με εὐνοίᾳ τοῦτο ποιεῖν,
πόρρω ὄντες τοῦ εἰδέναι ὅτι οὐδεὶς θεὸς δύσνους
ἀνθρώποις οὐδ᾽ ἐγὼ δυσνοίᾳ τοιοῦτον οὐδὲν δρῶ,
ἀλλά μοι ψεῦδός τε συγχωρῆσαι καὶ ἀληθὲς ἀ-
φανίσαι οὐδαμῶς θέμις."

Πότερον[8] οὖν τὴν ἑαυτοῦ φύσιν ὡς κριτικω-

[1] X, J, g, E, B, ε, n ; πλατωνικὰ ζητήματα ὧν οὐχ εὑρέθη
ἡ ἀρχή -α, Α, β, Bonon. C 3635, Voss. 16, Escorial T-11-5 (all
beginning with τοῦ νοητοῦ μόνον [1002 D]) and γ (beginning
with τί δήποτε τὴν ψυχὴν [1002 E]).

[2] μαιεύεσθαι -Plato (*Theaetetus* 150 c 7).　　　　[3] τε -J, g.

[4] τῷ -omitted by J and added superscript by J[4] ; τοῦ
-omitted by X, g, E, B, ε, n.

[5] ἤδη -Nogarola from *Theaetetus* 151 c 5.

[6] πρός με οὕτω -X, E, B, ε, n, Plato ; οὕτω πρός με -J, g.

[7] ⟨ἕτοιμοι εἶναι⟩ -added by Stephanus from *Theaetetus*
151 c 7.

18

PLATONIC QUESTIONS

QUESTION I

1. WHYEVER did god, as is stated in the *Theaetetus*,[a] bid Socrates act as midwife to others but prevent him from himself begetting? Certainly he would not have used the name of god in irony or jest [b] ; and besides in the *Theaetetus* Socrates has been made to say many arrogant and haughty things, among them this [c] : " For a great many men, my excellent friend, have got into such a state of mind towards me as practically to bite when I remove some silliness of theirs ; and they do not believe that I am doing this out of benevolence, for they are a long way from knowing that no god is malevolent towards men and that neither do I do any such deed out of malevolence but that it is quite illicit for me to admit falsehood and suppress truth."

Is it then his own nature, as being more dis-

---

[a] Plato, *Theaetetus* 150 c 7-8.

[b] *Cf.* Plato, *Symposium* 216 E 4-5 (εἰρωνευόμενος δὲ καὶ παίζων πάντα τὸν βίον πρὸς τοὺς ἀνθρώπους διατελεῖ). The tendency to dismiss as "irony" statements of Socrates that connected with god his behaviour in carrying on his elenchus is mentioned not only in *Anon. in Platonis Theaetetum* (Pap. Berl. 9782), col. 58, 39-49 (p. 39 [Diels-Schubart]) but also in the Platonic *Apology* 37 E 5—38 A 1.

[c] *Theaetetus* 151 c 5-D 3.

---

[8] πότερα -X, e, n.

PLUTARCH'S MORALIA

(999) τέραν ἢ[1] γονιμωτέραν οὖσαν θεὸν προσεῖπε, καθάπερ Μένανδρος " ὁ νοῦς γὰρ ἡμῶν ὁ θεός "
καὶ Ἡράκλειτος " ἦθος ἀνθρώπου[2] δαίμων "· ἢ
E θεῖόν τι καὶ δαιμόνιον ὡς ἀληθῶς αἴτιον ὑφηγήσατο Σωκράτει τοῦτο τῆς φιλοσοφίας τὸ γένος,
ᾧ τοὺς ἄλλους ἐξετάζων ἀεὶ τύφου καὶ πλάνου[3]
καὶ ἀλαζονείας καὶ τοῦ βαρεῖς εἶναι πρῶτον μὲν
αὐτοῖς εἶτα καὶ τοῖς συνοῦσιν ἀπήλλαττε; καὶ
γὰρ ὥσπερ ἐκ τύχης τότε φορὰν συνέβη γενέσθαι[4]
σοφιστῶν ἐν τῇ Ἑλλάδι· καὶ τούτοις οἱ νέοι
πολὺ τελοῦντες[5] ἀργύριον οἰήματος ἐπληροῦντο καὶ
δοξοσοφίας, καὶ λόγων ἐζήλουν[6] σχολὴν καὶ διατρι-

---

[1] ἢ -Turnebus, Nogarola ; καὶ -all mss.

[2] ἀνθρώπῳ -Bernardakis (cf. Stobaeus, Anth. iv, 40, 23 =
v, p. 925, 12 [Hense]) ; but cf. ἀνθρώπων in Alexander, De
Fato, p. 170, 18-19 and De An. Libri Mantissa, p. 185, 23
(Bruns).

[3] πλάνης -J, g.

[4] γενέσθαι συνέβη -J, g.

[5] πολυτελοῦντες -X[1], J[1], ε.

[6] ἐζήλουν -X, E, ε, n, B^corr. (ἐζήτουν -B[1] with λ superscript
over τ) ; ζήλου -J, g.

---

[a] Being predominantly, therefore, cognition (cf. τῷ κριτικῷ
in De An. Proc. in Timaeo 1024 B infra), the part or faculty
which exists without difference in the soul of gods also (cf.
Albinus, Epitome xxv, 7 [Louis] =p. 178, 32-33 [Hermann]).
For τὸ γόνιμον as part of the irrational soul cf. Philo Jud.,
De Agricultura 30-31 (ii, p. 101, 5-7 [Wendland]) and Quis
Rerum Div. Heres 232 (iii, p. 52, 13-15 [Wendland]) ;
Plutarch probably identified it with that fifth part which he
calls now θρεπτικόν and again φυτικόν (De E 390 F and
De Defectu Orac. 429 E ; cf. Aristotle, De Anima 415 a
23-26 and Eth. Nic. 1102 a 32-b 2).

[b] Cf. ὅτι εἰκάζει ἑαυτὸν θεῷ (Anon. in Platonis Theaetetum [Pap. Berl. 9782], col. 58, 42-43) and τῷ θεῷ συνέταξεν
ἑαυτόν (Olympiodorus, In Platonis Alcibiadem Priorem,
p. 53, 14-15 and pp. 173, 21–174, 9 [Creuzer]).

cerning than fertile,[a] that he called god,[b] as Menander said " for our intelligence is god " [c] and Heraclitus " the character of a man is his guardian spirit " [d] ; or did some truly divine and spiritual cause [e] guide Socrates to this kind of philosophy with which by continually subjecting others to examination he made them free of humbug and error and pretentiousness and of being burdensome first to themselves and then to their companions also ? [f] For at that time as if by chance there happened also to have sprung up in Greece a crop of sophists ; and the young men, paying these persons a large amount of money, were getting themselves filled full of self-conceit and sham-wisdom and were zealous for dis-

[c] Menander, frag. 749 (Koerte-Thierfelder)=frag. 762 (Kock) ; cf. frag. 64 (Koerte-Thierfelder)=frag. 70 (Kock).

[d] Heraclitus, frag. B 119 (D.-K. and Walzer)=frag. 121 (Bywater). For the implied polemic against the conventional notion of the δαίμων as the " destiny " assigned to a man cf. G. Misch, *A History of Autobiography in Antiquity* (London, 1950), pp. 94-95 ; and see Plato, *Republic* 617 E 1 and 620 D 8, where the soul of each selects its own δαίμων, and Apuleius, *De Deo Socratis* xv, 150 ("... animus humanus etiam nunc in corpore situs daemon nuncupatur ... daemon bonus id est animus virtute perfectus est ")=Xenocrates, frag, 81 (Heinze).

[e] This is surely a reference to the " divine sign," τὸ δαιμόνιον (cf. 1000 D *infra*), which in Plato's *Apology* 31 c 8–D 1 Socrates calls θεῖόν τι καὶ δαιμόνιον (cf. Proclus, *In Platonis Alcibiadem Priorem*, p. 79, 1-14 [Creuzer]=p. 35 [Westerink]) and the nature of which is discussed by Plutarch in *De Genio Socratis* 580 c—582 c and 588 c—589 F. ὑφηγήσατο could not properly be used of the sign which according to Plato ἀεὶ ἀποτρέπει ... προτρέπει δὲ οὔποτε (*Apology* 31 D 3-4, cf. *Phaedrus* 242 c 1), but Plutarch seems to have neglected this limitation (cf. *De Genio Socratis* 581 B : δαιμόνιον εἶναι τὸ κωλῦον ἢ κελεῦον ἔλεγε).

[f] Cf. Plato, *Theaetetus* 210 c 2-4 and *Sophist* 230 B 4–c 3.

21

(999) βὰς ἀπράκτους ἐν ἔρισι καὶ φιλοτιμίαις καλὸν δὲ
καὶ χρήσιμον οὐδ᾽ ὁτιοῦν. τὸν οὖν ἐλεγκτικὸν
λόγον ὥσπερ καθαρτικὸν ἔχων φάρμακον[1] ὁ Σω-
F κράτης ἀξιόπιστος ἦν ἑτέρους ἐλέγχων τῷ μηδὲν
ἀποφαίνεσθαι, καὶ μᾶλλον ἥπτετο δοκῶν ζητεῖν
κοινῇ τὴν ἀλήθειαν οὐκ αὐτὸς ἰδίᾳ δόξῃ[2] βοηθεῖν.

1000   2. Ἔπειτα τοῦ κρίνειν ὄντος ὠφελίμου τὸ γεννᾶν[3] ἐμπόδιόν ἐστι. τυφλοῦται γὰρ τὸ φιλοῦν
περὶ τὸ φιλούμενον· φιλεῖται δὲ τῶν ἰδίων οὐδὲν
οὕτως ὡς δόξα καὶ λόγος ὑπὸ τοῦ τεκόντος. ἡ
γὰρ λεγομένη τέκνων δικαιοτάτη διανομὴ[4] πρὸς
λόγους ἐστὶν ἀδικωτάτη· δεῖ γὰρ ἐκεῖ μὲν λαβεῖν[5] τὸ ἴδιον ἐνταῦθα δέ, κἂν ἀλλότριον ᾖ, τὸ
βέλτιστον. ὅθεν ὁ γεννῶν ἴδια γίγνεται φαυλότερος ἑτέρων κριτής. καὶ καθάπερ Ἠλείους τῶν
σοφῶν[6] τις ἔφη βελτίους ἂν εἶναι τῶν Ὀλυμπίων
ἀγωνοθέτας, εἰ μηδὲ εἷς Ἠλείων ἦν ἀγωνιστής,
οὕτως ὁ μέλλων ἐν λόγοις ὀρθῶς ἐπιστατήσειν

---

[1] φάρμακον ἔχων -B.   [2] δόξης -X, J¹ (? -η over erasure).
[3] γενναῖον -J, g.   [4] νομὴ -B.
[5] X, E, B, ε, n ; ἐκεῖ λαβεῖν μὲν -J, g.
[6] σοφιστῶν -J, g.

---

[a] See 1000 c-d *infra* (οὐ γὰρ σώματος ἡ Σωκράτους ἰατρεία
ψυχῆς δ᾽ ἦν . . . καθαρμός). The source is Plato's *Sophist* 230 c
3–e 3 and 231 b 3-8.   *Cf.* Philo of Larissa in Stobaeus, *Ecl.*
ii, 7, 2 (p. 40, 11-20 [Wachsmuth]) ; Albinus, *Prologue* vi
(p. 150, 15-35 [Hermann]) ; *Cebetis Tabula* xix ; Philo
Jud., *De Decalogo* 10-13 (iv, pp. 270, 23–271, 13 [Cohn]).

[b] *Theaetetus* 150 c 5-6 ; *cf. Anon. in Platonis Theaetetum*
(Pap. Berl. 9782), col. 54, 17-26.

[c] *Cf.* Plutarch, *Quomodo Adulator ab Amico Internoscatur*
72 a and *Adv. Colotem* 1117 d (*cf.* Pohlenz-Westman, *Moralia*
vi/2, p. 237, note to p. 194, 26-28) ; Plato, *Charmides* 165 b
5-8 and *Gorgias* 506 a 3-5 and *Cratylus* 384 c 1-3.

[d] So given as from Plato in *Quomodo Adulator ab Amico*

cussion of arguments and for disputations futile in
wranglings and ambitious rivalries but not for anything fair and serviceable at all. So Socrates with
his refutatory discourse like a purgative medicine [a]
by maintaining nothing [b] claimed the credence of
others when he refuted them, and he got the greater
hold on them because he seemed to be seeking the
truth along with them, not himself to be defending
an opinion of his own.[c]

2. In the second place, while the exercise of judgment is beneficial, begetting is an obstacle to it, for
what loves is blinded about the thing it loves [d] and
nothing of one's own is so beloved as is an opinion
or an argument by its parent. For the distribution
of offspring that is proverbially most just [e] is most
unjust when applied to arguments, for in the former
case one must take what is one's own but in the
latter what is best even if it be another's.[f] For this
reason the man who begets his own becomes a poorer
judge of others ; and just as one of the sages said
that Eleans would be better directors of the Olympic
games if not a single Elean were entered in the con-
test,[g] so one who is going to be an upright moderator

<hr/>

Internoscatur 48 E-F and in *De Capienda ex Inimicis Utili-
tate* 90 A and 92 E ; Plato in *Laws* 731 E has τυφλοῦται γὰρ
περὶ τὸ φιλούμενον ὁ φιλῶν.
    [e] I have not found the proverb or saying cited elsewhere.
    [f] *Cf.* Plato, *Philebus* 29 A (. . . δεῖν τἀλλότρια . . . λέγειν
. . .) and *Phaedo* 85 c 8-9 (. . . τὸν γοῦν βέλτιστον τῶν ἀνθρω-
πίνων λόγων λαβόντα . . .).
    [g] *Cf.* Herodotus, ii, 160 and Diodorus Siculus, i, 95, 2.
The impartiality with which the Eleans administered the
games was, nevertheless, held to be exemplary (*cf.* Plutarch,
Lycurgus xx, 6 [52 c-d]=*Reg. et Imp. Apophthegmata* 190
c-d and 215 E-F ; Dio Chrysostom, *Oratio* xiv =xxxi [von
Arnim], 111 ; Athenaeus, viii, 350 b-c).

(1000)
B καὶ βραβεύσειν[1] οὐ δίκαιός ἐστιν αὐτὸς φιλοστε-
φανεῖν οὐδ᾽ ἀνταγωνίζεσθαι τοῖς κρινομένοις. καὶ
γὰρ οἱ τῶν Ἑλλήνων στρατηγοὶ τὴν περὶ τῶν
ἀριστείων ψῆφον φέροντες αὑτοὺς ἀρίστους ἔκρι-
ναν ἅπαντες[2]· καὶ τῶν φιλοσόφων οὐδείς ἐστιν,
ὃς οὐ τοῦτο πέπονθε δίχα τῶν ὥσπερ Σωκράτης
ὁμολογούντων μηδὲν ἴδιον λέγειν· οὗτοι δὲ καθα-
ροὺς μόνοι καὶ ἀδεκάστους τῆς ἀληθείας παρέχου-
σιν ἑαυτοὺς δικαστάς. ὥσπερ γὰρ ὁ ἐν τοῖς ὠσὶν
ἀήρ, ἂν μὴ σταθερὸς ᾖ μηδὲ φωνῆς ἰδίας ἔρημος ἀλλ᾽
ἤχου καὶ ῥοίζου μεστός, οὐκ ἀκριβῶς ἀντιλαμβάνε-
ται τῶν φθεγγομένων, οὕτω τὸ[3] τοὺς λόγους ἐν φιλοσοφίᾳ[4] κρῖνον, ἂν ἔνδοθεν ἀντιπαταγῇ[5] ⟨τι⟩[6] καὶ
C ἀντηχῇ, δυσξύνετον ἔσται τῶν λεγομένων ἔξωθεν.
ἡ γὰρ οἰκεία δόξα καὶ σύνοικος οὐ προσδέξεται τὸ
διαφωνοῦν πρὸς αὑτήν, ὡς μαρτυρεῖ τῶν αἱρέσεων
τὸ πλῆθος,[7] ὧν, ἂν ἄριστα πράττῃ φιλοσοφία,
μίαν ἔχει[8] κατορθοῦσαν οἰομένας δὲ τὰς ἄλλας
ἁπάσας καὶ μαχομένας[9] πρὸς τὴν ἀλήθειαν.

3. Ἔτι τοίνυν, εἰ μὲν οὐδέν ἐστι καταληπτὸν
ἀνθρώπῳ καὶ γνωστόν, εἰκότως ὁ θεὸς ἀπεκώ-

[1] καὶ βραβεύσειν -omitted by J, g.
[2] ἅπαντας -J.
[3] τὸ -omitted by g.
[4] σοφίᾳ -E, B.
[5] ἀντιπαγῇ -g.
[6] Hubert ; ἔνδοθέν ⟨τι⟩ ἀντιπαταγῇ -Wyttenbach.
[7] οὐ προσδέξεται . . . τὸ πλῆθος -omitted by J.
[8] φιλοσοφία, μίαν ἔχει -X, E, B ; φιλοσοφίαν ἔχειν -J, g ;
φιλοσοφία μίαν ἔχειν -ε, n.
[9] καὶ μαχομένας -omitted by J, g.

---

[a] Cf. De Herodoti Malignitate 871 D-E and Themistocles
xvii, 2 ; Herodotus, viii, 123.
[b] Cf. Theophrastus, De Sensibus 19 (Dox. Graeci, pp. 504,

and umpire in arguments is bound not to crave the palm himself or to vie with the contenders. For even the generals of the Greeks when casting their ballot for the award of excellence all gave judgment for themselves as best[a]; and of philosophers there is none to whom this has not happened apart from those who like Socrates admit that they say nothing original, and these alone show themselves to be sound and incorruptible judges of the truth. For as the air in the ears does not accurately perceive utterances if it be not still and free from sound of its own but full of ringing and buzzing,[b] so what judges arguments in philosophy will have poor understanding of statements coming from without if they are muffled by the clatter and noise ⟨of something⟩ from within.[c] For personal opinion to which one is wedded will not accept what disagrees with her, as the multitude of systems testifies, of which philosophy, if she is faring her best, involves a single one being right and all the others guessing and being in conflict with the truth.

3. Furthermore, if nothing is apprehensible and knowable to man,[d] it was reasonable for god to have

29–505, 2) and 41 (*Dox. Graeci*, p. 511, 6-8) = Diogenes of Apollonia, frag. A 19 (ii, p. 55, 26-28 [D.-K.]).

[c] *Cf.* the explanation of Socrates' sensitivity to the " spiritual voice " given in *De Genio Socratis* 588 D-E and 589 C-D.

[d] The position of Arcesilaus (for whom see note *a* on *De Stoic. Repug.* 1036 A *infra*), ascribed by him to Socrates also (*cf. Adv. Colotem* 1121 F—1122 A ; Cicero, *Acad. Post.* i, 44-45 and *De Oratore* iii, 67 ; Lactantius, *Div. Inst.* iii, 6, 7 = p. 188, 11-14 [Brandt] ; A. Goedeckemeyer, *Die Geschichte des griechischen Skeptizismus* [Leipzig, 1905], pp. 33-34).

PLUTARCH'S MORALIA

(1000) λυσεν αὐτὸν ὑπηνέμια καὶ ψευδῆ καὶ ἀβέβαια
γεννᾶν ἐλέγχειν[1] δὲ τοὺς ἄλλους ἠνάγκαζε τοιαῦτα
δοξάζοντας. οὐ γὰρ μικρὸν ἦν ὄφελος ἀλλὰ μέγιστον ὁ τοῦ μεγίστου τῶν κακῶν, ἀπάτης καὶ
κενοφροσύνης, ἀπαλλάττων λόγος

οὐδ᾽[2] Ἀσκληπιάδαις τοῦτό γ᾽ ἔδωκε θεός.

οὐ γὰρ σώματος ἡ Σωκράτους ἰατρεία ψυχῆς δ᾽
D ἦν ὑπούλου καὶ διεφθαρμένης καθαρμός. εἰ δ᾽
ἔστιν ἐπιστήμη τοῦ ἀληθοῦς ἐν δὲ τὸ ἀληθές, οὐκ
ἔλαττον ἔχει τοῦ εὑρόντος ὁ μαθὼν παρὰ τοῦ
εὑρόντος· λαμβάνει δὲ μᾶλλον ὁ μὴ πεπεισμένος
ἔχειν, καὶ λαμβάνει τὸ βέλτιστον ἐξ ἁπάντων, ὥσπερ ὁ μὴ τεκὼν παῖδα ποιεῖται[3] τὸν ἄριστον.

4. Ὅρα δὲ μὴ τἆλλα μὲν οὐδεμιᾶς ἦν ἄξια
σπουδῆς ποιήματα καὶ μαθήματα καὶ λόγοι ῥητό-
ρων καὶ δόγματα σοφιστῶν, ἃ Σωκράτην[4] γεννᾶν
τὸ δαιμόνιον ἀπεκώλυσεν· ἦν δὲ μόνην ἡγεῖτο Σωκράτης σοφίαν, ⟨τὴν⟩[5] περὶ τὸ θεῖον καὶ νοητὸν[6]

---

[1] λέγειν -J, g.
[2] εἰ δ᾽ -Theognis (οὐ δ᾽ -Vat. gr. 915).
[3] Wyttenbach; παιδοποιεῖται -mss.
[4] J, g; Σωκράτη -X, E, B, ε, n.
[5] ⟨τὴν⟩ -added by Wilamowitz.
[6] νοητὴν -B.

---

[a] Cf. Plato, *Theaetetus* 151 E 5-6 and 160 E 6—161 A 4.
[b] Theognis, 432; cf. the use of the line (also with initial οὐδ᾽) by Dio Chrysostom, *Oratio* i, 8 (von Arnim).
[c] Cf. Plato, *Sophist* 230 c—231 B and note a on p. 22 *supra*; and with ψυχῆς ὑπούλου cf. *Gorgias* 480 B 1-2 and 524 E 5—525 A 2.
[d] Cf. Cicero, *Acad. Prior.* ii, 115 and 147 and *De Oratore* ii, 30 (" cum plus uno verum esse non possit "); Seneca, *Epistle* cii, 13; Lucian, *Hermotimus* 14 (τὸ δέ γε ἀληθὲς ... ἓν ἦν αὐτῶν ...); and Aristotle, *Anal. Prior.* 47 a 8-9.

26

prevented Socrates from begetting inane and false and baseless notions and to compel him to refute the others who were forming such opinions.[a] For the discourse that liberates from the greatest of evils, deception and vanity, was not a slight but a very great help—

This gift god didn't grant even Asclepius' sons.[b]

For the treatment given by Socrates was not of the body but was a purgation of the ulcerous and corrupted soul.[c] If, however, there is knowledge of what is true and what is true is single,[d] he who has learned it from the discoverer does not possess it less than he who discovered it [e]; but the one who acquires it is rather he who is not sure that he possesses it,[f] and he acquires what is best of all, just as he who is not a parent himself adopts the child that is best.

4. Consider too that, while the other things, poetry and mathematics and rhetorical speeches and sophistic doctrines, which the spiritual power [g] prevented Socrates from begetting, were worth no serious concern, what Socrates held to be alone wisdom, ⟨that⟩ which he called passion for the

---

[e] See, however, *De Recta Ratione Audiendi* 48 B-D and Plutarch's advice there ἀσκεῖν ἅμα τῇ μαθήσει τὴν εὕρεσιν. The proverbial alternative ἢ εὑρεῖν ἢ παρ' ἄλλου μαθεῖν (*cf.* Plato, *Laches* 186 c and 186 E—187 A; *Phaedo* 85 c 7-8 and 99 c 6-9; [*Alcibiades* i] 106 D, 109 D-E, and 110 D; [Demodocus] 381 E 6-8; Aristotle, *Topics* 178 b 34-35) was itself converted into a proof that μάθησις is ἀνάμνησις (Maximus of Tyre, *Philos.* x, v h -vi b =pp. 119, 8-120, 20 [Hobein]).

[f] Contrast the situation of those who . . . πρὶν ἢ λαβεῖν ἔχειν ὁμολογοῦντες οὐ λαμβάνουσιν (*De Recta Ratione Audiendi* 47 D).   [g] See note *e* on p. 21 *supra*.

PLUTARCH'S MORALIA

(1000) ἐρωτικὴν ὑπ' αὐτοῦ προσαγορευομένην, ταύτης οὐ
E γένεσις ἔστιν ἀνθρώποις οὐδὲ εὕρεσις ἀλλ' ἀνάμνησις. ὅθεν οὐδὲν ἐδίδασκε Σωκράτης, ἀλλ' ἐνδιδοὺς
ἀρχὰς ἀποριῶν ὥσπερ ὠδίνων τοῖς νέοις ἐπήγειρε
καὶ ἀνεκίνει καὶ συνεξῆγε τὰς ἐμφύτους νοήσεις·
καὶ τοῦτο μαιωτικὴν τέχνην ὠνόμαζεν, οὐκ ἐν-
τιθεῖσαν ἔξωθεν, ὥσπερ ἕτεροι προσεποιοῦντο, νοῦν
τοῖς ἐντυγχάνουσιν, ἀλλ' ἔχοντας οἰκεῖον ἐν
ἑαυτοῖς ἀτελῆ δὲ καὶ συγκεχυμένον καὶ δεόμενον[1]
τοῦ τρέφοντος καὶ βεβαιοῦντος[2] ἐπιδεικνύουσαν.

ZHTHMA B′

1. Τί δήποτε τὸν ἀνωτάτω θεὸν πατέρα τῶν[3]
πάντων καὶ ποιητὴν προσεῖπε;[4] πότερον ὅτι[5] τῶν
μὲν θεῶν τῶν γεννητῶν[6] καὶ τῶν ἀνθρώπων πα-

[1] καὶ δεόμενον -omitted by J, g.
[2] καὶ βεβαιοῦντος -omitted by J, g.
[3] τῶν -omitted by J, g.
[4] προσεῖπεν -J, g.
[5] πότερον ὅτι -omitted by J, g.
[6] J, g ; γενητῶν -X, E, B, ε, n.

---

[a] Cf. Plato, *Symposium* 204 B 2-5 and 210 E—212 A ; *Republic* 490 A 8-B 7 and 501 D 1-2 with 409 A (. . . ἦν μόνην δεῖ . . . σοφίαν καλεῖσθαι) and *Theaetetus* 176 C 3-D 1.
[b] Cf. Plutarch, *De Defectu Orac.* 422 B-C and the theses ascribed to him in Olympiodorus, *In Platonis Phaedonem*, pp. 155, 24–157, 12 and 212, 1-26 (Norvin). For parallels with this and the remainder of this section in Cicero, Albinus, Maximus of Tyre, and the anonymous commentator on Plato's *Theaetetus* cf. O. Luschnat, *Theologia Viatorum*, viii (1961/62), pp. 167-171 ; and for the Platonic doctrine of reminiscence cf. *Meno* 85 D—86 B, *Phaedo* 72 E—76 E and 91 E, and *Phaedrus* 249 B 5-c 4.
[c] Cf. *Theaetetus* 151 A 5-B 1 and 157 c 9-D 2. The ἔμφυτοι νοήσεις here are not " inbred " as are the Stoic ἔμφυτοι προλήψεις (see note b on *De Stoic. Repug.* 1041 E *infra*),

28

divine and intelligible,[a] is for human beings a matter not of generation or of discovery but of reminiscence.[b] For this reason Socrates was not engaged in teaching anything, but by exciting perplexities as if inducing the inception of labour-pains in young men he would arouse and quicken and help to deliver their innate conceptions [c] ; and his name for this was obstetric skill,[d] since it does not, as other men pretended to do, implant in those who come upon it intelligence from without but shows that they have it native within themselves but undeveloped and confused and in need of nurture and stabilization.

QUESTION II

1. WHYEVER did he call the supreme god father and maker of all things ? [e] Was it because he is of gods, the gods that are engendered,[f] and of men father, as

despite the Stoic terminology : *cf.* Cicero, *Tusc. Disp.* i, 57 : "... insitas ... notiones quas ἐννοίας vocant ..." ; *Anon. in Platonis Theaetetum* (Pap. Berl. 9782), col. 47, 42–45 : ... ἀναπτύσσων αὐτῶν τὰς φυσικὰς ἐννοίας ... ; and especially Albinus, *Epitome* iv, 6 (Louis) = p. 155, 17–29 (Hermann) : νόησις ... διττή ... ἡ μὲν πρὸ τοῦ ἐν σώματι γενέσθαι τὴν ψυχὴν ... γενομένης δ' αὐτῆς ἐν σώματι ἡ τότε λεγομένη νόησις νῦν ἐλέχθη φυσικὴ ἔννοια. ...

[d] *Cf. Theaetetus* 161 E 4–6, 184 A 8–B 2, 210 B 8–9 ; Olympiodorus, *In Platonis Phaedonem*, p. 159, 1-3 (Norvin) = Plutarch, *Moralia* vii, p. 33, 7-10 (Bernardakis).

[e] A paraphrase of *Timaeus* 28 C 3-4 (τὸν μὲν οὖν ποιητὴν καὶ πατέρα τοῦδε τοῦ παντός), the interpretation of which is discussed at length by Proclus (*In Platonis Timaeum* i, pp. 299, 13–319, 21 [Diehl], especially pp. 299, 21–300, 28 ; pp. 303, 24–304, 22 ; and pp. 311, 25–312, 9) and which is paraphrased somewhat differently by Plutarch in *Quaest. Conviv.* 718 A (... πατέρα καὶ ποιητὴν τοῦ τε κόσμου καὶ τῶν ἄλλων γεννητῶν ...). *Cf.* also *Timaeus* 37 C 7 and 41 A 5-7.

[f] *Cf. Timaeus* 40 D 4 (θεῶν ὁρατῶν καὶ γεννητῶν).

(1000) τήρ ἐστιν, ὡς[1] Ὅμηρος ἐπονομάζει, ποιητὴς δὲ
F τῶν ἀλόγων καὶ ἀψύχων; οὐδὲ γὰρ[2] χορίου[3] φησὶ Χρύσιππος πατέρα καλεῖσθαι τὸν παρασχόντα
τὸ σπέρμα, καίπερ ἐκ τοῦ σπέρματος γεγονότος.
ἢ[4] τῇ μεταφορᾷ χρώμενος, ὥσπερ εἴωθε, τὸν
αἴτιον πατέρα τοῦ κόσμου κέκληκεν; ὡς τῶν
ἐρωτικῶν λόγων πατέρα Φαῖδρον ἐν Συμποσίῳ
1001 προσεῖπεν, εἰσηγητὴν αὐτῶν[5] γενόμενον ἐν δὲ
τῷ ὁμωνύμῳ διαλόγῳ καλλίπαιδα[6]· πολλοὺς γὰρ
καὶ[7] καλοὺς λόγους ἐν φιλοσοφίᾳ γενέσθαι, τὴν
ἀρχὴν ἐκείνου παρασχόντος. ἢ[8] διαφέρει πατήρ
τε ποιητοῦ καὶ γεννήσεως γένεσις ;[9] ὡς γὰρ τὸ
γεγεννημένον καὶ γέγονεν,[10] οὐ μὴν ἀνάπαλιν, οὕτως ὁ γεννήσας καὶ πεποίηκεν[11]· ἐμψύχου γὰρ γένεσις[12] ἢ γέννησίς ἐστι. καὶ ποιητοῦ μέν, οἷος
οἰκοδόμος ἢ ὑφάντης ἢ λύρας δημιουργὸς ἢ ἀνδριάντος,[13] ἀπήλλακται γενόμενον τὸ ἔργον[14]· ἡ δ' ἀπὸ

[1] ὁ -ε ; ὡς -all other mss.
[2] X, E, B, n ; οὐ γὰρ -J, g ; οὐδὲ -ε.
[3] Leonicus ; χορείου -X, E, B ; χωρίου -J, g ; χωρείου -ε,
n.
[4] ἢ -Stephanus ; καὶ -E (added superscript), B ; omitted
by X, J, g, ε, n.
[5] αὐτὸν -J, g.
[6] Wyttenbach ; καλλιπῖδαν -X, J, g ; καλλιππίδαν -E, B,
ε, n.
[7] γὰρ καὶ -X, E, B, ε, n ; γὰρ ἦν καὶ -J, g.
[8] ἢ -J, g ; ἢ -X, B, n ; ἢ -E, ε.
[9] E, B, ε, n ; γένεσις -X (with ε superscript over η -X[1]) ;
γέννησις -J, g ; ποίησις -Leonicus.
[10] γέγονεν -mss. ; πεποίηται -Donato Polo.
[11] <οὐ μὴν ἀνάπαλιν> -added by Meziriac ; <οὐ μὴν ὁ
πεποιηκὼς γεγέννηκεν> -added by Pohlenz after πεποίηκεν.
[12] γένεσις -mss. ; ποίησις -Leonicus.
[13] ἀνδρίαν τε -J.   [14] τὸ γενόμενον ἔργον -J, g.

---

[a] Iliad i, 544 and often elsewhere.

Homer names him,[a] but maker of irrational beings
and of inanimate things ? [b] For not even of the
placenta, says Chrysippus,[c] though it is a product of
the seed, is he who provided the seed called father.
Or is it by his customary use of metaphor that he
has called him who is responsible for the universe
its father ? So in the *Symposium* [d] he called Phaedrus
father of the amatory discourses because he was in-
stigator of them and in the dialogue that bears his
name [e] called him blessed with fair children because
as a result of his initiative philosophy had been filled
with many fair discourses.[f] Or is there a difference
between father and maker and between birth [g] and
coming to be ? For as what has been born has *ipso
facto* come to be but not contrariwise so it is that he
who has begotten has *ipso facto* made, for birth is
the coming to be of an animate thing. Also in the
case of a maker, such as a builder is or a weaver or
one who produces a lyre or a statue, his work when
done is separated from him, whereas the principle

[b] This interpretation is mentioned and rejected by Proclus,
In Platonis Timaeum i, p. 319, 15-21 (Diehl).

[c] *S.V.F.* ii, frag. 1158.

[d] *Symposium* 177 D 4-5 (*cf.* 177 A 4).

[e] *Phaedrus* 261 A 3-4.

[f] *Cf. Phaedrus* 242 A 8-B 5 and Hermias, *In Platonis
Phaedrum*, p. 223, 18-19 (Couvreur) : . . . καλοὺς παῖδας
τίκτοντα τοὺς λόγους.

[g] For this passive meaning of γέννησις *cf. e.g.* Cornutus,
Theologia Graeca 30 (p. 58, 14 [Lang]) and Hippolytus,
Refutatio, vii, 29, 14 (p. 212, 18 [Wendland]). The erroneous
assumption that the word can have only the active meaning,
" procreation," was apparently responsible for the drastic
emendations of the passage made in the sixteenth century
and adopted by later editors. It should be noticed, moreover,
that Hubert's report of the readings of X in this passage is
erroneous.

(1001) τοῦ γεννήσαντος ἀρχὴ καὶ δύναμις ἐγκέκραται
τῷ τεκνωθέντι καὶ συνέχει τὴν φύσιν, ἀπόσπασμα
καὶ μόριον οὖσαν τοῦ τεκνώσαντος.[1] ἐπεὶ τοίνυν
B οὐ πεπλασμένοις ὁ κόσμος οὐδὲ συνηρμοσμένοις
ποιήμασιν ἔοικεν,[2] ἀλλ᾽ ἔνεστιν[3] αὐτῷ μοῖρα
πολλὴ ζωότητος[4] καὶ θειότητος, ἣν ὁ θεὸς ἐγ-
κατέσπειρεν ἀφ᾽[5] ἑαυτοῦ τῇ ὕλῃ[6] καὶ κατέμιξεν,
εἰκότως ἅμα πατήρ τε τοῦ κόσμου, ζῴου γεγονότος, καὶ ποιητὴς ἐπονομάζεται.[7]

2. Τούτων δὲ μάλιστα τῆς Πλάτωνος ἁπτο-
μένων δόξης, ἐπίστησον εἰ κἀκεῖνο[8] λεχθήσεται
πιθανῶς· ὅτι, δυεῖν[9] ὄντων ἐξ ὧν ὁ κόσμος συνέστηκε, σώματος καὶ ψυχῆς, τὸ μὲν οὐκ ἐγέννησε
θεὸς ἀλλά, τῆς ὕλης παρασχομένης, ἐμόρφωσε καὶ
συνήρμοσε, πέρασιν οἰκείοις καὶ σχήμασι δήσας
C καὶ ὁρίσας τὸ ἄπειρον· ἡ δὲ ψυχή, νοῦ μετασχοῦσα
καὶ λογισμοῦ καὶ ἁρμονίας, οὐκ ἔργον ἐστὶ τοῦ

---

[1] τοῦ τεκνώσαντος -omitted by n.
[2] ἔοικεν -omitted by B.
[3] ἔστιν -J.
[4] ζωότητος πολλὴ -B.
[5] ἐφ᾽ -J, g.
[6] τῇ ὕλῃ -X.
[7] ὀνομάζεται -ε.
[8] κἀκεῖ -J, g.
[9] X, E ; δυοῖν -J, g, B, ε, n.

---

a Cf. De Sera Numinis Vindicta 559 D (τὸ γεννηθὲν οὐχ
ὥς τι δημιούργημα πεποιημένον ἀπήλλακται τοῦ γεννήσαντος);
S.V.F. ii, p. 308, 15-18 ; [Galen], Ad Gaurum x, 4 (p. 47,
12-15 [Kalbfleisch]) ; and contra Philoponus, De Aeternitate
Mundi xiii, 9 (pp. 500, 26–501, 12 [Rabe]).

or force emanating from the parent is blended in the
progeny [a] and cohibits its nature, which is a fragment or part of the procreator.[b] Since, then, the
universe is not like products that have been moulded
or fitted together but has in it a large portion of
vitality and divinity, which god sowed from himself
in the matter [c] and mixed with it, it is reasonable
that, since the universe has come into being a living
thing, god be named at the same time father of it
and maker.

2. While this most nearly coincides with Plato's
opinion, consider whether there will be plausibility
in the following statement also : There are two constituent parts of the universe, body and soul.[d] The
former god did not beget ; but, matter having submitted itself to him, he formed and fitted it together [e] by binding and bounding the unlimited with
suitable limits and shapes.[f] The soul, however, when
it has partaken of intelligence and reason and con-

[b] Cf. S.V.F. i, frag. 128 including Plutarch, De Cohibenda
Ira 462 F.

[c] Cf. Quaest. Conviv. 718 A (. . . ἄλλη δὲ δυνάμει τοῦ θεοῦ
τῇ ὕλῃ γόνιμον ἀρχὴν . . . ἐντεκόντος) and Plato, Timaeus
41 c 7–D 1, where the figure of " sowing " is used but not in
connexion with the vitalization of the universe, for which cf.
Timaeus 36 D 8–E 5.

[d] Cf. Albinus, Epitome xiii, 1 (p. 73, 4-5 [Louis]=p. 168,
6-7 [Hermann]) ; Plato, Timaeus 34 A 8–B 4 and 36 D 8–
E 1.

[e] Cf. De An. Proc. in Timaeo 1014 B-C (τὴν δ' οὐσίαν καὶ
ὕλην . . . ἐμπαρασχεῖν. . . . ἔταξε καὶ διεκόσμησε καὶ συνήρμοσε
. . .) and De Iside 372 F (. . . χώρα καὶ ὕλη . . . παρέχουσα
γεννᾶν ἐξ ἑαυτῆς ἐκείνῳ . . .).

[f] Cf. Quaest. Conviv. 719 C-E and De An. Proc. in Timaeo
1023 C. For the figure of the " bond " cf. Timaeus 31 c 1—
32 c 4 and for the " binding " of the unlimited by limit
Philebus 27 D 9.

(1001) θεοῦ μόνον ἀλλὰ καὶ μέρος, οὐδὲ ὑπ' αὐτοῦ ἀλλὰ
καὶ[1] ἀπ' αὐτοῦ καὶ ἐξ αὐτοῦ γέγονεν.

ΖΗΤΗΜΑ Γ'[2]

1. Ἐν τῇ Πολιτείᾳ [γοῦν][3] τοῦ[3] παντὸς ὥσπερ
μιᾶς γραμμῆς τετμημένης εἰς[4] ἄνισα τμήματα,
πάλιν τέμνων ἑκάτερον τμῆμα εἰς δύο ἀνὰ τὸν
αὐτὸν λόγον, τό τε τοῦ ὁρωμένου γένους[5] καὶ τὸ
τοῦ νοουμένου, τέσσαρα τὰ[6] πάντα ποιήσας τοῦ
μὲν νοητοῦ πρῶτον ἀποφαίνει τὸ περὶ τὰ πρῶτα
εἴδη, δεύτερον τὸ μαθηματικόν,[7] τοῦ δ' αἰσθητοῦ
πρῶτον μὲν τὰ στερέμνια σώματα, δεύτερον δὲ
τὰς εἰκόνας καὶ τὰ εἴδωλα τούτων· καὶ κριτήριον[8]
D ἑκάστῳ τῶν τεσσάρων ἀποδίδωσιν ἴδιον, νοῦν μὲν
τῷ πρώτῳ διάνοιαν δὲ τῷ μαθηματικῷ[9] τοῖς δ'
αἰσθητοῖς πίστιν, εἰκασίαν δὲ τοῖς[10] περὶ τὰ εἴδωλα
καὶ τὰς εἰκόνας. τί οὖν διανοηθεὶς εἰς[11] ἄνισα τμή-

---

[1] καὶ -omitted by J, g ; ἀλλὰ καὶ -all other mss.
[2] New question distinguished by Wyttenbach.
[3] [γοῦν] -deleted by Wyttenbach ; γοῦν τοῦ -X, E, B, ε,
n ; γοῦν -J, g.   [4] εἰς -omitted by J, g.
[5] γένους -X, E[1], ε, n, Plato (*Republic* 509 D 8) ; γένος -J,
g, B, E[2] (ος superscript over ους).
[6] Hubert (τέτταρα [τὰ] -Wyttenbach) ; περὶ τὰ -J ; παρὰ τὰ
-all other mss. ; μέρη δ' (*i.e.* μέρη τέσσαρα) -Bernardakis, Papabasileios (*Athena*, x [1898], p. 225).   [7] μαθητικόν -J[1], ε.
[8] κριτηρίῳ -J, g.   [9] μαθητικῷ -J, g[1].
[10] δὲ τῆς -J, g, n.   [11] εἰς -omitted by J, g.

---

[a] Cf. 1003 A *infra* and *De An. Proc. in Timaeo* 1014 E and
1016 B (quoting *Timaeus* 36 E 6—37 A 1). ἁρμονία, which I
regularly translate " concord," means not " harmony " in
the modern sense of notes played or sung together as
" chords " but generally a " fitting together " and in music
such a fitting together of sequential sounds to produce a tune
or a " scale " (*e.g. De An. Proc. in Timaeo* 1021 B *infra*) ; and

34

cord,[a] is not merely a work but also a part of god and has come to be not by his agency but both from him as source and out of his substance.[b]

QUESTION III

1. In the *Republic* [c] he likens the sum of things to a single line that has been divided into unequal segments, again divides into two in the same ratio each of the two segments, that of the visible class and that of the conceptual, and, having made four in all, declares first of the intelligible segment that of the primary ideas, second the mathematical, and first of the perceptible segment the solid bodies and second the semblances and images of these. Also to each of the four he assigns its own peculiar criterion : intelligence to the first and thought to the mathematical segment and to the perceptibles belief and conjecture to matters of images and semblances. What, then, did he have in mind when he divided the sum of things into unequal [d] seg-

of harmony in this sense the theory is ἡ ἁρμονική (*e.g.* 1001 F *infra*).

[b] *Cf. De Sera Numinis Vindicta* 559 D (... ἐξ αὐτοῦ γάρ, οὐχ ὑπ᾽ αὐτοῦ, γέγονεν ὥστ᾽ ἔχει τι καὶ φέρεται τῶν ἐκείνου μέρος ἐν ἑαυτῷ ...) and see Jones, *Platonism of Plutarch*, p. 10, n. 15 and p. 105 ; H. Dörrie, *Museum Helveticum*, xxvi (1969), p. 222 and *Philomathes : Studies ... in Memory of Philip Merlan* (The Hague, 1971), pp. 40-41.

[c] *Republic* 509 D 6—511 E 5.

[d] Even in antiquity some, apparently reading ἀν᾽ ἴσα or ἴσα in *Republic* 509 D 6 (*cf.* ἄν, ἴσα -cod. F), tried to explain why Plato had divided the line into *equal* segments (Iamblichus, *De Comm. Math. Scientia*, p. 36, 15-23 [Pseudo-Archytas, frag. 3, Nolle] and p. 38, 15-28 [Festa] ; *Scholia in Platonis Rem Publicam* 509 D [vi, p. 350, 9-16, Hermann]) ; but contrast Proclus, *In Platonis Rem Publicam* i, p. 288, 18-20 and 26-27 (Kroll).

(1001) ματα[1] τὸ πᾶν ἔτεμε;[2] καὶ πότερον τῶν τμημά
των, τὸ νοητὸν ἢ τὸ αἰσθητόν, μεῖζόν ἐστιν; αὐτὸς
γὰρ οὐ δεδήλωκε.

Δόξει δ' αὐτόθεν μὲν εἶναι μεῖζον τὸ αἰσθητόν·
ἡ γὰρ ἀμέριστος οὐσία καὶ κατὰ ταὐτὸν ὡσαύτως
ἔχουσα τῶν νοητῶν ἐστιν εἰς βραχὺ συνηγμένη[3]
καὶ καθαρόν, ἡ δὲ σκεδαστὴ περὶ τὰ σώματα καὶ
περιπλανὴς τὸ αἰσθητὸν παρέσχεν. ἔτι τὸ μὲν ἀσώ
ματον πέρατος οἰκεῖον, τὸ δὲ σῶμα τῇ μὲν ὕλῃ[4]
ἄπειρον καὶ ἀόριστον αἰσθητὸν δὲ γιγνόμενον[5] ὅταν
Ε ὁρισθῇ μετοχῇ τοῦ νοητοῦ. ἔτι, καθάπερ αὐτῶν
τῶν αἰσθητῶν ἕκαστον εἰκόνας ἔχει πλείους καὶ
σκιὰς καὶ εἴδωλα καὶ ὅλως ἀφ' ἑνὸς παραδείγμα
τος πάμπολλα μιμήματα γίγνεσθαι καὶ φύσει καὶ
τέχνῃ δυνατόν ἐστιν, οὕτως ἀνάγκη τὰ ἐνταῦθα
τῶν ἐκεῖ πλήθει διαφέρειν κατὰ τὸν Πλάτωνα
παραδείγματα καὶ ἰδέας τὰ νοητὰ[6] τῶν αἰσθητῶν
ὥσπερ εἰκόνων ἢ ἐμφάσεων ὑποτιθέμενον.[7] ἔτι[8]
τῶν εἰδῶν ἡ νόησις ⟨· νόησιν δ'⟩[9] ἐξ ἀφαιρέσεως

---

[1] E, B ; τὰ τμήματα -X, J, g, ε, n.
[2] E, B ; ἔτεμνε -X, J, G, ε, n.
[3] συνηγμένη -ε.
[4] τῇ ὕλῃ μὲν -Benseler (but cf. Bolkestein, Adversaria, pp. 98-99 and p. 105).
[5] γίγνεται μόνον -Bernardakis (but cf. De Exilio 599 B-C and Wyttenbach, Animadversiones on 40 D).
[6] Stephanus ; νοήματα -MSS.
[7] ὑποτιθεμένων -J, g.   [8] ἔτι -Leonicus ; ἐν -MSS.
[9] H. C. ; ἡ νόησις ἐξ -MSS. ; τὴν νόησιν ἐξ -Leonicus ; νόησιν ἐξ -Stephanus.

---

[a] Cf. the argument of Pseudo-Brontinus, μεῖζον . . . τὸ διανοατὸν τῷ νοατῷ, quoted and commented upon by Iamblichus, De Comm. Math. Scientia, pp. 34, 20–35, 26 (Festa).

[b] This terminology comes from Timaeus 35 A 1-6 and 37 A 5-6. Cf. De An. Proc. in Timaeo 1012 B, 1014 D, and 1022

ments ? And which of the segments is larger, the
intelligible or the perceptible ? For he has not made
it clear himself.

On the face of it the perceptible segment would
seem to be larger,[a] for the indivisible and invariably
identical being of the intelligibles is narrowly and
purely concentrated but the perceptible segment was
provided by the dispersed and erratic being of
bodies.[b] Moreover, incorporeality is proper to
limit,[c] whereas body, while in matter it is unlimited
and indefinite, becomes perceptible whenever it is
bounded by virtue of participation in the intelligible.[d]
Moreover, just as each of the perceptibles themselves has a multiplicity of semblances and shadows
and images and as generally both in nature and in
art it is possible for numerous copies to come from a
single pattern, so the things of this world must surpass in number the things of that world according to
Plato's supposition that the intelligibles are patterns,
that is ideas, of which the perceptibles are as semblances or reflections.[e] Moreover, the ideas are the
objects of intellection [f] ⟨; and intellection⟩ he in-

e-f ; *De Defectu Orac.* 428 b and 430 f ; and further with ἡ
σκεδαστὴ . . . καὶ περιπλανής *De An. Proc. in Timaeo* 1023 c
and 1024 a, *Quaest. Conviv.* 718 d and 719 e.

 c *Cf. De Comm. Not.* 1080 e (τὸ δὲ πέρας σῶμα οὐκ ἔστιν).

 d See 1001 b *supra* and note *f* there but especially *De An.
Proc. in Timaeo* 1013 c (τῆς μὲν ὕλης τὸ μετοχῇ . . . τοῦ
νοητοῦ μορφωθὲν εὐθὺς ἁπτὸν καὶ ὁρατόν ἐστιν).

 e *Cf.* Areius Didymus, *Epitomes Frag. Phys.* 1 (*Dox.
Graeci*, p. 477 a 5-16 and b 4-12) = Eusebius, *Praep. Evang.*
xi, 23, 3-4 and Albinus, *Epitome* xii, 1 (Louis) = pp. 166, 37–
167, 5 (Hermann).

 f *Republic* 511 d 8 ; *cf. Timaeus* 52 a 1-4 and 28 a 1-2 with
Philebus 62 a 2-5, and *n.b. Republic* 534 a, where νόησις
refers to the two upper segments of the line together.

37

(1001) καὶ περικοπῆς¹ σώματος ἐπάγει, τῇ τῶν μαθημά-
των² τάξει καταβιβάζων ἀπὸ τῆς ἀριθμητικῆς ἐπὶ
γεωμετρίαν, εἶτα μετὰ ταύτην ἐπ᾽ ἀστρολογίαν,
F ἐπὶ πάσαις δὲ τὴν ἁρμονικὴν τιθείς· γίγνεται γὰρ
τὰ μὲν³ γεωμετρούμενα, τοῦ ποσοῦ μέγεθος προσ-
λαβόντος⁴· τὰ δὲ στερεά, τοῦ μεγέθους βάθος·
τὰ δ᾽ ἀστρολογούμενα, τοῦ στερεοῦ κίνησιν· τὰ
δὲ ἁρμονικά, τῷ κινουμένῳ σώματι φωνῆς προσ-
γενομένης. ὅθεν ἀφαιροῦντες φωνὴν μὲν τῶν κινουμένων κίνησιν δὲ τῶν στερεῶν βάθος δὲ τῶν
1002 ἐπιπέδων, μέγεθος δὲ τῶν ποσῶν, ἐν αὐταῖς γε-
νησόμεθα ταῖς νοηταῖς ἰδέαις, οὐδεμίαν διαφορὰν
ἐχούσαις⁵ πρὸς ἀλλήλας κατὰ τὸ ἓν καὶ μονάδα⁶
νοουμέν⟨αις⟩.⁷ οὐ γὰρ ποιεῖ μονὰς ἀριθμόν, ἂν

¹ περισκοπῆς -J, g.   ² Leonicus ; μαθητῶν -mss.
³ γίγνεται μὲν γὰρ τὰ γεωμετρούμενα -J, g.
⁴ προλαβόντος -J¹.   ⁵ E, B, ε ; ἐχούσας -X, J, g, n.
⁶ μονάδα -H. C. ; μόνον -mss. ; [καὶ] μόνον -Bury.
⁷ Pohlenz ; νοοῦμεν -X, E, B, ε, n ; omitted by J, g ;
νοούμενον -Dübner.

ᵃ The course of studies in *Republic* 525 b 3—531 d 6 is
meant. According to Plato (*Republic* 531 d 7—535 a 2) the
whole of this is a progressive course of training leading up to
dialectic, the method which alone reveals the ideas ; but
καταβιβάζων here implies that it is instead a graduated descent
and departure from the ideas, and hence it is inferred that
graduated abstraction in the reverse order (*cf.* ὅθεν ἀφαιροῦντες . . . [1001 F *infra*]) will bring one to the ideas themselves.

ᵇ Because of τὰ δὲ στερεά *infra* and *Republic* 528 a 6–e 2
it has been thought that stereometry must have been mentioned after γεωμετρίαν, but the latter by itself could have
been meant to include both plane and solid geometry (*cf.*
Non Posse Suaviter Vivi 1093 d and *Moralia* vii, p. 113,
11-14 [Bernardakis] =vii, p. 90, 11-14 [Sandbach] ; Proclus,
In Primum Euclidis El. Lib., p. 39, 8-10 [Friedlein]).

ᶜ With this use of μέγεθος for extension in a single plane

38

troduces as a result of abstraction or lopping away
of body when in the order of studies he leads down [a]
from arithmetic to geometry and then after this [b] to
astronomy and crowns all with the theory of harmony, for the objects of geometry are the result
when quantity has taken on extension,[c] the solids
when extension has taken on depth, the objects of
astronomy when solid body has taken on motion,
and the objects of harmonics when sound has been
added to the body in motion. Hence by abstracting
sound from the things in motion and motion from the
solids and depth from the planes and extension from
the quantities we shall arrive at the intelligible ideas
themselves,[d] which do not differ from one another
at all when conceived in respect of their singularity
and unity.[e] For unity does not produce number un-

cf. Sextus, *Adv. Math.* vii, 73 (=Gorgias, frag. B 3 [D.-K.]),
where σῶμα, characterized as having three dimensions, is distinguished from μέγεθος ; Aristotle, *Metaphysics* 1053 a 25-
26, where the particular examples of μέγεθος are only μῆκος
and πλάτος ; and the definition of line as μέγεθος ἐφ' ἓν
διαστατόν (Proclus, *In Primum Euclidis El. Lib.*, p. 97, 7-8
[Friedlein]).

[d] *Cf.* Albinus (*Epitome* x, 5 [Louis] =p. 165, 14-17 [Her-
mann]) for god like the point conceived κατ' ἀφαίρεσιν (also
Clement, *Stromata* v, xi, 71, 2-3 ; vi, xi, 90, 4). Plato did
not say or imply that the ideas can be reached by such a procedure, though Aristotle contended that those who posited
the ideas did so by an invalid extension of the kind of abstraction legitimately used in mathematics (*Physics* 193 b 35—
194 a 7 ; *cf.* Cherniss, *Aristotle's Criticism of Plato . . .*, pp.
203-204).

[e] *Cf.* [Plutarch], *De Placitis* 877 B =*Dox. Graeci*, p. 282,
17-25 (ὁ γὰρ νοῦς κατὰ μονάδα θεωρεῖται . . . τὰ γὰρ εἴδη ταῦτα
πάντα καὶ γένη κατὰ μονάδας εἰσί); Sextus, *Adv. Math.* x, 258
(ἑκάστη ἰδέα κατ' ἰδίαν μὲν λαμβανομένη ἓν εἶναι λέγεται . . .) ;
and Theon Smyrnaeus, p. 100, 4-8 (Hiller).

(1002) μὴ τῆς ἀπείρου δυάδος ἅψηται· ποιήσασα δὲ
οὕτως ἀριθμόν, εἰς στιγμὰς εἶτα γραμμὰς ἐκ δὲ[11]
τούτων εἰς ἐπιφανείας καὶ βάθη καὶ σώματα[2]
πρόεισι καὶ σωμάτων ποιότητας ἐν πάθεσι γιγνομένων. ἔτι τῶν μὲν νοητῶν[3] ἓν κριτήριον ὁ νοῦς·
καὶ γὰρ ἡ διάνοια νοῦς ἐστιν ἐν τοῖς μαθηματικοῖς
ὥσπερ ἐν[4] κατόπτροις ἐμφαινομένων[5] τῶν νοητῶν.
ἐπὶ δὲ τὴν τῶν σωμάτων γνῶσιν ὑπὸ πλήθους
πέντε δυνάμεις καὶ διαφορὰς αἰσθητηρίων ἡ φύσις
ἔδωκεν ἡμῖν· καὶ οὐ πάντα φωρᾶται ταύταις ἀλλ'
B ἐκφεύγει πολλὰ διὰ[6] μικρότητα[7] τὴν αἴσθησιν. ἔτι,
ὥσπερ[8] ἡμῶν ἑκάστου συνεστῶτος ἔκ τε τῆς[9] ψυχῆς καὶ τοῦ σώματος μικρόν ἐστι τὸ ἡγεμονικὸν
καὶ νοερὸν ἐν πολλῷ τῷ τῆς σαρκὸς ὄγκῳ κεκρυμ-

---

[1] δὲ -omitted by B ; three points superscript over δὲ -E.
[2] σώματος -J.   [3] τὸ μὲν νοητὸν -g[1].
[4] ἐν -omitted by B.
[5] B, E[2] (ἐμ superscript) ; ἐκφαινομένων -all other mss.
[6] εἰς -J ; διὰ -all other mss. (g over erasure).
[7] μακρότητα -J, B ; μικρότητα -all other mss. (μι over erasure -g).
[8] ἔτι, ὥσπερ -Wyttenbach ; ἐν ᾧ καίπερ -mss. ; ἐν ᾧ καὶ ὥσπερ -Nogarola.   [9] τῆς -omitted by B.

---

[a] Cf. De An. Proc. in Timaeo 1012 e and De Defectu Orac. 428 e—429 b ; Aristotle, Metaphysics 1081 a 14-15, 1088 b 28-35, and 1091 a 4-5. For the further derivation of points, lines, etc. which follows cf. Theophrastus, Metaphysics 6 a 23-b 5 ; Alexander Polyhistor in Diogenes Laertius, viii, 25 ; Sextus, Adv. Math. x, 276-283 and Pyrrh. Hyp. iii, 153-154.

[b] Cf. ποιότητα καὶ χρῶσιν . . . ἐν πεντάδι (Nicomachus in Iamblichus, Theolog. Arith., p. 74, 11-12 [De Falco]) and πε-ποιωμένῳ δὲ σώματι πεμπτάς (Proclus, In Platonis Timaeum iii, p. 382, 15 and ii, p. 270, 8 [Diehl]).

[c] Cf. Quaest. Conviv. 718 e (πᾶσι μὲν οὖν τοῖς καλουμένοις μαθήμασιν ὥσπερ . . . κατόπτροις ἐμφαίνεται τῆς τῶν νοητῶν ἀληθείας ἴχνη καὶ εἴδωλα) ; Syrianus, Metaph., p. 82, 22-25 ;

less it comes into contact with the unlimited dyad ; and, when it has thus produced number,[a] it passes on into points and then lines and from these into surfaces and depths and bodies and qualities [b] of bodies in process of modification. Moreover, of the intelligibles there is a single criterion, the intelligence, for thought too is intelligence concerning the intelligibles that are reflected in the mathematical objects as in mirrors.[c] For the cognition of bodies, however, nature, impelled by their multiplicity, gave us five faculties and distinctive sense-organs ; and these do not detect all bodies, but many by reason of their minuteness elude sense-perception. Moreover, just as in each of us, whose constituent parts are soul and body, the ruling and intellectual faculty is small, buried in the mass of flesh which is large,[d]

Proclus, *In Primum Euclidis El. Lib.*, p. 4, 18-24 and p. 11, 5-7 (Friedlein) ; *Anon. Proleg. to Platonic Philosophy* viii, 11-12 (p. 37 [Westerink]=*Platonis Dialogi* vi, p. 214, 1 [Hermann]) ; *Scholia in Rem Publicam* 509 D (vi, p. 350, 30 and p. 351, 2 [Hermann]). This notion that the objects of διάνοια are images of the ideas in the highest segment of the line still persists (*cf.* A. Wedberg, *Plato's Philosophy of Mathematics* [Stockholm, 1955], p. 105), although Plato never says this but asserts rather that, while διάνοια employs as likenesses sensible figures in the third segment, its objects in this procedure are the idea of the square or the idea of the diagonal, which are νοητὰ μετὰ ἀρχῆς (*Republic* 510 D 5— 511 A 1 and 511 D 2 ; *cf.* P. Shorey, *Plato's Republic* ii [*L.C.L.*], p. 116, note *b* and p. 206, note *a*).

[d] The souls that rise from the body after death, ἀχλύν τινα καὶ ζόφον ὥσπερ πηλὸν ἀποσειομένους (*De Genio Socratis* 591 F), are said to be τὸν ὄγκον εὐσταλεῖς (*De Sera Numinis Vindicta* 564 A, *cf. Non Posse Suaviter Vivi* 1105 D). *Cf.* . . . εἰς τὸν ὄγκον τὸν παχὺν τοῦτον εἰσκρίνονται (Proclus, *In Platonis Timaeum*, iii, p. 297, 23-24 [Diehl]) ; ὁ δῆμος πλέον ἢ ὁ ἄρχων, καὶ τὸ σῶμα πλέον ἢ ἡ ψυχή (Maximus of Tyre, *Philos.* vii, ii d =p. 77, 10-11 [Hobein]) ; and what Plutarch

(1002) μένον, οὕτως εἰκὸς ἔχειν ἐν τῷ παντὶ τὸ νοητὸν
πρὸς τὸ αἰσθητόν.[1] καὶ γὰρ ἄρχει τὰ νοητὰ τῶν
σωματικῶν, ἀρχῆς δὲ πάσης πλέον τὸ ἐξ αὐτῆς καὶ
μεῖζον.

2. Πρὸς δὲ τοὐναντίον εἴποι τις ἂν πρῶτον ὅτι[2]
συγκρίνοντες ⟨τὰ⟩[3] αἰσθητὰ τοῖς νοητοῖς τρόπον
τινὰ τὰ θνητὰ τοῖς θείοις[4] ἐξισοῦμεν· ὁ γὰρ θεὸς
ἐν τοῖς νοητοῖς. ἔπειτα πανταχοῦ δήπου τὸ
περιεχόμενον ἔλαττόν ἐστι τοῦ περιέχοντος, ἡ δὲ
C τοῦ παντὸς φύσις τῷ νοητῷ περιέχει τὸ αἰσθητόν·
ὁ γὰρ θεὸς τὴν ψυχὴν εἰς τὸ μέσον θεὶς διὰ παντός
τ᾽ ἔτεινε καὶ ἔτι ἔξωθεν[5] τὰ σώματα[6] αὐτῇ περιε-
κάλυψεν, ἔστι δ᾽ ἀόρατος ἡ ψυχὴ καὶ πάσαις ταῖς
αἰσθήσεσιν ἀναίσθητος ὡς ἐν τοῖς Νόμοις εἴρηται.
διὸ καὶ φθαρτὸς ἡμῶν εἷς ἕκαστός ἐστιν, ὁ δὲ

---

[1] παντὶ τὸ αἰσθητὸν καὶ τὸ νοητόν -J, g.
[2] ὅτι -omitted by J, g.   [3] ⟨τὰ⟩ -added by Stephanus.
[4] θείοις -Stephanus ; θεοῖς -X, J, g, ε, n ; νοητοῖς -E, B.
[5] ἔτι ἔξωθεν -Hubert (cf. Timaeus 34 B 4) ; ἐπέξωθεν -X,
E, B, ε, n ; ἔξωθεν -J, g.
[6] τὸ σῶμα -Timaeus 34 B 4.

---

says of the ἡγεμονικόν according to the Stoics (De Comm.
Not. 1084 B).

[a] For the argument from microcosm to macrocosm cf.
Plato, Philebus 29 A—30 A.

[b] Cf. Sextus, Adv. Math. x, 251-253.

[c] See 1003 E infra (τῆς μὲν ἀρχῆς ἐγγυτέρω τὸ ἔλαττον) and
cf. De Comm. Not. 1077 A-B and Quaest. Conviv. 636 A-B ;
Aristotle, De Gen. Animal. 788 a 13-17 ; De Caelo 271 b 11-
13 ; De Motu Animal. 701 b 24-28.

[d] See De An. Proc. in Timaeo 1016 B, where god is identified with τῶν νοητῶν . . . τοῦ ἀρίστου of Timaeus 37 A 1 (cf.,
however, for the meaning of νοητῶν in this phrase of Plato's
Cherniss, Aristotle's Criticism of Plato . . ., p. 605 and
Gnomon, xxv [1953], p. 372, n. 1).

such in the sum of things is likely to be the relation
of the intelligible to the perceptible.[a] For in fact
the intelligibles are principles of the corporeals,[b]
and every principle is exceeded in number and size
by that which comes from it.[c]

2. To the contrary, however, one might say first
that in comparing ⟨the⟩ perceptibles with the intelligibles we are in a way putting mortal things on
a level with the divine, for god is among the intelligible entities.[d] In the second place, what is encompassed is in all cases surely less than that which
encompasses ; and the nature of the sum of things
encompasses the perceptible with the intelligible,[e]
for god, having placed the soul in the middle,
stretched it out through everything and further enveloped the bodies with it on the outside,[f] and the
soul is invisible and imperceptible to all the senses,
as has been said in the *Laws*.[g] That is also why
each one of us is subject to destruction but the

[e] Cf. Proclus, *In Platonis Rem Publicam* i, p. 289, 6-18
(Kroll).

[f] *Timaeus* 34 B 3-4 (where διὰ παντός means through all
the body of the universe, referred to by αὐτοῦ which Plutarch
omits after εἰς τὸ μέσον, as he changes τὸ σῶμα in B 4 to τὰ
σώματα [cf. 34 B 2]) ; cf. *De An. Proc. in Timaeo* 1023 A
infra.

[g] *Laws* 898 E 1-2, where ἀναίσθητον πάσαις τοῦ σώματος
αἰσθήσεσι is followed by νοητὸν δ' εἶναι (for the meaning of
which cf. *Gnomon*, xxv [1953], p. 372, n. 1). The possible
influence of this passage upon Plutarch's treatment of the
soul as " intelligible " and upon the doxographical statements
that Plato held the soul to be οὐσία νοητή ([Plutarch], *De
Placitis* 898 c = *Dox. Graeci*, p. 386 A 16 ; cf. p. 386 t 5 [Theo-
doretus and Nemesius]) is overlooked by H. Dörrie, who
asserts " Niemals bezeichnet Platon die Seele als νοητόν . . ."
(*Porphyrios*' " *Symmikta Zetemata* " [München, 1959], p.
187).

43

(1002) κόσμος οὐ φθαρησόμενος· ἡμῶν μὲν γὰρ ἑκάστου[1]
τὴν ζωτικὴν δύναμιν ἐντὸς περιέχει τὸ θνητοει-
δὲς καὶ διαλυτόν, ἐν δὲ τῷ κόσμῳ τοὐναντίον ὑπὸ
τῆς κυριωτέρας ἀρχῆς[2] καὶ κατὰ ταὐτὰ ὡσαύτως
ἐχούσης ἀεὶ σῴζεται τὸ σωματικὸν ἐν μέσῳ περιεχόμενον. καὶ μὴν ἀμερές γε[3] λέγεται καὶ ἀμέριστον τὸ μὲν σῶμα μικρότητι, τὸ δ' ἀσώματον
D καὶ νοητὸν ὡς ἁπλοῦν καὶ εἰλικρινὲς καὶ καθαρὸν
ἁπάσης ἑτερότητος[4] καὶ διαφορᾶς. καὶ ἄλλως εὐ-
ηθές ἐστι τοῖς σωματικοῖς τεκμαίρεσθαι περὶ τῶν
ἀσωμάτων. τὸ γοῦν νῦν ἀμερὲς μὲν καλεῖται
καὶ ἀμέριστον ἅμα δὲ πανταχοῦ ἐνέστηκε καὶ
οὐδὲν αὐτοῦ[5] τῆς οἰκουμένης μέρος[6] ἔρημόν ἐστιν,
ἀλλὰ καὶ πάθη πάντα καὶ πράξεις φθοραί τε
πᾶσαι καὶ γενέσεις αἱ[7] ὑπὸ τὸν κόσμον[8] ἐν τῷ
νῦν περιέχονται. κριτήριον δὲ τοῦ νοητοῦ[9] μόνον
ἐστὶν ὁ νοῦς, ὡς φωτὸς ὄψις, διὰ ἁπλότητα καὶ

----

[1] ἑκάστου -Stephanus ; ἕκαστος -mss. ; ἑκάστῳ -Nogarola ;
ἑκάστοις -Bernardakis.
[2] ἀρχῆς -omitted by J, g.
[3] τε -J ; omitted by g.
[4] ἑτερότητος -Apelt (*Philologus*, lxii [1903], p. 287) ; στε-
ρεότητος -mss.
[5] αὐτοῦ -X, E, B, ε, n ; τι -J, g.
[6] μέρος -omitted by g.
[7] αἱ -E, B ; καὶ -X, J, g, ε, n.
[8] τοῦ κόσμου -J, g² (τ   κοσμ   -g¹).
[9] τοῦ νοητοῦ -with these words begin a, A, β, Bonon.
C 3635, Voss. 16, Escorial T-11-5 (see *app. crit.* 999 c *supra*
[title]) ; also the first words on folio 606 recto of E, where
above them stands erased the title : ΛΘ πλατωνικὰ ζητήματα ὧν οὐχ εὑρέθη ἡ ἀρχή.

----

[a] This reason why the universe will never be destroyed is
not that which is given in the *Timaeus* (41 A 7–B 6 ; *cf.* Plutarch, *Quaest. Conviv.* 720 B [ὁ θεὸς . . . ἐποίησε καὶ ποιεῖ καὶ

universe is not going to be destroyed, for in our case what is subject to mortality and dissolution encompasses the vital force that each one has within, whereas in the universe on the contrary what is corporeal is for ever preserved by the more sovereign and invariably identical principle, in the middle of which it is encompassed.[a] Moreover, body is said to be without parts and indivisible because of minuteness but the incorporeal and intelligible because of its simplicity and purity and freedom from all diversity and difference.[b] And, besides, it is silly to judge of things incorporeal from things corporeal. At any rate, the now, while it is said to be without parts and indivisible,[c] is present everywhere simultaneously,[d] and no part of the whole world is devoid of it ; but all incidents and actions, all cessations and commencements of being under heaven [e] are encompassed in the now. It is because of the simplicity and similarity of the intelligible, however, that its sole criterion is the intelligence as

φυλάττει διὰ παντὸς . . . τὸν κόσμον]) but may be an inference drawn from *Timaeus* 36 E 2-5.

[b] This is meant as a reply to the argument in 1001 D *supra* (ἡ γὰρ ἀμέριστος οὐσία . . . εἰς βραχὺ συνηγμένη καὶ καθαρόν . . .) ; *cf. De An. Proc. in Timaeo* 1022 E (chap. 21 *init.*). For the combination ἑτερότης καὶ διαφορά *cf. De Virtute Morali* 446 E (cited by Apelt) ; *De An. Proc. in Timaeo* 1015 E-F, 1026 A and c ; *De Comm. Not.* 1083 E ; *Numa* xvii, 2 (71 c).

[c] *Cf.* Aristotle, *Physics* 233 b 33—234 a 24 and Plutarch's criticism of the Stoics, *De Comm. Not.* 1081 c.

[d] *Cf.* Plato, *Parmenides* 131 B 3-5 (. . . ἡμέρα μία καὶ ἡ αὐτὴ οὖσα πολλαχοῦ ἅμα ἐστὶ . . .) ; Aristotle, *Physics* 218 b 13 and 220 b 5-6 (ὁ χρόνος . . . καὶ ὁ αὐτὸς δὲ πανταχοῦ ἅμα).

[e] *Cf.* ὑπὸ τὸν οὐρανόν in *Timaeus* 23 c 7–D 1 ; and for κόσμος in this sense *cf.* Isocrates, *Panegyricus* 179 ; Polybius, xii, 25, 7 (Timaeus) ; Sextus, *Adv. Math.* x, 174-175.

PLUTARCH'S MORALIA

(1002) ὁμοιότητα· τὰ δὲ σώματα, πολλὰς διαφορὰς ἔ-
χοντα καὶ ἀνομοιότητας, ἄλλα ἄλλοις[1] κριτηρίοις
E ὥσπερ ὀργάνοις ἁλίσκεσθαι πέφυκεν. ἀλλὰ μὴν
οὐδὲ τῆς[2] ἐν ἡμῖν νοητῆς καὶ νοερᾶς δυνάμεως
καταφρονοῦσιν ὀρθῶς· πολλὴ γὰρ οὖσα καὶ μεγάλη
περίεστι παντὸς τοῦ αἰσθητοῦ καὶ μέχρι τῶν θείων
ἐξικνεῖται. τὸ δὲ μέγιστον αὐτὸς ἐν Συμποσίῳ
διδάσκων πῶς δεῖ[3] τοῖς ἐρωτικοῖς χρῆσθαι, μετ-
άγοντα τὴν ψυχὴν ἀπὸ τῶν αἰσθητῶν καλῶν[4] ἐπὶ
τὰ νοητά, παρεγγυᾷ μήτε σώματός τινος μήτ᾽
ἐπιτηδεύματος μήτ᾽ ἐπιστήμης κάλλει μιᾶς[5] ὑπο-
τετάχθαι καὶ δουλεύειν, ἀλλ᾽ ἀποστάντα τῆς περὶ
ταῦτα μικρολογίας ἐπὶ τὸ πολὺ τοῦ καλοῦ πέλα-
γος τρέπεσθαι.

ΖΗΤΗΜΑ Δ΄

Τί δήποτε,[6] τὴν ψυχὴν ἀεὶ πρεσβυτέραν ἀποφαί-
νων τοῦ σώματος αἰτίαν τε τῆς ἐκείνου γενέσεως

[1] ἄλλοις ἄλλα -J (corrected by J⁴), g, Bonon. C 3635, Voss.
16, Escorial T-11-5.
[2] τῆς -omitted by J, g.
[3] δὴ -a¹, ε.
[4] καλῶν -omitted by J (added in margin -J⁴), g.
[5] μηδεμιᾶς -Escorial T-11-5.
[6] τί δήποτε -with these words begin γ, Tolet. 51, 5 (cf.
Class. Quart., xxi [1927], p. 167), Laurent. 80, 5 and 80, 22.

[a] This answers the argument in 1002 A supra (ἔτι τῶν μὲν
νοητῶν ἐν κριτήριον . . .) ; and, as the subsequent words show,
διὰ ἁπλότητα καὶ ὁμοιότητα refers to the homogeneity of the
intelligible (cf. Adv. Colotem 1114 D [. . . ὁμοιότητι πρὸς αὐτὸ
καὶ τῷ μὴ δέχεσθαι διαφορὰν . . .]) and not to a similarity of
intelligence and intelligible or of vision and light.
[b] The νοῦς is the νοερὰ δύναμις in us (cf. 1002 B supra : τὸ

46

that of light is vision *a* ; but, since bodies have many differences and dissimilarities, different ones are naturally apprehended by different criteria, as it were by different instruments. But furthermore it is not right of them to be disdainful even of the intelligible and intellectual faculty *b* in us men, for because it is ample and stout it transcends all that is perceptible and reaches as far as things divine.*c* The most important point, however, is that, when in the *Symposium* *d* Plato explains how one must manage the matter of love by diverting the soul from the beautiful objects that are perceptible to those that are intelligible, his own injunction is not to subjugate oneself and play the slave to the beauty of a particular body or practice or of a single science but to desist from petty concern about these things and turn to the vast sea of the beautiful.*e*

QUESTION IV

WHYEVER, when he declares that the soul is always senior to the body and the cause and origin of the

ἡγεμονικὸν καὶ νοερόν), and Plutarch thinks that he has the authority of Plato for treating this itself as a νοητόν (see note *g* on 1002 c *supra*). There is therefore no reason to read into this passage the distinction between νοητή and νοερά for which it is cited by H. Dörrie (*Porphyrios'* " *Symmikta Zetemata*," p. 189, n. 5).

c Cf. Philo Jud., *De Opificio Mundi* 70-71 (i, pp. 23, 18–24, 1 [Cohn]) and R. M. Jones, *Class. Phil.*, xxi (1926), pp. 101 ff.

d *Symposium* 210 D.

e Plutarch conveniently cuts short his paraphrase of the passage, for the end and purpose of the whole progress in the *Symposium* is the ἐπιστήμη μία of the idea of beauty (210 D 6–211 D 1 ; *cf.* Albinus, *Épitome* v, 5 [Louis] = p. 157, 14-18 [Hermann] and x, 6 [Louis] = p. 165, 24-29 [Hermann]).

47

(1002)

F καὶ ἀρχήν, πάλιν φησὶν οὐκ ἂν γενέσθαι ψυχὴν
ἄνευ σώματος οὐδὲ νοῦν ἄνευ ψυχῆς ἀλλὰ ψυχὴν
μὲν ἐν¹ σώματι νοῦν δ' ἐν τῇ ψυχῇ; δόξει γὰρ τὸ
σῶμα καὶ εἶναι καὶ μὴ εἶναι, συνυπάρχον ἅμα τῇ
ψυχῇ καὶ γεννώμενον ὑπὸ τῆς ψυχῆς.

1003 ᾺἩ² τὸ πολλάκις ὑφ' ἡμῶν λεγόμενον ἀληθές
ἐστιν· ἡ μὲν γὰρ ἄνους ψυχὴ καὶ τὸ ἄμορφον
σῶμα συνυπῆρχον³ ἀλλήλοις ἀεὶ καὶ οὐδέτερον
αὐτῶν γένεσιν ἔσχεν οὐδ' ἀρχήν· ἐπεὶ δὲ ἡ ψυχὴ
νοῦ μετέλαβε καὶ ἁρμονίας καὶ γενομένη διὰ συμφωνίας ἔμφρων⁴ μεταβολῆς αἰτία γέγονε⁵ τῇ ὕλῃ
καὶ κρατήσασα ταῖς αὐτῆς⁶ κινήσεσι τὰς ἐκείνης⁷
ἐπεσπάσατο καὶ ἐπέστρεψεν,⁸ οὕτω τὸ σῶμα τοῦ

---

¹ ἐν -omitted by J¹, g.
² ἦ -a.
³ συνυπάρχοντα (τα superscript over ον) -J¹ ; συνυπάρχον
-Voss. 16 ; συνυπάρχουσιν -Escorial T-11-5.
⁴ ἔμφρον -J¹.
⁵ αἰτία γέγονε -omitted by J¹, g.
⁶ κρατήσας αὐταῖς ταῖς -J¹, g.
⁷ ἐκείνας -Escorial T-11-5.
⁸ ἐπέστρεψαν -J.

ᵃ Plato, *Timaeus* 34 B 10—35 A 1 and *Laws* 896 A 5–C 8
(with 892 A 2–C 6) ; see *De An. Proc. in Timaeo* 1013 E-F
and 1016 A-B (where *Timaeus* 34 B 10—35 A 1 is quoted).
ᵇ *Timaeus* 30 B 3-5 (cf. Albinus, *Epitome* xiv, 4 [Louis] = p.
170, 2-3 [Hermann]: ἴσως οὐχ οἷόν τε ὄντος νοῦ ἄνευ ψυχῆς
ὑποστῆναι). Here as elsewhere Plato does say that νοῦς cannot exist apart from ψυχή (*Timaeus* 46 D 5-6, *Sophist* 249 A
4-8, *Philebus* 30 C 9-10 ; cf. Cherniss, *Aristotle's Criticism of
Plato* . . ., pp. 606-607) but neither here nor anywhere that
soul cannot exist without body. This is simply a false inference from the statement that the demiurge did put soul into
the body of the universe.
ᶜ See note c on *De Comm. Not.* 1075 F *infra*.
ᵈ With what follows cf. QUESTION II, 2 (1001 B-C) *supra* and
De An. Proc. in Timaeo 1014 B-E and 1017 A-B. In those

48

latter's generation,[a] does he again say that soul could not have come to be without body or intelligence without soul either,[b] but soul in body and intelligence in soul ? For it would seem that the body both exists and does not exist if it is at once coexistent with the soul and being generated by the soul.

Or [c] is that right which we frequently assert ? [d] For soul without intelligence [e] and amorphous body [f] were always coexistent with each other, and neither of them had generation or origin ; but, when the soul had partaken of intelligence and concord [g] and, grown rational through consonance, had become a cause of change for matter and had attracted and converted the motions of the latter [h] by having dominated them with its own motions,[i] this is the

passages god or the demiurge, who is not mentioned in the present QUESTION, is the subject of statements which here have for subject instead soul, *i.e.* intelligent soul ; but this latter according to 1001 c *supra* is not merely the work of god but also a part of him.

[e] *Cf. Timaeus* 44 A 8 : κατ' ἀρχάς τε ἄνους ψυχὴ γίγνεται, said, however, of the particular human soul when it enters the body.

[f] *Timaeus* 50 D 7 and 51 A 7 (see *De An. Proc. in Timaeo* 1014 F [τὸ τὴν ὕλην ἀεὶ μὲν ἄμορφον καὶ ἀσχημάτιστον ὑπ' αὐτοῦ λέγεσθαι . . .] and *cf.* Timaeus Locrus 94 A [ἄμορφον δὲ καθ' αὑτὰν καὶ ἀσχημάτιστον]).

[g] See note *a* on 1001 c *supra.*

[h] According to Plutarch's own doctrine these could be only motions induced by disorderly soul not yet grown rational, for amorphous matter of itself would be δυνάμεως οἰκείας ἔρημον, ἀργὸν ἐξ αὐτοῦ, ἄμοιρος αἰτίας ἁπάσης (*De An. Proc. in Timaeo* 1014 F—1015 A, *cf.* 1015 E).

[i] See the similar language used of the effect of νοῦς on ψυχή in *De An. Proc. in Timaeo* 1024 D : ἐγγενόμενος δὲ τῇ ψυχῇ καὶ κρατήσας εἰς ἑαυτὸν ἐπιστρέφει . . . (*cf.* Thévenaz, *L'Âme du Monde,* pp. 71-72) ; and *cf. Timaeus* 42 c 4–D 2 with Cornford's note *ad loc.* (*Plato's Cosmology,* p. 144, n. 2).

(1003) κόσμου γένεσιν ἔσχεν ὑπὸ τῆς ψυχῆς, καὶ κατα-
σχηματιζόμενον καὶ συνομοιούμενον. οὐ γὰρ ἐξ αὑτῆς ἡ ψυχὴ τὴν τοῦ σώματος ἐδημιούργει φύσιν
οὐδ' ἐκ τοῦ μὴ ὄντος, ἀλλ' ἐκ σώματος ἀτάκτου
καὶ ἀσχηματίστου σῶμα τεταγμένον ἀπειργά-
B σατο[1] καὶ πειθήνιον.[2] ὥσπερ οὖν, εἰ φαίη τις ἀεὶ
τὴν τοῦ σπέρματος[3] δύναμιν εἶναι μετὰ σώματος[4] γεγονέναι μέντοι τὸ σῶμα τῆς συκῆς ἢ[5] τῆς[6]
ἐλαίας ὑπὸ σπέρματος, οὐδὲν ἐρεῖ διάφωνον[7] (αὐτὸ
γὰρ τὸ σῶμα, κινήσεως αὐτῷ καὶ μεταβολῆς ὑπὸ
τοῦ σπέρματος ἐγγενομένης, ἔφυ τοιοῦτο καὶ δι-
εβλάστησεν) οὕτως ἡ ἄμορφος ὕλη καὶ ἀόριστος
ὑπὸ τῆς ψυχῆς[8] ἐνούσης[9] σχηματισθεῖσα μορφὴν
ἔσχε τοιαύτην καὶ διάθεσιν.

ΖΗΤΗΜΑ Ε΄

1. Διὰ τί, τῶν μὲν εὐθυγράμμων τῶν δὲ κυκλικῶν σωμάτων καὶ σχημάτων ὄντων, τὰς τῶν εὐθυγράμμων[10] ἀρχὰς[11] ἔλαβε τὸ ἰσοσκελὲς τρίγωνον
C καὶ τὸ σκαληνόν, ὧν τὸ μὲν τὸν κύβον συνέστησε
γῆς στοιχεῖον ὄντα τὸ δὲ σκαληνὸν τήν τε πυραμίδα καὶ τὸ ὀκτάεδρον καὶ τὸ εἰκοσάεδρον, τὸ μὲν

---

[1] ἀπεργάσατο -X.
[2] καὶ πειθήνιον ἀπειργάσατο -E[1].
[3] σώματος -γ.
[4] μετὰ τοῦ σώματος -Voss. 16, Escorial T-11-5.
[5] ἢ -omitted by g.
[6] καὶ -Escorial T-11-5.
[7] διαφέρειν -J[1]; διαφέρον -g (ἔρον over erasure); διάφορον
(ορ superscript over ων) -B[1].
[8] ὑπὸ τῆς ψυχῆς -omitted by X.
[9] ἐνούσας -Escorial T-11-5.
[10] τῶν δὲ κυκλικῶν . . . τῶν εὐθυγράμμων -omitted by J[1], g.
[11] ἀρχὴν -J[1], g.

way in which the body of the universe got generated
by the soul, in being fashioned by it and assimilated.
For it was not out of itself that the soul fabricated
the nature of body or out of what is non-existent
either, but out of disorderly [a] and shapeless body it
produced a well-ordered and disciplined [b] one. Therefore, just as there would be nothing inconsistent in
the assertion if one should say that the potency of
the seed is always associated with body and yet the
body of the fig or the olive has come to be by the
agency of seed (for the body itself had such and
such a growth and germination because by the
agency of the seed motion and change arose in it [c]),
so the amorphous and indefinite matter got such and
such a shape and disposition when it was fashioned
by the soul existing within it.

QUESTION V

1. Some bodies and figures being rectilinear and
others circular,[d] what was his reason for taking as
the principles of the rectilinear figures the isosceles
triangle and the scalene, the former of which produced the cube as element of earth while the scalene
produced the pyramid and the octahedron and the

---

[a] Cf. Quaest. Conviv. 720 B (ἡ μὲν ὕλη τῶν ὑποκειμένων
ἀτακτότατόν ἐστι . . .) and De An. Proc. in Timaeo 1024 A–B
(οὔτε γὰρ τὸ αἰσθητὸν εἰλήχει τάξεως . . .).

[b] Cf. De An. Proc. in Timaeo 1029 E for the word, there
applied to the soul ; but for the notion here cf. Timaeus 48 A
2–5 and 56 C 5–6.

[c] Cf. [Plutarch], De Placitis 905 A = Dox. Graeci, p. 417 A
2–5.

[d] Cf. Plato, Parmenides 137 D 8–E 6 and 145 B 3–5 ;
Aristotle, De Caelo 286 b 13–16 ; Proclus, In Primum
Euclidis El. Lib., p. 144, 10–18 (Friedlein).

PLUTARCH'S MORALIA

(1003) πυρὸς σπέρμα τὸ δ᾽ ἀέρος τὸ δὲ ὕδατος γενόμενον,
τὸ δὲ τῶν κυκλικῶν¹ ὅλως παρῆκε, καίτοι μνησθεὶς
τοῦ σφαιροειδοῦς ἐν οἷς φησι τῶν κατηριθμημένων
σχημάτων ἕκαστον σώματος περιφεροῦς εἰς ἴσα
διανεμητικὸν εἶναι;

Πότερον, ὡς ὑπονοοῦσιν ἔνιοι,² τὸ δωδεκάεδρον
τῷ σφαιροειδεῖ προσένειμεν, εἰπὼν ὅτι τούτῳ³
πρὸς τὴν τοῦ παντὸς ὁ θεὸς κατεχρήσατο φύσιν
ἐκεῖνο διαζωγραφῶν; καὶ γὰρ μάλιστα τῷ πλήθει
τῶν στοιχείων ἀμβλύτητι δὲ τῶν γωνιῶν τὴν
D εὐθύτητα διαφυγὸν⁴ εὐκαμπές ἐστι, καὶ τῇ περιτάσει καθάπερ αἱ δωδεκάσκυτοι σφαῖραι κυκλο-
τερὲς γίγνεται καὶ περιληπτικόν⁵· ἔχει γὰρ εἴκοσι
γωνίας στερεάς, ὧν ἑκάστην ἐπίπεδοι περιέχουσιν
ἀμβλεῖαι τρεῖς· ἑκάστη γὰρ ὀρθῆς ἐστι καὶ πέμπτου
μορίου· συνήρμοσται δὲ καὶ συμπέπηγεν ἐκ δώδεκα
πενταγώνων⁶ ἰσογωνίων καὶ ἰσοπλεύρων, ὧν ἕκα-

¹ κύκλων -Escorial T-11-5.
² ἕτεροι (νι superscript over τε) -ε.   ³ τοῦτο -Voss. 16.
⁴ διέφυγεν -J¹, g ; διαφυγῶν -Voss. 16¹.
⁵ παραληπτικόν -J¹, g.   ⁶ πανταγώνων -J¹.

ᵃ Timaeus 53 c 4—55 c 4 and 55 ᴅ 7—56 ʙ 6. For Plutarch's use of γῆς στοιχεῖον and πυρὸς σπέρμα in these lines
cf. Timaeus 56 ʙ 5 (στοιχεῖον καὶ σπέρμα) with Cornford's
note (Plato's Cosmology, p. 223, n. 1).
ᵇ Aristotle (De Caelo 286 b 27-33) interprets this as supporting evidence for his thesis that the sphere is the primary
solid figure.
ᶜ Timaeus 55 ᴀ 3-4. Plato's words there are ὅλου περιφεροῦς διανεμητικὸν εἰς ἴσα μέρη καὶ ὅμοια, and ὅλου περιφεροῦς
means " the whole circumference " of the sphere in which the
tetrahedron is inscribed. At this point in the Timaeus only
this, " the simplest solid figure," has been constructed, though
what is said of its division of the sphere in which it is inscribed
is undoubtedly meant to apply also to the four regular solids
mentioned immediately thereafter.

52

icosahedron, which became the seed of fire and of
air and of water respectively,[a] but for disregarding
altogether the question of the circular figures,[b] even
though he did mention the spherical in the passage
where he says [c] that each of the figures enumerated
has the property of dividing into equal parts an en-
circling body ?

Did he, as some surmise, associate the dodecahedron with what is spherical,[d] since he said [e] that
god employed the former for the nature of the sum
of things in tracing the design of this ? For, furthest
withdrawn from straightness by the multitude of its
elements [f] and obtuseness of its angles, it is flexible
and like the balls that are made of twelve pieces of
leather [g] by being distended becomes circular and
circumscriptive,[h] for it has twenty solid angles each
of which is contained by three plane angles that are
obtuse, since each consists of a right angle and a
fifth [i] ; and it has been assembled and constructed
out of twelve equiangular and equilateral pentagons,[j]

---

[a] Cf. " Timaeus Locrus " 98 E (τὸ δὲ δωδεκάεδρον εἰκόνα
τῶ παντὸς ἐστάσατο, ἔγγιστα σφαίρας ἐόν) and Philoponus, De
Aeternitate Mundi xiii, 18 (pp. 536, 27–537, 2 [Rabe]).

[e] Timaeus 55 c 4-6, more accurately quoted by Plutarch
in De Defectu Orac. 430 B.

[f] Cf. De Defectu Orac. 427 B (μέγιστον δὲ καὶ πολυμερέ-
στατον τὸ δωδεκάεδρον) ; and for στοιχεῖον as here used (the
ultimate constituent triangles) cf. Timaeus 54 D 6-7, 55 A 8,
55 B 3-4, and 57 c 9.

[g] Cf. Plato, Phaedo 110 B 5-7 and Proclus, In Platonis
Timaeum iii, p. 141, 19-24 (Diehl).

[h] Cf. De Defectu Orac. 428 D (ἡ δὲ τοῦ δωδεκαέδρου φύσις
περιληπτικὴ τῶν ἄλλων σχημάτων οὖσα . . .).

[i] Cf. Euclid, Elements xiii, Prop. 18, Lemma (iv, p. 340,
6-7 [Heiberg]).

[j] Cf. Euclid, Elements xi, Def. 28.

PLUTARCH'S MORALIA

(1003) στον[1] ἐκ τριάκοντα τῶν πρώτων σκαληνῶν τριγώνων συνέστηκε· διὸ καὶ δοκεῖ τὸν ζῳδιακὸν
ἅμα καὶ τὸν ἐνιαυτὸν ἀπομιμεῖσθαι ταῖς διανομαῖς
τῶν μοιρῶν[2] ἰσαρίθμοις οὔσαις.[3]

2. Ἦ πρότερόν ἐστι κατὰ φύσιν τὸ εὐθὺ τοῦ
περιφεροῦς, μᾶλλον δὲ ὅλως πάθος τι τῆς εὐθείας
E ἡ περιφερής; κάμπτεσθαι γὰρ λέγεται τὸ ὀρθὸν
καὶ ὁ κύκλος γράφεται κέντρῳ καὶ διαστήματι·
τοῦτο δ' ἐστὶν εὐθείας τόπος,[4] ὑφ' ἧς καὶ μετρεῖται·
τὸ γὰρ[5] περιέχον ἐκ τοῦ μέσου πανταχόθεν ἴσον
ἀφέστηκε. γεννᾶται δὲ καὶ κῶνος καὶ κύλινδρος
ἀπ' εὐθυγράμμων, ὁ μὲν τριγώνου περὶ[6] μίαν
πλευρὰν μένουσαν τῇ ἑτέρᾳ πλευρᾷ καὶ τῇ βάσει
περιενεχθέντος ὁ δὲ κύλινδρος παραλληλογράμμου
ταὐτὸ τοῦτο παθόντος.[7] ἔτι[8] τῆς μὲν ἀρχῆς ἐγγυτέρω τὸ ἔλαττον, ἐλαχίστη δὲ πασῶν[9] ἡ εὐθεῖα·
τῆς γὰρ περιφεροῦς τὸ μὲν ⟨ἐντός⟩[10] ἐστι κοῖλον

---

[1] ἕκαστος -Escorial T-11-5[1]. [2] μυρίων -J, g.
[3] οὕτως -Escorial T-11-5. [4] τύπος -X, ε, n.
[5] γὰρ -omitted by J[1], g. [6] περὶ -omitted by g.
[7] πεπονθότος -Escorial T-11-5.
[8] ἔτι -Leonicus ; ἔστι -Escorial T-11-5 ; ἐπεὶ -all other
MSS. [9] παθῶν -X, a, A[1], β[1], ε, n.
[10] ⟨ἐντός⟩ -added here by Bernardakis (. . . κοῖλον ⟨τὸ
ἐντός⟩ -Leonicus).

---

[a] This is erroneous (*cf.* Heath, *Manual*, pp. 177-178), and
Plutarch seems to make Ammonius call attention to the fact
in *De Defectu Orac.* 428 A (. . . τὸ τοῦ καλουμένου δωδεκαέδρου
στοιχεῖον ἄλλο ποιοῦσιν, οὐκ ἐκεῖνο τὸ σκαληνὸν ἐξ οὗ τὴν
πυραμίδα καὶ τὸ ὀκτάεδρον καὶ τὸ εἰκοσάεδρον ὁ Πλάτων
συνίστησιν). Albinus in his *Epitome* xiii, 2 (p. 77 [Louis]=
pp. 168, 37–169, 2 [Hermann]) says that each of the twelve
pentagons is divided into five triangles and each of these
consists of six triangles, but it should be observed that he
does not state what kind of triangles these are.

[b] Neither Plutarch here nor Albinus in his *Epitome* xiii, 2

54

each of which consists of thirty of the primary scalene triangles,[a] and this is why it seems to represent at once the zodiac and the year in that the divisions into parts are equal in number.[b]

2. Or is the straight naturally prior to the circular [c] or rather the circular line simply a modification of the straight line ? For we do speak of the bending of what is straight [d] and the circle is described by a centre and a distance, this latter being the location of a straight line by which it is measured as well,[e] for what contains the circle is at all points equally removed from the middle. Also, both cone and cylinder are generated by rectilinear figures, the former when one side and the base of a triangle are rotated about the other side, which remains fixed, and the cylinder when this same thing happens to a parallelogram.[f] Moreover, what is lesser is nearer to the principle [g] ; but the straight line is the least of all lines,[h] for the circular line has its ⟨interior⟩

(pp. 75-77 [Louis] =pp. 168, 34–169, 3 [Hermann]) refers to any relation between the zodiac and the dodecahedron other than the *numerical* similarity that both of them (and the year) consist of twelve parts, each of which consists of thirty parts.

[c] Cf. Proclus, *In Primum Euclidis El. Lib.*, pp. 106, 20–107, 10 (Friedlein).

[d] Cf. Aristotle, *De Incessu Animal.* 708 b 22-24 and *Meteorology* 386 a 1-7.

[e] Cf. Euclid, *Elements* i, Post. 3 and Proclus, *In Primum Euclidis El. Lib.*, p. 185, 22-25 (Friedlein) : . . . διάστημα δὲ ἡ εὐθεῖα. ὅση γὰρ ἂν αὕτη τυγχάνῃ τοσοῦτο ἔσται τὸ ἀπόστημα τοῦ κέντρου πρὸς πάντα τὰ μέρη τῆς περιφερείας.

[f] Cf. Euclid, *Elements* xi, Defs. 18 and 21.

[g] See 1002 в *supra* and note c there.

[h] Cf. Archimedes, *Opera Omnia* iterum ed. J. L. Heiberg, i, p. 8, 3-4 ; Proclus, *In Primum Euclidis El. Lib.*, p. 110, 10-26 (Friedlein) ; Theon Smyrnaeus, pp. 111, 22–112, 1 (Hiller).

(1003) κυρτὸν δὲ τὸ¹ ἐκτός. ἔτι τῶν σχημάτων οἱ
ἀριθμοὶ πρότεροι, καὶ γὰρ ἡ μονὰς τῆς στιγμῆς·
F ἔστι γὰρ ἡ στιγμὴ μονὰς ἐν θέσει.² καὶ μὴν ἡ
μονὰς τρίγωνός ἐστι· πᾶς γὰρ τρίγωνος ἀριθμὸς
ὀκτάκις γενόμενος καὶ μονάδα προσλαβὼν γίγνεται τετράγωνος· τοῦτο δὲ καὶ³ τῇ μονάδι συμ-
βέβηκε⁴· πρότερον οὖν τοῦ κύκλου τὸ τρίγωνον· εἰ
δὲ τοῦτο, καὶ εὐθεῖα τῆς περιφεροῦς. ἔτι τὸ στοιχεῖον εἰς⁵ οὐδὲν διαιρεῖται τῶν συνισταμένων ἐξ
αὐτοῦ, τοῖς δ' ἄλλοις⁶ εἰς τὸ στοιχεῖον ἡ διάλυ-
1004 σις. εἰ⁷ τοίνυν τὸ μὲν τρίγωνον εἰς οὐδὲν περιφε-
ρὲς διαλύεται, τὸν δὲ κύκλον εἰς τέσσαρα⁸ τρίγωνα

¹ τὸ -omitted by J¹, g.
² ἐνθέτως -J¹.
³ καὶ -omitted by J¹, g.
⁴ μονάδι οὐ συμβέβηκε -g.
⁵ ὡς -J, g.
⁶ τοὺς δὲ ἄλλους -J¹, g.
⁷ ἔτι -J¹, g.   ⁸ εἰς τὰ τέτταρα -g.

ᵃ Cf. Proclus, In Primum Euclidis El. Lib., p. 106, 24-25
(Friedlein) ; [Aristotle], Mechanica 847 b 23—848 a 3.
ᵇ Cf. Hero Alexandrinus, Def. a′ (iv, p. 14, 13-19 [Hei-
berg]) ; Theon Smyrnaeus, p. 111, 14-16 (Hiller) ; Proclus,
In Primum Euclidis El. Lib., p. 95, 21-26 (Friedlein) ;
Aristotle, Topics 108 b 26-31 and Metaphysics 1016 b 24-31
with Cherniss, Aristotle's Criticism of Plato . . ., pp. 131-132
and note 322 on p. 397. Contrast 1002 A supra, where unity
is said to produce numbers and then to pass on into points,
lines, and figures.
ᶜ The unit, being the ἀρχή of number and not itself a
number, is usually called " potentially triangular," 3 being the
first triangular number as in De An. Proc. in Timaeo 1020 D
(Theon Smyrnaeus, p. 33, 5-7 and p. 37, 15-19 [Hiller] ;
Nicomachus, Arithmetica Introductio, pp. 88, 23–89, 5
[Hoche] ; Iamblichus, In Nicomachi Arithmeticam Introductionem, p. 62, 2-5 [Pistelli]). For triangular numbers cf.

concave and its exterior convex.[a] Moreover,
numbers are prior to figures, for the unit is itself
prior to the point because the point is a unit in
position.[b] Now, the unit is triangular, for every
triangular number multiplied by eight and with
addition of a unit becomes a square number, and
this is characteristic of the unit also.[c] The triangle,
then, is prior to the circle [d] ; and, if so, the straight
line too is prior to the circular. Moreover, the
element is divided into none of the things that are
compounded out of it, whereas the other things are
subject to resolution into the element. If, then, the
triangle is resolved into nothing that is circular,
whereas the two diameters of the circle divide it into

Quaest. Conviv. 744 B (where 3 and 6 are the examples) ;
Theon Smyrnaeus, p. 33, pp. 37, 7–38, 14, and p. 41, 3-8
(Hiller) ; Nicomachus, *Arithmetica Introductio* II, viii (pp.
87, 22–89, 16 [Hoche]). The algebraic formula is $\frac{n(n+1)}{2}$;
and 1 conforms to this, being half of the product of itself and
2. The proposition that any triangular number multiplied
by 8 becomes a square number when 1 is added is repeated by
Iamblichus (*In Nicomachi Arithmeticam Introductionem*,
p. 90, 18-19 [Pistelli]) but is not by him explicitly applied to
the unit (*cf.* Heath, *History* i, p. 84 and ii, pp. 516-517 ; M. R.
Cohen and I. E. Drabkin, *A Source Book in Greek Science*
[New York, 1948], p. 9, n. 2).

[d] This does not follow, for not only is the unit " square " as
well as " triangular " (*De E* 391 A, *De Defectu Orac.* 429 E ;
Nicomachus, *Arithmetica Introductio*, p. 91, 4-5 [Hoche] ;
Iamblichus, *In Nicomachi Arithmeticam Introductionem*,
p. 60, 3-5 and p. 75, 11-13 [Pistelli]) but even its being triangular does not prove the triangle to be a unit prior to the
circle, which can itself be regarded as analogous to the unit
(Aristotle, *De Caelo* 286 b 33—287 a 2 ; Iamblichus, *op. cit.*,
p. 61, 6-24 and pp. 94, 27–95, 2 [Pistelli] ; Proclus, *In Primum
Euclidis El. Lib.*, pp. 146, 24–147, 5 and pp. 151, 20–152, 5
[Friedlein]).

(1004) τέμνουσιν αἱ δύο διάμετροι, πρότερον ἂν τῇ φύσει
καὶ στοιχειωδέστερον εἴη τοῦ κυκλικοῦ[1] τὸ εὐθύγραμμον. ὅτι τοίνυν προηγούμενον μέν ἐστι τὸ
εὐθύγραμμον[2] τὸ δὲ κυκλικὸν ἐπιγιγνόμενον[3] καὶ
συμβεβηκὸς αὐτὸς ὁ Πλάτων ἐνεδείξατο· τὴν γὰρ
γῆν[4] ἐκ κύβων συστησάμενος, ὧν ἕκαστον[5] εὐθύγραμμοι[6] περιέχουσιν ἐπιφάνειαι,[7] σφαιροειδὲς αὐτῆς γεγονέναι τὸ σχῆμά[8] φησι καὶ στρογγύλον.
ὥστ᾽ οὐδὲν ἔδει ποιεῖν τῶν περιφερῶν ἴδιον στοιχεῖον, εἰ καὶ τοῖς εὐθυγράμμοις πρὸς ἄλληλά πως
συναρμοττομένοις[9] ὁ σχηματισμὸς οὗτος ἐπιγίγνε-
σθαι πέφυκεν.

B   3. Ἔτι, εὐθεῖα[10] μὲν ἥ τε μείζων ἥ τε μικρο-
τέρα τὴν αὐτὴν εὐθύτητα διατηρεῖ, τὰς δὲ τῶν
κύκλων περιφερείας, ἂν ὦσι σμικρότεραι, καμπυλωτέρας[11] καὶ σφιγγομένας τῇ κυρτότητι μᾶλλον
ὁρῶμεν, ἂν δὲ μείζους, ἀνειμένας· ἱστάμενοι γοῦν
κατὰ τὴν κυρτὴν περιφέρειαν οἱ μὲν κατὰ σημεῖον

---

[1] κύκλου -J[1], g.

[2] ὅτι τοίνυν . . . τὸ εὐθύγραμμον -omitted by J[1], g, Escorial
T-11-5[1].

[3] κυκλικόν ἐστι γινόμενον -J[1], g ; κυκλικὸν ἐπιγενόμενον
-Escorial T-11-5.

[4] γῆν -omitted by J[1], g.

[5] ἕκαστος -J[1], g ; ἕκαστοι -ε.

[6] εὐθύγραμμον -J, g, Voss. 16.   [7] ἐπιφαίνεται -J, g.

[8] τὸ σχῆμα γεγονέναι -Escorial T-11-5.

[9] συναρμοττόμενος -J, g, Voss. 16[1].

[10] ἔστι γὰρ εὐθεῖα -J, g.   [11] καμπυλοτέρας -B, ε.

---

[a] Since the bases of the triangles into which the circle is
divided remain arcs of a circle, the conclusion here drawn

four triangles, the rectilinear would be naturally prior to the circular and more elementary than it.[a] Furthermore, that the rectilinear is antecedent and the circular supervenient and incidental was indicated by Plato himself, for after making the earth consist of cubes,[b] each of which is contained by rectilinear surfaces, he says that the shape of it has turned out to be spherical or round.[c] Consequently there was no need to postulate an element peculiar to circular figures if this configuration does naturally supervene upon rectilinears conjoined with one another in a particular way.

3. Moreover, while a straight line, whatever its length, keeps the same straightness throughout, we see that the circumferences of circles are more curved, that is are more highly concentrated in their convexity, if they are smaller, and more relaxed, if they are larger.[d] At any rate, when set up on their convex circumference, some circles touch the under-

does not follow from the argument, with which *cf.* Nicomachus, *Arithmetica Introductio* II, vii, 4 (p. 87, 7-19 [Hoche]) and Simplicius, *De Caelo*, pp. 613, 30–614, 10 on Aristotle, *De Caelo* 303 a 31–b 1.

[b] *Timaeus* 55 D 8—56 A 1.

[c] Despite φησι this is not a quotation. In fact, in the *Timaeus* after 55 D 8—56 A 1 the sphericity of the earth is referred to only by implication in 62 D 12—63 A 3 (*cf.* Cornford, *Plato's Cosmology*, p. 263, notes 1 and 2 with *Phaedo* 108 E 4—109 A 7 and 110 B 5-7). Misguided attempts have been made to deny that even these passages refer to the earth's sphericity (*cf. Lustrum*, IV [1959], Nos. 660-661 and V [1960], Nos. 1464 and 1465).

[d] *Cf.* John Wallis, *A Treatise of Angular Sections* (London, 1684), p. 90 : ". . . the lesser circumference is more crooked. For it hath as much of curvity in a shorter length. And therefore . . . it is more crooked intensively."

(1004) οἱ δὲ κατὰ γραμμὴν ἅπτονται τῶν ὑποκειμένων
ἐπιπέδων· ὥσθ᾽ ὑπονοήσειεν ἄν τις εὐθείας κατὰ
μικρὰ πολλὰς συντιθεμένας[1] τὴν περιφερῆ γραμμὴν
ἀποτελεῖν.

4. Ὅρα δὲ μὴ τῶν μὲν[2] ἐνταῦθα κυκλικῶν καὶ
σφαιροειδῶν οὐδέν ἐστιν ἀπηκριβωμένον ἀλλ᾽ ἐντάσει[3] καὶ περιτάσει τῶν εὐθυγράμμων ἢ μικρότητι
C τῶν μορίων τῆς διαφορᾶς λανθανούσης ἐπιφαίνεται
τὸ στρογγύλον καὶ κυκλοειδές, ὅθεν οὐδὲ κινεῖται
φύσει τῶν ἐνταῦθα σωμάτων ἐγκυκλίως οὐδὲν ἀλλ᾽
ἐπ᾽ εὐθείας ἅπαντα· τὸ δ᾽ ὄντως σφαιροειδὲς οὐκ
ἔστιν αἰσθητοῦ σώματος ἀλλὰ τῆς ψυχῆς καὶ τοῦ
νοῦ στοιχεῖον, οἷς καὶ τὴν κυκλοφορητικὴν[4] κίνησιν ὡς προσήκουσαν κατὰ φύσιν ἀποδίδωσιν.

---

[1] συντεθειμένας -Escorial T-11-5.

[2] μὲν -J¹, g, Voss. 16, Bonon., Escorial T-11-5 ; omitted
by all other mss.

[3] ἐντάσει -E, B, n, Escorial T-11-5 ; ἐνστάσει -all other
mss.

[4] κυκλοφορικὴν -E, B, n ; κυκλοφορητικὸν -Escorial T-11-5.

---

[a] This in fact has nothing to do with the preceding statement, for a circle however large will never touch the plane
at a line unless both are material, and then it will do so
however small it is (cf. Aristotle, *Metaphysics* 997 b 35—
998 a 4 and Alexander, *Metaph.*, p. 200, 15-21). It does not
then support the subsequent conclusion either, to which
Plutarch himself should not have subscribed anyway, for he
held that the curvature of a circle is uniform (cf. *De Facie*
932 f and *Class. Phil.*, xlvi [1951], p. 144).

[b] Cf. Proclus, *In Primum Euclidis El. Lib.*, p. 54, 11-13

lying planes at a point and others at a line.[a] Consequently one might surmise that many straight lines when put together bit by bit produce the circular line.

4. Consider too that none of the circular or spherical things in this world is exactly perfect [b] but there is a superficial appearance of roundness and circularity, the difference being unnoticed because of the tension and distension of the rectilinears or the minuteness of their parts, this being the reason why none of the bodies in this world moves naturally in a circle either but all move in a straight line, whereas the really spherical is an element not of perceptible body but of soul and intelligence,[c] to which he assigns as naturally befitting them circular motion as well.[d]

(Friedlein) ; [Plato], *Epistle* vii, 343 A 5-9 ; and Plato, *Philebus* 62 A 7–B 9.

[c] *Cf.* Atticus, frag. vi (Baudry) = Eusebius, *Praep. Evang.* xv, 8, 7 (ii, p. 367, 13-18 [Mras]) ; Proclus, *In Primum Euclidis El. Lib.*, p. 82, 7-12 and pp. 147, 22–148, 4 (Friedlein). In calling the spherical, of which the natural motion is circular (*cf. De E* 390 A), τῆς ψυχῆς . . . στοιχεῖον, however, Plutarch seems to be perilously close to the identification of soul with the Aristotelian πέμπτη οὐσία κυκλοφορητική (*cf.* Cherniss, *Aristotle's Criticism of Plato* . . ., pp. 601-602 ; P. Moraux, *R.-E.* xxiv [1963], cols. 1248, 37–1251, 12). Even " materialists " like the Atomists and Chrysippus had assigned the spherical to soul (*cf.* Aristotle, *De Anima* 404 a 1-9 and 405 a 8-13 ; *S.V.F.* ii, frag. 815).

[d] Plato, *Timaeus* 34 A 1-4, 36 E 2—37 C 3, 47 B 5–C 4 and *Laws* 898 A 3–B 3 (*cf.* Cherniss, *Aristotle's Criticism of Plato* . . ., pp. 404-405) ; *cf. De An. Proc. in Timaeo* 1024 C-D.

(1004)   ZHTHMA ϛ´

Πῶς ποτ' ἐν τῷ[1] Φαίδρῳ λέγεται τὸ τὴν τοῦ[2]
πτεροῦ φύσιν, ὑφ' ἧς ἄνω τὸ ἐμβριθὲς ἀνάγεται,[3]
κεκοινωνηκέναι μάλιστα τῶν περὶ τὸ σῶμα τοῦ
θείου;[4]

Πότερον ὅτι περὶ ἔρωτος ὁ λόγος ἐστί, κάλλους
δὲ τοῦ περὶ τὸ σῶμα ὁ ἔρως, τὸ δὲ κάλλος ὁμοιότητι τῇ πρὸς τὰ θεῖα κινεῖ καὶ ἀναμιμνήσκει τὴν
D ψυχήν; ἢ μᾶλλον οὐδὲν περιεργαστέον ἀλλὰ ἁπλῶς
ἀκουστέον ὅτι, τῶν περὶ τὸ σῶμα τῆς ψυχῆς δυνάμεων πλειόνων[5] οὐσῶν, ἡ λογιστικὴ[6] καὶ διανο-
ητικὴ μάλιστα τοῦ θείου κεκοινώνηκεν, ἣν τῶν
θείων καὶ οὐρανίων ἔφησεν;[7] ἣν οὐκ ἀπὸ τρόπου
πτερὸν προσηγόρευσεν, ὡς τὴν ψυχὴν ἀπὸ τῶν
ταπεινῶν καὶ θνητῶν ἀναφέρουσαν.

                      ZHTHMA Z´

1. Πῶς ποτέ φησιν ὁ Πλάτων τὴν ἀντιπερίστασιν τῆς κινήσεως διὰ τὸ μηδαμοῦ κενὸν ὑπάρχειν

    [1] τῷ -omitted by J[1], g.
    [2] τοῦ -omitted by Escorial T-11-5 (ἡ πτεροῦ δύναμις -Plato,
Phaedrus 246 D 6).
    [3] ἄγεται -J[1], g (ἄγειν ἄνω -Plato, Phaedrus 246 D 6 ; but
for ἀνάγειν ἄνω cf. Republic 533 D 2-3).
    [4] θείου -Kaltwasser (cf. 1004 D infra and Phaedrus 246
D 8) ; θεοῦ -mss.
    [5] πλειόνων -omitted by J[1].
    [6] λογιστικὴ -Ziegler (R.-E. xxi/i [1951], col. 748, 4) ; δια-
λογιστικὴ -mss.
    [7] ἔφυσεν -Escorial T-11-5.

────────────────────────────────────

    [a] Plato, Phaedrus 246 D 6-8.
    [b] Cf. Phaedrus 249 D 4—251 A 7 and 254 B 5-7 ; Plutarch,
Amatorius 765 B, D, F and 766 A, E-F ; Plotinus, Enn. VI,
vii, 22, lines 3-19,

QUESTION VI

In what sense is it asserted in the *Phaedrus* [a] that the pinion's nature, by which what is heavy is raised on high, is among things of the body most closely akin to the divine ?

Is it because the subject of the discourse is love and beauty of the body is the object of love and beauty by its similarity to things divine stirs the soul and makes it remember ? [b] Or should one rather not labour the point at all but understand quite simply that, while there are a good many faculties of the soul concerned with the body,[c] the faculty of reason or thought, whose objects he has said are things divine and celestial, is most closely akin to the divine ? [d] This faculty he not inappropriately called a pinion because it bears the soul up [e] and away from the things that are base and mortal.

QUESTION VII

1. In what sense does Plato say [f] that, because there is void nowhere, the cyclical replacement [g] of

---

[c] Cf. the interpretation given by Hermias, *In Platonis Phaedrum*, p. 133, 25-30 (Couvreur).

[d] Cf. *Phaedo* 80 b 1-3 and 84 a 7–b 4 ; *Symposium* 211 e 3—212 a 2 with *Phaedrus* 247 c 6-8, 248 b 7–c 2, and 249 c 4-6 and *Republic* 611 e 1-5 ; and also *Philebus* 62 a 7-8 for the ideas, the objects of reason or intelligence, as θεῖα.

[e] Cf. *An Seni Respublica Gerenda Sit* 786 d.

[f] *Timaeus* 79 e 10—80 c 8.

[g] The process is not called ἀντιπερίστασις by Plato, but Aristotle called it this (*Physics* 215 a 14-15 and 267 a 15-20 [cf. Simplicius, *Phys.*, p. 668, 32-34 ; p. 1350, 31-36 ; and p. 1351, 28-29]) as well as περίωσις (*Parva Naturalia* 472 b 6).

(1004) αἰτίαν εἶναι τῶν περὶ τὰς ἰατρικὰς σικύας[1] παθη-
μάτων[2] καὶ τῶν περὶ τὴν κατάποσιν[3] καὶ τὰ ῥι-
E πτούμενα βάρη[4] καὶ τὰ τῶν ὑδάτων ῥεύματα καὶ
κεραυνοὺς τήν τε φαινομένην πρὸς ἤλεκτρα καὶ τὴν
λίθον τὴν Ἡρακλείαν[5] ὁλκὴν τάς τε τῶν φθόγγων συμφωνίας·[6] δόξει γὰρ ἀτόπως αἰτίαν ⟨μίαν⟩[7]
παμπόλλων καὶ ἀνομοίων γένεσιν ἐπάγειν[8] παθῶν.

2. Τὸ μὲν γὰρ περὶ τὴν ἀναπνοὴν ὡς γίγνεται
τῇ ἀντιπεριστάσει τοῦ ἀέρος αὐτὸς[9] ἱκανῶς ἀποδέ-
δειχε· τὰ δὲ λοιπὰ πάντα φήσας θαυματουργεῖσθαι
τῷ κενὸν[10] εἶναι μηδὲν περιωθεῖν θ' αὐτὰ ταῦτ'
εἰς ἄλληλα καὶ διαμείβεσθαι πρὸς τὰς αὐτῶν ἕδρας
ἰόντα, τὴν καθ' ἕκαστον ἐξεργασίαν ἡμῖν ἀφῆκε.

3. Πρῶτον μὲν οὖν τὸ περὶ τὴν σικύαν[11] τοιοῦτόν ἐστιν· ὁ περιληφθεὶς ὑπ' αὐτῆς[12] πρὸς τῇ σαρ-
F κὶ μετὰ θερμότητος ἀὴρ ἐκπυρωθεὶς καὶ γενόμενος

---

[1] σικύας -J[1], g.
[2] μαθημάτων -J[1].
[3] κατάστασιν -J[1], g.
[4] βάρη -X, J, g, ε, n ; μέρη -all other mss.
[5] Hubert ; τὴν λίθον τὴν Ἡράκλειον -Escorial T-11-5 ;
τὸν λίθον τὸν (τὴν -Voss. 16) Ἡράκλειον -all other mss.
[6] συμφθονίας -J[1].
[7] ⟨μίαν⟩ -added by Fähse (implied by versions of Amyot
and Xylander) ; μίαν instead of αἰτίαν -Schellens (after Wyttenbach) ; αἰτίαν (αἰτϊ over erasure -a²) παμπόλλων -mss.
[8] ἐπάγειν -Turnebus, Xylander ; ὑπάγειν -mss.
[9] αὐτοῦ -J, g.
[10] H. C. ; καὶ τῷ κενὸν -Bernardakis ; τε καὶ (i.e. θαυμα-
τουργεῖσθαί τε καὶ εἶναι) -mss.
[11] σικύαν -J[1], g.
[12] αὐτοῦ -J[1], g.

---

[a] It was Plato's express purpose to banish ὁλκή from
physical theory (*Timaeus* 80 c 2-3 ; *cf.* Cherniss, *Aristotle's
Criticism of Plato* . . ., n. 306 on p. 387 *sub finem*). This
point is missed entirely in "Timaeus Locrus" 101 D—102 A,

motion is the cause of what happens in the case of
medical cupping-instruments and in that of swallowing and of weights that are thrown and of flowing
waters and of thunderbolts and of the apparent
attraction [a] to amber and the loadstone and of the
consonances of sounds ? For he would seem in extra-
ordinary fashion to be proposing a ⟨single⟩ cause as
the source of numerous and dissimilar occurrences.

2. For, while in the case of respiration he has
given an adequate exposition himself [b] of the way in
which it comes about by the cyclical replacement of
the air, for all the rest, after saying that these apparent wonders are produced because there is no
void and these objects push themselves around into
one another and interchange in going to their own
positions,[c] he left it to us to work out the particulars.

3. Well then, in the first place, the case of the
cupping-instrument is like this. The air, which along
with heat it has enclosed next to the flesh, having
become fiery and finer in texture than the pores of

where respiration occurs ἑλκομένω τῶ ἀέρος ἀντὶ τῶ ἀπορ-
ρέοντος, the cupping-instrument ἀπαναλωθέντος ὑπὸ τῶ
πυρὸς τῶ ἀέρος ἐφέλκεται τὸ ὑγρόν (cf. Hero Alexandrinus,
Pneumatica, Prooem., p. 16, 10-16 [Schmidt]), and amber
ἀναλαμβάνει τὸ ὅμοιον σῶμα.
    [b] Timaeus 79 A 5–E 9. Cf. Albinus, Epitome xxi (p. 107
[Louis] = p. 175, 20-27 [Hermann]) and " Timaeus Locrus "
101 D—102 A (see the last note supra) and the criticisms of the
exposition by Aristotle (Parva Naturalia 472 b 6-32) and by
Galen (De Placitis Hippoc. et Plat. viii, 8 = pp. 714, 14–720,
16 [Mueller] and In Plat. Timaeum Comment. Frag. xvii-
xix = pp. 22, 27–26, 2 ([Schröder]).
    [c] In this paraphrase of Timaeus 80 c 3-8 διακρινόμενα καὶ
συγκρινόμενα (c 4-5) is omitted, an omission which affects
the meaning of διαμειβόμενα in the original and obscures the
connexion of the passage with Timaeus 58 B 6–c 2.

(1004) τῶν τοῦ[1] χαλκοῦ πόρων[2] ἀραιότερος ἐξέπεσεν
οὐκ εἰς κενὴν χώραν (οὐ γὰρ ἔστιν) εἰς δὲ[3] τὸν
περιεστῶτα τὴν σικύαν[4] ἔξωθεν ἀέρα, κἀκεῖνον ἀπ-
έωσεν· ὁ δὲ τὸν πρὸ αὐτοῦ· καὶ τοῦτο πάσχων
ἀεὶ καὶ δρῶν[5] ὁ ἔμπροσθεν ὑποχωρεῖ,[6] τῆς κε-
νουμένης γλιχόμενος χώρας ἣν ὁ πρῶτος ἐξέλιπεν·
1005 οὕτω δὲ τῇ σαρκὶ περιπίπτων, ἧς ἡ σικύα[7] δέ-
δρακται, καὶ ἀναπιέζων[8] ἅμα[9] συνεκθλίβει τὸ ὑγρὸν
εἰς τὴν σικύαν.[10]

4. Ἡ δὲ κατάποσις γίγνεται τὸν αὐτὸν τρόπον·
αἱ γὰρ περὶ τὸ στόμα καὶ[11] τὸν στόμαχον κοι-
λότητες ἀέρος ἀεὶ πλήρεις εἰσίν. ὅταν οὖν ἐμ-
πιεσθῇ τὸ σιτίον ὑπὸ τῆς γλώττης, ἅμα καὶ τῶν
παρισθμίων ἐνταθέντων, ἐκθλιβόμενος ὁ ἀὴρ πρὸς
τὸν οὐρανὸν[12] ἕπεται τοῦ ὑποχωροῦντος καὶ συν-
επωθεῖ τὸ σιτίον.

5. Τὰ δὲ ῥιπτούμενα βάρη τὸν ἀέρα σχίζει μετὰ
πληγῆς ἐμπεσόντα[13] καὶ διίστησιν· ὁ δὲ περιρ-
ρέων ὀπίσω τῷ[14] φύσιν ἔχειν ἀεὶ τὴν ἐρημουμένην[15]

---

[1] τοῦ -omitted by J[1], g.
[2] πόρων ὡς -X ; σωρῶν -J[1], g.
[3] οὐδὲ -ε.
[4] σικύαν -J[1], g.
[5] δρῶν -Wyttenbach ; ἄγων -mss.
[6] ὑποχωρεῖ ‹ὁ δ' ὄπισθεν ἐπιχωρεῖ› -Wyttenbach.
[7] σικήα -J[1], g.
[8] ἀναπιέζων -Emperius (*Op. Philol.*, p. 340); ἀναξέων -J, g ; ἀναζέων -all other mss.
[9] ἅμα -omitted by n.
[10] σικήαν -J[1], g.
[11] τὸ στόμα καὶ -omitted by J[1], g.
[12] τὸν οὐρανὸν -Nogarola, Stephanus, a[1] (?); τὸ ἧκον -a[2],

66

the bronze escapes not into empty space (for there isn't any) but into the air surrounding the cupping-instrument from without and pushes this air aside, as this air does that before itself ; and at every step thus acted upon and acting the air that is in front gives way, making for the vacated space which the first had left, and so, falling upon the circumference of the flesh gripped by the cupping-instrument and pressing it up, it simultaneously squeezes the liquid out into the cupping-instrument.[a]

4. Swallowing occurs in the same way, for the cavities of the mouth and the oesophagus are always full of air. So, when the food is pressed in by the tongue, the fauces too having been stretched taut at the same time, the air, being squeezed out against the palate, follows closely upon that which gives way and helps to push the food on.[b]

5. Weights that are thrown cleave the air and separate it because of the impact with which they have fallen upon it ; and the air because of its nature always to seek out and fill up the space left empty

---

[a] Asclepiades of Bithynia, who compared the mechanism of respiration with the action of cupping-instruments, must have explained the latter also by a kind of περίωσις without the intervention of ὁλκή ([Plutarch], De Placitis 903 e-f = Dox. Graeci, pp. 412, 31–413, 1 ; cf. R. A. Fritzsche, Rhein. Mus., N.F. lvii [1902], p. 384).

[b] Cf. the view opposed by Galen (De Naturalibus Facultatibus iii, chap. 8 = pp. 176-177 [Kühn]) that in deglutition the food is merely pushed down from above without any ὁλκή.

---

n ; τὸ εἶκον -all other mss. (τὸ omitted by Voss. 16, Escorial T-11-5).

[13] All mss. (pace Hubert) ; ἐκπεσόντα -Aldine, Basil.

[14] τὸ -J.   [15] ἐρημωμένην -J[1].

(1005) χώραν διώκειν καὶ ἀναπληροῦν συνέπεται τῷ ἀφιεμένῳ[1] τὴν κίνησιν συνεπιταχύνων.[2]

B 6. Αἱ δὲ τῶν κεραυνῶν πτώσεις καὶ αὐταὶ ῥί-
ψεσιν ἐοίκασιν· ἐκπηδᾷ γὰρ ὑπὸ πληγῆς ἐν τῷ
νέφει γενομένης τὸ πυρῶδες εἰς τὸν ἀέρα, κἀκεῖνος
ἀντιρραγεὶς ὑποχωρεῖ καὶ πάλιν εἰς ταὐτὸ[3] συμπί-
πτων ἄνωθεν ἐξωθεῖ κάτω παρὰ φύσιν[4] ἀποβιαζό-
μενος τὸν κεραυνόν.

7. Τὸ δ' ἤλεκτρον[5] οὐδὲν ἕλκει τῶν παρακει-
μένων ὥσπερ οὐδὲ ἡ σιδηρῖτις λίθος, οὐδὲ προσ-
πηδᾷ τι τούτοις ἀφ' αὑτοῦ τῶν πλησίον· ἀλλὰ ἡ
μὲν λίθος τινὰς ἀπορροὰς[6] ἐξίησιν ἐμβριθεῖς καὶ
πνευματώδεις, αἷς ὁ συνεχὴς ἀναστελλόμενος ἀὴρ
ὠθεῖ τὸν πρὸ αὑτοῦ· κἀκεῖνος ἐν κύκλῳ περιιὼν
καὶ ὑπονοστῶν αὖθις ἐπὶ[7] τὴν κενουμένην χώραν
C ἀποβιάζεται καὶ συνεφέλκεται τὸν σίδηρον. τὸ δ'

---

[1] ἐφιεμένῳ -J[1], g, Voss. 16, Escorial T-11-5.
[2] ἐπιταχύνων -E, B, Escorial T-11-5.
[3] εἰς ταυτὰ -J, g.
[4] παρὰ τὴν φύσιν -J[1], g.
[5] τὸ δ' ἤλεκτρον . . . συνεφέλκεται τὸν σίδηρον -omitted by ε.
[6] Bernardakis ; ἀπορροίας -mss.
[7] ὑπὸ -X.

---

[a] Cf. Simplicius, Phys., p. 668, 25-32 on Aristotle, Physics
215 a 14-15 and the objections of Aristotle (Physics 267 a
15-20) and of Philoponus (Phys., pp. 639, 12—641, 6). Nothing is said in the Timaeus of the acceleration to which
Plutarch refers (cf. A. E. Taylor, A Commentary on Plato's
Timaeus, p. 572 on 80 a 1-2 ; F. Wehrli, Die Schule des
Aristoteles, Heft v[2], p. 63 on Strato, frag. 73).

[b] Cf. Aristotle's explanation of the downward motion of
the thunderbolt contrary to its nature (Meteorology 342 a 12-
16 and 369 a 17-24).

[c] i.e. τὴν λίθον τὴν Ἡρακλείαν of 1004 ε supra called ἡ
σιδηρῖτις as here by Plutarch in De Iside 376 β and Quaest.

flows around behind and follows along with the object discharged, helping to accelerate its motion.[a]

6. The falling of thunderbolts itself also resembles the hurling of missiles, for the impact that has occurred in the cloud makes the fiery substance leap out into the air, and the latter gives way when it has been rent asunder and, falling back together again, expels the thunderbolt from above, forcing it back downwards contrary to its nature.[b]

7. Amber does not attract any of the objects placed near it as the loadstone [c] does not either, nor does any of the things in their neighbourhood spring to them of itself; but the loadstone emits certain effluvia which are heavy and like wind, and the contiguous air, forced back by these, pushes the air that is before itself, and that air, moving around in a circle and settling again upon the vacated space, forces the iron back and drags it along with itself.[d]

Conviv. 641 c ; *cf.* Plato, *Ion* 533 d 3-5 and Pliny, *N.H.* xxxvi, 127.

[d] The similarity of the ancillary cause of the iron's motion given by Lucretius (vi, 1022-1041) led R. A. Fritzsche to assume a common source and to identify this as Asclepiades of Bithynia, who is known to have denied the occurrence of ὁλκή in nature (*Rhein. Mus.*, N.F. lvii [1902], pp. 369-373 and pp. 386-389) ; but *cf.* M. Bollack, *Rev. Études Latines*, xli (1963 [1964]), pp. 171-173 and pp. 183-184. Plutarch's συνεφέλκεται here and ἐφέλκεται in the next sentence are unfortunate expressions at least, for, although they refer to " traction " by the air which is driven from behind and not to any " attraction " by the magnet or amber, they might be thought to compromise the denial of ὁλκή, the original principle of the theory (*cf.* οὐδὲν ἕλκει at the beginning of this paragraph), and to represent a contamination with the Epicurean notions expressed by *ducitur ex elementis* (Lucretius, vi, 1012) and by συνεπισπᾶσθαι τὸν σίδηρον (Epicurus, frag. 293 [Usener, *Epicurea*, p. 208, 26-27]).

(1005) ἤλεκτρον ἔχει μέν τι[1] φλογοειδὲς ἢ πνευματικόν,
ἐκβάλλει δὲ τοῦτο τρίψει[2] τῆς ἐπιφανείας, τῶν
πόρων ἀναστομωθέντων· τὸ δὲ ταὐτὸ μὲν ἐκπεσὸν
ποιεῖ τῷ[3] τῆς σιδηρίτιδος, ἐφέλκεται δὲ τῶν πλησίον
τὰ κουφότατα καὶ ξηρότατα διὰ λεπτότητα καὶ
ἀσθένειαν· οὐ γάρ ἐστιν ἰσχυρὸν οὐδ' ἔχει βάρος
οὐδὲ ῥύμην πλῆθος ἀέρος ἐξῶσαι δυναμένην, ᾧ τῶν
μειζόνων, ὥσπερ ἡ σιδηρῖτις, ἐπικρατήσει. πῶς οὖν
οὔτε λίθον οὔτε ξύλον ὁ ἀὴρ ἀλλὰ μόνον τὸν σίδηρον[4] ὠθεῖ καὶ προσστέλλει[5] πρὸς τὴν[6] λίθον; αὕτη δ' ἐστὶ μὲν ἀπορία κοινὴ πρός τε τοὺς[7] ὁλκῇ
τῆς[8] λίθου καὶ τοὺς[9] φορᾷ τοῦ σιδήρου τὴν σύμ-
πηξιν οἰομένους γίγνεσθαι τῶν σωμάτων, εἴη λύσις
D δ' ἂν οὕτως ὑπὸ τοῦ Πλάτωνος.[10] ὁ σίδηρος οὔτ'
ἄγαν ἀραιός ἐστιν ὡς ξύλον οὔτ' ἄγαν πυκνὸς ὡς
χρυσὸς ἢ λίθος ἀλλ' ἔχει πόρους καὶ οἴμους[11] καὶ
τραχύτητας διὰ τὰς ἀνωμαλίας τῷ ἀέρι συμμέτρους,
ὥστε μὴ[12] ἀπολισθαίνειν ἀλλὰ ἕδραις τισὶν ἐνισχό-
μενον καὶ ἀντερείσεσι[13] περιπλοκὴν σύμμετρον ἐχού-

---

[1] μέντοι -A, Escorial T-11-5.
[2] τῇ τρίψει -A², β, γ, E, B, Voss. 16, Escorial T-11-5,
Bonon.   [3] τὸ -J, g, Voss. 16.
[4] τὸν σίδηρον μόνον -J, g.
[5] H. C. ; προστέλλει -mss.
[6] Wyttenbach ; τὸν -mss.
[7] τῇ -J, g.
[8] τῆς -Bernardakis ; τοῦ -mss.
[9] τῇ -J, g.
[10] H. C. ; σωμάτων εἰλυσπᾶν οὕτως ὑπὸ τοῦ Πλάτωνος -X,
ε, n ; σωμάτων . . . vac. 18 (erased) . . . ὁ σίδηρος -a ; σωμάτων . . . vac. 4 . . . ὁ σίδηρος (with εἰλυσπᾶν οὕτως ὑπὸ τοῦ
Πλάτωνος added in margin) -β ; σωμάτων . . . vac. 11 to
16 . . . ὁ σίδηρος -A, E, B ; between σωμάτων and ὁ σίδηρος: εἰλυσπᾶν -Voss. 16, καὶ εἰλυσπᾶν -Escorial T-11-5, εἰλυσπᾶν
(with οὕτως ὑπὸ τοῦ Πλάτωνος deleted) -Bonon. ; σωμάτων· ὁ

Amber contains a substance like flame or wind which
it ejects when its pores have been opened by friction
of its surface ; and this substance, when it has
escaped, has the same action as that from the loadstone has but because of its tenuousness and weak-
ness drags along the lightest and driest of the things
in the neighbourhood, for it is not strong and does
not have weight or impetus capable of expelling an
amount of air with which to master the larger objects
as the loadstone does. How is it then that the air
pushes and presses against the loadstone neither
stone nor wood but only iron ? This, to be sure, is a
difficulty that confronts equally those who think that
the cohesion of the bodies comes about by the loadstone's attraction and those who think that it comes
about by conveyance of the iron,[a] but Plato might
provide a solution in the following way. Iron is
neither exceedingly loose in texture like wood nor
exceedingly close like gold or stone but has pores
and passages and corrugations which by reason of
their irregularities conform to the air ; and the
result is for the air, however in its motion to the
loadstone it may fall upon the iron, not to slip off
but, intercepted by certain lodgements and counter-

---

[a] *i.e.* by the iron's being " carried " or propelled to the
magnet as in Plutarch's own explanation ; φορᾷ does not
here refer to any " impulse " of the iron itself, for such an
explanation (as *e.g.* in Alexander, *Quaestiones*, p. 74, 24-30
[Bruns]) would not be confronted by this difficulty.

σίδηρος (without lacuna) -J, g, γ; εὔλυτος δ' ἂν οὕτως ὑπὸ
(or μετὰ) τοῦ Πλάτωνος -Hubert ; ἐλύετο δ' ἂν οὕτως ὑπὸ τοῦ
Πλάτωνος -Bernardakis.
[11] X, ε, n ; οἴμας -all other mss.
[12] Dübner ; μήτε -mss.
[13] ἀντερείσεσι καὶ -J, g.

(1005) σαις, ὡς ἂν ἐμπέσῃ πρὸς τὴν¹ λίθον φερόμενος, ἀπο-
βιάζεσθαι καὶ προωθεῖν τὸν σίδηρον. τούτων μὲν
οὖν τοιοῦτός τις² ἂν εἴη λόγος.

8. Ἡ δὲ τῶν³ ἐπὶ γῆς ὑδάτων ῥύσις οὐχ ὁμοίως
εὐσύνοπτον ἔχει τὸν τῆς ἀντιπεριώσεως τρόπον.⁴
ἀλλὰ χρὴ καταμανθάνειν τὰ λιμναῖα τῶν ὑδάτων
ἀτρεμοῦντα καὶ μένοντα τῷ περικεχύσθαι καὶ συν-
Ε αγαγεῖν πανταχόθεν αὐτοῖς⁵ ἀκίνητον ἀέρα, μηδαμοῦ κενὴν ποιοῦντα χώραν. τὸ γοῦν ἐπιπολῆς
ὕδωρ ἔν τε ταῖς λίμναις καὶ ἐν τοῖς πελάγεσι δο-
νεῖται καὶ κυμαίνεται τοῦ ἀέρος σάλον λαμβάνον-
τος· ἕπεται γὰρ εὐθὺς μεθισταμένῳ καὶ συναπορρεῖ⁶
διὰ τὴν ἀνωμαλίαν· ἡ γὰρ κάτω πληγὴ τὴν κοιλό-
τητα ποιεῖ τοῦ κύματος ἡ δ' ἄνω τὸν ὄγκον, ἄχρι⁷
οὗ⁸ καταστῇ καὶ παύσηται, τῆς περιεχούσης⁹ τὰ
ὑγρὰ χώρας ἱσταμένης.¹⁰ αἱ ῥύσεις οὖν τῶν¹¹ φερομέ-
νων ἀεὶ τὰ ὑποχωροῦντα τοῦ ἀέρος διώκουσαι τοῖς
δ' ἀντιπεριωθουμένοις¹² ἐλαυνόμεναι τὸ ἐνδελεχὲς
καὶ ἀλώφητον ἔχουσι. διὸ καὶ φέρονται θᾶττον οἱ
F ποταμοὶ πληθύοντες¹³· ὅταν δ' ὀλίγον ᾖ καὶ κοῖλον,
⟨ἀν⟩ίεται¹⁴ τὸ ὑγρὸν ὑπ' ἀσθενείας, οὐχ ὑπείκοντος¹⁵

¹ Dübner (after Wyttenbach *supra*) ; τὸν -MSS.
² τις -omitted by J¹, g, ε.
³ τοῦ -g.   ⁴ τόπον -J, g.
⁵ Escorial T-11-5 ; αὐτοῖς -all other MSS.
⁶ συναπορεῖ -X, ε ; συναπορρεῖται -J, g.
⁷ Bernardakis ; ἄχρις -MSS.   ⁸ οὖν -n.
⁹ περιούσης -J¹, g, β (superscript over περιεχούσης) ; περι-
εχούσας -Escorial T-11-5 (σης over σας -corr.).
¹⁰ ἱστάμενος -J¹, Voss. 16, Escorial T-11-5, Bonon.ᶜᵒʳʳ· (ος
superscript over ης) ; ἱστάμενα -g ; ἐνισταμένης ("*impediente*")
-Wyttenbach.   ¹¹ τοῦ -Escorial T-11-5.
¹² τοῦ δ' ἀντιπεριπεριωθουμένου -Escorial T-11-5.
¹³ πληθύοντες -J, g, Voss. 16, Escorial T-11-5.

72

pressures with meshes that conform to it, to force
the iron back and push it on before itself.[a] Well
then, of these phenomena there might be some such
explanation.

8. It is not similarly easy to comprehend the way
in which cyclical propulsion is involved in the flowing
of waters upon the earth. It must be observed, however, that the water of pools is calm and at rest
because it has spread and collected about itself from
all sides motionless air that nowhere leaves an
empty space. At any rate, the water on the surface
in pools and in seas is agitated and undulates when
the air begins to surge, for it straightway follows
the latter as it changes position and flows off along
with it because of the irregularity, the downward
impact [b] producing the trough of the wave and the
upward impact the swell until it has settled down
and stopped as the space that encompasses the
waters comes to rest. The streams of running
waters, then, always pursuing the air that gives
way and being driven on by that which is pushed
around in turn, flow perpetually and unremittingly.
This is also why rivers run more swiftly when they
are full ; but, when the water is low and shallow, it
grows slack from feebleness, as the air does not

[a] Cf. Lucretius, vi, 1056-1064 with R. A. Fritzsche, Rhein.
Mus., N.F. lvii (1902), p. 370 and p. 372, n. 14 ; and especially for the terminology cf. the use of the theory of effluvia,
pores, and corrugations of a surface in Plutarch, Quaest.
Naturales 916 D-F.
[b] i.e. the impact of the air on the water.

---

[14] Wyttenbach ; ἵεται -X, J, g, β, B, ε, n ; ἵεται -all
other mss. ; ἵσταται -Wyttenbach, Apelt (Philologus, lxii
[1903], p. 287).   [15] ὑπήκοντος -J, ε, n.

(1005) τοῦ ἀέρος οὐδὲ πολλὴν ἀντιπερίστασιν λαμβάνοντος.
οὕτω δὲ καὶ τὰ πηγαῖα τῶν ὑδάτων ἀναγκαῖόν[1]
ἐστιν ἀναφέρεσθαι, τοῦ θύραθεν ἀέρος εἰς τὰς κενουμένας[2] ἐν βάθει χώρας[3] ὑποφερομένου καὶ πάλιν θύ-
1006 ραζε τὸ ὕδωρ ἐκπέμποντος. οἴκου δὲ βαθυσκίου
καὶ περιέχοντος ἀέρα νήνεμον[4] ὕδατι ῥανθὲν[5] ἔδαφος
πνεῦμα ποιεῖ καὶ ἄνεμον, μεθισταμένου τοῦ ἀέρος
ἐξ ἕδρας παρεμπίπτοντι τῷ ὑγρῷ καὶ πληγὰς
λαμβάνοντος.[6] οὕτως ἐξωθεῖσθαί θ' ὑπ' ἀλλήλων
καὶ ἀνθυπείκειν ἀλλήλοις πέφυκεν, οὐκ οὔσης κε-
νότητος ἐν ᾗ θάτερον ἱδρυθὲν[7] οὐ μεθέξει τῆς θατέρου μεταβολῆς.

9. Καὶ μὴν τὰ περὶ τῆς[8] συμφωνίας αὐτὸς εἴρηκεν ὃν τρόπον ὁμοι⟨οπαθεῖς αἱ κινήσεις ποι⟩[9]οῦσι
τοὺς φθόγγους. ὀξὺς μὲν γὰρ ὁ ταχὺς γίγνεται
βαρὺς δὲ ὁ βραδύς[10]· διὸ καὶ πρότερον κινοῦσι[11] τὴν
αἴσθησιν οἱ ὀξεῖς· ὅταν δὲ τούτοις ἤδη[12] μαραινομέ-
νοις[13] καὶ ἀπολήγουσιν οἱ βραδεῖς ἐπιβάλωσιν ἀρχό-
B μενοι, τὸ κραθὲν αὐτῶν διὰ ὁμοιοπάθειαν ἡδονὴν
τῇ ἀκοῇ παρέσχεν, ἣν συμφωνίαν καλοῦσιν. ὅτι
δὲ τούτων ὄργανον ὁ ἀήρ ἐστι ῥᾴδιον συνιδεῖν ἐκ
τῶν προειρημένων. ἔστι γὰρ ἡ φωνὴ πληγὴ τοῦ

---

[1] τὰ πηγαῖα τῶν ἀναγκαίων -J[1], g.

[2] κενουμένας -X[1]; κινουμένας -J[1].

[3] χώρας ἐν βάθει -X.

[4] Wyttenbach (ἢ νήνεμον -Leonicus, Nogarola) ; ἀέρα ἢ
ἄνεμον -mss.   [5] ῥαθὲν -J[1].

[6] λαμβάνοντι -J[1], g.

[7] J, g ; ἱδρυνθὲν -all other mss.

[8] τὰς -Voss. 16, Escorial T-11-5, Bonon.

[9] ⟨...⟩ -added by Pohlenz ; ὁμοιοῦσι -mss. ; ὁμολογοῦσι οἱ
φθόγγοι -Nogarola.   [10] βαρύς -J[1].

[11] X, ε, n ; πρότερον οὐ κινοῦσι -all other mss. (but οὐ erased
in a and cancelled in A).   [12] ἤδη -omitted by ε.

yield and does not undergo much cyclical replacement. It must be in this way too that the waters of
fountains run upwards, the air from outside running
down into the vacated underground spaces and
thrusting the water forth again. In a darkened
house where the air enclosed is still sprinkling the
floor with water produces a draught or breeze, as
the air shifts from its position before the moisture
when it intervenes and is subjected to its impacts.
Thus the two are naturally expelled by each other
and yield to each other in turn, for there is no vacuity
in which the one could be situated and so not partake of the change in the other.

9. And now as to the subject of consonance, he
has himself stated [a] how the sounds ⟨are made con-
gruous by the motions⟩. For the sound that is swift
turns out to be high, and that which is slow to be
low, which is also why the sense is set in motion
sooner by the high sounds ; and, when these as they
are already fading out and dying away are over-
taken by the slow sounds just beginning,[b] the product of their blending because of the congruity affords
the hearing pleasure which men call consonance.
That the air is the instrument of this process is easy
to see from what was previously stated.[c] Sound, in

[a] *Timaeus* 80 a 3–b 8. Of the genuine problems involved
in this passage Plutarch appears not to have been aware.
They are stated but not persuasively resolved by Cornford
(*Plato's Cosmology*, pp. 320-326) and Moutsopoulos (*La
Musique . . . de Platon*, pp. 36-42).

[b] *i.e.* just beginning to affect the percipient by setting the
sense in motion.

[c] *Timaeus* 67 b 2-6 ; *cf.* Plutarch, *De Fortuna* 98 b, *De E*
390 b, and *De Defectu Orac.* 436 d.

---

[13] φανερομένοις (with μαραινο superscript) -γ.

(1006) αἰσθανομένου δι' ὤτων ὑπ' ἀέρος· πλήττει γὰρ¹
πληγεὶς ὁ ἀὴρ ὑπὸ τοῦ κινήσαντος, ἂν μὲν ᾖ σφο-
δρόν, ὀξέως, ἂν δ' ἀμβλύ, μαλακώτερον· ὁ δὴ²
σφόδρα³ καὶ συντόνως πληγεὶς⁴ προσμίγνυσι τῇ
ἀκοῇ πρότερος,⁵ εἶτα περιὼν πάλιν⁶ καὶ καταλαμ-
βάνων τὸν⁷ βραδύτερον συνέπεται καὶ συμπαραπέμ-
πει⁸ τὴν αἴσθησιν.

ZHTHMA H'

1. Πῶς λέγει τὰς ψυχὰς ὁ Τίμαιος εἴς τε γῆν καὶ
σελήνην καὶ τἆλλα ὅσα ὄργανα χρόνου σπαρῆναι;
C   Πότερον οὕτως⁹ ἐκίνει τὴν γῆν ὥσπερ ἥλιον καὶ
σελήνην καὶ¹⁰ τοὺς πέντε πλάνητας, οὓς ὄργανα
χρόνου διὰ τὰς τροπὰς προσηγόρευε,¹¹ καὶ ἔδει τὴν
γῆν ἰλλομένην¹² περὶ τὸν διὰ πάντων πόλον τεταμέ-
νον¹³ μεμηχανῆσθαι μὴ¹⁴ συνεχομένην καὶ μένουσαν
ἀλλὰ στρεφομένην¹⁵ καὶ ἀνειλουμένην νοεῖν, ὡς

¹ τε -J¹, g ; τε superscript over γὰρ -X¹.
² ὁ δὴ -X, J, g, A, γ, E, B ; ὁ δὲ -n.
³ σφοδρὸς -g.   ⁴ σύντονος πληγὴ -J, g.
⁵ πρότερον -J¹, g.   ⁶ πάντα -J¹, g.
⁷ τὸ -J¹, g, ε.
⁸ παραπέμπει -Voss. 16, Escorial T-11-5.
⁹ ὄντως -X, J.
¹⁰ ἢ σελήνην ἢ -J¹, g.
¹¹ προσηγόρευσε -J¹, g.
¹² ἰλλομένην . . . ἀνειλουμένην -omitted by J¹, g ; εἰλλουμένην
(ει and ου superscript over ι and ο) -B^corr. ; εἰλουμένην -Voss.
16, Escorial T-11-5.
¹³ τεταγμένον -a, A, β¹ (γ erased -β²), γ, E, B, ε, n, Escorial
T-11-5.
¹⁴ X, β², Bonon., Voss. 16, Escorial T-11-5 ; μὴ μεμηχανῆσθαι -all other mss. ; [μεμηχανῆσθαι] -Hartman (De Plutarcho, p. 585).
¹⁵ συστρεφομένην -X.

fact, is the impact made by air through the ears upon the percipient, for the air, when struck by the agent that moved it, strikes sharply if that agent is vehement and more softly if it is dull. The air, then, that has been struck vehemently and intensely comes upon the hearing sooner and then, moving around again and catching up the slower air,[a] accompanies it and with it conveys the sensation.

QUESTION VIII

1. WHAT does Timaeus mean by saying [b] that the souls were sowed in earth and moon and all the rest of the instruments of time ?

Was he giving the earth motion like that of sun and moon and the five planets, which because they reverse their courses [c] he called instruments of time ; and ought the earth coiling about the axis extended through all [d] be understood to have been devised not as confined and at rest but as turning and whirl-

---

[a] This seems to contradict the statement just above, ὅταν δὲ τούτοις . . . οἱ βραδεῖς ἐπιβάλωσιν ἀρχόμενοι . . ., and is certainly not in accord with *Timaeus* 80 A 6–B 4.

[b] Plato, *Timaeus* 42 D 4-5 (see also 41 E 4-5) ; *cf.* [Plutarch], *De Fato* 573 E.

[c] *Cf. Timaeus* 39 D 7-8 (. . . τῶν ἄστρων ὅσα δι' οὐρανοῦ πορευόμενα ἔσχεν τροπάς . . .) and 40 B 6-7 (τὰ δὲ τρεπόμενα καὶ πλάνην τοιαύτην ἴσχοντα . . .) with Proclus, *In Platonis Timaeum* iii, pp. 127, 31–128, 1 (Diehl).

[d] *Timaeus* 40 B 8–c 2. Plutarch's μεμηχανῆσθαι represents Plato's ἐμηχανήσατο. Instead of διὰ πάντων (*i.e.* all the planetary orbits) the mss. of Plato have διὰ παντός, δι' ἅπαντος, or διὰ τοῦ παντός ; and instead of ἰλλομένην two of them (W, Y) have εἰλουμένην, while two (A, P) have ἰλλομένην (or εἰλλ-) τὴν (*cf.* Cornford, *Plato's Cosmology*, p. 120, n. 1 ; and for the textual tradition of Aristotle, *De Caelo* 293 b 31-32 *cf.* P. Moraux, *Hermes*, lxxxii [1954], pp. 176-178).

(1006) ὕστερον Ἀρίσταρχος καὶ Σέλευκος ἀπεδείκνυσαν, ὁ
μὲν ὑποτιθέμενος μόνον ὁ δὲ Σέλευκος καὶ ἀποφαι-
νόμενος ; Θεόφραστος δὲ καὶ προσιστορεῖ τῷ
Πλάτωνι πρεσβυτέρῳ γενομένῳ μεταμέλειν ὡς οὐ
προσήκουσαν ἀποδόντι τῇ γῇ τὴν μέσην χώραν
τοῦ παντός.

2. Ἦ τούτοις μὲν ἀντίκειται πολλὰ τῶν ὁμολο-
D γουμένως[1] ἀρεσκόντων τῷ ἀνδρί, μεταγραπτέον δὲ
τὸ " χρόνου " " χρόνῳ," λαμβάνοντας[2] ἀντὶ τῆς
γενικῆς[3] τὴν δοτικήν, καὶ δεκτέον ὄργανα μὴ τοὺς
ἀστέρας ἀλλὰ τὰ σώματα τῶν ζῴων λέγεσθαι
καθάπερ Ἀριστοτέλης ὡρίσατο τὴν ψυχὴν ἐντε-

---

[1] ὁμολογουμένων -J[1] (final ν remade to ς -J[2]), g.
[2] X, J[1], g, β, Bonon., Voss. 16, Escorial T-11-5[corr.] ; λαμβάνοντος -γ, Escorial T-11-5[1] ; λαμβάνοντα -a, A, E, B, ε, n.
[3] γενητικῆς -J[1], g.

---

[a] Cf. Plutarch, De Facie 923 a with the references in my
note ad loc. (L.C.L. xii, p. 54, note a).
[b] Cf. Heath, Aristarchus of Samos, pp. 305-307 ; S. Pines,
" Un fragment de Séleucus . . .," Rev. d'Histoire des
Sciences, xvi (1963), pp. 193-209 ; and N. Swerdlow, Isis,
lxiv (1973), pp. 242-243 in his review of B. L. van der
Waerden, ibid., pp. 239-243.
[c] Theophrastus, Phys. Opin., frag. 22 (Dox. Graeci, p.
494, 1-3) ; cf. Plutarch, Numa xi, 3 (67 D).
[d] Like Chalcidius (Platonis Timaeus, p. 187, 4-13 [Wro-
bel] =p. 166, 6-12 [Waszink]) Plutarch here recognizes only
two possible interpretations of ἰλλομένην περὶ τόν . . . πόλον :
one, that the earth is stationary at the centre (with συνεχομένην καὶ μένουσαν cf. Proclus, In Platonis Timaeum iii, p. 137,
6-7 and 13-20 [Diehl] and Plutarch's own usage in Quaest.
Conviv. 728 E : ἰλλομένην τὴν ὄπα καὶ καθειργομένην), and
the other, that the earth revolves like a planet around the
axis common to all the planetary orbits (with στρεφομένην
καὶ ἀνειλουμένην cf. Proclus, In Platonis Timaeum iii, p. 138,
7-8 [Diehl] : εἰλουμένην καὶ στρεφομένην ; cf. εἰλουμένων
[Simplicius, Phys., p. 292, 28-29] and ἀνείλησιν [Simplicius,
78

ing about in the way set forth later by Aristarchus [a] and Seleucus,[b] by the former only as an hypothesis but by Seleucus beyond that as a statement of fact ? In fact Theophrastus even adds the observation [c] that Plato, when he had grown older, repented of having assigned to the earth as not befitting her the midmost space of the sum of things.[d]

2. Or is this in opposition to many of the opinions that the man admittedly held ; and must we change " of time " to read " in time," adopting the dative instead of the genitive, and take instruments to mean not the stars but the bodies of living beings in the way that Aristotle defined the soul as actuality

De Caelo, p. 499, 15]). The way in which the second alternative is limited by the comparison with the hypothesis of Aristarchus is made clear by what Theophrastus is reported to have said and doubly clear by the reference in Numa xi, where . . . τῆς γῆς ὡς ἐν ἑτέρᾳ χώρᾳ καθεστώσης . . . shows it to be incompatible with the " more genuinely " Pythagorean theory of Simplicius which Cornford sought to identify as its true basis (Plato's Cosmology, pp. 127-129 ; K. Gaiser, Platons ungeschriebene Lehre [Stuttgart, 1963], p. 184, n. 155 [pp. 385-387]) but which is itself certainly post-Aristotelian (cf. W. Burkert, Weisheit und Wissenschaft [Nürnberg, 1962], pp. 216-217). Plutarch's two alternatives silently exclude the possibility that the Timaeus refers to a central earth with axial rotation (Aristotle, De Caelo 293 b 30-32 and 296 a 26-27) or with any sort of vibratory or oscillatory motion, discredited modern fantasies recently revived by K. Gaiser (op. cit., p. 183, n. 153 [pp. 381-385]) in the form of " wobbling motion about the axis . . . to produce a kind of nutation " and account for precession—which was unknown to Plato. On Timaeus 40 B 8-c 3, Aristotle's statements in the De Caelo, and the remark by Theophrastus cf. Cherniss, Aristotle's Criticism of Plato, pp. 545-564 ; I. Düring, Gnomon, xxvii (1955), pp. 156-157 ; F. M. Brignoli, Giornale Italiano di Filologia, xi (1958), pp. 246-260 ; W. Burkert, Weisheit und Wissenschaft, p. 305, n. 17.

(1006) λέχειαν[1] σώματος φυσικοῦ[2] ὀργανικοῦ δυνάμει
ζωὴν ἔχοντος, ὥστε τοιοῦτον εἶναι τὸν λόγον· αἱ
ψυχαὶ εἰς τὰ προσήκοντα ὀργανικὰ σώματα ἐν
χρόνῳ κατεσπάρησαν; ἀλλὰ καὶ τοῦτο παρὰ[3] τὴν
δόξαν ἐστίν· οὐ γὰρ ἅπαξ ἀλλὰ πολλάκις ὄργανα
χρόνου τοὺς ἀστέρας εἴρηκεν, ὅπου καὶ τὸν ἥλιον
αὐτὸν εἰς διορισμὸν καὶ φυλακὴν ἀριθμῶν χρόνου[4]
E γεγονέναι φησὶ μετὰ τῶν ἄλλων πλανήτων.

3. Ἄριστον οὖν τὴν γῆν ὄργανον ἀκούειν χρόνου,
μὴ κινουμένην ὥσπερ τοὺς ἀστέρας, ἀλλὰ τῷ[5]
περὶ αὐτὴν μένουσαν ἀεὶ παρέχειν ἐκείνοις φερο-
μένοις ἀνατολὰς καὶ δύσεις, αἷς τὰ πρῶτα μέτρα
τῶν χρόνων, ἡμέραι καὶ νύκτες, ὁρίζονται· διὸ
καὶ φύλακα καὶ δημιουργὸν αὐτὴν ἀτρεκῆ νυκτὸς
καὶ ἡμέρας προσεῖπε[6]· καὶ γὰρ οἱ τῶν ὡρολογίων
γνώμονες οὐ συμμεθιστάμενοι ταῖς σκιαῖς ἀλλὰ
ἑστῶτες ὄργανα χρόνου καὶ μέτρα[7] γεγόνασι, μι-
μούμενοι τῆς γῆς τὸ ἐπιπροσθοῦν τῷ ἡλίῳ περὶ

[1] ἐνδελέχειαν -J[1], g ; ἐντελέχειαν -all other mss. ; ⟨πρώτην⟩
ἐντελέχειαν -Bernardakis.
[2] ψυχικοῦ -J, g.
[3] περὶ -J[1].

[4] χρόνου -J[1], g ; χρόνου X[1] ; χρόνῳ -all other mss.
[5] τοῖς -J[1], g.
[6] προσῆκε -J, g.

[7] Pohlenz ; καὶ μέτρα χρόνου -X ; καὶ χρόνου μέτρα -all
other mss.

---

[a] Aristotle, *De Anima* 412 a 27-28 and 412 b 5-6 are here
conflated. In both the ἐντελέχεια is specified as ἡ πρώτη, but

of body that is natural, instrumental, and potentially possessed of life,[a] so that the meaning is like this : the souls in time were disseminated in the appropriate [b] instrumental bodies ? This too, however, is contrary to his thought, for it is not once but frequently that he has called the stars instruments of time, since he even says [c] that the sun itself along with the other planets came into being to distinguish and preserve the numbers of time.

3. It is best, then, to understand that the earth is an instrument of time not by being in motion as the stars are but by remaining always at rest as they revolve about her and so providing them with risings and settings, which define days and nights, the primary measures of times.[d] That is also why he called her strict guardian and artificer of night and day,[e] for the pins of sun-dials too have come to be instruments and measures of time not by changing their position along with the shadows but by standing still, imitating the earth's occultation of the sun when

Plutarch need not therefore have written πρώτην ἐντελέχειαν (cf. Dox. Graeci, p. 387 A 14-15 as against A 1-3). The crucial word for Plutarch here, ὀργανικοῦ, comes from the second passage and in order to support the proposed interpretation of ὄργανα in Timaeus 42 D 4-5 should be taken to mean not "furnished with instruments " (cf. De Anima 412 a 28–b 4) but " instrumental."

[b] Cf. Timaeus 41 E 5.

[c] Timaeus 38 c 5-6.

[d] Cf. " Timaeus Locrus " 97 D (γᾶ δ' ἐν μέσῳ ἱδρυμένα . . . ὥρός τε ὄρφνας καὶ ἁμέρας γίνεται δύσιάς τε καὶ ἀνατολὰς γεννῶσα . . .) ; Proclus, In Platonis Timaeum iii, pp. 139, 23–140, 5 (Diehl).

[e] Timaeus 40 c 1-2 ; cf. Plutarch, De Facie 937 E and 938 E with my notes ad loc. (L.C.L. xii, p. 157, note c and p. 165, note c).

PLUTARCH'S MORALIA

(1006) αὐτὴν ὑποφερομένῳ, καθάπερ εἶπεν Ἐμπεδοκλῆς

νύκτα δὲ γαῖα τίθησιν, ὑφισταμένη¹ φαέεσσι.

F τοῦτο μὲν οὖν τοιαύτην ἔχει τὴν ἐξήγησιν.

4. Ἐκεῖνο δὲ² μᾶλλον ἄν τις ὑπίδοιτο,³ μὴ παρὰ
τὸ εἰκὸς ὁ ἥλιος καὶ ἀτόπως λέγεται⁴ μετὰ τῆς
σελήνης καὶ τῶν πλανήτων εἰς διορισμὸν χρόνου
γεγονέναι. καὶ γὰρ ἄλλως μέγα τοῦ ἡλίου τὸ ἀξίωμα καὶ ὑπ' αὐτοῦ Πλάτωνος ἐν Πολιτείᾳ βασι-
λεὺς ἀνηγόρευται παντὸς τοῦ αἰσθητοῦ καὶ κύριος,
1007 ὥσπερ τοῦ νοητοῦ τἀγαθόν· ἐκείνου γὰρ⁵ ἔκγονος⁶
λέγεται, παρέχων τοῖς ὁρατοῖς μετὰ τοῦ φαίνεσθαι
τὸ γίγνεσθαι, καθάπερ ἀπ' ἐκείνου τὸ εἶναι καὶ τὸ
γιγνώσκεσθαι τοῖς νοητοῖς ὑπάρχει. τὸν δὴ τοιαύτην φύσιν ἔχοντα καὶ δύναμιν τηλικαύτην θεὸν
ὄργανον χρόνου γεγονέναι καὶ μέτρον ἐναργὲς τῆς⁷
πρὸς ἀλλήλας⁸ βραδυτῆτι καὶ τάχει τῶν ὀκτὼ
σφαιρῶν διαφορᾶς οὐ πάνυ δοκεῖ πρεπῶδες οὐδ'
ἄλλως εὔλογον εἶναι. ῥητέον οὖν τοὺς ὑπὸ τούτων

---

¹ ἐφισταμένη -Scaliger; ὑφισταμένοιο φάεσσι -Diels (*Po-
etarum Philos. Fragmenta* [1901], p. 126).
² ἐκεῖ δὲ -J¹ (corrected J¹), g.
³ ὑπείδοιτο -J¹ (before erasure), g; ὑπόδοιτο -Voss. 16 (ὁ
over erasure).
⁴ λέγεται -n; λέγηται -all other mss.
⁵ δὲ -J¹, g.
⁶ ἔγγονος -X¹; ἔκγονος -α, ε, n, Escorial T-11-5; ἔγγονος
-all other mss.
⁷ τῆς -omitted by X, J¹, g, α (but added superscript by
X¹ and α¹).
⁸ ἀλλήλαις -X (α superscript over αι -X¹), J¹, g.

ᵃ Empedocles, frag. B 48 (D.-K.). There is no good reason
to emend ὑφισταμένη (cf. Aeschylus, *Persae* 87 ; Thucydides,
vii, 66, 2) as Scaliger and Diels did ; but Kranz, who retains

82

he moves down around her, as Empedocles said

> Night is produced by the earth when she stands in the way of the daylight.[a]

Such, then, is the explanation of this point.

4. One might rather have misgivings about that other point, whether it is not unlikely and absurd to assert of the sun that along with the moon and the planets he came into being to distinguish time.[b] For the sun is generally rated high in dignity and especially by Plato who himself in the *Republic* [c] has proclaimed him king and sovereign of all that is perceptible just as the good is of the intelligible, for of that good he is said to be the offspring, affording to things visible with their coming to light their coming to be even as that good is for things intelligible the source of their being and of being known. Now certainly for the god with such a nature and so much power to have come to be as an instrument of time and evident measure of the relative difference in speed and slowness of the eight spheres [d] seems to be not very proper and to be unreasonable besides. It must be stated, then, that because of ignorance

it, is mistaken in insisting that it must imply motion of the earth (*Rhein. Mus.*, c [1957], pp. 122-124).

   [b] *i.e. Timaeus* 38 c 5-6, which was appealed to at the end of section 2 *supra* (1006 d *sub finem*).

   [c] *Republic* 506 e 3—507 a 4, 508 a 4-6, 508 b 12–c 2, 509 b 2-8, and 509 d 1-4 ; see also Plutarch, *De Facie* 944 e with my note *ad loc.* (*L.C.L.* xii, p. 213, note *g*).

   [d] *Timaeus* 39 b 2-5, where Plato says φοράς, however, and not " spheres " (*cf.* Cornford, *Plato's Cosmology*, pp. 78-79 and 119 ; Cherniss, *Aristotle's Criticism of Plato*, p. 555). So the " circles " of *Republic* 617 b 4-7 are called " spheres " by Plutarch in *Quaest. Conviv.* 745 c and in *De An. Proc. in Timaeo* 1029 c. *Cf.* also Albinus, *Epitome* xiv, 7 (p. 87, 1-8 [Louis] =pp. 170, 36–171, 7 [Hermann]).

(1007) ταραττομένους δι' ἄγνοιαν οἴεσθαι τὸν χρόνον[1]
μέτρον εἶναι κινήσεως καὶ ἀριθμὸν κατὰ πρότερον
καὶ ὕστερον,[2] ὡς Ἀριστοτέλης εἶπεν, ἢ τὸ ἐν
B κινήσει ποσόν, ὡς Σπεύσιππος, ἢ διάστημα κινήσεως ἄλλο[3] δ'[4] οὐδέν, ὡς ἔνιοι τῶν Στωικῶν ἀπὸ
συμβεβηκότος[5] ὁριζόμενοι τὴν δ' οὐσίαν αὐτοῦ καὶ
τὴν δύναμιν οὐ συνορῶντες, ἣν ὅ γε[6] Πίνδαρος
ἔοικεν οὐ φαύλως ὑπονοῶν εἰπεῖν

> ἄνακτα[7] τὸν πάντων ὑπερβάλλοντα χρόνον[8] μα-
> κάρων

ὅ τε Πυθαγόρας, ἐρωτηθεὶς τί χρόνος ἐστί, τὴν
τοὐρανοῦ[9] ψυχὴν εἰπεῖν. οὐ γὰρ πάθος οὐδὲ συμβεβηκὸς ἧς ἔτυχε κινήσεως ὁ χρόνος ἐστίν, αἰτία
δὲ καὶ δύναμις καὶ ἀρχὴ τῆς πάντα συνεχούσης τὰ
γιγνόμενα συμμετρίας καὶ τάξεως, ἣν ἡ τοῦ ὅλου
φύσις ἔμψυχος οὖσα κινεῖται· μᾶλλον δὲ κίνησις

---

[1] τῶν χρόνων -J, g.
[2] κατὰ τὸ πρότερον καὶ τὸ ὕστερον -Escorial T-11-5 ; κατὰ
⟨τὸ⟩ πρότερον καὶ ὕστερον -Bernardakis.
[3] ἄλλα -J[1], g.   [4] δὴ -g.
[5] συμβεβηκότα -J[1].
[6] ἣν ὅ γε -J[1], g ; ἣν ὅ τε -Stephanus.
[7] Heyne ; ἄνα -J, g ; ἀνὰ -all other mss.
[8] τῶν . . . χρόνων -J, g.
[9] Turnebus ; τούτου -mss. ; τοῦ ὅλου -Nogarola.

---

[a] Physics 219 b 1-2 and 220 a 24-25 (ἀριθμὸς κινήσεως κατὰ
τὸ πρότερον καὶ ὕστερον), 220 b 32—221 a 1 and 221 b 7
(μέτρον κινήσεως) ; cf. Plotinus, Enn. iii, vii, 9, lines 1-2
and J. F. Callahan, Four Views of Time in Ancient Philosophy (Harvard Univ. Press, 1948), pp. 50-53.
[b] Speusippus, frag. 53 (Lang). Cf. Strato's τὸ ἐν ταῖς
πράξεσι ποσόν (Simplicius, Phys., pp. 789, 34-35 and 790, 1-2
=Strato, frag. 76 [Wehrli]).
[c] S.V.F. ii, frag. 515 ; cf. ii, frags. 509-510 and i, frag. 93
and Dox. Graeci, p. 461, 15-16 (Posidonius).

those who are disturbed by these considerations
think time to be a measure or number of motion
according to antecedent and subsequent, as Aristotle
said,[a] or what in motion is quantitative, as Speusippus
did,[b] or extension of motion and nothing else, as did
some of the Stoics,[c] defining it by an accident and not
comprehending its essence and potency,[d] of which
no mean surmise seems to have been expressed
by Pindar in the words,

The lord, the lofty, time, who excels all the beatified gods,[e]

and by Pythagoras, when asked what time is, in the
reply, the soul of the heavens.[f] For time is not an
attribute or accident of any chance motion[g] but
cause and potency and principle of that which holds
together all the things that come to be, of the symmetry and order in which the nature of the whole
universe, being animate, is in motion; or rather,

[d] Cf. Proclus, *In Platonis Timaeum* iii, p. 20, 10-15 and
p. 95, 7-20 (Diehl); V. Goldschmidt, *Le système stoïcien*, pp.
41-42.

[e] Pindar, frag. 33 (Bergk, Schroeder, Snell) =24 (Turyn)
=14 (Bowra).

[f] Assigned to the Pythagorean Ἀκούσματα by A. Delatte
(*Études sur la littérature pythagoricienne* [Paris, 1915], p.
278); but cf. Zeller, *Phil. Griech.* i/1, p. 524, n. 2 and p. 546,
n. 2. A fanciful interpretation is given by R. B. Onians,
Origins of European Thought . . . (Cambridge, 1954), pp.
250-251; but the definition here ascribed to Pythagoras
might be connected with the theory mentioned by Aristotle
(frag. 201 [Rose]), for which cf. Cherniss, *Crit. Presoc. Phil.*,
pp. 214-216.

[g] Contrast Aristotle, *Physics* 251 b 28 (. . . ὁ χρόνος πάθος
τι κινήσεως), 219 b 15-16, and 220 b 24-28; and cf. Proclus,
In Platonis Timaeum iii, p. 21, 5-6 (Diehl): οὐκ ἄρα ἀκολου-
θητέον τοῖς ἐν ψιλαῖς ἐπινοίαις αὐτὸν ἱστᾶσιν ἢ συμβεβηκός τι
ποιοῦσιν.

(1007)
C οὖσα καὶ τάξις αὐτὴ[1] καὶ συμμετρία χρόνος καλεῖται,

πάντα γὰρ δι᾽ ἀψόφου
βαίνων κελεύθου κατὰ δίκην τὰ θνήτ᾽ ἄγει.

καὶ γὰρ ἡ ψυχῆς οὐσία κατὰ τοὺς παλαιοὺς ἀριθμὸς ἦν αὐτὸς ἑαυτὸν κινῶν. διὸ δὴ καὶ Πλάτων
ἔφη χρόνον ἅμα μετ᾽ οὐρανοῦ γεγονέναι κίνησιν δὲ[2]
καὶ πρὸ τῆς τοῦ[3] οὐρανοῦ[4] γενέσεως. χρόνος δ᾽[5]
οὐκ ἦν· οὐδὲ γὰρ τάξις[6] οὐδὲ μέτρον οὐδὲν οὐδὲ
διορισμὸς ἀλλὰ κίνησις ἀόριστος ὥσπερ ἄμορφος
ὕλη χρόνου καὶ ἀσχημάτιστος· ἐφελκύσασα δὲ

---

[1] Hartman (*De Plutarcho*, p. 586), implied by the versions
of Amyot and Xylander ; αὐτὴ -X ; αὕτη -all other mss.

[2] δὲ -omitted by J[1], g.

[3] τοῦ -omitted by β, Voss. 16, Escorial T-11-5, Bonon.

[4] ἀνοῦ (*i.e.* ἀνθρώπου) -J.

[5] δ᾽ -omitted by J[1], g.   [6] τάξεις -J[1].

---

[a] This practical identification of time with the activity of
the rational world-soul prefigures the doctrine of Plotinus
(*e.g. Enn.* III, vii, 12, lines 1-3 and 20-25 ; *cf.* H. Leisegang,
Die Begriffe der Zeit und Ewigkeit im späteren Platonismus
[Münster i.W., 1913], pp. 9 and 23-24 ; Thévenaz, *L'Âme
du Monde*, p. 96). It is with a very different emphasis upon
the Platonic contrast of time and eternal being that Plutarch
in *De E* 392 E makes his teacher, Ammonius, say : κινητὸν
γάρ τι καὶ κινουμένη συμφανταζόμενον ὕλη . . . ὁ χρόνος,
οὗ γε δὴ τὸ μὲν ἔπειτα καὶ τὸ πρότερον . . . αὐτόθεν ἐξομολόγη-
σίς ἐστι τοῦ μὴ ὄντος (*cf.* C. Andresen, *Logos und Nomos*
[Berlin, 1955], pp. 284-287).

[b] Euripides, *Troiades* 887-888, adapted by Plutarch in *De
Iside* 381 B also (ἄγεις -Euripides).

[c] The definition is ascribed to Pythagoras in [Plutarch],
De Placitis 898 c = *Dox. Graeci*, p. 386 A 13-15 (*cf.* 386 B 8-11
[" Pythagoras . . . and similarly also Xenocrates "] and W.
Burkert, *Weisheit und Wissenschaft* [Nürnberg, 1962], p. 57,
n. 73) ; but Plutarch himself, ascribing it to Xenocrates,
rejects it as a misinterpretation of the *Timaeus* (*De An. Proc.*

being motion and order itself and symmetry, it is
called time,[a]

> For all that mortal is,
> Going his noiseless path, he guides aright.[b]

In fact, the ancients even held that the essence of
soul is number itself moving itself.[c] That is just the
reason too why Plato said that time had come to be
simultaneously with heaven [d] but there had been
motion even before the generation of the heaven.[e]
Time there was not, however, for there was not
order either or any measure or distinction [f] but motion indeterminate, amorphous and unwrought matter, as it were, of time [g] ; but providence,[h] when

in Timaeo 1012 D-F =Xenocrates, frag. 68 [Heinze] and 1013
C-D), which may account for his vague ascription of it to
" the ancients " here where he cites it as testimony in support
of an interpretation (cf. Thévenaz, L'Âme du Monde, p. 96).

[d] Timaeus 38 B 6.

[e] This refers, of course, to Timaeus 30 A 3-5 and 52 D—
53 A ; cf. De An. Proc. in Timaeo 1014 B, 1016 D-F, and
1024 C.

[f] Cf. Macrobius, Sat. I, viii, 7 (". . . cum chaos esset,
tempora non fuisse, siquidem tempus est certa dimensio
quae ex caeli conversione colligitur") ; and contrast the
formula of Atticus (Proclus, In Platonis Timaeum iii, p. 37,
12-13 [Diehl]) : χρόνος μὲν ἦν καὶ πρὸ οὐρανοῦ γενέσεως, τεταγ-
μένος δὲ χρόνος οὐκ ἦν.

[g] In view of C. Andresen's misinterpretation (Logos und
Nomos [Berlin, 1955], p. 285 and n. 28) it must be emphasized that χρόνου depends upon ὕλη, which is modified by
ἄμορφος καὶ ἀσχημάτιστος (cf. De An. Proc. in Timaeo 1014
F: τὸ τὴν ὕλην ἀεὶ μὲν ἄμορφον καὶ ἀσχημάτιστον ὑπ' αὐτοῦ
λέγεσθαι).

[h] Cf. ἐκ προνοίας (De Facie 926 F), κατὰ θαυμασιωτάτην
πρόνοιαν (Albinus, Epitome xii, 1 =p. 67, 20 [Louis] =p. 167,
10 [Hermann]) ; and [Plutarch], De Placitis 884 F (Dox.
Graeci, p. 321 A 10-11) with Proclus, In Platonis Timaeum i,
p. 415, 18-20 (Diehl).

PLUTARCH'S MORALIA

(1007) πρόνοια[1] καὶ καταλαβοῦσα[2] τὴν μὲν ὕλην σχήμασι
τὴν δὲ κίνησιν περιόδοις τὴν μὲν κόσμον ἅμα τὴν
δὲ χρόνον ἐποίησεν. εἰκόνες[3] δ' εἰσὶν ἄμφω τοῦ
D θεοῦ, τῆς μὲν οὐσίας ὁ κόσμος τῆς δ' ἀιδιότητος
⟨ὁ⟩[4] χρόνος ἐν κινήσει καθάπερ ἐν γενέσει θεὸς ὁ
κόσμος. ὅθεν ὁμοῦ γεγονότας φησὶν ὁμοῦ καὶ λυ-
θήσεσθαι πάλιν,[b] ἄν τις αὐτοὺς καταλαμβάνῃ λύσις·
οὐ γὰρ οἷόν τ' ⟨εἶναι⟩[6] χωρὶς χρόνου τὸ γενητὸν[7]
ὥσπερ οὐδὲ τὸ νοητὸν αἰῶνος,[8] εἰ μέλλει τὸ μὲν[9]
ἀεὶ μένειν τὸ δὲ μηδέποτε διαλύεσθαι γιγνόμενον.
οὕτως οὖν[10] ἀναγκαίαν πρὸς τὸν οὐρανὸν ἔχων
συμπλοκὴν καὶ συναρμογὴν ὁ χρόνος οὐχ ἁπλῶς
ἐστι[11] κίνησις ἀλλὰ ὥσπερ εἴρηται κίνησις ἐν τάξει
μέτρον ἐχούσῃ καὶ πέρατα καὶ περιόδους· ὧν ὁ

[1] H. C.; ἐπικλύσασα δ' ἐν χρόα (δ' ἐν χρόνω -J[1], g; δ'
ἡ τάξις -Escorial T-11-5) -mss.; ἐπικλώσασα δὲ Μοῖρα -Em-
perius (*Op. Philol.*, p. 340); ἐπικλύσασα δ' ἡ χορεία -Apelt
(*Philologus*, lxii [1903], p. 287); ⟨ἣν ὁρίσασ' ἡ ψυχή,⟩ ἐγ-
κλείσασα δ' ἐν χώρᾳ -Pohlenz.
       λ β
[2] καταβαλοῦσα -X[1]; περιβαλοῦσα -Escorial T-11-5; κατα-
βαλλοῦσα -n; καταβαλοῦσα -all other mss.; μεταβαλοῦσα
-Pohlenz.
[3] Leonicus; εἰκότως -mss.
[4] ⟨ὁ⟩ -added by Stephanus.
[5] πάντα -J[1]; πάντας -g.
[6] ⟨εἶναι⟩ -added by Wyttenbach.
[7] γεννητὸν -J, g.   [8] ἄνευ αἰῶνος -Escorial T-11-5.
[9] μὲν -β[2] (added superscript), Bonon., Voss. 16, Escorial
T-11-5; omitted by all other mss.
[10] οὖν -omitted by g.
[11] ἐστι -omitted by a, A, β[1] (but added superscript), γ,
E, B, ε, n.

  [a] *Cf. Quaest. Conviv.* 719 E (. . . τοῦ λόγου καταλαμβά-
νοντος αὐτὴν . . .) and 1001 b-c *supra* with note *f* there.
  [b] This like [Plutarch], *De Placitis* 881 A (*Dox. Graeci*, p.
299 A 11-12) suggests a misinterpretation of *Timaeus* 92 c 7
88

she took in tow and curbed matter with shapes [a]
and motion with revolutions, simultaneously made
of the former a universe and of the latter time.
They are both semblances of god, the universe of his
essence [b] and time a semblance in motion of his
eternity,[c] even as in the realm of becoming the universe is god.[d] Hence he says [e] that, as they came
into being together, together they will also be dissolved again if any dissolution overtake them, for
what is subject to generation cannot ⟨be⟩ apart from
time just as what is intelligible cannot apart from
eternity either if the latter is always to remain fixed
and the former never to be dissolved in its process
of becoming.[f] Time, then, since it is thus necessarily implicated and connected with the heaven, is
not simply motion but, as has been said, motion in
an orderly fashion that involves measure and limits

or even the reading ποιητοῦ there instead of νοητοῦ (though
the latter is implied by *De Iside* 373 B, . . . εἰκόνα τοῦ νοητοῦ
κόσμου αἰσθητὸν ὄντα) possibly supported by the misinterpretation of *Timaeus* 29 E 3 (*cf. De Sera Numinis Vindicta* 550
D and *De An. Proc. in Timaeo* 1014 B [. . . πρὸς αὐτὸν
ἐξομοίωσιν . . .]) ; but it may also have been inferred that,
since γένεσις is an εἰκὼν οὐσίας ἐν ὕλῃ (*De Iside* 372 F), if, as
Plutarch proceeds to assert, the universe is god in the realm
of γένεσις (see note *d infra*), that of which it is the semblance
must be god in the realm of οὐσία.

[c] *Cf. Timaeus* 37 D 5-7. Plutarch himself in *De Defectu
Orac.* 422 B-C assigns eternity to the ideas (περὶ αὐτὰ τοῦ αἰῶνος ὄντος οἷον ἀπορροὴν ἐπὶ τοὺς κόσμους φέρεσθαι τὸν χρόνον) ;
cf. Albinus, *Epitome* xiv, 6 (p. 85, 5-6 [Louis] = p. 170, 21-23
[Hermann]).

[d] *Cf. Timaeus* 34 A 8–B 1 and B 8-9, 92 C 4-9, and *Critias*
106 A 3-4 (one of the passages cited by Plutarch himself in
De An. Proc. in Timaeo 1017 C).

[e] *Timaeus* 38 B 6-7.

[f] *Cf. Timaeus* 27 D 6—28 A 4 and 38 C 1-3.

(1007) ἥλιος ἐπιστάτης ὢν καὶ σκοπὸς[1] ὁρίζειν καὶ βρα-
Ε βεύειν καὶ ἀναδεικνύναι καὶ ἀναφαίνειν μεταβολὰς καὶ ὥρας, αἳ πάντα φέρουσι καθ' Ἡράκλειτον,
οὐ[2] φαύλων οὐδὲ μικρῶν ἀλλὰ τῶν μεγίστων καὶ
κυριωτάτων τῷ ἡγεμόνι καὶ πρώτῳ[3] θεῷ γίγνεται
συνεργός.

ΖΗΤΗΜΑ Θ′

1. Περὶ τῶν τῆς ψυχῆς[4] δυνάμεων ἐν Πολιτείᾳ
Πλάτωνος τὴν τοῦ λογιστικοῦ[5] καὶ θυμοειδοῦς
καὶ ἐπιθυμητικοῦ συμφωνίαν ἁρμονίᾳ[6] μέσης καὶ
ὑπάτης καὶ νήτης εἰκάσαντος ἄριστα διαπορήσειεν
ἄν τις πότερον κατὰ τῆς μέσης τὸ θυμοειδὲς ἢ
τὸ λογιστικὸν[7] ἔταξεν· αὐτὸς[8] γὰρ ἔν γε τούτοις
οὐ δεδήλωκεν. ἡ μὲν οὖν κατὰ τόπον[9] τῶν μερῶν
F τάξις εἰς τὴν τῆς μέσης χώραν τίθεται τὸ θυμοειδὲς τὸ δὲ λογιστικὸν εἰς τὴν τῆς ὑπάτης. τὸ
γὰρ ἄνω καὶ πρῶτον ὕπατον οἱ παλαιοὶ προσ-

---

[1] ⟨ἐπιταχθεὶς ἐπί⟩σκοπος -Reinhardt (*Hermes*, lxxvii
[1949], p. 229, n. 1).

[2] οὐδὲ -J[2] (δὲ added superscript), a, A, β[1] (δὲ erased -β[2]),
γ, Ε, Β, ε, n.

[3] καὶ πρώτῳ -omitted by ε; καὶ πρωτίστῳ -Escorial
T-11-5.

[4] περὶ τῆς ψυχῆς τῶν -J[1], g; περὶ -deleted by Hartman
(*De Plutarcho*, p. 586).

[5] Bernardakis; λογικοῦ -mss.

[6] ἁρμονίαν -B.   [7] λογικὸν -X, ε, n.

[8] Wyttenbach (*cf.* 1001 D *supra*); οὗτος -mss.

[9] κατὰ τὸν τόπον -Voss. 16, Escorial T-11-5.

---

[a] *Cf. Homeric Hymn* ii (*Demeter*), 62, cited by Hubert for
σκοπός used of Helios.

[b] Heraclitus, frag. B 100 (D.-K. and Walzer)=frag. 34
(Bywater) with G. S. Kirk, *Heraclitus: The Cosmic Fragments* (Cambridge, 1954), pp. 294-305.

and revolutions. The sun, being overseer and sentinel *a* of these for defining and arbitrating and revealing and displaying changes and seasons which according to Heraclitus *b* bring all things, turns out to be collaborator with the sovereign and primary god *c* not in paltry or trivial matters but in those that are greatest and most important.

QUESTION IX

1. About the faculties of the soul in the *Republic,* where *d* Plato likened excellently well the consonance of the rational and mettlesome and appetitive to a concord of intermediate and topmost and nethermost strings,*e* one might raise the question whether it is the mettlesome or the rational that he gave the rank of intermediate, for in this passage he has not made it clear himself. Now, the local disposition of the parts does put the mettlesome in the position of the intermediate and the rational in that of the topmost string. For what is above and first the ancients styled topmost,*f* even as Xenocrates calls

---

c Cf. τὸν ἀνωτάτω θεόν (1000 E [Question II *init.*] *supra*).

d *Republic* 443 D 5-7.

e The note of lowest pitch in the scale was called " topmost " (*scil.* string) ; and its octave, that of highest pitch, was called " nethermost " : cf. Nicomachus, *Harmonices Man.* 3 (*Musici Scriptores Graeci,* p. 241, 19-23 [Jan]) ; Theon Smyrnaeus, p. 51, 12-14 (Hiller) ; Chalcidius, *Platonis Timaeus,* p. 111, 7-11 (Wrobel) =p. 93, 8-11 (Waszink) ; and Plutarch, *De An. Proc. in Timaeo* 1021 A *infra* (. . . βαρύτερον φθέγγεται ὡς ὑπάτη πρὸς νήτην . . . ὀξύτερον ὡς νήτη πρὸς ὑπάτην).

f Cf. [Aristotle], *De Mundo* 397 b 24-26 ; Aristides Quintilianus, *De Musica* i, 6 (p. 8, 8-9 and 27-28 [Winnington-Ingram]).

91

PLUTARCH'S MORALIA

(1007) ἠγόρευον· ᾗ¹ καὶ Ξενοκράτης Δία τὸν ἐν μὲν
τοῖς² κατὰ ταὐτὰ καὶ³ ὡσαύτως ἔχουσιν ὕπατον καλεῖ νέατον δὲ τὸν⁴ ὑπὸ σελήνην,⁵ πρότερον⁶ δὲ
Ὅμηρος τὸν τῶν ἀρχόντων ἄρχοντα θεὸν ὕπατον
1008 κρειόντων προσεῖπε. καὶ⁷ δικαίως τῷ κρατίστῳ ἀποδέδωκε τὴν ἄνω⁸ χώραν ἡ φύσις, ὥσπερ
κυβερνήτην ἐνιδρύσασα τῇ κεφαλῇ τὸν λογισμὸν
ἔσχατον δὲ καὶ νέατον ἀποικίσασα πόρρω τὸ
ἐπιθυμητικόν. ἡ γὰρ κάτω νεάτη προσαγορεύεται
τάξις, ὡς δηλοῦσιν αἱ τῶν νεκρῶν κλήσεις νερτέρων
καὶ ἐνέρων προσαγορευομένων· ἔνιοι δὲ καὶ τῶν
ἀνέμων φασὶ τὸν κάτωθεν ἐκ τοῦ ἀφανοῦς πνέοντα

---

¹ ᾗ -omitted by J¹, g.
² τὸν μὲν ἐν τοῖς -J¹, g ; τὸν μὲν τοῖς -B.
³ καὶ -omitted by X ; κατὰ αὐτὰ καὶ -γ ; κατὰ τὰ αὐτὰ
καὶ -all other mss.   ⁴ τὸ -J.   ⁵ τὴν σελήνην -E, B.
⁶ πρότερον -X, a, ε, n ; πρῶτον -J¹, g ; πρότερος -all
other mss.
⁷ καὶ -omitted by J¹, g.   ⁸ τὴν ἄνω -omitted by J¹, g.

ᵃ Xenocrates, frag. 18 (Heinze). " Nethermost Zeus " is
the chthonian Zeus or Hades (cf. Aeschylus, Supplices 156-
158 and 230-231 [with E. Fraenkel on Agamemnon 1386-
1387] ; Euripides, frag. 912, 1-3 and 6-8 [Nauck, Trag.
Graec. Frag.², p. 655] ; Pausanias, ii, 24, 4 with Proclus, In
Platonis Cratylum, pp. 83, 24–84, 1 [Pasquali]), whose
domain, however, is no longer subterranean but is the whole
sublunar region of the universe (cf. De Facie 942 F and 943 C
[L.C.L. xii, p. 195, note d and p. 201, note c] ; P. Boyancé,
Rev. Études Grecques, lxv [1952], pp. 334-335 ; W. Burkert,
Weisheit und Wissenschaft [Nürnberg, 1962], pp. 344-346).
By " topmost Zeus " Xenocrates may have meant to refer
to the monad which he is said to have given the station of
father reigning ἐν οὐρανῷ, to have styled Zeus and νοῦς, and
to have regarded as πρῶτος θεός (frag. 15 [Heinze] = Dox.
Graeci, p. 304 B 1-7). To establish strict correspondence
between the present passage (frag. 18) and frags. 15 and 5,
however, one must assume that Xenocrates posited a Ζεὺς

92

Zeus who is among things invariable and identical topmost but nethermost him who is beneath the moon [a] and earlier Homer styled the god who is ruler of rulers topmost of lords.[b] Nature has also duly assigned the position above to what is most excellent by establishing the reason like a pilot in the head and making the appetitive part dwell last and nethermost in distant banishment.[c] For the station underneath is styled nethermost, as is made clear by the appellations of the dead, who are styled nether and infernal; and some people say that of the winds too it is the one blowing from underneath out of the unseen pole [d] that has been named

μέσος also (cf. A. B. Krische, Die theologischen Lehren der griechischen Denker [Göttingen, 1840], p. 324; H. J. Krämer, Der Ursprung der Geistmetaphysik [Amsterdam, 1964], p. 37, n. 58 and p. 82, n. 209; H. Happ, Parusia: Festgabe für Johannes Hirschberger [Frankfurt am Main, 1965], p. 178, n. 101); and, had he done so, it is unlikely that Plutarch would have omitted mention of it in this context. In Quaest. Conviv. 745 B the Delphian muses are said to have been named Ὑπάτη, Μέση, and Νεάτη from the regions of the universe guarded by each of them and not—as, in fact, is asserted by Censorinus (frag. 12 = p. 65, 13-15 [Hultsch])—from the musical notes or strings; but, even if this passage too derived from Xenocrates (Heinze, Xenokrates, p. 76), the latter may well have treated Zeus only in his two commonly recognized aspects as ὕψιστος and χθόνιος (cf. Pausanias, ii, 2, 8).
   [b] Iliad viii, 31; Odyssey i, 45 and 81 and xxiv, 473.
   [c] From Timaeus 44 D 3-6 and 69 D 6—71 A 3 (n.b. 70 E 6-7), but the figure of reason as a pilot comes from Phaedrus 247 C 7-8; cf. Albinus, Epitome xxiii (p. 111 [Louis] = p. 176, 9-19 [Hermann]) and Apuleius, De Platone i, 13 (p. 97, 2-12 [Thomas]) and Philo Jud., Leg. Allegor. iii, 115-118 (i, pp. 138, 27-139, 17 [Cohn]).
   [d] Cf. [Aristotle], De Mundo 394 b 31-32; Joannes Lydus, De Mensibus iv, 119 (p. 157, 14-15 [Wuensch]).

(1008) νότον ὠνομάσθαι. ἦν οὖν τὸ ἔσχατον ἔχει πρὸς¹
τὸ πρῶτον ἀντίθεσιν καὶ τὸ νέατον πρὸς τὸ ὕπατον ταύτην τοῦ ἐπιθυμητικοῦ πρὸς τὸ λογιστικὸν
ἔχοντος, οὐκ ἔστιν ἀνωτάτω μὲν εἶναι καὶ πρῶτον
ὕπατον δὲ μὴ² εἶναι τὸ λογιστικὸν³ ἀλλὰ ἕτερον.⁴
Β οἱ γὰρ ὡς κυρίαν δύναμιν αὐτῷ τὴν τῆς μέσης
ἀποδιδόντες ἀγνοοῦσιν ὅτι τὴν κυριωτέραν ἀφαι-
ροῦνται τὴν⁵ τῆς ὑπάτης, μήτε τῷ θυμῷ μήτε τῇ
ἐπιθυμίᾳ προσήκουσαν· ἑκάτερον γὰρ ἄρχεσθαι
καὶ ἀκολουθεῖν οὐδέτερον δ' ἄρχειν ἢ⁶ ἡγεῖσθαι
τοῦ λογιστικοῦ πέφυκεν. ἔτι δὲ μᾶλλον τῇ φύσει
φανεῖται τὸ θυμοειδὲς τῷ τόπῳ⁷ τὴν μέσην ἔχον
ἐκείνων τάξιν⁸· εἴ γε δὴ τῷ μὲν⁹ λογιστικῷ τὸ
ἄρχειν τῷ δὲ θυμοειδεῖ τὸ ἄρχεσθαι καὶ τὸ¹⁰ ἄρχειν
κατὰ φύσιν ἐστίν, ὑπηκόῳ μὲν ὄντι τοῦ λογισμοῦ
κρατοῦντι δὲ καὶ κολάζοντι τὴν ἐπιθυμίαν ὅταν

---

¹ ἔχει καὶ -J¹, g.
² μὴ -omitted by J¹, g.
³ λογικὸν -J, g.
⁴ After these words at the end of folio 6 v the remainder
of n from οἱ γὰρ is by a different hand.
⁵ τὴν -omitted by J¹, g (ἀφαιροῦντα τὴν -Bonon.).
⁶ ἢ -omitted by J, g.
⁷ ⟨ἢ⟩ τῷ τόπῳ -Hubert.
⁸ τάξιν -omitted by Voss. 16, Escorial T-11-5.
⁹ μὲν -omitted by J¹, g.
¹⁰ ἄρχεσθαι καὶ τὸ -omitted by J¹, g.

ᵃ The derivation of νότος (the " moist " wind or rain-wind)
from νέατος, as false as would be that of "thunder" from
" under," is probably reflected in τοῦ νότου πνέοντος ἀπὸ
τῶν κάτω τόπων of *Heracliti Quaestiones Homericae* 47 (*cf.*
Hermias, *In Platonis Phaedrum*, p. 29, 7-8 [Couvreur]) and
in " Auster . . . qui et Notus, ex humili flans, . . ." of Isidore
(*De Natura Rerum* xxxvii, 3) and persists in the etymological
verses of Johannes Mauropus (R. Reitzenstein, *Geschichte der
griechischen Etymologika* [Leipzig, 1897], p. 174, lines 37-38).

thunder-gust.[a] Since, then, the opposition of last
to first and of nethermost to topmost is the relation
in which the appetitive part stands to the rational,
it is not possible for the rational to be furthest above
and first and yet for another than it to be topmost.
For those who assign it the rôle of the intermediate
on the ground that this is a sovereign function [b] fail
to understand that they are eliminating the more
sovereign function of the topmost, which befits
neither mettle nor appetite, for to be ruled and to
follow is natural to either of these but to rule or to
lead the rational is natural to neither.[c] From their
nature it will be still more apparent that the mettlesome part has the locally intermediate station among
them,[d] if in fact ruling is natural to the rational but
being ruled and ruling to the mettlesome, which,
while obedient to the reason, dominates and chastises
the appetite whenever it disobeys the reason.[e] Also,

[b] Cf. 1009 A infra : τὴν δὲ πρώτην ἔχει καὶ κυριωτάτην
δύναμιν ὡς μέση. . . .

[c] Cf. De Virtute Morali 442 A with Plato, Republic 441
E 4—442 D 1 ; and De Virtute Morali 442 c (τὸ δὲ παθητικὸν
. . . τοῦ λογιζομένου καὶ φρονοῦντος εἰσακούειν . . . καὶ ὑπείκειν
. . . πέφυκεν) with Aristotle, Eth. Nic. 1102 b 25-31, with
Eth. Eud. 1219 b 28-31, and with Iamblichus, Protrepticus,
p. 41, 20-22 (Pistelli).

[d] The argument, which hitherto has turned on the meaning
of ὕπατον and νέατον, now is based upon the nature of the
parts of the soul ; but its purpose is still to prove that the
mettlesome part is in the locally middle position of the three.
Hubert was mistaken, therefore, in wishing to construe τῷ
τόπῳ as an " instrumental " in comparison with τῇ φύσει and
in emending the text to this end.

[e] Cf. Proclus, In Platonis Rem Publicam i, pp. 211, 7-212,
20 (Kroll) and Stobaeus, Ecl. i, 49, 27 (p. 355, 10-12 [Wachs-
muth]) ; and for the characterization of the mettlesome part
cf. Plato, Republic 441 E 5-6 and Timaeus 70 A 2-7.

(1008) ἀπειθῇ τῷ λογισμῷ. καὶ[1] καθάπερ ἐν γράμμασι
τὰ ἡμίφωνα μέσα[2] τῶν ἀφώνων ἐστὶ καὶ τῶν
C φωνηέντων τῷ πλέον ἐκείνων ἠχεῖν[3] ἔλαττον δὲ
τούτων, οὕτως ἐν τῇ ψυχῇ τοῦ ἀνθρώπου τὸ θυμοειδὲς οὐκ ἀκράτως παθητικόν ἐστιν ἀλλὰ φαντασίαν καλοῦ πολλάκις ἔχει μεμιγμένην ἀλόγῳ[4] τῇ[5]
τῆς τιμωρίας[6] ὀρέξει.[7] καὶ Πλάτων αὐτὸς εἰκάσας
συμφύτῳ ζεύγει καὶ ἡνιόχῳ τὸ τῆς ψυχῆς εἶδος
ἡνίοχον μέν, ὡς παντὶ δῆλον, ἀπέφηνε τὸ λογιστικὸν τῶν δὲ ἵππων τὸ μὲν περὶ τὰς[8] ἐπιθυμίας
ἀπειθὲς καὶ ἀνάγωγον παντάπασι περὶ ὦτα λάσιον,[9] κωφόν, μάστιγι μετὰ κέντρων μόγις[10] ὑπεῖ-
κον τὸ δὲ θυμοειδὲς εὐήνιον τὰ πολλὰ τῷ λογισμῷ
καὶ σύμμαχον.[11] ὥσπερ οὖν συνωρίδος οὐχ ὁ
D ἡνίοχός ἐστιν ἀρετῇ καὶ δυνάμει μέσος ἀλλὰ τῶν
ἵππων ὁ φαυλότερος μὲν τοῦ ἡνιόχου βελτίων δὲ
τοῦ ὁμοζύγου, οὕτω τῆς ψυχῆς οὐ τῷ[12] κρατοῦντι
τὴν μέσην[13] ἀπένειμε τάξιν ἀλλὰ ᾧ πάθους μὲν

[1] καί -omitted by J[1], g, a[1].
[2] καί (instead of μέσα) -J[1], g.
[3] Leonicus ; ἔχειν -MSS.
[4] Xylander, Stephanus ; ἀλόγως -MSS.
[5] τῇ -omitted by J[1], g, n.
[6] μωρίας -A, β, E, B, Voss. 16, Escorial T-11-5, Bonon.
[7] ἕξει -B.
[8] τὰς -omitted by g.
[9] περὶ ᾧ ταλάσιον -J ; περὶ τὰ ὦτα λάσιον -γ.
[10] μόγις -J, g (so Plato, *Phaedrus* 253 E 4) ; μόλις -all
other MSS.
[11] καὶ σύμμαχον τῷ λογισμῷ -B ; καὶ λογισμῷ σύμμαχον -n.
[12] οὕτω n.
[13] τὴν τῆς μέσης -X, J, g, β[2].

[a] Cf. *Quaest. Conviv.* 738 D-E ; Plato, *Philebus* 18 B 8–c 6
(*n.b.* τά τε ἄφθογγα καὶ ἄφωνα . . . καὶ τὰ φωνήεντα καὶ τὰ
μέσα) with *Cratylus* 424 c 5-8 and *Theaetetus* 203 B 2-7.

just as among letters the semivowels are intermediate between the mutes and the vowels by having
more sound than the former and less than the latter,[a]
so in the soul of man the mettlesome part is not
purely affective but frequently has a mental image
of what is fair,[b] though one commingled with what
is irrational, the yearning for retribution.[c]   Plato
too, when he likened the structure of the soul to a
composite of team and charioteer,[d] represented, as
is clear to everyone, the rational part as charioteer
and in the team of horses represented as shaggy
about the ears, deaf, scarcely yielding to whip and
goads [e] the contumacy and utter indiscipline of the
appetites but the mettlesome part as mostly tract-
able to the reason and allied with it.[f]   Now, as in the
car and pair it is not the charioteer that is intermediate in virtue and function but that one of the
horses which is worse than the charioteer but better
than its yoke-fellow, so in the soul Plato allotted the
intermediate station not to the dominant part but

[b] Cf. ὁ θυμὸς ὑπερορᾷ μὲν σώματος εἰς ἀσώματον δὲ ἀγαθὸν
βλέπει τὴν τιμήν (Proclus, In Platonis Rem Publicam, i, p.
235, 16-18 [Kroll] with i, p. 211, 25-26 and p. 225, 27-30 and
p. 226, 13-17 [Kroll]).

[c] Cf. ὄρεξις τιμωρητική (Proclus, In Platonis Rem Publicam
i, p. 208, 14-18 [Kroll]) and τὸ ἀντιλυπήσεως ὀρέγεσθαι (ibid.)
with Plutarch, De Virtute Morali 442 B (ὄρεξιν ἀντιλυπήσεως)
and Aristotle, De Anima 403 a 30-31.

[d] Phaedrus 246 A 6-7.

[e] Phaedrus 253 E 4-5.

[f] In Phaedrus 247 B 2 the vehicles of the gods are called
εὐήνια and in Republic 441 E 5-6 the mettlesome part of the
soul is characterized as ὑπήκοον καὶ σύμμαχον τοῦ λογιστικοῦ
(see note e on 1008 B supra); but in the Phaedrus these terms
are not used of the nobler horse, though he is said to be
εὐπειθὴς τῷ ἡνιόχῳ (Phaedrus 254 A 1) and to be guided
κελεύσματι μόνον καὶ λόγῳ (253 D 7-E 1).

(1008) ἧττον¹ ἢ τῷ ⟨τρίτῳ μᾶλλον δ᾽ ἢ τῷ⟩² πρώτῳ
λόγου δὲ μᾶλλον ἢ τῷ τρίτῳ ⟨ἧττον δ᾽ ἢ τῷ
πρώτῳ⟩³ μέτεστιν. αὕτη γὰρ ἡ τάξις καὶ τὴν
τῶν συμφωνιῶν ἀναλογίαν φυλάττει, τοῦ μὲν θυμοειδοῦς πρὸς τὸ λογιστικὸν⁴ ὡς ὑπάτην τὸ διὰ τεσσάρων πρὸς δὲ⁵ τὸ ἐπιθυμητικὸν ὡς νήτην τὸ διὰ
πέντε τοῦ δὲ λογιστικοῦ πρὸς⁶ τὸ ἐπιθυμητικὸν
ὡς ὑπάτη⁷ πρὸς νήτην τὸ διὰ πασῶν. ἐὰν δὲ τὸν
λογισμὸν εἰς τὸ μέσον ἕλκωμεν, ἔσται πλέον ὁ
E θυμὸς ἀπέχων τῆς ἐπιθυμίας, ὃν⁸ ἔνιοι τῶν φιλοσόφων ἐπιθυμίᾳ ταὐτὸν εἶναι διὰ ὁμοιότητα νο-
μίζουσιν.

2. Ἦ τὸ μὲν τοῖς τόποις ἀπονέμειν⁹ τὰ πρῶτα
καὶ τὰ μέσα καὶ τὰ τελευταῖα γελοῖόν ἐστιν, αὐτὴν
τὴν ὑπάτην ὁρῶντας ἐν μὲν λύρᾳ¹⁰ τὸν ἀνωτάτω¹¹
καὶ πρῶτον ἐν δ᾽ αὐλοῖς τὸν κάτω καὶ τὸν τελευ-

---

¹ πλέον -Emperius (*Op. Philol.*, p. 340).
² ⟨. . .⟩ -added by Wyttenbach.
³ ⟨. . .⟩ -added by Wyttenbach.
⁴ λογικὸν -a, A, β¹, E, B, ε.
⁵ δὲ -omitted by J¹.
⁶ πρὸς -omitted by J, g ; τὸ δὲ λογιστικὸν πρὸς -Escorial
T-11-5.   ⁷ ὑπάτην -B.
⁸ ὧν -n, Voss. 16, Bonon.
⁹ νέμειν -X.
¹⁰ ἐν μὲν τῇ λύρᾳ -J, g.
¹¹ ἀνώτερον -J¹, g ; τερον superscript over ωτά -X¹.

ᵃ Proclus (*In Platonis Rem Publicam* i, pp. 212, 26–213,
16 [Kroll]) also makes the mettlesome part intermediate ; but
according to him its relation to the rational part is that of the
fifth and to the appetitive that of the fourth, which implies
that the appetitive part is ὑπάτη and the rational part νήτη
(*cf. e.g. De An. Proc. in Timaeo* 1019 D-E *infra*), the argument
for this being that, while it makes the interval between
mettlesome and rational greater than that between mettle-

to that in which the affective component is less than in the ⟨third but greater than in the⟩ first and the component of reason greater than in the third ⟨but less than in the first⟩. The fact is that this disposition also preserves the proportion of the consonances, of the mettlesome to the rational as topmost string the fourth and to the appetitive as nethermost the fifth and of the rational to the appetitive as topmost to nethermost the octave [a] ; but if we pull the reason into the middle, it will remove to a greater distance from the appetite the mettle, which because of its similarity to appetite some of the philosophers believe to be identical with it.[b]

2. Or [c] is it ridiculous to allot to local positions the status of first and intermediate and last, seeing that the topmost itself, while on the lyre it occupies the position furthest above and first, on the pipes occupies the one underneath and last [d] and that the

some and appetitive, it preserves the greater consonance of the mettlesome with the rational, the fifth being $\mu\hat{a}\lambda\lambda o\nu$ $\sigma\nu\mu\phi\omega\nu\iota\alpha$ than the fourth. Yet elsewhere, in the divine $\dot{a}\rho\mu o\nu\iota\alpha$ of mind, soul, and body it is $\sigma\hat{\omega}\mu\alpha$ that is $\nu\dot{\eta}\tau\eta$ and $\nu o\hat{\upsilon}s$ that is $\dot{\upsilon}\pi\dot{a}\tau\eta$ to the $\mu\acute{e}\sigma\eta$ of soul (*In Platonis Rem Publicam* ii, p. 4, 15-21 [Kroll]).

[b] Cf. *De Virtute Morali* 442 b ('Αριστοτέλης . . . τὸ μὲν θυμοειδὲς τῷ ἐπιθυμητικῷ προσένειμεν ὡς ἐπιθυμίαν τινὰ τὸν θυμὸν ὄντα . . .). It is less likely that Plutarch had in mind here such classifications as those of *S.V.F.* iii, frag. 396, to which Hubert refers, especially since what he emphasizes as characteristic of Stoic doctrine is the denial that τὸ παθητικὸν καὶ ἄλογον is distinct from τὸ λογικόν (*De Virtute Morali* 441 c-d and 446 f—447 a, *De Sollertia Animalium* 961 d, *De An. Proc. in Timaeo* 1025 d).

[c] See note c on 1003 a *supra* and note c on *De Comm. Not.* 1075 f *infra*.

[d] Cf. Aelian Platonicus quoted by Porphyry, *In Ptolemaei Harmonica*, p. 34, 22-28 (Düring).

(1008) ταῖον ἐπέχουσαν[1] ἔτι δὲ τὴν μέσην, ἐν ᾧ τις ἂν[2]
χωρίῳ τῆς λύρας θέμενος ὡσαύτως ἁρμόσηται,[3]
φθεγγομένην ὀξύτερον μὲν ὑπάτης βαρύτερον δὲ
νήτης ; καὶ γὰρ ὀφθαλμὸς οὐκ ἐν παντὶ ζῴῳ τὴν
αὐτὴν ἔχει τάξιν, ἐν παντὶ δὲ καὶ πανταχοῦ
κείμενος κατὰ φύσιν ὁρᾶν ὁμοίως πέφυκεν. ὥσπερ
F οὖν ὁ παιδαγωγὸς οὐ πρόσθεν ἀλλ' ὄπισθεν βαδίζων[4]
ἄγειν λέγεται, καὶ ὁ τῶν Τρώων στρατηγὸς

ὁτὲ μέν τε μετὰ[5] πρώτοισι φάνεσκεν
ἄλλοτε δ' ἐν πυμάτοισι κελεύων

ἑκατέρωθι[6] δ' ἦν πρῶτος καὶ τὴν πρώτην δύναμιν
εἶχεν, οὕτω τὰ τῆς ψυχῆς μόρια δεῖ μὴ τοῖς τόποις
καταβιάζεσθαι μηδὲ τοῖς ὀνόμασιν ἀλλὰ τὴν δύνα-
1009 μιν καὶ τὴν ἀναλογίαν ἐξετάζειν. τὸ γὰρ τῇ θέσει
πρῶτον ἱδρῦσθαι τὸ λογιστικὸν ἐν τῷ σώματι τοῦ
ἀνθρώπου κατὰ συμβεβηκός ἐστι· τὴν δὲ πρώτην
ἔχει καὶ κυριωτάτην δύναμιν ὡς μέση πρὸς ὑπάτην
μὲν τὸ ἐπιθυμητικὸν νήτην δὲ τὸ θυμοειδές, τῷ[7]
χαλᾶν καὶ ἐπιτείνειν καὶ ὅλως συνῳδὰ καὶ σύμφωνα ποιεῖν ἑκατέρου τὴν ὑπερβολὴν ἀφαιρῶν καὶ
πάλιν οὐκ ἐῶν ἀνίεσθαι παντάπασιν οὐδὲ κατα-
δαρθάνειν· τὸ γὰρ μέτριον καὶ τὸ[8] σύμμετρον

---

[1] τελευταῖον, ἀποφαίνοντα -n.
[2] ἑνώσῃ ἂν -J[1], g.
[3] θοῖτο ὡσαύτως ἁρμόσεται -Escorial T-11-5.
[4] ἀλλ' ἔμπροσθεν βαδίζειν -J[1], g.
[5] ὁτὲ . . . vac. 5 . . . μετὰ -J[1] ; ὁτὲ μετὰ -g (no lacuna
indicated) ; ὁτὲ μὲν μετὰ -B.
[6] ἑκατέρωθεν -ε, Escorial T-11-5 ; ἑκατέρωθε -n, Voss. 16.
[7] τὸ -J, g, a, A, γ, E, B, ε.
[8] τὸ -omitted by g.

intermediate moreover, wherever it is located on the
lyre, if tuned in the same way, sounds higher than
the topmost string and lower than the nethermost ? [a]
For the situation of the eye too is not the same in
every animal ; but, as in all and everywhere it is
naturally placed, seeing is similarly natural to it.[b]
As, then, the children's tutor is said to lead, though
he walks behind them and not before, and the general
of the Trojans

Now would appear in the foremost ranks of the battle,
Then in the rearmost, urging them forward,[c]

but in either place was first and had the foremost
function, so the parts of the soul must not be con-
strained by location or by nomenclature but their
function and their proportion must be scrutinized.
In fact it is incidental that in the body of man the
rational part has been situated as first in local position ; but the foremost and most sovereign function
belongs to it as intermediate in relation to the appetitive as topmost and to the mettlesome as nethermost inasmuch as it slackens and tightens and
generally makes them harmonious and concordant
by removing the excess from either and again not
permitting them to relax entirely and to fall asleep,[d]
for the moderate and the commensurate [e] are

[a] Cf. De Virtute Morali 444 e-f ; Aristotle, Physics 224
b 33-34 ; Chalcidius, Platonis Timaeus, p. 106, 13-17
(Wrobel) =p. 89, 10-14 (Waszink).
[b] Cf. De Facie 927 d—928 b.
[c] Iliad xi, 64-65.
[d] Cf. De Virtute Morali 444 c ; Plato, Republic 441 e 9—
442 a 2.
[e] Cf. Plato, Philebus 64 e 6 (μετριότης καὶ συμμετρία) and
66 a 6–b 1 (summarized by Plutarch, De E 391 c-d), where
τὸ μέτριον is prior to τὸ σύμμετρον.

(1009) ὁρίζεται μεσότητι.¹ μᾶλλον δὲ τοῦτο² τέλος³ ἐστὶ
τῆς τοῦ λόγου δυνάμεως, μεσότητας⁴ ἐν τοῖς
πάθεσι ποιεῖν, ἃς ἱερὰς καλοῦσι ⟨συν⟩ουσίας,⁵
Β ἐχούσας τὴν τῶν ἄκρων πρὸς τὸν λόγον καὶ πρὸς
ἄλληλα διὰ τοῦ λόγου σύγκρασιν.⁶ οὐ γὰρ ἡ
συνωρὶς μέσον ἔχει τῶν ὑποζυγίων τὸ κρεῖττον,
οὐδὲ τὴν ἡνιοχείαν ἀκρότητα θετέον ἀλλὰ μεσότητα
τῆς ἐν ὀξύτητι καὶ βραδυτῆτι τῶν ἵππων ἀμετρίας,
ὥσπερ ἡ τοῦ λόγου⁷ δύναμις ἀντιλαμβανομένη⁸
κινουμένων ἀλόγως τῶν παθῶν καὶ συναρμότ-
τουσα περὶ αὐτὴν εἰς τὸ μέτριον,⁹ ἐλλείψεως καὶ
ὑπερβολῆς μεσότητα, καθίστησιν.

¹ μεσότητα -J¹, g.
² δὲ αὐτὸ τοῦτο -n, Voss. 16, Escorial T-11-5, Bonon.;
αὐτό τε (superscript after τοῦτο) -β².
³ τέλος implied by Amyot's version, Wyttenbach (αὐτὸ
τοῦτο τέλος); ἀτελές (ἀταλές -Voss. 16) -mss.
⁴ δυνάμεως, ὡς μεσότητας Ε, Β.
⁵ Η. C.; καλοῦσιν οὐσίας -mss.; καλοῦσι καὶ ὁσίας -Em-
perius (Op. Philol., p. 340), and implied by Amyot's version.
⁶ συγκρίνειν -g.   ⁷ ἡλίου -J¹, g.
⁸ ἀντιλαμβανομένους -n, Voss. 16, Escorial T-11-5.
⁹ τὸ μέτριον -deleted by Hartman (De Plutarcho, p. 586).

ᵃ Cf. Albinus, Epitome xxx, 6 (p. 151, 4-7 [Louis] =p. 184,
27-30 [Hermann]).
ᵇ Cf. De Virtute Morali 443 c-d (. . . τοῦ λόγου . . . ὅρον
τινὰ καὶ τάξιν ἐπιτιθέντος αὐτῷ καὶ τὰς ἠθικὰς ἀρετάς, . . . συμ-

defined by a mean [a]—or rather this is the purpose of
the faculty of reason, to produce in the affections
means,[b] which are called [c] sacred unions because
they involve the combination of the extremes with
the ratio and through the ratio with each other.[d]
For in the case of the car and pair it is not the
better of the yoked beasts that is intermediate, and
the management of the reins must be reckoned not as
an extreme but as a mean between the immoder-
ate keenness and sluggishness of the horses, just as
the faculty of reason, laying hold of the affections
when they are in irrational motion and ranging
them in concord about herself, reduces them to mo-
deration,[e] a mean between deficiency and excess.[f]

μετρίας παθῶν καὶ μεσότητας, ἐμποιοῦντος) and 444 c (. . . ἐμποιεῖ τὰς ἠθικὰς ἀρετὰς περὶ τὸ ἄλογον . . . μεσότητας οὔσας).
    [c] I am unable to identify the subject of καλοῦσι.
    [d] Cf. Proclus, In Platonis Timaeum ii, p. 22, 22-26 (Diehl):
τοῦτο (scil. τὸ μέσον) γάρ ἐστι δι’ οὗ πᾶσα ἀναλογία συνέστηκε,
συνάγον τοὺς ἄκρους κατὰ τὸν λόγον καὶ διαπορθμεῦον τὸν λόγον
ἀπὸ τῆς ἑτέρας δυνάμεως ἐπὶ τὴν λοιπήν . . . δι’ αὐτοῦ γὰρ ἡ
ἀναλογία συνδεῖ τοὺς ἄκρους.
    [e] Cf. De Virtute Morali 444 b, 445 a (. . . εἰς τὸ μέτριον . . .
καθιστᾶσα τῶν παθῶν ἕκαστον), 451 f (. . . ἐγγενομένης ὑπὸ λόγου
ταῖς παθητικαῖς δυνάμεσι καὶ κινήσεσιν ἐπιεικείας καὶ μετριότητος).
    [f] Cf. [Plato], Definitions 415 a 4 (μέτριον τὸ μέσον
ὑπερβολῆς καὶ ἐλλείψεως) ; Aristotle, De Part. Animal. 652
b 17-19 and Politics 1295 b 4 ; Plutarch, Quomodo Quis
Suos in Virtute Sentiat Profectus 84 a (. . . εἰς τὸ μέσον
καθίστασθαι καὶ μέτριον).

(1009)

ZHTHMA I'

1. Διὰ τί Πλάτων εἶπε τὸν λόγον ἐξ ὀνομάτων
καὶ ῥημάτων κεράννυσθαι; δοκεῖ γὰρ πάντα[1]
πλὴν δυεῖν τούτων τὰ μέρη τοῦ λόγου Πλάτωνα
μὲν μεθεῖναι Ὅμηρον δὲ καὶ[2] νεανιευσάμενον εἰς
C ἕνα στίχον ἐμβαλεῖν ἅπαντα τοῦτον

αὐτὸς ἰὼν[3] κλισίηνδε, τὸ σὸν γέρας· ὄφρ' εὖ
εἰδῆς.[4]

καὶ γὰρ ἀντωνυμία καὶ μετοχὴ καὶ ὄνομα καὶ
ῥῆμα καὶ πρόθεσις καὶ ἄρθρον καὶ σύνδεσμος καὶ
ἐπίρρημα ἔνεστι· τὸ γὰρ " δε " μόριον νῦν ἀντὶ
τῆς " εἰς " προθέσεως τέτακται· τὸ γὰρ " κλισίηνδε " τοιοῦτόν ἐστιν οἷον τὸ " Ἀθήναζε." τί[5]
δὴ ῥητέον ὑπὲρ τοῦ Πλάτωνος;

"Ἢ[6] ὅτι " πρῶτον[7] λόγον " οἱ παλαιοὶ τὴν τότε

---

[1] πάντα -omitted by g.
[2] H. C. (μεθεῖναι -R. G. Bury, *Proc. Cambridge Philol.
Soc. for 1950–1951*, N.S. 1, p. 31); λόγου μηθὲν Ὅμηρον δὲ
καὶ -J, g; λόγου μερῶν μηθὲν ἅμα καὶ -X, β, ε, n, Voss. 16,
Bonon.; λόγου μερῶν μηθὲν ἅμα . . . vac. 13 . . . καὶ -E;
λόγου . . . vac. 32 -α (erasure), 27 -A, 28 -γ, 34 -B . . . καὶ;
λόγου παραλιπόντα μηθὲν καὶ -Escorial T-11-5.
[3] αὐτὸς δὲ ἰὼν -J.
[4] εἰδὼς -X.
[5] τὸ -J[1], g.
[6] ἢ -mss.; ἤ -Dübner.
[7] πρῶτον -omitted by J[1], g; πρῶτον ὅτι -β[2], n, Voss. 16,
Bonon., Escorial T-11-5.

---

[a] This question is translated and discussed by J. J. Hartman in *De Avondzon des Heidendoms* (Leiden, 1910), ii,
pp. 22-30 and translated in part by A. von Mörl in *Die
Grosse Weltordnung* (Berlin/Wien/Leipzig, 1948), ii, pp.
85-89; it is commented on in detail by O. Göldi, *Plutarchs
sprachliche Interessen* (Diss. Zürich, 1922), pp. 2-10.
[b] *Sophist* 262 c 2-7; cf. *Cratylus* 425 a 1-5 and 431 b 5-c
1, *Theaetetus* 206 d 1-5, and [Plato], *Epistle* vii, 342 b 6-7 and
343 b 4-5; O. Apelt, *Platonis Sophista* (Lipsiae, 1897),

QUESTION X [a]

1. WHAT was Plato's reason for saying [b] that speech is a blend of nouns and verbs ? For it seems that except for these two Plato dismissed all the parts of speech whereas Homer in his exuberance went so far as to pack all together into a single line, the following :

Tentward going myself take the guerdon that well you may know it.[c]

In this there are in fact a pronoun and participle and noun and verb and preposition and article and conjunction and adverb,[d] for the suffix " ward " has here been put in place of the preposition " to," the expression " tentward " being of the same kind as the expression " Athensward." [e] What, then, is to be said on behalf of Plato ?

Or [f] is it that the ancients styled " primary

p. 189 and F. M. Cornford, *Plato's Theory of Knowledge* (London, 1935), pp. 307-308.

[c] *Iliad* i, 185.

[d] For these eight parts of speech *cf.* Dionysius Thrax, *Ars Grammatica* § 11 (p. 23 1-2 [Uhlig]). As the Homeric line containing all of them the grammarians cite *Iliad* xxii, 59 (*Scholia in Dionysii Thracis Artem Grammaticam*, p. 58, 13-19 and p. 357, 29-36 [Hilgard] ; Eustathius, *Commentarii ad Homeri Iliadem* 1256, 60-61) ; and there the noun is δύστηνον, for the adjective (" noun adjective " in older grammars [*cf.* *O.E.D.* *s.v.* " noun " 3]) was considered to be a kind of noun, ὄνομα ἐπίθετον (Dionysius Thrax, *op. cit.*, § 12 [p. 33, 1 and pp. 34, 3–35, 2] with *Scholia . . .*, p. 233, 7-33 and p. 553, 11-17 ; *cf.* H. Steinthal, *Geschichte der Sprachwissenschaft bei den Griechen und Römern²*, ii [Berlin, 1891], pp. 251-256).

[e] *Cf. Etym. Magnum* 761, 30-32 and 809, 8-9 (Gaisford) and further for μόριον as " prefix " or " suffix " 141, 47-52.

[f] See 1003 A and 1008 E *supra* and note c on *De Comm. Not.* 1075 F *infra.*

(1009) καλουμένην πρότασιν[1] νῦν δ' ἀξίωμα προσηγόρευον, ὃ πρῶτον λέγοντες ἀληθεύουσιν ἢ ψεύδονται; τοῦτο δ' ἐξ ὀνόματος καὶ ῥήματος συνέστηκεν, ὧν τὸ μὲν πτῶσιν οἱ διαλεκτικοὶ τὸ δὲ
D κατηγόρημα καλοῦσιν. ἀκούσαντες γὰρ ὅτι Σωκράτης φιλοσοφεῖ καὶ πάλιν ὅτι Σωκράτης πέτεται,[2] τὸν μὲν ἀληθῆ λόγον εἶναι τὸν δὲ ψευδῆ φήσομεν, οὐδενὸς ἄλλου προσδεηθέντες. καὶ γὰρ εἰκὸς ἀνθρώπους ἐν χρείᾳ λόγου τὸ πρῶτον[3] καὶ φωνῆς ἐνάρθρου γενέσθαι, τάς τε πράξεις καὶ τοὺς πράττοντας αὐτὰς καὶ τὰ πάθη καὶ τοὺς πάσχοντας ἀλλήλοις διασαφεῖν καὶ ἀποσημαίνειν βουλομένους. ἐπεὶ τοίνυν τῷ μὲν ῥήματι τὰ

[1] πρόφασιν -J[1], g.   [2] πέτεται -Pohlenz ; τρέπεται -mss.

[3] τὸ πρῶτον ἐν χρείᾳ λόγου -J[1], g ; τὸ πρῶτον -omitted by a[1].

---

a Plato, Sophist 262 c 6-7 (τῶν λόγων ὁ πρῶτός τε καὶ σμικρότατος) and 9-10 (λόγον . . . ἐλάχιστόν τε καὶ πρῶτον); cf. Ammonius, De Interpretatione, p. 67, 20-30 and pp. 78, 29-79, 9.

b Cf. [Apuleius], Περὶ ἑρμηνείας i (pp. 176, 15-177, 2 [Thomas]); Galen, Institutio Logica i, 5 (with J. Mau's note ad loc., Galen, Einführung in die Logik [Berlin, 1960], pp. 3-4); and Proclus, In Primum Euclidis El. Lib., pp. 193, 18-194, 4 (Friedlein). For πρότασις used in the general sense of " proposition " cf. Albinus, Epitome vi, 1 and 3 (p. 29, 1-4 and 19-20 [Louis] =p. 158, 4-7 and 21-22 [Hermann]) and Aristotle himself (Anal. Prior. 24 a 16-17 with Alexander, Anal. Prior., p. 44, 16-23); and for ἀξίωμα as the Stoic term for this cf. besides the passage of Proclus just cited Ammonius, De Interpretatione, p. 2, 26 and Mates, Stoic Logic, pp. 27-33 and p. 132, s.v. ἀξίωμα.

c Plato, Sophist 262 e 8-9 and 263 a 11-b 3; cf. [Apuleius], Περὶ ἑρμηνείας iv (p. 178, 1-7 [Thomas]) and Ammonius, De Interpretatione, p. 18, 2-22 and pp. 26, 31-27, 4. It

speech " [a] what then was called a pronouncement
and now is called a proposition,[b] that in the enuncia-
tion of which a truth or falsehood is first expressed ? [c]
And this consists of a noun and a verb, the former
of which the dialecticians call subject and the latter
predicate.[d] For upon hearing " Socrates philoso-
phizes " and again " Socrates flies " we should say
without requiring anything else besides that the
former is true speech and the latter false.[e] Moreover, it is likely that men first felt need of speech
and articulate sound [f] in desiring to designate and
make quite clear to one another actions and their
agents and patients and what they undergo. Since,
then, with the verb we do make adequately clear

was express Stoic doctrine that every proposition is either
true or false (cf. Mates, Stoic Logic, pp. 28-29).

[d] Cf. [Apuleius], Περὶ ἑρμηνείας iv (p. 178, 12-15
[Thomas]) ; Martianus Capella, iv, 393 ; and Mates, Stoic
Logic, pp. 16-17 with notes 34-41 and p. 25 with notes 79-81.
Notice the difference between Diogenes Laertius, vii, 58 and
Plutarch's statement (Mates, p. 16, n. 34) ; and with πτῶσις
as used by Plutarch here cf. besides Sextus, Adv. Math. xi,
29 (Mates, p. 17, n. 40) Clement of Alexandria, Stromata
viii, ix, 26, 4-5, cited by Pearson (Fragments, p. 75) in connexion with Stobaeus, Ecl. i, 12, 3 (p. 137, 3-6 [Wachsmuth])
=S.V.F. i, p. 19, 24-26. οἱ διαλεκτικοί in the present passage
as in 1011 A and 1011 D infra are the Stoics (cf. Aulus
Gellius, xvi, viii, 1 and 8 ; Sextus, Pyrrh. Hyp. ii, 146 and
247 and Adv. Math. viii, 93 ; Cicero, Acad. Prior. ii, 97;
and see note d on De Stoic. Repug. 1045 F infra).

[e] Plato, Sophist 263 A 8-B 3.

[f] i.e. λόγος in the sense of speech. Cf. De Sollertia
Animalium 973 A (προφορικοῦ λόγου καὶ φωνῆς ἐνάρθρου) with
S.V.F. ii, p. 43, 18-20 (τῷ προφορικῷ λόγῳ=ἐνάρθρους φωνάς
[but in S.V.F. iii, p. 215, 35-36 ἡ σημαίνουσα ἔναρθρος
φωνή, with which cf. S.V.F. ii, frag. 143]) ; and De An.
Proc. in Timaeo 1026 A (λόγος δὲ λέξις ἐν φωνῇ σημαντικῇ
διανοίας).

(1009) πράγματα καὶ τὰ[1] πάθη τῷ δ' ὀνόματι τοὺς πράττοντας αὐτὰ καὶ πάσχοντας ἀποχρώντως δηλοῦμεν,
ὡς[2] αὐτὸς εἴρηκε, ταῦτα σημαίνειν ἔδοξε[3]· τὰ δ'
ἄλλα φαίη τις ἂν οὐ σημαίνειν, οἷον οἱ στεναγμοὶ
E καὶ ὀλολυγμοὶ τῶν ὑποκριτῶν· καὶ νὴ Δία πολλάκις[4] ἐπιμειδίασις[5] καὶ[6] ἀποσιώπησις ἐμφαντι-
κώτερον ποιεῖ τὸν λόγον, οὐ μὴν ἀναγκαίαν[7] ἔχει[8]
πρὸς τὸ σημαίνειν ὡς τὸ ῥῆμα καὶ τοὔνομα
δύναμιν ἀλλ' ἐπίθετόν τινα ποικίλλουσαν τὸν λόγον·
ὥσπερ τὰ στοιχεῖα ποικίλλουσιν οἱ τὰ πνεύματα
καὶ τὰς δασύτητας αὐτῶν ἐκτάσεις[9] τε καὶ
συστολὰς ἐνίων αὐτὰ καθ' αὑτὰ[10] στοιχεῖα τιθέμε-
νοι, πάθη μᾶλλον ὄντα καὶ συμβεβηκότα[11] καὶ
διαφορὰς[12] στοιχείων, ὡς ἐδήλωσαν οἱ παλαιοὶ[13]
διὰ τῶν ἑκκαίδεκα φράζοντες ἀποχρώντως καὶ[14]
γράφοντες.

2. Ἔπειτα σκόπει μὴ παρακούωμεν τοῦ Πλάτω-
F νος, ἐκ τούτων κεράννυσθαι τὸν λόγον οὐ διὰ

---

[1] τὰ -omitted by J[1], g.
[2] καὶ -ε.   [3] ἔνδοξος -J[1], g.
[4] δία πολλὰ πολλάκις -X.   [5] ἐπιμειδιάσης -J[1].
[6] καὶ -X, a, ε; omitted by all other mss.
[7] ἀνάγκην -J[1], g.   [8] ἔχειν -J.
[9] ἐκστάσεις -J[1].
[10] καθ' αὑτὰ (ἑαυτὰ -X) τὰ -X, a, A, γ, E, B, ε.
[11] συμβεβηκότως -J.   [12] διαφθορὰς -J[1], g.
[13] πολλοὶ -g.   [14] καὶ -omitted by g.

---

[a] *Sophist* 262 A 3-7, B 6, and B 10-c 1; but Plato here
speaks only of πράξεις and πράττοντες as signified by verbs
and nouns. For Plutarch's substitution of πράγματα for
πράξεις cf. *Scholia in Dionysii Thracis Artem Grammaticam*,
p. 215, 28-30 (Hilgard); Apollonius Dyscolus, *De Constructione* i, 130 and iii, 58 (p. 108, 11-14 and pp. 323, 9–324,
9 [Uhlig]).

acts and what is undergone and with the noun the
agents and patients, as Plato has said himself,[a] it
seemed that these signify, whereas one might say
that the rest like the groans and shouts of actors do
not signify ; and, by heaven, suddenly falling silent
with a smile often makes speech more expressive
and yet has not the force requisite for signifying as
do the verb and the noun but a certain supplementary
force embellishing speech in the way that the letters
are embellished by those who make independent
ones of their breathings and aspirates and in some
cases of their long and short quantities,[b] although
these are rather modifications and incidental characteristics and variations of letters,[c] as the ancients
showed by adequately expressing themselves in
actually writing with sixteen letters.[d]

2. In the second place, take care lest we fail to
heed what Plato has said, that speech is a blend of

[b] τὰ πνεύματα are the two " breathings," δασὺ καὶ ψιλόν
(cf. Dionysius Thrax, Ars Grammatica, Suppl. i, p. 107, 4
[Uhlig] and for the argument that such marks are letters cf.
Scholia in Dionysii Thracis Artem Grammaticam, pp. 187,
26–188, 21 and p. 496, 11-13 [Hilgard]) ; but τὰς δασύτητας
refers to the aspirates θ, φ, χ (cf. Dionysius Thrax, Ars
Grammatica § 6, p. 12, 5 [Uhlig] ; Sextus, Adv. Math. i,
103 ; Priscian, Inst. Grammatica i, 24-25 = i, p. 19, 3-8
[Hertz]) and ἐκτάσεις τε καὶ συστολὰς ἐνίων to the distinction
of η from ε and of ω from o (cf. Sextus, Adv. Math. i, 115).

[c] Cf. Scholia in Dionysii Thracis Artem Grammaticam,
p. 496, 19-24 (Hilgard).

[d] Cf. Plutarch, Quaest. Convic. 738 F ; Demetrius of
Phaleron, frag. 196 (Wehrli) ; Varro, De Antiquitate Lit-
terarum, frag. 2 (Funaioli, Grammaticae Romanae Fragmenta i, p. 184 ; cf. pp. 2 and 120 for L. Cincius, frag. 1 and
Cn. Gellius, frag. 1) ; Pliny, N.H. vii, 192 ; Tacitus, Ann.
xi, 14 ; Scholia in Dionysii Thracis Artem Grammaticam,
pp. 34, 27–35, 13 and pp. 184, 7-12 and 185, 3-7 (Hilgard).

(1009) τούτων εἰρηκότος, εἶθ᾽ ὥσπερ ὁ¹ τὸν λέγοντα² τὸ
φάρμακον ἐκ κηροῦ μεμῖχθαι καὶ χαλβάνης συκο-
φαντῶν, ἐπεὶ τὸ πῦρ παρέλιπε καὶ τὸ ἀγγεῖον ὧν
χωρὶς οὐκ ἐνῆν μεμῖχθαι, καὶ ἡμεῖς ὁμοίως ἐγκα-
λῶμεν³ ὅτι συνδέσμους καὶ προθέσεις καὶ τὰ
τοιαῦτα παρῆκεν· οὐ γὰρ ἐκ τούτων ὁ λόγος ἀλλ᾽,
εἴπερ ἄρα, διὰ τούτων καὶ οὐκ ἄνευ τούτων κεράν-
1010 νυσθαι πέφυκεν. οὐ γάρ, ὥσπερ ὁ τὸ " τύπτει "⁴
φθεγξάμενος ἢ τὸ " τύπτεται "⁵ καὶ πάλιν τὸ
" Σωκράτης " ἢ τὸ " Πυθαγόρας " ἁμωσγέπως
νοῆσαί τι καὶ διανοηθῆναι παρέσχηκεν,⁶ οὕτω
τοῦ " μέν " ἢ " γάρ " ἢ " περί " καθ᾽ αὑτὸ⁷
ἐκφωνηθέντος⁸ ἔστιν ἔννοιάν τινα λαβεῖν⁹ ἢ πράγματος ἢ σώματος· ἀλλ᾽ ἐὰν μὴ περὶ ἐκεῖνα καὶ
μετ᾽ ἐκείνων ἐκφέρηται, ψόφοις κενοῖς καὶ ἤχοις
ἔοικεν· ὅτι ταῦτα μὲν οὔτε καθ᾽ αὑτὰ σημαίνειν
οὔτε μετ᾽ ἀλλήλων οὐδὲν πέφυκεν, ἀλλ᾽ ὅπως ἂν
συμπλέκωμεν ἢ μιγνύωμεν εἰς ταὐτὸ συνδέσμους
καὶ ἄρθρα καὶ προθέσεις, ἔν τι¹⁰ πειρώμενοι κοινὸν
ἐξ αὐτῶν ποιεῖν,¹¹ τερετίζειν μᾶλλον ἢ διαλέγε-

¹ ὁ -omitted by J¹, g.
² λέγον (τὸν and τα omitted) -a¹.
³ ἐγκαλοῦμεν -J¹, g.
⁴ τύπτει -mss. ; τύπτειν -Basiliensis.
⁵ τύπτεσθαι -Aldine, Basiliensis.
⁶ παρέσχεν -J, g.
⁷ καθ᾽ αὑτὸ -omitted by E, B.
⁸ φωνήεντός -J, g.
⁹ λαβεῖν τινα -X, ε.
¹⁰ ἔν τινι -n.
¹¹ κοινὸν ποιεῖν ἐξ αὐτῶν -X.

ᵃ The phrase, σῶμα ἢ πρᾶγμα σημαῖνον, occurs in the
definition of ὄνομα given by Dionysius Thrax, Ars Gram-

these, not that it is blended by means of them, and
lest then like one who, when the medicine is said
to be a mixture of wax and galbanum, carps at the
omission of the fire and the receptacle, without
which it could not have been mixed, we too similarly
object that Plato disregarded conjunctions and prepositions and the like, for it is not of these that
speech is naturally blended but, if at all, by means
of them and not without them. For it is not the case
that as one by uttering " strikes " or " is struck "
and again " Socrates " or " Pythagoras " has provided something to conceive and have in mind somehow so, when " indeed " or " for " or " about " has
been pronounced by itself, it is possible to get some
conception of an act or an object [a]; but, unless
these are expressions about those other words and
in association with them, they resemble senseless
sounds and noises. The reason is that they naturally
signify nothing either by themselves or in association
with one another; but, however we may combine
or mix together conjunctions and articles and prepositions in trying to make of them a single thing
in common, it will seem that we are babbling gib-

---

matica § 12 (p. 24, 3-4 [Uhlig]). Since Plutarch has just
given both verbs and nouns as counter-examples, however,
πράγματος here is probably meant in the sense of τὰ πράγματα
in 1009 D *supra* (page 108, note *a*); *cf.* also Dionysius Hal.,
De Comp. Verb. xii, 69-70 (p. 46, 21 f. [Usener-Rader-
macher]), ᾧ σημαίνει τι σῶμα ἢ πρᾶγμα, where the preceding
οὔτε ὄνομα οὔτε ῥῆμα (*ibid.*, p. 46, 18) indicates that πρᾶγμα
means " act " and not " thing." The use of σῶμα for " object " generally reflects the Stoic doctrine that all agents and
patients—and so all entities—are σώματα (see notes *f* and *g*
on *De Comm. Not.* 1073 E *infra* and *cf.* Apollonius Dyscolus,
De Constructione i, 16 = p. 18, 5-8 [Uhlig]).

(1010)
B σθαι[1] δόξομεν· ῥήματος δ' ὀνόματι[2] συμπλεκομέ-
νου, τὸ γενόμενον εὐθὺς διάλεκτός[3] ἐστι καὶ λόγος.
ὅθεν εἰκότως ἔνιοι μόνα ταῦτα μέρη τοῦ λόγου τί-
θενται· καὶ Ὅμηρος ἴσως τοῦτο βούλεται δηλοῦν
ἑκάστοτε λέγων

ἔπος τ' ἔφατ' ἔκ τ' ὀνόμαζεν·

ἔπος γὰρ τὸ ῥῆμα καλεῖν εἴωθεν, ὥσπερ ἐν τούτοις

ὦ γύναι, ἦ μάλα τοῦτο ἔπος θυμαλγὲς[4] ἔειπες

καὶ

χαῖρε, πάτερ ὦ ξεῖνε, ἔπος δ' εἴπερ τι[5] λέλεκ-
ται[6]

δεινόν, ἄφαρ τὸ φέροιεν ἀναρπάξασαι ἄελλαι.

οὔτε γὰρ σύνδεσμον οὔτ' ἄρθρον[7] οὔτε πρόθεσιν[8]
δεινόν ἐστι καὶ θυμαλγὲς εἰπεῖν ἀλλὰ ῥῆμα[9]
C πράξεως ἐμφαντικὸν[10] αἰσχρᾶς ἢ[11] πάθους τινὸς
ἀνεπιτηδείου. διὸ καὶ ποιητὰς καὶ συγγραφεῖς
εἰώθαμεν ἐπαινεῖν ἢ ψέγειν οὕτω πως λέγοντες

[1] διαλογίζεσθαι -J, g.   [2] ὀνόματος -J[1].
[3] διάλογος -β[1], n, Voss. 16, Escorial T-11-5, Bonon.
[4] θυμαλγὲς -J[1].
[5] ἔπος τ' εἴπερ τε -β, n, Voss. 16, Escorial T-11-5, Bonon.
[6] βέβακται -Homer.
[7] ἄθερον -J[1].
[8] πρότερον -J[1], g.
[9] ῥίζα -J[1], g.
[10] ἐμφατικὸν -e.
[11] ἢ -Meziriac ; ἐκ -MSS.

[a] Plato, Sophist 262 c 4-7 and D 2-6.
[b] Cf. [Apuleius], Περὶ ἑρμηνείας iv (p. 178, 4-7 [Thomas]) ;
Apollonius Dyscolus, De Constructione i, 30 (p. 28, 6-9
[Uhlig] with Priscian, Inst. Grammatica xvii, 22 =ii, pp. 121,
21–122, 1 [Hertz]) ; and Scholia in Dionysii Thracis Artem
Grammaticam, pp. 515, 19–517, 32 (Hilgard), where the

berish rather than speaking a language. When a
verb is combined with a noun, however, the result
is straightway language and speech.[a] Wherefore it
is reasonable that some people consider these alone
to be parts of speech [b] ; and this perhaps is what
Homer wants to make clear each time he says

> gave word to the thought and announced it,[c]

for it was his custom to call the verb " word," as in
these lines :

> Verily, woman, a heart-breaking word is this thou hast
>   spoken [d]

and

> Joy to thee, reverend guest ; if offensive words have been
>   spoken,
> May they be gone forthwith swept up and away by a
>   whirlwind.[e]

For what is offensive and heart-breaking to speak is
not a conjunction or an article or a preposition but a
verb expressive of a shameful action or of some im-
proper experience. This is also why we customarily
praise or censure writers of poetry and prose in

doctrine is ascribed to the Peripatetics and some of the
supporting arguments are answered (cf. Priscian, op. cit.,
ii, 15 and xi, 6-7 = i, p. 54, 5-7 and pp. 551, 17-552, 14
[Hertz]). An elaborate defence of the doctrine, in many
particulars like Plutarch's, is given by Ammonius (De
Interpretatione, pp. 11, 1-15, 13), who with explicit reference
to the Cratylus and the Sophist asserts that Plato anticipated
Aristotle in holding it (De Interpretatione, p. 40, 26-30 ;
p. 48, 30-32 ; p. 60, 1-3 and 17-23). Cf. Aristotle, Rhetoric
1404 b 26-27 ; Theophrastus and Boethus of Sidon in
Simplicius, Categ., p. 10, 24-27 and p. 11, 23-25 ; and
Adrastus in Theon Smyrnaeus, p. 49, 7-9 (Hiller).

[c] Iliad vi, 253 and 406 ; vii, 108 ; and passim.

[d] Odyssey xxiii, 183.

[e] Odyssey viii, 408-409.

(1010) " Ἀττικοῖς ὀνόμασιν ὁ δεῖνα κέχρηται καὶ[1] καλοῖς
ῥήμασιν " ἢ πάλιν " πεζοῖς " τὸ δέ γε " πεζοῖς "[2]
ἢ " καλοῖς " πάλιν " καὶ Ἀττικοῖς ἄρθροις "
οὐκ ἂν εἴποι τις Εὐριπίδην ἢ Θουκυδίδην διει-
λέχθαι.

3. " Τί οὖν ; "—φήσαι τις ἄν—" οὐδὲν ταῦτα
συμβάλλεται πρὸς λόγον ; " ἔγωγε φήσαιμ' ἂν
ὥσπερ ἅλας[3] συμβάλλεσθαι πρὸς ὄψον ὕδωρ δὲ
πρὸς μᾶζαν. Εὔηνος[4] δὲ καὶ τὸ πῦρ ἔφασκεν
ἡδυσμάτων εἶναι κράτιστον. ἀλλ' οὔθ' ὕδωρ μάζης
ἢ ἄρτου μέρος εἶναι λέγομεν[5] οὔτε πῦρ οὔθ' ἅλας
ἑψήματος ἢ βρώματος,[6] ὧν ἀεὶ τυγχάνομεν δεόμε-
νοι, οὐχ ὥσπερ ὁ λόγος πολλάκις ἐκείνων ἀπροσ-
D δεής ἐστιν, ὡς δοκεῖ μοι [περὶ Ῥωμαίων] ἔχειν ὁ
Ῥωμαίων, ⟨ᾧ⟩[7] νῦν ὁμοῦ τι πάντες ἄνθρωποι
χρῶνται· προθέσεις τε γὰρ ἀφήρηκε πλὴν ὀλίγων[8]

[1] καὶ -J[1], g ; omitted by all other mss.
[2] Dübner (τὸ δὲ πεζοῖς -Wyttenbach) ; ὁ δέ γε πεζοῖς -J[1],
g ; πεζοῖς δὲ -Escorial T-11-5 ; ὅδε δὲ πεζοῖς -all other mss.
[3] ἅλλας -J[1], g.
[4] εὔωνος -n, Voss. 16, ε[1] (?).
[5] κράτιστον . . . μέρος εἶναι -omitted by J, g, a, A, γ, E,
B ; κράτιστον . . . εἶναι λέγομεν -omitted by β[1] (added in
margin by β[2]).
[6] ἀρώματος -X, ε.
[7] Dübner (μοι ὁ Ῥωμαίων ἔχειν, ᾧ -Wyttenbach) ; μοι
περὶ ῥωμαίων λέγειν ὁρῶ μέλλω (μέλλων -β, n, Voss. 16, Bonon.) νῦν -all mss. except Escorial T-11-5 (μοι περὶ ρω-
μαίων λέγειν ὁρῶ . . . vac. 30 . . . ἀλλ' ὥσπερ ὁμοῦ πάντες).
[8] ὀλίγον -J.

[a] In such expressions ὄνομα (and the same could be said
of ῥῆμα) is used in a different sense, i.e. τὸ κοινῶς ἐπὶ πᾶν μέρος
λόγου διατεῖνον (cf. Simplicius, Categ., p. 25,[1] 14-17 ; Scholia
in Dionysii Thracis Artem Grammaticam, p. 522, 21-28
[Hilgard]).
[b] Evenus, frag. 10 (Bergk, Poetae Lyr. Graec. ii[4], p. 271 ;

terms like these, " the nouns employed by so-and-so
are ' Attic ' and the verbs are ' elegant ' " or again
" pedestrian," [a] whereas it would not be said by
anyone that in the language of Euripides or Thucydides " pedestrian " or again " elegant and Attic
articles " are used.

3. " What then ? "—one might say—" Do these
words contribute nothing to speech ? " I should say
that they do make a contribution to it just as salt
does to a dish of food and water to a barley-cake.
Evenus even said that fire is the best of sauces.[b]
Nevertheless, we do not say either that water is a
part of barley-cake or wheat-bread or that fire or
salt is a part of greens or victuals, although we do
always require fire and salt, whereas speech unlike
this often has no need of those additional words.
So it is, it seems to me, with the speech of the
Romans, which now is used by nearly all men, for it
has eliminated all prepositions except for a few [c]

Edmonds, *Elegy and Iambus* i, p. 476). The remark is
ascribed to Evenus in *Quomodo Adulator ab Amico Internoscatur* 50 A and in *Quaest. Conviv.* 697 c-D but to Prodicus
in *De Tuenda Sanitate* 126 D.

    [c] According to Hartman (*De Plutarcho*, p. 583) this is an
erroneous generalization from those Latin expressions of
relations of place in which no preposition is used ; according
to H. J. Rose (*The Roman Questions of Plutarch* [Oxford,
1924], p. 198 *ad* lxvii [208 A]) it is rather an exaggeration
suggested by the contemporary fondness for archaic and
poetical constructions which omitted the prepositions of
Ciceronian grammar ; and both these observations may be
partial explanations of Plutarch's " odd statement," but it
should be remembered also that many Latin " prepositions "
were regarded by the Greeks as not being prepositions at all
(Priscian, *Inst. Grammatica* xiv, 9-10 and 23=ii, pp. 28,
19-29, 11 and pp. 36, 20-37, 6 [Hertz]). From a different
point of view Plutarch's statement without being noticed is

(1010) ἀπάσας, τῶν τε καλουμένων ἄρθρων οὐδὲν προσ-
δέχεται τὸ παράπαν, ἀλλὰ ὥσπερ ἀκρασπέδοις[1]
χρῆται τοῖς ὀνόμασι. καὶ οὐ θαυμαστόν ἐστιν,
ὅπου καὶ Ὅμηρος ἐπέων κόσμῳ περιγενόμενος
ὀλίγοις τῶν ὀνομάτων ἄρθρα ὥσπερ λαβὰς ἐκπώμασι μὴ[2] δεομένοις ἢ λόφους[3] κράνεσιν ἐπιτίθησι·
διὸ καὶ[4] παράσημα τῶν ἐπῶν ἐν οἷς ταῦτα ποιεῖ[5]
γέγονεν, ὡς τὸ

Αἴαντι δὲ μάλιστα δαΐφρονι θυμὸν ὄρινε
τῷ Τελαμωνιάδῃ

καὶ τὸ

ποίεεν,[6] ὄφρα τὸ κῆτος ὑπεκπροφυγὼν[7] ἀλέοιτο[8]

καὶ βραχέα πρὸς τούτοις ἕτερα. τοῖς δ' ἄλλοις
Ε μυρίοις οὖσιν ἄρθρου μὴ[9] προσόντος οὐδὲν εἰς
σαφήνειαν οὐδὲ κάλλος ἡ φράσις βλάπτεται.

[1] Meziriac; κρασπέδοις -MSS.
[2] μὴ -β², n, Voss. 16, Escorial T-11-5, Bonon.; omitted
by all other MSS.
[3] λόφοις -J¹, g.　　　　[4] καὶ -omitted by g.
[5] ποιεῖν -ε; προ (i.e. προγέγονεν) -Escorial T-11-5.
[6] ποιεῖν n; ποίεον -Homer.　　　[7] ὑπερπροφυγὼν -n.
[8] ἀλλέοιτο -Escorial T-11-5; ἀλέαιτο -Homer.
[9] ἄρθρου δὲ μὴ -J, g.

supported by R. Poncelet (Cicéron Traducteur de Platon
[Paris, 1957]), who characterizes the Latin penury of analy-
tical instruments as " pas d'articles, peu de prépositions, peu
de participes " (p. 18) and considers the rudimentary prepo-
sitional system of Latin along with its lack of an article to be
one of the principal reasons for Cicero's difficulties in trans-
lating the philosophical Greek of Plato (pp. 52-61, pp. 105-
129, p. 139).
    [a] Cf. Quintilian, Instit. Orat. i, 4, 19 ; Priscian, Inst.
Grammatica ii, 16 and xvii, 27 (i, p. 54, 13-16 and ii, p. 124,
16-18 [Hertz]).
    [b] Cf. Democritus, frag. B 21 (D.-K.) and Pausanias, ix, 30,

and of the words called articles admits none at all [a]
but employs nouns without tassels, as it were. This
is not surprising either, since Homer too, who ex-
celled in marshalling words,[b] attaches articles to
few of his nouns, as it were crests to helmets or
handles to goblets that do not require them [c] ; and
that is the very reason why critical marks [d] have
been put at the verses in which he does so, for
example :

> Wrathful fury he chiefly excited in fiery Ajax,
> The Telamonian one,[e]

and

> Built it to let him elude and evade the notorious monster [f]

and a few others besides. In the rest, however,
countless as they are, though an article is not
present, the expression suffers nothing in clarity or
beauty.

4 and 12. The phrase κόσμον ἐπέων occurs in a line of
Solon's quoted by Plutarch himself (*Solon* viii, 2 [82 c]) ; *cf.*
also Parmenides, frag. B 8, 52 (D.-K.) and Philetas of Cos,
frag. 8 (Diehl, *Anth. Lyr. Graec.* ii, p. 211) = 10 (Powell,
Collectanea Alexandrina, p. 92).

[c] There were ἐκπώματα of countless kinds (Clement of
Alexandria, *Paedagogus* ii, iii, 35, 2), many without handles
(Athenaeus, xi, 783 a, 478 b, and 481 d).

[d] *Cf.* Aristotle, *Soph. Elench.* 177 b 6 (κἀκεῖ . . . παράσημα
ποιοῦνται).

[e] *Iliad* xiv, 459-460. Leaf (*The Iliad* ii², p. 97 *ad* 458-459)
calls the use of τῷ in 460 " hardly Homeric." *Cf.* in general
Scholia Graeca in Homeri Iliadem ed. Dindorf i, p. 70, 10-11
ad B 1 and p. 339, 14-15 *ad* K 1 (ἔστι γὰρ ὁ ποιητὴς παρα-
ληπτικὸς τῶν ἄρθρων).

[f] *Iliad* xx, 147. For the use of the article here *cf. Scholia
Graeca in Homeri Iliadem* ed. Dindorf ii, p. 199, 19-20 ;
Leaf (*The Iliad* ii², p. 359) calls it very rare in Homer and
says that " instances such as this are confined to late passages
in the *Iliad*."

117

(1010)   4. Καὶ μὴν οὔτε ζῷον οὔτ' ὄργανον οὔθ' ὅπλον
οὔτ' ἄλλο τῶν ὄντων οὐδὲν οἰκείου μέρους ἀφαι-
ρέσει καὶ στερήσει πέφυκε γίγνεσθαι κάλλιον[1] οὐδ'
ἐνεργέστερον οὐδὲ ἥδιον· λόγος δέ, συνδέσμων ἐξ-
αιρεθέντων, πολλάκις ἐμπαθεστέραν καὶ κινητικω-
τέραν ἔχει δύναμιν· ὡς ὁ τοιοῦτος

ἄλλον ζωὸν ἔχουσα[2] νεούτατον, ἄλλον ἄουτον,
ἄλλον τεθνειῶτα[3] κατὰ μόθον ἕλκε ποδοῖιν·

καὶ τὰ τοῦ Δημοσθένους ταυτὶ "πολλὰ γὰρ ἂν
ποιήσειεν ὁ τύπτων, ὧν[4] ὁ παθὼν ἔνι' οὐδ' ἂν
F ἀπαγγεῖλαι δύναιθ' ἑτέρῳ, τῷ σχήματι τῷ βλέμ-
ματι τῇ φωνῇ, ὅταν ὑβρίζων, ὅταν ἐχθρὸς[5] ὑπ-
άρχων, ὅταν κονδύλοις,[6] ὅταν ἐπὶ κόρρης[7]· ταῦτα
κινεῖ,[8] ταῦτ' ἐξίστησιν αὐτῶν ἀνθρώπους[9] ἀήθεις
τοῦ[10] προπηλακίζεσθαι." καὶ πάλιν "ἀλλ' οὐ[11]
Μειδίας· ἀλλ' ἀπὸ ταύτης τῆς ἡμέρας[12] λέγει, λοι-
δορεῖται, βοᾷ. χειροτονεῖταί τις;[13] Μειδίας Ἀνα-
1011 γυράσιος[14] προβέβληται. Πλουτάρχου[15] προξενεῖ,

---

[1] κάλλιστον -J, g.   [2] ἔχουσα -omitted by J[1], g.

[3] τεθνηῶτα -Homer (cf. *Scholia Graeca in Homeri Iliadem* ed. Dindorf ii, p. 176 *ad* 537).

[4] τύπτων, ὦ ἄνδρες Ἀθηναῖοι, ὧν -Demosthenes.

[5] ὅταν ὡς ὑβρίζων, ὅταν ὡς ἐχθρὸς -Demosthenes.

[6] ὅταν κονδύλοις -omitted by J[1], g.

[7] κόρης -J, g; κόρης τύπτῃ -Escorial T-11-5.

[8] κινῇ -J, g, Escorial T-11-5.

[9] αὐτῶν ἐξίστησιν ἀνθρώπους -J; αὐτοῦ ἐξίστησιν ἀνθρώπους -g; ἐξίστησιν αὐτοὺς ἀνθρώπους -Escorial T-11-5; ἐξίστησιν ἀνθρώπους αὐτῶν -Demosthenes.

[10] ἀήθους τοῦ -ε; ἀήθεις ὄντας τοῦ -Demosthenes.

[11] οὐδὲ -g.

[12] τῆς ἡμέρας ταύτης -Demosthenes S and Y (but A and F agree with Plutarch).   [13] Demosthenes; τι -MSS.

[14] Escorial T-11-5 and Demosthenes; ἀναγυράσιος -all other MSS.   [15] Demosthenes; πλουτάρχῳ -MSS.

4. Moreover, it is not natural for any living being or instrument or weapon or any other existing thing to become more beautiful or more effective or more pleasant by the removal or loss of a part that belongs to it[a] ; but frequently when conjunctions have been eliminated speech has a force more emotional and more stirring,[b] as in a case like this :

> One just wounded alive in her clutches, another unwounded,
> Dead already another she dragged by the feet through the turmoil[c]

and this by Demosthenes : " He who strikes one might do many things, some of which his victim could not even report to another, by his posture, by his look, by his tone of voice, when insultingly, when in hostility, when with the fist, when with a slap in the face ; these are the things that stir up, that drive to distraction men unused to contemptuous treatment." [d] And again : " Not Meidias, however ; but from this day forth he talks, reviles, shouts. Is someone to be elected ? Meidias of Anagyrus is a candidate. He represents the interests

---

[a] Cf. Scholia in Dionysii Thracis Artem Grammaticam, pp. 516, 37–517, 4 (Hilgard).

[b] Cf. [Plutarch], De Vita Homeri 40 (vii, pp. 355, 20–356, 5 [Bernardakis]) ; for Plutarch, Caesar 1, 3-4 (731 f) cf. R. Jeuckens, Plutarch von Chaeronea und die Rhetorik (Strassburg, 1908), pp. 162-163.

[c] Iliad xviii, 536-537 =[Hesiod], Scutum 157-158 (cf. F. Solmsen, Hermes, xciii [1965], pp. 1-6).

[d] Demosthenes, Oratio xxi, 72. The passage is quoted and analysed by " Longinus " (De Sublimitate xx-xxi) for the combination of several figures, asyndeton included ; cf. also Tiberius Rhetor, Περὶ σχημάτων 40 (Rhetores Graeci iii, p. 78, 1-4 [Spengel]).

(1011) τἀπόρρητ᾽ οἶδεν, ἡ πόλις αὐτὸν οὐ χωρεῖ.'' διὸ καὶ
σφόδρα τὸ ἀσύνδετον σχῆμα παρὰ τοῖς[1] τὰς[2]
τέχνας γράφουσιν εὐδοκιμεῖ· τοὺς[3] δ᾽ ἄγαν νομί-
μους ἐκείνους καὶ μηδένα σύνδεσμον ἐκ τῆς
συνηθείας ἀφιέντας ὡς ἀργὴν καὶ ἀπαθῆ καὶ
κοπώδη τῷ ἀμεταβλήτῳ τὴν φράσιν ποιοῦντας
αἰτιῶνται. τὸ δὲ τοὺς διαλεκτικοὺς μάλιστα συνδέσμων δεῖσθαι πρὸς τὰς τῶν ἀξιωμάτων συναφὰς
καὶ συμπλοκὰς καὶ διαζεύξεις ὥσπερ ἡνιόχους
ζυγῶν καὶ τὸν ⟨ἐν⟩[4] Κύκλωπος Ὀδυσσέα λύγων
πρὸς τὴν τῶν προβάτων σύν⟨δεσιν . . .⟩ οὐ[5] μέρος
λόγου τὸν[6] σύνδεσμον ἀλλ᾽ ὄργανόν τι[7] συνδετικὸν[8]
B ἀποφαίνει, καθάπερ ὠνόμασται, καὶ συνεκτικὸν οὐ

---

[1] παρ᾽ οἷς -n, Voss. 16.
[2] τὰς -omitted by a, A, γ, E, B, ε.
[3] τῆς -J[1] ; τοὺς -all other mss.
[4] ⟨ἐν⟩ -added by Emperius (Op. Philol., p. 340).
[5] Hubert after Bernardakis (λύγων πρὸς τῶν προβάτων τὴν
σύνδεσιν ⟨Odyssey ix, 425 and 427⟩ οὐ); λυγῶν πρὸς τὴν
τῶν προβάτων οὐ -J, g ; λυγῶντα πρὸς τὴν τῶν προβάτων συν
. . . vac. 83 (first 5 erased) . . . οὐ -β (σὺν . . . vac. 57 . . . οὐ
-Bonon.) ; λυγῶντα πρὸς τὴν τῶν προβάτων . . . vac. 58 . . .
οὐ -n, Voss. 16 ; λέγοντα πρὸς τὴν τῶν προβάτων . . . vac.
64 . . . οὐ -Escorial T-11-5 ; Ὀδυσσέα . . . vac. 30 -X ; 62 -a;
100 -A ; 84 -γ ; 87 -E ; 88 -B ; 69 -ε . . . οὐ.
[6] τὸν -omitted by J, g ; τοῦ -a.
[7] τι -J, g ; omitted by all other mss.
[8] συνδεκτικὸν -J, g.

---

[a] Plutarch, the tyrant of Eretria (cf. Plutarch, Phocion
xii-xiii [747 A-E] ; Demosthenes, Oratio v, 5 [with scholion
ad loc.] and xxi, 110).
[b] Demosthenes, Oratio xxi, 200. Part of this passage is
quoted for asyndeton by [Aristides], Libri Rhetorici i, 28
(pp. 13, 23–14, 1 [W. Schmid]).
[c] Cf. Demetrius, De Elocutione 193-194 and 268-269 ;
" Longinus," De Sublimitate xxi ; Tiberius Rhetor, Περὶ

of Plutarch,[a] knows the secrets of state, is too big for the city."[b] This is just the reason why the figure of asyndeton is very highly esteemed by the writers of the rhetorical manuals, and those who abide too strictly by the rules and leave out no conjunction of the ordinary language they censure for making their style dull and unemotional and wearisome from lack of variety.[c] That the dialecticians have special need of conjunctions for the connexions and combinations and disjunctions of propositions,[d] as charioteers have of yokes and as Odysseus ⟨in the cave⟩ of Cyclops had of withes for binding the sheep together[e] ⟨. . .⟩, this shows not that the conjunction is a part of speech[f] but that it is a kind of instrument for conjoining, just as its name indicates, that

σχημάτων 40 (*Rhetores Graeci* iii, p. 78, 11-15 [Spengel]); [Cicero], *Ad Herennium* iv, 41. For *αἱ τέχναι* = "rhetorical manuals" *cf.* Isocrates, *Adv. Sophistas* 19 (*τὰς καλουμένας τέχνας*) with the scholion *ad loc.*

[d] The dialecticians are the Stoics (see note *d* on page 107 *supra*). The propositions in question are the conditional (*συνημμένον*), the conjunctive (*συμπεπλεγμένον*), and the disjunctive (*διεζευγμένον*); and the *σύνδεσμοι* required for these are respectively *ὁ συναπτικός* (*εἰ*), *ὁ συμπλεκτικός* (*καί*), and *ὁ διαζευκτικός* (*ἤτοι* or *ἤ*): *cf.* Diogenes Laertius, vii, 71-72 (*S.V.F.* ii, frag. 207); Galen, *Institutio Logica* iii, 3-4 and iv, 4-6 (pp. 8, 13-9, 8 and pp. 10, 13-11, 12 [Kalbfleisch] = *S.V.F.* ii, frags. 208 and 217); and Plutarch, *De E* 386 F—387 A, *De Sollertia Animalium* 969 A-B, and *De An. Proc. in Timaeo* 1026 B-C.

[e] *Cf. Odyssey* ix, 427 and Euripides, *Cyclops* 225.

[f] As the Stoics held it to be: *cf.* Diogenes Laertius, vii, 57-58 (*S.V.F.* ii, frag. 147 and iii, p. 214, 1-2); *S.V.F.* ii, frag. 148; *Scholia in Dionysii Thracis Artem Grammaticam*, p. 356, 13-15 and p. 517, 33-34 with p. 519, 26-32 (Hilgard). Posidonius wrote against those who said that conjunctions *οὐ δηλοῦσι μέν τι αὐτὸ δὲ μόνον τὴν φράσιν συνδέουσι* (Apollonius Dyscolus, *De Conjunctionibus*, p. 214, 4-8 [Schneider]).

(1011) πάντων ἀλλὰ τῶν οὐχ ἁπλῶς λεγομένων, εἰ μὴ
καὶ τοῦ φορτίου τὸν ἱμάντα καὶ τοῦ βιβλίου τὴν
κόλλαν ἀξιοῦσι μέρος εἶναι καὶ νὴ Δία[1] τὰς δια-
νομὰς τοῦ πολιτεύματος, ὡς ἔλεγε Δημάδης, κόλλαν ὀνομάζων τὰ θεωρικὰ[2] τῆς δημοκρατίας.
ποῖος δὲ σύνδεσμος οὕτως ἐν ἐκ πολλῶν ἀξίωμα
ποιεῖ συμπλέκων καὶ συνάπτων ὡς ἡ μάρμαρος[3]
τὸν συλλιπαινόμενον[4] διὰ τοῦ πυρὸς σίδηρον; ἀλλ'
οὐκ ἔστιν οὐδὲ λέγεται τοῦ σιδήρου μέρος· καίτοι
⟨τὰ⟩ τοιαῦτά[5] γε τοῖς κεραννυμένοις ἐνδυόμενα
καὶ συντηκόμενα ποιεῖ τι [καὶ πάσχει][6] κοινὸν ἐκ
C πλειόνων.[7] τοὺς δὲ συνδέσμους εἰσὶν οἱ μὴ νό-

---

[1] νὴ Δία -X, β², n, Voss. 16, Bonon., Escorial T-11-5 ;
εἶναι νὴ Δία καὶ -e ; νὴ Δία -omitted by all other mss.

[2] θεωρητικὰ -J, g, Voss. 16, Escorial T-11-5.

[3] μάρμερος -J, Escorial T-11-5[1] ; μάμερ -g.

[4] σύλανλιπαινόμενον -J.

[5] H. C. ; καὶ τοιαῦτα -J, g ; καίτοι ταῦτα -all other mss.

[6] [καὶ πάσχει] -deleted by Hartman (De Plutarcho, p. 588).

[7] πλοιόνων -J.

---

[a] That is even for the Stoics the conjunction holds together
only a molecular proposition, this consisting of two or more
atomic (simple) propositions, each of which itself consists of
a subject and predicate not connected by any conjunction :
cf. Sextus, Adv. Math. viii, 93-95 and 108-109 (S.V.F. ii,
p. 66, 28-37 and pp. 70, 36–71, 2) with Mates, Stoic Logic,
pp. 95-96 ; and Diogenes Laertius, vii, 68-69 and 71-72
(S.V.F. ii, frags. 203 and 207).

[b] Cf. [Apuleius], Περὶ ἑρμηνείας iv (p. 178, 7-11 [Thomas]) ;
Ammonius, De Interpretatione, pp. 12, 25–13, 6 and p. 67,
15-19 and p. 73, 19-22 ; Simplicius, Categ., p. 64, 23-25 ;
Scholia in Dionysii Thracis Artem Grammaticam, p. 515,
19-29 (Hilgard).

[c] Demades, frag. 13 (Baiter-Sauppe, Oratores Attici ii,
p. 315 B 38-42)=xxxvi (De Falco, Demade Oratore², p. 31).

[d] See note d on 1011 A supra.

PLATONIC QUESTIONS x, 1011

is for holding together not all statements but those
that are non-simple,[a]—unless one also maintains
that the strap is part of the load and the glue part
of the book [b] and the dole, by heaven, part of the
government, as Demades said when he called the
festival-grants the glue of the democracy.[c] What
kind of conjunction, moreover, by combining and con-
necting [d] makes of many a proposition so thoroughly
one as the marble makes the iron that is smelted with
it in the fire ? The marble, however, is not and is
not said to be a part of the iron ; and yet things of
this kind make something common out of a multiplicity [e] by permeating the objects that are being
blended and by being fused with them.[f] As to conjunctions, however, there are people who believe

---

[e] *Cf.* 1010 A *supra* : ἕν τι πειρώμενοι κοινὸν ἐξ αὐτῶν ποιεῖν.
[f] The marble is not fused with the iron, as Plutarch
apparently believed it is, but supplies the limestone which
unites with the non-ferrous minerals of the ore (the " gan-
gue ") and with the ash of the fuel to form the " cinder " or
" slag." It may be such a flux to which reference is made by
[Aristotle], *De Mirabilibus Auscultationibus* 833 b 24-28 and
by Theophrastus, *De Lapidibus* 9 (*cf.* H. Blümner, *Techno-
logie und Terminologie der Gewerbe und Künste bei Griechen
und Römern* iv [Leipzig, 1887], pp. 219-220 ; A. W. Persson,
Eisen und Eisenbereitung in ältester Zeit [Lund, 1934], pp.
15-17 ; E. R. Caley and J. F. C. Richards, *Theophrastus on
Stones* [Columbus, 1956], p. 77) ; but in no ancient text, so
far as I know, is an explanation of the process offered,
although the purpose of the flux used in refining gold is
mentioned (*cf.* Agatharchides in Photius, *Bibliotheca*, cod.
250, p. 448, 19-30 [Bekker] ; Pliny, *N.H.* xxxiii, 60 ; H.
Blümner, *op. cit.*, pp. 131-135). It is to a different stage in
the working of the iron that Plutarch refers in *Quaest.
Conviv.* 660 c and *De Primo Frigido* 954 A-B; *cf.* also
H. D. P. Lee on Aristotle, *Meteorologica* 383 a 32-b 7 (*L.C.L.*,
pp. 324-329).

(1011) μίζοντες ἕν τι ποιεῖν ἀλλ' ἐξαρίθμησιν εἶναι τὴν
διάλεκτον, ὥσπερ ἀρχόντων ἐφεξῆς ⟨ἢ⟩[1] ἡμερῶν
καταλεγομένων.

5. Καὶ μὴν τῶν γε λοιπῶν ἡ μὲν ἀντωνυμία
περιφανῶς γένος[2] ὀνόματός ἐστιν, οὐχ ᾗ πτώσεων
μετέχει μόνον ἀλλὰ καὶ τῷ κυριωτάτην ἅμα τῇ
φάσει[3] ποιεῖν δεῖξιν ἐνίας ἐπὶ τῶν ὡρισμένων ἐκ-
φερομένας· καὶ οὐκ οἶδα ὅτι μᾶλλον ὁ " Σωκράτην "[4] φθεγξάμενος ἢ ὁ " τοῦτον " εἰπὼν ὀνομαστὶ[5]
πρόσωπον δεδήλωκεν.

6. Ἡ δὲ καλουμένη μετοχή, μῖγμα ῥήματος
οὖσα καὶ ὀνόματος,[6] καθ' ἑαυτὴν[7] μὲν οὐκ ἔστιν,
ὥσπερ οὐδὲ τὰ κοινὰ θηλυκῶν καὶ ἀρρενικῶν ὀνό-
D ματα, συντάττεται δ' ἐκείνοις, ἐφαπτομένη τοῖς μὲν
χρόνοις τῶν ῥημάτων ταῖς δὲ πτώσεσι τῶν ὀνομάτων. οἱ δὲ διαλεκτικοὶ τὰ τοιαῦτα καλοῦσιν

---

[1] ⟨ἢ⟩ -added by Meziriac ; implied by Amyot's version.
[2] γένος περιφανῶς -J, g.
[3] Wyttenbach ; φύσει -mss.
[4] Σωκράτη -X.   [5] ὀνόματι -J, g.
[6] καὶ ὀνόματος -omitted by J[1], g.
[7] ἑαυτὸ -X.

[a] Cf. the sceptical argument that a statement or proposition cannot exist, because the expressions, which must be
its constituent parts, do not coexist but are at most successive
(Sextus, Adv. Math. i, 132-138 with Pyrrh. Hyp. ii, 109 and
Adv. Math. viii, 81-84, 132, and 136).
[b] i.e. demonstratives (cf. Apollonius Dyscolus, De Prono-
mine, pp. 9, 17-10, 7 and p. 10, 18-26 [Schneider] ; Scholia

PLATONIC QUESTIONS x, 1011

that they do not make anything one but that language is an enumeration like that of annual magistrates ⟨or⟩ of days listed one after another.[a]

5. Now, of the rest the pronoun is patently a kind of noun, not only as it shares the cases of the noun but also by reason of the fact that some pronouns,[b] being expressions of definite reference, make an indication fully decisive as soon as they are spoken ; and I do not know that a speaker uttering " Socrates " has by calling a name more clearly indicated a person than has one saying " this man." [c]

6. And as for what is called the participle, since it is a mixture of verb and noun,[d] it does not exist of itself,[e] to be sure, as the nouns of common feminine and masculine gender do not either [f] ; but it is ranked with those parts of speech, since through its tenses it borders on the verbs and through its cases on the nouns. Terms of this kind, moreover, are

in Dionysii Thracis Artem Grammaticam, pp. 77, 25–78, 6 with p. 86, 7-13 and p. 260, 21-24 [Hilgard]).

[c] *Cf.* Sextus, *Adv. Math.* viii, 96-97 (*S.V.F.* ii, frag. 205 [pp. 66, 38–67, 9]) : according to the Stoics Σωκράτης κάθηται is intermediate between the indefinite τὶς κάθηται and the definite οὗτος κάθηται.

[d] *Cf.* Dionysius Thrax, *Ars Grammatica* § 15 (p. 60, 2-4 [Uhlig]) ; *Scholia in Dionysii Thracis Artem Grammaticam*, pp. 255, 25–256, 7 (Hilgard) ; Ammonius, *De Interpretatione*, p. 15, 2-4.

[e] *Cf.* Priscian, *Inst. Grammatica* xi, 2 (i, p. 549, 3-6 [Hertz] : " ideo autem participium separatim non tradebant [*scil.* Stoici] partem orationis . . .") and ii, 16 (i, p. 54, 9-10 [Hertz]) ; *Scholia in Dionysii Thracis Artem Grammaticam*, p. 518, 17-22 (Hilgard).

[f] *Cf. Scholia in Dionysii Thracis Artem Grammaticam*, pp. 218, 18–219, 15 and especially pp. 525, 32–526, 11 (Hilgard) ; R. Schneider, *Apollonii Dyscoli Quae Supersunt* i, 2 (*Commentarium . . . in Apollonii Scripta Minora*), pp. 24-25.

(1011) ἀντανακλάστους,[1] οἷον ὁ φρονῶν ἀντὶ[2] τοῦ φρο-
νίμου καὶ ὁ σωφρονῶν[3] ἀντὶ[4] τοῦ σώφρονός ἐστιν,
ὡς ὀνομάτων καὶ προσηγοριῶν δύναμιν ἔχοντα.

7. Τάς γε μὴν προθέσεις ἔστιν ἐπικράνοις καὶ
βάσεσι καὶ ὑποθέμασιν, ὡς οὐ λόγους ἀλλὰ περὶ
τοὺς λόγους μᾶλλον οὔσας, ὁμοιοῦν. ὅρα δὲ[5] μὴ
κόμμασι καὶ θραύσμασιν ὀνομάτων ἐοίκασιν, ὥσπερ
γραμμάτων σπαράγμασι[6] καὶ κεραίαις οἵ[7] σπεύ-
δοντες γράφουσι· τὸ γὰρ "ἐμβῆναι" καὶ "ἐκ-
βῆναι" συγκοπὴ προφανής[8] ἐστι τοῦ "ἐντὸς
E βῆναι" καὶ τοῦ "ἐκτὸς βῆναι," καὶ τὸ "προ-
γενέσθαι" τοῦ "πρότερον γενέσθαι," καὶ τὸ
"καθίζειν" τοῦ "κάτω ἴζειν"[9] ὥσπερ ἀμέλει
τὸ "λίθους βάλλειν" καὶ "τοίχους ὀρύσσειν"

---

[1] R. T. Schmidt (*Stoicorum Grammatica* [Halle, 1839],
p. 46, n. 66); ἀνακλάστους -MSS.
[2] ἀντὶ -G. F. Shoemann (*Die Lehre von den Redetheilen*
[Berlin, 1862], p. 39, n. 1); ἀπό -MSS.
[3] σώφρων -J, g.
[4] ἀντὶ -G. F. Shoemann (*loc. cit.*); ἀπό -MSS.
[5] ὅρα δὴ -J[1], g ; ὅσα δὲ -e.
[6] σπαράγματα -J[1].   [7] οἷον -J[1], g.
[8] περιφανῶς -J[1], g ; προφανῶς -β[2], n, Voss. 16, Bonon.,
Escorial T-11-5.

[9] καταίζειν -X ; καταΐζειν -all other MSS.

---

[a] *Cf.* Priscian, *Inst. Grammatica* xi, 1 (i, pp. 548, 14–549,
1 [Hertz]) : " sic igitur supra dicti philosophi [*scil.* Stoici]
etiam participium aiebant appellationem esse reciprocam, id
est ἀντανάκλαστον προσηγορίαν, hoc modo : legens est lector
et lector legens, cursor est currens et currens cursor, amator
est amans et amans amator, vel nomen verbale vel modum
verbi casualem."
[b] The correction, καὶ προσηγοριῶν, is required because the
Stoics had restricted ὄνομα to proper nouns and had made a
separate part of speech called προσηγορία to cover common
nouns and noun adjectives (Diogenes Laertius, vii, 57-58

called reciprocals by the dialecticians [a] on the ground
that they have the force of nouns, that is of appel-
latives,[b] as for example the reflecting instead of re-
flective and the abstaining instead of abstinent man.[c]

7. The prepositions, for their part, can be likened
to capitals and pedestals and bases as being not
speech but rather appurtenances of speech. Consider
too that they resemble bits and pieces of words [d]
like the fragmentary letters and dashes used by
those who write in haste. For " incoming " and
" outgoing " are plainly contractions of " coming
within " and " going without," " foregoing " of
" going before," and " undersetting " of " setting
underneath," just as it is, of course, by quickening
and abridging the expression that for " pelting with

[S. V.F. ii, frag. 147 and iii, p. 213, 27-31]), which the grammarians, however, continued to call ὀνόματα or treated as a
sub-class of ὄνομα (Dionysius Thrax, *Ars Grammatica*, p. 23,
2-3 and pp. 33, 6–34, 2 [Uhlig] with *Scholia in Dionysii
Thracis Artem Grammaticam*, pp. 214, 17–215, 3 and p. 356,
7-23 and pp. 517, 33–518, 16 [Hilgard]).

[c] The Stoics, for whom the sage alone is φρόνιμος and
σώφρων and alone φρονεῖ and σωφρονεῖ, could hold that ὁ
φρονῶν must always be ὁ φρόνιμος and ὁ σωφρονῶν ὁ σώφρων and
even that ὁ φρόνιμος is always ὁ φρονῶν, since the sage's
exercise of virtue is continual and unremitting (*S. V.F.* i,
frags. 216 [p. 52, 25-33] and 569 ; iii, p. 149, 16-18). Nevertheless, they did distinguish between ὁ φρόνιμος and ὁ φρονῶν
(*S. V.F.* iii, p. 64, 3-5 ; *cf.* iii, frag. 244) ; and the same
distinction between the appellative and the participle is
implied by Chrysippus in *S.V.F.* iii, frag. 243 (*De Stoic.
Repug.* 1046 F—1047 A *infra*).

[d] ὀνομάτων here must have been meant in this general
sense, since Plutarch proceeds to represent the prepositions in
composition as fragments of adverbs and not of what he calls
nouns. Varro also appears to have taken the prepositions,
which he called " praeverbia," to be adverbs (frag. 267, 4-7
[Funaioli, *Grammaticae Romanae Fragmenta* i, p. 286]).

(1011) " λιθοβολεῖν " καὶ " τοιχωρυχεῖν "¹ ἐπιταχύνοντες
καὶ σφίγγοντες τὴν φράσιν λέγουσι.

8. Διὸ χρείαν μέν τινα τῷ λόγῳ παρέχεται
τούτων ἕκαστον, μέρος δὲ λόγου καὶ στοιχεῖον
οὐδέν ἐστι, πλὴν ὥσπερ εἴρηται τὸ ῥῆμα καὶ
τοὔνομα, ποιοῦντα τὴν πρώτην τό τ' ἀληθὲς καὶ
τὸ ψεῦδος δεχομένην σύνθεσιν, ἣν οἱ μὲν πρότασιν
οἱ δ' ἀξίωμα Πλάτων δὲ λόγον προσηγόρευκεν.

¹ τυχωρυχεῖν -X ; τοιχορυχεῖν -ε.

ᵃ Cf. Ammonius, De Interpretatione, p. 12, 27-30 and for
the στοιχεῖον added by Plutarch in explanation of μέρος ibid.,
p. 64, 26-27 and S.V.F. ii, frag. 148 (p. 45, 9-11) with
Scholia in Dionysii Thracis Artem Grammaticam, p. 356,
1-4 and pp. 514, 35–515, 12 (Hilgard).

ᵇ See 1009 c supra. Of the six " parts of speech " besides
noun and verb which had there been listed as present in

stones " and " breaking into houses " men say
" stoning " and " housebreaking."

8. Consequently, while each of these renders some
service to speech, none is a part of speech, that is a
constituent element of it,[a] except, as has been said,[b]
the verb and the noun, for these produce the first
combination admitting of truth and falsity, that
combination which has been styled pronouncement
by some and proposition by others but by Plato
speech.

Iliad i, 185 Plutarch has accounted for all except the adverb
(ἐπίρρημα). With his neglect of this *cf.* what is said of the
Stoics, τὰ ἐπιρρήματα οὔτε λόγου οὔτε ἀριθμοῦ ἠξίωσαν, παρα-
φυάδι καὶ ἐπιφυλλίδι αὐτὰ παρεικάσαντες (*Scholia in Dionysii
Thracis Artem Grammaticam*, p. 356, 15-16 and p. 520, 16-18
[Hilgard]), for whose treatment of the adverb *cf.* M. Pohlenz,
Kleine Schriften i (Hildesheim, 1965), p. 55.

ON THE GENERATION OF
THE SOUL IN THE
TIMAEUS
(DE ANIMAE PROCREATIONE
IN TIMAEO)

INTRODUCTION

THIS essay, Plutarch says at the very beginning, was written because the two sons to whom he addresses it thought that he ought to bring together in a separate treatise what he had frequently said and had here and there written of the way he understood Plato's doctrine of the soul, since this interpretation of his was not easy to manage otherwise and was in need of vindication.

The two sons addressed, who were themselves not the oldest of Plutarch's children (*cf. Consolatio ad Uxorem* 608 c and 609 D), could not have been much less than twenty years old when they made this suggestion, for it is assumed that they are familiar both with their father's earlier writings and also with most of the extensive literature about the disputed passage of the *Timaeus* (*cf.* 1012 D and 1027 A [chap. 29 *init.*] *infra*). Plutarch, therefore, could not have been much less than forty-five years old and probably was a good deal older when he wrote the essay. In it he refers (1013 E *infra*) to an earlier treatise of his on the cosmogony as Plato meant it; and what in *Plat. Quaest.* IV is together with II the essence of the interpretation developed in the present essay he there had already called τὸ πολλάκις ὑφ' ἡμῶν λεγόμε-νον (1003 A). Aspects of it or parallels to certain aspects of it appear in the *Quaest. Conviv.*, the *De E*, and the

De Iside ; but there is no conclusive evidence to prove that any of these is earlier or later than the present essay.[a]

The essay is in form a commentary on *Timaeus* 35 A 1—36 B 5 and falls into two parts, each of which is begun by way of preface with the quotation of that section of the Platonic passage with which it deals, the first (chaps. 1-28 [1012 B—1027 A]) with the quotation of *Timaeus* 35 A 1–B 4 and the second (chaps. 29-33 [1027 A—1030 c])[b] with that of *Timaeus* 35 B 4—36 B 5.

This second part is expressly divided into three sections, in each of which one specific question is discussed and answered (1027 c-D) : first, what the whole numbers are that Plato adopts in the double and triple intervals and that will permit the insertion of the means described by him (1027 D-F and 1017 c—1022 c [chaps. 30 and 11-19]) ; second, whether these numbers are to be arranged in a single row or in the figure of a lambda (1022 c-E and 1027 F— 1028 A [chaps. 20 and 30 b]) ; and, third, what is their function or for what effect are they employed in the composition of the soul (1028 A—1030 c

[a] In 1029 D here Plutarch asserts what in *Quaest. Conviv.* 745 c-F he denies in his own person but then has Ammonius assert. It would be equally easy to make out a specious but inconclusive case for the priority of either passage to the other.

[b] The traditional numbers of the chapters and the pagination of Stephanus are retained, though they are confusing because they antedate the discovery and correction of the displacement in the MSS. The order in the text as rearranged is : chaps. 1-10 (1012 A—1017 c), chaps. 21-30 (1022 E— 1027 F), chaps. 11-20 (1017 c—1022 E), chaps. 30 b-33 (1027 F—1030 c).

[chaps. 31-33]). All this by Plutarch's own admission (1027 A [chap. 29 *init.*] and 1022 C [chap. 20 *init.*]) contains little that is original; and it is of interest chiefly for the information that it provides about earlier treatments of *Timaeus* 35 B 4—36 B 5 and about the arithmological, musicological, and astronomical speculations related to them. With regard to the third question Plutarch rejects all the astronomical interpretations that he reports in chaps. 31-32 and says that the ratios and numbers in this passage of the *Timaeus* are meant to signify the harmony and concord of the soul itself (chap. 33 [1029 D-E and 1030 B-C]). As to the second question, which receives the briefest treatment, he accepts Crantor's arrangement because he thinks it almost explicitly prescribed by the order of the numbers in Plato's text. The treatment of the first question is the longest, and in the course of it Plutarch reveals some of his characteristic weaknesses. He is aware of the correct contention that Plato is concerned not with any particular integers but with the ratios that alone are specified; and yet he rejects it, "even if it be true," not only because it makes the matter harder to understand but also because it would prevent him from indulging himself in the arithmological speculations about the " remarkable numbers " to which he devotes several chapters (1027 D-F and 1017 C—1019 B [chaps. 30 and 11-14]). Then as the base for the intervals into which the means are inserted he chooses 192 instead of 384 because " the ' leimma ' will have its ratio expressed in the numbers that Plato has given, 256 to 243, if 192 is made the first number," thus arguing with misplaced literalness as if it were the very numbers and not just the ratio

that Plato intended and at the same time showing
that he could not have worked out the problem,
since 192 will not serve the purpose of clearing the
fractions after the first fourth (1020 c-d [chap. 16 *sub
finem*] and 1022 A [chap. 18 *sub finem*]).

The originality of the first part of the essay is
emphasized by Plutarch himself. At the very beginning he says that the interpretation here advocated
requires vindication because it is opposed to that of
most Platonists (1012 B), and after criticizing the
interpretations of *Timaeus* 35 A 1–B 4 by Xenocrates
and Crantor he repeats in beginning his own that he
must vindicate what is unusual and paradoxical about
it (1014 A). In the first place, he insists that contrary
to what the Platonists contend Plato must have
meant the generation of the universe and its soul to
be understood literally as a beginning, for otherwise
soul could not be senior to body and so there would
be nothing to Plato's argument against the atheists
in the *Laws* (chap. 4, *cf.* chap. 3 *init.*). Plutarch
holds, therefore, that according to Plato god did
literally bring into being the soul and the body of
the universe, though not from nothing, which is
impossible, but from precosmic principles that had
always existed, an amorphous and chaotic corporeality and a self-moved and irrational motivity that
kept the former in disorderly turmoil (chap. 5). This
irrational psychic principle Plutarch identifies with
the " infinitude " of the *Philebus*, the " congenital
desire " and " inbred character " of the *Politicus*, the
" necessity " and even (1024 c) the precosmic
γένεσις of *Timaeus* 52 D and says is openly called in
the *Laws* " disorderly and maleficent soul " (1014 D—
1015 A [chap. 6]). It is, moreover, this, he maintains,

that is the principle of evil whereby Plato avoided the absurdity into which the Stoics later fell, for the evil in the universe must have a cause and this cause cannot be god, who is entirely good, or matter, which is inert and without quality, but must be soul, which is the cause and principle of motion (1015 A-E [chaps. 6-7]) ; and this irrational soul, " soul in itself," it is that in the *Phaedrus* is proved to be indestructible because not subject to generation and not subject to generation because self-moved, the precosmic principle from which god by introducing into it intelligence and reason created the soul of the universe (chaps. 8-9), as he created its body out of precosmic matter by removing from this the cause of its turbulence and introducing into it form and symmetry (*cf.* 1015 E and 1016 D—1017 A).

The " creation " in the *Timaeus* had already been taken literally by Aristotle and others but so far as is known not by anyone regarded as a Platonist,[a] and no one at all is known to have anticipated Plutarch in interpreting it with a theory of the cosmic soul such as his.[b] This theory of his, despite all narrow literalism [c] and despite his protest against interpret-

[a] See note a on 1013 E (chap. 4 *init.*) *infra.*

[b] Plutarch's claim to the originality of his interpretation was accepted by Thévenaz (*L'Âme du Monde*, pp. 55-56), and Helmer argued that there is no reason to doubt it (*De An. Proc.*, pp. 69-70), though Plutarch's " general lack of originality " made R. M. Jones doubt that he could have been the author of the theory (*Platonism of Plutarch*, p. 80).

[c] Such as the assumption that ἰδέα in the Posidonian interpretation must mean " idea " (see 1023 B-C [chap. 22] with note c on 1023 B) and the crucial assumption that πρεσβυτέρα used of soul must mean senior in the sense of earlier in origin (see 1013 E-F [chap. 4] and 1016 A-B [chap. 8]), concerning which *cf.* Cherniss, *Aristotle's Criticism of*

ing Plato for the promotion of one's own doctrines (1013 B), was not the consequence of his literal interpretation of the *Timaeus* but was the formulation of his own theology and theodicy, which, to be plausibly represented as in his words " something that agrees with Plato," required the " creation " in the *Timaeus* to be taken literally. This is indicated by the very reasons that he here gives for adopting this interpretation (1013 E-F and 1015 A-E) [a] and even more clearly by his way of manipulating Platonic texts to support it. Not only is there nothing in those texts to justify him in identifying with soul, as he does here, the " infinitude " of the *Philebus* or the " necessity " or γένεσις of the *Timaeus*, but these identifications are incompatible even with what he says in other passages himself.[b] When he identifies

---

Plato . . ., pp. 424-426 and note 365 on pp. 429-431 and E. de Strycker in *Aristotle and Plato in the Mid-Fourth Century*, ed. I. Düring and G. E. L. Owen (Göteborg, 1960), pp. 90-91. F. Romano is mistaken, however, in supposing that Plutarch's interpretation was simply the consequence of his " cieco e pedissequo ossequio al verbo di Platone," which made him incapable of distinguishing *logos* from *mythos* (*Sophia*, xxxiii [1965], p. 119 *sub finem*).

[a] *Cf.* Zeller, *Phil. Griech.* III, 2, p. 191 ; Andresen, *Logos und Nomos*, pp. 281, 284, and 290 ; H. Dörrie, *Philomathes : Studies . . . in Memory of Philip Merlan* (The Hague, 1971), p. 46 ; and especially Babut, *Plutarque et le Stoïcisme*, p. 287, who considers this essay to be primarily a polemic against Stoic monism and a continuation of Plutarch's anti-Stoic works (*op. cit.*, pp. 139-142).

[b] For the ἀπειρία of the *Philebus* see page 185, note *d* (chap. 6) ; for the γένεσις of *Timaeus* 52 D see notes *c* and *d* on 1024 c (chap. 24) and the comparison with *De Facie* 926 F in note *a* on 1016 F (chap. 9) ; and for the ἀνάγκη of the *Timaeus* see note *c* on 1014 E (chap. 6) with Cherniss, *Aristotle's Criticism of Plato . . .*, pp. 446-450. As to the

with irrational soul the "congenital desire" and
"inbred character" in the myth of the *Politicus*,
adapting for this a quotation of *Politicus* 273 B 4-6,
he suppresses Plato's phrase, τὸ σωματοειδὲς τῆς
συγκράσεως, which would have embarrassed his interpretation[a]; when he insists that in the proof of
Phaedrus 245 c 5—246 A 2 the soul that is not subject
to generation is meant to be only "the soul that
before the generation of the universe keeps all things
in disorderly motion" (1016 A, 1016 c, 1017 A-B
[chaps. 8-9]), he ignores both the words ψυχὴ πᾶσα
with which that proof begins (*Phaedrus* 245 c 5) and
of which the conclusion is certainly meant to hold
and the express statement that it is impossible for
the self-moving mover that sustains the universe, *i.e.*
the cosmic soul, either to perish or to come to be

last, were ἀνάγκη, as Plutarch here maintains, the precosmic
irrational soul from which by mixture with νοῦς the soul of
the cosmos was created, his interpretation would be open
to the objection that he opposes to Crantor's (1013 B-C,
1023 A), for what he calls the psychogony would not be dis-
tinguishable from the cosmogony, since Plato says μεμειγμένη
γὰρ οὖν ἡ τοῦδε τοῦ κόσμου γένεσις ἐξ ἀνάγκης τε καὶ νοῦ συστά-
σεως ἐγεννήθη (*Timaeus* 47 E 5—48 A 2).

[a] See note *f* on 1015 A (chap. 6). In this passage he also
substitutes ἀνάγκη for the εἱμαρμένη of the *Politicus* (see
note *e* on 1015 A); *cf.* his substitution of σφαῖρα for Plato's
φορά or κύκλος (see note *f* on 1029 c [chap. 32]) and his
insertion of ὕλη into quasi-quotations of the *Timaeus* (see the
end of note *c*, page 173 [chap. 3]). Sometimes by omitting
words or curtailing the original he alters the meaning of a
passage (see note *c* on *Plat. Quaest.* 1004 E *supra*), thereby
eliminating what would otherwise impugn his interpretation
(see note *d* on 1016 F [chap. 9] and notes *f*, *b*, and *c* on 1023
E-F [chap. 23]); and sometimes he inserts into an apparent
quotation what is in fact an erroneous inference of his own
(see note *b* on *Plat. Quaest.* 1002 F *supra*).

(*Phaedrus* 245 D 7–E 2) ; and, when he asserts that
by all these Plato meant what in the *Laws* he called
disorderly and maleficent soul and that this is " soul
in itself," which became the soul of the universe
(1014 D-E [chap. 6] and 1015 E [chap. 7]), he disregards
the fact that the evil kind or aspect of soul there
posited is never said to be precosmic or antecedent
to beneficent soul or that out of which a single
cosmic soul was created but to the contrary is represented as being coeval with the good souls, the
movers of the celestial bodies and the universe, and
distinct from them.[a]

All this is far from literal interpretation of Plato's
words ; and so is the identification of the " divisible
being " in the psychogony of the *Timaeus* with the
irrational and maleficent soul elicited from the *Laws*
(1014 D-E [chap. 6] and 1015 E [chap. 7]). Neither in
the psychogony nor elsewhere in the *Timaeus* is
there any mention of such an irrational soul or of
any irrational element in the cosmic soul[b] ; and

---

[a] *Cf. Laws* 896 D 10–E 6, 898 C 6—899 B 9, 904 A 6–C 4
and E 5-7, 906 A 2-7 ; see Cherniss, *Proceedings of the
American Philosophical Society*, xcviii (1954), p. 26, n. 29.
In *De Iside* 370 F Plutarch himself implies that what he takes
to be the maleficent soul of the *Laws* is not antecedent to
the beneficent soul but that the two are coeval and distinct,
for he says that according to Plato there (*i.e. Laws* 896 D 10–
E 6) *the universe is moved* by at least two souls, one beneficent
and the other adverse to this.

[b] *Cf.* Cherniss, *Aristotle's Criticism of Plato . . .*, p. 446
with notes 386 and 387 and *Proceedings of the American
Philosophical Society*, xcviii (1954), p. 26 with notes 26-28.
The soul that in *Timaeus* 44 A 7–B 1 is said to become ἄνους
is only the human soul when disturbed in consequence of its
embodiment (*cf.* 86 B 2—87 A 7) ; even in that soul there
is no irrationality in the " immortal part " produced by the

140

GENERATION OF THE SOUL

Plutarch's assertion that this is what Plato meant by
οὐσίας ... τῆς αὖ περὶ τὰ σώματα γιγνομένης μεριστῆς
(*Timaeus* 35 A 2-3) is made without any supporting
argument [a] and apparently in reliance upon the mere
assumption that in the *Laws* the proper name is used
for that to which Plato elsewhere must have been
referring covertly in enigmatic and metaphorical
terms,[b] a principle so pliable that in the very passage
where it is enunciated this maleficent soul of the
Laws is identified not, as it is in this essay, with the
" divisible being " but with the " difference," the
θάτερον, of the psychogony.[c]

Identifying the " divisible being " of the psychogony with precosmic irrational soul from which god
by introducing into it intelligence and reason created
the soul of the universe ought to imply moreover
that the " indivisible being " there is νοῦς ; and Plutarch does explicitly make this identification also,[d]

---

demiurge, the circles of sameness and difference, when not so
disturbed (44 B 1-7), while the " mortal and passible part "
of it (*i.e.* the θυμοειδές and ἐπιθυμία), which Plutarch derives
from the " divisible being," is in the *Timaeus* a confection
of the " created gods " and is unrelated to the ingredients
or the result of the psychogony (see note *c* on 1026 D [chap.
27 *sub finem*]).

[a] The later attempts to account for the term μεριστή (1024 A
[chap. 23] and 1024 C [chap. 24]) are not arguments in support of this identification and would not be cogent if they
were intended to be so.

[b] *Cf.* 1014 D (. . . ἐν δὲ τοῖς Νόμοις ἄντικρυς . . . εἴρηκε
. . .) with *De Iside* 370 E-F (πολλαχοῦ μὲν οἷον . . . παρα-
καλυπτόμενος . . . ἐν δὲ τοῖς Νόμοις . . . οὐ δι' αἰνιγμῶν οὐδὲ
συμβολικῶς ἀλλὰ κυρίοις ὀνόμασιν . . .).

[c] *De Iside* 370 E-F; see page 251, note *c* on 1025 F *infra*.

[d] See *infra* 1014 D-E (ἐν δὲ Τιμαίῳ τὴν τῇ ἀμερίστῳ συγκεραννυμένην . . . αὕτη . . . νοῦ . . . μετέσχεν, ἵνα κόσμου ψυχὴ

141

PLUTARCH'S MORALIA

although in the *Timaeus* not only is there no mention of precosmic νοῦς as an ingredient in the constitution of soul but in a passage from which Plutarch conveniently omits νοῦς [a] the latter is said to arise in the soul after its constitution and organization and as a result of its contact with the ideas. Plutarch's one attempt to justify his identification is an explication of the sense in which the terms ἀμερὲς καὶ ἀμέριστον are used ; but in this sense even according to him they characterize the incorporeal and intelligible as such, and so they are in fact more appropriately used of the being of the ideas and can be supposed to refer to νοῦς only because he takes νοῦς to be a νοητόν.[b] Since for him it is god, however, the νοητόν *par excellence* [c] and the only true being,[d] that is νοῦς,[e] although in arguing against the Posidonians he contends that god's relation to soul is that of artificer to finished product (1023 c *infra*), he nevertheless asserts that the νοῦς introduced by

---

γένηται), 1016 c with note c, 1024 A (page 229, note d), 1024 c-D (ὁ δὲ νοῦς . . . ἐγγενόμενος δὲ τῇ ψυχῇ . . . ἡ κοινωνία γέγονεν αὐτῶν, τῷ ἀμερίστῳ τὸ μεριστὸν . . .) with note c there for an additional misrepresentation of the Platonic text.

[a] *Timaeus* 37 c 1-3 ; see *infra* 1023 F with note c there.

[b] See *infra* page 214, note a and the references there to *Plat. Quaest.* 1002 c-D and 1002 E.

[c] See *infra* 1016 B with note d and the reference there to *Plat. Quaest.* 1002 B ; and cf. *De Iside* 372 A, where Osiris is the οὐσία νοητή of which the sun is the visible light.

[d] Cf. *De E* 392 A (. . . μόνην μόνῳ προσήκουσαν τὴν τοῦ εἶναι προσαγόρευσιν . . .) and 393 A-B.

[e] Cf. *De Iside* 371 A (in the soul of the universe Osiris is νοῦς καὶ λόγος), 373 B (Osiris is λόγος αὐτὸς καθ᾽ ἑαυτὸν ἀμιγὴς καὶ ἀπαθής), and 376 c (ὁ τοῦ θεοῦ νοῦς καὶ λόγος ἐν τῷ ἀοράτῳ καὶ ἀφανεῖ βεβηκὼς εἰς γένεσιν ὑπὸ κινήσεως προῆλθεν).

god into the irrational soul is itself a part of god [a];
and so he implicitly makes the " indivisible being "
of the *Timaeus* substantially identical with the
demiurge, which is itself to renounce the literal
interpretation of Plato's text. Moreover, in 1024
c-d (chap. 24), where of the three, ὄν and χώρα and
γένεσις, said in *Timaeus* 52 D 2-4 to have been
before heaven came to be, Plutarch identifies the
last with the irrational soul, the second with matter,
and the first with the intelligible, the real existence
that always remains fixed and of which semblances
are dispersed in this world, he introduces without
explanation or reference to the text that he has
quoted a νοῦς which was " abiding and immobile all
by itself " before it got into the soul ; and this νοῦς
he explicitly identifies with the " indivisible being "
of the psychogony. This must be the νοῦς that is
substantially identical with god,[b] added as a fourth
to the precosmic three of *Timaeus* 52 D 2-4, for it
cannot be identical with the ὄν, which Plutarch himself here clearly—and correctly (*cf. Timaeus* 52 A 1-4
and c 5–D 1 with 48 E 5-6)—treats as the being of
the ideas, the stable and real existence with which,
as he says, the circular motion of the soul made
rational is most closely in contact ; but this is to
make Plato omit from the three that he lists as precosmic the " indivisible being " which he clearly
treats as such in the psychogony and which must be the
ὄν among the three that he here lists, not a fourth
such as that gratuitously introduced by Plutarch.

[a] See *infra* 1016 c with note d and *Plat. Quaest.* 1001 c
referred to there.
[b] See 1016 c, *Plat. Quaest.* 1001 c, and the passages of the
De Iside, which are cited in the last two preceding notes.

That the " indivisible being " of the psychogony
is the being of the ideas and the " divisible being "
the dispersed being of phenomena, not νοῦς and the
irrational soul, as Plutarch insists, and not ingredients
of soul but external to soul, which after it has been
constituted judges them by coming into contact now
with the one and again with the other, this is clear
from another passage of the *Timaeus*, which is
partially paraphrased and partially quoted by
Plutarch himself but for his own purpose and in a
mutilated form that obscures its significance.[a] At
the beginning of this passage which he omits (*Timaeus* 37 A 2-4) it is emphasized that the ingredients of soul were three. This was twice said in the
passage of the psychogony (*Timaeus* 35 A 6-7 and B 1)
quoted by him at the beginning of his essay (1012
B-C *infra*), where it was explained that of these three
ingredients one is a " third kind of being " blended
by the demiurge between the " indivisible being "
and the " divisible being " and the other two are a
sameness and a difference also constructed between
the indivisible and the divisible sameness and
difference. This intermediacy of the ingredients
sameness and difference eluded Plutarch altogether,

---

[a] *Timaeus* 37 A 2-c 5, where in 37 A 5-B 3 the soul of the
universe is said now to touch something that has οὐσία
σκεδαστή, *i.e.* μεριστή (*cf.* Plotinus, *Enn.* IV, ii, 1, line 12
and Proclus, *In Platonis Timaeum* ii, p. 298, 24-25 [Diehl]),
which is one of τὰ γιγνόμενα, *i.e.* the perceptible of 37 B 6,
and now something that has οὐσία ἀμέριστος, which is one of
τὰ κατὰ ταὐτὰ ἔχοντα ἀεί, *i.e.* the rational of 37 c 1 (*cf.*
Proclus, *ibid.*, p. 300, 5-10 and 17-19 [Diehl] and Cherniss,
Aristotle's Criticism of Plato . . ., pp. 407-408) ; for Plutarch's paraphrase of 37 A 5-B 3 and quotation of 37 B 3-
c 5 see *infra* pages 225, note *f* and 227, notes *b* and *c*.

GENERATION OF THE SOUL

as it has eluded many modern interpreters ; and
that of the " third kind of being " he misinterpreted
by neglecting the statement that this is only one
ingredient of soul and by taking it to be the literal
mixture of " indivisible " and " divisible being " [a]
identified with νοῦς and the irrational soul, with the
result that in fact he made the soul of the universe a
mixture of these two ingredients alone [b] or again a

---

[a] The " blending " (συνεκεράσατο [*Timaeus* 35 a 3]) of
the " third kind of being " like the construction of the intermediate sameness and difference (κατὰ ταὐτὰ συνέστησεν
[35 a 5]) is a figurative expression for the construction of a
mean between two extremes (*cf.* Porphyry in Proclus, *In
Platonis Timaeum* ii, pp. 162, 31–163, 1 [Diehl] and Proclus,
ibid., ii, pp. 149, 14–150, 24 and p. 156, 16-24 [Diehl] ;
Themistius, *De Anima*, p. 11, 1-4 ; Simplicius, *De Anima*,
p. 259, 11-29 ; [Philoponus], *De Anima* iii [*i.e.* Stephanus],
p. 504, 8-12). The figure is used by Plutarch himself when
he says that means involve τὴν τῶν ἄκρων . . . πρὸς ἄλληλα διὰ
τοῦ λόγου σύγκρασιν (*Plat. Quaest.* 1009 a-b) ; and yet,
when he uses as a " likeness of the proportion " in the
psychogony the insertion of two means between extremes
in *Timaeus* 31 b 4—32 c 4, he makes of the mathematical
procedure in that passage a physical " fusion " and employs
in his résumé of it the words ἐκέρασεν and συνέμιξε, which
Plato there does not use in any form (see *infra* 1025 a-b
[chap. 25] with note *f* there).

[b] See 1014 e (chap. 6) : αὕτη γὰρ ἦν ψυχὴ καθ᾿ ἑαυτήν, νοῦ
δὲ . . . μετέσχεν, ἵνα κόσμου ψυχὴ γένηται and 1024 a (chap. 23) :
. . . κόσμου ψυχὴν συνίστησιν ἐξ ὑποκειμένων τῆς τε κρείττονος
οὐσίας καὶ ἀμερίστου καὶ τῆς χείρονος, ἣν περὶ τὰ σώματα μεριστὴν
κέκληκεν. . . . A striking modern parallel is provided by P.
Friedländer (*Plato* iii [Princeton University Press, 1969], p.
366), who without reference to Plutarch and despite his bibliography (pp. 543-544) in obvious ignorance of the correct
construction of *Timaeus* 35 a 1-b 4 says : " The ingredients
. . . are, first, the being that is indivisible . . . and second,
the being that is divisible. . . . That would be enough, but
in order to emphasize the difficulty of the mixture . . . he

145

blend of four ingredients when to account for the obvious presence of sameness and difference in the psychogony he took these to be two extremes with the " indivisible being " and the " divisible " as two intermediates between them.[a] Plato's emphatic warning that the ingredients of soul are three he simply disregarded.

Similar treatment of Plato's text and similar internal contradictions characterize Plutarch's literal interpretation of the generation of the physical universe. A single example will suffice. Timaeus begins his account of the creation by saying in a passage on which Plutarch lays much stress that god took over all that was visible [b] but later says that he constructed the world visible and tangible.[c] Instead of explaining how these two statements can both be

---

adds as a third component the mixture of the previous two— or, as it may be put differently (35 A 3-4), the mixture of ' the same ' and ' the different.' "

[a] See 1025 B (chap. 25, where the proportion of four terms in *Timaeus* 32 B 3-7 is expressly cited as parallel to this) and note *b* there with references. It is the " divisible being " itself that Plutarch elsewhere calls intermediate, transferring to it, which identified with irrational soul or " soul in itself " he makes an ingredient of " created soul," the intermediacy of the three ingredients in the psychogony (see 1015 B [chap. 6] with note *c*, 1024 B [chap. 23] with note *d*, and 1024 C [chap. 24] with note *d*), two of which, sameness and difference, his interpretation fits so ill that in trying to explain them he flagrantly contradicts himself (see 1024 D [chap. 24] with note *f*, 1025 A [chap. 24] with note *b*, and 1027 A [chap. 28] with note *a*).

[b] *Timaeus* 30 A 3-4 (πᾶν ὅσον ἦν ὁρατὸν παραλαβὼν . . .); see *infra* 1016 D with note *g*.

[c] *Timaeus* 32 B 7-8 (. . . συνεστήσατο οὐρανὸν ὁρατὸν καὶ ἁπτόν); cf. 36 E 5-6.

taken literally [a] Plutarch simply omits " visible and
tangible " from his quotation of the latter passage,[b]
for he maintains that god did not create the tangibility of the matter out of which he formed the
physical universe but that this was perceptible and
corporeal [c] ; and yet elsewhere he insists that
Platonic " matter " is entirely without quality and
becomes tangible and visible by participating in the
intelligible and simulating it.[d]

So Plutarch's interpretation upon closer inspection
proves to be far from " literal." His motive was not
strict fidelity to Plato's words but concern to enlist
Plato's authority for the proposition that the universe
was brought into being by god ; and, since he says
himself why he thought it necessary to insist upon
such a beginning of the universe, the course of his
reasoning can be plausibly explicated in the following
manner. Soul as such must have existed without
beginning, for, as Plato says himself, soul is self-
moving motion, which itself is not subject to generation or destruction. This soul cannot be the soul of
the universe, however, for, if it were, it would without
beginning have always been producing in body the
motions of the corporeal universe just as they are
now organized by the soul of the universe [e] ; and this

[a] For the bearing of the contradiction on the question
whether the creation was meant to be taken literally cf.
L. Tarán in *Essays in Ancient Greek Philosophy* edited by
J. P. Anton with G. L. Kustas (Albany, State Univ. of New
York Press, 1971), pp. 382-384 with notes 98-104.

[b] See *infra* 1016 F with note d.

[c] See *infra* pages 183, note d ; 185, note c ; 229, note i.

[d] See *infra* 1014 F with note e and 1013 c with note d.

[e] See *infra* 1030 c (chap. 33 *sub finem*), and *Plat. Quaest.*
1003 A-B.

corporeal universe, if it had been so organized always
and without beginning, would be coeval with soul, in
which case there would be neither cogent evidence
for the existence of god (see *infra* 1013 E-F) nor any
need of his existence.[a] Therefore the existence of
god requires that the soul of the universe have had
a beginning antecedent to that of the corporeal universe organized by it. This beginning, however,
could not have been a coming to be from what was
not soul, since as soul it is without beginning, and so
could have been only a change in preexisting soul
such as would account for the regular motions of an
ordered corporeal universe, *i.e.* a change in self-
motion from the disorderly or demented to the
orderly and rational, which must have been caused
by the introduction of νοῦς into the soul already
existing. Therefore Plato, despite what he seems to
say in the *Timaeus*, must have meant not that the
demiurge created the substance of soul but that he
compounded the soul of the universe by blending
νοῦς with irrational soul, the vestigial irrationality of
which is the cause of the evil in the universe as the
rationality imposed upon it by god is the cause of
the good[b]; and consequently the essential ingredients in the psychogony must be these two, both

---

[a] According to Atticus, who adopted Plutarch's interpretation (see note *a* on 1013 E *infra*), Plato, reasoning that what
has not come to be needs no creator or guardian for its well-
being, ἵνα μὴ ἀποστερήσῃ τὸν κόσμον τῆς προνοίας ἀφεῖλε τὸ
ἀγένητον αὐτοῦ (Atticus, frag. iv [Baudry]=Eusebius, *Praep.
Evang.* xv, 6, 2 [ii, p. 359, 14-18, Mras]); and Plutarch is said
to have called the divine cause πρόνοια (Proclus, *In Platonis
Timaeum* i, p. 415, 18-20 [Diehl]; see *Plat. Quaest.* 1007 c
with note *h* there).

[b] See *infra* 1026 D-E (chap. 27) and 1027 A (chap. 28).

148

preexisting and without beginning, νοῦς and the self-motion that is soul in itself.

This interpretation has won for Plutarch the praise of some modern scholars for acuteness and ingenuity and even for " fathoming the thought of Plato better than did Plato's immediate disciples." [a] In fact, it is instructive chiefly because it shows how Plutarch could manipulate for his own purpose philosophical texts still available for comparison with his treatment of them and what arbitrariness and contradictions are involved in an attempt to prove Platonic the dogma of " creation " as an historical beginning.

A Latin translation of the essay made by Turnebus was published in 1552.[b] The first edition of the Greek text restored to its original order was published in 1848 by A. D. Maurommates [c] ; and in 1873 B. Müller, who in 1870 had independently

---

[a] So Thévenaz, L'Âme du Monde, p. 95. Helmer (De An. Proc., p. 66) says that Plutarch's " Scharfsinn " can seldom be refused recognition. R. Del Re tries to defend Plutarch's interpretation even in the crucial and embarrassing matter of the " divisible being " (Studi Italiani di Filologia Classica, N.S. xxiv [1949], pp. 51-64 [n.b. pp. 56-57]) ; and J. B. Skemp, while taking the " ' analytic ' view of the Timaeus . . . as at any rate the more probable," nevertheless treats Plutarch's interpretation very seriously (The Theory of Motion in Plato's Later Dialogues, Enlarged Edition [Amsterdam, 1967], pp. x, xiv, 26-27, 59, 76, 111-112, and 149).

[b] Plutarchi Chaeronei De Procreatione Animi in Timaeo Platonis Adriano Turnebo interprete. Parisiis, Ex officina Adriani Turnebi Typographi Regis. M.D. LII.

[c] Πλουτάρχου περὶ τῆς ἐν Τιμαίῳ ψυχογονίας, ἐκδόντος καὶ εἰς τὴν ἀρχαίαν συνέχειαν ἀποκαταστήσαντος Ἀνδρέου Δ. Μαυρομμάτου Κορκυραίου, Ἐν Ἀθήναις, 1848. The text, based chiefly on that of Dübner, is preceded by an essay on the restoration of the proper order and followed by ten pages of notes.

discovered this order, published another edition of
it.[a] There are two monographs devoted entirely to
the essay. One of them by Joseph Helmer is entitled
*Zu Plutarchs " De animae procreatione in Timaeo " :
Ein Beitrag zum Verständnis des Platon-Deuters
Plutarch* (Würzburg, 1937 [Diss. München]). The
other by Pierre Thévenaz, *L'Âme du Monde, le
Devenir et la Matière chez Plutarque* (Paris, 1938), is a
systematic study preceded by an annotated translation into French of the first part of the essay, *i.e.*
chaps. 1-10 (1012 B—1017 c) and 21-28 (1022 E—
1027 A). There are two earlier monographs of wider
range in which the study of this essay is an important
part, *Plutarchi Chaeronensis studia in Platone explicando posita* by Herbert Holtorf (Stralesundiae,
1913 [Diss. Greifswald]) and *The Platonism of
Plutarch* by Roger M. Jones (Menasha, 1916 [Diss.
Chicago]). Unfortunately none of these four authors
was aware of the correct construction of *Timaeus*
35 A 1-B 1, first pointed out in modern times apparently by G. M. A. Grube (*Class. Phil.*, xxvii
[1932], pp. 80-82), the crucial passage with which
Plutarch begins his exposition.

The *De Animae Procreatione in Timaeo* is No. 65 in
the Catalogue of Lamprias and No. 77 in the Planudean order. The text of it here printed is based
upon E B e u f m r [b] Escor. 72, all of which have been

---

[a] Plutarch über die Seelenschöpfung im Timaeus, von
Berthold Müller, Breslau, 1873 (Gymnasium zu St. Elisabet.
Bericht über das Schuljahr 1872–1873). The text is based
chiefly on E, and the *apparatus* reports mainly the readings
of that MS., the *Epitome*, and the Aldine.

[b] r is Leiden B.P.G. 59 and not Voss. 59 as it is called in
Hubert-Drexler, *Moralia* vi/1, pp. XVI and XX; *cf. Bibliotheca Universitatis Leidensis* : Codices Manuscripti—VIII :

collated from photostats.[a] In all these MSS. there is the same displacement of chapters 21-30 (1022 E— 1027 F) from their proper place immediately after chapter 10, a displacement discovered first by A. D. Maurommates (Πλουτάρχου περὶ τῆς ἐν Τιμαίῳ ψυχογονίας . . . [Athens, 1848], pp. ιβ´-ιε´) and later independently by B. Müller (Hermes, iv [1870], pp. 390-403[b] ; cf. v [1871], p. 154) and again still later by P. Tannery (Rev. Études Grecques, vii [1894], pp. 209-211). All these MSS., therefore, derive from one ancestor, but their differences at the junctures resulting from the displacement show that they were not all copied from a single archetype and suggest the division of them into groups that is confirmed by their variations throughout the essay. At these junctures E and B are alike ; e and u are alike and

---

Codices Bibliothecae Publicae Graeci descripsit K. A. de Meyier adiuvante E. Hulshoff Pol (Lugduni Batavorum, 1965), p. 82. For confirmation of this fact as well as for the correct photostats I am obliged to the generosity of Dr. de Meyier.

[a] I report the readings of Escor. 72 because they seem to have remained unknown hitherto. From Oxoniensis Coll. Corp. Christi 99 (C.C.C. 99) I report only one correct reading, for my collation of this MS. has confirmed the statement (Hubert-Drexler, Moralia vi/1, p. xvi) that it is close to f, m, r and especially close to r, with which in fact it agrees against all others seventy-six times, though it cannot be their source, since it disagrees with all of them at least eighteen times, in five of which it lacks words that they preserve. For Marciani 184, 187, and 523, which I have not collated, cf. B. Müller (1873), pp. 3-4 and Hubert-Drexler, op. cit., pp. xv-xvi.

[b] Here (p. 403, n. 1) Müller reports that the correct order had already been indicated in a marginal note made by Deodat Gröhe ; but, since Gröhe published his doctoral dissertation in 1867, his note could scarcely have been made before Maurommates' publication.

different from E, B ; f, m, r are substantially alike
and different from both E, B and e, u ; and Escor. 72
agrees in part with e, u and in part with f, m, r (see
the critical *apparatus* on 1022 E following 1017 C,
chapter 21 *init.*). The text of the Aldine at one
juncture is closest to that of e, u and at the other
two agrees with that of m, r.

B agrees with E (or with E corrected) against all
the other MSS. more than eighty times, indicating
lacunae where all the others show none but instead
have words or letters missing from E and B (*cf.*
1015 C [τοῦ . . . θέντος], 1015 D [ὡς . . . τὴν], 1024 E
[τῶν . . . ἐπικρατεῖ]), omitting words that all the
others preserve (*cf.* 1014 A [περὶ τούτων], 1025 B
[ἀλλά], 1018 B [ὧν]), and preserving words omitted
by all the others (*cf.* 1027 C [καὶ τριπλασίοις], 1018 A
[καὶ ποιοῦσαι . . .]). B alone or in agreement with
others differs from E in forty-nine places ; but the
negligence of the scribe of B might be held to
account for many of these differences [a] and his own
acumen for others,[b] although he must have been
more than acute to have added the καὶ that E and
all the others omit in διὰ τὸ καὶ τὰς ἀρχάς. . . (1025 E).[c]

[a] It is difficult to believe that negligence alone can explain
εὐρύθμως for the εὐσήμως of E (1019 A) or συνήθειαν (unrecorded in Hubert-Drexler, *Moralia* vi/1, p. 179) for the per-
fectly clear συνήχησιν of E (1021 B).

[b] *e.g.* for τῇ ὕλῃ καὶ ὑπ' ἐκείνης (1016 D), where E alone
omits καὶ (unrecorded in Hubert-Drexler, *ibid.*, p. 153), and
for Ἄρεος (1029 B), where E with all others except f, m, r
has ἀέρος.

[c] One of the eight cases of difference added by D. A.
Russell (*Class. Rev.*, N.S. v [1955], p. 161) to the " crucial
instance " (p. 170, 9 f. [Hubert-Drexler] = 1018 B : ἐν ὅσαις
ἡμέραις [μοίραις]) adduced in Hubert-Drexler, *ibid.*, p. xvi as
proof that B is independent of E. Of Russell's seven remain-

This and the ἦν δὴ ὁ θεὸς αὐτὸς of B in 1017 A-B, where E has τὴν δὲ αὐτὸς ὁ θεὸς,[a] look like genuine variants rather than mere " slips " or arbitrary emendations ; and so does the καὶ that B alone has between τῷ ἐπογδόῳ and τῷ ἐπιτρίτῳ in 1022 c (chapter 19 *sub finem*), for something is certainly missing here and the erroneous καὶ may be a misreading by B of some sign to that effect in his original. There are indications, then, that this essay in B was not copied directly from E, though it must be admitted that none of them is tantamount to definitive proof.

While e and u are frequently in agreement with f, m, r against E and B [b] and more frequently in agreement with E, B against f, m, r,[c] it is still more

---

ing cases two (171. 3 and 176. 20, *i.e.* [ἀφ'/ἐφ' in 1018 B and ἀντί/ὄντι in 1020 A) are merely errors in the critical *apparatus* of Hubert-Drexler, four others (150. 13, 159. 12, 163. 10, 187. 21 [Hubert-Drexler]) are cases in which the text of B might be accounted for by the corrections in E, and the seventh (156. 8 [Hubert-Drexler] = 1022 E : θήγουσα for θιγοῦσα) is an error shared by B with u[1], a fact not recorded by Hubert-Drexler, as four other cases of the agreement of u with B in error against all the others have also gone unrecorded, though to many these might seem to be more significant than the " crucial instance " of 1018 B where B neglects two letter-spaces left vacant in E between ὅσαις and μοίραις.

[a] ἦν δὲ αὐτὸς ὁ θεὸς is the reading of e[1]. Neither this nor the reading of B is recorded in Hubert-Drexler (*ibid.*, p. 154, 26).

[b] Besides such cases as 1025 B and 1027 c already mentioned for the agreement of E and B against all the others see especially 1018 B (καὶ τὰ ιβ') and 1028 A (μονονουχὶ οὖν).

[c] There are more than a score of cases, among which see τρίτα for ἐπίτριτα and the omission of πρὸς τὰ γ' καὶ μ' καὶ σ' in 1021 E.

common for e and u or for e and u with Escor. 72 to be in agreement against all the others.[a] Nevertheless, e and u are clearly independent of each other, for they differ from each other in more than sixty places, in forty of which u is alone in error but in at least one of which it agrees with f, m, r in correctly preserving a word that is not in e or in the others (1017 F [καὶ τοῦ ιβ′]), while in several places e preserves words that are lacking in u, most notably a passage of 21 words that the latter omits (1019 F [ἐν δὲ τοῖς τριπλασίοις ... οὕτω γίγνεται μέσος]).

While in agreement with e and u against E and B at least a dozen times and in five of these with words that are not in E or B at all,[b] f, m, and r are clearly independent of e and u, since in about a dozen passages all three of them agree in having words that are absent from both e and u[c]; but f, m, and r, although they agree against all the others in more than sixty places and in more than a score of these alone preserve the correct text, are themselves independent of one another, for besides other striking differences each of them preserves words that the other two do not have.[d] Of the three the

[a] Of the two score cases and more see 1015 D (ὡς οὐκ εὖ τὴν), 1017 B (see the critical *apparatus* on μέγα), 1023 E (λέγειν), 1027 B-C (καὶ ὑπερεχομένην ... ὑπερέχουσαν omitted by e, u, Escor. 72).

[b] See 1014 A, 1018 B (twice), 1025 B, and 1028 A.

[c] Of these the most significant are 1027 B-C (καὶ ὑπερεχομένην ... ὑπερέχουσαν), 1018 A (see the critical *apparatus* on καὶ ποιοῦσαι), 1020 A (καὶ τοῖς τριπλασίοις), and 1021 E (πρὸς τὰ γ′ καὶ μ′ καὶ σ′). In all these cases the Aldine also lacks the words preserved by f, m, r.

[d] Of the many cases see *e.g.* 1020 D and 1028 D for words in f and m that are not in r; 1025 F, 1019 D, and 1021 C for

GENERATION OF THE SOUL

text of m is most nearly intact and the best by far.

Escor. 72,[a] though it often agrees with f, m, and r against e and u and more often with e and u against f, m, and r and in both cases frequently agrees with E and B, was not copied from any of these MSS. From E and B it differs more than eighty times and in at least seven of these exhibits in agreement with e and u or with f, m, and r or with all five of them words that are absent from both E and B.[b] So also, while f, m, and r have words that it lacks,[c] it preserves words that are missing from them,[d] as it does others that are missing from e or from u.[e] Although like f, m, and r more recent than the Aldine, like them (see page 154, note *c supra*) it too preserves words that are lacking in the Aldine,[f] from which it

---

words in m and r that are not in f ; 1024 A, 1025 D, and 1019 E for words in f or r that are not in m.

[a] The contents of this MS. (Σ-Ι-12) are of different dates, the *De Animae Procreatione in Timaeo* (ff. 75ʳ-87ʳ) being of the 16th century according to P. A. Revilla, *Catálogo de los Códices Griegos de la Biblioteca de El Escorial* I (Madrid, 1936), p. 253 and p. 255 (No. 13).

[b] See 1012 B, 1014 A, 1015 D, 1024 E, 1025 B, 1018 B, 1028 A.

[c] There are more than a dozen such cases to testify that f, m, and r do not derive from Escor. 72 ; see especially 1020 A (καὶ τοῖς τριπλασίοις) and 1021 E (πρὸς τὰ γ΄ καὶ μ΄ καὶ σ΄).

[d] There are half a dozen cases of this, the most striking being 1022 B, where a whole clause is missing from f, m, r ; in 1025 F it is f alone that omits eleven words, and in 1025 C f and r that omit ten.

[e] See 1027 D (περὶ δὲ τῆς τάξεως) and 1029 A (πέντε τετραχόρδων), and for u alone 1019 F (ἐν δὲ τοῖς τριπλασίοις . . .).

[f] See the critical *apparatus* on 1016 E (καὶ τὴν), 1017 B (τεκμήριόν ἐστι μέγα), and 1024 A (καὶ τῆς χείρονος).

differs in more than thirty passages [a] and with which
it is alone in agreement against all the other mss.
only twice.[b] When it agrees with the Aldine against
other mss., it is usually at the same time in agreement with e and u or at least with e.

The Aldine itself cannot have been taken from E
or B, with both of which it disagrees more than a
hundred times and with neither of which it ever
agrees against all the other mss.[c] In at least a dozen
places it exhibits words that are in other mss. but
are missing from E and B [d]; and at 1027 B-C it agrees
exactly with e, u, and Escor. 72 in a mutilated text
entirely different from the text of E and B, although
other passages prove that it could not have been
taken from e or u either.[e] Nor could it have been

[a] See e.g. the critical apparatus on 1016 B (συνέρξας),
1024 E (κρίσις), 1018 A (τὰ μὲν γὰρ), 1022 A (ἀναλόγως ἤδη),
1030 C (ἐμμέλειαν).

[b] See the critical apparatus on 1017 A (ταῦτα δὴ δεῖ) and
1021 E (κατὰ τὸν βαρύτατον). In 1020 D (υπϛ′) Escor. 72 has
δ superscript over ϛ′, a miscorrection that might have come
from the Aldine (υπδ′) or from the source of f, m, r (υοδ′).
There are more than half a dozen cases in which Escor. 72
has been corrected to a reading in which the Aldine and
f, m, r agree.

[c] The nearest it comes to this is at 1029 D where for the
first word in chapter 33 (σκοπεῖτε) it agrees with E, B, and
r against all the others.

[d] See e.g. the critical apparatus on 1014 A (περὶ τούτων),
1015 D (ὡς οὐκ εὖ τὴν), 1024 E (πλανήτων), 1025 B (ἄδεκτον
οὖσαν ἀλλὰ), 1018 B (ἐπόγδοος ὤν), 1028 A (μονονουχί).

[e] In half a dozen passages it agrees with u alone against
all the other mss. (see especially 1024 E on κρίσις: κίνησις -u,
Aldine); and yet in 1019 F it preserves twenty-one words
that are not in u (ἐν δὲ τοῖς τριπλασίοις . . .), while in at least
two places it agrees with f, m, r in words that are not in e or u
(see 1014 B on πρὸ τῆς τοῦ and 1029 C on τῇ ὑπάτῃ τόνου).
In more than thirty other passages it disagrees with e and u,

taken from C.C.C. 99, which in many passages lacks words that it preserves.[a]

---

for which *e.g.* see the critical *apparatus* on 1023 E (λέγειν), 1025 F (χωρὶς τούτων), 1018 A (τὰ μὲν γὰρ), 1018 B (διὰ τοῦτο καὶ), 1022 A (ἀναλόγως ἤδη), and 1028 B (τὸν Ἑρμοῦ).

[a] To mention none of the other cases, words that the Aldine preserves and r omits in the following passages are also wanting in C.C.C. 99 : 1017 A, 1017 B, 1020 D, 1022 B, 1025 C, 1026 B, 1028 D.

ΠΕΡΙ ΤΗΣ
ΕΝ ΤΙΜΑΙΩΙ[1] ΨΥΧΟΓΟΝΙΑΣ

Ὁ πατὴρ Αὐτοβούλῳ καὶ Πλουτάρχῳ εὖ
πράττειν

B 1. Ἐπεὶ τὰ πολλάκις εἰρημένα καὶ γεγραμμένα
σποράδην ἐν ἑτέροις ἕτερα τὴν Πλάτωνος ἐξηγουμένοις δόξαν ἣν εἶχεν ὑπὲρ ψυχῆς, ὡς ὑπενοοῦμεν
ἡμεῖς, οἴεσθε δεῖν εἰς ἓν συναχθῆναι καὶ τυχεῖν
ἰδίας ἀναγραφῆς τὸν λόγον τοῦτον, οὔτ' ἄλλως εὐ-
μεταχείριστον ὄντα καὶ διὰ τὸ τοῖς πλείστοις τῶν
ἀπὸ Πλάτωνος ὑπεναντιοῦσθαι δεόμενον παραμυθίας, προεκθήσομαι τὴν λέξιν ὡς ἐν Τιμαίῳ γέγρα-
πται. "τῆς ἀμεροῦς[2] καὶ ἀεὶ κατὰ[3] ταὐτὰ ἐχούσης
οὐσίας καὶ τῆς αὖ περὶ τὰ σώματα γιγνομένης

---

[1] ἐν τῷ Τιμαίῳ -Ε, B, e, u, Escor. 72.
[2] ἀμερίστου -Timaeus 35 A 1.
[3] καὶ ἀεὶ καὶ κατὰ -e, u, Escor. 72.

---

[a] Concerning these two sons of Plutarch's cf. K. Ziegler,
R.-E. xxi/1 (1951), col. 649, 9-63.

[b] Timaeus 35 A 1–B 4. The passage is here translated in
such a way as to make it compatible with the construction
of it implied by Plutarch's subsequent interpretation. The
correct construction and interpretation of Plato's text are
given by G. M. A. Grube (Class. Phil., xxvii [1932], pp. 80-
82) and by F. M. Cornford (Plato's Cosmology, pp. 59-61),
who might have cited in their own support not only Proclus, as they do (cf. especially In Platonis Timaeum ii, pp.

ON THE GENERATION OF
THE SOUL IN THE TIMAEUS

To Autobulus and Plutarch [a] *from their Father
with his Wishes for their Welfare*

1. SINCE you think that there ought to be a unified
collection of the various statements that I have
frequently made and have set down sporadically in
various writings explaining what I supposed to be
the opinion held by Plato concerning the soul and
that a separate treatise ought to be devoted to this
account, as it is both difficult to deal with otherwise
and in need of vindication because of its opposition
to most of the Platonists, I shall make my preface
the passage as it is written in the *Timaeus.* [b] " Of
the indivisible [c] and ever invariable being and of the

155, 20–156, 24 and p. 162, 6–14 [Diehl]), but also the clear
and concise paraphrases of the passage by Hermias (*In
Platonis Phaedrum*, p. 123, 4–12 [Couvreur]) and by Aristi-
des Quintilianus (*De Musica* iii, 24 = p. 126, 1–7 [Winnington-
Ingram]). Proclus (*ibid.*, pp. 162, 25–163, 3) implies that
Porphyry understood the passage in the same way.

[c] Plato wrote ἀμερίστου here (*Timaeus* 35 A 1), and Plutarch usually employs that word in referring to this passage
(1012 E, 1014 D, 1022 E and F, 1025 B and E *infra*; *cf. Plat.
Quaest.* 1001 D *supra*) ; but a few lines below (*Timaeus* 35
A 5) Plato himself used ἀμεροῦς in the same sense (*cf. Theaetetus* 205 C 2 and D 1–2 with E 2), and in 1022 E *infra*
Plutarch remarks τὸ . . . μονοειδὲς ἀμερὲς εἴρηται καὶ ἀμέριστον.

(1012)
C μεριστῆς τρίτον ἐξ ἀμφοῖν ἐν μέσῳ συνεκεράσατο[1]
οὐσίας εἶδος, τῆς τε ταὐτοῦ φύσεως αὖ πέρι καὶ τῆς
τοῦ ἑτέρου[2] καὶ κατὰ ταῦτα[3] συνέστησεν ἐν μέσῳ
τοῦ τ' ἀμεροῦς αὐτὴν[4] καὶ τοῦ κατὰ τὰ σώματα
μεριστοῦ. καὶ τρία λαβὼν αὐτὰ ὄντα συνεκεράσατο[5] εἰς μίαν πάντα ἰδέαν, τὴν θατέρου φύσιν δύσμικτον οὖσαν εἰς ταὐτὸ[6] συναρμόττων βίᾳ μιγνὺς
δὲ μετὰ τῆς οὐσίας. καὶ ἐκ τριῶν ποιησάμενος ἐν
πάλιν ὅλον τοῦτο μοίρας εἰς ἃς[7] προσῆκε διένειμεν
ἑκάστην δὲ τούτων[8] ἔκ τε ταὐτοῦ καὶ θατέρου καὶ
τῆς οὐσίας μεμιγμένην· ἤρχετο δὲ διαιρεῖν ὧδε.''
D ταῦτα πρῶτον ὅσας παρέσχηκε τοῖς ἐξηγουμένοις

[1] συνεκεκράσατο -u.
[2] τοῦ ἑτέρου -E, B (cf. 1012 E infra : τοῦ δὲ ταὐτοῦ καὶ τοῦ
ἑτέρου), Timaeus 35 A 4-5 (in A, P, W, Y but θατέρου
in F) ; τοῦ θατέρου -e, u ; θατέρου -f, m, r, Escor. 72.
[3] ταῦτὰ -r, Timaeus 35 A 5 (in F but ταῦτα in A, P, W, Y).
[4] αὐτῶν -m, r, Timaeus 35 A 6.
[5] συνεκεκράσατο -u.
[6] ταὐτὸν -Timaeus 35 A 8.
[7] μοίρας ὅσας -Timaeus 35 B 2.
[8] Omitted in Timaeus 35 B 3 by A, P, W, Y.

[a] Plato wrote κατὰ ταὐτὰ . . . αὐτῶν ; but instead of the
former Plutarch probably read κατὰ ταῦτα, and instead of
the latter he certainly read αὐτὴν and construed τοῦ τ'
ἀμεροῦς . . . καὶ τοῦ . . . μεριστοῦ as a genitive of material
with συνέστησεν αὐτήν instead of as governed by ἐν μέσῳ.
for in 1025 B and 1025 E—1026 A infra he says that between
sameness and difference there was placed as a receptacle
for them the mixture of the indivisible and the divisible.
The change of αὐτῶν to αὐτὴν may have been occasioned
by the same desire for an expressed object of συνέστησεν
that led Hackforth (Class. Rev., N.S. vii [1957], p. 197),
while adopting Cornford's construction of the passage, to

divisible on the other hand that comes to pass in the case of bodies he blended together out of both a third kind of being in the middle, and in regard to the nature of sameness again and that of difference he also in this way compounded it *a* in the middle of the indivisible and what is divisible among bodies. And he took them, three as they were, and blended them all together into a single entity,*b* forcibly fitting into sameness the nature of difference, which is refractory to mixture, and mixing them together with being.*c*   And, when out of three he had made one, he again distributed the whole of this into fractions *d* that were appropriate and each of these a blend of sameness and difference and being ; and he began the division in the following way." To recount at present all the dissensions that these words have

propose κατὰ ταῦτα ⟨ταὐτὸ⟩ ; but κατὰ ταὐτὰ συνέστησεν here needs a separately expressed object no more than does μιγνύς five lines below (*Timaeus* 35 B 1) or περί τε ψυχῆς φύσεως διιδὼν κατὰ ταὐτά in *Phaedrus* 277 B 8.

b For Plato's use of ἰδέα in this sense *cf. Theaetetus* 184 D 3, 203 E 4, 204 A 1-2, 205 C 1-2, 205 D 5 ; *Parmenides* 157 D 7–E 2 ; *Politicus* 308 C 6-7 (and with this *cf. Timaeus* 28 A 8).

c As Proclus saw (*In Platonis Timaeum* ii, p. 159, 5-14 [Diehl]), Plato meant simply " and mixing them (*i.e.* both of them) with being " (*cf. Timaeus* 37 A 2-4 ; and for this use of μετά *cf.* 83 B 5-6, 85 A 5, and *Laws* 961 D 9-10) ; but from 1025 B *infra* it appears that Plutarch took it to mean " and mixing them (*i.e.* the two of them) together with the help of being," as do Taylor (*Commentary on Plato's Timaeus*, p. 109) and Thévenaz (*L'Âme du Monde*, pp. 13, 39, 42).

d The εἰς ἅς, which here replaces Plato's ὅσας (*cf. Laws* 737 E 3-4 and 756 B 8–c 1), is in accordance with Plutarch's own usage (*cf. De Comm. Not.* 1081 C–D *infra*, *De Defectu Orac.* 422 E, *Quaest. Conviv.* 719 E).

(1012) διαφορὰς ἄπλετον ἔργον ἐστὶ διελθεῖν ἐν τῷ παρ-
όντι, πρὸς δὲ ὑμᾶς ἐντετυχηκότας[1] ὁμοῦ ⟨τι⟩[2] ταῖς
πλείσταις καὶ περιττόν. ἐπεὶ δὲ τῶν δοκιμωτάτων
ἀνδρῶν τοὺς μὲν Ξενοκράτης προσηγάγετο, τῆς
ψυχῆς τὴν οὐσίαν ἀριθμὸν αὐτὸν ὑφ' ἑαυτοῦ κινούμενον ἀποφηνάμενος,[3] οἱ δὲ Κράντορι τῷ Σολεῖ[4]
προσέθεντο, μιγνύντι τὴν ψυχὴν ἔκ τε τῆς νοητῆς
καὶ τῆς περὶ τὰ αἰσθητὰ δοξαστῆς φύσεως, οἶμαί τι
τὴν τούτων ἀνακαλυφθέντων σαφήνειαν ὥσπερ ἐν-
δόσιμον ἡμῖν[5] παρέξειν.

2. Ἔστι δὲ βραχὺς ὑπὲρ ἀμφοῖν ὅ[6] λόγος. οἱ
μὲν γὰρ οὐδὲν ἢ γένεσιν ἀριθμοῦ δηλοῦσθαι νομί-
E ζουσι τῇ μίξει τῆς ἀμερίστου καὶ μεριστῆς οὐσίας·
ἀμέριστον μὲν γὰρ εἶναι τὸ ἓν μεριστὸν δὲ τὸ πλῆ-

---

[1] ἐντυχόντας -f, m, r.
[2] ⟨τι⟩ -added by Hartman (De Plutarcho, p. 589, n. 1);
ἐμοῦ ταῖς -r ; ὁμοῦ ταῖς -all other mss.
[3] ἀποφηναμένους -Escor. 72.
[4] f, m ; σωλεῖ -r ; σολιεῖ -E, B, e, u, Escor. 72.
[5] E, B, e ; ὑμῖν -u, f, m, r, Escor. 72.
[6] ὁ -omitted by e, u, Escor. 72.

---

[a] Sextus according to the mss. of Adv. Math. i, 301 asserts
that πάντες οἱ Πλάτωνος ἐξηγηταί were silent about the
passage ; but cf. W. Theiler's suggestion (Gnomon, xxviii
[1956], p. 286).

[b] Xenocrates, frag. 68 (Heinze [p. 187, 6-8]); cf. Plat.
Quaest. 1007 c supra with note c there and Xenocrates,
frags. 60-61 with Cherniss, Aristotle's Criticism of Plato
. . ., p. 396, n. 321.

[c] Crantor, frag. 3 (Kayser)=frag. 3 (Mullach, Frag.
Philos. Graec. iii, p. 140). With the formulation, τῆς νοητῆς
καὶ τῆς . . . δοξαστῆς φύσεως, cf. Plutarch, Adv. Colotem
1114 c ; Albinus, Epitome ix, 4 (p. 55, 1-3 [Louis]=p. 164,
1-3 [Hermann]) and Apuleius, De Platone i, 9 (p. 92, 10-15
[Thomas]) referring to Timaeus 51 d-e ; Sextus, Adv.
Math. vii, 141 referring to Timaeus 27 d 6—28 a 4 ; and

occasioned their interpreters [a] is in the first place an immense task and to do so to you superfluous as well, as you have read pretty nearly the most of them. Since, however, of the men most highly esteemed some were won over by Xenocrates, who declared the soul's essence to be number itself being moved by itself,[b] and others adhered to Crantor of Soli, who makes the soul a mixture of the intelligible nature and of the opinable nature of perceptible things,[c] I think that the clarification of these two when exposed will afford us something like a key-note.[d]

2. The statement concerning both is concise.[e] The former believe [f] that nothing but the generation of number is signified by the mixture of the indivisible and divisible being, the one being indivisible

---

see Plato, *Republic* 534 A 6-7. Crantor, the pupil of Xenocrates (Diogenes Laertius, iv, 24), is called by Proclus (*In Platonis Timaeum* i, p. 76, 1-2 [Diehl]) ὁ πρῶτος τοῦ Πλάτωνος ἐξηγητής.

[d] *Cf. De Defectu Orac.* 420 F and 421 F, *Quaest. Conviv.* 704 E ; Athenaeus, xiii, 556 a.

[e] The expression suggests that what follows was taken not directly from Xenocrates and Crantor but from a report of their interpretations.

[f] Xenocrates, frag. 68 (Heinze [p. 187, 11-23]). *Cf.* Cherniss, *The Riddle*, pp. 45-46 and p. 73 and *Aristotle's Criticism of Plato . . .*, pp. 396-402 ; and Merlan, *Platonism to Neoplatonism*, pp. 34-35, who on pp. 45-48 argues that Xenocrates' interpretation of *Timaeus* 35 A 1–B 4 is not " so thoroughly mistaken " although on p. 13 he had himself accepted as correct the interpretation given by Cornford (see note *b* on 1012 B *supra*), whereas it is by neglect of the latter and consequent misconstruction of *Timaeus* 35 A 1–B 4 that Xenocrates' interpretation is vindicated by H. J. Krämer (*Geistmetaphysik*, p. 328 ; *cf.* his *Arete*, p. 314, lines 1-3).

PLUTARCH'S MORALIA

(1012) θος ἐκ δὲ τούτων γίγνεσθαι τὸν ἀριθμὸν τοῦ ἑνὸς
ὁρίζοντος τὸ πλῆθος καὶ τῇ ἀπειρίᾳ πέρας ἐντιθέντος,[1] ἣν καὶ δυάδα καλοῦσιν ἀόριστον (καὶ Ζαράτας ὁ
Πυθαγόρου διδάσκαλος ταύτην μὲν ἐκάλει τοῦ ἀριθμοῦ μητέρα τὸ δὲ ἓν πατέρα· διὸ καὶ βελτίονας
εἶναι τῶν ἀριθμῶν ὅσοι τῇ μονάδι προσεοίκασι),
τοῦτον δὲ μήπω ψυχὴν τὸν ἀριθμὸν[2] εἶναι· τὸ γὰρ
κινητικὸν καὶ τὸ κινητὸν ἐνδεῖν αὐτῷ. τοῦ δὲ ταύ-

---

[1] mss. (cf. 1014 D infra [ἀπειρίαν ... ἐν αὐτῇ πέρας οὐδὲν
... ἔχουσαν] and 1026 A infra with Quaest. Conviv. 719 E
[ἀπείρῳ πέρατος ἐγγενομένου] ; Iamblichus, Theolog. Arith.,
p. 9, 1 [de Falco]) ; ἐπιτιθέντος -Bernardakis.
[2] τὸν ἀριθμόν -deleted as a gloss by Papabasileios (Athena,
x [1898], p. 226).

---

[a] Cf. De Defectu Orac. 429 A (τότε γὰρ ἀριθμὸς γίγνεται
τῶν πληθῶν ἕκαστον ὑπὸ τοῦ ἑνὸς ὁριζόμενον).
[b] Cf. Proclus, In Platonis Timaeum ii, p. 153, 19-21 and
23-25 (Diehl)=Numenius, Test. 31 (p. 97 [Leemans]) ; Themistius, De Anima, p. 12, 13-27 (cf. Gnomon, xxxi [1959],
pp. 42-43) ; and for number as the product of the one and
the indefinite dyad see the references in note a on Plat.
Quaest. 1002 A supra (where the terms used are μονάς and
ἡ ἄπειρος δυάς).
[c] Plutarch mentions " Zaratas " only here and must have
been unaware that this is just another form of " Zoroaster "
(cf. Bidez-Cumont, Les Mages Hellénisés i, pp. 36-38), to
whom he refers at 1026 B infra and for whom he accepted
the date of 5,000 years before the Trojan War (De Iside
369 D-E ; cf. Hermodorus in Diogenes Laertius, i, 2 and
Hermippus in Pliny, N.H. xxx, 4). With the first part of
Plutarch's parenthesis here cf. Hippolytus in Refutatio vi,
23, 2 (p. 149, 29-30 [Wendland] : καὶ Ζαράτας ὁ Πυθαγόρου
διδάσκαλος ἐκάλει τὸ μὲν ἓν πατέρα τὸ δὲ δύο μητέρα), who
for this cites no authority but who in Refutatio i, 2, 12
(p. 7, 2-5 [Wendland]) as his source for a highly con-
taminated account of the doctrine expounded to Pythagoras
by Zaratas cites Aristoxenus (frag. 13 [Wehrli] ; cf. F.
Jacoby, F. Gr. Hist. III a, pp. 295, 20-298, 14 [ad 273 F 94]

164

and multiplicity divisible and number being the
product of these when the one bounds multiplicity *a*
and inserts a limit in infinitude, which they call
indefinite dyad too *b* (this Zaratas too, the teacher of
Pythagoras, called mother of number ; and the one
he called father,*c* which is also why he held those
numbers to be better that resemble the monad *d*) ;
but they believe that this number is not yet soul,
for it lacks motivity and mobility,*e* but that after the

and W. Spoerri, *Rev. Études Anciennes*, lvii [1955], pp. 267-
290 [especially pp. 272-273]) and an otherwise unknown
Diodorus of Eretria. The explanation of this latter name
attempted by J. Bidez (*Eos* [Bruxelles, 1945], pp. 16-17) is
implausible even on chronological grounds ; and it is more
probable that behind this " Diodorus " lurks the name of
Eudorus (*cf.* J. Roeper, *Philologus*, vii [1852], pp. 532-535),
who is cited by Plutarch at 1013 B, 1019 E, and 1020 C
infra and who is therefore likely to have been his source
not only for the parenthetical reference to Zaratas here but
also for the summary in which it stands (see note *e* on 1012 D
supra and Helmer, *De An. Proc.*, p. 13, n. 18).

d *i.e.* the odd numbers (*cf.* Nicomachus, *Arithmetica
Introductio* II, xx, 2 [p. 118, 4-6, Hoche] ; Syrianus, *Metaph.*,
p. 181, 23-25), which are called male (*cf.* Plutarch, *Quaest.
Romanae* 264 A and 288 C-D, *De E* 388 A-B) and " better "
(*cf. Quaest. Romanae* 264 A *init.* ; Demetrius in Proclus,
In Platonis Rem Publicam ii, p. 23, 13-22 [Kroll] ; Aristides
Quintilianus, *De Musica* iii, 24 [p. 126, 24-27, Winnington-
Ingram]). Plutarch himself speaks of their derivation from
the monad as from " the better principle " (*De Defectu Orac.*
429 B), and Xenocrates seems to have identified with odd-
ness the monad which as male he gave the rank of father
(Xenocrates, frag. 15 [Heinze] and Aristotle, *Metaphysics*
1084 a 32-37 with 1083 b 28-30 ; *cf. A.J.P.*, lxviii [1947],
pp. 245-246 in note 86).

e *Cf. infra* τοῦ κινεῖσθαι καὶ κινεῖν (" of being in motion
and setting in motion ") and Aristotle's objection, *De Anima*
409 a 3 (εἰ [ἦ] γάρ ἐστι κινητικὴ καὶ κινητή, διαφέρειν δεῖ) with
De Generatione 326 b 3-5.

(1012) τοῦ καὶ τοῦ ἑτέρου συμμιγέντων, ὧν τὸ μέν ἐστι
κινήσεως ἀρχὴ καὶ μεταβολῆς τὸ δὲ μονῆς, ψυχὴν[1]
γεγονέναι, μηδὲν ἧττον τοῦ ἱστάναι καὶ ἵστασθαι
F δύναμιν ἢ τοῦ κινεῖσθαι καὶ κινεῖν οὖσαν. οἱ δὲ
περὶ τὸν Κράντορα μάλιστα τῆς ψυχῆς ἴδιον ὑπολαμβάνοντες ἔργον εἶναι τὸ[2] κρίνειν τά τε νοητὰ καὶ
τὰ αἰσθητὰ τάς τε τούτων ἐν αὑτοῖς καὶ πρὸς ἄλληλα γιγνομένας διαφορὰς καὶ ὁμοιότητας ἐκ πάντων φασίν, ἵνα πάντα γιγνώσκῃ, συγκεκρᾶσθαι τὴν
1013 ψυχήν· ταῦτα δ' εἶναι τέσσαρα, τὴν νοητὴν φύσιν

----

[1] μονὴν (μόνην -f) ψυχῆς -f, m, r, Escor. 72corr. (ν and s
superscript over s and ν), Aldine.

[2] τὸ -f, m, r ; τοῦ -E, B, e, u, Escor. 72, Aldine.

----

[a] For difference and sameness as the principles of motion
and rest respectively cf. Aristotle, *Physics* 201 b 19-21
(= *Metaphysics* 1066 a 11) and *Metaphysics* 1084 a 34-35
with Cherniss, *Aristotle's Criticism of Plato* . . ., note 305
on p. 385 and pp. 11-12, p. 122, p. 443. Aristotle argues
that a self-mover must have an internal principle of motion
(cf. Cherniss, *op. cit.*, pp. 389-390) and that soul must be
στατική as well as κινητική (*Topics* 127 b 15-16 ; cf. *De Anima*
406 b 22-24 with 409 b 7-11) ; and Xenocrates mistakenly
tried to make soul as self-motion satisfy both these require-
ments (cf. Cherniss, *op. cit.*, note 366 [especially pp. 432-
433]). In " Timaeus Locrus " 95 E—96 A the sameness and
difference mixed with the blend of indivisible form and
divisible being are called δύο δυνάμιας ἀρχὰς κινασίων without
further specification.

[b] Crantor, frag. 4 (Kayser)=frag. 4 (Mullach, *Frag.
Philos. Graec.* iii, p. 140), with the whole of which cf.
Albinus, *Epitome* xiv, 1-2 (p. 79, 3-14 [Louis]=p. 169, 16-26
[Hermann]). Unlike Xenocrates Crantor did not read into
the psychogony any principle of motion or any identification
of soul with number (Taylor, *Commentary on Plato's
Timaeus*, p. 113) ; and P. Merlan in saying that " Crantor
. . . interpreted the ' psychogony ' of the *Timaeus* as being
simply ' arithmogony ' . . ." (Armstrong, *Later Greek* . . .

commingling of sameness and difference, the latter of which is the principle of motion and change while the former is that of rest,[a] then the product is soul, soul being a faculty of bringing to a stop and being at rest no less than of being in motion and setting in motion. Crantor and his followers, on the other hand,[b] supposing that the soul's peculiar function is above all to form judgments of the intelligible and the perceptible objects [c] and the differences and similarities occurring among these objects both within their own kind and in relation of either kind to the other,[d] say that the soul, in order that it may know all, has been blended together out of all [e] and

Philosophy, pp. 17-18) erroneously ascribes to him the very interpretation that he in fact rejected.

[c] Cf. Albinus, loc. cit., p. 79, 3 (Louis)=p. 169, 16 (Hermann) and Proclus, In Platonis Timaeum i, p. 254, 29-31 with ii, p. 135, 24-25 (Diehl). This use of κρίνειν is frequent in Aristotle (e.g. De Anima 427 a 17-21, 428 a 3-5, cf. 432 a 15-16 and 404 b 25-27); for Plato cf. Republic 523 B 1-2 (ὡς ἱκανῶς ὑπὸ τῆς αἰσθήσεως κρινόμενα).

[d] That is the difference and similarity (1) of intelligibles to one another or of perceptibles to one another and (2) of intelligible and perceptible to each other. Cf. Timaeus 37 A 5-B 3 and Proclus, In Platonis Timaeum ii, pp. 304, 22-305, 4 (Diehl).

[e] Because " like is known by like " (cf. Albinus, loc. cit.), the assumption underlying the psychogony according to Aristotle (De Anima 404 b 16-18) and later interpreters generally (cf. Sextus, Adv. Math. i, 303 [cf. vii, 92-93 and 116-120]; Chalcidius, Platonis Timaeus, pp. 119, 14–120, 11 [Wrobel]=p. 100, 8-22 [Waszink]; Proclus, In Platonis Timaeum ii, p. 135, 23-30 and p. 298, 2-31 [Diehl]); but see Cherniss, Aristotle's Criticism of Plato . . ., pp. 408-411 (with note 339 sub finem on Crantor) and G. M. Stratton, Theophrastus and the Greek Physiological Psychology before Aristotle (London/New York, 1917), pp. 156-157 on De Sensibus 1 (Dox. Graeci, p. 499, 3).

PLUTARCH'S MORALIA

(1013) ἀεὶ κατὰ ταὐτὰ καὶ ὡσαύτως ἔχουσαν καὶ τὴν περὶ
τὰ σώματα παθητικὴν[1] καὶ μεταβλητὴν ἔτι δὲ τὴν
ταὐτοῦ καὶ τοῦ ἑτέρου διὰ τὸ κἀκείνων ἑκατέραν
μετέχειν ἑτερότητος καὶ ταὐτότητος.

3. Ὁμαλῶς δὲ πάντες οὗτοι χρόνῳ μὲν οἴονται
τὴν ψυχὴν μὴ γεγονέναι μηδ' εἶναι γενητὴν[2] πλεί-
ονας δὲ δυνάμεις ἔχειν, εἰς ἃς ἀναλύοντα θεωρίας[3]
ἕνεκα τὴν οὐσίαν αὐτῆς λόγῳ τὸν Πλάτωνα γιγνομένην ὑποτίθεσθαι καὶ συγκεραννυμένην· τὰ δ' αὐτὰ

---

[1] mss. (cf. 1023 b infra [τῶν νοητῶν τὸ ἀίδιον καὶ τῶν αἰσθητῶν τὸ παθητικόν] and Dox. Graeci, p. 281 a 11 and b 9);
παθητὴν -Bernardakis (cf. De E 392 b from Eusebius, Praep.
Evang. xi, 11, 4 [τῶν παθητῶν καὶ μεταβλητῶν]).
[2] γεννητὴν -f, m, Aldine.　　　　[3] θεωρίαν -r[1].

---

[a] Plato emphatically stated that the ingredients of the soul
are *three* (*Timaeus* 35 a 6-7 and 37 a 2-4).

[b] Called τῆς περὶ τὰ αἰσθητὰ δοξαστῆς φύσεως in 1012 d
supra (see note c there) and in 1013 b *infra* simply τῆς
αἰσθητῆς οὐσίας. With the expression used here (περὶ τὰ
σώματα may have been taken directly from *Timaeus* 35 a
2-3, but *cf.* τῷ περὶ τὰ σώματα πλανητῷ καὶ μεταβλητῷ in
Quaest. Conviv. 718 d) *cf.* τῶν αἰσθητῶν τὸ παθητικόν in 1023
b-c *infra*, (φύσεως) οὔσης ἐν πάθεσι παντοδαποῖς καὶ μεταβολαῖς
ἀτάκτοις in 1015 e *infra*, τὴν δὲ σωματικὴν καὶ παθητικὴν
(φύσιν) in De Defectu Orac. 428 b, and also *Adv. Colotem*
1115 e (τῆς ὕλης . . . πάθη πολλὰ καὶ μεταβολὰς . . . δεχομένης)
and 1116 d (ταύταις αἷς ἐν τῷ πάσχειν καὶ μεταβάλλειν τὸ εἶναι).

[c] *Cf.* Albinus, *loc. cit.*, p. 79, 10-11 (Louis)=p. 169, 22-24
(Hermann): . . . ἐπὶ τῶν νοητῶν ταὐτότητά τε καὶ ἑτερότητα καὶ ἐπὶ τῶν μεριστῶν. . . .

[d] Xenocrates, frag. 68 (Heinze [p. 187, 23-27]) and
Crantor, frag. 4 (Kayser [p. 19])=frag. 4 (Mullach, *Frag.
Philos. Graec.* iii, p. 140).

[e] *Cf.* 1017 b *infra* (οὐ θεωρίας ἕνεκα) and οὐ τοῦ θεωρῆσαι
ἕνεκεν (Aristotle, *Metaphysics* 1091 a 28-29; contrast
Speusippus, frag. 46, 17-20 [Lang]), διδασκαλίας χάριν ὡς
μᾶλλον γνωριζόντων (Aristotle, *De Caelo* 280 a 1, with Taurus
in Philoponus, *De Aeternitate Mundi*, p. 187, 1 and p. 224,

168

that these are four,[a] the intelligible nature, which is
ever invariable and identical, and the passive and
mutable nature of bodies [b] and furthermore that of
sameness and of difference because each of the
former two also partakes of diversity and identity.[c]

3. All these interpreters are alike in thinking [d]
that the soul did not come to be in time and is not
subject to generation but that it has a multiplicity of
faculties and that Plato in analysing its essence into
these for the sake of examination [e] represents it
verbally as coming to be [f] and being blended to-

[1] [Rabe]; Alexander, *ibid.*, p. 217, 23-24; Simplicius,
De Caelo, p. 304, 4-6; [Alexander], *Metaph.*, p. 819, 38
and p. 820, 5), σαφηνείας χάριν (Theophrastus, *Phys. Opin.*,
frag. 11 [*Dox. Graeci*, pp. 485, 18–486, 2], with Taurus in
Philoponus, *De Aeternitate Mundi*, p. 187, 5 [Rabe] and
Alexander, *ibid.*, p. 216, 13), ἐπὶ τοῦ σαφοῦς χρείᾳ (Atticus
in Eusebius, *Praep. Evang.* xv, 6, 4=ii, p. 360, 7 [Mras]),
and various combinations of these expressions in Plotinus
(*Enn.* iv, iii, 9, lines 14-15), Proclus (*In Platonis Timaeum*
i, p. 290, 9-10 [Diehl]), and Philoponus (*De Aeternitate
Mundi*, p. 186, 14-16 and p. 189, 10-13 [Rabe]). With
εἰς ἃς ἀναλύοντα . . . τὴν οὐσίαν αὐτῆς *cf.* especially Proclus,
In Platonis Timaeum ii, pp. 123, 27–124, 10 (Diehl) and
Chalcidius, *Platonis Timaeus*, p. 97, 5-7 (Wrobel)=pp. 81,
26–82, 1 (Waszink), on which *cf.* J. H. Waszink, *Studien
zum Timaioskommentar des Calcidius* i (Leiden, 1964), p. 7,
n. 3. For similar language used of the cosmogony *cf.*
Taurus, Porphyry, and Alexander in Philoponus, *De
Aeternitate Mundi*, p. 146, 13-20, pp. 148, 9-23 with 153,
23–154, 5, and pp. 217, 25–218, 10 (Rabe); Plotinus, *Enn.*
iv, iii, 9, lines 15-20; and Simplicius, *De Caelo*, p. 304, 7-13.
[f] *Cf.* "Timaeus Locrus" 94 c (cap. ii *init.* [7] ed. W. Marg):
πρὶν ὧν ὠρανὸν λόγῳ γενέσθαι . . . with Proclus, *In Platonis
Timaeum* ii, p. 101, 1-14 (Diehl); *cf.* also Plotinus, *Enn.*
vi, vii, 35, lines 28-29 (ὁ δὲ λόγος διδάσκων γινόμενα ποιεῖ)
with *Enn.* iv, iii, 9, lines 13-15 and viii, 4, lines 40-42 and
in general *Enn.* iii, v, 9, lines 24-29 (. . . καὶ οἱ λόγοι καὶ
γενέσεις τῶν ἀγεννήτων ποιοῦσι . . .).

(1013) καὶ περὶ τοῦ κόσμου διανοούμενον ἐπίστασθαι μὲν
ἀίδιον ὄντα καὶ ἀγένητον[1] τὸ δὲ ᾧ τρόπῳ συντέ-
B τακται καὶ διοικεῖται καταμαθεῖν οὐ ῥᾴδιον ὁρῶντα
τοῖς μήτε γένεσιν αὐτοῦ μήτε[2] τῶν γενητικῶν[3] σύν-
οδον ἐξ ἀρχῆς προϋποθεμένοις[4] ταύτην τὴν ὁδὸν
τραπέσθαι. τοιούτων δὲ τῶν καθόλου λεγομένων,
ὁ μὲν Εὔδωρος οὐδετέρους ἀμοιρεῖν οἴεται τοῦ εἰκότος[5]· ἐμοὶ δὲ δοκοῦσι τῆς Πλάτωνος ἀμφότεροι

[1] ἀγέννητον -f, m, r, Aldine.
[2] μήτε -f, m, r ; μηδὲ -E, B, e, u, Escor. 72, Aldine.
[3] γεννητικῶν -f, m, r, Aldine.
[4] προυποθεμένην -r.   [5] εἰκότως -u.

---

[a] Xenocrates, frag. 54 (Heinze [p. 180, 21-26]) and
Crantor, frag. 4 (Kayser [p. 19])=frag. 4 (Mullach, *Frag.
Philos. Graec.* iii, p. 140) ; *cf.* in Xenocrates, frag. 54
(Heinze) and Speusippus, frag. 54 a-b (Lang) Aristotle,
De Caelo 279 a 32—280 a 8 with Simplicius, *De Caelo*,
pp. 303, 33–304, 15 (*cf.* [Alexander], *Metaph.*, p. 819, 37-38)
and *Scholia in Aristotelem* 489 a 4-12 (Brandis).   For
Crantor's further explanation of γενητόν as meaning not
that the universe had a beginning but that it is dependent
upon an extrinsic cause (frag. 2 [Kayser=Mullach, *Frag.
Philos. Graec.* iii, p. 139]=Proclus, *In Platonis Timaeum*
i, p. 277, 8-10 [Diehl]) *cf.* later Albinus, *Epitome* xiv, 3
(p. 81, 14 [Louis]=p. 169, 26-30 [Hermann]) with Proclus,
In Platonis Timaeum i, p. 219, 2-11 (Diehl) ; Taurus in
Philoponus, *De Aeternitate Mundi*, p. 147, 5-9 (Rabe) ;
Plotinus, *Enn.* ii, ix, 3, lines 12-14 and *Enn.* iii, ii, 1, lines
22-26 and vii, 6, lines 52-54 ; Chalcidius, *Platonis Timaeus*,
p. 89, 20-21 (Wrobel)=p. 74, 18-19 (Waszink) ; Simplicius,
Phys., p. 1154, 9-11 ; and Proclus, *In Platonis Timaeum* i,
p. 277, 10-17 (Diehl).
[b] *Cf.* Taurus in Philoponus, *De Aeternitate Mundi*, p. 187,
15-16 (Rabe) with Alexander, *ibid.*, p. 216, 13-15 ; Chalcidius, *Platonis Timaeus*, pp. 91, 22–92, 3 (Wrobel)=p. 77,
8-13 (Waszink) ; Simplicius, *De Caelo*, p. 304, 6-10.
[c] That is neither Xenocrates in his arithmological explication of the psychogony nor Crantor in his epistemological
explication of it, the two explications that Plutarch proceeds

gether ; and they think[a] that with the same thing
in mind concerning the universe too, while he knows
it to be everlasting and ungenerated, yet seeing the
way of its organization and management not to be
easy for those to discern who have not presupposed
its generation and a conjunction of the generative
factors at the beginning,[b] this course is the one that
he took. Such being on the whole what they say,
Eudorus thinks that neither party is without all
title to likelihood[c] ; but to me they both seem to

to say are *both* wrong. The passage has been misinterpreted
to mean that Eudorus reconciled the interpretation of the
cosmogony by Xenocrates with the " literal " interpretation of it by Crantor (H. Dörrie, *Hermes*, lxxix [1944],
pp. 27-28 in his article on Eudorus, *ibid.*, pp. 25-39),
although Plutarch has just asserted that Crantor and
Xenocrates and all their followers alike rejected the " literal "
interpretation of both the psychogony and the cosmogony.
He has also ascribed to all of them alike the same explanation of both, θεωρίας ἕνεκα, and has not mentioned Crantor's
additional interpretation of γενητόν (see note *a* on p. 170
supra) ; and so C. Moreschini must be mistaken in supposing him to refer to these as the two different explications to
both of which Eudorus gave some title to likelihood (*Annali
della Scuola Norm. Sup. di Pisa* [Lettere . . .], 2 Ser. xxxiii
[1964], pp. 31-32). For Plutarch's use of Eudorus in this
essay see note *c* on 1012 E *supra* ; and for Eudorus himself
besides Dörrie's article *cf.* E. Martini, *R.-E.* vi (1909), cols.
915, 41–916, 66 and G. Luck, *Der Akademiker Antiochos*
(Bern/Stuttgart, 1953), pp. 27-28. *Pap. Oxyrh.* 1609 (xiii,
pp. 94-96 ; *cf.* Diels-Kranz, *Frag. Vorsok.*[6] i, p. 352, 1-6),
in which the author refers to his own commentary on the
Timaeus, has for this reason been ascribed to Eudorus, who
has recently been proposed as the source of an ever-increasing
number of later texts (*cf.* P. Boyancé, *Rev. Études Grecques*,
lxxiii [1959], pp. 378-380 and lxxvi [1963], pp. 85-89, 95,
and 98 ; M. Giusta, *I Dossografi di Etica* i [Torino, 1964],
pp. 151 ff. ; W. Theiler, *Parusia : Festgabe für Johannes
Hirschberger* [Frankfurt am Main, 1965], pp. 204 ff.).

(1013) διαμαρτάνειν δόξης, εἰ κανόνι τῷ¹ πιθανῷ χρη-
στέον οὐκ ἴδια δόγματα περαίνοντας ἀλλ' ἐκείνῳ τι
βουλομένους λέγειν ὁμολογούμενον. ἡ μὲν ⟨γὰρ⟩²
ἐκ τῆς νοητῆς³ καὶ τῆς αἰσθητῆς⁴ οὐσίας λεγομένη
μῖξις⁵ οὐ διασαφεῖται πῇ ποτε ψυχῆς μᾶλλον ἢ τῶν
ἄλλων, ὅ τι ἄν τις εἴπῃ,⁶ γένεσίς ἐστιν. αὐτός τε
C γὰρ ὁ κόσμος οὗτος⁷ καὶ τῶν μερῶν ἕκαστον συνέστηκεν ἔκ τε σωματικῆς οὐσίας καὶ νοητῆς, ὧν ἡ
μὲν ὕλην καὶ ὑποκείμενον ἡ δὲ⁸ μορφὴν καὶ εἶδος
τῷ γενομένῳ⁹ παρέσχε· καὶ τῆς μὲν ὕλης τὸ μετοχῇ καὶ εἰκασίᾳ τοῦ¹⁰ νοητοῦ μορφωθὲν εὐθὺς ἁπτὸν

---

¹ τῷ -omitted by f, m, r, u¹.
² ⟨γὰρ⟩ added by Maurommates (" nam " -Turnebus :
" car " -Amyot).
³ Marcianus 187ᶜᵒʳʳ· ; νοητικῆς -all other MSS.
⁴ Marcianus 187 ; αἰσθητικῆς -all other MSS.
⁵ μίξης -u.   ⁶ εἴποι -B, r.
⁷ f, m, r, Escor. 72ᶜᵒʳʳ· ; οὕτως -all other MSS.
⁸ οἱ δὲ -B.   ⁹ τῶν γενομένων -r.   ¹⁰ τοῦ -omitted by u.

ᵃ See 1014 A infra (πιστούμενος τῷ εἰκότι) ; and cf. De
Defectu Orac. 430 B (. . . πρὸς τὴν ἐκείνου διάνοιαν ἐπάγειν τὸ
εἰκός . . .), Quaest. Conviv. 728 F (. . . τοῦ δὲ πιθανοῦ καὶ
εἰκότος . . .) with 700 B, and contrast 719 F (. . . δόξας ὡς
ἰθαγενεῖς καὶ ἰδίας . . . ἐπήνεσα καὶ τὸ εἰκὸς ἔφην ἔχειν ἱκανῶς).
ᵇ For τῆς αἰσθητῆς οὐσίας, an abbreviation of the formula-
tions given in 1012 D and 1013 A supra (see note b there),
cf. Proclus, In Platonis Timaeum ii, p. 154, 1-3 (Diehl) with
Plotinus, Enn. iv, viii, 7 and Simplicius, De Anima, p. 28, 1-2.
ᶜ Crantor may not have meant to make the μεριστὴ οὐσία
of Timaeus 35 A 2-3 a constituent part of the soul and
probably did not identify it with corporeal being or matter
(cf. Helmer, De An. Proc., p. 11 ; Thévenaz, L'Âme du
Monde, p. 61) ; but the present refutation assumes that he
did, and the assumption may have been the easier for
Plutarch to make because such an interpretation had
already been adopted by others : it is attributed to Eratosthenes by Proclus (In Platonis Timaeum ii, p. 152, 24-27 ;

be utterly mistaken about Plato's opinion if as a standard plausibility is to be used, not in promotion of one's own doctrines but with the desire to say something that agrees with Plato.[a] ⟨For⟩, as to what the one party calls the mixture of the intelligible and the perceptible being,[b] it is not made clear how in the world this is generation of soul rather than of anything else one may mention, for this universe itself and each of its parts consist of corporeal and intelligible being, of which the former provided matter or substrate and the latter shape or form for what has come to be,[c] and any matter that by participating in the intelligible and simulating it has got shape is straightway tangible ⟨and⟩ visible,[d]

cf. F. Solmsen, *T.A.P.A.*, lxxiii [1942], pp. 198 and 202) and is recorded by Chalcidius (*Platonis Timaeus*, p. 94, 4-10 [Wrobel]=p. 79, 9-14 [Waszink]), whose ultimate source for it is probably pre-Plutarchean (*cf.* " Timaeus Locrus " 94 A-B). Later (1023 A *infra*), when against those who interpret the psychogony as a commingling of corporeal matter with indivisible being the present refutation of Crantor is repeated, it is preceded by the argument that Plato in that passage uses none of the expressions by which he was accustomed to designate corporeal matter. In fact, like Aristotle (*Physics* 209 b 11-13) Plutarch identified with ὕλη the χώρα or receptacle of the *Timaeus* (1024 c *infra*; *cf.* 1015 D *infra* and *Quaest. Conviv.* 636 D), confusing this further with " precosmic " corporeal chaos (*cf.* 1014 B-C and 1016 D—1017 A *infra*; Jones, *Platonism of Plutarch*, p. 81, n. 34; Thévenaz, *L'Âme du Monde*, pp. 110-113); and, though he apparently knew that Plato had not used ὕλη in this sense (*De Defectu Orac.* 414 F; *cf.* Chalcidius, *Platonis Timaeus*, pp. 304, 4-7 and 336, 8-12 [Wrobel]=pp. 277, 18–278, 2 and 309, 3-6 [Waszink]), he even went so far as to insert the term into quasi-quotations of the *Timaeus* (*cf.* 1016 D *infra* and *De Defectu Orac.* 430 C-D).

[a] Cf. *Plat. Quaest.* 1001 D-E *supra*; and for ἁπτὸν ⟨καὶ⟩ ὁρατόν *cf.* Plato, *Timaeus* 28 B 7-8, 31 B 4, and 32 B 7-8.

(1013) ⟨καὶ⟩[1] ὁρατόν ἐστιν, ἡ ψυχὴ δὲ πᾶσαν αἴσθησιν
ἐκπέφευγεν. ἀριθμόν γε μὴν ὁ Πλάτων οὐδέποτε
τὴν ψυχὴν προσεῖπεν ἀλλὰ κίνησιν αὐτοκίνητον ἀεὶ
καὶ κινήσεως πηγὴν καὶ ἀρχήν· ἀριθμῷ δὲ καὶ
λόγῳ καὶ ἁρμονίᾳ διακεκόσμηκε τὴν οὐσίαν[2] αὐτῆς
ὑποκειμένην καὶ δεχομένην τὸ κάλλιστον εἶδος ὑπὸ
τούτων ἐγγιγνόμενον. οἶμαι δὲ μὴ ταὐτὸν εἶναι τῷ
D κατ' ἀριθμὸν συνεστάναι τὴν ψυχὴν τὸ τὴν οὐσίαν
αὐτῆς ἀριθμὸν ὑπάρχειν, ἐπεὶ ⟨καὶ⟩[3] καθ' ἁρμονίαν συνέστηκεν ἁρμονία δ' οὐκ ἔστιν, ὡς αὐτὸς ἐν
τῷ περὶ Ψυχῆς ἀπέδειξεν. ἐκφανῶς δὲ τούτοις
ἠγνόηται τὸ περὶ τοῦ ταὐτοῦ καὶ τοῦ ἑτέρου· λέγουσι γὰρ ὡς τὸ μὲν στάσεως τὸ δὲ κινήσεως συμβάλλεται δύναμιν εἰς τὴν τῆς ψυχῆς γένεσιν, αὐτοῦ
Πλάτωνος ἐν τῷ Σοφιστῇ τὸ ὂν καὶ τὸ ταὐτὸν καὶ
τὸ ἕτερον πρὸς δὲ τούτοις στάσιν καὶ κίνησιν ὡς

[1] ⟨καὶ⟩ -added by Xylander, implied by versions of
Turnebus and Amyot.

[2] διακόσμηκεν οὐσίαν -r.   [3] ⟨καὶ⟩ -added by Hubert.

---

[a] Plato, *Laws* 898 E 1-2 (see *Plat. Quaest.* 1002 c *supra*
with note *g* there) and *Timaeus* 36 E 5-6 and 46 D 6-7 ; *cf.*
Albinus, *Epitome* xiii, 1 (p. 73, 4-7 [Louis]=p. 168, 6-9
[Hermann]).

[b] *Phaedrus* 245 c 9 (πηγὴ καὶ ἀρχὴ κινήσεως). The preceding κίνησιν αὐτοκίνητον ἀεί is not a quotation but a
formulaic summary of *Phaedrus* 245 c 7-8 and 245 E 2-4
influenced by the phraseology of *Laws* 894 B 9-c 1, 895 B 1-6,
and 895 E 10—896 A 5 (*cf. infra* 1014 D [αὐτοκίνητον δὲ καὶ
κινητικὴν ἀρχήν], 1016 A [τῷ δ' αὐτοκινήτῳ πιστουμένη τὸ
ἀγένητον αὐτῆς], 1017 A [δύναμιν αὐτοκίνητον καὶ ἀεικίνητον],
1023 c [ἡ μὲν γὰρ ἀεικίνητος]), and it does not indicate that
Plutarch knew αὐτοκίνητον as a variant of ἀεικίνητον in
Phaedrus 245 c 5 (*cf. Lustrum*, iv [1959], p. 137, # 692 and
693). Others also, who certainly read ἀεικίνητον there, say
that in this passage of the *Phaedrus* soul is defined as τὸ
αὐτοκίνητον (*e.g.* Hermias, *In Platonis Phaedrum*, p. 108,

whereas soul is beyond the range of all sense-perception.[a] Then as for number, that Plato never called the soul; but he called it motion perpetually self-moved and motion's source and principle.[b] By means of number and ratio and concord he did arrange its substance[c] underlying and receiving the fairest form, which by their agency arises in it; but it is not the same, I think, to say that the soul is put together on a numerical pattern and to say that its essence is number, since ⟨in fact⟩ it is put together on the pattern of a concord but is not a concord, as he himself proved in the work on the Soul.[d] It is manifest too that these interpreters[e] have failed to understand the part about sameness and difference, for they say that to the generation of the soul the former contributes the faculty of rest and the latter that of motion,[f] whereas by Plato himself in the *Sophist*[g] existence and sameness and difference and besides these rest and motion are distinguished and

6-17 and p. 118, 14-16 [Couvreur]; Philoponus, *De Aeternitate Mundi*, p. 271, 18-23 and pp. 246, 27-247, 2 [Rabe]; cf. Fernanda Decleva Caizzi, *Acme*, xxiii (1970), pp. 91-97.

[c] See 1023 D *infra* (. . . τὴν οὐσίαν . . . τῆς ψυχῆς . . . ταττομένην ὑπ' ἀριθμοῦ). That is the procedure of *Timaeus* 35 B 4—36 D 7, after which the soul is described as λογισμοῦ μετέχουσα καὶ ἁρμονίας . . . καὶ ἀνὰ λόγον μερισθεῖσα καὶ συνδεθεῖσα (36 E 6—37 A 4). With Plutarch's expression here cf. *infra* 1015 E (. . . ἁρμονίᾳ καὶ ἀναλογίᾳ καὶ ἀριθμῷ χρώμενος ὀργάνοις), 1017 B (διαρμοσάμενος τοῖς προσήκουσιν ἀριθμοῖς καὶ λόγοις), 1027 A, 1029 D-E, and 1030 C.

[d] *Phaedo* 92 A 6—95 A 3. For ἁρμονία, translated as "concord," see note a on *Plat. Quaest.* II, 1001 C *supra*.

[e] Xenocrates and his followers.

[f] See 1012 E *supra* with note a on page 166.

[g] *Sophist* 254 D 4—259 B 7 (especially 255 B 5-E 2 and 256 C 5-D 4), to which Plutarch refers in *De E* 391 B and *De Defectu Orac.* 428 C also.

(1013) ἕκαστον ἑκάστου διαφέρον καὶ πέντε ὄντα χωρὶς
ἀλλήλων τιθεμένου καὶ διορίζοντος.

4. Ὅ¹ γε μὴν οὗτοί τε κοινῇ καὶ οἱ πλεῖστοι τῶν
Ε χρωμένων Πλάτωνι φοβούμενοι καὶ παραλυπού-
μενοι² πάντα μηχανῶνται καὶ παραβιάζονται καὶ
στρέφουσιν, ὥς τι δεινὸν καὶ ἄρρητον οἰόμενοι δεῖν
περικαλύπτειν καὶ ἀρνεῖσθαι, τήν τε τοῦ κόσμου
τήν τε τῆς ψυχῆς αὐτοῦ γένεσιν καὶ σύστασιν, οὐκ
ἐξ ἀιδίου συνεστώτων³ οὐδὲ τὸν ἄπειρον χρόνον
οὕτως ἐχόντων, ἰδίᾳ τε λόγου τέτευχε καὶ νῦν ἀρκέ-
σει ῥηθὲν ὅτι τὸν περὶ θεῶν ἀγῶνα καὶ λόγον, ᾧ
Πλάτων ὁμολογεῖ φιλοτιμότατα⁴ καὶ παρὰ ἡλικίαν
πρὸς τοὺς ἀθέους κεχρῆσθαι, συγχέουσι μᾶλλον δὲ
ὅλως ἀναιροῦσιν.⁵ εἰ γὰρ ἀγένητος⁶ ὁ κόσμος

¹ οἱ -r. ² παραμυθούμενοι -Turnebus. ³ συνεστότων -r.
⁴ φιλοτιμότατα -r. ⁵ ἀνεροῦσιν -u. ⁶ ἀγέννητος -f, m, r.

ᵃ According to Proclus (In Platonis Timaeum i, pp. 276,
31–277, 1 [Diehl]) Plutarch, Atticus, and "many other
Platonists" took the cosmogony of the Timaeus literally;
but Plutarch is the earliest of these named either by him
(cf. op. cit., i, pp. 381, 26–382, 12 and for the psychogony
ii, pp. 153, 25–154, 1 [Diehl]) or by Philoponus (De Aeternitate Mundi, p. 211, 10-20 and p. 519, 22-25 [Rabe]), and
his "many others" are probably later Platonists like
Harpocration (Scholia Cod. Vat. f. 34ʳ in Proclus, In
Platonis Rem Publicam ii, p. 377, 15-23 [Kroll]), who was
a pupil of Atticus (cf. Proclus, In Platonis Timaeum i, p. 305,
6-7 [Diehl]), the anonymous source of Diogenes Laertius,
iii, 71-72 and 77 (cf. C. Andresen, Logos und Nomos [Berlin,
1955], p. 283), and possibly even Severus with his "cyclical"
interpretation (Proclus, In Platonis Timaeum i, p. 289, 7-13
and ii, pp. 95, 29-96, 1; cf. iii, p. 212, 7-9 [Diehl]) and the
"eclectic" Galen (Compendium Timaei Platonis, p. 39,
11-13 [Kraus-Walzer]). Before Plutarch, however, the
literal interpretation of the Timaeus, on which Aristotle had
insisted (De Caelo 280 a 28-32 and 300 b 16-18, Physics

set apart from one another as being five things different each from each.

4. In any case, what frightens and embarrasses these men in common with most of those who study Plato *a* so that they manipulate and force and twist everything in the belief that they must conceal and deny it as something dreadful and unspeakable is the generation and composition *b* of the universe and of its soul which have not been compounded from ever-lasting or in their present state for infinite time. To this a treatise by itself has been devoted *c*; and now it will suffice to state that these people confuse or rather utterly ruin the reasoning of Plato's case for the gods,*d* which he admits he made against the atheists with a zeal extreme and unsuited to his years.*e* For, if the universe is ungenerated, there is

251 b 17-19, *Metaphysics* 1071 b 37—1072 a 3) but about which Theophrastus was uncertain (*Phys. Opin.*, frag. 11 [*Dox. Graeci*, pp. 485, 17-486, 2]), seems to have been adopted not only by the Peripatetics generally (*cf.* Philoponus, *De Aeternitate Mundi*, p. 135, 9-14 and his quotations from Alexander, *ibid.*, pp. 213, 17-222, 17 [Rabe]) and the Epicureans (*cf.* Cicero, *De Nat. Deorum* i, 18-21 [Usener, *Epicurea*, pp. 245-246]) but also by Cicero (*Timaeus* 5, p. 159, 2-3 [Plasberg]; *cf. Tusc. Disp.* i, 63 and 70 and *Acad. Prior.* ii, 118) and by Philo Judaeus (*De Aeternitate Mundi* 13-16=vi, pp. 76, 16-77, 20 [Cohn-Reiter]), who like Philoponus later appeals to Aristotle as the decisive authority for this interpretation.

b For σύστασιν here *cf.* Plato, *Timaeus* 32 c 5-6 and 36 D 8-9.

c Presumably the lost work, No. 66 in the *Catalogue of Lamprias*, Περὶ τοῦ γεγονέναι κατὰ Πλάτωνα τὸν κόσμον (vii, p. 474 and frag. xxviii on p. 140 [Bernardakis]).

d *Laws* 891 E 4—899 D 4.

e A somewhat inexact reminiscence of *Laws* 907 B 10–c 5, on which see E. B. England, *The Laws of Plato* (Manchester, 1921), ii, p. 503.

(1013) ἐστίν, οἴχεται τῷ Πλάτωνι τὸ πρεσβυτέραν[1] τοῦ
F σώματος τὴν ψυχὴν οὖσαν ἐξάρχειν μεταβολῆς καὶ
κινήσεως πάσης, ἡγεμόνα καὶ πρωτουργόν, ὡς
αὐτὸς εἴρηκεν, ἐγκαθεστῶσαν. τίς δ' οὖσα καὶ
τίνος ὄντος ἡ ψυχὴ τοῦ σώματος προτέρα καὶ πρεσβυτέρα λέγεται γεγονέναι, προϊὼν ὁ λόγος ἐνδεί-
ξεται· τοῦτο γὰρ ἠγνοημένον ἔοικε τὴν πλείστην
ἀπορίαν καὶ ἀπιστίαν παρέχειν τῆς ἀληθοῦς δόξης.

1014   5. Πρῶτον οὖν ἣν ἔχω περὶ τούτων[2] διάνοιαν ἐκ-
θήσομαι, πιστούμενος τῷ εἰκότι καὶ παραμυθού-
μενος, ὡς ἔνεστι, τὸ ἀηθὲς[3] τοῦ λόγου καὶ παρά-
δοξον· ἔπειτα ταῖς[4] λέξεσιν ἐπάξω συνοικειῶν ἅμα
τὴν ἐξήγησιν καὶ τὴν ἀπόδειξιν. ἔχει γὰρ οὕτως
κατά γε τὴν ἐμὴν τὰ πράγματα δόξαν. "κόσμον
τόνδε" φησὶν Ἡράκλειτος "οὔτε τις θεῶν οὔτ'

---

[1] Hubert (cf. 1013 F infra and 1002 F supra; Timaeus
34 c 4-5; Laws 892 c 6 and 896 c 6); πρεσβύτερον -MSS.
(cf. Epinomis 980 D 6 and E 3).
[2] περὶ τούτων -omitted by E, B.
[3] Wyttenbach (after the versions of Turnebus and Amyot);
ἀληθὲς -MSS.   [4] ἔπειτ' αὐταῖς -Bernardakis.

---

[a] Laws 896 A 5-c 8 (n.b. 896 B 1: μεταβολῆς τε καὶ
κινήσεως ἁπάσης αἰτία ἅπασιν) with 892 A 2-c 6 (cf. in [Plato],
Epinomis 980 D 6-E 3 the reference to " the main point ");
and see Plat. Quaest. 1002 E-F supra with page 48, note a.
[b] Cf. infra 1016 c (. . . ἡγεμόνα τοῦ παντὸς ἐγκατέστησαν)
and 1017 B (. . . ἐγκατέστησαν ἡγεμόνα τοῦ κόσμου . . .), in
both places used of the created soul, i.e. the soul after it had
been made rational by god. The title is not quoted from
Plato, but cf. Timaeus 41 c 7 (θεῖον λεγόμενον ἡγεμονοῦν τε)
with Phaedo 80 A 3-9 and 94 c 10-D 2 and ὡς δεσπότιν in
Timaeus 34 c 5 (quoted in 1016 B infra).
[c] This is not an exact quotation either but a reminiscence
of Laws 897 A 4, where the soul's motions are called πρω-
τουργοὶ κινήσεις.

an end of Plato's contention that the soul, being
senior to the body, initiates all change and motion [a]
installed in her position of chief [b] and, as he has said
himself, of primary agent.[c] What is meant by soul
and what by body when she is said to have been
prior and senior to it,[d] this will be made plain by our
account as it proceeds, for it is the failure to understand this that seems to occasion most of the per-
plexity and incredulity about the true doctrine.

5. First, therefore, I shall set down what I think
about these matters, confirming and vindicating as
far as may be by probability [e] what is unusual and
paradoxical about my account [f] ; and then I shall apply the interpretation and the demonstration to the
texts, at the same time bringing them into accord
with one another.[g] For in my opinion this is the
way matters stand. " This universe was not made
by anyone either god or man," says Heraclitus [h]

[d] *Cf. Timaeus* 34 c 4-5 (. . . καὶ γενέσει καὶ ἀρετῇ προτέραν
καὶ πρεσβυτέραν ψυχὴν σώματος . . . συνεστήσατο).

[e] See 1013 B *supra* and page 172, note *a*.

[f] See 1012 B *supra* (διὰ τὸ τοῖς πλείστοις . . . ὑπεναντιοῦσθαι
δεόμενον παραμυθίας), and *cf.* Atticus, frag. vi *init.* (Baudry)
=Eusebius, *Praep. Evang.* xv, 6, 3 (ii, pp. 359, 18–360, 4
[Mras]).

[g] The object of συνοικειῶν is the texts, τὰς λέξεις " understood " from ταῖς λέξεσιν (*cf.* Kühner-Gerth, ii, pp. 575-576),
and not, as Thévenaz has it, the interpretation and the demonstration ; the reconciliation of apparently incompatible
passages (1016 A and E *infra*) is itself taken to be an ἀπόδειξις
of Plutarch's interpretation (1015 F *infra* [chap. 8 *init.*]), a
point overlooked by C. Theander in his treatment of this passage (*Plutarch und die Geschichte* [Lund, 1951], pp. 42-43).

[h] Heraclitus, frag. B 30 (D.-K. and Walzer)=frag. 20
(Bywater), quoted more fully by Clement of Alexandria,
Stromata v, xiv, 104, 2 ; *cf.* M. Marcovich, *R.-E.* Supple-
ment x (1965), cols. 261, 23-37 and 293, 51-66.

(1014) ἀνθρώπων ἐποίησεν,'' ὥσπερ[1] φοβηθεὶς μὴ θεοῦ[2]
ἀπογνόντες ἄνθρωπόν τινα γεγονέναι τοῦ κόσμου
δημιουργὸν ὑπονοήσωμεν.[3] βέλτιον οὖν Πλάτωνι
πειθομένους τὸν μὲν κόσμον ὑπὸ θεοῦ γεγονέναι
λέγειν καὶ ᾄδειν '' ὁ μὲν γὰρ κάλλιστος τῶν γεγο-
B νότων ὁ δ᾽ ἄριστος τῶν αἰτίων ''[4] τὴν δ᾽ οὐσίαν καὶ
ὕλην, ἐξ ἧς γέγονεν, οὐ γενομένην ἀλλὰ ὑποκειμένην ἀεὶ τῷ δημιουργῷ εἰς διάθεσιν καὶ τάξιν
αὐτὴν[5] καὶ πρὸς αὐτὸν ἐξομοίωσιν ὡς δυνατὸν ἦν
ἐμπαρασχεῖν.[6] οὐ γὰρ ἐκ τοῦ μὴ ὄντος ἡ γένεσις
ἀλλ᾽ ἐκ τοῦ μὴ καλῶς μηδὲ ἱκανῶς ἔχοντος, ὡς
οἰκίας καὶ ἱματίου καὶ ἀνδριάντος. ἀκοσμία γὰρ
ἦν τὰ πρὸ τῆς τοῦ[7] κόσμου γενέσεως, ἀκοσμία δ᾽
οὐκ ἀσώματος οὐδ᾽ ἀκίνητος οὐδ᾽ ἄψυχος ἀλλ᾽

---

[1] ὡς -r.

[2] θεὸν -Benseler (De Hiatu, p. 528).

[3] ὑπονοήσομεν -u.

[4] Dübner (from Timaeus 29 A 6); αἰτιῶν -MSS.

[5] Wyttenbach (after Xylander's version); αὐτῆς -MSS.

[6] E, B, e, u; παρασχεῖν -f, m, r, Escor. 72.

[7] τοῦ -omitted by e, u, Escor. 72.

---

[a] Timaeus 29 A 5-6; cf. Plutarch, Quaest. Conviv. 720 B
(ὁ δὲ θεὸς τῶν αἰτίων ἄριστον).

[b] The identification, οὐσία καὶ ὕλη, is Stoic according to
Plutarch himself (see De Comm. Not. 1085 E-F infra with
note a on F, and cf. De Amicorum Multitudine 97 A-B) ;
but he so far adopts this terminology as even to use οὐσία
alone for what he considers to be Platonic ὕλη (e.g. De
Defectu Orac. 430 E [οὐ γὰρ ὁ θεὸς διέστησεν . . . τὴν οὐσίαν
ἀλλὰ . . . αὐτὴν . . . ἔταξε]), for which cf. Diogenes Laertius,
iii, 70 (p. 149, 16-17 [Long]) and Dox. Graeci, p. 447 A 27
(Areius Didymus) in contrast to p. 447 B 22 (Albinus).

[c] See Plat. Quaest. 1001 B supra with note e there.

[d] The Platonic source of this is Timaeus 29 E 3—30 A 3
(cf. 1015 B infra [. . . πάντα βουλόμενος αὐτῷ κατὰ δύναμιν

as if afraid lest by absolving god we get the notion that some human being had been the artificer of the universe. It is better, then, to be persuaded by Plato and, chanting " for it is the fairest of things that have come to be and he the best of causes,"*a* to assert that the universe has been brought into being by god whereas the substance or matter *b* out of which it has come into being did not come to be but was always available to the artificer to whom it submitted itself for disposing and ordering *c* and being made as like to him as was possible,*d* for the source of generation is not what is non-existent *e* but, as in the case of a house and a garment and a statue, what is not in good and sufficient condition. In fact, what preceded the generation of the universe was disorder,*f* disorder not incorporeal or immobile or

ἐξομοιῶσαι]). For the tendency to take that passage as identifying the demiurge with the model of the sensible universe see *Plat. Quaest.* 1007 c-d *supra* (εἰκόνες . . . τοῦ θεοῦ, τῆς μὲν οὐσίας ὁ κόσμος . . .) with page 89, note *b*; cf. H. Dörrie, *Museum Helveticum*, xxvi (1969), pp. 222-223 and *Philomathes : Studies . . . in Memory of Philip Merlan* (The Hague, 1971), pp. 41-42.

e Cf. Plutarch, *Quaest. Conviv.* 731 D (τὴν ἐκ μὴ ὄντος παρανόμως ἐπεισάγουσα γένεσιν τοῖς πράγμασιν) and *Adv. Colotem* 1111 A, 1112 A, and 1113 c ; for the general acceptance of the principle *cf.* Aristotle, *Physics* 187 a 27-29 and 34-35 and 191 b 13-14 and Chalcidius, *Platonis Timaeus*, p. 323, 1-2 (Wrobel)=p. 296, 5-6 (Waszink).

f Cf. *Dion* x, 2 (962 b [. . . ᾧ τὸ πᾶν ἡγουμένῳ πειθόμενον ἐξ ἀκοσμίας κόσμος ἐστί]), *Quaest. Conviv.* 615 F (τὸν μέγαν θεὸν ὑμεῖς πού φατε τὴν ἀκοσμίαν εὐταξίᾳ μεταβαλεῖν εἰς κόσμον . . .), and with the rest of this paragraph *Plat. Quaest.* 1003 A-B *supra* and Chalcidius, *Platonis Timaeus*, pp. 95, 18–96, 4 (Wrobel)=pp. 80, 20–81, 7 (Waszink) with J. C. M. van Winden, *Calcidius on Matter*² (Leiden, 1965), pp. 256-258.

(1014) ἄμορφον μὲν καὶ ἀσύστατον τὸ σωματικὸν ἔμπληκτον δὲ καὶ ἄλογον τὸ κινητικὸν ἔχουσα· τοῦτο
δ᾽ ἦν ἀναρμοστία ψυχῆς οὐκ ἐχούσης λόγον. ὁ γὰρ
θεὸς οὔτε σῶμα τὸ ἀσώματον οὔτε ψυχὴν τὸ ἄψυ-
C χον ἐποίησεν. ἀλλὰ ὥσπερ ἁρμονικὸν ἄνδρα καὶ
ῥυθμικὸν[1] οὐ φωνὴν ποιεῖν οὐδὲ κίνησιν ἐμμελῆ δὲ
φωνὴν καὶ κίνησιν εὔρυθμον ἀξιοῦμεν οὕτως ὁ θεὸς
οὔτε τοῦ σώματος τὸ ἁπτὸν καὶ ἀντίτυπον οὔτε τῆς
ψυχῆς τὸ φανταστικὸν καὶ κινητικὸν αὐτὸς ἐποίησεν ἀμφοτέρας δὲ τὰς ἀρχὰς παραλαβών, τὴν μὲν
ἀμυδρὰν καὶ σκοτεινὴν τὴν δὲ ταραχώδη καὶ ἀνόητον ἀτελεῖς δὲ[2] τοῦ προσήκοντος ἀμφοτέρας καὶ

[1] ἄνδρα, ῥυθμητικὸν (with η changed to ι) -r.
[2] δὲ -omitted by r.

---

[a] In *Timaeus* 50 D 7 and 51 A 7 ἄμορφος is used of the
" receptacle," whereas ἀσύστατον (used by Plato only in a
different and irrelevant context [*Timaeus* 61 A 1]) shows
that Plutarch is here referring to the " precosmic " chaos of
Timaeus 53 A 8–B 4 (see 1016 E-F *infra*).

[b] For the expression *cf.* De Iside 371 B (τῆς ψυχῆς τὸ . . .
ἄλογον καὶ ἔμπληκτον) ; the motivity is τὴν κινητικὴν τῆς ὕλης
καὶ . . . ἄτακτον καὶ ἄλογον οὐκ ἄψυχον δὲ κίνησιν (1015 E
infra).

[c] *i.e.* ψυχὴν τὴν πρὸ τῆς κόσμου γενέσεως πλημμελῶς πάντα
καὶ ἀτάκτως κινοῦσαν (1016 C *infra*). ἀναρμοστία ψυχῆς is
interpretation of τὸ τῆς παλαιᾶς ἀναρμοστίας πάθος (Plato,
Politicus 273 C 7–D 1), quoted by Plutarch at 1015 D *infra* ;
see also 1017 C (ἐκ τῆς προτέρας ἕξεως ἀναρμόστου καὶ ἀλόγου)
and 1029 E *infra* (. . . ἀταξίαν καὶ πλημμέλειαν ἐν ταῖς κινήσεσι
τῆς ἀναρμόστου καὶ ἀνοήτου ψυχῆς . . .).

[d] See 1017 A *infra* (. . . οὐχὶ σώματος ἁπλῶς οὐδ᾽ ὄγκου καὶ
ὕλης) and De E 390 D (σῶμα . . . ἁπτὸν ὄγκον καὶ ἀντίτυπον)
with the definition, σῶμα . . . ὄγκος ἀντίτυπος in [Plutarch],
De Placitis 882 F (*Dox. Graeci*, p. 310 A 10-11) and Sextus,

inanimate but of corporeality amorphous and incoherent [a] and of motivity demented and irrational,[b] and this was the discord of soul that has not reason.[c] For god made neither the incorporeal into body nor the inanimate into soul ; but just as a man skilled in attunement and rhythm is expected not to create sound or movement either but to make sound tuneful and movement rhythmical so god did not himself create either the tangibility and resistance of body [d] or the imagination and motivity of soul,[e] but he took over [f] both the principles, the former vague and obscure [g] and the latter confused and stupid [h] and both of them indefinite and without their appropriate

Adv. Math. i, 21 (p. 603, 12 [Bekker]). From *Timaeus* 31 B 4-6 taken with 62 c 1-2 it could be inferred that corporeality entails tangibility and tangibility resistance (*cf.* Proclus, *In Platonis Timaeum* ii, p. 12, 20-23, p. 13, 2-12, and p. 17, 13-17 [Diehl]) ; but the explicit assertion that ἀντιτυπία is the distinctive property of corporeality as differentiated from the geometrical solid is Epicurean and Stoic (see page 824, note *a* on *De Comm. Not.* 1080 c *infra* [especially Sextus, *Adv. Math.* i, 21 and x, 221-222 ; *S.V.F.* ii, p. 127, 5-11 and p. 162, 29-31]).

[e] See *infra* 1017 A (. . . τινα φανταστικῆς . . . φορᾶς . . . δύναμιν αὐτοκίνητον καὶ ἀεικίνητον) and 1024 A (. . . τὴν . . . φανταστικὴν . . . κίνησιν . . .). *Cf. De Sollertia Animalium* 960 D (πᾶν τὸ ἔμψυχον αἰσθητικὸν εὐθὺς εἶναι καὶ φανταστικὸν πέφυκεν) ; and for Plutarch's conception of τὸ φανταστικόν *cf. Quomodo Quis . . . Sentiat Profectus* 83 A-c, *De Defectu Orac.* 437 E, and *Coriolanus* xxxviii, 4 (232 c).

[f] παραλαβών is from *Timaeus* 30 A 3-5 (*cf.* 68 E 1-3), cited by Plutarch at 1016 D *infra* (see also 1029 E *infra* and *De Defectu Orac.* 430 E [. . . παραλαβὼν ἔταξε . . .]).

[g] *Cf.* Plotinus, *Enn.* II, iv, 10, line 30 (τοῦτο νοεῖ ἀμυδρῶς ἀμυδρὸν καὶ σκοτεινῶς σκοτεινόν . . .) ; in *Timaeus* 49 A 3-4 χαλεπὸν καὶ ἀμυδρὸν εἶδος refers to the receptacle, χώρα.

[h] See *infra* 1015 E (ὑπὸ τῆς ἀνοήτου ταραττομένην αἰτίας) and 1026 c (ἐμφαίνεται . . . αὐτῆς τῷ μὲν ἀλόγῳ τὸ ταραχῶδες).

PLUTARCH'S MORALIA

(1014) ἀορίστους, ἔταξε καὶ διεκόσμησε καὶ συνήρμοσε,
τὸ κάλλιστον ἀπεργασάμενος καὶ τελειότατον ἐξ
αὐτῶν ζῷον. ἡ μὲν οὖν σώματος οὐσία τῆς λεγομένης ὑπ' αὐτοῦ¹ πανδεχοῦς φύσεως ἕδρας τε καὶ
D τιθήνης τῶν γενητῶν² οὐχ ἑτέρα τίς ἐστιν.³
6. Τὴν δὲ τῆς ψυχῆς ἐν Φιλήβῳ μὲν ἀπειρίαν
κέκληκεν, ἀριθμοῦ καὶ λόγου στέρησιν οὖσαν ἐλλεί-

¹ E, B ; ἀπ' αὐτοῦ -e, u, f, m, r, Escor. 72.
² γεννητῶν -f, m, r, Escor. 72.
³ Aldine ; ἐστι -MSS.

ᵃ This idiomatic use of ἀτελές with the genitive is so
frequent in Plutarch that its occurrence here is not likely
to be a reminiscence of the pun in *Phaedrus* 248 B 4 (ἀτελεῖς
τῆς τοῦ ὄντος θέας) or to have any of the profound significance seen in it by Thévenaz (*L'Âme du Monde*, p. 18, n. 47).
ᵇ *Cf. Timaeus*, 30 B 4–c 1, 30 D 1—31 A 1, 32 D 1 f., 68 E
1-6, 69 B 8–c 3, 92 c 5-9 ; with Plutarch's συνήρμοσε *cf.*
Timaeus 36 E 1 (συναγαγὼν προσήρμοττεν).
ᶜ *Timaeus* 51 A 7 (πανδεχές [*cf.* 50 B 6 : τῆς τὰ πάντα
δεχομένης σώματα φύσεως]), 52 B 1 (ἕδραν δὲ παρέχον ὅσα ἔχει
γένεσιν πᾶσιν), 49 A 5-6 (πάσης εἶναι γενέσεως ὑποδοχὴν αὐτὴν
οἷον τιθήνην). It is to describe the rôle of χώρα, itself incorporeal and imperceptible to sense (*Timaeus* 51 A 4–B 2 and
52 A 8–B 2), that Plato uses these terms ; but to Plutarch
they are indifferently designations of ὕλη (see *infra* 1015 D,
1023 A, 1024 c ; *cf. Quaest. Conviv.* 636 D and *De Iside*
372 E-F) and, as in this chapter, of corporeality, with which
ὕλη is thus identified (see 1023 A *infra* : δεξαμενὴν . . .
ἐκείνην [*scil.* σωματικὴν ὕλην] . . . μᾶλλον δὲ σῶμα . . .) and
which is taken to have existed in precosmic disorder (see
1017 A *infra* [οὐχὶ σώματος ἁπλῶς . . . ἦν ὁ θεὸς . . .
δημιουργός] ; *cf. Plat. Quaest.* 1003 A *supra* [. . . τὸ ἄμορφον
σῶμα . . . and ἐκ σώματος ἀτάκτου . . .], and see page 173,
note c *supra*). This precosmic matter Plutarch even calls
perceptible (1024 B *infra* [τὸ αἰσθητὸν . . . ἦν ἄμορφον καὶ
ἀόριστον]), although he had already insisted that Platonic
matter is entirely devoid of quality (1014 F—1015 D *infra*)
and had asserted that ὕλη becomes tangible and visible, *i.e.*

184

perfection,[a] and he ordered and arrayed and fitted
them together, producing from them the living being
supremely fair and perfect.[b] So the substance of
body is none other than what is called by Plato the
omnirecipient nature, abode and nurse of the things
that are subject to generation.[c]

6. As for the substance of soul, in the *Philebus* he
has called it infinitude[d] as being privation of number

perceptible body, only when shaped by participation in the
intelligible (see 1013 c *supra* with *Plat. Quaest.* 1001 D-E).
When in [Plutarch], *De Placitis* 882 c (*Dox. Graeci*, p. 308
A 4-9 and B 5-9 ; *cf.* Theodoret, *Graec. Affect. Curatio*
iv, 13) the Platonic " receptacle " is called ὕλη and characterized as at once corporeal and without quality, it may
be an example of the identification of Platonic " primary
matter " with the Stoic ἄποιον σῶμα (*cf.* Simplicius, *Phys.*,
p. 227, 23-26=*S.V.F.* ii, frag. 326). Others, however, who
identified the receptacle with ὕλη, asserted that, being
without quality, it is neither corporeal nor incorporeal but
potentially corporeal (Albinus, *Epitome* viii, 3 [Louis]=
p. 163, 3-7 [Hermann] ; Apuleius, *De Platone* i, 5=p. 87,
10-20 [Thomas] ; Hippolytus, *Refutatio* i, 19, 3=pp. 19,
13-20, 1 [Wendland] ; Chalcidius, *Platonis Timaeus*,
pp. 342, 16-344, 20 [Wrobel]=pp. 314, 17-316, 13 [Wa-
szink]), an expedient obviously borrowed from Aristotle (*De
Generatione* 329 a 33 ; *cf.* Areius Didymus, *Epitomes Frag.
Phys.* 2 [*Dox. Graeci*, p. 448, 3-12] and " Ocellus Lucanus "
ii, 6 [24]=p. 16, 22-24 [Harder]).

[d] This assertion (see 1014 E *infra* : ἐν δὲ Φιλήβῳ . . .
ἀπειρίαν . . . τῇ ψυχῇ) is justified by nothing in the *Philebus*,
not even by *Philebus* 26 B 6-10 (the limitless appetites of
wantonness and vice) or 27 E 1—28 A 4 and 52 c (pleasures
and pains in the class of τὸ ἄπειρον), for the nature of soul
is not in question there and such " psychic infinitude " is
expressly just one example among many of the ἀπειρία in the
world (*cf. Philebus* 16 c 9-10, 24 A—25 A, 25 c 5-D 1). In
De E 391 B-c the ἄπειρον of the *Philebus*, though taken to
correspond to the κίνησις of the *Sophist*, is said by its combination with the πέρας to constitute πᾶσαν γένεσιν.

(1014) ψεώς¹ τε καὶ ὑπερβολῆς καὶ διαφορᾶς καὶ ἀνομοιότητος ἐν αὑτῇ πέρας οὐδὲν οὐδὲ μέτρον ἔχουσαν·
ἐν δὲ Τιμαίῳ τὴν τῇ ἀμερίστῳ συγκεραννυμένην
φύσει καὶ περὶ τὰ σώματα γίγνεσθαι λεγομένην
μεριστὴν οὔτε πλῆθος ἐν μονάσι καὶ στιγμαῖς οὔτε
μήκη καὶ πλάτη λέγεσθαι νομιστέον, ἃ σώμασι
προσήκει καὶ σωμάτων μᾶλλον ἢ τῆς ψυχῆς ἐστιν,
ἀλλὰ τὴν ἄτακτον καὶ ἀόριστον αὐτοκίνητον δὲ καὶ
κινητικὴν ἀρχὴν ἐκείνην, ἣν πολλαχοῦ μὲν ἀνάγ-
E κην ἐν δὲ τοῖς Νόμοις ἄντικρυς ψυχὴν ἄτακτον
εἴρηκε καὶ κακοποιόν· αὕτη γὰρ ἦν ψυχὴ καθ᾽ ἑαυτήν, νοῦ δὲ καὶ λογισμοῦ καὶ ἁρμονίας ἔμφρονος
μετέσχεν, ἵνα κόσμου ψυχὴ γένηται. καὶ γὰρ τὸ

¹ ἐλλήψεως -r.

ᵃ Timaeus 35 A 1-3.
ᵇ See μεριστὸν δὲ τὸ πλῆθος in the Xenocratean interpretation (1012 E supra) and in 1023 D infra ἐκ μονάδων corresponding to the preceding μήτε τοῖς ἀριθμοῖς as οὐδὲ
γραμμῶν οὐδ᾽ ἐπιφανειῶν corresponds to the preceding μήτε
τοῖς πέρασι. For καὶ στιγμαῖς in a reference to the Xenocratean
interpretation cf. Aristotle, De Anima 409 a 3-7 with
Cherniss, Aristotle's Criticism of Plato . . ., p. 396 and n. 322
and W. Theiler, Aristoteles über die Seele (Berlin, 1959),
p. 101 ad 18, 1.
ᶜ As in the Posidonian interpretation of chap. 22 infra
(see in 1023 B δεξάμενοι τὴν τῶν περάτων οὐσίαν περὶ τὰ σώματα
λέγεσθαι μεριστήν and in 1023 D οὐδὲ γραμμῶν οὐδ᾽ ἐπιφανειῶν
corresponding to μήτε τοῖς πέρασι [see the last note supra]).
For the distinction between the arithmetical and the geometrical interpretations cf. Iamblichus in Stobaeus, Ecl. i,
49, 32 (pp. 363, 26–364, 12 [Wachsmuth]) and Proclus, In
Platonis Timaeum ii, p. 153, 18-25 (Diehl).
ᵈ Cf. Proclus, In Platonis Timaeum ii, pp. 153, 25–154, 1
(Diehl) : . . . μεριστὴν μὲν οὐσίαν λέγουσι τὴν ἄλογον προοῦσαν
τῆς λογικῆς . . ., καθάπερ Πλουτάρχος καὶ Ἀττικός, . . .
ᵉ See 1014 E infra (τὴν ἐν Τιμαίῳ λεγομένην ἀνάγκην) and

and ratio and having in itself no limit or measure of
deficiency and excess and difference and dissimilitude;
and in the *Timaeus* that which is blended together
with the indivisible nature and is said to become
divisible in the case of bodies[a] must be held to mean
neither multiplicity in the form of units and points[b]
nor lengths and breadths,[c] which are appropriate to
bodies and belong to bodies rather than to soul, but
that disorderly and indeterminate but self-moved
and motive principle[d] which in many places he has
called necessity[e] but in the *Laws* has openly called
disorderly and maleficent soul.[f] This, in fact, was
soul in itself[g]; but it partook of intelligence and reason and rational concord[h] that it might become the
soul of the universe. For the aforesaid omnireci-

1015 A *infra* (ὥσπερ ἐν Πολιτικῷ λέγεται . . . ἀνάγκη . . .)
with the notes there.

[f] In 1015 E *infra* Plato is said to have called it ψυχὴν
ἐναντίαν καὶ ἀντίπαλον τῇ ἀγαθουργῷ (*cf. De Iside* 370 F),
which is closer to the terminology of *Laws* 896 D 5—898 c 8
(especially 896 E 5-6, 897 B 3-4, 897 D 1, and 898 c 4-5),
the passage that Plutarch has in mind. For his interpretation of it, which Atticus adopted, *cf.* Proclus, *In Platonis
Timaeum* i, p. 382, 2-12 and p. 391, 8-12 (Diehl); *cf.* also
that of Numenius (p. 94, 6-11 [Leemans] in Chalcidius,
Platonis Timaeus, p. 326, 12-17 (Wrobel)=p. 299, 14-18
(Waszink). In fact, the passages of the *Laws* envisage no
such evil " world-soul " as Plutarch reads into them and
lend no support to the identification of evil soul or of soul at
all with the " necessity " or with the " divisible being " of
the *Timaeus* (*cf.* Cherniss, *Proceedings of the American
Philosophical Society*, xcviii [1954], c [1957], pp. 334-335 ; H. Görgemanns, *Beiträge zur Interpretation von Platons Nomoi* [München,
1960], p. 200, n. 1).

[g] See 1024 A *infra*: νῦν οὐχ ἁπλῶς ψυχὴν. . . .

[h] *Cf. Timaeus* 36 E 6—37 A 1; see 1016 B *infra* and *Plat.
Quaest.* 1001 c with note a and 1003 A *supra*.

PLUTARCH'S MORALIA

(1014) πανδεχὲς καὶ ὑλικὸν ἐκεῖνο μέγεθος μὲν ἐκέκτητο
καὶ διάστημα καὶ χώραν, κάλλους δὲ καὶ μορφῆς
καὶ σχημάτων μετριότητος ἐνδεῶς εἶχεν· ἔλαχε δὲ
τούτων, ἵνα γῆς καὶ θαλάττης καὶ οὐρανοῦ καὶ
ἀστέρων φυτῶν τε καὶ ζῴων παντοδαπὰ σώματα
καὶ ὄργανα γίγνηται[1] κοσμηθέν. οἱ δὲ τὴν ἐν Τιμαίῳ λεγομένην ἀνάγκην ἐν δὲ Φιλήβῳ περὶ τὸ
μᾶλλον καὶ ἧττον ἐλλείψεως[2] καὶ ὑπερβολῆς ἀμε-
τρίαν καὶ ἀπειρίαν τῇ ὕλῃ προστιθέντες ἀλλὰ μὴ
F τῇ ψυχῇ, ποῦ[3] θήσονται τὸ τὴν ὕλην ἀεὶ μὲν ἄμορφον καὶ ἀσχημάτιστον ὑπ' αὐτοῦ λέγεσθαι καὶ πάσης ποιότητος καὶ δυνάμεως οἰκείας ἔρημον εἰκά-

[1] γένηται -Bernardakis.
[2] ἐλλήψεως -r ; [ἐλλείψεως καὶ ὑπερβολῆς] -deleted by
Thévenaz (*L'Âme du Monde*, p. 19, n. 62).
[3] Turnebus ; ψυχῇ γε οὐ -mss. (ψυχῇ . . . vac. 16 -f ; vac.
17 -m ; vac. 10 -r . . . γε οὐ).

---

[a] See 1014 c *supra* with page 185, note c.
[b] For χώρα in this sense of " room " in which to hold
something *cf. De Comm. Not.* 1077 E *infra* (τοῦ διάστασιν
οὐκ ἔχοντος οὐδὲ χώραν ἐν αὐτῷ) and *Quaest. Conviv.* 707 B
(χώραν πλακοῦντι καταλιπεῖν).
[c] *Timaeus* 47 E 4—48 A 7, 56 C 3-7, and 68 E 1—69 A 5.
For the attribution to which Plutarch here objects *cf.*
" Timaeus Locrus " 93 A ; Diogenes Laertius, iii, 75-76
(p. 151, 17-24 [Long]) ; Aëtius i, 26, 3 (*Dox. Graeci*, p. 321 A
18-19 and B 19-20) ; Numenius (p. 97, 1-5 [Leemans]) in
Chalcidius, *Platonis Timaeus*, p. 328, 8-11 (Wrobel)=p. 301,
18-20 (Waszink) and *ibid.*, pp. 299, 14—301, 22 (Wrobel)=
pp. 273, 15—275, 17 (Waszink) ; Plotinus, *Enn.* I, viii, 7,
lines 4-7 ; Proclus, *In Platonis Cratylum*, p. 112, 25-28
(Pasquali). Even Lamprias in *De Defectu Orac.* 435 F—
436 A is made to interpret Plato as οὐκ ἀποστερῶν τὴν ὕλην

pient and material principle [a] too already possessed
magnitude and dimension and spaciousness [b] ; but it
was in want of beauty and shape and regularity of
figures, and these were allotted to it that it might be
reduced to order and then become all the various
bodies and organs of plants and animals and of earth
and sea and sky and stars. Those, however, who
attribute to matter and not to the soul what in the
Timaeus is called necessity [c] and in the *Philebus*
measurelessness and infinitude in the varying degrees
of deficiency and excess,[d] what will they make of
the fact that by Plato matter is said always to be
amorphous and shapeless and devoid of all quality
and potency of its own [e] and is likened to odourless

τῶν ἀναγκαίων πρὸς τὸ γιγνόμενον αἰτιῶν, and in *Quaest.
Conviv.* 720 b-c Plutarch in his own person interpreting the
Timaeus speaks of the universe as perpetually involved in
generation and change διὰ τὴν σύμφυτον ἀνάγκην τοῦ σώματος.

[d] *Philebus* 24 a—25 a and 25 c 5-d 1 (see page 185, note
d *supra*). For the attribution to which Plutarch here ob-
jects *cf.* Hermodorus according to Dercyllides as reported
from Porphyry by Simplicius, *Phys.*, p. 247, 34-35 ; Proclus,
In Platonis Timaeum i, p. 263, 10-14 and p. 384, 29-30
(Diehl) and *De Malorum Subsistentia*, col. 236, 21-24
(Cousin)=§ 35, 19-21 (Boese) ; Aristides Quintilianus, *De
Musica* iii, 11 (p. 110, 2-9 [Winnington-Ingram]).

[e] *Timaeus* 50 b 6-c 2, 50 d 7-e 1, 50 e 4-5, and 51 a 4-7,
where as in the following simile (*Timaeus* 50 e 5-8) the
subject is the receptacle, *i.e.* χώρα, and not ὕλη (see τὸ
πανδεχὲς καὶ ὑλικόν [1014 e *supra*] and page 185, note c
supra). With Plutarch's statement here *cf.* Albinus, *Epitome*
viii, 2 (p. 49, 6-11 [Louis]=p. 162, 30-36 [Hermann]) ; *Dox.
Graeci*, p. 308 a 4-9 and b 5-9 ; and Chalcidius, *Platonis
Timaeus*, p. 356, 8-12 (Wrobel)=p. 326, 3-6 (Waszink).
With his δυνάμεως οἰκείας ἔρημον *cf.* ἀργὸν ἐξ αὐτοῦ (1015 a
infra) ; Proclus, *Elements of Theology* 80 (p. 76, 5-6 [Dodds]) ;
Simplicius, *Categ.*, p. 249, 26-27 ; Olympiodorus, *In Platonis
Phaedonem*, p. 40, 19-21 (Norvin).

(1014) ζεσθαι δ' ἀώδεσιν ἐλαίοις ἃ πρὸς τὰς βαφὰς οἱ
1015 μυρεψοὶ λαμβάνουσιν; οὐ γὰρ οἷόν τε τὸ ἄποιον
καὶ ἀργὸν ἐξ αὐτοῦ καὶ ἀρρεπὲς[1] αἰτίαν κακοῦ καὶ
ἀρχὴν[2] ὑποτίθεσθαι τὸν Πλάτωνα καὶ καλεῖν ἀπειρίαν αἰσχρὰν καὶ κακοποιὸν αὖθις δ' ἀνάγκην πολλὰ
τῷ θεῷ δυσμαχοῦσαν καὶ ἀφηνιάζουσαν.[3] ἡ γὰρ
ἀναστρέφουσα τὸν οὐρανόν, ὥσπερ ἐν Πολιτικῷ
λέγεται, καὶ ἀνελίττουσα πρὸς τοὐναντίον ἀνάγκη
καὶ " σύμφυτος[4] ἐπιθυμία " καὶ " τὸ τῆς πάλαι ποτὲ
φύσεως σύντροφον πολλῆς μετέχον ἀταξίας πρὶν
εἰς τὸν νῦν κόσμον ἀφικέσθαι," πόθεν ἐγγέγονε[5]
τοῖς πράγμασιν εἰ τὸ μὲν ὑποκείμενον ἄποιος[6] ἦν
ὕλη καὶ ἄμοιρον[7] αἰτίας ἁπάσης ὁ δὲ δημιουργὸς
B ἀγαθὸς καὶ πάντα βουλόμενος αὑτῷ κατὰ δύναμιν
ἐξομοιῶσαι τρίτον δὲ παρὰ ταῦτα μηδέν; αἱ γὰρ

---

[1] Ε, Β ; ἀρεπὲς -e, u, f, m, r, Escor. 72.
[2] καὶ ἀρχὴν καὶ ἀρχὴν -f.
[3] ἀφανίζουσαν -r.
[4] συμφύτοις -e, u (corrected in margin).
[5] Ε, Β, u ; ἐγέγονε -e ; ἐγεγόνει -f, m, r, Escor. 72.
[6] ἄποιος -B ; ἄποιον -E ; ἄποιον -all other mss.
[7] ἄμοιρος -Wyttenbach.

---

[a] This substitution for τὰ δεξόμενα ὑγρὰ τὰς ὀσμάς of
Timaeus 50 ε 7-8 is made by Albinus too in *Epitome* viii, 2
(p. 49, 12-13 [Louis]=p. 162, 37 f. [Hermann]). For oil as
the base of perfumes *cf.* with Plutarch, *De Iside* 374 ε and
Quaest. Conviv. 661 c especially Theophrastus, *De Odoribus*
§§ 14-20 and Pliny, *N.H.* xiii, 7.

[b] The terminology is Stoic. See *infra De Stoic. Repug.*
1054 A and *De Comm. Not.* 1076 c-d with note c there ; and
cf. De Iside 374 ε, where ὕλη, which in 372 f was characterized as ῥέπουσα ἀεὶ πρὸς τὸ βέλτιον ἐξ ἑαυτῆς, is expressly used *not* in the Stoic sense of ἄψυχόν τι σῶμα καὶ
ἄποιον ἀργόν τε καὶ ἄπρακτον ἐξ ἑαυτοῦ.

[c] This expression, not used by Plato, combines Plutarch's

190

oils [a] which makers of perfume take for their in-
fusions ? For what is without quality and of itself
inert and without propensity [b] Plato cannot suppose
to be cause and principle of evil and call ugly and
maleficent infinitude [c] and again necessity which is
largely refractory and recalcitrant to god.[d] In fact,
the necessity and " congenital desire " whereby the
heaven is reversed, as is said in the *Politicus*,[e] and
rolled back in the opposite direction and " its
ancient nature's inbred character which had a large
share of disorder before reaching the state of the
present universe," [f] whence did these come to be in
things if the substrate was unqualified matter and
so void of all causality and the artificer good and so
desirous of making all things resemble himself as far
as possible [g] and third besides these there was
nothing ? For we are involved in the difficulties of

interpretations of the *Philebus* and the *Laws* in 1014 D-E
supra (see pages 185, note *d* and 187, note *f*). In contrast
to Plutarch *cf.* Proclus, *In Platonis Timaeum* i, p. 175, 8-10
(Diehl) with Plotinus, *Enn.* ii, iv, 16, lines 19-24 and Olympiodorus, *In Platonis Phaedonem*, p. 40, 19-20 (Norvin).

[d] *Cf. De Iside* 371 A-B (. . . πρὸς τὴν βελτίονα ἀεὶ δυσμαχοῦσαν . . . and . . . ἀφηνιασμοὶ Τυφῶνος) ; *De Virtute
Morali* 442 A-B and 451 D.

[e] *Politicus* 272 E 5-6 (ἀνελίττουσα from ἀνείλιξις in 270
D 3 and 286 B 9), for the εἱμαρμένη of which Plutarch here
substitutes ἀνάγκη, a substitution which he may have thought
justified by *Politicus* 269 D 2-3 (. . . αὐτῷ τὸ ἀνάπαλιν ἰέναι
. . . ἐξ ἀνάγκης ἔμφυτον γέγονε) or on the ground alleged in
1026 B *infra* (. . . ἀνάγκην, ἣν εἱμαρμένην οἱ πολλοὶ καλοῦσιν).

[f] *Politicus* 273 B 4-6 with slight adaptation but with the
significant omission of the immediately preceding τὸ σωματοειδὲς τῆς συγκράσεως (contrast *Quaest. Conviv.* 720 B-C , . .·
διὰ τὴν σύμφυτον ἀνάγκην τοῦ σώματος . . ., cited in note *c* on
1014 E *supra*).

[g] *Timaeus* 29 E 1—30 A 3 (see note *d* on 1014 B *supra*).

PLUTARCH'S MORALIA

(1015) Στωικαὶ καταλαμβάνουσιν ἡμᾶς ἀπορίαι, τὸ κακὸν
ἐκ τοῦ μὴ ὄντος ἀναιτίως καὶ ἀγενήτως¹ ἐπεισ-
άγοντας, ἐπεὶ τῶν γ᾽ ὄντων οὔτε τἀγαθὸν οὔτε τὸ
ἄποιον εἰκός ἐστιν οὐσίαν κακοῦ καὶ γένεσιν παρασχεῖν. ἀλλὰ ταὐτὸ Πλάτων² οὐκ ἔπαθε τοῖς ὕστερον, οὐδὲ παριδὼν ὡς ἐκεῖνοι τὴν μεταξὺ τῆς ὕλης
καὶ τοῦ θεοῦ τρίτην ἀρχὴν καὶ δύναμιν ὑπέμεινε
τῶν λόγων τὸν³ ἀτοπώτατον, ἐπεισόδιον οὐκ οἶδα
ὅπως ποιοῦντα τὴν τῶν κακῶν φύσιν ἀπ᾽ αὐτο-
μάτου κατὰ συμβεβηκός. Ἐπικούρῳ μὲν γὰρ οὐδ᾽
C ἀκαρὲς ἐγκλῖναι τὴν ἄτομον συγχωροῦσιν, ὡς ἀν-
αίτιον ἐπεισάγοντι⁴ κίνησιν ἐκ τοῦ μὴ ὄντος· αὐτοὶ
δὲ κακίαν καὶ κακοδαιμονίαν τοσαύτην ἑτέρας τε
περὶ σῶμα μυρίας ἀτοπίας καὶ δυσχερείας, αἰτίαν
ἐν ταῖς ἀρχαῖς οὐκ ἐχούσας, κατ᾽ ἐπακολούθησιν
γεγονέναι λέγουσιν.

7. Ὁ δὲ Πλάτων οὐχ οὕτως, ἀλλὰ τήν γε⁵ ὕλην

¹ ἀγεννήτως -f, m, r.   ² πλάττων -Escor. 72.
³ τὸ -f, m, r.   ⁴ ἐπειάγοντες -r.
⁵ ἀλλά γε καὶ -f, m, r.

ᵃ See De Comm. Not. 1076 c-d infra ; cf. De Iside 369 d
(εἰ γὰρ οὐδὲν ἀναιτίως πέφυκε γενέσθαι αἰτίαν δὲ κακοῦ τἀγαθὸν
οὐκ ἂν παράσχοι, δεῖ γένεσιν ἰδίαν καὶ ἀρχὴν ὥσπερ ἀγαθοῦ καὶ
κακοῦ τὴν φύσιν ἔχειν) and Numenius (p. 93, 13-16 [Lee-
mans]) in Chalcidius, Platonis Timaeus, pp. 325, 22–326,
3 (Wrobel)=p. 299, 5-7 (Waszink).
ᵇ For οὐδέ in this sense cf. W. J. Verdenius, Mnemosyne,
4 Ser. vi (1953), p. 109 ; vii (1954), p. 68 ; and ix (1956),
p. 249.
ᶜ This " third principle " is ψυχὴ καθ᾽ ἑαυτήν (1014 e
supra), whereas the τρίτην τινὰ μεταξὺ φύσιν . . . of De Iside
370 f—371 a is Platonic " matter," there said to be οὐκ
ἄψυχον . . . οὐδ᾽ ἀκίνητον ἐξ αὑτῆς.
ᵈ i.e. the Stoics, who themselves ὅμοιόν τε εἶναί φασιν καὶ
192

GENERATION OF THE SOUL, 1015

the Stoics by bringing in evil without cause and
process of generation out of what is non-existent,[a]
since of things that do exist neither what is good nor
what is without quality is likely to have occasioned
evil's being or coming to be. The same thing did not
happen to Plato, however, as did to those who came
later, for [b] he did not as they did by overlooking the
third principle and potency, which is intermediate
between matter and god,[c] acquiesce in the most
absurd of doctrines that makes the nature of evils
supervenient I know not how in a spontaneously
accidental fashion. The fact is that they,[d] while
conceding to Epicurus not even the slightest swerve
of the atom, on the ground that he thus brings in
uncaused motion from what is non-existent,[e] do
themselves assert that vice and so much unhappiness
as there is and countless other monstrous and dis-
agreeable features of body are without any cause
among the principles but have arisen by way of
incidental consequence.[f]

7. This is not Plato's way, however ; but, exempt-

ὁμοίως ἀδύνατον τὸ ἀναιτίως τῷ γίνεσθαί τι ἐκ μὴ ὄντος (Alexander, *De Fato*, p. 192, 14-15 [Bruns] = *S. V.F.* ii, p. 273,
14-15). See also next note *infra*.

[e] Usener, *Epicurea*, p. 201, 21-23 (in frag. 281). *Cf.* the
passages cited in note *a* on *De Stoic. Repug.* 1045 b-c and
in note *c* on 1050 c *infra*, among them especially *De Sollertia
Animalium* 964 c ; Cicero, *De Fato* 18, 20, and 22-23 ;
Galen, *De Placitis Hippoc. et Plat.* iv, 4 (p. 361, 14-16
[Müller]).

[f] *Cf. S. V.F.* i, p. vi, lines 7-10 and ii, frag. 1170 (Aulus
Gellius, vii, i, 7-13) ; Marcus Aurelius, vi, 36 ; [Plutarch],
Consolatio ad Apollonium 117 d-e (. . . οὔτε τῶν κατὰ
προηγούμενον λόγον συμβαινόντων οὔτε τῶν κατ' ἐπακολούθησιν);
Philo Jud. in Eusebius, *Praep. Evang.* viii, 14, 45-59 (espe-
cially i, p. 474, 20-22 and p. 476, 7-8 [Mras]).

(1015) διαφορᾶς ἁπάσης ἀπαλλάττων καὶ τοῦ θεοῦ τὴν
τῶν κακῶν αἰτίαν ἀπωτάτω τιθέμενος ταῦτα περὶ
τοῦ κόσμου γέγραφεν ἐν τῷ Πολιτικῷ. "παρὰ
μὲν γὰρ τοῦ ξυνθέντος[1] πάντα τὰ καλὰ[2] κέκτηται·
παρὰ δὲ τῆς ἔμπροσθεν ἕξεως ὅσα χαλεπὰ καὶ
ἄδικα ἐν οὐρανῷ γίγνεται, ταῦτ' ἐξ ἐκείνης αὐτός
D τε ἔχει καὶ τοῖς ζῴοις ἐναπεργάζεται." καὶ μικρὸν ἔτι προελθὼν "προϊόντος δέ" φησι "τοῦ χρόνου[3] καὶ λήθης ἐγγιγνομένης ἐν αὐτῷ μᾶλλον δυναστεύει[4] τὸ τῆς παλαιᾶς ἀναρμοστίας πάθος" καὶ
κινδυνεύει "διαλυθεὶς εἰς τὸν τῆς ἀνομοιότητος
ἄπειρον ὄντα τόπον" δῦναι πάλιν. ἀνομοιότης δὲ
περὶ τὴν ὕλην, ἄποιον καὶ ἀδιάφορον οὖσαν, οὐκ
ἔστιν. ἀλλὰ μετὰ πολλῶν ἄλλων καὶ Εὔδημος
ἀγνοήσας κατειρωνεύεται τοῦ Πλάτωνος ὡς οὐκ
εὖ τὴν[5] πολλάκις ὑπ' αὐτοῦ μητέρα καὶ τιθήνην
προσαγορευομένην αἰτίαν κακῶν καὶ ἀρχὴν[6] ἀποφαί-

---

[1] ξυνθέντος -r ; ξελθέντος -e, u, f, m, Escor. 72, Aldine ;
τοῦ . . . vac. 10 -E ; vac. 6 -B . . . θέντος -E, B.

[2] πάντα τὰ καλὰ -mss. (so Cod. B, Vat. 225, and Ven. 185
of Plato ; and Clement, Stromata iii, iii, 19, 5) ; πάντα καλὰ
-all other mss. of Plato (so Theodoret, Proclus, Philoponus,
Simplicius).

[3] δὲ τοῦ χρόνου φησὶ -B.

[4] μᾶλλον καὶ δυναστεύει -Plato, Politicus 273 c 7.

[5] ὡς οὐκ εὖ τὴν -e, u ; ὡς οὐκ αὐτὴν -f, m, r, Escor. 72,
Aldine ; ὡς . . . vac. 7-8 . . . τὴν -E, B.

[6] E, B ; κακῶν ιζ̅' ἀρχὴν -e, u, Escor. 72 (ῥίζαν in margin) ;
κακῶν ῥίζαν ἀρχὴν -f, m, r, Aldine.

---

[a] Politicus 273 b 6–c 2.
[b] Politicus 273 c 6–d 1.

ing matter from all differentiation and putting the
cause of evils at the farthest remove from god, he
has written about the universe as follows in the
Politicus [a] : " For it has got from him who constructed
it all it has that is fair but from its previous state
whatever troubles and iniquities occur in the universe
—from that source it has these itself and produces
them in its living beings." And a little further on
still he says : " But with the passage of time and the
setting in of forgetfulness the effect of the ancient
discord becomes more potent," [b] and it is in danger
of sinking again " dissolved into the boundless region
of dissimilitude." [c] Dissimilitude, however, is not
connected with matter, since matter is without
quality or differentiation.[d] Yet from misapprehen-
sion shared with many others even Eudemus rallies
Plato for not doing right in declaring her to be the
cause and principle of evils whom he frequently calls
by the name of mother and nurse.[e] In fact, while

[c] *Politicus* 273 d 6–e 1. In Plato's sentence πάλιν goes
with the words that follow (πάλιν ἔφεδρος . . . γιγνόμενος)
and not with the preceding δύῃ as in Plutarch's paraphrase,
κινδυνεύει . . . δῦναι πάλιν. On the other hand, all the mss.
of Plato like all those of Plutarch have τόπον (*cf.* also
Plotinus, *Enn.* i, viii, 13, lines 16-17 ; Eusebius, *Praep.
Evang.* xi, 34, 4) and not the πόντον adopted by Burnet,
Taylor, and Diès on the authority of Proclus and Simplicius
(*cf.* the articles listed in *Lustrum*, iv [1959], p. 148 [# 746]
and v [1960], p. 602 [# 1987]).

[d] See 1014 f *supra* with note *e* there.

[e] Eudemus, frag. 49 (Wehrli) ; *cf.* U. Schöbe, *Quaestiones
Eudemeae* (Diss. Halle, 1931), pp. 43-45 and Cherniss,
Aristotle's Criticism of Plato . . ., note 62 (pp. 95-97,
especially p. 97). Eudemus is called by Simplicius (*Phys.*,
p. 411, 15-16 ; *cf.* p. 133, 21-22) the most genuine disciple
of Aristotle.

PLUTARCH'S MORALIA

(1015) νοντος. ὁ γὰρ Πλάτων μητέρα μὲν καὶ τιθήνην καλεῖ
E τὴν ὕλην αἰτίαν δὲ κακοῦ τὴν κινητικὴν τῆς ὕλης
καὶ περὶ τὰ σώματα γιγνομένην μεριστὴν ἄτακτον
καὶ ἄλογον οὐκ ἄψυχον δὲ κίνησιν, ἣν ἐν Νόμοις
ὥσπερ εἴρηται ψυχὴν ἐναντίαν καὶ ἀντίπαλον τῇ
ἀγαθουργῷ προσεῖπε. ψυχὴ γὰρ αἰτία κινήσεως καὶ
ἀρχή, νοῦς δὲ τάξεως καὶ συμφωνίας περὶ κίνησιν.
ὁ γὰρ θεὸς οὐκ ἀνέστησε τὴν ὕλην ἀργοῦσαν ἀλλ᾽
ἔστησεν ὑπὸ τῆς ἀνοήτου ταραττομένης¹ αἰτίας· οὐδ᾽
ἀρχὰς τῇ φύσει μεταβολῆς καὶ παθῶν παρέσχεν,
ἀλλ᾽ οὔσης ἐν πάθεσι παντοδαποῖς καὶ μεταβολαῖς
ἀτάκτοις ἐξεῖλε τὴν πολλὴν ἀοριστίαν καὶ πλημμέλειαν ἁρμονίᾳ καὶ ἀναλογίᾳ καὶ ἀριθμῷ χρώμενος
ὀργάνοις, ὧν ἔργον ἐστὶν οὐ μεταβολῇ καὶ κινήσει²
F ἑτερότητος πάθη καὶ διαφορᾶς³ παρέχειν τοῖς

¹ πραττομένην -f.
² ἔργον μεταβολὴν καὶ κίνησιν -r (μεταβολὴν καὶ κίνησιν -f¹
[in margin], m¹ [in margin]).
³ διαφορᾶς -H. C. (" diversitatis et differentiae " -Turne-
bus) : διαφορὰς -mss.

ᵃ For " mother " cf. Timaeus 50 D 2-4 and 51 A 4-5 and
for " nurse " Timaeus 49 A 5-6, 52 D 4-E 1, and 88 D 6.
With Plutarch's statement cf. " Timaeus Locrus " 94 A (τὰν
δ᾽ ὕλαν ἐκμαγεῖον καὶ ματέρα τιθάναν τε . . .) ; Albinus,
Epitome viii, 2 (p. 49, 1-2 [Louis] = p. 162, 25-27 [Hermann]) ;
Chalcidius, Platonis Timaeus, p. 304, 4-7 and p. 336, 18-19
(Wrobel) = pp. 277, 18–278, 2 and p. 309, 11-12 (Waszink) ;
and see page 185, note c supra.
ᵇ Timaeus 35 A 2-3 as interpreted in 1014 D supra (see
page 187, notes a and d).
ᶜ See 1014 D-E supra with note f there.
ᵈ Cf. Plato, Phaedrus 245 c 5—246 A 2 and Laws 896 A 5-
B 3 (see supra 1013 c with note b and 1013 F with note a) ;
and for the argument that follows here cf. Galen, Compendium Timaei Platonis iv b (pp. 43, 7–44, 13 [Kraus-

196

Plato calls matter mother and nurse,[a] what he calls the cause of evil is the motion that moves matter and becomes divisible in the case of bodies,[b] the disorderly and irrational but not inanimate motion, which in the *Laws*, as has been said,[c] he called soul contrary and adverse to the one that is beneficent. For soul is cause and principle of motion,[d] but intelligence of order and consonance in motion[e]; and the fact is that god did not arouse matter from torpor[f] but put a stop to its being disturbed by the mindless cause[g] and did not impart to nature the origins of change and of modifications but from her, who was involved in modifications of every kind and in disorderly changes,[h] removed the vast indefinitude and jangle, using as tools concord and proportion and number,[i] the function of which is not by change and motion to impart to things the modifications of

Walzer]) and Proclus, *In Platonis Timaeum* i, p. 382, 2-12 (Diehl).

[e] For the relation of τάξις in motion to νοῦς and the lack of it to ἄνοια *cf.* Plato, *Laws* 898 A 8–B 8. The distinction between ἁπλῶς κίνησις and κίνησις ἐν τάξει is drawn in *Plat. Quaest.* 1007 D *supra*.

[f] *Cf.* 1015 A *supra* (ἀργόν) with note b there; and for what follows see 1014 B-C *supra* and *Plat. Quaest.* 1003 A with notes.

[g] See 1014 c *supra* (τὴν δὲ ταραχώδη καὶ ἀνόητον) and 1016 c *infra* (ψυχὴν τὴν ... πλημμελῶς πάντα καὶ ἀτάκτως κινοῦσαν).

[h] *Cf.* Plato, *Timaeus* 52 D 4–E 1 (τὴν δὲ δὴ γενέσεως τιθήνην ... ὅσα ἄλλα ... πάθη ... πάσχουσαν παντοδαπὴν μὲν ἰδεῖν φαίνεσθαι ...) with 1024 c *infra* (γένεσιν ... τὴν ἐν μεταβολαῖς καὶ κινήσεσιν οὐσίαν); *Quaest. Conviv.* 720 c (ἐν γενέσει καὶ μετατροπῇ καὶ πάθεσι παντοδαποῖς ...).

[i] *Cf. Quaest. Conviv.* 720 B (ἐβούλετ' οὖν μηδὲν ... ὑπολιπεῖν ... ἀόριστον ἀλλὰ κοσμῆσαι λόγῳ καὶ μέτρῳ καὶ ἀριθμῷ τὴν φύσιν ...); and see 1013 c *supra* with the passages referred to in page 175, note c, especially 1029 D-E and 1030 c in chap. 33 *infra*.

(1015) πράγμασιν ἀλλὰ μᾶλλον ἀπλανῆ καὶ στάσιμα καὶ
τοῖς κατὰ ταὐτὰ[1] ὡσαύτως ἔχουσιν ὅμοια ποιεῖν. ἡ
μὲν οὖν διάνοια τοιαύτη κατά γε τὴν ἐμὴν δόξαν
τοῦ Πλάτωνος.

8. Ἀπόδειξις δὲ πρώτη μὲν ἡ τῆς λεγομένης καὶ
δοκούσης αὐτοῦ πρὸς ἑαυτὸν ἀσυμφωνίας καὶ δια-
1016 φορᾶς λύσις. οὐδὲ γὰρ σοφιστῇ κραιπαλῶντι, πόθεν γε δὴ Πλάτωνι, τοιαύτην ἄν τις ἀναθείη περὶ
οὖς ἐσπουδάκει μάλιστα τῶν λόγων ταραχὴν καὶ
ἀνωμαλίαν ὥστε τὴν αὐτὴν φύσιν ὁμοῦ καὶ ἀγένητον[2] ἀποφαίνειν[3] καὶ γενομένην, ἀγένητον[4] μὲν ἐν
Φαίδρῳ τὴν ψυχὴν ἐν δὲ Τιμαίῳ γενομένην.[5] ἡ
μὲν οὖν ἐν Φαίδρῳ διάλεκτος ὀλίγου δεῖν ἅπασι
διὰ στόματός ἐστι, τῷ ἀγενήτῳ[6] τὸ ἀνώλεθρον τῷ[7]
δ' αὐτοκινήτῳ πιστουμένη τὸ ἀγένητον[8] αὐτῆς· ἐν
δὲ Τιμαίῳ "τὴν δὲ[9] ψυχὴν" φησιν "οὐχ ὡς νῦν
ὑστέραν ἐπιχειροῦμεν λέγειν οὕτως ἐμηχανήσατο
καὶ ὁ θεὸς νεωτέραν—οὐ γὰρ ἂν ἄρχεσθαι πρεσβύ-
B τερον ὑπὸ νεωτέρου συνέρξας[10] εἴασεν—ἀλλά πως[11]

[1] κατὰ τὸ αὐτὸ -r.   [2] ἀγέννητον -f, m, r.
[3] ἀποφαίνει -r.
[4] ἀγέννητον -f, m, r.
[5] Wyttenbach ; γινομένην -MSS. (γιγνομένην -r).
[6] ἀγεννήτῳ -f, m, r.
[7] τὸ -u.
[8] ἀγέννητον -f, m, r.
[9] δὲ -omitted by B ; δὲ δὴ -Plato (Timaeus 34 b 10).
[10] Stephanus from Timaeus 34 c 2 ; ξυνέρξας -f, m, r ;
συνέρξεν -e (sic) ; συνεῖρξεν -u ; συνεῖρξ . . . vac. 3 -E, vac.
2 -B ; συναρ . . . vac. 3 -Escor. 72 ; συνῆρξεν -Aldine.
[11] ἀλλὰ πῶς -E, B, e, u, Escor. 72.

[a] For this collocation see supra Plat. Quaest. 1002 d,
note b.
[b] See supra 1014 A, note g.
[c] Cf. Proclus, In Platonis Timaeum ii, p. 119, 29-30

198

diversity and difference [a] but rather to make them
inerrant and stable and similar to the entities that
are invariably identical. Such, then, in my opinion
is Plato's meaning.

8. A first proof of it is that it resolves what is
called and seems to be his inconsistency and self-
contradiction.[b] For one would not attribute even to
a drunken sophist and it is nonsense then to attribute
to Plato in regard to the doctrines about which he
had been most seriously concerned such confusion
and capriciousness as to declare of the same entity
both that it is unsubject to generation and that it
did come to be, in the *Phaedrus* that the soul is
unsubject to generation and in the *Timaeus* that it
came to be.[c] Now, almost everyone has at the tip of
his tongue the discourse in the *Phaedrus* [d] confirming
the soul's indestructibility by the fact that it is not
subject to generation and its not being subject to
generation by the fact that it is self-moved ; but in
the *Timaeus* [e] he says : " The soul, however, now
later in the account that we are attempting, was not
thus junior also in god's devising—for he would not
have permitted the senior of those that he had
coupled to be ruled by the junior—, but we, as we

(Diehl) ; Chalcidius, *Platonis Timaeus*, pp. 91, 9-12 and
92, 3-11 (Wrobel)=pp. 76, 10-12 and 77, 13-20 (Waszink).
[d] *Phaedrus* 245 c 5—246 a 2. With Plutarch's summary
of the argument here *cf.* Albinus, *Epitome* xxv, 4 (p. 121,
3-6 [Louis]=p. 178, 12-15 [Hermann]) ; Hermias, *In Platonis
Phaedrum*, p. 115, 1-3 (Couvreur) ; and Macrobius, *In
Somnium Scipionis* ii, xiii, 12.
[e] *Timaeus* 34 b 10—35 a 1. See 1013 f *supra* and the
notes there ; and observe that Plutarch in his quotation
here stops short of ἐκ τῶνδε . . ., which modifies συνεστήσατο
in *Timaeus* 35 a 1.

(1016) ἡμεῖς πολὺ μετέχοντες¹ τοῦ προστυχόντος τε² καὶ
εἰκῇ ταύτῃ πῃ καὶ λέγομεν, ὁ δὲ καὶ γενέσει καὶ
ἀρετῇ προτέραν³ ⟨καὶ πρεσβυτέραν⟩⁴ τὴν⁵ ψυχὴν
σώματος ὡς δεσπότιν καὶ ἄρξουσαν ἀρξομένου
συνεστήσατο." καὶ πάλιν, εἰπὼν ὡς " αὐτὴ ἐν
ἑαυτῇ στρεφομένη θείαν ἀρχὴν ἤρξατο ἀπαύστου
καὶ ἔμφρονος βίου," "τὸ μὲν δὴ σῶμά" φησιν
" ὁρατὸν οὐρανοῦ⁶ γέγονεν, αὐτὴ⁷ δ' ἀόρατος μὲν⁸
λογισμοῦ δὲ μετέχουσα καὶ ἁρμονίας ψυχὴ τῶν
νοητῶν ἀεί τ' ὄντων ὑπὸ τοῦ ἀρίστου ἀρίστη γενομένη τῶν γεννηθέντων."⁹ ἐνταῦθα γὰρ τὸν μὲν
θεὸν ἄριστον εἰπὼν τῶν ἀεὶ ὄντων τὴν δὲ ψυχὴν
C ἀρίστην τῶν γεννηθέντων,¹⁰ σαφεστάτῃ ταύτῃ τῇ
διαφορᾷ καί ἀντιθέσει τὸ ἀίδιον αὐτῆς καὶ τὸ
ἀγένητον¹¹ ἀφῄρηται.

9. Τίς οὖν τούτων ἐπανόρθωσις ἑτέρα πλὴν ἧς
αὐτὸς δίδωσι τοῖς δέχεσθαι βουλομένοις; ἀγένη-
τον¹² μὲν γὰρ ἀποφαίνει ψυχὴν τὴν πρὸ τῆς κόσμου
γενέσεως πλημμελῶς πάντα καὶ ἀτάκτως κινοῦσαν

¹ μετέχοντες πολὺ -r.   ² τε -omitted by r.
³ πρότερον -r.
⁴ ⟨. . .⟩ added by Turnebus from *Timaeus* 34 c 4-5 (*cf.*
1013 F *supra*).
⁵ τὴν -not in *Timaeus* 34 c 5.
⁶ ὁρατὸν τοῦ οὐρανοῦ -f, m, r.
⁷ αὐτὴ -B. Müller from *Timaeus* 36 e 6 ; αὕτη -mss.
(αὕτη -u).
⁸ αὕτη μὲν ἀόρατος -f, m, r ; αὕτη μὲν ἀόρατος μὲν -Escor. 72.
⁹ γενηθέντων -E, B, u, Escor. 72.
¹⁰ f, m ; γεννηθέν -r (at end of line) ; γεννηθέντων -E, B, e, u,
Escor. 72.
¹¹ ἀγέννητον -f, m, r.   ¹² ἀγέννητον -f, m, r.

ᵃ *Timaeus* 36 e 3-4. Plutarch stops short of πρὸς τὸν
σύμπαντα χρόνον which in the *Timaeus* follows ἔμφρονος βίου.
ᵇ *Timaeus* 36 e 5—37 a 2.

partake largely of the casual and random, express ourselves in this way too, whereas he constructed the soul prior ⟨and senior⟩ to body in generation and excellence to be mistress and ruler of it as her subject." And again, after having said *a* that " herself revolving within herself she made a divine beginning of ceaseless and rational life," he says *b* : " So the body of heaven has come to be visible ; but soul herself, invisible but participant in reason and concord,*c* is become best of the things generated by the best of intelligible and everlasting beings."*d* For here he has called god best of everlasting beings but the soul best of the things generated, and by this most manifest distinction and opposition he has removed from her the character of being everlasting and ungenerated.

9. What way of adjusting these statements *e* is there, then, other than what he provides himself for those who will accept it ? For unsubject to generation is said of the soul that before the generation of the universe keeps all things in disorderly and jangling motion,*f* but come to be and so subject to

---

c See *supra* 1014 E and note *h* there.

d What follows shows that Plutarch construed the passage in this way, the second of the three ways considered by Proclus (*In Platonis Timaeum* ii, p. 294, 1-18 [Diehl]) ; see also *Plat. Quaest.* 1002 B (ὁ γὰρ θεὸς ἐν τοῖς νοητοῖς) with note *d* on page 42.

e See 1014 A, note *g* supra on συνοικειῶν.

f Cf. κινούμενον πλημμελῶς καὶ ἀτάκτως in *Timaeus* 30 A 3-5 (paraphrased in 1016 D *infra*), the cause of which motion according to Plutarch must have been precosmic soul (see 1015 E *supra* with notes *d* and *g* there ; cf. Proclus, *In Platonis Timaeum* i, p. 382, 3-4 and p. 391, 8-12 [Diehl] and Chalcidius, *Platonis Timaeus*, pp. 326, 15-17 and 328, 16-20 [Wrobel]=pp. 299, 16-18 and 302, 3-6 [Waszink]).

(1016) γενομένην[1] δὲ καὶ γενητὴν[2] πάλιν ἦν ὁ θεὸς ἔκ τε
ταύτης καὶ τῆς μονίμου τε καὶ ἀρίστης οὐσίας ἐκείνης ἔμφρονα[3] καὶ τεταγμένην ἀπεργασάμενος καὶ[4]
καθάπερ εἶδος καὶ τῷ αἰσθητικῷ τὸ νοερὸν καὶ τῷ
κινητικῷ τὸ τεταγμένον ἀφ᾽ αὑτοῦ[5] παρασχὼν ἡγε-
D μόνα τοῦ παντὸς ἐγκατέστησεν. οὕτως γὰρ καὶ τὸ
σῶμα τοῦ κόσμου πῇ μὲν ἀγένητον ἀποφαίνει πῇ
δὲ γενητόν[6]· ὅταν μὲν γὰρ εἴπῃ πᾶν ὅσον ἦν ὁρατὸν
οὐχ ἡσυχίαν ἄγον ἀλλὰ κινούμενον ἀτάκτως τὸν
θεὸν παραλαβόντα διακοσμεῖν καὶ πάλιν τὰ τέσσαρα γένη, πῦρ καὶ ὕδωρ καὶ γῆν καὶ ἀέρα, πρὶν ἢ[7]
τὸ πᾶν ἀπ᾽ αὐτῶν[8] διακοσμηθὲν γενέσθαι, σεισμὸν
ἐμποιεῖν[9] τῇ ὕλῃ καὶ[10] ὑπ᾽ ἐκείνης τινάσσεσθαι διὰ
τὴν ἀνωμαλίαν, ὄντα που ποιεῖ καὶ ὑποκείμενα τὰ

----

[1] γιγνομένην -r. 　　　　　　[2] γεννητὴν -f, m, r.
[3] ἔμφρονον -r.
[4] καὶ -omitted by B and deleted by Dübner.
[5] B. Müller (" de suo " -Turnebus ; " ex se " -Dübner) ;
ἀπ᾽ αὐτοῦ -mss.
[6] ἀγέννητον . . . γεννητόν -f, m, r.
[7] πρὶν καὶ -Timaeus 53 A 7.
[8] ἀπ᾽ αὐτῶν -H. C. (cf. De Defectu Orac. 430 D [ἐπ᾽ αὐτῶν
-mss.] and Babbitt ad loc. [L.C.L. v, p. 458, n. 5]) ; ὑπ᾽
αὐτῶν -mss. ; ἐξ αὐτῶν -Timaeus 53 A 7.
[9] Stephanus ; ἐμποιοῦν -mss.
[10] καὶ -omitted by E.

----

[a] Cf. γενομένη τῶν γεννηθέντων (Timaeus 37 A 1-2) quoted
in 1016 B supra ; but καὶ γενητὴν is Plutarch's own explication, probably suggested by Timaeus 28 c 1-2 cited in
1016 E infra (γιγνόμενα καὶ γενητά).
[b] See 1013 F, note b supra.
[c] i.e. the indivisible being of Timaeus 35 A 1-2 ; see
1024 A infra : τῆς τε κρείττονος οὐσίας καὶ ἀμερίστου . . . περὶ
τὴν ἀεὶ μένουσαν . . . οὐσίαν. . . . For the connotation of ἔκ τε

GENERATION OF THE SOUL, 1016

generation [a] is said on the other hand of soul that
god installed as chief of the sum of things [b] when out
of this soul here and that abiding and most excellent
being yonder [c] he had produced a rational and orderly
one and from himself [d] had provided intellectuality
and orderliness as form [e] for her perceptivity and
motivity. For thus it is that the body of the universe
too is said in one context to be ungenerated and in
another to be subject to generation [f] : when Plato
says that [g] everything visible, being not at rest but
in disorderly motion, was taken over by god who
arranges it and says again that [h] the four kinds, fire
and water and earth and air, before the sum of
things has come to be arranged from them cause
matter [i] to be agitated and are shaken by it because
of the irregularity, he posits bodies as existing, no

ταύτης καὶ . . . ἐκείνης see *infra* 1023 F (. . . δοξαστικὴν ταύτην
. . . νοητικῆς ἐκείνης) and 1024 c (διαδιδοῦσαν ἐνταῦθα τὰς ἐκεῖθεν
εἰκόνας) ; and for μόνιμος cf. 1024 c-d *infra* and *Adv. Colotem*
1116 b with Plato, *Timaeus* 29 b 5-7 and 49 e 3-4.

[d] See *Plat. Quaest.* 1001 c (. . . καὶ ἀπ' αὐτοῦ καὶ ἐξ αὐτοῦ
γέγονεν) with note *b* there.

[e] See 1013 c *supra* (. . . τὴν οὐσίαν αὐτῆς ὑποκειμένην καὶ
δεχομένην τὸ κάλλιστον εἶδος . . .) and Proclus, *In Platonis
Timaeum* ii, pp. 153, 28–154, 1 (Diehl) ; cf. also Plotinus,
Enn. ii, iv, 3, lines 4-6 and iii, ix, 5, line 3.

[f] Cf. Apuleius, *De Platone* i, 8 (p. 91, 12-13 [Thomas]) ;
Numenius (p. 91, 9-17 [Leemans]) in Chalcidius, *Platonis
Timaeus*, p. 324, 4-11 (Wrobel)=p. 297, 10-16 (Waszink) ;
Hippolytus, *Refutatio* i, 19, 4 (p. 20, 2-6 [Wendland]).

[g] *Timaeus* 30 a 3-5. For the stress laid on this passage by
Plutarch and Atticus cf. Proclus, *In Platonis Timaeum* i,
p. 381, 26-28 (Diehl).

[h] *Timaeus* 52 e 3-5 and 53 a 2-7 ; cf. Plutarch, *De Defectu
Orac.* 430 c-d (τὰ στοιχεῖα σείοντα τὴν ὕλην . . .).

[i] For the insertion of this term see *supra* 1013 c, note *c*
on page 173.

(1016) σώματα πρὸ τῆς τοῦ κόσμου γενέσεως· ὅταν δὲ
πάλιν λέγῃ τῆς ψυχῆς νεώτερον γεγονέναι τὸ σῶμα
καὶ τὸν κόσμον εἶναι γενητὸν[1] ὅτι ὁρατὸς καὶ
E ἁπτὸς καὶ σῶμα ἔχων ἐστὶ τὰ δὲ τοιαῦτα γιγνόμενα καὶ γενητὰ[2] ἐφάνη, παντὶ δῆλον ὡς γένεσιν
τῇ φύσει τοῦ σώματος ἀποδίδωσιν. ἀλλὰ πολλοῦ
δεῖ τἀναντία λέγειν καὶ διαφέρεσθαι πρὸς αὐτὸν[3]
οὕτως ἐκφανῶς[4] ἐν τοῖς μεγίστοις. οὐ γὰρ ὡσαύτως οὐδὲ ταὐτὸ σῶμα γίγνεσθαί τέ φησιν ὑπὸ τοῦ
θεοῦ καὶ εἶναι πρὶν ἢ[5] γενέσθαι· ταῦτα γὰρ ἄντικρυς
φαρμακῶντός ἐστιν. ἀλλὰ τί δεῖ νοεῖν[6] καὶ τὴν[7]
γένεσιν αὐτὸς διδάσκει. "τὸ μὲν γὰρ[8] πρὸ τούτου"[9] φησὶ "ταῦτα πάντα[10] εἶχεν ἀλόγως καὶ ἀμέ-
τρως· ὅτε δ' ἐπεχειρεῖτο κοσμεῖσθαι τὸ πᾶν, πῦρ
πρῶτον καὶ ὕδωρ καὶ γῆν καὶ ἀέρα, ἴχνη μὲν
ἔχοντα[11] ἄττα αὐτῶν,[12] παντάπασι μὴν[13] διακείμενα

---

[1] γεννητὸν -f, m, r.
[2] γεννητὰ -f, m, r (A[1], F, P in *Timaeus* 28 c 2).
[3] m, Aldine ; αὐτὸν -all other mss. (αὐτὸν αὐτὸν -u).
[4] ἀφανῶς -m, r.
[5] ἢ -omitted by f, m, r, Escor. 72.
[6] νοεῖν -omitted by f, m, r (added in margin of f and m).
[7] καὶ τὴν -omitted by Aldine, Basiliensis ; καὶ ταύτην
τὴν or καὶ τὸ γινόμενον καὶ τὴν -B. Müller ; καὶ τίνα (?)
-Bernardakis.
[8] τὸ μὲν δὴ -*Timaeus* 53 a 8.
[9] τούτου -Bernardakis from *Timaeus* 53 a 8 ; τοῦ -mss.
[10] πάντα ταῦτ' -*Timaeus* 53 a 8.
[11] u, f, r ; ἔχον τὰ -E, B, e, m, Escor. 72.
[12] ἄττα αὐτῶν -Dübner (implied by Xylander's version)
from *Timaeus* 53 b 2 (ἔχοντα αὐτῶν ἄττα [αὐτὰ -A, F, Y ;
Simplicius, *Phys.*, p. 228, 6]) ; αὐτὰ αὐτῶ -mss.

doubt, and ready to hand [a] before the generation of the universe ; but, when again he says that [b] body has come to be junior to soul and that [c] the universe is subject to generation because it is visible and tangible and has body and such things had been shown to be in process of becoming and subject to generation, it is clear to everyone that he attributes a genesis to the nature of body.[d] Nevertheless, he is far from contradicting himself and being so manifestly at odds with himself in matters of the greatest moment, for it is not in the same way and not the same body that he says is brought into being by god and exists before it came to be ; it takes a downright sot [e] for that, whereas he himself explains the sense in which the genesis too must be understood. " For before this," he says,[f] " all these were without ratio or measure ; and, when it was undertaken to reduce the sum of things to order, fire first and water and earth and air, while having some traces of themselves, were nevertheless in the very condition that is likely to be the state of everything

---

[a] See 1014 в supra : οὐ γενομένην ἀλλὰ ὑποκειμένην ἀεὶ τῷ δημιουργῷ. . . .

[b] Timaeus 34 в 10—35 a 1 ; see supra 1016 a-b with note e on page 199.

[c] Timaeus 28 в 7–c 2.

[d] See against this conclusion Proclus, In Platonis Timaeum i, pp. 283, 27–285, 6 and ii, pp. 117, 3–119, 10 (Diehl) on Timaeus 28 в 7–c 2 and 34 c 4—35 a 1 respectively.

[e] Cf. σοφιστῇ κραιπαλῶντι (1016 a supra) and εἰ γὰρ οὐ κραιπαλῶντες οὐδὲ φαρμακῶντες . . . (Adv. Colotem 1123 ғ).

[f] Timaeus 53 a 8–в 5.

---

[13] Dübner (implied by Xylander's version) from Timaeus 53 в 3 (μὴν -F, Y ; γε μὴν -A ; μὲν -Simplicius, Phys., p. 228, 7) ; παντάπασιν ἦν -mss.

(1016)

F ὥσπερ εἰκὸς ἔχειν ἅπαν ὅταν ἀπῇ τινος θεός, οὕτω
δὴ τότε πεφυκότα ταῦτα πρῶτον διεσχηματίσατο
εἴδεσι καὶ[1] ἀριθμοῖς.'' ἔτι δὲ πρότερον, εἰπὼν ὡς
οὐ μιᾶς ἔργον[2] ἦν ἀναλογίας ἀλλὰ δυεῖν τὸ συν-
δῆσαι στερεὸν ὄντα καὶ βάθος ἔχοντα τὸν τοῦ
παντὸς ὄγκον καὶ διελθὼν ὅτι πυρὸς καὶ γῆς ὕδωρ
ἀέρα τε ὁ θεὸς ἐν μέσῳ θεὶς συνέδησε καὶ συνεστήσατο τὸν οὐρανόν, '' ἔκ τε δὴ τούτων '' φησὶ[3] '' τοι-

1017 ούτων καὶ τὸν ἀριθμὸν τεττάρων τὸ τοῦ κόσμου
σῶμα ἐγεννήθη[4] δι' ἀναλογίας ὁμολογῆσαν, φιλίαν
τ' ἔσχεν ἐκ τούτων, ὥστ' εἰς ταὐτὸν αὐτῷ συνελ-
θὸν ἄλυτον ὑπὸ τῶν ἄλλων[5] πλὴν ὑπὸ τοῦ συνδή-
σαντος γενέσθαι,'' σαφέστατα διδάσκων ὡς οὐχὶ
σώματος ἁπλῶς οὐδ' ὄγκου καὶ ὕλης ἀλλὰ συμμετρίας περὶ σῶμα[6] καὶ κάλλους καὶ[7] ὁμοιότητος
ἦν ὁ θεὸς πατὴρ καὶ δημιουργός. ταῦτα[8] δὴ δεῖ[9]

---

[1] εἴδεσί τε καὶ -A in Timaeus 53 в 5.
[2] ἔργου -e, u¹ (corrected by u²).
[3] δή φησι τούτων -r.
[4] ἐγενήθη -E, B, u¹ (corrected by u²).
[5] ὑπό του ἄλλου -A and P in Timaeus 32 c 3.
[6] περὶ σῶμα -omitted by r.
[7] καὶ -omitted by B, u¹ (added superscript by u²).
[8] ταὐτὰ -Hubert (dub., cf. " quod idem . . ." -Turnebus).
[9] δὴ -omitted by f, m, r ; δεῖ -omitted by Escor. 72,
Aldine, Basiliensis.

---

[a] Cf. Plutarch, De Facie 926 F (L.C.L. xii, p. 84, note b);
but there the absence of god is said to mean absence of

whenever god is absent from it,[a] and so, this being then their natural state, god first gave them definite shape with figures and numbers." Still earlier, after saying that[b] it took not one proportion but two to bind together the mass of the sum of things since it is a solid and has depth and after explaining that[c] god put water and air between fire and earth and so bound together and constructed the heaven,[d] he says[e]: " from these, being such in kind and four in number, was the body of the universe engendered consentient through proportion, and from these it acquired amity so that banded in union with itself it came to be indissoluble by others than by him who had bound it together." So he most manifestly teaches that god was father and artificer not of body in the absolute sense,[f] that is to say not of mass and matter, but of symmetry in body and of beauty and similarity.[g] This, then, is what one must suppose in

νοῦς καὶ ψυχή, whereas here it is assumed to be absence of νοῦς only with ψυχὴ καθ᾽ ἑαυτήν (see 1014 E, note g supra), i.e. irrational soul, present and moving the precosmic chaos (see supra 1016 c with note f there and Plat. Quaest. 1003 A, note h).

[b] Timaeus 32 A 7–B 3.

[c] Timaeus 32 B 3-7.

[d] In fact Plato says συνεστήσατο οὐρανὸν ὁρατὸν καὶ ἁπτόν (Timaeus 32 B 7-8 ; cf. 31 B 4-8 and 36 E 5-6 [quoted in 1016 B supra]), although in Timaeus 30 A 3-5 (see 1016 D supra) the supposed precosmic chaos had been called ὁρατόν and Plutarch asserts that the tangibility of body was not created by the demiurge (1014 c supra with note d there).

[e] Timaeus 32 B 8–C 4.

[f] See supra pages 183, note d and 185, note c; and with σώματος ἁπλῶς cf. ἁπλῶς ψυχήν in 1024 A infra.

[g] Cf. 1014 E supra (... κάλλους δὲ καὶ μορφῆς καὶ σχημάτων μετριότητος ἐνδεῶς εἶχεν) and Plato, Timaeus 53 B 5-6 and 69 B 2-5.

(1017) διανοεῖσθαι καὶ περὶ ψυχῆς, ὡς τὴν μὲν οὔθ' ὑπὸ τοῦ θεοῦ γενομένην οὔτε κόσμου ψυχὴν οὖσαν ἀλλά τινα φανταστικῆς[1] καὶ δοξαστικῆς ἀλόγου δὲ καὶ ἀτάκτου φορᾶς καὶ ὁρμῆς δύναμιν αὐτοκίνητον καὶ B ἀεικίνητον τὴν δ'[2] αὐτὸς ὁ θεὸς διαρμοσάμενος[3] τοῖς προσήκουσιν ἀριθμοῖς καὶ λόγοις ἐγκατέστησεν ἡγεμόνα τοῦ κόσμου γεγονότος γενητὴν[4] οὖσαν.

10. Ὅτι δὲ περὶ τούτων διενοεῖτο ταῦτα καὶ οὐ θεωρίας ἕνεκα τοῦ τε κόσμου [μὴ][5] γενομένου καὶ τῆς ψυχῆς ὁμοίως[6] ὑπετίθετο σύστασιν καὶ γένεσιν[7] ἐκεῖνο πρὸς πολλοῖς τεκμήριόν ἐστι μέγα[8] τὸ τὴν μὲν ψυχὴν ὑπ' αὐτοῦ καὶ ἀγένητον[9] ὥσπερ εἴρηται

[1] φανταστικὴν -r.
[2] ἣν δὴ -B ; ἣν δὲ -e^1 (ἣν remade to τὴν by e^2).
[3] ὁ θεὸς αὐτὸς διαρμοσάμενος -B ; αὐτὸς ὁ δημιουργησάμενος -r.
[4] γεννητὴν -f, m, r.
[5] μὴ -omitted by B, f, m, r ; μὴ -E ; μὴ -e, u ; μὴ -Escor. 72.
[6] MSS. ; ὅμως -Wyttenbach (with μὴ γενομένου *supra*).
[7] καὶ γένεσιν -omitted by r.
[8] μέγα -H. C. (*cf. Moralia* 91 D, 624 F, 1101 E) ; μετὰ -e, Escor. 72; μετὰ -u ; ἐστι . . . vac. 5 -E ; vac. 6 -B . . . τὸ ; ἐστι τὸ -f, m, r, Aldine.
[9] ἀγέννητον -f, m, r (so also *infra* γεννητὴν and γεννητὸν ἀγέννητον δὲ).

---

[a] *Cf.* Thévenaz (*L'Âme du Monde*, p. 22, note 92): " Dans tout ce passage (*scil.* chap. 9) Plutarque applique aussi à l'âme ce que Platon ne disait que du corps." Plutarch in fact here abandons the literal interpretation that he professes to maintain, for the *Timaeus* speaks not of a precosmic soul regulated or organized by the demiurge but of soul produced by him " substance " and all (*cf.* Proclus, *In Platonis Timaeum* i, p. 383, 25-31 and ii, p. 119, 10-24 [Diehl] with insistence upon the ἐκ τῶνδε . . ., omitted by Plutarch in

the case of soul also,[a] that, whereas the one [b] neither was brought into being by god nor is the soul of the universe [c] but is a certain self-moved and so perpetually activated potency [d] of imaginative and opinionative but irrational and disorderly transport and impulse,[e] the other was regulated by god himself with the appropriate numbers and ratios [f] and then being generated was installed by him as chief [g] of the universe that had come to be.

10. That this is what he really thought about these matters and that he was not for the sake of examination supposing in like manner a composition and generation of the soul and of the universe which has come to be,[h] of this a strong indication in addition to many is the notorious fact that, while, as has been said,[i] he speaks of the soul both as ungenerated and his quotation of *Timaeus* 34 B 10—35 A 1 [see *supra* page 199, note *e*]).

[b] See 1016 c *supra*: ἀγένητον μὲν ... ψυχὴν τὴν πρὸ τῆς κόσμου γενέσεως ... γενομένην δὲ ... ἦν ὁ θεός. ...

[c] Contrast 1024 A *infra*: νῦν οὐχ ἁπλῶς ψυχὴν ἀλλὰ κόσμου ψυχήν. ...

[d] For δύναμιν see 1015 B *supra* (τὴν ... τρίτην ἀρχὴν καὶ δύναμιν) ; for the implication of καί cf. Hermias, *In Platonis Phaedrum*, p. 103, 20-21 (with p. 104, 7-8) and p. 112, 33-34 (Couvreur) and see *supra* 1016 A, note *d*.

[e] See 1024 A *infra* (τὴν δοξαστικὴν καὶ φανταστικὴν ... κίνησιν ...) and *supra* 1014 c, note *e*.

[f] See *supra* page 175, note *c*.

[g] See *supra* 1013 F, note *b*.

[h] See *supra* 1013 A (chap. 3 *init.*).

[i] 1016 A *supra* (... ὁμοῦ καὶ ἀγένητον ... καὶ γενομένην, ἀγένητον μὲν ἐν Φαίδρῳ τὴν ψυχὴν ἐν δὲ Τιμαίῳ γενομένην). Resolved by Plutarch in his fashion in 1016 c *supra* (chap. 9 *init.*), this was used by Proclus (*In Platonis Timaeum* i, p. 287, 18-23 [Diehl]) as evidence that Plato in the *Timaeus* could call the universe γενητόν also though holding it to be ἀγένητον κατὰ χρόνον.

(1017) καὶ γενητὴν λέγεσθαι τὸν δὲ κόσμον ἀεὶ μὲν γεγονότα καὶ γενητὸν ἀγένητον δὲ μηδέποτε μηδ' ἀΐδιον. τὰ μὲν οὖν ἐν Τιμαίῳ τί δεῖ προφέρειν;[1]
ὅλον γὰρ καὶ πᾶν τὸ σύγγραμμα περὶ κόσμου γενέσεως ἄχρι τέλους ἀπ' ἀρχῆς[2] ἐστι. τῶν δ' ἄλλων
C ἐν μὲν Ἀτλαντικῷ προσευχόμενος ὁ Τίμαιος ὀνομάζει τὸν πάλαι μὲν ἔργῳ γεγονότα νῦν δὲ λόγῳ[3]
θεόν, ἐν Πολιτικῷ δὲ ὁ Παρμενίδειος ξένος τὸν
κόσμον ὑπὸ τοῦ θεοῦ συντεθέντα φησὶ πολλῶν ἀγαθῶν μεταλαβεῖν, εἰ δέ τι φλαῦρόν ἐστιν ἢ χαλεπόν,
ἐκ τῆς προτέρας ἕξεως ἀναρμόστου καὶ ἀλόγου συμ-
μεμιγμένον ἔχειν· ἐν δὲ τῇ Πολιτείᾳ περὶ τοῦ
ἀριθμοῦ, ὃν γάμον ἔνιοι καλοῦσιν, ὁ Σωκράτης ἀρχόμενος λέγειν "ἔστι δέ" φησι "θείῳ
μὲν γενητῷ[4] περίοδος ἦν[5] ἀριθμὸς περιλαμβάνει

---

[1] B (προ -E in margin) ; προσφέρειν -all other mss.
[2] ἀπ' ἀρχῆς ἄχρι τέλους -B.
[3] λόγοις -Plato, *Critias* 106 A 4.
[4] γεννητῷ -f, m, r, Escor. 72, Plato (*Republic* 546 B 3).
[5] ἦ -u.

---

[a] Contrast Joannes Lydus, *De Mensibus* iii, 3 (p. 38,
13-16 [Wuensch]). What Plutarch here states as a fact
(*cf.* Philoponus, *De Aeternitate Mundi* vi, 24 [pp. 199, 26–
200, 3, Rabe]), taking it to be compatible with his previous
assertion that Plato τὸ σῶμα τοῦ κόσμου πῆ μὲν ἀγένητον
ἀποφαίνει πῆ δὲ γενητόν (1016 D *supra* with note *f* there),
would have been denied by those who read *Timaeus* 27 c 5
in the way reported and rejected by Proclus (*In Platonis
Timaeum* i, p. 219, 13-18 [Diehl]) ; and it would be untrue
also if *Timaeus* 40 B 5 in the version of A, adopted by modern
editors, were surely right, but the ἀΐδια there used of the
" fixed stars " was not in the texts read by Cicero, Proclus,
and Chalcidius and so may not have been in that known to
Plutarch.
[b] *Critias* 106 A 3-4 : τῷ δὲ πρὶν μὲν πάλαι ποτ' ἔργῳ νῦν

as generated, he always speaks of the universe as
having come to be and as generated and never as
ungenerated or everlasting.[a] As to the *Timaeus*,
what need to cite passages in it ? For the whole
work in its entirety from beginning to end is about
the generation of the universe.   Among his other
writings, however, in the *Account of Atlantis* Timaeus
invokes by name the god that in fact of old but now
in word has come to be,[b] and in the *Politicus* the
Parmenidean Stranger says [c] that the universe constructed by god partook of much good and that
anything defective or troublesome in it is an ingredient retained from its prior discordant and irrational state ; and in the *Republic* Socrates, when
he begins to speak about the number that some call
Nuptial,[d] says : " A divine object of generation has
a period that is comprised by a perfect number," [e]

δὲ λόγοις ἄρτι θεῷ γεγονότι προσεύχομαι (*cf.* P. Frutiger, *Les
Mythes de Platon*, p. 209, n. 1 and p. 195, n. 2 on *Timaeus*
20 D 7 and 26 E 4-5). Plutarch's transposition of the words
tends to diminish their ambiguity and so may not have been
unintentional.

[c] *Cf. Politicus* 269 D 8-9 and 273 B 4–D 1 (see 1015 c-D
supra [chap. 7 *init.*]).

[d] *Republic* 546 B 3–D 3. With Plutarch's expression here
cf. Nicomachus, *Arithmetica Introductio* II, xxiv, 11 (p. 131,
8-9 [Hoche]) : κατὰ τὸν τοῦ λεγομένου γάμου τόπον ἐν τῇ
Πολιτείᾳ. . . . Iamblichus refers to the passage as τὸν ἐν τῇ
Πλάτωνος πολιτείᾳ γαμικὸν ἀριθμόν (*In Nicomachi Arithmeticam Introductionem*, p. 82, 20-21 [Pistelli]), and Plutarch
himself in *De Iside* 373 F speaks of τὸ γαμήλιον διάγραμμα
there formulated.

[e] *Republic* 546 B 3-4. In 1018 c *infra* Plutarch says that
six is τέλειος and is called γάμος but does not suggest any
connexion between that and this sentence of Plato's, the
ἀριθμὸς τέλειος of which is not the " nuptial number " anyway but is distinguished from it.

211

(1017) τέλειος," οὐκ ἄλλο καλῶν θεῖον γενητὸν¹ ἢ τὸν
κόσμον.

1022 Ε   21. ⟨Ἀλλ' οὐδὲ περὶ τοῦ κόσμου καὶ τῆς ψυχῆς
ὁμοίως⟩ ἐν⟨ταῦθα λέγει τὸ ἀμέριστον καὶ ἀεὶ⟩²
κατὰ ταὐτὰ ἔχον³ ὡς μορφὴν καὶ εἶδος, τὸ δὲ περὶ
τὰ σώματα⁴ γιγνόμενον μεριστὸν ὡς ὑποδοχὴν καὶ
ὕλην, τὸ δὲ μῖγμα κοινὸν ἐξ ἀμφοῖν ἀποτετελεσμέ-
νον.⁵ ἡ μὲν οὖν ἀμέριστος οὐσία καὶ ἀεὶ κατὰ
ταὐτὰ καὶ ὡσαύτως ἔχουσα μὴ μικρότητι καθάπερ
τὰ ἐλάχιστα τῶν σωμάτων νοείσθω φεύγουσα τὸν

¹ γεννητὸν -f, m, r, Escor. 72.
² ⟨...⟩ ἐν⟨...⟩ -supplied by H. C.; κόσμον. ... vac. 4
-E; vac. 8 -B ... followed by δὲ ἡ τῶν τριῶν (chap. 11 [1017
c] infra) through ἀρτίων καὶ π (chap. 20 [1022 Ε] infra) ...
vac. 4-1/2 lines -E; vac. 2-1/2 lines -B ... followed by
κατὰ τὰ αὐτὰ (chap. 21 [1022 Ε] here) through τῶν δυεῖν
δευτέρα (chap. 30 [1027 F] infra) followed immediately by
περιττῶν. τὴν γὰρ (chap. 30 b [1027 F] infra) to the end -E,
B; κόσμον ... vac. 5 -f, m; vac. 3 -r ... ἐν ... vac. 4 ...
followed by δὲ ἡ τῶν τριῶν through ἀρτίων καὶ ἐπὶ ... vac.
14 -f; vac. 13 -m, r ... followed by κατὰ τὰ αὐτὰ through
τῶν δυοῖν. δευτέρα (δευτέρα δὲ -f) τῶν περιττῶν. τὴν γὰρ -f,
m, r; κόσμον. ἔνθα (ἐν ... vac. 2 -Escor. 72) δὲ ἡ τῶν τριῶν
through ἀρτίων καὶ ἐπὶ κατὰ (κατὰ -Escor. 72; ἐπϊκατὰ -u) τὰ
αὐτὰ through τῶν δυοῖν δευτεριττῶν (ρατῶνπε -Escor. 72 in
margin) τὴν γὰρ -e, u, Escor. 72; κατὰ τὰ αὐτὰ ... τῶν δυεῖν
δευτέρα (chaps. 21-30) and δὲ ἡ τῶν τριῶν ... ἀρτίων καὶ
(chaps. 11-20) transposed by Maurommates (1848) and B.
Müller (1870 and 1873).
³ B; ἔχων -all other mss.
⁴ περὶ σῶμα -f.
⁵ ἀποτελεσμένον -e, u, f.

ᵃ Cf. Proclus, In Platonis Rem Publicam ii, pp. 14, 8–15,
20 and p. 30, 6-10 (Kroll); and In Platonis Timaeum i,
p. 292, 6-9 (Diehl).
ᵇ The supplements proposed by B. Müller (1870 [p. 398]

what he calls a divine object of generation being nothing other than the universe.[a]

21.[b] ⟨Nor in our passage [c] either does he with regard to the universe and the soul alike speak of what is indivisible and ever⟩ invariable as shape or form, of what becomes divisible in the case of bodies as receptacle or matter, and of the mixture as having been produced from both in common.[d] Now, the indivisible and ever invariable and identical being is to be thought of as eluding division not because of minuteness as do the smallest of bodies,[e] for it is the

and 1873 [p. 33]), which like the earlier one by Maurommates (1848 [p. 38]) introduce the name of Crantor, were criticized by H.-R. Schwyzer (*Rhein. Mus.*, lxxxiv [1935], pp. 361-363) and by Thévenaz (*L'Âme du Monde*, pp. 61-62), who later (*Rev. Études Grecques*, lii [1939], pp. 358-366) gave in French paraphrase a supplement of his own, gratuitously assuming on the basis of *De Iside* 373 E—374 A that Plutarch here too had introduced the triangle supposedly used in the nuptial number and had confused the latter with the τέλειος ἀριθμός just mentioned but correctly observing that chap. 21 must continue the theme introduced at the beginning of chap. 10 by οὐ . . . τοῦ τε κόσμου . . . καὶ τῆς ψυχῆς ὑπετίθετο σύστασιν καὶ γένεσιν.

[c] *i.e. Timaeus* 35 A 1-B 4 (1012 B-C *supra*); see νῦν in 1023 A *infra*.

[d] For identification of the indivisible with shape or form and of the divisible with matter H.-R Schwyzer (*Rhein. Mus.*, lxxiv [1935], p. 363) cites "Timaeus Locrus" 94 A (ὕλαν . . . τὰν δὲ περὶ τὰ σώματα μεριστὰν εἶμεν . . .) and 97 E (ἀρχαὶ . . . ὡς μὲν ὑποκείμενον ἁ ὕλα ὡς δὲ λόγος μορφᾶς τὸ εἶδος), to which add 95 E (. . . κρᾶμα . . . ἔκ τε τᾶς ἀμερίστω μορφᾶς καὶ τᾶς μεριστᾶς οὐσίας, ὡς ἐν κρᾶμα ἐκ δύο τουτέων εἶμεν).

[e] This does not imply that anyone had taken the " indivisible being " of *Timaeus* 35 A to mean " minimal body " (though it is treated as quantitatively indivisible, *i.e.* as a spatial point, by Aristotle in his criticism of *Timaeus* 37 A [*cf.* Cherniss, *Aristotle's Criticism of Plato* . . ., n. 316 on

(1022) μερισμόν· τὸ γὰρ ἁπλοῦν καὶ ἀπαθὲς καὶ καθαρὸν[1]
αὐτῆς καὶ μονοειδὲς ἀμερὲς εἴρηται καὶ ἀμέριστον,
ᾧ καὶ τῶν συνθέτων καὶ μεριστῶν καὶ διαφερο-
μένων ἀμωσγέπως θιγοῦσα[2] παύει τὸ πλῆθος καὶ
F καθίστησιν εἰς μίαν διὰ ὁμοιότητος ἕξιν. τὴν δὲ
περὶ τὰ σώματα γιγνομένην[3] μεριστὴν εἰ μέν τις
ἐθέλοι[4] καλεῖν ὕλην ὡς καὶ ὑποκειμένην ἐκείνῃ καὶ
μεταληπτικὴν ἐκείνης φύσιν, ὁμωνυμίᾳ χρώμενος,
οὐ διαφέρει πρὸς τὸν λόγον· οἱ δὲ σωματικὴν ἀξι-
οῦντες ὕλην συμμίγνυσθαι τῇ ἀμερίστῳ διαμαρ-

---

[1] καθαρὸν καὶ ἀπαθὲς -B.
[2] θιγοῦσα -Dübner ; θήγουσα -B, u[1] ; θίγουσα -all other mss.
[3] Maurommates ; γενομένην -mss.
[4] ἐθέλει -B, u, r.

---

p. 394 and p. 407]) but is a warning against the common
association of ἀμερές and ἐλάχιστον (cf. Xenocrates, frag. 51
[Heinze] ; Alexander, *Metaph.*, p. 247, 22-24 ; Simplicius,
Categ., p. 39, 12-16) and, as is indicated by *Plat. Quaest.*
1002 c-d (see note *b* there), was probably suggested by such
misleading expressions as ἡ ἀμέριστος οὐσία . . . ἐστιν εἰς
βραχὺ συνηγμένη . . . (*Plat. Quaest.* 1001 d): *cf.* the warning
against taking indivisibly one to mean ἓν ὡς ἐλάχιστον (Da-
mascius, *Dub. et Sol.*, pp. 2, 24–3, 2 [Ruelle]=Speusippus,
frag. 36 [Lang] and *Anon. in Platonis Parmenidem* i, 20-
24=*Rhein. Mus.*, xlvii [1892], p. 602=P. Hadot, *Porphyre
et Victorinus* ii [Paris, 1968], p. 66).

a Cf. the characteristics ascribed to the νοῦς of Anaxagoras
by Plutarch (*Pericles* iv, 6 [154 c]) and by Aristotle (*Physics*
256 b 24-25 ; *De Anima* 405 a 16-17, 405 b 19-21, 429 b 23-
24) and by the latter to his own νοῦς ποιητικός (*De Anima*
430 a 17-18) ; and for Plutarch himself see *infra* 1024 a
(τὸ γὰρ νοερὸν . . . ἀπαθές . . .) and 1026 d (. . . ἐκ τε τῆς θείας
καὶ ἀπαθοῦς . . .) and *De Facie* 945 c-d (ὁ δὲ νοῦς ἀπαθής).
In *Plat. Quaest.* 1002 c-d ἁπλοῦν καὶ εἰλικρινὲς καὶ καθαρὸν
ἁπάσης ἑτερότητος καὶ διαφορᾶς (=μονοειδές here) characterizes
the incorporeal and intelligible (as does ἀπαθές in *Amatorius*
765 a, τὰ νοητά . . . τῆς ἀσωμάτου καὶ ἀπαθοῦς οὐσίας εἴδη), but
Plutarch treats νοῦς itself as a νοητόν (see note *g* on *Plat.
Quaest.* 1002 c and note *b* on 1002 e *supra*).

214

simplicity and impassivity and purity and uniformity
of it [a] that is meant by its being without parts and
indivisible, that with which when it somehow just
touches [b] objects composite and divisible and differing
it puts a stop to their multiplicity and reduces it to a
state that is single through similarity. [c] As to the
being that becomes divisible in the case of bodies, if
anyone should wish to call it matter homonymously
in the sense of a nature underlying the former and
capable of participating in it, [d] this use of the term
makes no difference to the meaning ; but those who
maintain that corporeal matter is mixed with the
indivisible being are utterly mistaken, [e] first because

---

[b] *Cf. Timaeus* 37 A 5-6 (ὅταν . . . ἐφάπτηται . . .) and
Aristotle's criticism (*De Anima* 407 a 15-18) as well as his
own use of the metaphor (*Metaphysics* 1072 b 20-21 and
1051 b 24-25) ; *cf.* also Theophrastus, *Metaph.* 9 B 13-16
and Speusippus, frag. 30, 10-11 (Lang) and among the many
later occurrences especially Hermias, *In Platonis Phaedrum*,
p. 64, 15-17 (Couvreur).

[c] *Cf.* Themistius, *Anal. Post.*, p. 64, 18-20 (τὴν δὲ καθόλου
ἐπιφορὰν ὁ νοῦς ποιήσεται. τούτου γὰρ ἔργον ἤδη τὰ πολλὰ ἑνοῦν
καὶ τὰ ἄπειρα, ὅπερ φησὶ Πλάτων, πέρατι συνδήσασθαι [*Philebus*
27 D 9]) and at 1025 c *infra* the description of the function
of " sameness " : ὧν ἂν ἅψηται . . . συνάγειν καὶ συνιστάναι
διὰ ὁμοιότητος ἐκ πολλῶν μίαν ἀναλαμβάνοντος μορφὴν καὶ δύναμιν.

[d] So Plutarch himself has called it : see 1013 c *supra*
with note e on page 203 *supra* and *cf. De Iside* 374 E (τὴν
ψυχὴν . . . ὡς ὕλην . . . τῷ λόγῳ . . . παρέχομεν).

[e] See 1013 B-c *supra* with note c there. So here Crantor,
while not the only one (see note d on 1022 E *supra*), is,
however unjustifiably and Schwyzer to the contrary not-
withstanding (*Rhein. Mus.*, lxxxiv [1935], p. 362), one
among those whom Plutarch has in mind. In addition to
the subsequent arguments of Plutarch's see the one adduced
against Eratosthenes by Proclus (*In Platonis Timaeum* ii,
p. 152, 28-29 [Diehl]) : κρᾶσις γὰρ οὐκ ἄν ποτε γένοιτο . . .
ἀμερίστου καὶ σώματος.

PLUTARCH'S MORALIA

1023 τάνουσι, πρῶτον μὲν¹ ὅτι τῶν ἐκείνης ὀνομάτων
οὐδενὶ νῦν ὁ Πλάτων κέχρηται (δεξαμενὴν γὰρ
εἴωθε καὶ πανδεχῆ καὶ τιθήνην ἀεὶ καλεῖν ἐκείνην,
οὐ περὶ τὰ σώματα μεριστὴν μᾶλλον δὲ σῶμα
μεριζόμενον εἰς τὸ καθ' ἕκαστον) ἔπειτα τί διοίσει
τῆς τοῦ κόσμου γενέσεως ἢ² τῆς ψυχῆς, εἴπερ ἀμφοτέροις ἔκ τε τῆς ὕλης καὶ τῶν νοητῶν γέγονεν ἡ
σύστασις; αὐτός γε μὴν ὁ Πλάτων, ὥσπερ ἀπ-
ωθούμενος³ τῆς ψυχῆς τὴν ἐκ σώματος γένεσιν,
ἐντὸς αὐτῆς φησιν ὑπὸ τοῦ θεοῦ τεθῆναι τὸ σωματικὸν εἶτ' ἔξωθεν ὑπ' ἐκείνης περικαλυφθῆναι⁴· καὶ
B ὅλως ἀπεργασάμενος τῷ λόγῳ τὴν ψυχὴν ὕστερον⁵
ἐπεισάγει τὴν περὶ τῆς ὕλης ὑπόθεσιν, μηδὲν αὐτῆς πρότερον ὅτε τὴν ψυχὴν ἐγέννα δεηθείς, ὡς
χωρὶς ὕλης γενομένην.

22. Ὅμοια δὲ τούτοις ἔστιν ἀντειπεῖν καὶ τοῖς περὶ
Ποσειδώνιον. οὐ γὰρ μακρὰν τῆς ὕλης ἀπέστη-

¹ μὲν -omitted by f, m, r, Escor. 72.
² ἢ -u.
³ E, B ; ἀποθέμενος -all other mss.
⁴ περικεκαλυφθῆναι -r.
⁵ ὕστερος -u.

---

a See page 213, note *c* supra ; and for νῦν in this sense see 1024 A infra, Plat. Quaest. 1009 c supra, and J. H. Quincey (J.H.S., lxxxvi [1966], p. 149, n. 17) on Moralia 22 F.

b δεξαμενή occurs in Timaeus 53 A 3 (cf. Plutarch, De Iside 374 B ; [Plutarch], De Placitis 882 c=Dox. Graeci, p. 308 A 4-9 and B 5-9), πανδεχές in Timaeus 51 A 7, and τιθήνη in Timaeus 49 A 6, 52 D 5, 88 D 6. See pages 185, note c and 197, note a supra.

c This last (cf. De Defectu Orac. 429 B, εἰς πλείονα μέρη τοῦ αἰσθητοῦ καὶ σωματικοῦ μεριζομένου διὰ τὴν σύμφυτον ἀνάγκην τῆς ἑτερότητος) is implicitly denied by Plato in Timaeus 51 A 4-7, where the receptacle is declared to be " not earth or air or fire or water μήτε ὅσα ἐκ τούτων μήτε ἐξ ὧν ταῦτα γέγονεν."

216

Plato in the present passage [a] has used none of the names for the former (for that it is his custom always to call receptacle and omnirecipient and nurse,[b] not divisible in the case of bodies but rather body that is divided into particularity [c]) and secondly wherein would the generation of the soul differ from that of the universe if both have had as constituents of their composition matter and the intelligibles? [d] In any case, Plato himself, as if warding off from soul the coming to be out of body, says that the corporeal was placed by god within her and then enveloped with her on the outside [e]; and, quite generally, it is after having produced the soul in his account that he introduces in addition the theory about matter,[f] having had no need of it before when he was generating the soul, as it presumably came to be apart from matter.

22. Similar objections can be made also to Posidonius and his followers.[g] For they did not withdraw

[d] See 1013 B-C and note e on 1022 F supra.

[e] Timaeus 34 B 3-4 and 36 D 9-E 3 (cf. Cherniss, Aristotle's Criticism of Plato . . ., pp. 406-407 and n. 334), and see supra Plat. Quaest. 1002 B-C with note f there.

[f] Plutarch means the account of the receptacle, which is introduced at Timaeus 48 E 2—49 A 6 ; but he conveniently forgets both the earlier treatment of the corporeality of the universe (31 B 4—32 C 4), to which he had himself referred at 1016 F—1017 A supra, and the warning about the sequence given in Timaeus 34 B 10—35 A 1 and quoted by himself at 1016 A-B supra (cf. Helmer, De An. Proc., p. 15 and Cherniss, Aristotle's Criticism of Plato . . ., pp. 424-425).

[g] For this chapter (=F 141 a [Edelstein-Kidd]) cf. especially Thévenaz, L'Âme du Monde, pp. 63-67 and in P. Merlan's last extensive treatment, Platonism to Neoplatonism, pp. 34-58, the bibliography on pp. 55 and 57, to which add Marie Laffranque, Poseidonios d'Apamée (Paris, 1964), pp. 373-374, pp. 379-380, and pp. 431-432. The

(1023) σαν,[1] ἀλλὰ δεξάμενοι τὴν τῶν περάτων οὐσίαν περὶ
τὰ σώματα λέγεσθαι μεριστὴν καὶ ταῦτα τῷ νοητῷ
μίξαντες ἀπεφήναντο τὴν ψυχὴν ἰδέαν εἶναι τοῦ
πάντῃ διαστατοῦ κατ' ἀριθμὸν συνεστῶσαν ἁρμο-

―――――――――
[1] ἀπέστησαν τὴν ψυχήν -Epitome 1030 f infra.
―――――――――

phrase τοῖς περὶ Ποσειδώνιον (cf. Wyttenbach, Animadversiones on De E 385 A) might of itself mean only " Posidonius "
(so Turnebus, Xylander, and Amyot) or only his pupils or
" circle " (cf. Laffranque, op. cit., p. 379, n. 37) ; but, as by
οἱ περὶ τὸν Κράντορα (1012 F supra) after οἱ δὲ Κράντορι . . .
προσέθεντο, μιγνύντι . . . (1012 D supra) Plutarch must have
meant " Crantor and his followers," so here too he probably
meant to refer both to Posidonius himself and to his followers. His immediate source for the subsequent Posidonian
interpretation, then, may have been something by one of
those followers such as the work of Phanias (cf. Diogenes
Laertius, vii, 41) or even the work by Eudorus that seems
to have been his source for the interpretations given by
Xenocrates and Crantor (see note c on 1012 E and note c
on 1013 B supra ; cf. P. Merlan, Philologus, lxxxix [1934],
p. 211 and Helmer, De An. Proc., p. 17, n. 22). Such use
of a secondary source, however, would not of itself prove that
he did not know the original as well (cf. W. Crönert's
observation concerning Galen, Gnomon, vi [1930], p. 155).

    [a] i.e. so interpreting τῆς αὖ περὶ τὰ σώματα γιγνομένης μερι-
στῆς (οὐσίας) of Timaeus 35 A 2-3, which, contrary to Marie
Laffranque's assertion (op. cit., p. 379), is tantamount to
saying that the following definition is " une glose posi-
donienne du Timée," though not that it stood in a " commentary " on the Timaeus. For the controversy about the
existence of such a commentary see L. Edelstein, A.J.P.,
lvii (1936), p. 304, n. 72 ; E. Bickel, Rhein. Mus., N.F. ciii
(1960), pp. 8-10 ; K. Abel, Rhein. Mus., N.F. cvii (1964),
pp. 371-373.
    [b] i.e. τὰ πέρατα, " the limits." Merlan (Platonism to
Neoplatonism, p. 38) calls this " Plutarch's somewhat care-
less reference to ' the substance of the limits,' " i.e. τὴν τῶν
περάτων οὐσίαν, and insists that this phrase means " that
which is within the πέρατα," " the kind of being which ' has '
or ' accepts ' limits," οὐσία itself being " the πεπερασμένον

far from matter; but, having taken divisible in the case of bodies to mean [a] the being of the limits and having mixed these [b] with the intelligible, they declared the soul to be the idea of what is everyway extended, [c] herself constituted according to number

without its limits," that is, in fact, for a Stoic ὕλη. This cannot be what the phrase meant to Plutarch, however, any more than τῆς ψυχῆς . . . τὴν οὐσίαν a few lines below means "the kind of being that ' has ' or ' accepts ' soul," for his first refutation of the Posidonians explicitly assumes that in their interpretation of the psychogony they use the limits themselves (τοῖς τῶν σωμάτων πέρασιν [1023 c *infra*]) and not any "substance of the limits" in Merlan's sense, while at the beginning of the next chapter again (1023 D *infra*) the two constitutive factors of soul ascribed to them are the intelligible and the limits *tout court* (τοῖς πέρασι). Nor does this leave unexplained, as Merlan contends it would do, Plutarch's imputation of " materialism " to the Posidonians, for it has already been said in reference to their interpretation (1014 D *supra*, page 187, note c) that the nature said in the *Timaeus* to become divisible in the case of bodies must not be held to be μήκη καὶ πλάτη . . . ἃ σώμασι προσήκει καὶ σωμάτων μᾶλλον ἢ τῆς ψυχῆς ἐστιν. Whether Plutarch's imputation is justified is another question. He knew that according to the Stoics limits are incorporeal (*De Comm. Not.* 1080 E *infra*) but probably knew also that, while existing only in thought for the Stoics (*S.V.F.* ii, frag. 488), they exist in reality (καθ᾽ ὑπόστασιν) as well for Posidonius (Diogenes Laertius, vii, 135); and, since according to the latter being that is κατὰ τὴν ὑπόστασιν differs from matter only in thought (*Dox. Graeci*, p. 458, 10-11), one might reasonably suppose that for him the limits, which exist in reality, must also be material.

[c] So much of the definition is identical with that ascribed by Iamblichus to Speusippus (frag. 40 [Lang]); in an obviously Stoic version it is ascribed to Plato himself (Diogenes Laertius, iii, 67 : ἰδέαν τοῦ πάντῃ διεστῶτος πνεύματος [*cf. ibid.* vii, 157 : soul is πνεῦμα ἔνθερμον for Posidonius *et al.*]); and the first word by itself, *idea*, is the Posidonian definition in the list given by Macrobius (*In Somnium*

(1023) νίαν[1] περιέχοντα· τά τε γὰρ μαθηματικὰ τῶν πρώτων νοητῶν μεταξὺ καὶ τῶν αἰσθητῶν τετάχθαι,
τῆς τε ψυχῆς, τῶν νοητῶν τὸ ἀίδιον καὶ τῶν αἰσθη-
C τῶν[2] τὸ παθητικὸν ἐχούσης, προσῆκον[3] ἐν μέσῳ τὴν
οὐσίαν ὑπάρχειν. ἔλαθε γὰρ καὶ τούτους ὁ θεὸς
τοῖς τῶν σωμάτων πέρασιν ὕστερον, ἀπειργασμένης ἤδη τῆς ψυχῆς, χρώμενος ἐπὶ τὴν τῆς ὕλης
διαμόρφωσιν, τὸ σκεδαστὸν αὐτῆς καὶ ἀσύνδετον
ὁρίζων καὶ περιλαμβάνων ταῖς ἐκ τῶν τριγώνων
συναρμοττομένων ἐπιφανείαις. ἀτοπώτερον δὲ τὸ[4]

---

[1] ἁρμονίαν -B and *Epitome* 1030 F *infra*; a . . . vac. 5 . . .
ίαν -E (ἁμαρτίαν εἶχε: ἁρμονίαν ἢ οὐσίαν -in margin); ἁμαρτίαν
-all other mss.

[2] αἰσθητῶν -E (τῶν over erasure), B; αἰσθητικῶν -all other
mss.

[3] προσῆκον -mss. and *Epitome* 1031 A *infra* (cf. Philo Jud.,
De Vita Mosis ii, § 69 = iv, p. 216, 18-19 [Cohn]); προσήκειν
-Bernardakis (cf. 1022 D *infra*).   [4] τὸν -e, u, Escor. 72[1].

Scipionis I, xiv, 19). That Plutarch took ἰδέα to mean a
Platonic " idea " is clear from his second refutation (1023 c
infra: ἀτοπώτερον δὲ . . .); but that it was not so meant is
equally clear if, as he here reports, the soul according to
the Posidonians has her being between the intelligibles and
the perceptibles. The word is used in *Timaeus* 35 A 7 itself
and not in the sense of " idea " (see 1012 c *supra* with note
b there), as Plutarch himself knew (see 1025 B *infra*: . . .
τὸ πᾶν . . . τῆς ψυχῆς εἶδος) ; and that passage of the *Timaeus*
whether directly or through Speusippus is the source of its
use in the Posidonian definition, where, if the exegesis of
Plato was meant to be Posidonian doctrine as well, the meaning intended was " rational configuration " (cf. Proclus, *In
Primum Euclidis El. Lib.*, p. 143, 8-21 [Friedlein] : . . . τὸν
λόγον τοῦ σχήματος . . . αἴτιον . . . τῆς περιοχῆς with L. Edelstein, *A.J.P.*, lvii [1936], p. 303) of the tridimensional (for
πάντῃ [cf. *Timaeus* 36 E 2: πάντῃ διαπλακεῖσα]=τριχῇ cf.
Aristotle, *De Caelo* 268 a 7-10 and 24-28 with Simplicius,
De Caelo, p. 9, 17-29 ; Philo Jud., *De Opificio Mundi* 36 = i,
p. 11, 9-10 [Cohn]). As to the intention of Speusippus see

that embraces concord,[a] for (they said) the mathematicals have been ranked between the primary
intelligibles and the perceptibles[b] and it is an
appropriate thing for the soul likewise, possessing as
she does the everlastingness of the intelligibles and
the passivity of the perceptibles,[c] to have her being
in the middle.[d] In fact these people too failed to
notice that only later, after the soul has already been
produced, does god use the limits of the bodies for
the shaping of matter[e] by bounding and circumscribing its dispersiveness and incoherence with the
surfaces made of the triangles fitted together.[f]

Cherniss, *Aristotle's Criticism of Plato* . . ., pp. 509-511 and
The Riddle, pp. 73-74 with the rejoinder by Merlan, *Platonism to Neoplatonism*, pp. 40-48 and p. 56.

[a] *Cf.* Iamblichus, *De Comm. Math. Scientia*, p. 40, 15-23
(Festa) : . . . κατ' ἀριθμοὺς ἁρμονίαν περιέχοντας ὑφεστώσης
. . . and *Theolog. Arith.*, p. 30, 7-9 (De Falco)=Anatolius,
p. 32, 21-22 (Heiberg)=Sextus, *Adv. Math.* iv, 8 (p. 723,
17-20 [Bekker]).

[b] For this doctrine, which Aristotle ascribes to Plato by
name in *Metaphysics* 987 b 14-18 and 1028 b 19-21, *cf.*
Cherniss, *The Riddle*, pp. 75-78 and E. M. Manasse,
Philosophische Rundschau, Beiheft 2 (1961), pp. 96-97 and
pp. 149-156 ; see also note c on *Plat. Quaest.* 1002 a *supra*.

[c] See note b on 1013 a *supra*.

[d] *Cf.* Proclus, *In Platonis Timaeum* ii, p. 153, 18-19
(Diehl) without reference, however, to the Posidonians or
Speusippus : οἱ μὲν μαθηματικὴν ποιοῦντες τὴν οὐσίαν τῆς ψυχῆς
ὡς μέσην τῶν τε φυσικῶν καὶ τῶν ὑπερφυῶν. . . .

[e] *Timaeus* 53 c 4—56 b 6 (*cf.* 53 b 4 : . . . πρῶτον διεσχηματίσατο . . .), the fabrication of the soul having been
completed at 36 d 7 (*cf.* 36 d 8-9). For this argument of
Plutarch's see the end of the preceding chapter (1023 b
supra with note f on page 217).

[f] See *Plat. Quaest.* 1001 b-c *supra* with note f there ;
and for τὸ σκεδαστόν see *infra* 1023 e (= *Timaeus* 37 a 5-6)
and 1024 a (. . . φερομένης καὶ σκεδαννυμένης . . . ὕλης) and
Plat. Quaest. 1001 d *supra* with note b there.

(1023) τὴν ψυχὴν ἰδέαν ποιεῖν· ἡ μὲν γὰρ ἀεικίνητος[1]
ἡ δ' ἀκίνητος, καὶ ἡ μὲν ἀμιγὴς πρὸς τὸ αἰσθητὸν ἡ
δὲ τῷ[2] σώματι συνειργμένη. πρὸς δὲ τούτοις ὁ θεὸς
τῆς μὲν ἰδέας ὡς παραδείγματος γέγονε μιμητὴς
τῆς δὲ ψυχῆς ὥσπερ ἀποτελέσματος δημιουργός.
D ὅτι δ' οὐδ' ἀριθμὸν ὁ Πλάτων τὴν οὐσίαν τίθεται[3]
τῆς ψυχῆς ἀλλὰ ταττομένην ὑπ' ἀριθμοῦ, προείρηται.

23. Πρὸς δ' ἀμφοτέρους τούτους κοινόν ἐστι τὸ
μήτε τοῖς πέρασι μήτε τοῖς ἀριθμοῖς μηδὲν ἴχνος
ἐνυπάρχειν ἐκείνης τῆς δυνάμεως ᾗ τὸ αἰσθητὸν

---

[1] Wyttenbach from *Epitome* 1031 A *infra*; εὐκίνητος
-mss.
[2] τῷ -omitted by f, m, r.
[3] τίθεται τὴν οὐσίαν -B.

---

[a] See 1013 c *supra* with note *b* on page 174.
[b] Cf. *Timaeus* 38 A 3 (τὸ δὲ ἀεὶ κατὰ ταὐτὰ ἔχον ἀκινήτως)
and Aristotle, *Topics* 148 a 20-21 (ἀπαθεῖς γὰρ καὶ ἀκίνητοι
. . . αἱ ἰδέαι . . .).
[c] Cf. *Symposium* 211 E 1-3 (. . . εἰλικρινές, καθαρόν, ἄμεικτον
. . .), *Phaedrus* 247 c 6-7, and *Timaeus* 52 A 1-4 (. . . οὔτε αὐτὸ
εἰς ἄλλο ποι ἰόν, . . . ἀναίσθητον). The ideas are " separate,"
by which is meant τὸ ἀμιγὲς πάσης ὕλης καὶ μηδενὶ παθητῷ
συμπεπλεγμένον (*Dox. Graeci*, p. 304 A 6-8 and B 27-31; *cf.*
Olympiodorus, *In Platonis Phaedonem*, pp. 103, 25–104, 2
[Norvin]).
[d] Cf. συνέρξας in *Timaeus* 34 c 2, quoted in 1016 B *supra*,
where the soul is mistress of the body, so that the verb here
is not likely, as Thévenaz supposes (*L'Âme du Monde*,
p. 26, n. 121), to refer to the notion that the body is the
prison of the soul, the less so since the envelopment of the
corporeal by the world-soul has just been emphasized by
Plutarch (1023 A *supra* with note *e* there).
[e] Cf. *Timaeus* 28 A 6–B 2, 28 c 6—29 A 6, 37 c 6–D 1,
and 39 E 3-7 with Plutarch, *Quaest. Conviv.* 720 B–C.
[f] See 1014 c and 1016 c *supra* and 1027 A *infra*, but

What is more absurd, however, is to make the soul an idea, for the former is perpetually in motion [a] but the latter is immobile [b] and the latter cannot mix with the perceptible [c] but the former has been coupled with body [d]; and, besides, god's relation to the idea is that of imitator to pattern [e] but his relation to the soul is that of artificer to finished product.[f] As to number, however, it has been stated above [g] that Plato regards the substance of soul not as number either but as being ordered by number.

23. It is an argument against both of these in common,[h] moreover, that neither in limits nor in numbers is there any trace of that faculty with which the soul naturally forms judgments of what is

notice also *Plat. Quaest.* 1001 c (. . . οὐκ ἔργον ἐστὶ τοῦ θεοῦ μόνον ἀλλὰ καὶ μέρος . . .).

[g] In 1013 c-d *supra* (see page 175, note c). By this reference Plutarch cannot mean, as both Helmer (*De An. Proc.*, p. 18 [3]) and Thévenaz (*L'Âme du Monde*, p. 67) think he must, that the earlier refutation of Xenocrates is somehow applicable to the Posidonian definition too, for, as Thévenaz himself remarks, κατ' ἀριθμὸν συνεστῶσαν in this definition (1023 b *supra*) corresponds to κατ' ἀριθμὸν συνεστάναι (1013 d *supra*), which Plutarch used in refuting the Xenocratean identification of soul with number. He recurs to Xenocrates now because, as the Posidonian definition unlike the Xenocratean was obnoxious to the charge of materialism brought against others in the preceding chapter, so both the Xenocratean and the Posidonian are open to quite different objections about to be advanced in the subsequent chapter, where, as will be seen, the two interpretations are referred to as distinct despite the common defect imputed to them.

[h] *i.e.* the Posidonians and the Xenocrateans. Thévenaz (*L'Âme du Monde*, p. 27, n. 124) adopts from the *Epitome* 1031 b the erroneous reading ἀμφοτέροις τούτοις and so cannot account for κοινόν, which in his translation is omitted or disguised as " il va de soi."

(1023) ἡ ψυχὴ πέφυκε κρίνειν. νοῦν μὲν γὰρ αὐτῇ καὶ
⟨τὸ⟩¹ νοητὸν² ἡ τῆς νοητῆς μέθεξις ἀρχῆς ἐμπε-
ποίηκε· δόξας δὲ καὶ πίστεις καὶ τὸ φανταστικὸν
καὶ τὸ παθητικὸν³ ὑπὸ⁴ τῶν περὶ τὸ σῶμα ποιοτήτων, τοῦτ'⁵ οὐκ ἄν τις ἐκ μονάδων οὐδὲ γραμμῶν
οὐδ' ἐπιφανειῶν ἁπλῶς νοήσειεν ἐγγιγνόμενον. καὶ
μὴν οὐ μόνον αἱ τῶν θνητῶν ψυχαὶ⁶ γνωστικὴν τοῦ
αἰσθητοῦ⁷ δύναμιν ἔχουσιν, ἀλλὰ καὶ τὴν τοῦ
E κόσμου φησὶν⁸ ἀνακυκλουμένην αὐτὴν πρὸς ἑαυτήν,
ὅταν οὐσίαν σκεδαστὴν ἔχοντός τινος ἐφάπτηται
καὶ ὅταν ἀμέριστον, λέγειν⁹ κινουμένην διὰ πάσης
ἑαυτῆς, ὅτῳ τ' ἄν τι¹⁰ ταὐτὸν ᾖ¹¹ καὶ ὅτου¹² ἂν
ἕτερον, πρὸς ὅ τι τε μάλιστα καὶ ὅπῃ καὶ ὅπως¹³
συμβαίνει κατὰ τὰ γιγνόμενα¹⁴ πρὸς ἕκαστον

¹ ⟨τὸ⟩ -added by H. C.
² mss. and *Epitome* 1031 в *infra*; νοητικὸν -Turnebus;
νόησιν -Wyttenbach; but *cf. Plat. Quaest.* 1002 e *supra* (τῆς
ἐν ἡμῖν νοητῆς καὶ νοερᾶς δυνάμεως) with note *b* there.
³ παθητὸν -E (with τ dotted and cross in margin), B.
⁴ ὑπὲρ -r.
⁵ τοῦτ' -H. C.; ὁ -mss.; [ὁ] -deleted by Dübner.
⁶ ἡ τῶν θνητῶν ψυχὴ -e.
⁷ αἰσθητοῦ -Turnebus (so *Epitome* 1031 c); αἰσθητικοῦ
-mss.
⁸ φύσιν -B, u¹.
⁹ λέγειν -e, u, Escor. 72¹; λέγῃ -E, B, f, m, r, Escor.
72corr.
¹⁰ τι -Wyttenbach from *Timaeus* 37 a 7 (so Bcorr. in
Epitome 1031 c); τις -mss.
¹¹ ᾖ -Stephanus from *Timaeus* 37 a 7 (so Bcorr. in *Epitome*
1031 c); ἢ -mss.
¹² ὅτου -Bernardakis from *Timaeus* 37 a 7 (so Bcorr. in
Epitome 1031 c); ὅτῳ -mss.
¹³ ὅπως ⟨καὶ ὁπότε⟩ -Pohlenz from *Timaeus* 37 b 1 (*cf. quid
quoque loco aut modo aut tempore* -Turnebus).
¹⁴ Dübner from *Timaeus* 37 b 2; καταγινόμενα -mss.; καὶ
τὰ γινόμενα -*Epitome* 1031 c.

GENERATION OF THE SOUL, 1023

perceptible.*ª* Intelligence and intelligibility have been produced in her by participation in the intelligible principle *ᵇ* ; but opinions and beliefs,*ᶜ* that is to say what is imaginative and impressionable by the qualities in body,*ᵈ* there is not anyone who could conceive of this arising in her simply from units or from lines or surfaces.*ᵉ* Now, not only do the souls of mortal beings have a faculty that is cognizant of the perceptible ; but he says *ᶠ* that the soul of the universe also as she is revolving upon herself, whenever she touches anything that has being either dispersed or indivisible, is moved throughout herself and states of anything's being the same and different with regard to whatever it is so precisely the respect and context and manner of its happening to be or to have as attribute ⟨either of these⟩ in relation to each

ª Whereas this had been taken into account by Crantor and his followers, μάλιστα τῆς ψυχῆς ἴδιον ὑπολαμβάνοντες ἔργον εἶναι τὸ κρίνειν τά τε νοητὰ καὶ τὰ αἰσθητὰ . . . (1012 ꜰ *supra* with note *c* there on this use of κρίνειν).

ᵇ In the account of the Posidonian interpretation (1023 ʙ *supra*) this would be represented by ταῦτα τῷ νοητῷ μίξαντες. With Plutarch's expression here *cf.* τοῦ δὲ νοῦ μετέσχεν ἀπὸ τῆς κρείττονος ἀρχῆς ἐγγενομένου (1026 ᴇ *infra* [chap. 27 *sub finem*]).

ᶜ *Timaeus* 37 ʙ 8 quoted in 1023 ᴇ *infra*.

ᵈ See 1024 ᴀ *infra* : τὴν δοξαστικὴν καὶ φανταστικὴν καὶ συμπαθῆ τῷ αἰσθητῷ κίνησιν.

ᵉ The " units " and the " lines or surfaces " here refer respectively to the " numbers " of the Xenocratean and the " limits " of the Posidonian interpretations just above (see 1014 ᴅ *supra* with notes *b* and *c* there).

ᶠ *Timaeus* 37 ᴀ 5–ʙ 3, from which Plutarch omits as irrelevant to his argument the καὶ πρὸς τὰ κατὰ ταὐτὰ ἔχοντα ἀεί (ʙ 3) and so the τε after γιγνόμενα (ʙ 2) ; but then he ought also to have omitted the καὶ ὅταν ἀμέριστον in 37 ᴀ 6.

225

(1023) ⟨ἕκαστα⟩[1] εἶναι καὶ πάσχειν. ἐν τούτοις ἅμα καὶ
τῶν δέκα κατηγοριῶν ποιούμενος ὑπογραφὴν ἔτι
μᾶλλον τοῖς ἐφεξῆς διασαφεῖ. "λόγος" γάρ φησιν
"ἀληθὴς ὅταν μὲν περὶ τὸ αἰσθητὸν γίγνηται καὶ
ὁ τοῦ[2] θατέρου κύκλος ὀρθὸς[3] ἰὼν εἰς πᾶσαν αὐτοῦ
τὴν ψυχὴν διαγγείλῃ, δόξαι καὶ πίστεις γίγνονται
F βέβαιοι καὶ ἀληθεῖς· ὅταν δ' αὖ περὶ τὸ λογιστικὸν[4] ᾖ καὶ ὁ τοῦ ταὐτοῦ[5] κύκλος εὔτροχος ὢν
αὐτὰ μηνύσῃ, ἐπιστήμη[6] ἐξ ἀνάγκης ἀποτελεῖται·
τούτῳ[7] δ' ἐν ᾧ τῶν ὄντων ἐγγίγνεσθον, ἐάν ποτέ
τις αὐτὸ ἄλλο πλὴν ψυχὴν προσείπῃ, πᾶν μᾶλλον
ἢ τὸ ἀληθὲς ἐρεῖ." πόθεν οὖν ἔσχεν ἡ ψυχὴ τὴν
ἀντιληπτικὴν τοῦ αἰσθητοῦ καὶ δοξαστικὴν ταύτην
1024 κίνησιν, ἑτέραν τῆς νοητικῆς[8] ἐκείνης καὶ τελευτώσης εἰς ἐπιστήμην, ἔργον εἰπεῖν μὴ θεμένους
βεβαίως ὅτι νῦν οὐχ ἁπλῶς ψυχὴν ἀλλὰ κόσμου
ψυχὴν συνίστησιν ἐξ ὑποκειμένων[9] τῆς τε κρείττονος οὐσίας καὶ ἀμερίστου[10] καὶ τῆς[11] χείρονος, ἣν

---

[1] Added by Maurommates from *Epitome* 1031 c and
Timaeus 37 в 2.
[2] τοῦ -omitted by E, B.
[3] ὀρθῶς -r[corr].
[4] λογικὸν -r.
[5] τοῦ αὐτοῦ -u.
[6] νοῦς ἐπιστήμη τε -*Timaeus* 37 c 2.
[7] τοῦτο -E, B ; τούτῳ -u, r, Aldine.
[8] νοητῆς -*Epitome* 1031 D.
[9] ὑποκειμένης -*Epitome* 1031 D-E.
[10] καὶ τῆς ἀμερίστου -r.
[11] τῆς -omitted by f, m, r, Aldine.

---

[a] *Cf.* Albinus, *Epitome* vi, 10 (p. 159, 34-35 [Hermann] =
p. 37, 1-2 [Louis]), where they are said to have been adum-
brated by Plato in the *Parmenides* and elsewhere. A work
by Plutarch entitled Διάλεξις περὶ τῶν δέκα κατηγοριῶν is
No. 192 in the *Catalogue of Lamprias*.

among the things that come to be. As in these words he is simultaneously giving an outline of the ten categories [a] too, in those that follow he states the case more clearly still, for he says [b] : " Whenever true discourse is concerning itself about the perceptible and the circle of difference running aright conveys the message through all its soul, there arise opinions and beliefs steadfast and true ; but, whenever on the other hand it is concerned about the rational and the circle of sameness running smoothly gives the information, knowledge [c] is of necessity produced ; and, if anyone ever calls by another name than soul that one of existing things in which these two come to be, he will be speaking anything but the truth." Whence, then, did the soul get this motion that can apprehend what is perceptible and form opinions of it, a motion different from that which is intellective and issues in knowledge ? It is difficult to say without steadfastly maintaining that in the present passage [d] he is constructing not soul in the absolute sense but the soul of the universe out of entities already available, the superior, that is to say indivisible, being and the inferior, which he has

[b] *Timaeus* 37 B 3–C 5, from which Plutarch omits δὲ ὁ κατὰ ταὐτόν in B 3–4 and γιγνόμενος . . . ἠχῆς in B 4–6 and reduces νοῦς ἐπιστήμη τε in C 2 to ἐπιστήμη.

[c] By reducing Plato's νοῦς ἐπιστήμη τε to ἐπιστήμη alone Plutarch suppresses the embarrassing fact that νοῦς here is clearly treated as a state of soul and not a transcendent entity made an ingredient of it (*cf.* Proclus, *In Platonis Timaeum* ii, pp. 313, 24–314, 5 [Diehl] and Cherniss, *Aristotle's Criticism of Plato . . .*, p. 607).

[d] This is not the last two passages cited (*Timaeus* 37 A 5–B 3 and B 3–C 5) but the central passage under discussion, *Timaeus* 35 A 1–B 4 (1012 B–C *supra*); for νῦν see note *a* on 1023 A *supra*.

(1024) περὶ τὰ σώματα μεριστὴν κέκληκεν, οὐχ ἑτέραν
οὖσαν ἢ τὴν δοξαστικὴν καὶ φανταστικὴν καὶ συμπαθῆ τῷ αἰσθητῷ[1] κίνησιν, οὐ γενομένην ἀλλὰ
ὑφεστῶσαν ἀίδιον ὥσπερ ἡ ἑτέρα. τὸ γὰρ νοερὸν
ἡ φύσις ἔχουσα καὶ τὸ δοξαστικὸν εἶχεν ἀλλ'
ἐκεῖνο μὲν ἀκίνητον ⟨καὶ⟩[2] ἀπαθὲς καὶ περὶ τὴν ἀεὶ
μένουσαν ἱδρυμένον[3] οὐσίαν τοῦτο δὲ μεριστὸν καὶ
πλανητόν, ἅτε δὴ φερομένης καὶ σκεδαννυμένης
B ἐφαπτόμενον ὕλης. οὔτε γὰρ τὸ αἰσθητὸν εἰλήχει
τάξεως ἀλλ' ἦν ἄμορφον καὶ ἀόριστον, ἥ τε περὶ
τοῦτο τεταγμένη δύναμις οὔτε δόξας[4] ἐνάρθρους[5]

---

[1] τῶν αἰσθητῶν -Epitome 1031 E.
[2] ⟨καὶ⟩ -supplied by Müller (1873) from Epitome 1031 E.
[3] ἱδρυμένην -u, Escor. 72[1].
[4] δόξαν -u.
[5] ἀνάρθρους -e, u, Escor. 72, Aldine.

---

[a] See supra 1015 E with note b and 1014 D referred to
there.

[b] See supra page 209 with notes a to e and 1014 c referred
to there.

[c] ἡ φύσις (called " wohl corrupt " by B. Müller [1873]
ad loc.) is used here to designate the precosmic state as it is
in 1015 E supra (οὐδ' ἀρχὰς τῇ φύσει . . . παρέσχεν, ἀλλ' οὔσης
ἐν πάθεσι . . .).

[d] i.e. " the former " just mentioned, the " indivisible being "
of Timaeus 35 A 1-2 ; cf. 1024 D infra, where νοῦς=τῷ
ἀμερίστῳ . . . καὶ τῷ μηδαμῇ κινητῷ.

[e] See 1024 c infra : ὁ δὲ νοῦς αὐτὸς μὲν . . . μόνιμος ἦν
καὶ ἀκίνητος. Plato says nothing of the kind ; but, since
immobility and impassivity are characteristics of the intelligible being of the ideas (see page 223 supra with note b
there), Plutarch, who identifies the indivisible being of the
intelligibles (cf. Plat. Quaest. 1001 D supra : ἡ γὰρ ἀμέριστος
οὐσία . . . τῶν νοητῶν) with precosmic νοῦς (see the immediately
preceding note), naturally ascribes to the latter these characteristics of the former (see 1016 c supra with note c [τῆς
μονίμου τε καὶ ἀρίστης οὐσίας ἐκείνης] and 1026 A infra [τῷ

called divisible in the case of bodies,[a] this latter
being none other than the opinionative and imaginative motion sensitive to what is perceptible, not
brought into being but having subsisted everlastingly
just like the former.[b] For nature [c] possessing intellectuality [d] possessed the opinionative faculty also,
the former, however, immobile [e] ⟨and⟩ impassive [f]
and settled about the being that always remains
fixed [g] but the latter divisible and erratic inasmuch
as it was in contact with matter, which was in motion
and in dispersion.[h] The fact is that the perceptible
had not got any portion of order but was amorphous
and indefinite [i] ; and the faculty stationed about this
had neither articulate opinions nor motions that were

περὶ τὰ νοητὰ μονίμῳ]). Since at the same time he regards
god as the source of rationality in the soul (see *supra* 1016 c
with note *d*), he was perhaps not uninfluenced by the Aristotelian notion of god as νοῦς ἀκίνητος, which is read into Plato
by Albinus in *Epitome* x, 2 (p. 57, 5-9 [Louis]=p. 164, 20-
24 [Hermann]). The νοῦς as πρῶτος θεός may have been
called μόνιμος even by Xenocrates, since he identified it with
the μονάς (frag. 15 [Heinze] ; and for νοῦς=μονὰς διὰ τὸ
μόνιμον *cf.* Alexander, *Metaph.*, p. 39, 14-15 and A. Delatte,
Études sur la littérature pythagoricienne [Paris, 1915], p.
167, 3-4).

[f] See *supra* 1022 E, page 215, note *a*.

[g] *Cf.* 1024 D *infra* (περὶ τὸ μένον ἀεί) and *Plat. Quaest.*
1007 D *supra* (τὸ νοητὸν . . . ἀεὶ μένειν).

[h] See *supra* 1023 c, note *f* and *Plat. Quaest.* 1001 D, note
b with the references there. The combination of μεριστὸν καὶ
πλανητόν here (the former referring to σκεδαννυμένης, the
latter to φερομένης) recalls the identification as precosmic
disorderly soul of both the divisible being and the necessity
of the *Timaeus* (1014 D-E *supra*), since the latter is called
a πλανωμένη αἰτία (*Timaeus* 48 A 6-7).

[i] For the confusion involved in speaking of " the perceptible " and of " corporeality " (just below) in this precosmic state taken literally see page 184, note *c supra*.

(1024) οὔτε κινήσεις ἁπάσας εἶχε¹ τεταγμένας ἀλλὰ τὰς
πολλὰς ἐνυπνιώδεις καὶ παραφόρους καὶ ταραττούσας τὸ σωματοειδές, ὅσα μὴ κατὰ τύχην τῷ
βελτίονι περιέπιπτεν· ἐν μέσῳ γὰρ ἦν ἀμφοῖν καὶ
πρὸς ἀμφότερα συμπαθῆ καὶ συγγενῆ φύσιν εἶχε,
τῷ μὲν αἰσθητικῷ τῆς ὕλης ἀντεχομένη τῷ δὲ
κριτικῷ τῶν νοητῶν.

24. Οὕτω δέ πως καὶ αὐτὸς² διασαφεῖ τοῖς ὀνό-
μασιν· " οὗτος " γάρ φησι " παρὰ τῆς ἐμῆς ψήφου
λογισθεὶς ἐν κεφαλαίῳ δεδόσθω λόγος, ὅν τε καὶ
C χώραν καὶ γένεσιν εἶναι τρία τριχῇ καὶ πρὶν οὐρανὸν γενέσθαι." χώραν τε γὰρ καλεῖ τὴν ὕλην

¹ Ε¹ (in margin), Β ; ἔχουσα -all other mss., Aldine,
Epitome 1031 f.
² Πλάτων -Epitome 1032 a.

ᵃ Cf. in 1026 e infra the period ἐν ᾗ τὸ μὲν φρόνιμον . . .
καταδαρθάνει . . . and De Facie 944 e-f, where the substance
of soul from which νοῦς has been separated is said to retain
ἴχνη τινὰ βίου καὶ ὀνείρατα.
ᵇ See 1015 e supra (τὴν ὕλην . . . ὑπὸ τῆς ἀνοήτου ταραττομένην αἰτίας) with note g there.
ᶜ Cf. Timaeus 69 b 6 (. . . οὔτε τούτων, ὅσον μὴ τύχῃ, τι
μετεῖχεν . . .), referring to the ἴχνη of Timaeus 53 b quoted
by Plutarch in 1016 e-f supra.
ᵈ The subject of ἐν μέσῳ ἦν as of the preceding περιέπιπτεν
must be the precosmic disorderly soul, the δοξαστικὴ καὶ φαντα-
στικὴ . . . κίνησις identified by Plutarch with ἡ περὶ τὰ σώματα
μεριστὴ οὐσία of Timaeus 35 a (see also 1024 c infra : τὴν ἐν
μεταβολαῖς καὶ κινήσεσιν οὐσίαν . . . μεταξὺ τεταγμένην . . . μεριστὴ
προσηγορεύθη . . .), though in the Timaeus it is not this being
that is ἐν μέσῳ but rather that produced by the demiurge
between it and indivisible being to be the οὐσία that is an
ingredient of soul. See the next note infra.
ᵉ Though τὸ κριτικόν can refer to the exercise of αἴσθησις
as well as of νοῦς (see 1024 e infra with note e there), here
it can mean only the latter, for it is explicitly distinguished

all orderly, but most of them were dreamlike [a] and
deranged and were disturbing corporeality [b] save in so
far as it would by chance encounter that which is the
better,[c] for it was intermediate between the two [d]
and had a nature sensitive and akin to both, with its
perceptivity laying hold on matter and with its
discernment on the intelligibles.[e]

24. In terms that go something like this [f] he states
the case clearly himself, for he says [g] : " Let this be
he account rendered in summation as reckoned from
my calculation, that real existence and space and
becoming were three and distinct [h] even before
heaven came to be." Now, it is matter that he calls

from τῷ αἰσθητικῷ and moreover κριτήριον τοῦ νοητοῦ μόνον ἐστὶν
ὁ νοῦς (*Plat. Quaest.* 1002 D *supra*). Thus Plutarch's precosmic disorderly soul, though called ἀνόητος (1014 C and 1015 E
supra) and just distinguished (1024 A *supra*) as τὸ δοξαστικόν
from the precosmic νοερόν, which comes to the former he
maintains only by the action of god in the psychogony (see
1016 C *supra* [τῷ αἰσθητικῷ τὸ νοερὸν . . . ἀφ' αὑτοῦ παρασχὼν
. . .] ; *cf.* 1026 E *infra* [τοῦ δὲ νοῦ μετέσχεν ἀπὸ τῆς κρείττονος
ἀρχῆς ἐγγενομένου]), is here given the intermediate position
that properly belongs to the " created " soul (see the immediately preceding note) and with it the faculty of νοῦς that it
should not have at all until after the psychogony. Similarly
it is said in the next chapter (1024 C *infra*) to disperse in this
world the semblances of the intelligible ideas, which in its
context shows that the attempt to interpret literally the
" precosmic chaos " of *Timaeus* 52 D—53 B was what con-
strained Plutarch here to contradict his own literal interpretation of the psychogony by ascribing to his precosmic disorderly soul characteristics proper according to his own
account only to the " created " soul.

    [f] *Cf.* P. Shorey, *Class. Phil.*, xvii (1922), pp. 261-262 on
Euthydemus 304 E.
    [g] *Timaeus* 52 D 2-4.
    [h] *Cf.* Proclus, *In Platonis Timaeum* i, p. 358, 11-12
(Diehl) : ὅταν λέγῃ τρία ταῦτα εἶναι χωρίς. . . .

(1024) ὥσπερ ἕδραν ἔστιν ὅτε καὶ ὑποδοχήν, ὃν δὲ τὸ
νοητόν, γένεσιν δὲ τοῦ κόσμου μήπω γεγονότος
οὐδεμίαν ἄλλην ἢ τὴν ἐν μεταβολαῖς καὶ κινήσεσιν
οὐσίαν, τοῦ τυποῦντος καὶ τοῦ τυπουμένου μεταξὺ
τεταγμένην, διαδιδοῦσαν[1] ἐνταῦθα τὰς ἐκεῖθεν εἰκόνας. διά τε δὴ ταῦτα μεριστὴ προσηγορεύθη
καὶ ὅτι τῷ αἰσθητῷ τὸ αἰσθανόμενον καὶ τῷ φανταστῷ τὸ φανταζόμενον ἀνάγκη συνδιανέμεσθαι
καὶ συμπαρήκειν· ἡ γὰρ αἰσθητικὴ κίνησις, ἰδίᾳ
ψυχῆς οὖσα, κινεῖται πρὸς τὸ αἰσθητὸν ἐκτός· ὁ δὲ
νοῦς αὐτὸς μὲν ἐφ' ἑαυτοῦ[2] μόνιμος ἦν καὶ ἀκίνητος,

[1] διαδιδοῦσαν -r.
[2] E, B, e, u ; ἀφ' ἑαυτοῦ -f, m, r, Escor. 72, Aldine.

---

[a] See note c on page 184 supra.

[b] Cf. Timaeus 52 A 1-4 with c 5–D 1, 48 E 5-6, 27 D 6—
28 A 4.

[c] Taking Timaeus 52 D—53 B literally, Plutarch had to
identify the precosmic soul that he posited with one of the
three alone there named as being " before heaven came to
be." Of these there remained to him only γένεσις, and he
may even have thought this identification supported by
ψυχὴν . . . τὴν πρώτην γένεσιν of Laws 896 A 5–B 1 and 899 c
6-7 (see 1013 F supra with note a there). Yet he must have
understood that γένεσις in the Timaeus is not an entity
transmitting to this world or dispersing in it the semblances
of the other but is itself τὰ γιγνόμενα, the " offspring " of
the intelligible and the receptacle and only in this sense
something " between " them (cf. Timaeus 50 c 7–D 4), for
this is the conception that he elsewhere himself ascribes to
Plato (De Iside 373 E [ὁ μὲν οὖν Πλάτων τὸ μὲν νοητὸν . . .
πατέρα, τὴν δὲ ὕλην καὶ μητέρα . . . καὶ χώραν γενέσεως, τὸ δ'
232

space, as he sometimes calls it abode and receptacle,[a] and the intelligible that he calls real existence [b]; and what he calls becoming, the universe not yet having come to be, is nothing other than that being involved in changes and motions which, ranged between what makes impressions and what receives them, disperses in this world the semblances from that world yonder.[c] For this very reason it was called divisible [d] and also because it is necessary for that which is perceiving and that which is forming mental images to be divided in correspondence with what is perceptible and with what is imaginable and to be coextensive with them,[e] for the motion of sense-perception, which is the soul's own,[f] moves towards what is perceptible without [g] but the intelligence, while it was abiding and immobile all by itself,[h] upon having got into the soul

ἐξ ἀμφοῖν ἔκγονον καὶ γένεσιν ὀνομάζειν εἴωθεν] and 372 F [εἰκὼν γάρ ἐστιν οὐσίας ἐν ὕλῃ γένεσις . . .]). In any case, Plutarch's precosmic soul, here identified with γένεσις, is irrational; and his giving it access to the intelligible world is an inconsistency resulting from his attempt to account for the "traces" and "modifications" in the chaos of *Timaeus* 52 D—53 B as literally precosmic (see note *e* on 1024 B *supra*).

[d] *i.e. Timaeus* 35 A, where, however, the μεριστὴ οὐσία is explicitly not μεταξὺ τεταγμένη (see note *d* on 1024 B *supra*).

[e] See 1024 A *supra* (μεριστὸν . . . ἅτε . . . σκεδαννυμένης ἐφαπτόμενον ὕλης) and *cf.* Simplicius, *De An.*, p. 45, 8-10; for the term συμπαρήκειν *cf.* Boethus in Simplicius, *Categ.*, p. 434, 3-4.

[f] Because τὴν . . . συμπαθῆ τῷ αἰσθητῷ κίνησιν is ἁπλῶς ψυχή (1024 A *supra*; *cf.* ψυχὴ καθ᾽ ἑαυτήν in 1014 D-E *supra*).

[g] *Cf.* [Plutarch], *De Placitis* 899 E = *Dox. Graeci*, p. 394 A 15-20; Porphyry, *Sententiae* xliii (pp. 41, 24–42, 1 and 42, 13-14 [Mommert]) = Stobaeus, *Ecl.* i, 48, 5 (pp 313, 15-17 and 314, 5-7 [Wachsmuth]).

[h] See note *e* on 1024 A *supra*.

(1024)
D
ἐγγενόμενος δὲ τῇ ψυχῇ καὶ κρατήσας εἰς ἑαυτὸν
ἐπιστρέφει καὶ συμπεραίνει τὴν ἐγκύκλιον φορὰν
περὶ τὸ μένον ἀεὶ[1] μάλιστα ψαύουσαν τοῦ ὄντος.
διὸ καὶ δυσανάκρατος ἡ κοινωνία γέγονεν αὐτῶν,
τῷ ἀμερίστῳ τὸ[2] μεριστὸν καὶ τῷ μηδαμῇ κινητῷ[3] τὸ πάντῃ φορητὸν μιγνύουσα καὶ καταβιαζο-
μένη[4] θάτερον εἰς ταὐτὸν[5] συνελθεῖν. ἦν δὲ τὸ
θάτερον οὐ κίνησις,[6] ὥσπερ οὐδὲ ταὐτὸν[7] στάσις,
ἀλλ' ἀρχὴ διαφορᾶς καὶ ἀνομοιότητος. ἑκάτερον
γὰρ ἀπὸ τῆς ἑτέρας ἀρχῆς κάτεισι, τὸ μὲν ταὐτὸν
ἀπὸ τοῦ ἑνὸς τὸ δὲ θάτερον[8] ἀπὸ τῆς δυάδος· καὶ
μέμικται πρῶτον ἐνταῦθα περὶ τὴν ψυχήν, ἀριθ-
E μοῖς καὶ λόγοις συνδεθέντα καὶ μεσότησιν ἐναρμο-

[1] τὸ μὲν ἀεὶ -u ; τὸ ἀεὶ -f.   [2] τὸν -e, u, Escor. 72[1].
[3] κινητὸν -r.
[4] καταβιβαζομένη -m[1], r.
[5] ταὐτὸ -E[1], B[1] (ν superscript -E[1], B[1]), r.
[6] ἦν δὲ τὸ θάτερον οὐ κίνησις -margin of f[1] (τὸ omitted) and
of m[1], *Epitome* 1032 c ; ἦν δὲ τὸ ἕτερον κίνησις -E (οὐκ ἦν in
margin -E[1], ἡ superscript between ν and κ -E[2]) ; οὐκ (two
dots over ὐ) ἦν δὲ τὸ ἕτερον ἡ κίνησις -B ; ἦν δὲ τὸ θάτερον ἡ
κίνησις -e, u, f, m, r, Escor. 72, Aldine.
[7] ὥσπερ δὲ ταὐτὸν (ὥσπερ δὲ οὐ ταὐτὸν in margin) -f, m ;
ὥσπερ δὴ ταὐτὸν (οὐ ταὐτὸν in margin) -r.
[8] τὸ δὲ ἕτερον -E, B (θάτερον in margin -B[1]).

[a] See *Plat. Quaest.* 1003 A with note *i* there for κρατήσασα
. . . ἐπέστρεψεν used of the rational soul's action upon the
motions of matter. Similar language to describe the influence of god upon the world-soul and its νοῦς is used by
Albinus in *Epitome* x, 3 and xiv, 3 (pp. 59, 5-7 and 81, 4-9
[Louis]=pp. 165, 1-3 and 169, 30-35 [Hermann]), with
which *cf.* also Chalcidius, *Platonis Timaeus*, p. 226, 8-9
(Wrobel)=p. 205, 1-2 (Waszink).
[b] *Cf.* Proclus, *In Primum Euclidis El. Lib.*, p. 147, 15-18
(Friedlein). For περὶ τὸ μένον ἀεὶ see 1024 A, note *g supra*,
and for the "circular motion" see *Plat. Quaest.* 1004 c
with note *d* there.

and taken control makes her turn around to him[a]
and with her accomplishes about that which always
remains fixed the circular motion most closely in
contact with real existence.[b] This is also why the
union of them proved to be a difficult fusion, being a
mixing of the divisible with the indivisible [c] and of
the altogether transient with the utterly immobile
and a constraining of difference to unite with sameness. Difference is not motion, however, as sameness is not rest either,[d] but the principle of differentiation and dissimilitude.[e] In fact, each of the
two derives from another of two principles, sameness
from the one and difference from the dyad[f]; and it
is first here in the soul that they have been commingled, bound together by numbers and ratios and

---

[c] In *Timaeus* 35 A (see 1012 c *supra*) δύσμικτον is used
not of the " divisible " or the " indivisible " but of " difference " alone, and this Plutarch himself later emphasizes and
defends just after having distinguished the " divisible " and
the " indivisible " from " difference " and " sameness "
(1025 B-C *infra*).

[d] See *supra* 1013 D with notes f and g there; ἦν here is
the " philosophical imperfect."

[e] *Cf.* 1025 c *infra* (τὸ μὲν ταὐτὸν ἰδέα τῶν ὡσαύτως ἐχόντων
ἐστὶ τὸ δὲ θάτερον τῶν διαφόρως . . .) and *De Defectu Orac.* 428 c
(ἡ τοῦ ἑτέρου δύναμις . . . ἐνείργασται . . . τὰς . . . ἀνομοιότητας).

[f] *Cf.* Nicomachus, *Arithmetica Introductio* ii, xvii, 1
(p. 109, 2-6 [Hoche] and on this passage Philoponus,
B, νε, lines 12-15 [Hoche] and Asclepius, ii, ιη, lines 17-19
[Tarán]; Moderatus in Porphyry, *Vita Pythagorae*, 49-50
(p. 44, 8-18 [Nauck]); Plutarch, *De Garrulitate* 507 A
(ἡ δὲ δυὰς ἀρχὴ διαφορᾶς ἀόριστος). With the derivation from
these principles introduced here and reflected in the reference
to " dyadic " and " monadic " parts in 1025 D *infra* Plutarch comes near to giving soul an arithmetical character
not unlike that to which he objects in the Xenocratean interpretation (1013 c-D and 1023 c-D [chap. 22 *sub finem*] *supra*).
See similarly note b on 1025 A *infra*.

PLUTARCH'S MORALIA

(1024) νίοις, καὶ ποιεῖ¹ θάτερον μὲν ἐγγενόμενον τῷ ταὐτῷ
διαφορὰν τὸ δὲ ταὐτὸν ἐν τῷ ἑτέρῳ τάξιν, ὡς δῆλόν ἐστιν ἐν ταῖς πρώταις τῆς ψυχῆς δυνάμεσιν· εἰσὶ
δὲ αὗται τὸ κριτικὸν καὶ τὸ κινητικόν.² ἡ μὲν οὖν
κίνησις εὐθὺς ἐπιδείκνυται περὶ τὸν οὐρανὸν ἐν
μὲν³ τῇ ταὐτότητι τὴν ἑτερότητα τῇ περιφορᾷ τῶν
ἀπλανῶν⁴ ἐν δὲ τῇ ἑτερότητι τὴν ταὐτότητα τῇ τάξει
τῶν πλανήτων⁵· ἐπικρατεῖ γὰρ ἐν ἐκείνοις τὸ ταὐτὸν ἐν δὲ τοῖς περὶ γῆν τοὐναντίον. ἡ δὲ κρίσις⁶
ἀρχὰς μὲν ἔχει δύο, τόν τε νοῦν ἀπὸ τοῦ⁷ ταὐτοῦ
πρὸς τὰ καθόλου καὶ τὴν αἴσθησιν ἀπὸ τοῦ ἑτέρου
F πρὸς τὰ καθ' ἕκαστα. μέμικται δὲ λόγος ἐξ ἀμ-

¹ ποῖ -r. ² κινητόν -u. ³ ἐν δὲ -f, m, r, Aldine.
⁴ ἀπλανῶν -mss.; under this word πλανητῶν -E¹, and in
margin as correction -B¹.
⁵ τῶν πλανήτων -Epitome 1032 D; τῶν . . . vac. 6 . . . -E,
B; τῶν ἀπλανῶν -e, u, Escor. 72, Aldine; τῶν πλανωμένων
-f, m, r. ⁶ κίνησις -u, Aldine.
⁷ τοῦ -E¹ (added superscript), B, Epitome 1032 D;
omitted by all other mss. and Aldine.

---

[a] Not "harmonic," for which Plutarch uses the regular
technical expression, ἁρμονικὴ μεσότης, and which he knows
is only one of the two means used in Timaeus 36 A (see
1019 D and 1028 A infra); see page 175 supra with note c
there on ἀριθμῷ καὶ λόγῳ καὶ ἁρμονίᾳ.
[b] Cf. 1025 F and 1027 A (τῇ δὲ ταὐτοῦ καὶ τῇ ἑτέρου δυνάμει
τάξιν . . . καὶ διαφορὰν . . .) infra; and for another use
of the distinction between difference in sameness and sameness in difference cf. Porphyry, Sententiae xxxvi and xxxvii
(p. 31, 1-9 and pp. 32, 15-33, 8 [Mommert]) and Marius
Victorinus, Adv. Arium i, 48, 22-28 (Henry-Hadot).
[c] Cf. Aristotle, De Anima 432 a 15-17.
[d] Cf. De Virtute Morali 441 E-F. In Timaeus 36 c 4–D 7
the single and undivided outer revolution, into which all the
"fixed stars" are set (40 A 2–B 6), is called the motion of
sameness; and the inner revolution of seven circles, unequal and with speeds different but rationally related (and

236

harmonious means,[a] and that difference come to be in sameness produces differentiation but sameness in difference order,[b] as is clear in the case of the soul's primary faculties. These are the faculties of discernment and motivity.[c] Now, directly in the heaven motion exhibits diversity in identity by the revolution of the fixed stars and identity in diversity by the order of the planets, for in the former sameness predominates but its opposite in the things about the earth.[d] Discernment, however, has two principles,[e] intelligence proceeding from sameness to universals and sense-perception from difference to particulars [f] ;

so " ordered "), into each of which one of the planets is set (38 c 7–d 1), is called the motion of difference. All these circles, however, are homogeneous in constitution (35 b 1-3 and 36 b 5–c 4) ; and their designations are not meant to distinguish as their respective constituents the sameness and difference that were ingredients in the blending of soul (so apparently " Timaeus Locrus " 96 c [. . . τάπερ αἰθέρια . . . τὰ μὲν τᾶς ταὐτῶ φύσιος εἶμεν τὰ δὲ τᾶς τῶ ἑτέρω.]) or to indicate any predominance of one or the other of the latter in each of the two revolutions such as Plutarch here assumes and for which even Proclus tries to account though recognizing that the constitution of the two revolutions is homogeneous (In Platonis Timaeum ii, pp. 253, 23–255, 8 and p. 255, 13-16 [Diehl]).

[e] Cf. Aristotle, De Anima 432 a 16 (. . . τῷ τε κριτικῷ [see note c supra] ὁ διανοίας ἔργον ἐστὶ καὶ αἰσθήσεως) and see supra 1012 f, note c and 1023 d, note a on κρίνειν. With ἀρχὰς . . . δύο here cf. Albinus, Epitome iv, 4 (p. 13, 14-15 [Louis]=p. 154, 28-29 [Hermann]).

[f] Cf. Timaeus 37 b 6–c 3 (1023 e-f supra), where from the reports of the circle of sameness concerning the rational and of the circle of difference concerning the perceptible arise respectively knowledge and opinion ; but the characters of these circles Plutarch here, as in the preceding sentence (see note d supra), equates with the sameness and difference that are ingredients of soul. For universals as

(1024) φοῖν, νόησις ἐν τοῖς νοητοῖς καὶ δόξα γιγνόμενος ἐν
τοῖς αἰσθητοῖς ὀργάνοις τε μεταξὺ[1] φαντασίαις τε
καὶ μνήμαις[2] χρώμενος, ὧν τὰ μὲν ἐν τῷ ταὐτῷ
τὸ ἕτερον τὰ δ' ἐν τῷ ἑτέρῳ ποιεῖ τὸ ταὐτόν. ἔστι
γὰρ ἡ μὲν νόησις κίνησις τοῦ νοοῦντος περὶ τὸ
μένον, ἡ δὲ δόξα μονὴ τοῦ αἰσθανομένου περὶ τὸ
1025 κινούμενον. φαντασίαν δὲ συμπλοκὴν δόξης πρὸς
αἴσθησιν οὖσαν ἵστησιν ἐν μνήμῃ τὸ ταὐτὸν τὸ δὲ

---

[1] τε καὶ μεταξὺ -Aldine ; τε ταῖς μεταξὺ -Stephanus.
[2] γνώμαις -r.

---

the objects of knowledge or intelligence contrasted to particulars as the objects of sense-perception see 1025 E *infra*
(. . . νοεῖν μὲν ἐκεῖνα ταῦτα δ' αἰσθάνεσθαι . . .) and *cf.* Aristotle,
De Anima 417 b 22-23 and *Physics* 189 a 5-8 ; Areius
Didymus, *Epitomes Frag. Phys.* 16 (*Dox. Graeci*, p. 456,
9-12) ; Proclus, *In Primum Euclidis El. Lib.*, p. 30, 11-15
(Friedlein).

[a] *i.e.* the λόγος of *Timaeus* 37 B 3 (*ratio* in Cicero, *Timaeus*
28, p. 177, 2 [Plasberg] and *motus rationabilis* in Chalcidius,
Platonis Timaeus, p. 172, 11 and 19-21 [Wrobel]=p. 153,
16 and 23-25 [Waszink]), which there, however, means
" discourse " (see 1023 E *supra*) but discourse which is
articulate thought (*cf. Theaetetus* 189 E 6-7 and *Sophist*
263 E 3-6).

[b] *Cf.* Proclus, *In Platonis Timaeum* i, p. 255, 2-24 and
ii, p. 299, 16-24 (Diehl) ; and *cf.* also the διττὸς λόγος of
Albinus, *Epitome* iv, 3 (p. 13, 8-11 [Louis]=p. 154, 22-25
[Hermann]) with the *duplex virtus* of the rational part of the
soul in Chalcidius, *Platonis Timaeus*, p. 198, 22-26 (Wrobel)
=p. 177, 14-17 (Waszink).

[c] For the connexion of μνήμη and φαντασία *cf.* Aristotle,
De Memoria 450 a 22-25 and 451 a 14-17 ; with ὀργάνοις *cf.*
Plutarch, frag. xv (vii, p. 111, 12-14 [Bernardakis])=frag.
23, 9-11 (Sandbach) and *Adv. Colotem* 1119 A (τὰ δὲ λοιπὰ

and reason *a* is a blend of both, becoming intellection
in the case of the intelligibles and opinion in the case
of the perceptibles *b* and employing between them
mental images and memories as instruments,*c* of
which the former are produced by difference in sameness and the latter by sameness in difference.*d* For
intellection is motion of what is cognizing about what
remains fixed,*e* and opinion fixity of what is perceiving about what is in motion *f* ; but mental
imagining, which is a combination of opinion with
sense-perception,*g* is brought to a stop in memory

. . . ὄργανα τῆς τούτου δυνάμεως); and with μεταξύ cf.
Plotinus, *Enn.* iv, iv, 13, line 13 and Proclus, *In Primum
Euclidis El. Lib.*, p. 52, 10-21 (Friedlein).

d The antecedent of ὧν τὰ μὲν . . . τὰ δ' is not, as Thévenaz
thought (*L'Âme du Monde*, pp. 29 and 81), τοῖς νοητοῖς . . .
τοῖς αἰσθητοῖς but φαντασίαις τε καὶ μνήμαις treated as neuter
because of ὀργάνοις. Their dependence upon difference and
sameness is explained in the second half of the next sentence,
as was that of νοῦς and αἴσθησις in the preceding one (page
237, note *f*). The whole of this exposition has to do with the
rôles of sameness and difference not in the existence of intelligibles and perceptibles but in the constitution of the
soul's faculties (see 1024 E *supra*).

e See 1024 D *supra* with note *b* there ; and cf. Aristotle,
De Anima 407 a 20-22 (on the *Timaeus*) : νοῦ μὲν γὰρ κίνησις
νόησις. . . .

f Contrast τὸ δοξαστικὸν . . . πλανητόν, ἅτε δὴ φερομένης . . .
ἐφαπτόμενον ὕλης (1024 A *supra*) and τῷ αἰσθητῷ τὸ αἰσθανόμενον
. . . ἀνάγκη . . . συμπαρήκειν (1024 C *supra*) ; but cf. δόξαι . . .
βέβαιοι of *Timaeus* 37 B 8 (1023 E *supra*) and the interpretation by Proclus, *In Platonis Timaeum* ii, p. 310, 5-10 (Diehl).

g Cf. Aristotle, *De Anima* 428 a 25-26 (οὐδὲ συμπλοκὴ
δόξης καὶ αἰσθήσεως) against Plato, *Sophist* 264 b 1-2 (σύμμειξις
αἰσθήσεως καὶ δόξης), where δόξα means " judgment," however, διανοίας ἀποτελεύτησις, in distinction from its meaning in
Timaeus 37 B 8 (cf. Proclus, *In Platonis Rem Publicam* i, pp.
262, 25-263, 8 [Kroll]).

PLUTARCH'S MORALIA

(1025) θάτερον¹ κινεῖ πάλιν ἐν διαφορᾷ² τοῦ πρόσθεν καὶ νῦν, ἑτερότητος ἅμα καὶ ταὐτότητος ἐφαπτομένην.³

25. Δεῖ δὲ τὴν περὶ τὸ σῶμα τοῦ κόσμου γενομένην σύντηξιν⁴ εἰκόνα λαβεῖν τῆς ἀναλογίας ἐν ᾗ διηρμόσατο⁵ ψυχήν.⁶ ἐκεῖ μὲν γὰρ ἦν ἄκρα τὸ⁷ πῦρ καὶ ἡ⁸ γῆ, χαλεπὴν⁹ πρὸς ἄλληλα κραθῆναι φύσιν ἔχοντα μᾶλλον δὲ ὅλως ἄκρατον καὶ ἀσύστατον· ὅθεν ἐν μέσῳ θέμενος αὐτῶν τὸν μὲν ἀέρα πρὸ τοῦ πυρὸς τὸ δὲ ὕδωρ πρὸ τῆς γῆς, ταῦτα πρῶτον ἀλλήλοις ἐκέρασεν εἶτα διὰ τούτων ἐκεῖνα πρός τε

B ταῦτα καὶ πρὸς¹⁰ ἄλληλα συνέμιξε καὶ συνήρμοσεν. ἐνταῦθα δὲ πάλιν τὸ ταὐτὸν καὶ τὸ θάτερον,¹¹ ἐναν-

¹ τὸ δὲ ἕτερον -E, B. ² ἐκ διαφορᾶς -u.
³ ἐφαπτομένην -B. Müller (1873) ; ἐφαπτόμενον -mss.
⁴ σύνταξιν -r, Epitome 1032 e. ⁵ διηρμήσατο -e, u.
⁶ ⟨τὴν⟩ ψυχήν -Bernardakis (vi, p. 531 : Addenda) from Epitome 1032 e.
⁷ ἄκρα τὸ -Wyttenbach from Epitome 1032 e ; ἄκρατον -mss. ⁸ ἡ -omitted by f. ⁹ χαλεπὸν -r.
¹⁰ πρὸς -omitted in Epitome 1032 e.
¹¹ τὸ ἕτερον -E, B.

ᵃ Cf. Aristotle, De Memoria 451 a 14-16 (μνήμη . . . φαντάσματος . . . ἕξις) and 450 a 27-b 11 with Themistius (Sophonias), Parva Nat., p. 5, 13 ad loc. (μνήμη δ' ἐστὶν ἡ ταύτης [scil. φαντασίας] μονὴ καὶ σωτηρία). For μνήμη referred to μονή cf. Plato, Cratylus 437 b 3 and the note on the Stoic definition in De Comm. Not. 1085 a infra, μνήμας δὲ μονίμους καὶ σχετικὰς τυπώσεις (=φαντασίας).
ᵇ As Thévenaz observed (L'Âme du Monde, p. 82), ἵστησιν . . . τὸ ταὐτὸν τὸ δὲ θάτερον κινεῖ (cf. τῇ ἑτέρου δυνάμει . . . μεταβολὴν . . . in 1027 a infra) asserts what Plutarch criticized Xenocrates for asserting (see supra page 167, note a and 1013 d with notes f and g). For a similar inconsistency see note f on 1024 d supra.
ᶜ Cf. Aristotle, De Memoria 449 b 22-30, 450 a 19-22,

240

by sameness [a] and by difference again set moving [b] in the distinction of past and present, [c] as it is in contact with diversity and identity at once.

25. The fusion [d] that was carried out in the case of the body of the universe must be taken as a likeness of the proportion with which he [e] regulated soul. In the former case, because there were extremes, fire and earth, of a nature difficult to blend together or rather utterly immiscible and incohesive, he accordingly put between them air in front of the fire and water in front of the earth and blended these with each other first and then by means of these commingled and conjoined those extremes with them and with each other. [f] And in the latter case again he

and 452 b 28-29 ; and the Stoic definition of memory mentioned by Plutarch, *De Sollertia Animalium* 961 c.

[d] For the noun σύντηξις in this sense *cf.* Proclus (commenting on *Timaeus* 43 A 3), *In Platonis Timaeum* iii, p. 321, 14-19 and p. 323, 9-12 (Diehl), where the erroneous variant σύνταξ- appears in some MSS. also.

[e] *i.e.* god, the demiurge : *cf.* ἐν μέσῳ θέμενος in the next sentence *infra* with ὁ θεὸς ἐν μέσῳ θείς of *Timaeus* 32 B 4.

[f] *Timaeus* 32 B 3-7. The " blending " and " mingling " of Plutarch's interpretation here (*cf.* also *De Fortuna Romanorum* 316 E-F and the rôle assigned to air between fire and water in *De Primo Frigido* 951 D-E) are entirely absent from *Timaeus* 31 B 4—32 C 4 ; and the reason given there for inserting two means between the extremes of fire and earth is purely mathematical (see 1016 F—1017 A *supra*), as it remains in " Timaeus Locrus " 99 A-B and Albinus, *Epitome* xii, 2 (pp. 69, 14–71, 4 [Louis]=p. 167, 25-32 [Hermann]). For other " physical " interpretations *cf.* Theon Smyrnaeus, p. 97, 8-12 (Hiller) ; Macrobius, *In Somnium Scipionis* i, vi, 23-34 (*n.b. permisceri* in 24) ; Chalcidius, *Platonis Timaeus*, pp. 86, 10–88, 7 (Wrobel)= pp. 71, 24–73, 4 (Waszink) ; Proclus, *In Platonis Timaeum* ii, pp. 39, 14–42, 2 (Diehl) ; Philoponus, *De Aeternitate Mundi* xiii, 13 (pp. 514, 24–516, 23 [Rabe]) and *In Nico-*

(1025) τίας δυνάμεις καὶ ἀκρότητας ἀντιπάλους, συνήγα-
γεν οὐ δι᾽ αὑτῶν,[1] ἀλλ᾽ οὐσίας ἑτέρας μεταξύ, τὴν
μὲν ἀμέριστον πρὸ τοῦ ταὐτοῦ[2] πρὸ δὲ τοῦ θατέρου[3] τὴν μεριστήν, ἔστιν ᾗ προσήκουσαν ἑκατέραν
ἑκατέρᾳ τάξας εἶτα μιχθείσαις[4] ἐκείναις ἐπεγκεραν-
νύμενος, οὕτως τὸ πᾶν συνύφηνε[5] τῆς ψυχῆς
εἶδος, ὡς ἦν ἀνυστόν, ἐκ διαφόρων ὅμοιον ἔκ τε
πολλῶν ἓν ἀπειργασμένος.[6] οὐκ εὖ δέ τινες εἰρῆ-
σθαι λέγουσι δύσμικτον ὑπὸ τοῦ Πλάτωνος τὴν
θατέρου φύσιν, οὐκ ἄδεκτον οὖσαν ἀλλὰ[7] καὶ φίλην
C μεταβολῆς· μᾶλλον δὲ τὴν τοῦ[8] ταὐτοῦ, μόνιμον καὶ
δυσμετάβλητον οὖσαν, οὐ ῥᾳδίως προσίεσθαι μῖξιν
ἀλλ᾽ ἀπωθεῖσθαι καὶ φεύγειν, ὅπως ἁπλῆ διαμείνῃ[9]

Υ

[1] αὑτῶν -B ; αυτῶν -E ; αὐτῶν -all other mss.
[2] πρὸ τοῦ ταὐτοῦ -Stephanus from *Epitome* 1032 f ; πρὸ
ταυτοῦ -Leonicus ; πρὸ τούτου -mss.
[3] πρὸ δὲ τοῦ ἑτέρου -E, B.
[4] μιχθείσας -Dübner.
[5] E, B, f, m, r, Escor. 72 (ε over erasure) ; συνύφην ἐν -e ;
συνύφην ἐν -u, Aldine ; συνύφηνεν -Basiliensis ; συνύφηνε ἐν
-Stephanus ; συνύφηνεν ἐν -Hutten.
[6] ἀπειργασάμενος -f ; ἀπεργασάμενος -*Epitome* 1032 f.
[7] ἀλλὰ -omitted by E, B.
[8] τοῦ -Maurommates ; τῆς -mss.
[9] διαμένῃ -r.

---

machi Arith. Introd. B xxiv, 11 (p. 28 [Hoche, 1867]) ;
Nemesius, *De Natura Hominis* v (pp. 153-154 [Matthaei]) ;
J. H. Waszink, *Studien zum Timaioskommentar des Calcidius* I (1964), pp. 74-82.
    [a] *Cf.* Philoponus, *In Nicomachi Arith. Introd.* B xviii,
1=ξ, lines 12-16 (p. 18 [Hoche, 1867]) : . . . τὸ γὰρ ταὐτὸν
ἀδιαίρετον. . . . So some derived sameness in the psychogony
from the indivisible being and difference from the divisible
or identified the two pairs (*cf.* Proclus, *In Platonis Timaeum*

united sameness and difference, contrary forces and
antagonistic extremes, not just by themselves ; but
by first interposing other beings, the indivisible in
front of sameness and in front of difference the
divisible, as each of the one pair is in a way akin to
one of the other,[a] and by then making an additional
blend with those between after they had been commingled [b] he thus fabricated the whole structure of
the soul,[c] from what were various having made it as
nearly uniform and from what were many as nearly
single as was feasible. Some [d] say that it was not
right of Plato to use " refractory to mixture " as an
epithet of the nature of difference,[e] since it is not
unreceptive of change but is positively friendly to it,
and that it is rather the nature of sameness which,
being constant and hard to change, does not readily
submit to mixture but rejects and shuns it in order

ii, p. 155, 20-23 [Diehl] ; Themistius, *De Anima*, p. 11,
10-12 ; A. E. Taylor, *A Commentary on Plato's Timaeus*,
p. 128).

[b] See *infra* 1025 E (τὴν ἐκ τῆς ἀμερίστου καὶ τῆς μεριστῆς ὁ
θεὸς ὑποδοχὴν τῷ ταὐτῷ καὶ τῷ θατέρῳ συνέστησεν) and 1025 F
(δεῖται τρίτης τινὸς οἷον ὕλης ὑποδεχομένης . . .). For the way in
which Plutarch elicited this misinterpretation from *Timaeus*
35 A 4-B 1 see notes *a* and *c* on 1012 c *supra* with the reference in the latter note to Proclus (*In Platonis Timaeum*
ii, p. 159, 5-14 [Diehl]), who construed the text correctly,
inferring from it, however, contrary to Plutarch that (the
intermediate) sameness and difference were combined first
and the blend of them was then combined with (the intermediate) being.

[c] Cf. τὸ τῆς ψυχῆς εἶδος in *Plat. Quaest.* 1008 c, and for
συνεκεράσατο εἰς μίαν πάντα ἰδέαν of *Timaeus* 35 A 7 see *supra*
1012 c with note *b* there and 1023 B, note *c*.

[d] They have not yet been identified.

[e] *Timaeus* 35 A 7-8 (see 1012 c *supra* and note *c* on 1024 D
supra).

PLUTARCH'S MORALIA

(1025) καὶ εἰλικρινὴς[1] καὶ ἀναλλοίωτος. οἱ δὲ ταῦτ᾽[2]
ἐγκαλοῦντες ἀγνοοῦσιν ὅτι τὸ μὲν ταὐτὸν ἰδέα τῶν
ὡσαύτως ἐχόντων ἐστὶ τὸ δὲ θάτερον[3] τῶν διαφόρως καὶ τούτου μὲν ἔργον, ὧν ἂν ἅψηται, διιστάναι[4] καὶ[5] ἀλλοιοῦν καὶ πολλὰ ποιεῖν ἐκείνου δὲ
συνάγειν καὶ συνιστάναι διὰ ὁμοιότητος ἐκ[6] πολλῶν μίαν ἀναλαμβάνοντος[7] μορφὴν καὶ δύναμιν.

26. Αὗται μὲν οὖν δυνάμεις τῆς τοῦ παντός εἰσι
ψυχῆς εἰς δὲ θνητὰ καὶ παθητὰ παρεισιοῦσαι[8] ὄργανα ⟨σωμάτων⟩.[9] ἄφθαρτα καὶ αὐτὰ[10] [σωμάτων][11]
D ἐν ταύταις[12] τὸ τῆς δυαδικῆς[13] καὶ ἀορίστου μερίδος
ἐπιφαίνεται[14] μᾶλλον εἶδος, ⟨τὸ⟩[15] δὲ τῆς ἁπλῆς καὶ
μοναδικῆς ἀμυδρότερον ὑποδέδυκεν. οὐ μὴν ῥᾳδίως ἄν τις οὔτε πάθος ἀνθρώπου παντάπασιν

   [1] εἰληκρινὴς -f, m. r.
   [2] ταῦτα -E, B ; ταύτας -all other mss. (ṡ -r).
   [3] τὸ δὲ ἔτερον -E, B.
   [4] διεστάναι -u, Aldine.
   [5] διιστάναι δι᾽ ὁμοιότητος (omitting καὶ ἀλλοιοῦν . . . καὶ
συνιστάναι) -f, r.
   [6] ἐκ -E, B ; ἐκεῖ -all other mss., Aldine.
   [7] H. C. ; ἀναλαμβάνοντα -mss. ; ἀναλαμβανόντων -Turnebus,
Stephanus.
   [8] E, B, f, m, r, Basiliensis ; παρεισιοῦται -e, u, Escor. 72,
Aldine ; ⟨αἱ⟩ παρεισίασιν -B. Müller (1873) ; αἱ δ᾽ εἰς . . .
παρεισίασιν -Bernardakis.
   [9] ⟨σωμάτων⟩ -added by H. C.
   [10] ἄφθαρτα καὶ αὐτὰ -mss. ; φθαρτῶν καὶ αὐτὰ -Stephanus ;
⟨φθαρτῶν⟩ ἄφθαρτοι αὐταὶ -Dübner ; ἄφθαρτοι καὶ αὐταὶ -B.
Müller (1873) ; ἄφθαρτοι ⟨φθαρτῶν⟩ αὐταὶ -Bernardakis.
   [11] [σωμάτων] -deleted by H. C.
   [12] τούτοις -Stephanus.
   [13] τῆς ἁπλῆς δυαδικῆς -f.
   [14] ἐπιφέρεται -B¹ (ρ remade to ν -B²).

to remain simple and pure and unsubject to altera-
tion. They who make these objections fail to understand, however, that sameness is the idea [a] of things
identical and difference of things various and that the
function of the latter is to divide and diversify and
make many whatever it touches but of the former
is to unite and combine,[b] recovering from many by
means of similarity a single form and force.[c]

26. Now, these are faculties of the soul of the sum
of things [d] but enter besides [e] into mortal and passible
organs ⟨of bodies⟩. Indestructible as they are
themselves, in these faculties [f] the form of the dyadic
and indefinite part makes itself more apparent, while
⟨that⟩ of the simple and monadic part is submerged
in greater obscurity.[g] It would not be easy, however, to observe in man either an emotion entirely

[a] Cf. Plato, Sophist 255 E 5-6 and 256 A 12–B 3 (see 1013 D
supra with note g there) and see ἰδέα in 1023 c supra.

[b] See note e on 1024 D supra with De Defectu Orac. 428 c
referred to there and De E 391 c (... ταὐτοῦ δὲ τὴν μιγνύου-
σαν ἀρχὴν θατέρου δὲ τὴν διακρίνουσαν) ; and cf. Proclus, In
Platonis Timaeum ii, p. 155, 14-20 and p. 158, 18-31 (Diehl).

[c] See 1022 F supra with note c there ; cf. Plato, Phaedrus
265 D 3-4 and Hermias, In Platonis Phaedrum, p. 171, 8-11
(Couvreur).

[d] Cf. Timaeus 41 D 4-5 (τὴν τοῦ παντὸς ψυχὴν . . .) and De
Virtute Morali 441 F (ἥ τ' ἀνθρώπου ψυχὴ μέρος ἢ μίμημα τῆς
τοῦ παντὸς οὖσα . . .).

[e] The text has been thought to be corrupt chiefly because
of the failure to recognize παρεισιοῦσαι as a periphrastic
present (cf. Weissenberger, Die Sprache Plutarchs I, p. 9 :
H. Widmann, Beiträge zur Syntax Epikurs, p. 135).

[f] i.e. in these that have entered into the mortal organs of
bodies.

[g] The dyadic part is manifested as difference and the
monadic as sameness (see 1024 D supra with note f there).

---

[15] ⟨τὸ⟩ -added by Wyttenbach.

(1025) ἀπηλλαγμένον λογισμοῦ κατανοήσειεν οὔτε διανοίας
κίνησιν ᾗ μηδὲν ἐπιθυμίας ἢ φιλοτιμίας ἢ τοῦ
χαίροντος ἢ λυπουμένου πρόσεστι. διὸ τῶν φιλοσόφων οἱ μὲν τὰ πάθη λόγους ποιοῦσιν, ὡς πᾶσαν
ἐπιθυμίαν καὶ λύπην καὶ ὀργὴν κρίσεις οὔσας· οἱ δὲ
τὰς ἀρετὰς ἀποφαίνουσι παθητικάς, καὶ γὰρ ἀν-
δρείᾳ[1] τὸ φοβούμενον καὶ σωφροσύνη τὸ ἡδόμενον
καὶ δικαιοσύνη τὸ κερδαλέον εἶναι.[2] καὶ μὴν θεω-
E ρητικῆς γε τῆς ψυχῆς οὔσης ἅμα καὶ πρακτικῆς
καὶ θεωρούσης μὲν τὰ καθόλου πραττούσης δὲ[3] τὰ
καθ᾽ ἕκαστα καὶ νοεῖν μὲν ἐκεῖνα ταῦτα δ᾽ αἰσθά-

---

[1] ἀνδρία -B, u.
[2] ἐνεῖναι -Bernardakis.
[3] καὶ θεωρούσης μὲν τὰ καθόλου πραττούσης δὲ -f[1] (in margin),
m[1] (in margin) ; καὶ θεωρούσης δὲ (δὲ -omitted by E, B) τὰ καθ᾽
ἕκαστα -mss., Aldine.

---

[a] See 1024 F *supra* (ἡ μὲν νόησις κίνησις τοῦ νοοῦντος . . .).
For διάνοια used of the intellectual faculty of the soul *cf.*
De Virtute Morali 441 c (Stoics) and 448 B-c (Plutarch himself of τὸ θεωρητικόν, *cf.* 451 B [τὸ διανοητικόν] and *Plat.
Quaest.* 1004 D *supra*) ; Galen, *De Placitis Hippoc. et Plat.*
ix, 1 (p. 733, 11-14 [Mueller]).
[b] *Cf. De Virtute Morali* 443 B-c (. . . τὸ θυμούμενον ἐν
ἡμῖν καὶ ἐπιθυμοῦν . . . οὐκ ἀποικοῦν οὐδ᾽ ἀπεσχισμένον [*scil.* τοῦ
φρονοῦντος] . . . ἀλλὰ φύσει μὲν ἐξηρτημένον ἀεὶ δὲ ὁμιλοῦν . . .).
[c] Stoic doctrine (*cf. De Virtute Morali* 441 c-D and
446 F—447 A, *De Sollertia Animalium* 961 D ; and Diogenes
Laertius, vii, 111 [*S.V.F.* i, frag. 202 and iii, frags. 382,
456, 459, 461, and 462]).
[d] *Cf. De Virtute Morali* 443 c-D (. . . τὰς ἠθικὰς ἀρετάς, οὐκ
ἀπαθείας οὔσας ἀλλὰ συμμετρίας παθῶν καὶ μεσότητας, . . . [*cf.*
Aristotle, *Eth. Nic.* 1104 b 24-26]) and Albinus, *Epitome*,
xxxii, 1 (p. 155, 1-5 [Louis]=p. 185, 21-25 [Hermann]) : αἱ
πλεῖσται ἀρεταὶ περὶ πάθη γίνονται . . . The doctrine is originally
Peripatetic : *cf.* Aristotle, *Eth. Nic.* 1104 b 13-16, 1109 b 30,

divorced from reason or a motion of the mind [a] in which there is present nothing of desire or ambition or rejoicing or grieving.[b] This is why some of the philosophers make the emotions varieties of reason, on the ground that all desire and grief and anger are judgments,[c] while others declare that the virtues have to do with emotions,[d] for fearing is the province of courage and enjoyment that of sobriety and acquisitiveness that of justice.[e] Now, as the soul is at once contemplative and practical [f] and contemplates the universals but acts upon the particulars [g] and apparently cognizes the former but perceives the

and 1178 a 10-21 with Aspasius, *Eth. Nic.*, p. 42, 21-24 ; [Aristotle], *Magna Moralia* 1206 a 36–b 29 ; Areius Didymus in Stobaeus, *Ecl.* ii, 7, 20 (p. 142, 6-7 [Wachsmuth]) ; and the Pseudo-Pythagoreans, Metopus and Theages, in Stobaeus, *Anth.* iii, 1, 115, and 118 (pp. 71, 16–72, 1 and p. 81, 11-14 [Hense]).

  [e] For courage and sobriety *cf. Eth. Nic.* 1104 a 18–b 8 and *Magna Moralia* 1185 b 21-32, and for justice *cf. Eth. Eud.* 1221 a 4 and 23-24 ; *cf.* also Stobaeus, *Ecl.* ii, 7, 20 (p. 141, 5-18 [Wachsmuth]) and Plutarch, *De Virtute Morali* 445 A (Babut, *Plutarque de la Vertu Éthique*, p. 78 and *Plutarque et le Stoïcisme*, pp. 331-332).

  [f] *Cf.* Albinus, *Epitome* ii, 2 and iv, 8 (pp. 7, 1-2 and 21, 4-8 [Louis]=pp. 153, 2-4 and 156, 13-17 [Hermann]) ; Proclus, *In Platonis Timaeum* iii, p. 335, 2-10 (Diehl) on *Timaeus* 43 c 7–D 4 ; Simplicius, *De Anima*, p. 95, 26-27. This bipartition, foreshadowed in Plato's *Politicus* 258 E 4-7, goes back to Xenocrates (frag. 6 [Heinze]) and Aristotle (*De Anima* 407 a 23-25 and 433 a 14-15, *Politics* 1333 a 24-25) ; and despite the tripartition frequently used by the latter (*Metaphysics* 1025 b 25, *Eth. Nic.* 1139 a 26-31) it became the conventional Peripatetic distinction ([Plutarch], *De Placitis*, 874 F—875 A=*Dox. Graeci*, pp. 273 A 25—274 A 17 ; Diogenes Laertius, v, 28).

  [g] *Cf.* Aristotle, *Metaphysics* 981 a 15-24 ; *Eth. Nic.* 1141 b 16 and 1143 a 32-33.

(1025) νεσθαι δοκούσης, ὁ κοινὸς λόγος ἀεὶ περί τε
ταὐτὸν ἐντυγχάνων τῷ θατέρῳ¹ καὶ ταὐτῷ² περὶ
θάτερον ἐπιχειρεῖ μὲν ὅροις καὶ διαιρέσεσι χωρίζειν τὸ ἓν καὶ τὰ πολλὰ καὶ τὸ ἀμερὲς καὶ τὸ
μεριστὸν³ οὐ δύναται δὲ καθαρῶς ἐν οὐδετέρῳ γενέσθαι διὰ τὸ καὶ⁴ τὰς ἀρχὰς ἐναλλὰξ⁵ ἐμπεπλέχθαι
καὶ καταμεμῖχθαι δι' ἀλλήλων. καὶ διὰ τοῦτο τῆς
οὐσίας τὴν ἐκ τῆς ἀμερίστου καὶ τῆς μεριστῆς ὁ
θεὸς ὑποδοχὴν τῷ ταὐτῷ⁶ καὶ τῷ θατέρῳ⁷ συν-
F έστησεν ἵν' ἐν διαφορᾷ τάξις γένηται· τοῦτο γὰρ
ἦν γενέσθαι, ἐπεὶ χωρὶς τούτων⁸ τὸ μὲν ταὐτὸν
οὐκ εἶχε διαφορὰν ὥστ' οὐδὲ κίνησιν οὐδὲ γένεσιν
τὸ θάτερον⁹ δὲ τάξιν οὐκ εἶχεν ὥστ' οὐδὲ σύστασιν
οὐδὲ γένεσιν. καὶ γὰρ εἰ τῷ ταὐτῷ συμβέβηκεν

¹ τῷ ἑτέρῳ -E, B.   ² καὶ ταυτὸ -B.
³ καὶ τὸ μεριστὸν -f, m ; καὶ τὸ ἀμεριστὸν -r¹ ; καὶ μεριστὸν
-E, B, e, u, Escor. 72, Aldine.
⁴ καὶ -B ; omitted by all other mss.
⁵ ἐναναλλαξ` (sic) -f, m.
⁶ E, B ; τῷ αὐτῷ -all other mss., Aldine.
⁷ f, m, r ; τῷ ἑτέρῳ -all other mss., Aldine.
⁸ τούτων -f, m, r, Aldine ; ὄντων -all other mss.
⁹ τὸ θάτερον -C.C.C. 99, Dübner ; θάτερον (τὸ omitted) -e,
u, m, r, Escor. 72, Aldine ; τὸ ἕτερον -E, B ; τὸ θάτερον . . .
οὐδὲ σύστασιν οὐδὲ γένεσιν -omitted by f.

ᵃ See 1024 E-F supra with note f on page 237.
ᵇ i.e. common to both the contemplative aspect and the
practical (cf. De Virtute Morali 443 E [. . . τοῦ λόγου . . .
τὸ μὲν . . . θεωρητικόν ἐστι τὸ δ' . . . πρακτικόν] with Aristotle,
Politics 1333 a 25 and Eth. Nic. 1139 a 6-15 [cf. Gauthier
et Jolif ad loc., ii, pp. 440-442]) ; but it is so just because
it is a blend of both principles, the one proceeding to universals and the other to particulars, and so becomes νόησις
ἐν τοῖς νοητοῖς, i.e. contemplative, and δόξα ἐν τοῖς αἰσθητοῖς,
i.e. practical (1024 F supra with notes a and b there). So
both Thévenaz (L'Âme du Monde, p. 31, note 159) and

latter,[a] the reason common to both,[b] as it is continually coming upon difference in sameness and upon sameness in difference, tries with definitions and divisions [c] to separate the one and the many, that is the indivisible and the divisible,[d] but cannot arrive at either exclusively,[e] because the very principles have been alternately intertwined and thoroughly intermixed with each other. It was just for this reason that god made from being the compound of the indivisible and the divisible as a receptacle for sameness and difference,[f] that order might come to be in differentiation; in fact, "come to be" amounted to this, since without these sameness had no differentiation so that it had no motion either and so no coming to be and difference had no order so that it had no coherence either and so no coming to be.[g]

Helmer (*De An. Proc.*, p. 53), whose interpretation he rejects and Hubert here adopts, are partially right.

[c] See 1026 D *infra*: ἡ δὲ ὁριστικὴ δύναμις . . . καὶ τοὐναντίον ἡ διαιρετική. . . .

[d] Cf. Plato, *Sophist* 245 A 8-9 with ἕν τε καὶ ἀμερές in *Theaetetus* 205 E 2 and *Parmenides* 138 A 5-6; and Aristotle, *Metaphysics* 1054 a 20-23 on τὸ ἓν καὶ τὰ πολλά as the indivisible and the divisible.

[e] Cf. Plato, *Philebus* 15 D 4-8.

[f] See 1025 B *supra* with note b there.

[g] See 1024 E *supra* with note b there. The next sentence shows that χωρὶς τούτων means without the compound of indivisible and divisible being as a receptacle. The οὐδὲ in both occurrences of οὐδὲ γένεσιν, the second of which Hubert mistakenly daggers, is consecutive (cf. *infra De Comm. Not.* 1070 E, note a): γένεσις presupposes motion (cf. Alexander, *Quaestiones*, p. 82, 3-4 [Bruns]; Philoponus, *De Generatione*, p. 306, 3-4), but it also implies something coherent that comes to be (cf. in *Adv. Colotem* 1114 B the objection to infinitude as a principle for coming to be: ἡ δ' ἄτακτος . . . ἀπερίληπτος, αὐτὴν ἀναλύουσα καὶ ταράττουσα . . .).

(1025) ἑτέρῳ εἶναι[1] τοῦ ἑτέρου καὶ τῷ ἑτέρῳ πάλιν αὐτῷ[2]
ταὐτόν, οὐδὲν ἡ τοιαύτη μέθεξις ἀλλήλων ποιεῖ
γόνιμον, ἀλλὰ δεῖται τρίτης τινὸς οἷον ὕλης ὑπο-
1026 δεχομένης καὶ διατιθεμένης ὑπ' ἀμφοτέρων. αὕτη
δ' ἐστὶν ἣν πρώτην συνέστησε τῷ περὶ τὰ νοητὰ
μονίμῳ τοῦ περὶ τὰ σώματα κινητικοῦ τὸ ἄπειρον
ὁρίσας.

27. Ὡς δὲ φωνή τίς ἐστιν ἄλογος καὶ ἀσήμαν-
τος λόγος δὲ λέξις ἐν φωνῇ σημαντικῇ[3] διανοίας,
ἁρμονία δὲ τὸ[4] ἐκ φθόγγων καὶ διαστημάτων καὶ

[1] ἕτερον εἶναι -Benseler (*De Hiatu*, p. 529).
[2] f, m ; αὐτῶ -E[1], e, u (αὐτῶι), Escor. 72 ; ταὐτῶ -E[2],
B ; αὐτὸς -r[1].
[3] σημαντικὴ -B, u.
[4] δέ τι -u.

[a] For συμβέβηκε in this sense see *Plat. Quaest.* 1003 F
supra (τοῦτο δὲ καὶ τῇ μονάδι συμβέβηκε). Even Aristotle
at times uses συμβέβηκε and συμβεβηκός *simpliciter* (*De Anima*
402 a 8-10, *De Part. Animal.* 643 a 30-31 with *Metaphysics*
1025 a 30-32) in referring to what he calls more exactly συμβεβηκότα καθ' αὑτά (*Anal. Post.* 75 b 1-2 and 83 b 19-20, *Metaphysics* 995 b 19-20). *Cf.* 1018 D *infra* (chap. 14) : ἴδιον τῷ
τελευταίῳ συμβέβηκε, τῷ κζ'. . . .
[b] *i.e.* the intercommunion of ideas in Plato, *Sophist* 254
D 4—259 B 7 (*cf.* 256 B 1 and 259 A 7 for the term μέθεξις) :
by such " participation " in difference sameness like all the
ideas is different from difference as it is from all the others,
and difference like all the others is the same as itself by
" participation " in sameness (*cf.* Proclus, *In Platonis
Parmenidem*, cols. 756, 33–757, 8 [Cousin[2]]). For the ideas,
sameness and difference, see *supra* 1025 c with note *a* there.
[c] In *Timaeus* 48 E 3—49 A 6 the γενέσεως ὑποδοχὴ καὶ
τιθήνη is introduced as a τρίτον γένος ; and Aristotle refers
to his substrate of contraries, themselves ἀπαθῆ ὑπ' ἀλλήλων,
i.e. to matter, as τρίτον τι (*Metaphysics* 1069 b 8-9 and
1075 a 30-32, *cf. Physics* 190 b 33—191 a 1). Plutarch in
De Iside 370 F—371 A also ascribes to Plato τρίτην τινὰ
φύσιν between ταὐτόν and θάτερον (see note *c* on 1015 B *supra*) ;

For, even if it is a characteristic [a] of sameness to be different from difference and of difference again to be the same as itself, mutual participation of this kind [b] has no fruitful result; but a third term is required, a kind of matter serving as a receptacle for both and being modified by them,[c] and this it is that he first compounded when with that which abides about the intelligibles [d] he bounded the limitlessness of that which is motive in the case of bodies.[e]

27. As some sound is not speech and not significant but speech is an utterance in sound that signifies thought,[f] and as concord is what consists of sounds and intervals and a sound is one and the same thing,[g]

but there he takes ταὐτόν to be the good principle and θάτερον the evil, *i.e.* the evil " world-soul " that he professes to find in the *Laws* and which in the present essay (1014 D-E *supra*) he identifies instead with the " divisible being " here compounded with the " indivisible " to be itself the " third term," the receptacle for both ταὐτόν and θάτερον.

[d] See note *e* on pages 228 f. *supra*.

[e] See 1015 E *supra* (τὴν κινητικὴν τῆς ὕλης καὶ περὶ τὰ σώματα γιγνομένην μεριστὴν . . . κίνησιν) with notes *b* and *c* there and 1027 A *infra* (τῷ μὲν ἑνὶ τὴν ἀπειρίαν ὁρίσαντος ἵν' οὐσία γένηται πέρατος μετασχοῦσα) with note *a* there.

[f] Cf. *S.V.F.* iii, p. 213, 18-21 and ii, p. 48, 28-30. The use of φωνή for " sound " in the generic sense (so *Plat. Quaest.* 1000 B, 1001 F, and 1006 B; cf. *Timaeus* 67 B 2-4 and *Divisiones Aristoteleae* § 30 [24]=pp. 37, 23-38, 14 [Mutschmann]) is called catachrestic by [Plutarch], *De Placitis* 902 B=*Dox. Graeci*, p. 408 A 3-8 (cf. Aristotle, *De Anima* 420 b 5-16 and 27-33). For speech (λόγος) as articulate sound that is " significant " see also *Plat. Quaest.* 1009 D-E.

[g] Cf. Nicomachus, *Harmonices Man.* 12 (*Musici Scriptores Graeci*, p. 261, 4-6 [Jan]); Aristoxenus, *Elementa Harmonica* i, 15, 15-16 with P. Marquard's note *ad loc.*, pp. 224-227; Theon Smyrnaeus, pp. 49, 18-20 from Adrastus and 60, 13-16 (Hiller).

(1026) φθόγγος μὲν ἓν καὶ ταὐτὸν διάστημα δὲ φθόγγων
ἑτερότης καὶ διαφορά, μιχθέντων δὲ τούτων ᾠδὴ
γίγνεται καὶ μέλος· οὕτως τὸ παθητικὸν τῆς ψυχῆς
ἀόριστον ἦν καὶ ἀστάθμητον, εἶθ' ὡρίσθη πέρατος
ἐγγενομένου[1] καὶ εἴδους τῷ μεριστῷ καὶ παντο-
δαπῷ τῆς κινήσεως. συλλαβοῦσα δὲ τὸ ταὐτὸν καὶ
τὸ θάτερον[2] ὁμοιότησι καὶ ἀνομοιότησιν ἀριθμῶν
B ἐκ[3] διαφορᾶς ὁμολογίαν ἀπεργασαμένων[4] ζωῆς[5] τε
τοῦ παντός ἐστιν ἔμφρων καὶ ἁρμονία καὶ λόγος
ἄγων πειθοῖ μεμιγμένην[6] ἀνάγκην, ἣν εἱμαρμένην
οἱ πολλοὶ καλοῦσιν, Ἐμπεδοκλῆς δὲ φιλίαν ὁμοῦ
καὶ νεῖκος, Ἡράκλειτος δὲ παλίντροπον[7] ἁρμονίην

[1] ἐγγινομένου -f, m, r.
[2] ἕτερον -E, B, u.
[3] καὶ -r.
[4] E, B ; ἐπεργασαμένων -e, u, Escor. 72, Aldine ; ἐπεργα-
σμένων -f, m, r.
[5] E, B ; ζῶν -all other mss., Aldine.
[6] μεμιγμένων -r.
[7] mss. (so in De Tranquillitate Animi 473 f—474 a all
mss. except D, which has παλίντονος as do all mss. in De Iside
369 b) ; παλίντονον -Turnebus.

---

[a] Cf. Aelian Platonicus and Thrasyllus in Porphyry, In
Ptolemaei Harmonica, p. 35, 15-22 and p. 91, 13-18 (Düring) ;
Bacchius, Isagoge 6 (Musici Scriptores Graeci, p. 292, 20-21
[Jan]). In 1020 e infra it is defined as πᾶν τὸ περιεχόμενον
ὑπὸ δυεῖν φθόγγων ἀνομοίων τῇ τάσει.
[b] So also Quaest. Conviv. 747 c ; cf. τὸ ἐκ φθόγγων καὶ
διαστημάτων καὶ χρόνων συγκείμενον in Bacchius, Isagoge 78
(Musici Scriptores Graeci, p. 309, 13-14 [Jan]) and the
objection of Aristoxenus, Elementa Harmonica i, 18, 16–19, 1.
[c] See the end of the preceding chapter with note e on
1026 a and 1016 c supra with note e on page 203.
[d] Probably a reference to similar and dissimilar numbers,
for which cf. Theon Smyrnaeus, pp. 36, 12–37, 6 (Hiller)
and Iamblichus, In Nicomachi Arithmeticam Introductionem,

an interval the diversity and difference of sounds,[a]
and the mixture of these results in song and melody,[b]
so the affective part of the soul was indeterminate and
unstable and then was bounded when there came to
be limit and form in the divisible and omnifarious
character of the motion.[c] And, once having compre-
hended sameness and difference with the similarities
and dissimilarities of numbers [d] that produced con-
sensus out of dissension, it is for the sum of things
rational life and concord [e] and reason guiding necessity that has been tempered with persuasion [f] and
which by most people is called destiny,[g] by Empedocles love together with strife,[h] by Heraclitus
concord of the universe retroverse like that of lyre

pp. 82, 10-18 and 84, 10–88, 15 (Pistelli) ; see 1017 ε *infra* :
αἱ συζυγίαι τῶν ὁμοίων ἔσονται πρὸς τοὺς ὁμοίους.

    [e] See 1030 c *infra* ; for ζωή . . . ἔμφρων *cf. Timaeus* 36 ε
3-4, quoted by Plutarch at 1016 β *supra*.

    [f] An inexact reminiscence of *Timaeus* 47 ε 5—48 α 5 ;
cf. Plutarch's *Phocion* ii, 9 (742 ε), and for his interpretation
of ἀνάγκη in the *Timaeus* see 1014 ᴅ —1015 α *supra*.

    [g] *Cf.* Iamblichus, *De Mysteriis* viii, 7 (p. 269, 13-14
[Parthey]) and *Corpus Hermeticum* xvi, 11 (ii, p. 235, 22
[Nock-Festugière]). Plutarch himself substitutes ἀνάγκη
for εἱμαρμένη (see *supra* 1015 ᴀ, note *e*) ; *cf.* also [Plutarch],
De Placitis 884 ᴇ-ꜰ (*Dox. Graeci*, p. 321 ᴀ 6-9 and p. 322
ᴀ 1-3) and Cicero, *De Natura Deorum* i, 55 (" illa fatalis
necessitas quam εἱμαρμένην dicitis ").

    [h] Empedocles, frag. A 45 (D.-K.) ; *cf.* Empedocles, frag.
B 115, 1-2 (D.-K.) with Hippolytus, *Refutatio* vii, 29, 23
(p. 214, 17-24 [Wendland]) and frags. A 32 and A 38 (D.-K.)
with Simplicius, *Phys.*, p. 197, 10-13, p. 465, 12-13, and
p. 1184, 5-17. Zeller's estimate of this evidence (*Phil.
Griech.* i, 2, p. 969, note 2) is still valid despite such attempts
at rehabilitation and embellishment as that of J. Bollack's
(*Empédocle* i [Paris, 1965], pp. 153-158 and 161) ; *cf.*
H. Schreckenberg, *Ananke* (München, 1964), pp. 111-113
with note 97.

PLUTARCH'S MORALIA

(1026) κόσμου ὄκωσπερ λύρης καὶ τόξου, Παρμενίδης δὲ
φῶς καὶ σκότος, Ἀναξαγόρας δὲ νοῦν καὶ ἀπειρίαν,
Ζωροάστρης δὲ θεὸν καὶ δαίμονα, τὸν μὲν Ὠρο-
μάσδην καλῶν τὸν δ' Ἀρειμάνιον.[1] Εὐριπίδης δ'
οὐκ ὀρθῶς ἀντὶ τοῦ συμπλεκτικοῦ τῷ διαζευκτικῷ
κέχρηται

Ζεὺς εἴτ'[2] ἀνάγκη φύσεος[3] εἴτε νοῦς[4] βροτῶν·

C καὶ γὰρ ἀνάγκη καὶ νοῦς ἐστιν ἡ διήκουσα διὰ
πάντων δύναμις. Αἰγύπτιοι μὲν οὖν μυθολογοῦν-

[1] ἀριμάνιον -B[1]; ἀριμάνιον -all other mss.
[2] ἤτε -u.
[3] Stephanus; φύσεως -mss.
[4] νοῦς -omitted by r.

---

[a] Heraclitus, frag. B 51 (D.-K. and Walzer)=frags. 45
and 56 (Bywater); cf. Dox. Graeci, p. 303 b 8-10 (. . .
εἱμαρμένην δὲ λόγον ἐκ τῆς ἐναντιοδρομίας δημιουργὸν τῶν ὄντων)
and Diogenes Laertius, ix, 7 (p. 440, 2-3 [Long]). Both in
De Tranquillitate Animi 473 f—474 a and in De Iside 369
b the quotation from Heraclitus is followed by that of Euripides, frag. 21, 3-4 (Nauck, Trag. Graec. Frag.², p. 369).
Neither in the former of these nor in the present passage is
there reason to doubt that Plutarch wrote παλίντροπος, whether it was this or παλίντονος, as in the De Iside, that Heraclitus had written (cf. W. K. C. Guthrie, A History of Greek
Philosophy i [Cambridge, 1962], p. 439, note 3 with references; M. Marcovich, Heraclitus [Merida, 1967], pp. 125-
126).

[b] See Plutarch, Adv. Colotem 1114 b. Cf. Simplicius,
Phys., p. 38, 18-24 (quoting Alexander); p. 25, 15-16;
pp. 30, 14–31, 2; and pp. 179, 20–180, 12 with Parmenides,
frag. B 8, 53-61 and B 9 (D.-K.). The belief that the second
part of Parmenides' poem, called the κοσμογονία by Plutarch
in Amatorius 756 e, was meant to be a valid account of the
phenomenal world (Adv. Colotem 1114 c-e) goes back to
Aristotle (Metaphysics 986 b 31-34; cf. Cherniss, Crit.
Presoc. Phil., p. 48, note 192); but Plutarch is alone in
identifying its two " principles " with ἀνάγκη, for which see

254

and bow,[a] by Parmenides light and darkness,[b] by Anaxagoras intelligence and infinitude,[c] and by Zoroaster god and spirit, the former called by him Oromasdes and the latter Areimanius.[d] Euripides has erred in using the disjunctive instead of the copulative conjunction in the prayer,

> Zeus, whether natural necessity
> Or the intelligence of mortal men,[e]

for the power that pervades all things [f] is both necessity and intelligence. Now, the Egyptians in a mythical account say enigmatically that, when

rather Parmenides, frag. B 10, 6-7 (D.-K) and frag. A 37 (p. 224, 7-9 [D.-K.]) with frag. B 12 (D.-K.).

[c] See *De Iside* 370 E (νοῦν καὶ ἄπειρον). *Cf.* Theophrastus, *Phys. Opin.*, frag. 4 (*Dox. Graeci*, p. 479, 14-15); and for Plutarch's ἀπειρία here *cf.* Aristotle, *Metaphysics* 988 a 28. Against the identification with ἀνάγκη see Plutarch himself in *Pericles* iv, 6 (154 B-C); but on the other hand see *De Defectu Orac.* 435 F (. . . τὸ κατ᾽ ἀνάγκην . . . μετιὼν ἀεὶ . . .) and Aristotle, *Metaphysics*, 985 a 18-21 (*cf.* Cherniss, *Crit. Presoc. Philos.*, pp. 234-235).

[d] See *supra* 1012 E with note *c* there on " Zaratas "; *De Iside* 369 D—370 C; and Diogenes Laertius, i, 8. *Cf.* Bidez-Cumont, *Les Mages Hellénisés* i, pp. 58-66 and ii, pp. 70-79; and J. Hani, *Rev. Études Grecques*, lxxvii (1964), pp. 489-525.

[e] Euripides, *Troiades*, 886. For the " correction " suggested by Plutarch in Stoic fashion *cf.* Babut, *Plutarque et le Stoïcisme*, p. 141.

[f] For this phrase *cf.* Cornutus, xi (p. 11, 21 [Lang]) and [Aristotle], *De Mundo* 396 B 28-29. It is used of the Platonic world-soul by Atticus, frag. viii (Baudry)=Eusebius, *Praep. Evang.* xv, 12, 3 (ii, p. 375, 17-19 [Mras]), though it is Stoic in origin : *cf.* Plutarch, *De Iside* 367 c with Diogenes Laertius, vii, 147 ; [Plutarch], *De Placitis* 882 A and 885 A (*Dox. Graeci*, p. 306 A 5-8 and p. 323 A 1-6) ; Alexander, *De Mixtione*, p. 225, 1-3 (Bruns) ; Plotinus, *Enn.* III, i, 4, lines 1-9.

(1026) τες[1] αἰνίττονται, τοῦ Ὥρου[2] δίκην ὀφλόντος,[3] τῷ
μὲν πατρὶ τὸ πνεῦμα καὶ τὸ αἷμα τῇ δὲ μητρὶ τὴν
σάρκα καὶ τὴν πιμελὴν προσνεμηθῆναι. τῆς δὲ
ψυχῆς οὐδὲν μὲν εἰλικρινὲς οὐδ᾽ ἄκρατον οὐδὲ χωρὶς
ἀπολείπεται τῶν ἄλλων· ἁρμονίη γὰρ ἀφανὴς φα-
νερῆς κρείττων καθ᾽ Ἡράκλειτον, ἐν ᾗ τὰς διαφορὰς καὶ τὰς ἑτερότητας ὁ μιγνύων θεὸς ἔκρυψε
καὶ κατέδυσεν· ἐμφαίνεται δὲ ὅμως αὐτῆς τῷ μὲν
ἀλόγῳ τὸ ταραχῶδες τῷ δὲ λογικῷ τὸ εὔτακτον,
ταῖς δ᾽ αἰσθήσεσι τὸ κατηναγκασμένον τῷ δὲ νῷ
D τὸ αὐτοκρατές. ἡ δὲ ὁριστικὴ δύναμις τὸ καθόλου
καὶ τὸ ἀμερὲς διὰ συγγένειαν ἀγαπᾷ, καὶ τοὐναντίον ἡ διαιρετικὴ πρὸς τὰ καθ᾽ ἕκαστα φέρεται τῷ
μεριστῷ· χαίρει δὲ ὁλότητι[4] διὰ τὸ ταὐτὸν ἐφήδεταί ⟨τε⟩[5] μεταβολῇ[6] διὰ τὸ θάτερον.[7] οὐχ ἥκιστα
δὲ ἥ τε πρὸς τὸ καλὸν διαφορὰ καὶ τὸ αἰσχρὸν ἤ

---

[1] μυθολογοῦνται -r. [2] r ; ὥρου -all other mss.
[3] Dübner ; ὀφλόντος -mss.
[4] ὁλότητι -Bury (Proc. Cambridge Philol. Soc., N.S. i
[1950–51], p. 31) ; ὅλον τῇ -mss.
[5] ἐφήδεταί ⟨τε⟩ -Bury (loc. cit.) ; ἐφ᾽ ᾷ δεῖται -mss.
[6] f, m, r, Aldine ; μεταβολῆς -all other mss.
[7] διὰ τὸ ἕτερον -E, B.

---

[a] See De Iside 358 E and De Libidine et Aegritudine 6 (vii,
p. 7, 2-16 [Bernardakis]=vi, 3, p. 56, 7-20 [Ziegler-Pohlenz,
1966]) ; cf. J. Hani, Rev. Études Grecques, lxxvi (1963),
pp. 111-120.
[b] See 1025 D supra with note b there and Plat. Quaest.
1008 C supra. In De Tranquillitate Animi 474 A, De Sollertia Animalium 964 D-E, and De Iside 369 C it is rather
human affairs or life, nature, and the sublunar world that
are said to contain nothing pure or unmixed.
[c] Heraclitus, frag. B 54 (D.-K. and Walzer)=frag. 47
(Bywater).
[d] Cf. τὴν δὲ ταραχώδη καὶ ἀνόητον (1014 C supra) and ἡμῶν
τὸ ταραχῶδες (Quaest. Conviv. 746 A).

Horus was convicted, the breath and blood were assigned to his father and the flesh and fat to his mother.[a] Of the soul, however, nothing remains pure or unmixed or separate from the rest,[b] for stronger than manifest concord according to Heraclitus is the unmanifest,[c] wherein god, making the mixture, sank and concealed the differences and the diversities ; but nevertheless turbulence makes itself evident in the irrational part of it [d] and orderliness in the rational,[e] necessitation in the senses [f] and independence in the intelligence.[g] Its faculty for defining has a fondness for the universal and the indivisible by reason of kinship, and contrariwise that for dividing is moved to particulars by the divisible [h] ; and it rejoices in integrity by reason of sameness ⟨and⟩ exults in change by reason of difference.[i] More than anything else, however, the dissension in regard to fair and foul and again in regard to pleasant

---

[e] Cf. τὸ νοερὸν καὶ . . . τὸ τεταγμένον (1016 c supra).

[f] Cf. Plato, Timaeus 42 A 3–B 1 and 69 c 7–D 6 ; the senses are dependent upon external stimuli (Timaeus 43 c 4-7 and Philebus 33 D 2—34 A 9).

[g] Cf. De Facie 945 D (ὁ δὲ νοῦς . . . αὐτοκράτωρ) and De Amore Prolis 493 D-E (. . . αὐτοκρατὴς λόγος) with Anaxagoras, frag. B 12 (ii, p. 37, 18-20 [D.-K.]) and Plato, Cratylus 413 c 5-7.

[h] See 1025 E supra (ἐπιχείρει μὲν ὅροις καὶ διαιρέσεσι χωρίζειν . . . τὸ ἀμερὲς καὶ τὸ μεριστὸν . . .) and cf. Iamblichus, De Comm. Math. Scientia, p. 65, 11-15 and 23-24 (Festa). For τὸ καθόλου καὶ τὸ ἀμερές cf. Aristotle, Anal. Post. 100 b 2 ; Platonic diaeresis does not extend to τὰ καθ' ἕκαστα, of course, save in the sense of " infimae species " sometimes given this term by Aristotle (Anal. Post. 97 b 28-37, De Part. Animal. 642 b 35-36).

[i] Of the many emendations proposed for the corrupt text of this clause only Bury's, which is here adopted, has any plausibility in the context.

PLUTARCH'S MORALIA

(1026) τε πρὸς τὸ ἡδὺ καὶ τὸ ἀλγεινὸν αὖθις οἵ τε τῶν
ἐρώντων ἐνθουσιασμοὶ καὶ πτοήσεις καὶ διαμάχαι
τοῦ φιλοκάλου πρὸς τὸ ἀκόλαστον ἐνδείκνυνται τὸ
μικτὸν ἔκ τε τῆς θείας καὶ ἀπαθοῦς ἔκ τε τῆς
θνητῆς καὶ περὶ τὰ σώματα παθητῆς μερίδος, ὧν
καὶ αὐτὸς ὀνομάζει τὸ μὲν ἐπιθυμίαν ἔμφυτον
E ἡδονῶν τὸ δ᾽ ἐπείσακτον δόξαν ἐφιεμένην τοῦ ἀρίστου. τὸ γὰρ παθητικὸν ἀναδίδωσιν ἐξ ἑαυτῆς
ἡ ψυχή, τοῦ δὲ νοῦ μετέσχεν ἀπὸ τῆς κρείττονος
ἀρχῆς ἐγγενομένου.¹

28. Τῆς δὲ διπλῆς κοινωνίας ταύτης οὐδὲ ἡ
περὶ τὸν οὐρανὸν ἀπήλλακται φύσις, ἀλλὰ² ἑτερορ-
ρεπούσα νῦν μὲν ὀρθοῦται³ τῇ ταὐτοῦ περιόδῳ
κράτος ἐχούσῃ καὶ διακυβερνᾷ τὸν κόσμον· ἔσται⁴
δέ τις χρόνου μοῖρα καὶ γέγονεν ἤδη πολλάκις, ἐν

---

¹ mss.; ἐγγινομένου -Aldine.　　² ἀλλ᾽ ἡ -r.
³ E, B; ὁρᾶται -all other mss., Aldine.　　⁴ ἔστι -B.

ᵃ See De Virtute 447 c (οὐχ ἑνός τινος μεταβολῆς ἀλλὰ δυεῖν
ἅμα μάχης καὶ διαφορᾶς) with Quomodo Adulator ab Amico
Internoscatur 61 D-F; cf. Galen, De Placitis Hippoc. et Plat.
iv, 7 (p. 401, 7-8 [Mueller]).
ᵇ See 1029 E infra (τῷ κρατίστῳ καὶ θειοτάτῳ μέρει) and
supra 1024 A (τὸ γὰρ νοερὸν . . . ἐκεῖνο μὲν . . . ἀπαθὲς . . .)
with note a on page 215.
ᶜ See 1023 D supra (τὸ παθητικὸν ὑπὸ τῶν περὶ τὸ σῶμα
ποιοτήτων). For this part of the human soul as mortal cf.
Timaeus 61 c 7-8 and 69 c 7-E 4, where, however, it is a
confection of the " created gods " (cf. also Timaeus 42 D 5-
E 4) and not derived from " the divisible being " of the psychogony as it is according to Plutarch (see with what follows
in this paragraph 1024 A supra [. . . οὐχ ἑτέραν οὖσαν ἢ τὴν
. . . συμπαθῆ τῷ αἰσθητῷ κίνησιν . . .]; cf. Jones, Platonism
of Plutarch, p. 12, note 36 and p. 85, note 41).
ᵈ Plato, Phaedrus 237 D 7-9, cited by Plutarch in Quaest.
Conviv. 746 D, where as here he writes ἐπείσακτον instead of
Plato's ἐπίκτητος and where he explicitly identifies the latter
258

and painful and the raptures and ecstasies of passionate lovers and the conflicts of probity with incontinence *a* make plain the mixture of the divine and impassive part *b* with the part that is mortal and passible in the case of bodies.*c* Of these Plato himself denominates the latter an innate desire of pleasures and the former an extraneous sentiment longing for what is best,*d* for the soul puts forth of herself the affective part *e* but partook of intelligence because it got into her from the superior principle.*f*

28. From this dual association the nature of the heavens is not exempt either; but it inclines this way or that, at present being kept straight by the dominant revolution of sameness *g* and piloting the universe, whereas there will be and often has already been a period of time in which its prudential part

with λόγος and the former with πάθος. For the meaning of δόξα in this passage of the *Phaedrus cf.* G. J. de Vries, *A Commentary on the Phaedrus of Plato*, p. 85 *ad* 237 E 2-3 and J. Sprute, *Der Begriff der Doxa in der platonischen Philosophie* (Göttingen, 1962), p. 113.

e See 1027 A *infra* (σύμφυτον ἔχουσαν ἐν ἑαυτῇ τὴν τοῦ κακοῦ μοῖραν) and 1024 C *supra* (ἡ γὰρ αἰσθητικὴ κίνησις, ἰδία ψυχῆς οὖσα, . . .) with note *f* there. Contrast *De Virtute Morali* 451 A (ὥσπερ ἐκ ῥίζης τοῦ παθητικοῦ τῆς σαρκὸς ἀναβλαστάνοντος).

f See 1024 C *supra* (ὁ δὲ νοῦς . . . ἐγγενόμενος δὲ τῇ ψυχῇ) and 1023 D *supra* (νοῦν . . . αὐτῇ . . . ἡ τῆς νοητῆς μέθεξις ἀρχῆς ἐμπεποίηκε); and see also 1016 C *supra* (ὁ θεὸς . . . καθάπερ εἶδος . . . τὸ νοερὸν . . . ἀφ' αὑτοῦ παρασχών . . .) with *Plat. Quaest.* 1001 c and note *b* there. There is no reason to suppose, however, as Thévenaz does (*L'Âme du Monde*, p. 71), that by "the superior principle" here Plutarch meant τὸ ἕν which in 1024 D *supra* he called the principle of sameness; but see *infra* 1027 A, note *a* on page 263.

g Cf. Timaeus 36 C 7–D 1 (κράτος δ' ἔδωκεν τῇ ταὐτοῦ . . . περιφορᾷ); on the "revolution of sameness" see *supra* 1024 E, note *d*.

259

PLUTARCH'S MORALIA

(1026) ᾗ τὸ μὲν φρόνιμον ἀμβλύνεται καὶ καταδαρθάνει
λήθης ἐμπιπλάμενον[1] τοῦ οἰκείου τὸ δὲ σώματι
σύνηθες ἐξ ἀρχῆς καὶ συμπαθὲς ἐφέλκεται καὶ
βαρύνει καὶ ἀνελίσσει τὴν ἐν δεξιᾷ τοῦ παντὸς
πορείαν ἀναρρῆξαι δ' οὐ δύναται παντάπασιν,
F ἀλλ' ἀνήνεγκεν αὖθις τὰ βελτίω καὶ ἀνέβλεψε
πρὸς τὸ παράδειγμα θεοῦ συνεπιστρέφοντος καὶ
1027 συναπευθύνοντος.[2] οὕτως ἐνδείκνυται πολλαχόθεν
ἡμῖν τὸ μὴ πᾶν ἔργον εἶναι θεοῦ τὴν ψυχὴν ἀλλὰ
σύμφυτον ἔχουσαν ἐν ἑαυτῇ τὴν τοῦ κακοῦ μοῖραν
ὑπ' ἐκείνου διακεκοσμῆσθαι, τῷ μὲν ἑνὶ τὴν ἀπει-

---

[1] ἐμπιμπλάμενον -f, m.

[2] Ε corr. (*i.e.* συνεπ -Ε[1]), B ; συνεπευθύνοντος -all other
mss., Aldine.

---

[a] *Cf. Politicus* 273 c 6–d 1, quoted by Plutarch at 1015 d
supra, and with Plutarch's ἀμβλύνεται *cf.* ἀμβλύτερον in
Politicus 273 b 3. In *Phaedrus* 248 c 7 the subject of λήθης
τε καὶ κακίας πλησθεῖσα βαρυνθῇ is the individual soul. In
neither case does Plato mention " falling asleep " ; but in
1024 b *supra* (see note *a* there) " dreamlike " is applied to
the precosmic soul, and Albinus speaks of the soul of the
universe or its intelligence as being awakened by god, who
turns it to himself (*Epitome* x, 3 and xiv, 3 = pp. 59, 6
and 81, 6-7 [Louis] = pp. 165, 2 and 169, 31-33 [Hermann]).
Cf. R. M. Jones, *Class. Phil.*, xxi (1926), pp. 107-108 ; and
J. H. Loenen, *Mnemosyne*, 4 Ser. x (1957), pp. 51-52, who
argues that Albinus got this notion from Plutarch.

[b] See 1024 a *supra* (. . . τὴν δοξαστικὴν . . . καὶ συμπαθῆ
τῷ αἰσθητῷ κίνησιν . . . ὑφεστῶσαν ἀΐδιον . . .).

[c] *Cf. Timaeus* 36 c 5-6 (τὴν μὲν δὴ ταὐτοῦ . . . ἐπὶ δεξιὰ
περιήγαγεν . . ., on which *cf. Lustrum*, iv [1959], pp. 220-221
[♯1039]) and Plutarch, *De Iside* 369 c (δυεῖν ἀντιπάλων δυνάμεων, τῆς μὲν ἐπὶ τὰ δεξιὰ . . . ὑφηγουμένης τῆς δ' ἔμπαλιν ἀνα-
στρεφούσης καὶ ἀνακλώσης).

[d] *Cf. Politicus* 270 d 3-4 and 286 b 9, and see 1015 a
supra with note *e* there.

[e] For the " pattern " see *supra* 1023 c (page 223, note *e*)

becomes dull and falls asleep, filled with forgetfulness of what is proper to it,[a] while the part intimate with body and sensitive to it from the beginning [b] puts a heavy drag upon the right-hand course of the sum of things [c] and rolls it back [d] without being able, however, to disrupt it entirely, but the better part recovers again and looks up at the pattern [e] when god helps with the turning and guidance.[f] Thus many considerations make it plain to us that the soul is not god's work entirely [g] but that with the portion of evil inherent in her [h] she has been arranged by god, who

and *cf.* Plato, *Republic* 540 A 7-9 of the individual soul. The " pattern " here for Plutarch is not god or the " thoughts of god " (*cf.* Jones, *Platonism of Plutarch*, p. 102, note 72), whereas according to Albinus in *Epitome* xiv, 3 (p. 81, 6-9 [Louis]=p. 169, 31-35 [Hermann]) the soul or its intelligence is awakened by god ὅπως ἀποβλέπουσα πρὸς τὰ νοητὰ αὐτοῦ δέχηται τὰ εἴδη καὶ τὰς μορφάς, ἐφιεμένη τῶν ἐκείνου νοημάτων (*cf.* in x, 3, p. 59, 2-4 [Louis]=p. 164, 35-37 [Hermann]).

[f] *Cf. Politicus* 269 c 4-6 (τὸ πᾶν τόδε ποτὲ μὲν αὐτὸς ὁ θεὸς συμποδηγεῖ πορευόμενον καὶ συγκυκλεῖ . . .), 270 A 3, and 273 E 1-4 ; and *Republic* 617 c 5-7 (τὴν μὲν Κλωθὼ τῇ δεξιᾷ χειρὶ ἐφαπτομένην συνεπιστρέφειν . . . τὴν ἔξω περιφοράν). Plutarch in *De Defectu Orac.* 426 c speaks of the gods τῶν κόσμων . . . τῇ φύσει συναπευθύνοντας ἕκαστον. In the present passage the unexpressed object of συνεπιστρέφοντος καὶ συναπευθύνοντος is to be understood from τὴν . . . τοῦ παντὸς πορείαν *supra*, though the phrase has sometimes been interpreted in the light of εἰς ἑαυτὸν ἐπιστρέφει (1024 D *supra* with note a there) as " conversion " of the soul or intelligence itself (Jones, *Platonism of Plutarch*, p. 83, note 35 ; Witt, *Albinus*, p. 131 ; Thévenaz, *L'Âme du Monde*, p. 72). In *De Iside* 376 B it is the rational motion of the universe itself that ἐπιστρέφει ποτὲ καὶ προσάγεται . . . πείθουσα τὴν . . . τυφώνειον εἶτ' αὖθις . . . ἀνέστρεψε. . . .

[g] See 1014 c and 1016 c cited in note f, page 223 *supra* ; *cf.* J. H. Loenen, *Mnemosyne*, 4 Ser. x (1957), p. 47.

[h] See *supra* 1026 E (with note e there), 1015 A (with note f there) and 1015 E.

(1027) ρίαν ὁρίσαντος ἵν᾽ οὐσία γένηται πέρατος μετασχοῦσα τῇ δὲ ταὐτοῦ καὶ τῇ ἑτέρου[1] δυνάμει τάξιν
᾽᾽αὶ μεταβολὴν καὶ διαφορὰν καὶ ὁμοιότητα συμμί-
ξαντος πᾶσι δὲ τούτοις, ὡς ἀνυστὸν ἦν, κοινωνίαν
πρὸς ἄλληλα καὶ φιλίαν ἐργασαμένου δι᾽ ἀριθμῶν
καὶ ἁρμονίας.

29. Περὶ ὧν εἰ καὶ πολλάκις ἀκηκόατε καὶ πολλοῖς ἐντετύχηκατε λόγοις καὶ γράμμασιν, οὐ χεῖρόν
ἐστι κἀμὲ βραχέως διελθεῖν, προεκθέμενον τὸ τοῦ
B Πλάτωνος· "μίαν ἀφεῖλε τὸ[2] πρῶτον ἀπὸ παντὸς
μοῖραν, μετὰ δὲ ταύτην ἀφῄρει διπλασίαν ταύτης,
τὴν δ᾽ αὖ τρίτην ἡμιολίαν μὲν τῆς δευτέρας τρι-
πλασίαν δὲ τῆς πρώτης, τετάρτην δὲ τῆς δευτέρας
διπλῆν, πέμπτην δὲ τριπλῆν τῆς τρίτης, τὴν δὲ[3]
ἕκτην τῆς πρώτης ὀκταπλασίαν, ἑβδόμην δὲ[4] ἑπτα-
καιεικοσαπλασίαν[5] τῆς πρώτης. μετὰ δὲ ταῦτα
συνεπληροῦτο τά τε διπλάσια καὶ τριπλάσια διαστήματα, μοίρας ἔτι ἐκεῖθεν ἀποτέμνων καὶ τιθεὶς
εἰς τὸ μεταξὺ τούτων, ὥστ᾽ ἐν ἑκάστῳ διαστήματι
δύο εἶναι μεσότητας, τὴν μὲν ταὐτῷ μέρει τῶν
ἄκρων αὐτῶν ὑπερέχουσαν καὶ ὑπερεχομένην τὴν
C δ᾽ ἴσῳ μὲν κατ᾽ ἀριθμὸν ὑπερέχουσαν ἴσῳ δὲ ὑπερ-

---

[1] θατέρου -Mau.
[2] B. Müller (1873) from *Timaeus* 35 B 4 ; ἀφείλετο -mss.
[3] τῆς δὲ -e, u, Escor. 72[1].
[4] τὴν δὲ ἑβδόμην δὲ -E ; τὴν δὲ ἑβδόμην -B.
[5] f (but with ι instead of α before π), m, r ; ἑπτακαιεικο-
σαπλασίω -E, B ; ἑπτὰ καὶ εἰκοσαπλασίω -e, u, Escor. 72,
Aldine.

---

[a] See *supra* 1014 D (page 185, note *d*), the end of chap. 26
(1026 A with note *e* there), and τοῦ ἑνὸς ὁρίζοντος τὸ πλῆθος
καὶ τῇ ἀπειρίᾳ πέρας ἐντιθέντος (1012 E *supra*) in the Xenocratean interpretation of the psychogony, which Plutarch

with the one bounded her infinitude that by participation in limit it might become substance *a* and
through the agency of sameness and of difference
commingled order and change and differentiation
and similarity *b* and in all these produced, so far as
was feasible, amity and union with one another by
means of numbers and concord.*c*

29. These last, though you have often heard and
read much talk and writing on the subject, it is as
well for me to explain briefly too after giving Plato's
passage *d* as a preface : " First from the total amount
he subtracted one portion, and thereafter he subtracted one twice as large as this, and then the third
half as large again as the second and three times the
first, and the fourth double of the second, and the
fifth triple of the third, and the sixth eight times the
first, and the seventh twenty-seven times the first.
After that he filled in the double and triple intervals
by putting in between the former portions portions
that he continued to cut off from that original source
so as to have in each interval two means, one that
exceeds and falls short of the extremes by the same
fraction of them and one that exceeds and falls short

rejects (1013 c-d and 1023 d *supra*) but from this part of
which his own present formulation differs only in that the
product for Xenocrates was ἀριθμός while for him it is now
οὐσία. It is noteworthy moreover that in 1024 d *supra* (see
note *f* there) Plutarch in opposition to the Xenocratean interpretation declared τὸ ἕν to be the principle of sameness as
distinguished from the ἀμέριστος οὐσία of the psychogony.

b See *supra* 1024 E (with note *b* there) and 1025 F.
c See *supra* 1013 c (page 175, note *c*).
d *Timaeus* 35 B 4—36 B 5, which follows immediately the
passage quoted by Plutarch at the beginning of this essay,
1012 B-c *supra*.

(1027) ἐχομένην.¹ ἡμιολίων δὲ διαστάσεων καὶ ἐπιτρίτων
καὶ ἐπογδόων γενομένων ἐκ τούτων τῶν δεσμῶν ἐν
ταῖς πρόσθεν διαστάσεσι, τῷ τοῦ ἐπογδόου διαστήματι τὰ ἐπίτριτα πάντα συνεπληροῦτο λείπων² αὐτῶν ἑκάστου μόριον, τῆς τοῦ³ μορίου ταύτης διαστάσεως λειφθείσης⁴ ἀριθμοῦ πρὸς ἀριθμὸν ἐχούσης
τοὺς ὅρους ἓξ καὶ πεντήκοντα καὶ διακοσίων⁵ πρὸς
τρία⁶ καὶ τετταράκοντα καὶ διακόσια.''⁷ ἐν τούτοις
ζητεῖται πρῶτον περὶ τῆς ποσότητος τῶν ἀριθμῶν,
δεύτερον περὶ τῆς τάξεως, τρίτον περὶ τῆς δυνά-
μεως· περὶ μὲν τῆς ποσότητος τίνες εἰσίν, οὓς ἐν
τοῖς διπλασίοις καὶ τριπλασίοις⁸ διαστήμασι λαμ-
D βάνει· περὶ δὲ τῆς⁹ τάξεως πότερον ἐφ᾽ ἑνὸς στί-
χου¹⁰ πάντας¹¹ ἐκθετέον ὡς Θεόδωρος ἢ μᾶλλον ὡς
Κράντωρ ἐν τῷ Λ¹² σχήματι, τοῦ πρώτου κατὰ
κορυφὴν τιθεμένου καὶ χωρὶς μὲν τῶν διπλασίων
χωρὶς δὲ τῶν τριπλασίων ἐν δυσὶ¹³ στίχοις¹⁴ ὑποτατ-

---

¹ τὴν μὲν ταὐτῷ . . . ἴσῳ δὲ ὑπερεχομένην -f, m, r (but with
ἄκρων repeated and ὑπερέχουσαν ἴσῳ δὲ omitted by r), Timaeus
36 A 3-5 ; καὶ ὑπερεχομένην τὴν δ᾽ ἴσῳ μὲν κατ᾽ ἀριθμὸν ὑπερέχουσαν -omitted by e, u, Escor. 72, Aldine ; τὴν μὲν ἑκατέρω τῶν
ἄκρων ἴσῳ τε ὑπερέχουσαν καὶ ὑπερεχομένην τὴν δὲ ταὐτῷ μέρει
τῶν ἄκρων αὐτῶν ὑπερέχουσαν καὶ ὑπερεχομένην Ε, Β.

² Dübner from Timaeus 36 B 1-2 (Α), see 1020 B infra (f,
m, r) and Proclus (In Platonis Timaeum ii, pp. 227, 30 and
230, 8 [Diehl]) ; συνεπλήρου τὸ λεῖπον -Ε, Β, e, u^corr.
(συνεπλήρον τὸ λειπὸν -u¹), Escor. 72 ; συνεπλήρου λείπων -f,
m, r.   ³ τῆς δὲ τοῦ -f, m, r.

⁴ ληφθείσης -Ε, Β¹ (ει superscript over first η -Β^corr.),
Proclus (In Platonis Timaeum ii, p. 230, 29 [Diehl]).

⁵ ς καὶ ν καὶ σ -Β.   ⁶ τρία -omitted by f.

⁷ πρὸς γ καὶ μ καὶ σ -Β.

⁸ καὶ τριπλασίοις -omitted by e, u, f, m, r, Escor. 72,
Aldine.   ⁹ τῆς -omitted by e, u.

¹⁰ στείχου -u (cf. ad ἐν δυσὶ στίχοις infra).

¹¹ Ε, Β ; πάντα -all other mss., Aldine.

by amounts numerically equal.[a] Since as a result of these links in the previous intervals there came to be intervals of three to two and of four to three and of nine to eight, he filled in all the intervals of four to three with the interval of nine to eight leaving a fraction of each of them, this remaining interval of the fraction having the terms of the numerical ratio 256 to 243." [b] Here the first question is concerned with the quantity, the second with the arrangement, the third with the function of the numbers [c] : concerning the quantity what numbers they are that he adopts in the double and triple intervals, concerning the arrangement whether one is to set them out as Theodorus [d] does all in a single row or rather as Crantor [e] does in the figure of a lambda with the first placed at the apex and the double and triple numbers ranged separately from each other in two

[a] The former is the harmonic mean and the latter the arithmetical mean (see 1019 c-e and 1028 a *infra*).

[b] For the procedure described and the numerical values resulting from it *cf.* B. Kytzler, *Hermes*, lxxxvii (1959), pp. 405-406.

[c] Three but not quite the same three questions are posed by Chalcidius, *Platonis Timaeus*, pp. 99, 17–100, 2 (Wrobel)= p. 83, 20-27 (Waszink) ; *cf.* B. W. Switalski, *Des Chalcidius Kommentar zu Plato's Timaeus* (Münster, 1902), pp. 81-82.

[d] Theodorus of Soli ; see chap. 20 (1022 c-d) *infra* and *De Defectu Orac.* 427 a-e.

[e] Crantor, frag. 7 (Kayser)=frag. 7 (Mullach, *Frag. Philos. Graec.* iii, p. 145) ; see chap. 20 (1022 c-e) *infra*, and for Crantor as the first exegete of Plato see 1012 d, note c *supra*.

---

[12] λάμβδα -E, B.

[13] ἐν τρισὶ -r.

[14] στείχοις -u (*cf. ad* στίχου *supra* and 1022 c *infra*: δύο στίχους [στοίχους -f, m, r]).

(1027) τομένων· περὶ δὲ τῆς χρείας καὶ τῆς δυνάμεως τί
ποιοῦσι παραλαμβανόμενοι πρὸς τὴν σύστασιν τῆς
ψυχῆς.

30. Πρῶτον οὖν περὶ τοῦ πρώτου παραιτησό-
μεθα[1] τοὺς λέγοντας ὡς ἐπὶ τῶν λόγων αὐτῶν
ἀπόχρη θεωρεῖν ἣν ἔχει τά τε διαστήματα φύσιν
αἵ τε ταῦτα συμπληροῦσαι μεσότητες, ἐν οἷς ἄν τις
ἀριθμοῖς ὑπόθηται χώρας ἔχουσι δεκτικὰς[2] μεταξὺ
τῶν εἰρημένων ἀναλογιῶν ὁμοίως περαινομένης
E τῆς διδασκαλίας. κἂν γὰρ ἀληθὲς[3] ᾖ τὸ λεγόμενον, ἀμυδρὰν ποιεῖ τὴν μάθησιν ἄνευ παραδειγ-
μάτων ἄλλης τε θεωρίας ἀπείργει χάριν ἐχούσης
οὐκ ἀφιλόσοφον. ἂν οὖν ἀπὸ τῆς μονάδος ἀρξά-
μενοι τοὺς διπλασίους καὶ τριπλασίους ἐν μέρει τι-
θῶμεν, ὡς αὐτὸς ὑφηγεῖται,[4] γενήσονται κατὰ τὸ[5]
ἑξῆς ὅπου μὲν τὰ δύο καὶ τέσσαρα καὶ ὀκτὼ[6] ὅπου
δὲ τρία καὶ ἐννέα καὶ εἰκοσιεπτά,[7] συνάπαντες μὲν

---

[1] ἀπαραιτησόμεθα -e, u (αρ cancelled -u^corr·), Escor. 72
(ἀπαιτησόμεθα -in margin) ; ἀπαρτησόμεθα -Aldine.
[2] δέ τινας -e¹ (corrected e²), u.
[3] E, B ; καὶ γὰρ ἂν ἀληθὲς -e, f, m, r, Escor. 72, Aldine ;
καὶ γὰρ ἀληθὲς -u.
[4] E, B ; ἀφηγεῖται -e, u, f, m, Escor. 72, Aldine ;
ά
ὑφηγεῖται -r.
[5] τὸ -Wyttenbach ; τὸν -E, B, e, u, Escor. 72, Aldine ;
τοὺς -f, m, r.
[6] τὰ δύο καὶ τὰ τέσσαρα καὶ ὀκτὼ -Maurommates (so also
the versions of Xylander and Amyot) ; τὸ δεύτερον καὶ τὸ
τέταρτον καὶ ὄγδοον -mss.
[7] τρία καὶ ἐννέα καὶ εἰκοσιεπτά -Maurommates (so also the
versions of Xylander and Amyot) ; τρίτον καὶ ἔνατον (ἔννατον
-E, B) καὶ εἰκοστοέβδομον -mss.

rows underneath, and concerning their use or function what effect is produced by their employment for
the composition of the soul.

30. First, then, with regard to the first question
we shall decline to follow those who say [a] that it
suffices to observe in the ratios themselves the nature
of the intervals and of the means with which they
are filled in, as the directions are carried out alike
with whatever numbers one may assume that have
spaces between them to receive the prescribed proportions.[b] Our reason is that, even if what they say
be true, by the absence of examples it obscures the
understanding of the subject [c] and debars us from
another speculation that has a charm not unphilo-
sophical.[d] So, if beginning from the unit we place
the double and triple numbers alternately [e] as
indicated by Plato himself,[f] the result will be in
succession on one side two, four, and eight and on
the other side three, nine, and twenty-seven, seven

[a] Perhaps Eudorus, following Crantor (see 1020 c-d
infra).

[b] See 1020 A *infra* (. . . τῶν αὐτῶν λόγων διαμενόντων, ὑποδοχὰς ποιοῦσιν ἀρκούσας . . .) and 1020 D *infra* (λόγον μὲν ἔχον
τὸν αὐτὸν ἀριθμὸν δὲ τὸν διπλάσιον) ; and with the latter *cf.*
Theon Smyrnaeus, p. 69, 7-9 (Hiller) in the same context :
οὐδὲν δὲ κωλύει καὶ ἐφ' ἑτέρων ἀριθμῶν τὸν αὐτὸν εὑρίσκειν λόγον
. . . οὐ γὰρ ἀριθμὸν ὡρισμένον ἔλαβεν ὁ Πλάτων ἀλλὰ λόγον
ἀριθμοῦ.

[c] *Cf. e.g.* Plato, *Politicus* 277 D 1-2.

[d] *i.e.* the arithmological speculations about the " remarkable numbers " (1017 E *infra*), to which Plutarch devotes
most of the next three chapters (*cf.* Burkert, *Weisheit und
Wissenschaft*, p. 375, n. 59).

[e] See 1017 E *infra* (ἐναλλὰξ καὶ ἰδίᾳ τάττεσθαι . . . τοὺς ἀρτίους . . . καὶ πάλιν τοὺς περιττούς.

[f] See 1017 E *infra* (ᾗ καὶ δῆλός ἐστι βουλόμενος . . .) and
1027 F—1028 A *infra* (μονονουχὶ δεικνύων ἡμῖν . . .).

(1027) ἑπτὰ κοινῆς δὲ λαμβανομένης τῆς μονάδος ἄχρι
τεσσάρων[1] τῷ πολλαπλασιασμῷ προιόντες.[2] οὐ
γὰρ ἐνταῦθα μόνον ἀλλὰ πολλαχόθι τῆς τετράδος ἡ[3]
F πρὸς τὴν ἑβδομάδα συμπάθεια γίγνεται κατάδηλος.
ἡ μὲν οὖν ὑπὸ τῶν Πυθαγορικῶν ὑμνουμένη τετρα-
κτύς, τὰ ἓξ καὶ τριάκοντα,[4] θαυμαστὸν ἔχειν δοκεῖ
τὸ[5] συγκεῖσθαι μὲν ἐκ πρώτων ἀρτίων τεσσάρων
καὶ πρώτων περιττῶν τεσσάρων γίγνεσθαι[6] δὲ συζυγία τετάρτη τῶν ἐφεξῆς συντιθεμένων[7]· πρώτη
μὲν γάρ ἐστι[8] συζυγία ἡ τοῦ ἑνὸς καὶ τῶν δυεῖν
1017 C δευτέρα[9] (11.) δὲ ἡ τῶν τριῶν[10] καὶ τεσσάρων[11]
D τρίτη δὲ ἡ τῶν ε' καὶ ς', ὧν[12] οὐδεμία ποιεῖ τετράγωνον οὔτ' αὐτὴ καθ' ἑαυτὴν οὔτε μετὰ τῶν ἄλλων·
⟨ἡ δὲ τῶν ζ' καὶ η'⟩[13] τετάρτη μέν ἐστι συντιθεμένη

[1] mss. ; τεσσαράκοντα in margin of f, m, r.
[2] προιόντες -Maurommates ; προιόντων -mss.
[3] ἤ -f, m, Aldine.
[4] καὶ τριάκοντα -B (cf. De Iside 381 F—382A) ; καὶ τὰ
τριάκοντα -all other mss.   [5] τῷ -f, m, r.
[6] γίνεται -f, m, r, Aldine.
[7] E, B, cf. De Iside 382 A ; συντεθειμένων -all other mss,
Aldine.   [8] ἐστι -omitted by r.
[9] δευτέρα περιττῶν (chap. 30 b [1027 F] infra) -E, B ;
δευτέρα (δευτέρα δὲ -f) τῶν περιττῶν -f, m, r, Aldine ; δευτεριττῶν -e, u, Escor. 72 (ρατῶνπε -Escor. 72 in margin) ; see 1022
E supra (chap. 21 init.), apparatus criticus, page 212, note 2.
[10] δὲ ἡ τῶν τριῶν -all mss., following 1017 C supra (chap. 10
ad finem) : κόσμον . . . vac. 4 -E, vac. 8 -B ; κόσμον . . . vac.
5 -f, m, vac. 3 -r . . . ἐν . . . vac. 4 . . . -f, m, r ; κόσμον. ἔνθα†
-e, u ; κόσμον. ἐν . . . vac. 2 . . . -Escor. 72 ; see 1022 E
supra (chap. 21 init.), apparatus criticus, page 212, note 2.
[11] τεσσάρων -Wyttenbach (τετράδος -Xylander) ; καὶ μιᾶς
-mss. (μιᾶς . . . vac. 3 . . . -E with illegible correction in
margin).   [12] καὶ -r.
[13] ⟨ἡ δὲ τῶν ζ' καὶ η'⟩ -added by Maurommates ; ⟨ζ' καὶ
η'⟩ added after τετάρτη μέν ἐστι -Xylander, and similarly
Amyot's version.
268

numbers in all but, the unit being taken as common,[a]
progressing to four by multiplication.[b] Not only
here, in fact, but in many cases does the affinity of
the tetrad with the hebdomad become manifest.[c]
So thirty-six, the tetractys celebrated by the Pythagoreans, is thought to have a remarkable property
in being the sum of the first four even and the first
four odd numbers and in coming to be as the fourth
pair of the successive numbers added together [d] : for
the first pair is that of one and two and the second
(11.) that of three and four and the third that of five
and six, none of which pairs either by itself or together with the others produces a square number ;
⟨but that of seven and eight⟩ is the fourth, and being

---

[a] See *infra* 1017 D (τὴν μὲν μονάδα, κοινὴν οὖσαν ἀρχὴν . . .),
1018 F (ἡ μονὰς ἐπίκοινος οὖσα . . .), 1027 D (τὴν γὰρ μονάδα
κοινὴν οὖσαν ἀμφοῖν προτάξας . . .) ; *cf.* Chalcidius, *Platonis
Timaeus*, p. 104, 20 (Wrobel)=pp. 87, 26–88, 1 (Waszink) :
" communi videlicet accepta singularitate."

[b] *Cf.* Theon Smyrnaeus, p. 95, 2-13 (Hiller).

[c] *Cf.* Philo Jud., *Quaestiones in Exodum* ii, 87 (p. 527
[Aucher]=p. 137 (*L.C.L.*]) and *De Specialibus Legibus* ii,
40 (v, p. 95, 15-20 [Cohn]) ; Nicomachus, *Excerpta* 6
(*Musici Scriptores Graeci*, p. 277, 18-19 [Jan]) and Nicomachus in Iamblichus, *Theolog. Arith.*, p. 58, 10-19 and
p. 59, 10-18 (De Falco).

[d] *Cf.* *De Iside* 381 F—382 A ; Chalcidius, *Platonis
Timaeus*, p. 104, 10-15 (Wrobel)=p. 87, 19-22 (Waszink) ;
Philo Jud., *Quaestiones in Genesin* iii, 49 (p. 233 [Aucher]=
pp. 247-248 [*L.C.L.*]). In all these passages, as here, one is
explicitly an odd number (*cf.* Theon Smyrnaeus, pp. 21,
24–22, 5 [Hiller] ; Speusippus, frag. 4, 22-25 [Lang]),
whereas for Plutarch ordinarily three is the first odd number
(see 1018 C *infra* : . . . ἔκ τε τῆς ἀρχῆς καὶ . . . τοῦ πρώτου
περιττοῦ). For 36 as the sum of a " tetractys " formed in a
different way *cf.* Nicomachus, *Excerpta* 7 and 10 (*Musici
Scriptores Graeci*, pp. 279, 8-15 and 282, 10-14 [Jan]) ; and
for the special properties of 36 see 1018 C-D *infra*.

(1017) δὲ ταῖς προτέραις τριακονταὲξ[1] τετράγωνον παρέσχεν. ἡ δὲ τῶν ὑπὸ Πλάτωνος ἐκκειμένων ἀριθμῶν τετρακτὺς ἐντελεστέραν ἔσχηκε τὴν γένεσιν, τῶν μὲν ἀρτίων ἀρτίοις διαστήμασι τῶν δὲ περιττῶν περιττοῖς πολλαπλασιασθέντων· περιέχει δὲ τὴν μὲν μονάδα, κοινὴν[2] οὖσαν ἀρχὴν ἀρτίων καὶ περιττῶν, τῶν δὲ ὑπ' αὐτῇ τὰ μὲν δύο καὶ τρία πρώτους ἐπιπέδους, τὰ δὲ[3] τέσσαρα καὶ ἐννέα πρώτους τετραγώνους, τὰ δ' ὀκτὼ καὶ εἰκοσιεπτὰ
E πρώτους κύβους ἐν[4] ἀριθμοῖς, ἔξω λόγου τῆς μονάδος τιθεμένης.[5] ᾗ καὶ δῆλός ἐστι βουλόμενος οὐκ ἐπὶ μιᾶς εὐθείας ἅπαντας ἀλλ' ἐναλλὰξ καὶ ἰδίᾳ τάττεσθαι τοὺς ἀρτίους μετ' ἀλλήλων καὶ πάλιν τοὺς περιττούς, ὡς[6] ὑπογέγραπται.[7] οὕτως αἱ συζυγίαι τῶν ὁμοίων ἔσονται πρὸς τοὺς ὁμοίους

---

[1] προτέραις τριακονταὲξ -Dübner ; προ . . . vac. 2 . . . τ
. . . vac. 3 . . . τριακοντα εξ (ἐξ -B) . . . vac. 2 . . . τετράγωνον -E, B ; πρώταις τριάκοντα ἕξ (λϛ -f, m, r) τετράγωνον -all other mss., Aldine.
[2] κοινὴν -omitted by r.
[3] τὰ δὲ τὰ δὲ -B.
[4] ἐν -omitted by r.
[5] θεμένης -f, m, r, Aldine.
[6] ὡς -Xylander (so Amyot's version) ; καὶ -mss. ; ὡς καὶ -B. Müller (1873).
[7] The figure as below in the margins of E, e, u, Escor. 72 ; Λ with the same numbers in the margins of B, f, m ; omitted altogether by r and Aldine (see page 272 infra).

---

[a] For the term " tetractys " used of this figure cf. Theon Smyrnaeus, p. 94, 12-14 and p. 95, 2-8 (Hiller) and Chalcidius, Platonis Timaeus, p. 104, 15-22 (Wrobel)=pp. 87, 22–88, 2 (Waszink) : ". . . quadratura cognominatur quia continet quattuor quidem limites in duplici latere. . . ."

added to the preceding pairs it gives thirty-six, a square number. The tetractys of the numbers set out by Plato,[a] however, has been generated in a more consummate way,[b] the multiplication of the even by even intervals and of the odd by odd ; and it contains the unit, to be sure, as being the common principle of even and odd numbers,[c] but of the numbers under the unit contains two and three, the first plane numbers,[d] and four and nine, the first square numbers, and eight and twenty-seven, the first cubic numbers,[e] the unit being left out of account, which makes it quite obvious that he wishes [f] them to be arranged not all in one straight line but alternately, that is the even numbers together by themselves and on the other hand the odd numbers as drawn below.[g] In this way numbers that are similar to one another

[b] See 1019 B *infra* (chap. 14 *sub finem*) : ὥστε πολὺ τῆς Πυθαγορικῆς . . . τελειοτέραν.

[c] *Cf.* Theon Smyrnaeus, p. 94, 15-16 (Hiller) and Chalcidius, *Platonis Timaeus*, p. 104, 24-25 (Wrobel)=p. 88, 3-4 (Waszink).

[d] See also 1022 D *infra* (ἐπιπέδων ἐπιπέδοις . . .) and *De Defectu Orac.* 415 E, where in the same context two and three are referred to as " the first two plane numbers." According to Nicomachus (*Arithmetica Introductio* II, vii, 3 [pp. 86, 21–87, 7, Hoche]) the plane numbers begin with three ; and Theon Smyrnaeus in this context calls both two and three " linear " (p. 95, 17-19 [Hiller], *cf.* p. 23, 11-14), although elsewhere he calls two itself " oblong " (p. 31, 15-17). In *De Iside* 367 E-F Plutarch himself treats square and oblong numbers as species of plane numbers.

[e] For the expression, ἐπιπέδους . . . τετραγώνους . . . κύβους ἐν ἀριθμοῖς, *cf.* Iamblichus, *Theolog. Arith.*, p. 82, 17 (De Falco)=Speusippus, frag. 4, 8-9 (Lang).

[f] See 1027 E *supra* with note f there.

[g] *i.e.* in accordance with Crantor's interpretation (see 1027 D *supra* with note e there), page 273 *infra*.

PLUTARCH'S MORALIA

(1017) καὶ ποιήσουσιν ἀριθμοὺς ἐπιφανεῖς κατά τε¹ σύνθεσιν καὶ πολλαπλασιασμὸν ἐξ ἀλλήλων.

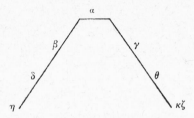

12. Κατὰ σύνθεσιν οὕτως· τὰ δύο καὶ τὰ τρία²
πέντε γίγνεται, τὰ τέσσαρα καὶ τὰ ἐννέα³ τριακαίδεκα,⁴ τὰ δ' ὀκτὼ καὶ εἰκοσιεπτὰ πέντε καὶ τριάκοντα. τούτων γὰρ τῶν ἀριθμῶν οἱ Πυθαγορικοὶ
τὰ μὲν πέντε τρόμον,⁵ ὅπερ ἐστὶ φθόγγον,⁶ ἐκά-
F λουν, οἰόμενοι τῶν τοῦ τόνου διαστημάτων πρῶτον
εἶναι φθεγκτὸν τὸ πέμπτον.⁷ τὰ δὲ τριακαίδεκα
λεῖμμα, καθάπερ Πλάτων τὴν εἰς ἴσα τοῦ τόνου
διανομὴν ἀπογιγνώσκοντες, τὰ δὲ πέντε καὶ τριά-

---

¹ τε -omitted by f, m, r, Escor. 72.
² καὶ τρία -f, m, r.   ³ καὶ ἐννέα -f, m, r, Aldine.
⁴ Aldine ; ιγ -E, B, f, m, r ; τρισκαίδεκα -e, u, Escor. 72.
⁵ Tannery (*Mémoires Scientifiques* ix [1929], pp. 379-
380) ; τροφόν -mss.   ⁶ φθόγγου -u.
⁷ τὸ πέμπτον -omitted by B ; τὸν πέμπτον -f, m, r.

ᵃ See 1022 D *infra* (chap. 20 *sub finem*): ἐπιπέδων ἐπιπέδοις
. . . συζυγούντων, and page 253, note *d supra*.
ᵇ Despite the " five tetrachords " of 1029 A-B *infra* and
the musical significance ascribed to five in *De E* 389 D-F
and *De Defectu Orac.* 430 A there is to my knowledge no
relevant parallel to this enigmatic passage ; and in default
of one I adopt Tannery's emendation and explanation as the
most plausible yet suggested, adding only that the use of
τόνος alone as here for " mode " or " scale " is well estab-

272

will form the pairs [a] and both by addition and by multiplication with each other will produce remarkable numbers.

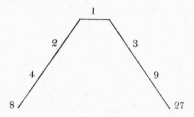

12. By addition as follows : two plus three are five, four plus nine are thirteen, and eight plus twenty-seven are thirty-five. These numbers are remarkable, for of them the Pythagoreans called five " tremor," which is to say " sound," thinking that the fifth of the scale's intervals is first to be sounded,[b] called thirteen " leimma," denying as did Plato that the tone is divisible into equal parts,[c] and called

lished (*cf. De E* 389 E [. . . τοὺς πρώτους εἴτε τόνους ἢ τρόπους εἴθ' ἁρμονίας χρὴ καλεῖν . . .]; Cleonides, *Introductio* 12 [*Musici Scriptores Graeci*, pp. 202, 6-8 and 203, 4-6, Jan]; Porphyry, *In Ptolemaei Harmonica*, p. 82, 3-6 [Düring]), though it is disturbing to find it used in a different sense in the very next clause. For a different interpretation of τὸ πέμπτον *cf.* H. Weil et Th. Reinach, *Plutarque : De la Musique* (Paris, 1900), p. LVI, note 5.

  [c] See 1018 E *infra* with note *d* there (. . . διὸ καὶ τὰ τριακαίδεκα λεῖμμα καλοῦσιν . . .) and 1020 E-F *infra* (. . . οἱ δὲ Πυθαγορικοὶ τὴν μὲν εἰς ἴσα τομὴν ἀπέγνωσαν αὐτοῦ . . .). As for καθάπερ Πλάτων, I take it with what follows (see 1021 D-E *infra* [. . . καὶ τοῦτ' ἐστὶν ὅ φησιν ὁ Πλάτων . . .]), giving Plutarch the benefit of the doubt, for Plato did not " call thirteen ' leimma,' " although some said that he had done so (*cf.* Theon Smyrnaeus, p. 69, 4-6 [Hiller]).

(1017) κοντα ἁρμονίαν, ὅτι συνέστηκεν ἐκ δυεῖν κύβων
πρώτων¹ ἀπ᾽ ἀρτίου καὶ περιττοῦ γεγονότων ἐκ
τεσσάρων δ᾽ ἀριθμῶν, τοῦ ς΄ καὶ τοῦ η΄ καὶ τοῦ θ΄
καὶ τοῦ² ιβ΄, τὴν ἀριθμητικὴν καὶ τὴν ἁρμονικὴν
1018 ἀναλογίαν περιεχόντων. ἔσται δὲ³ μᾶλλον ἡ⁴ δύναμις ἐκφανὴς ἐπὶ διαγράμματος. ἔστω τὸ α β γ δ
παραλληλόγραμμον ὀρθογώνιον ἔχον τῶν πλευρῶν
τὴν α β πέντε τὴν δὲ α δ ἑπτά· καὶ τμηθείσης τῆς
μὲν ἐλάττονος εἰς δύο καὶ τρία κατὰ τὸ κ τῆς δὲ
μείζονος εἰς τρία καὶ τέσσαρα κατὰ τὸ λ διήχθωσαν
ἀπὸ τῶν τομῶν εὐθεῖαι τέμνουσαι ἀλλήλας κατὰ τὸ
κ μ ν καὶ κατὰ τὸ λ μ ξ⁵ καὶ ποιοῦσαι⁶ τὸ μὲν α κ
μ λ⁷ ἕξ τὸ δὲ κ β ξ μ⁸ ἐννέα τὸ δὲ λ μ ν δ ὀκτὼ τὸ
δὲ μ ξ γ ν δώδεκα τὸ δὲ ὅλον παραλληλόγραμμον τριάκοντα καὶ πέντε, τοὺς τῶν συμφωνιῶν
τῶν πρώτων λόγους ἐν τοῖς τῶν χωρίων ἀριθμοῖς
Β εἰς ἃ διῄρηται περιέχον. τὰ μὲν γὰρ⁹ ἓξ καὶ ὀκτὼ
τὸν ἐπίτριτον ἔχει λόγον, ἐν ᾧ τὸ διὰ τεσσάρων,
τὰ δὲ ἓξ καὶ ἐννέα τὸν ἡμιόλιον, ἐν ᾧ τὸ διὰ πέντε,
τὰ δὲ ἓξ καὶ ιβ΄¹⁰ τὸν διπλάσιον, ἐν ᾧ τὸ διὰ πασῶν.

---

¹ πρῶτον -r.
² τοῦ -omitted by E, B, e, Escor. 72, Aldine.
³ δὲ -omitted by B.
⁴ ἡ -omitted by f.
⁵ λμζ -r.
⁶ ποιοῦσαι -omitted by f, r ; καὶ ποιοῦσαι . . . τὸ δὲ κβξμ
-omitted by e, u, Escor. 72, m (καὶ [ποιοῦσαι omitted] τὸ μὲν
ακλμ ἓξ τὸ δὲ κβμξ -m¹ in margin), Aldine.
⁷ ακλμ -f, m (in margin), r.
⁸ κβμξ -f, m (in margin) ; κβμζ -r.
⁹ γὰρ -E, B, e, u, Escor. 72 ; οὖν -f, m, r, Aldine.
¹⁰ E, B ; καὶ τὰ ιβ΄ -e, u, f, m, r, Escor. 72, Aldine.

ᵃ With this and the rest of the chapter through διὰ τοῦτο
καὶ ἁρμονίαν . . . ἐκάλεσαν cf. Iamblichus, Theolog. Arith.,

thirty-five " concord "[a] because it consists of the first
two cubes produced from even and odd [b] and of four
numbers, six and eight and nine and twelve, which
comprise the arithmetical and the harmonic proportion.[c] The force of this will be more evident in a
diagram. Let $\alpha\beta\gamma\delta$ be a rectangular parallelogram
with five as the side $\alpha\beta$ and seven as the side $\alpha\delta$;
and, the lesser having been divided into two and
three at κ and the greater into three and four at λ,
from the points of section let there be produced
along $\kappa\mu\nu$ and $\lambda\mu\xi$ straight lines that intersect and
make $\alpha\kappa\mu\lambda$ six, $\kappa\beta\xi\mu$ nine, $\lambda\mu\nu\delta$ eight, $\mu\xi\gamma\nu$ twelve,
and the whole parallelogram thirty-five, comprising
in the numbers of the areas into which it has been
divided the ratios of the primary consonances.[d] For
the areas six and eight have the sesquitertian ratio,
in which the fourth consists ; the areas six and nine
the sesquialteran, in which the fifth consists ; the
areas six and twelve the duple, in which the octave

p. 63, 7-23 (De Falco), *i.e.* Nicomachus (*cf. ibid.*, p. 56, 8-9
and *Gnomon*, V [1929], p. 554).

[b] $2^3 + 3^3 = 35$; *cf.* Iamblichus, *Theolog. Arith.*, p. 63, 7-9
(De Falco).

[c] *i.e.* $35 = 6 + 8 + 9 + 12$, in which 8 is the harmonic mean
and 9 is the arithmetical mean of the extremes, 6 and 12 ;
see 1019 c-d *infra* and *cf.* Nicomachus, *Arithmetica Introductio* ii, xxix, 3-4 (p. 146, 2-23 [Hoche]) and Iamblichus,
In Nicomachi Arithmeticam Introductionem, pp. 122, 12–
125, 13 (Pistelli).

[d] See 1019 d *infra* ($\tau\grave{\alpha}$ $\pi\rho\tilde{\omega}\tau\alpha$ $\sigma\acute{\upsilon}\mu\phi\omega\nu\alpha$) ; *cf.* Theon
Smyrnaeus, p. 51, 18-20 (Hiller), [Alexander], *Metaph.*,
p. 834, 1-2, and [Plutarch], *De Musica* 1139 c-d (. . . $\tau\grave{\alpha}$
$\kappa\upsilon\rho\iota\acute{\omega}\tau\alpha\tau\alpha$ $\delta\iota\alpha\sigma\tau\acute{\eta}\mu\alpha\tau\alpha$ . . .). Since the octave consists of a
fourth and a fifth, only the latter two were usually considered
to be strictly " primary " in the sense of " simple " consonances (*cf.* Ptolemy, *Harmonica*, p. 11, 24-25 [Düring] ;
Porphyry, *In Ptolemaei Harmonica*, p. 96, 12-20 [Düring]).

(1018) ἔνεστι δὲ καὶ ὁ τοῦ τόνου λόγος ἐπόγδοος ὢν[1] ἐν τοῖς ἐννέα καὶ ὀκτώ.[2] διὰ τοῦτο καὶ[3] ἁρμονίαν τὸν

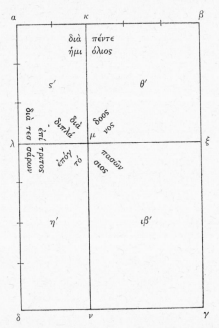

περιέχοντα τοὺς λόγους τούτους ἀριθμὸν ἐκάλεσαν. ἑξάκις δὲ[4] γενόμενος τὸν τῶν[5] δέκα ποιεῖ καὶ δια-

---

[1] ὢν -omitted by E, B.

[2] The figure *infra* set into text -E ; in margin (ἐπίτριτος omitted and ἐπόγδοος τόνος along the line γξβ in the rectangles ιβ and θ) -B ; in margin with letters only -f, m ; in margin (right angled parallelogram divided into four equal parts

consists; and the ratio of the tone, being sesquioctavan, is present too in the areas nine and eight. This

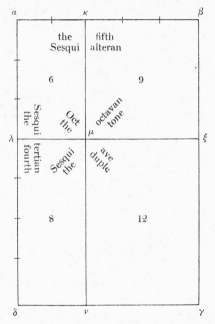

is precisely the reason why they called "concord" the
number that comprises these ratios. When multiplied by six, moreover, it produces the number 210,

---

with letters only, κ and ν omitted) -e, u, Escor. 72 (cancelled); figure omitted by r.

[3] καὶ -f, m, r, Aldine; μὲν -E, B, e, u, Escor. 72.

[4] δὲ -omitted by r. [5] τὸν τὸν -r.

(1018) κοσίων ἀριθμόν, ἐν ὅσαις ἡμέραις λέγεται[1] τὰ
ἑπτάμηνα τῶν βρεφῶν τελεογονεῖσθαι.

13. Πάλιν δ' ἀφ'[2] ἑτέρας ἀρχῆς, κατὰ πολλαπλα-
σιασμόν· ὁ μὲν δὶς γ' τὸν ϛ' ποιεῖ,[3] ὁ δὲ τετράκις
C ἐννέα τὸν λϛ',[4] ὁ δ' ὀκτάκις κζ' τὸν σιϛ'. καὶ
ἔστιν ὁ μὲν ϛ' τέλειος, ἴσος ὢν τοῖς ἑαυτοῦ μέρεσι,
καὶ γάμος καλεῖται διὰ τὴν τοῦ ἀρτίου καὶ περιττοῦ σύμμιξιν. ἔτι δὲ συνέστηκεν ἔκ τε τῆς ἀρχῆς
καὶ τοῦ ⟨πρώτου⟩[5] ἀρτίου καὶ τοῦ πρώτου περιττοῦ.[6] ὁ δὲ λϛ' πρῶτός ἐστι τετράγωνος ἅμα καὶ
τρίγωνος, τετράγωνος μὲν ἀπὸ τῆς ἑξάδος τρίγωνος
δ' ἀπὸ τῆς ὀγδοάδος· καὶ γέγονε πολλαπλασιασμῷ
μὲν τετραγώνων δυεῖν, τοῦ τέσσαρα τὸν ἐννέα

---

[1] Dübner (ὅσαις λέγεται ἡμέραις -Xylander); ὅσαις (. . .
vac. 2 . . . -E; no lacuna -B) μοίραις λέγεται -E, B; ὅσαις
(ὅσεσι -e, Escor. 72 [ἐν ὅσαις in margin]; ὅσησι -u; ὅσεσι
-Aldine) λέγεται μοίραις -e, u, f, m, r, Escor. 72.

[2] Xylander; ἐφ'-mss.   [3] ποιοῦσιν -e, u, Escor. 72.

[4] E, B, f, m, r; τριάκοντα καὶ ἕξ -e, u; τριακονταέξ
-Escor. 72.

[5] ⟨πρώτου⟩ -added in margin of Aldine from codex of
Donatus Polus and implied by Amyot's version; misplaced
by Xylander before the ἀρτίου of διὰ τὴν τοῦ ἀρτίου just above.

[6] καὶ τοῦ πρώτου ἀρτίου καὶ περιττοῦ -Wyttenbach; καὶ τοῦ
ἀρτίου καὶ τοῦ περιττοῦ πρώτου -B. Müller (1873).

---

[a] Cf. Iamblichus, Theolog. Arith., p. 51, 16-19 and p. 64,
5-13 (De Falco); Censorinus, De Die Natali xi, 5 (pp. 19,
28-20, 2 [Hultsch]); Macrobius, In Somnium Scipionis i,
vi, 15-16; Proclus, In Platonis Rem Publicam ii, pp. 34,
28-35, 23 (Kroll).

[b] i.e. the pairs of numbers in the triangle of Crantor
(1017 E supra [chap. 11 sub finem]), which in the preceding
chapter gave the sums 5, 13, and 35, now by multiplication
yield the products 6, 6², and 6³.

[c] See Quaest. Conviv. 738 F and Lycurgus v, 13 (42 F)
and cf. Euclid, Elements vii, Def. 22; Nicomachus, Arith-

GENERATION OF THE SOUL, 1018

the number of days in which it is said seven months' babes are born fully formed.[a]

13. And again making a fresh start, by multiplication: twice three makes six, four times nine thirty-six, and eight times twenty-seven 216.[b] Now, six is a perfect number, being equal to the sum of its factors,[c] and is called marriage by reason of the commixture of the even and odd[d]; and furthermore it consists of the principle and the ⟨first⟩ even and the first odd number.[e] Thirty-six is the first number at once square and triangular, square from six and triangular from eight[f]; and it is the result of the multiplication of two squares, nine multiplied by

metica Introductio I, xvi, 2-3 (pp. 39, 14-40, 22 [Hoche]); Theon Smyrnaeus, p. 45, 10-22 and p. 101, 6-9 (Hiller); Anatolius in Iamblichus, *Theolog. Arith.*, p. 17, 12-13 and p. 42, 19-20 (De Falco).

[d] *Cf.* Philo Jud., *Quaestiones in Genesin* iii, 38 (p. 206 [Aucher]=pp. 224-225 [*L.C.L.*]) with Joannes Lydus, *De Mensibus* ii, 11 (p. 32, 4-14 [Wuensch]); Clement of Alexandria, *Stromata* vi, xvi, 139, 3; Anatolius in Iamblichus, *Theolog. Arith.*, p. 43, 3-9 (De Falco).

[e] For two as the first even number and three as the first odd number see *Quaest. Romanae* 264 A, *De E* 388 A, *De Defectu Orac.* 429 B; and for unity or the monad as ἀρχὴ ἀριθμοῦ see *De Defectu Orac.* 415 E (ἔκ τε τῆς ἀρχῆς καὶ τῶν πρώτων . . .) and 1017 D *supra* with note c there (*cf.* also Nicomachus, *Arithmetica Introductio* I, viii, 2-3=p. 14, 18-19 [Hoche]; Iamblichus, *Theolog. Arith.*, p. 1, 4 [De Falco]; and Macrobius, *In Somnium Scipionis* I, vi, 7), but for one treated as the first odd number see 1027 F *supra* with note d there.

[f] For triangular numbers see the references in note c on *Plat. Quaest.* 1003 F *supra*. The expression $\frac{n(n+1)}{2}$ is satisfied for 36 by $n=8$, and none of the preceding triangular numbers (with the exception of 1) is a square (*cf.* Theon Smyrnaeus, p. 33, 16-17 [Hiller]).

279

(1018) πολλαπλασιάσαντος, συνθέσει δὲ τριῶν κύβων, τὸ
γὰρ ἓν καὶ τὰ ὀκτὼ καὶ τὰ εἰκοσιεπτὰ συντεθέντα

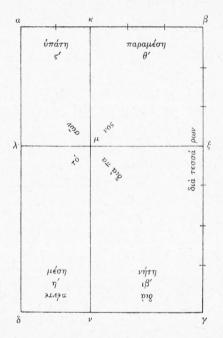

ποιεῖ τὸν προγεγραμμένον ἀριθμόν. ἔτι δὲ ἑτερο-
D μήκης ἀπὸ δυεῖν πλευρῶν, τῶν μὲν δώδεκα τρὶς

---

a For 1 as a cubic number see *Quaest. Conviv.* 744 B with
Iamblichus, *Theolog. Arith.*, p. 77, 9 (De Falco), and *cf.*
Nicomachus, *Arithmetica Introductio* II, xv, 3 and xx, 5
280

four, and of the addition of three cubic numbers, for one[a] and eight and twenty-seven added together

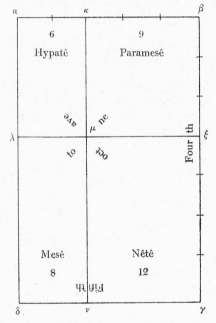

produce the aforesaid number. Moreover, it is an oblong number from two sides, from twelve multi-

(pp. 106, 6-7 and 119, 12-15 [Hoche]); Plutarch himself, however, calls eight the first cubic number (1017 D *supra*, 1020 D *infra*, and *Quaest. Conviv.* 738 F), for which *cf.* Iamblichus, *Theolog. Arith.*, p. 72, 2 (De Falco): πρῶτον ἐνεργείᾳ κύβον.

PLUTARCH'S MORALIA

(1018) γιγνομένων[1] τῶν δ' ἐννέα τετράκις. ἂν οὖν ἐκτε-
θῶσιν[2] αἱ τῶν σχημάτων πλευραί, τοῦ τετραγώνου
τὰ ϛ' καὶ τοῦ τριγώνου τὰ ὀκτὼ καὶ παραλληλογράμμων τοῦ μὲν ἑτέρου τὰ ἐννέα τοῦ δὲ ἑτέρου
τὰ ιβ', τοὺς[3] τῶν συμφωνιῶν ποιήσουσι λόγους.
ἔσται γὰρ τὰ δώδεκα πρὸς μὲν τὰ ἐννέα διὰ τεσσάρων ὡς νήτη πρὸς παραμέσην, πρὸς δὲ τὰ ὀκτὼ
διὰ πέντε ὡς νήτη πρὸς μέσην, πρὸς δὲ τὰ ϛ' διὰ
πασῶν ὡς νήτη πρὸς ὑπάτην. ὁ δὲ σις''[4] κύβος
ἐστὶν ἀπὸ ἑξάδος ἴσος τῇ ἑαυτοῦ περιμέτρῳ.

14. Τοιαύτας δὲ δυνάμεις τῶν ἐκκειμένων ἀριθμῶν ἐχόντων ἴδιον τῷ τελευταίῳ συμβέβηκε, τῷ
Ε κζ', τὸ τοῖς πρὸ αὐτοῦ συντιθεμένοις[5] ἴσον εἶναι
πᾶσιν. ἔστι δὲ καὶ περιοδικὸς σελήνης. καὶ τῶν

---

[1] γ . . . vac. 2 . . . ομένων -r.
[2] ἐντεθῶσιν -r. The figure *supra* set into text -E; in
margin -B ; in margin (right angled parallelogram divided
into four equal parts with letters and numbers only) -e, u,
Escor. 72 ; figure omitted by f, m, r.
[3] Between ιβ' and τοὺς f, m, r, and Aldine repeat καὶ τοῦ
τριγώνου . . . παραλληλογράμμων *supra* ; and Escor. 72 repeats
(but brackets) καὶ τοῦ τριγώνου . . . τοῦ μὲν ἑ.
[4] f, m, r, Escor. 72, Aldine (*cf.* ὁ μὲν ϛ' and ὁ δὲ λϛ' in
1018 c *supra*) ; ὁ δὲ τῶν σις' -E, B, e, u (τῶν σιβ').
[5] Maurommates ; συντιθέμενον -mss. (συντιθέμενος -r).

---

[a] Number of this kind is προμήκης and only that of the
type n(n +1) is ἑτερομήκης according to Nicomachus,
Arithmetica Introductio II, xvii, 1 and xviii, 2 (pp. 108, 8–
109, 11 and 113, 6-18 [Hoche]) and Theon Smyrnaeus,
pp. 30, 8-31, 8 (Hiller). Theon himself at least once, however, uses ἑτερομήκης for *any* oblong number (p. 36, 13-20
[Hiller]), just as Plutarch does here (see also *De Iside* 367 F,

282

GENERATION OF THE SOUL, 1018

plied by three and from nine multiplied by four.[a]
Now, if the sides of the figures be set out, six the
side of the square and eight of the triangular number
and of the parallelogrammic numbers [b] nine the side
of one and twelve of the other, they will produce the
ratios of the consonances, for twelve to nine will be a
fourth as nêtê to paramesê, to eight a fifth as nêtê
to mesê, and to six an octave as nêtê to hypatê.[c]
The number 216 is a cube from six equal to its own
perimeter.[d]

14. Of the numbers set out,[e] which possess such
properties, the last, twenty-seven, has the peculiar
characteristic [f] of being equal to the sum of all those
before it.[g] It is also the periodic number of the

where eighteen [*i.e.* 6 ×3 or 9 ×2] is called ἑτερομήκης), as
Euclid is supposed by Iamblichus to have done (*In Nico-machi Arithmeticam Introductionem*, pp. 74, 23–75, 4
[Pistelli]), and as Aristotle apparently did (*Anal. Post.*
73 a 40–b 1 with Philoponus, *Anal. Post.*, p. 62, 15-20).
Plato in *Theaetetus* 148 A 1–B 2 used both προμήκης and
ἑτερομήκης indifferently of all oblong numbers.

  [b] *i.e.* the oblongs, 12 ×3 and 9 ×4, *supra*. *Cf.* Theon
Smyrnaeus (pp. 27, 23–28, 2 [Hiller]), who uses the term
for those numbers that in his sense are προμήκεις but *not*
ἑτερομήκεις, *i.e.* those of the type n(n +m) where m is not
less than 2.

  [c] *Cf.* [Plutarch], *De Musica* 1138 E—1139 B and 1140 A ;
Nicomachus, *Harmonices Man.* 6 and *Excerpta* 7 (*Musici
Scriptores Graeci*, pp. 247, 7-26 and 248, 18-26 ; p. 279,
8-15 [Jan]). For the meaning of nêtê and hypatê see note
e on *Plat. Quaest.* 1007 E *supra* ; the paramesê is one tone
higher in pitch than the mesê (*cf.* Nicomachus in *Musici
Scriptores Graeci*, p. 248, 21-22 [Jan]).

  [d] *i.e.* 216=6³=the sum of the six bounding planes, each
of which is 6².

  [e] *i.e.* τῶν ὑπὸ Πλάτωνος ἐκκειμένων ἀριθμῶν (1017 D *supra*).

  [f] See page 251, note a *supra*.

  [g] *Cf.* Theon Smyrnaeus, p. 96, 5-8 (Hiller).

(1018) ἐμμελῶν διαστημάτων οἱ Πυθαγορικοὶ τὸν τόνον
ἐν τούτῳ τῷ ἀριθμῷ τάττουσι· διὸ καὶ[1] τὰ τριακαίδεκα λεῖμμα καλοῦσιν, ἀπολείπει γὰρ μονάδι τοῦ
ἡμίσεος. ὅτι δὲ οὗτοι[2] καὶ τοὺς τῶν συμφωνιῶν
λόγους περιέχουσι ῥᾴδιον καταμαθεῖν. καὶ γὰρ
διπλάσιος λόγος ἐστὶν ὁ τῶν δύο πρὸς τὸ ἓν ἐν ᾧ
τὸ διὰ πασῶν, καὶ ἡμιόλιος ὁ πρὸς τὰ δύο τῶν
τριῶν ἐν ᾧ τὸ διὰ πέντε, καὶ ἐπίτριτος ὁ πρὸς τὰ
τρία τῶν τεσσάρων ἐν ᾧ τὸ διὰ τεσσάρων, καὶ
τριπλάσιος ὁ πρὸς τὰ τρία τῶν ἐννέα ἐν ᾧ τὸ διὰ
F πασῶν καὶ διὰ πέντε, καὶ τετραπλάσιος ὁ πρὸς τὰ
δύο τῶν ὀκτὼ ἐν ᾧ τὸ δὶς[3] διὰ πασῶν[4]· ἔνεστι δὲ καὶ

----

[1] καὶ -omitted by r.
[2] οὗτοι -omitted by r.
[3] δὶς -omitted by u.
[4] δὶς διὰ πασῶν καὶ διὰ πέντε -r.

----

[a] *Cf.* Aulus Gellius, i, xx, 6 ; Favonius Eulogius, *De
Somnio Scipionis*, p. 12, 2-4 (Holder) ; and Chalcidius,
Platonis Timaeus, p. 180, 20-21 (Wrobel)=p. 160, 9-10
(Waszink). The period of 27⅓ days, also mentioned by
Chalcidius (p. 137, 17-20 [Wrobel]=p. 117, 11-13 [Waszink]),
is the approximate tropical month : *cf.* Geminus, *Elementa
Astronomiae* i, 30 (p. 12, 24-27 [Manitius]) ; Pliny, *N.H.* ii,
44 ; Theon Smyrnaeus, p. 136, 1-3 (Hiller) ; Macrobius,
In Somnium Scipionis i, vi, 50.

[b] See τὰ μελῳδούμενα . . . διαστήματα in 1019 A *infra* with
note *f* there ; and for τὰ ἐμμελῆ διαστήματα *cf.* Dionysius
Musicus in Porphyry, *In Ptolemaei Harmonica*, p. 37, 19-20
(Düring) and Gaudentius, *Harmonica Introductio* 3 (*Musici
Scriptores Graeci*, p. 330, 11-16 [Jan]).

[c] *Cf.* Boethius, *De Institutione Musica* iii, v (pp. 276,
15-277, 1 and p. 277, 16-18 [Friedlein])=Philolaus, frag.
A 26 (I, p. 405, 8-15 and 27-28 [D.-K.]). In fact, if the fifth,

moon *a* ; and of the melodious intervals *b* the tone is assigned to this number by the Pythagoreans, *c* which is also why they call thirteen " leimma," *d* for it falls short of the half by a unit. *e* And it is easy to see that these numbers also comprise the ratios of the consonances. *f* For the ratio of two to one is duple, in which the octave consists, and that of three to two is sesquialteran, in which the fifth consists, and that of four to three is sesquitertian, in which the fourth consists, and that of nine to three is triple, in which consists the octave plus a fifth, and that of eight to two is quadruple, in which the double octave consists ;

fourth, and tone be raised to their least common denominator, the numerator of the tone is 27.

d See 1017 F *supra* (page 273, note *c*). The " leimma " is the *ratio* 256·243 but was then identified with the difference between these two numbers, as is stated in 1022 A *infra* (τὸ μεταξὺ τῶν σμγ′ καὶ τῶν σνς′ . . .) and Boethius, *De Institutione Musica* III, v (p. 277, 5-7 [Friedlein])=Philolaus, frag. A 26 (I, p. 405, 19-20 [D.-K.]), a mistake of which Theon Smyrnaeus was aware despite his tendency to fall into it himself (p. 67, 13-16 and p. 69, 3-14 [Hiller]).

e The same explanation of the term " leimma," though without the additional mistake of μονάδι (for not thirteen but that of which it is a half falls short of twenty-seven by a unit), is given in 1020 F *infra* (. . . ὅτι τοῦ ἡμίσεος ἀπολείπει) and by Chalcidius (*Platonis Timaeus*, p. 112, 11-12 [Wrobel]= p. 94, 10-11 [Waszink]) and Gaudentius (*Harmonica Introductio* 14= *Musici Scriptores Graeci*, p. 343, 6-10 [Jan]) ; but the correct explanation, *i.e.* that it means " the remainder " after two tones have been measured off from a fourth (*cf.* Proclus, *In Platonis Timaeum* ii, p. 177, 10-13 and pp. 182, 30–183, 2 [Diehl] ; Theon Smyrnaeus, p. 70, 3-6 [Hiller]), is given in 1022 A *infra* (. . . περίεστι . . . διὸ καὶ λεῖμμα ὠνόμαζον).

f *Cf.* Theon Smyrnaeus, p. 95, 14-16 (Hiller) ; for what follows see *De E* 389 D and *cf.* Proclus, *In Platonis Timaeum* ii, p. 168, 2-8 (Diehl) and Macrobius, *In Somnium Scipionis* II, i, 15-20.

(1018) ἐπόγδοος ὁ¹ τῶν ἐννέα πρὸς τὰ ὀκτὼ² ἐν ᾧ τὸ τονιαῖον. ἂν τοίνυν ἡ μονὰς ἐπίκοινος οὖσα καὶ τοῖς
ἀρτίοις συναριθμῆται³ καὶ τοῖς περιττοῖς, ὁ μὲν
ἅπας ἀριθμὸς τὸ τῆς δεκάδος παρέχεται πλῆθος
(οἱ γὰρ ἀπὸ μονάδος μέχρι τῶν δέκα συντιθέμενοι
⟨πέντε καὶ πεντήκοντα ποιοῦσι⟩ τούτου δὲ ὁ μὲν
1019 ἄρτιος)⁴ πεντεκαίδεκα, τρίγωνον ἀπὸ πεντάδος, ὁ
δὲ περιττὸς τὸν τεσσαράκοντα κατὰ σύνθεσιν μὲν
ἐκ τῶν δεκατριῶν καὶ τῶν κζ΄ γεννώμενον, οἷς τὰ
μελῳδούμενα μετροῦσιν εὐσήμως⁵ οἱ μαθηματικοὶ
διαστήματα τὸ μὲν δίεσιν τὸ δὲ τόνον καλοῦντες,
κατὰ τὸν πολλαπλασιασμὸν δὲ τῇ τῆς τετρακτύος
δυνάμει γιγνόμενον, τῶν γὰρ πρώτων τεσσάρων
καθ' αὑτὸν ἑκάστου τετράκις λαμβανομένου γίγνε-

---

¹ ὁ -E, B ; omitted by all other mss. and Aldine.

² τῶν ἐννέα πρὸς τὰ ὀκτὼ -Bernardakis (πρὸς τὰ ὀκτὼ τῶν
ἐννέα -Maurommates) ; τῶν ὀκτὼ (η΄ -B, f, m, r) πρὸς τὰ θ΄
(ἐννέα -E) -mss.

³ E, B (first ι over erasure), f, m ; συναριθμεῖται -e, Aldine ; συναρθμεῖται -r ; συναρίμειται -u ; συναριθεῖται -Escor.
72.

⁴ ⟨. . .⟩ added by H. C. after Bernardakis (τὰ πέντε καὶ
πεντήκοντα ποιοῦσι· τούτου δὲ πάλιν ὁ μὲν ἄρτιος τὰ) and
similar supplements by Wyttenbach and B. Müller (1873) ;
συντιθέμενοι . . . vac. 50 -E ; vac. 48 -B . . . πεντεκαίδεκα -E,
B ; συντιθέμενοι† πεντεκαίδεκα -e, u, Escor. 72 ; συντιθέμενοι
ιε΄ (without lacuna) -f, m, r, Aldine.

⁵ εὐρύθμως -B.

ᵃ See De E 388 A (. . . ἡ μὲν μονὰς ἀμφοτέρων ἐπίκοινός
ἐστι τῇ δυνάμει) and 1027 E supra (page 269, note a) ; cf.
Theon Smyrnaeus, p. 95, 8-9 (Hiller) and Chalcidius,
Platonis Timaeus, p. 104, 16-25 (Wrobel)=pp. 87, 23-88, 4
(Waszink).

ᵇ With what follows, i.e. 1+2+3 . . . +10=55=(1+2+4
+8 [=15])+(1+3+9+27 [=40]) cf. Anatolius in Iamblichus, Theolog. Arith., p. 86, 10-18 (De Falco).

and among them also that of nine to eight is sesquioctavan, in which the interval of the tone consists. If,
then, the unit, which is common to the even numbers
and the odd,[a] be counted along with both, the number
taken all together [b] gives the sum of the decad (for
the numbers from one to ten added together ⟨make
fifty-five⟩, and of this the even number gives⟩ fifteen,
a triangular number from five,[c] while the odd number
gives forty, by addition produced from thirteen and
twenty-seven, numbers which the mathematicians,[d]
calling the former " diesis " and the latter " tone,"[e]
make distinct measures of the melodic intervals,[f] but
by multiplication arising in virtue of the tetractys,[g]
for, when each of the first four by itself is multiplied

[c] *i.e.* $15 = \dfrac{5(5+1)}{2}$. *Cf.* Theon Smyrnaeus, p. 38, 11-14
(Hiller) and see note *c* on *Plat. Quaest.* 1003 F *supra*.

[d] *i.e.* οἱ Πυθαγορικοί of 1018 E *supra*. See 1020 E-F *infra*,
where οἱ μὲν ἁρμονικοί . . . οἱ δὲ Πυθαγορικοί = τοῖς μὲν ἁρμονικοῖς . . . τοῖς δὲ μαθηματικοῖς, and 1021 D *infra* (. . . ὀρθῶς ὑπὸ
τῶν μαθηματικῶν λεῖμμα προσηγόρευται).

[e] See 1018 E *supra* with notes *c* and *d* there. As to the use
of " diesis " here for what is there called " leimma " *cf.*
Theon Smyrnaeus, pp. 55, 13-15 and 56, 18-57, 1 (Hiller) ;
Chalcidius, *Platonis Timaeus*, p. 112, 9-10 (Wrobel) = p. 94,
8-9 (Waszink) ; Macrobius, *In Somnium Scipionis* II, i, 23 ;
Boethius, *De Institutione Musica* II, xxviii (p. 260, 21-25
[Friedlein]) and III, v (p. 277, 1-5 [Friedlein] = Philolaus,
frag. A 26 [i, p. 405, 15-19, D.-K.]) with Philolaus, frag. B 6
(i, p. 410, 2-8 [D.-K.]).

[f] *Cf.* τῶν ἐμμελῶν διαστημάτων . . . τὸν τόνον . . . (1018 E
supra) and διάστημα ἐν μελῳδίᾳ . . . τῶν δὲ διαστημάτων . . .
τόνος (1020 E *infra*). In *De E* 389 E-F and *De Defectu Orac.*
430 A Plutarch counts five μελῳδούμενα διαστήματα, distinguishing δίεσις as the quarter-tone from ἡμιτόνιον (*cf.* Theon
Smyrnaeus, p. 55, 11-13 [Hiller]).

[g] Not the Platonic " tetractys " but, as is clear from what
follows, the quaternary of the first four numbers.

287

(1019) ται δ' καὶ η' καὶ ιβ' καὶ ιϛ'. ταῦτα τὸν[1] μ' συν-
τίθησι περιέχοντα τοὺς τῶν συμφωνιῶν λόγους· τὰ
μὲν γὰρ ιϛ' ἐπίτριτα τῶν δεκαδύο ἐστὶν τῶν δ'
ὀκτὼ διπλάσια, τῶν δὲ τεσσάρων[2] τετραπλάσια, τὰ
B ⟨δὲ⟩[3] ιβ' τῶν ὀκτὼ ἡμιόλια τῶν δὲ τεσσάρων τριπλάσια. οὗτοι δὲ οἱ λόγοι τὸ διὰ τεσσάρων καὶ τὸ
διὰ πέντε καὶ τὸ διὰ πασῶν καὶ τὸ δὶς διὰ πασῶν
περιέχουσιν. ἴσος γε μήν ἐστιν ὁ τῶν τεσσαράκοντα δυσὶ[4] τετραγώνοις[5] καὶ δυσὶ κύβοις ὁμοῦ
λαμβανομένοις· τὸ γὰρ ἓν καὶ τὰ τέσσαρα καὶ τὰ
ὀκτὼ καὶ τὰ κζ' κύβοι καὶ τετράγωνοι ⟨μ'⟩[6] γίγνονται συντεθέντες.[7] ὥστε πολὺ τῆς Πυθαγορικῆς
τὴν Πλατωνικὴν τετρακτὺν ποικιλωτέραν εἶναι τῇ
διαθέσει καὶ τελειοτέραν.

15. Ἀλλὰ ταῖς εἰσαγομέναις μεσότησι τῶν ὑποκειμένων ἀριθμῶν χώρας οὐ διδόντων, ἐδέησε μείζονας ὅρους λαβεῖν ἐν τοῖς αὐτοῖς λόγοις. καὶ
C λεκτέον τίνες εἰσὶν οὗτοι. πρότερον δὲ περὶ τῶν
μεσοτήτων· ὧν τὴν μὲν ἴσῳ κατ' ἀριθμὸν ὑπερ-

---

[1] ταῦτα δὲ τὸν -E, B. [2] τῶν δ' -E, B.
[3] ⟨δὲ⟩ -added by B. Müller (1873).
[4] δυσὶ -Bernardakis ; δυοῖν -E, B, f, m, r ; δυεῖν -e, u,
Escor. 72.
[5] τετραγώνοιν -f (-γωνοῖν), m[1], r.
[6] ⟨μ'⟩ -added by Maurommates.
[7] E ; συντιθέντες -all other mss., Aldine.

---

[a] The octave plus a fifth (12·4), though expressly included
in 1018 E-F *supra* as the ratio of nine to three, the triple
ratio, is (inadvertently ?) omitted here, as it is by the mss. of
Chalcidius, *Platonis Timaeus*, p. 101, 4-5 (Wrobel)=p. 84,
22-23 (Waszink).

[b] Since eight and twenty-seven are cubic numbers, one
and four must be the two square numbers (*cf. De Defectu
Orac.* 429 E [. . . πρώτων δυεῖν τετραγώνων . . . τῆς τε μονάδος

by four, the result is four and eight and twelve and sixteen. These make up the number forty while comprising the ratios of the consonances, for sixteen is four thirds of twelve and twice as much as eight and four times as much as four, ⟨and⟩ twelve is half again as much as eight and three times as much as four ; and these ratios comprise the fourth and the fifth and the octave and the double octave.[a] Then, as to the number forty, it is equal to two square and two cubic numbers taken together, for one and four and eight and twenty-seven are cubic and square numbers[b] amounting to ⟨forty⟩ when they have been added together. Consequently the Platonic tetractys is much more intricate and consummate in organisation than is the Pythagorean.[c]

15. Since, however, the numbers postulated do not provide room for the means that are being inserted, it was necessary to take higher terms in the same ratios.[d] So one must say what these are. Before that, however, about the means[e] : of these the one

καὶ τῆς τετράδος] and *De E* 391 A), though one has just been treated as a cubic number (see 1018 c *supra* with note *a* on page 281).

   [c] See 1017 D, note *b supra*.

   [d] The " numbers postulated " are τῶν ὑπὸ Πλάτωνος ἐκκει-μένων ἀριθμῶν (1017 D *supra*). See 1020 A *infra*, where after the digression on the means the substance of the present sentence is rephrased more clearly ; and *cf.* Chalcidius, *Platonis Timaeus*, pp. 106, 24–107, 2 (Wrobel)= p. 89, 19-21 (Waszink).

   [e] With what follows *cf.* Nicomachus, *Harmonices Man.* 8 (*Musici Scriptores Graeci*, pp. 250, 12–251, 3 and p. 251, 10-13 [Jan]) ; Philo Jud., *De Opificio Mundi* 108-110 (i, pp. 38, 19–39, 11 [Cohn]) ; Chalcidius, *Platonis Timaeus*, p. 107, 2-20 (Wrobel)=pp. 89, 22-90, 12 (Waszink) ; Martianus Capella, vii, 737.

(1019) ἔχουσαν ἴσῳ δὲ ὑπερεχομένην ἀριθμητικὴν οἱ νῦν
καλοῦσι τὴν δὲ ταὐτῷ μέρει τῶν ἄκρων αὐτῶν
ὑπερέχουσαν καὶ ὑπερεχομένην ὑπεναντίαν. ὅροι
δ᾽ εἰσὶ τῆς μὲν ἀριθμητικῆς ς΄ καὶ θ΄ καὶ ιβ΄, τὰ
γὰρ ἐννέα τῷ ἴσῳ κατ᾽ ἀριθμὸν τῶν ἒξ ὑπερέχει
καὶ τῶν ιβ΄ λείπεται· τῆς δὲ ὑπεναντίας ς΄ η΄ ιβ΄,
τὰ γὰρ ὀκτὼ δυσὶ¹ μὲν τῶν ς΄ ὑπερέχει τέσσαρσι
δὲ τῶν ιβ΄ λείπεται, ὧν τὰ μὲν δύο τῶν ἒξ τὰ δὲ
τέσσαρα τῶν δώδεκα τριτημόριόν ἐστι. συμβέβηκεν οὖν ἐν² μὲν τῇ ἀριθμητικῇ ταὐτῷ³ μέρει τὸ⁴
D μέσον⁵ ὑπερέχεσθαι καὶ ὑπερέχειν ἐν δὲ τῇ ὑπεν-
αντίᾳ ταὐτῷ μέρει τῶν ἄκρων τοῦ μὲν ἀποδεῖν
τὸ⁶ δὲ ὑπερβάλλειν, ἐκεῖ μὲν γὰρ τὰ τρία τοῦ μέσου
τρίτον ἐστὶ μέρος⁷ ἐνταῦθα δὲ τὰ δ΄ καὶ τὰ β΄ τῶν
ἄκρων ἑκάτερον ἑκατέρου· ὅθεν ὑπεναντία κέκλη-

¹ E, B; δύο -all other mss., Aldine. ² ἡ -r.
³ τῷ ἄκρῳ -u; τῷ αὐτῷ -all other mss.
⁴ μέρει τῶν ἄκρων τὸ -E, B.
⁵ μέσον -correction in margin -f¹, m¹, r¹, Leonicus; ἴσον
(or ἴσον) -mss.
⁶ τὸ -Turnebus; τοῦ -r; τὸν -all other mss., Aldine.
⁷ μέσον (with final ν remade to ς) -u.

[a] *i.e.* exceeds one extreme and falls short of the other.
This is clear in *Timaeus* 36 A 4-5 (quoted in 1027 B-C *supra*)
because this clause is preceded by that which defines the
harmonic mean and which contains τῶν ἄκρων.

[b] Though Plutarch here says that ὑπεναντία is the term
used for the harmonic mean by his contemporaries and so
uses it in paraphrasing Eudorus (1019 E *infra*), Iamblichus
says (*In Nicomachi Arithmeticam Introductionem*, pp. 100,
22–101, 5 and p. 113, 16-22 [Pistelli]) that what was originally
called ὑπεναντία was renamed ἁρμονική by the circle of
Archytas and Hippasus (*cf.* Archytas, frag. B 2 [D.-K.]=
Porphyry, *In Ptolemaei Harmonica*, p. 93, 7 and 13-17
[Düring]) and that afterwards the name ὑπεναντία was
applied to a new, fourth mean, thought to be contrary to the

that exceeds and falls short [a] by amounts numerically
equal men today call arithmetical, and the one that
exceeds and falls short of the extremes by the same
fraction of them they call subcontrary. [b] Of the
arithmetical six and nine and twelve are terms, for
nine exceeds six and falls short of twelve by numerical
equality ; and of the subcontrary six, eight, twelve
are terms, for eight exceeds six by two and falls
short of twelve by four, and of these two is a third
of six and four a third of twelve. So it is characteristic
in the arithmetical for the middle to exceed and fall
short by the same fraction [c] and in the subcontrary
for it to be inferior to one of the extremes and to
surpass the other by the identical fraction of them,
for in the former case three is a third of the middle
and in the latter four and two are thirds, one of one
extreme and the other of the other, for which reason
it has been called subcontrary. [d] And to this they

harmonic (*cf.* Nicomachus, *Arithmetica Introductio* ii,
xxviii, 3=p. 141, 4-16 [Hoche] and Theon Smyrnaeus,
p. 115, 9-11 [Hiller]).

[c] *i.e.* by the same fraction of itself. *Cf.* Nicomachus,
Arithmetica Introductio ii, xxv, 3 (p. 132, 18-20 [Hoche]
and for the whole of Plutarch's sentence *ibid.*, pp. 132,
18-133, 2) ; Iamblichus, *In Nicomachi Arithmeticam Introductionem*, p. 114, 5-8 (Pistelli).

[d] *Cf.* Iamblichus, *In Nicomachi Arithmeticam Introductionem*, p. 110, 17-23 with pp. 100, 25-101, 1 (Pistelli)
and Nicomachus, *Arithmetica Introductio* ii, xxv, 3 (p. 132,
21-22 [Hoche]). The contrariety is identified with another
characteristic by Iamblichus, *op. cit.*, p. 111, 18-26 and
Boethius, *De Institutione Arithmetica* ii, xlvii (p. 152, 27-31
[Friedlein]) ; *cf.* Nicomachus, *op. cit.* ii, xxiii, 6 and xxv,
2 (pp. 126, 1-6 and 132, 11-15 [Hoche]). E. de Strycker
(*Antiquité Classique*, xxi [1952], p. 531, n. 1) defended the
latter explanation ; Burkert (*Weisheit und Wissenschaft*,
p. 418, n. 98) proposed still another.

(1019) ται.   ταύτην δὲ[1] ἁρμονικὴν ὀνομάζουσιν ὅτι τοῖς
ὅροις τὰ πρῶτα σύμφωνα παρέχεται, τῷ μὲν με-

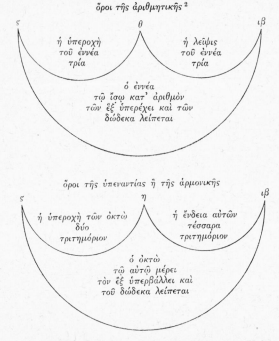

ὅροι τῆς ἀριθμητικῆς [2]

ς   θ   ιβ

ἡ ὑπεροχὴ   ἡ λεῖψις
τοῦ ἐννέα   τοῦ ἐννέα
τρία   τρία

ὁ ἐννέα
τῷ ἴσῳ κατ' ἀριθμὸν
τῶν ἕξ ὑπερέχει καὶ τῶν
δώδεκα λείπεται

ὅροι τῆς ὑπεναντίας ἢ τῆς ἁρμονικῆς

ς   η   ιβ

ἡ ὑπεροχὴ τῶν ὀκτὼ   ἡ ἔνδεια αὐτῶν
δύο   τέσσαρα
τριτημόριον   τριτημόριον

ὁ ὀκτὼ
τῷ αὐτῷ μέρει
τὸν ἐξ ὑπερβάλλει καὶ
τοῦ δώδεκα λείπεται

---

[1] τὴν αὐτὴν δὲ -B. Müller (1873) ; ταύτην δὲ ⟨καὶ⟩ -Hubert.
[2] The two figures as here -E (lower margin) ;

ς ⌣ Γ θ ⌣ Γ τ ιβ and ς ⌣ β η ⌣ δ ιβ -e, Escor. 72 (both

in side margin) ; figures omitted by all other mss.

give the name harmonic because by its terms it
exhibits the primary concords,[a] by the greatest in

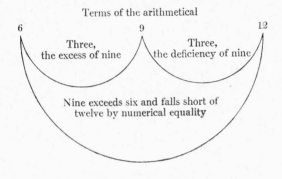

Terms of the arithmetical

6   9   12

Three,
the excess of nine

Three,
the deficiency of nine

Nine exceeds six and falls short of
twelve by numerical equality

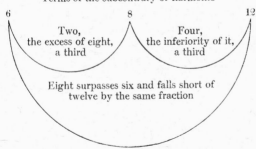

Terms of the subcontrary or harmonic

6   8   12

Two,
the excess of eight,
a third

Four,
the inferiority of it,
a third

Eight surpasses six and falls short of
twelve by the same fraction

[a] *Cf.* Iamblichus, *In Nicomachi Arithmeticam Introductionem*, p. 100, 23-25 (Pistelli) and Nicomachus, *Arithmetica
Introductio* II, xxvi, 2 (pp. 135, 10–136, 11 [Hoche]); for
τὰ πρῶτα σύμφωνα see page 275, note *d supra*.

(1019) γίστῳ πρὸς τὸν ἐλάχιστον τὸ διὰ πασῶν τῷ δὲ
μεγίστῳ¹ πρὸς τὸν² μέσον τὸ διὰ πέντε τῷ δὲ
μέσῳ πρὸς τὸν³ ἐλάχιστον τὸ διὰ τεσσάρων, ὅτι⁴
τοῦ μεγίστου τῶν ὅρων κατὰ νήτην τιθεμένου τοῦ
δ' ἐλαχίστου καθ' ὑπάτην ὁ μέσος γίγνεται ὁ⁵
E κατὰ μέσην πρὸς μὲν⁶ τὸν μέγιστον⁷ τὸ⁸ διὰ πέντε
ποιοῦσαν πρὸς δὲ τὸν ἐλάχιστον⁹ τὸ¹⁰ διὰ τεσσάρων·
ὥστε γίγνεσθαι τὰ ὀκτὼ κατὰ τὴν μέσην τὰ δὲ
δώδεκα κατὰ νήτην¹¹ τὰ δὲ ἐξ καθ' ὑπάτην.

16. Τὸν δὲ τρόπον ᾧ λαμβάνουσι τὰς εἰρημένας
μεσότητας ἁπλῶς καὶ σαφῶς Εὔδωρος ἀποδείκ-
νυσι. σκόπει δὲ πρότερον ἐπὶ τῆς ἀριθμητικῆς.
ἂν γὰρ ἐκθεὶς τοὺς ἄκρους λάβῃς ἑκατέρου¹² τὸ
ἥμισυ μέρος καὶ συνθῇς, ὁ συντεθεὶς ἔσται μέσος ἔν
τε τοῖς¹³ διπλασίοις καὶ τοῖς τριπλασίοις ὁμοίως.
ἐπὶ δὲ τῆς ὑπεναντίας, ἐν μὲν τοῖς διπλασίοις ἂν
τοὺς ἄκρους ἐκθεὶς¹⁴ τοῦ μὲν ἐλάττονος τὸ τρίτον
F τοῦ δὲ μείζονος τὸ ἥμισυ λάβῃς, ὁ συντεθεὶς¹⁵
γίγνεται μέσος· ἐν δὲ τοῖς τριπλασίοις¹⁶ ἀνάπαλιν
τοῦ μὲν ἐλάττονος ἥμισυ δεῖ λαβεῖν τοῦ δὲ μείζονος τρίτον, ὁ γὰρ συντεθεὶς οὕτω γίγνεται μέσος.
ἔστω γὰρ ἐν τριπλασίῳ λόγῳ τὰ ϛ' ἐλάχιστος ὅρος

---

¹ πρὸς τὸν ἐλάχιστον τὸ διὰ πασῶν τῷ δὲ μεγίστῳ -omitted
by f.
² τὸν -E (ν superscript -E¹), B ; τὸ -all other mss., Aldine.
³ τὸ -r.
⁴ ὅθεν -B. Müller (1873) ; ἔτι -Hubert (who also suggests
deleting ὅτι . . . τὰ δὲ ἐξ καθ' ὑπάτην as a marginal note).
⁵ ὁ -deleted by B. Müller (1873).
⁶ μὲν -omitted by r.
⁷ πρὸς μὲν τὴν νήτην -B. Müller (1873).   ⁸ τὸν -r, Aldine.
⁹ τὸ ἐλάχιστον -r ; τὴν ὑπάτην -B. Müller (1873).
¹⁰ τὸ -E, B, r ; omitted by all other mss. and Aldine.
¹¹ κατὰ τὴν νήτην -f, m, r.   ¹² ἑκάτερον -r.

relation to the least the octave and by the greatest in relation to the middle term the fifth and by the middle term in relation to the least the fourth, because, the greatest of the terms being placed at nêtê and the least at hypatê, the middle term turns out to be that at mesê, mesê in relation to the greatest making the fifth and in relation to the least the fourth, so that eight turns out to be at the mesê and twelve at nêtê and six at hypatê.

16. The way the aforesaid means are found is set forth simply and clearly by Eudorus.[a] Of the two consider first the arithmetical. If you set out the extreme terms and take the half of each and add the two halves together, the resulting sum will be the middle term in the case of the double numbers and of the triple alike.[b] In the case of the subcontrary,[c] however, if in the double numbers you set out the extreme terms and take the third of the lesser and the half of the greater, their sum turns out to be the middle term ; but in the triple numbers contrariwise you must take half of the lesser and a third of the greater, for the sum of this addition turns out to be the middle term. For let six be least term and

---

[a] See note c on 1013 b *supra*.

[b] *Cf.* Plutarch, *Quaest. Conviv.* 738 d (. . . συντεθέντα δ' ἀλλήλοις διπλασιάζει τὸν μέσον) ; Nicomachus, *Arithmetica Introductio* ii, xxvii, 7 (pp. 139, 23–140, 2 [Hoche]) ; Theon Smyrnaeus, p. 113, 22-25 and p. 116, 11-13 and 20-22 (Hiller).

[c] See note b on 1019 c *supra*.

---

13 τοῖς -omitted by f, m, r.

14 ἂν θεὶς -r.

15 συντιθεὶς -r.

16 ἐν δὲ τοῖς τριπλασίοις . . . οὕτω γίγνεται μέσος -omitted by u.

(1019) τὰ δὲ ιη′ μέγιστος· ἂν οὖν τῶν ϛ′ τὸ ἥμισυ λαβὼν
τὰ τρία καὶ τῶν ὀκτὼ καὶ δέκα τὸ τρίτον τὰ ϛ′
συνθῇς,[1] ἕξεις τὰ θ′[2] ταὐτῷ μέρει τῶν ἄκρων ὑπερ-
έχοντα καὶ ὑπερεχόμενα.[3] οὕτως μὲν αἱ μεσότητες
1020 λαμβάνονται. δεῖ δ᾿ αὐτὰς ἐκεῖ παρεντάξαι[4] καὶ
ἀναπληρῶσαι τὰ διπλάσια καὶ τριπλάσια διαστήματα. τῶν δ᾿ ἐκκειμένων ἀριθμῶν οἱ μὲν οὐδὲ
ὅλως μεταξὺ χώραν ἔχουσιν οἱ δ᾿ οὐχ ἱκανήν·
αὔξοντες οὖν αὐτούς,[5] τῶν αὐτῶν λόγων διαμενόντων, ὑποδοχὰς ποιοῦσιν ἀρκούσας ταῖς εἰρημέναις
μεσότησι. καὶ πρῶτον μὲν ἐλάχιστον ἀντὶ[6] τοῦ
ἑνὸς τὰ ἓξ θέντες, ἐπεὶ πρῶτος ἥμισύ τε καὶ τρίτον
ἔχει μέρος, ἅπαντας ἑξαπλασίους τοὺς ὑποτεταγ-
μένους ἐποίησαν,[7] ὡς ὑπογέγραπται,[8] δεχομένους
τὰς μεσότητας ἀμφοτέρας καὶ τοῖς διπλασίοις διαστήμασι καὶ τοῖς τριπλασίοις.[9] εἰρηκότος δὲ τοῦ

---

[1] E, B, e$^{corr.}$ (ϛ added over cancellation), u ; συνθῇ -f, m,
r, e[1], Escor. 72.
[2] τὰ θ′ -e, u, f, m, r, Escor. 72, Aldine ; τὸν ἐννέα -E ;
τὸν θ′ -B.
[3] e, u, f, m, r, Escor. 72, Aldine ; ὑπερεχόμενον -E, B.
[4] παρεντέξαι -e, u, Escor. 72[1].
[5] αὐτοὺς -omitted by B[1] (added superscript -B[2]).
[6] f, m, r ; ὄντι -all other mss., Aldine.
[7] ἐποίησεν -E, B.
[8] The figure (p. 298) -E (lower margin) ; the figure with
numbers but without words -e, u, f, m, Escor. 72 (all in side
margins) ; figure omitted by B, r.
[9] καὶ τοῖς τριπλασίοις -f, m (added in margin by m[1]), r ;
omitted by all other mss.

---

[a] The general method of finding the harmonic mean (m),
where of the extremes $c > a$, is given as $\dfrac{(c-a)a}{a+c} + a$ by Nico-

eighteen greatest in a triple ratio : then, if of six you take the half, three, and of eighteen the third, six, and add them together, you will have nine, which exceeds and falls short of the extremes by the same fraction of them.[a] This is the way the means are found ; but one must insert them in that designated position and fill up the double and triple intervals.[b] Of the numbers set out,[c] however, some do not have any room at all between them and others do not have enough ; so by increasing them with the same ratios preserved people produce sufficient accommodations for the aforesaid means.[d] First, for one they substituted as the smallest number six, since it is the first that has both a half and a third ; and all those ranged underneath, as drawn below, they made six times as large with room to admit both the means to the double intervals and the triple too.[e] Plato has

machus (*Arithmetica Introductio* ii, xxvii, 7 = p. 140, 8-13 [Hoche]), Theon Smyrnaeus (p. 119, 3-16 [Hiller]), and Proclus (*In Platonis Timaeum* ii, p. 172, 11-18 and pp. 172, 21-173, 4 [Diehl]). None of them gives the simpler formulation, $m = \dfrac{2ac}{a+c}$, although this is implicit in the statement that the sum of the extremes multiplied by the mean equals twice the product of the extremes, *i.e.* $m(a+c) = 2ac$, made both by Nicomachus (*op. cit.* ii, xxv, 4 = p. 133, 5-8 [Hoche] and *Harmonices Man.* 8 = *Musici Scriptores Graeci*, p. 251, 3-10 [Jan]) and by Theon Smyrnaeus (pp. 114, 25-115, 4 [Hiller]).

[b] *Cf. Timaeus* 35 c 2—36 a 5 quoted at 1027 b-c *supra.*

[c] See 1019 b *supra* (chap. 15 *init.*) with note *d* there.

[d] *Cf.* 1027 d *supra* (chap. 30 *init.*): . . . ἀριθμοῖς . . . χώρας ἔχουσι δεκτικὰς μεταξὺ τῶν εἰρημένων ἀναλογιῶν. . . .

[e] *Cf.* Proclus, *In Platonis Timaeum* ii, pp. 175, 22-176, 27 (Diehl) ; Iamblichus, *Theolog. Arith.*, p. 51, 8-15 and pp. 51, 25-52, 5 (De Falco) ; Chalcidius, *Platonis Timaeus*, pp. 106, 24-110, 2 (Wrobel) = pp. 89, 19-92, 5 (Waszink).

(1020)

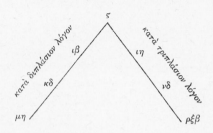

Πλάτωνος " ἡμιολίων δὲ διαστάσεων καὶ ἐπιτρίτων
B καὶ ἐπογδόων γενομένων ἐκ¹ τούτων τῶν δεσμῶν
ἐν ταῖς πρόσθεν διαστάσεσι, τῷ² τοῦ ἐπογδόου διαστήματι τὰ ἐπίτριτα πάντα συνεπληροῦτο λείπων³
αὐτῶν ἑκάστου⁴ μόριον, τῆς τοῦ⁵ μορίου ταύτης
διαστάσεως λειφθείσης⁶ ἀριθμοῦ πρὸς ἀριθμὸν ἐχούσης τοὺς ὅρους ϛ' καὶ ν' καὶ σ'⁷ πρὸς γ'⁸ καὶ μ'⁹
καὶ σ',"¹⁰ διὰ ταύτην τὴν λέξιν ἠναγκάζοντο πάλιν
τοὺς ἀριθμοὺς ἐπανάγειν καὶ μείζονας ποιεῖν. ἔδει
μὲν γὰρ ἐφεξῆς ἐπόγδοα γίγνεσθαι δύο· τῆς δὲ
ἑξάδος οὔτ' αὐτόθεν ἐπόγδοον ἐχούσης, εἴ τε τέμ-
νοιτο, κερματιζομένων εἰς μόρια τῶν μονάδων,
δυσθεωρήτου τῆς μαθήσεως ἐσομένης, αὐτὸ¹¹ τὸ
C πρᾶγμα τὸν πολλαπλασιασμὸν¹² ὑπηγόρευσεν, ὥσ-

---

¹ E, B, f, m, r ; εἰς -e, u, Escor. 72, Aldine.
² διαστάσαισι τὸ -u.
³ f, m, r ; συνεπλήρου τὸ λεῖπον -all other mss.
⁴ f, m, r ; ἑκάστῳ -all other mss.
⁵ τῆς δὲ τοῦ -f, m, r.
⁶ ληφθείσης -E, B.
⁷ ἐξ καὶ πεντήκοντα καὶ διακόσια -E, B ; ... διακοσίων -1027 c
supra and *Timaeus* 36 B 4.
⁸ πρὸς τρία πρὸς τρία -E¹ (first two words cancelled).
⁹ πρὸς τρία μ̄ -u.
¹⁰ πρὸς τρία καὶ τεσσαράκοντα καὶ διακόσια -E, B.

298

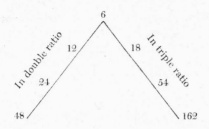

said,[a] however, " since as a result of these links in the previous intervals there came to be intervals of three to two and of four to three and of nine to eight, he filled in all the intervals of four to three with the interval of nine to eight leaving a fraction of each of them, this remaining interval of the fraction having the terms of the numerical ratio 256 to 243 " ; and because of this passage they were compelled again to raise the numbers and make them larger. For next in succession there had to come two sesquioctavans [b] ; but, as six of itself does not have a sesquioctavan and, if it should be divided with the units broken up into fractions,[c] understanding the subject would be an obscure matter,[d] the situation itself prescribed the multiplication, just as in har-

[a] *Timaeus* 36 A 6–B 5 quoted at 1027 c *supra*.

[b] *Cf.* Proclus, *In Platonis Timaeum* ii, pp. 176, 27–177, 3 (Diehl) ; Theon Smyrnaeus, p. 67, 16-21 (Hiller) ; Chalcidius, *Platonis Timaeus*, pp. 115, 6–116, 8 (Wrobel)=p. 97, 3-24 (Waszink).

[c] *Cf.* Proclus, *In Platonis Timaeum* ii, p. 177, 21 (Diehl) : . . . τοῖς ἄτμητον τὴν μονάδα φυλάττειν ἀεὶ βουλομένοις.

[d] *Cf.* 1027 E *supra* : . . . ἀμυδρὰν ποιεῖ τὴν μάθησιν . . . .

---

[11] αὐτῷ -u.

[12] f, m, r ; πολυπλασιασμὸν -all other mss.

(1020) περ ἐν ἁρμονικῇ μεταβολῇ τοῦ διαγράμματος ὅλου
συνεπιτεινομένου τῷ πρώτῳ τῶν ἀριθμῶν. ὁ μὲν
οὖν Εὔδωρος ἐπακολουθήσας Κράντορι πρῶτον
ἔλαβε τὸν τπδ', ὃς γίγνεται τοῦ ἐξ ἐπὶ τὰ ξδ' πολ-
λαπλασιασθέντος· ἐπηγάγετο δ' αὐτοὺς ὁ τῶν ξδ'
ἀριθμὸς[1] ἐπόγδοον ἔχων τὸν οβ'.[2] τοῖς δὲ ὑπὸ τοῦ
Πλάτωνος λεγομένοις συμφωνότερόν ἐστιν ὑπο-
θέσθαι τὸ ἥμισυ τούτου· τὸ γὰρ[3] λεῖμμα τὸ[4] τῶν
ἐπογδόων ἕξει λόγον ἐν ἀριθμοῖς οὓς ὁ Πλάτων
εἴρηκεν ϛ' καὶ ν' καὶ σ' πρὸς γ' καὶ μ' καὶ σ', τῶν
D ρϞβ' πρώτων τιθεμένων. ἂν δὲ ὁ τούτου διπλάσιος τεθῇ[5] πρῶτος, ἔσται τὸ λεῖμμα λόγον μὲν ἔχον
τὸν αὐτὸν ἀριθμὸν δὲ τὸν διπλάσιον, ὃν ἔχει τὰ φιβ'
πρὸς υπϛ'[6]· γίγνεται γὰρ ἐπίτριτα τῶν μὲν ρϞβ'[7]

---

[1] ἀριθμοὺς -u.
[2] τὸν οβ' -B ; τὸν ̅ο̅η̅ πρὸς τὸν ̅ο̅β̅ -E[1] (τὸν ̅ο̅η̅ πρὸς cancelled) ; τὸν ̅η̅ καὶ ̅ο̅ (ὁ -f, m, r) πρὸς τὸν ̅ο̅β̅ -all other mss.
[3] τούτου, τὸ γὰρ -f, m, r ; τούτου (τρίτου -B) γὰρ τὸ -all
other mss.
[4] τὸ -Maurommates ; τὸν -mss.
[5] τιθῇ -r.
[6] E, B, e, u, Escor. 72 (with δ superscript over ϛ) ; νοδ'
-f, m, r ; υπδ' -Aldine.
[7] ρϛβ' -u.

---

[a] Cf. Ptolemy, Harmonica, pp. 54, 13–55, 1 and p. 55,
4-5 and 7-9 (Düring).
[b] Crantor, frag. 5 (Kayser)=frag. 5 (Mullach, Frag.
Philos. Graec. iii, pp. 141-143). Plutarch's expression suggests that his immediate source was Eudorus (see note a on
1019 e supra).
[c] Cf. "Timaeus Locrus" 96 b ; Theon Smyrnaeus,
pp. 68, 12–69, 3 (Hiller) ; Proclus, In Platonis Timaeum ii,
p. 178, 2-11 (Diehl). The integer 384 is mentioned by
Chalcidius too (Platonis Timaeus, pp. 116, 19–117, 1
[Wrobel]=p. 98, 9-11 [Waszink]) but only in passing as

monic transposition the whole scale is raised in pitch
along with the first of the numbers.[a] Eudorus, then,
following Crantor [b] took as the first of the numbers
384,[c] which is the product of six multiplied by 64 ;
and they were attracted by the number 64 because
it has 72 as sesquioctavan.[d] It is more in accord with
Plato's words, however, to assume the half of this
number, for the " leimma " that is left after the
sesquioctavans are taken [e] will have its ratio expressed in the numbers that Plato has given, 256 to
243, if 192 is made the first number.[f] If the double
of this be made the first number, the " leimma " will
be the same in ratio, to be sure, but double in number,
being as 512 is to 486, for four thirds of 192 come to

another possibility. Severus adopted 768, twice 384, in
order to make the whole scale end with a " leimma "
(Proclus, *op. cit.*, ii, pp. 191, 1–192, 12 [Diehl]).

[d] Contrast Theon Smyrnaeus, pp. 68, 13–69, 1 (Hiller)
and Proclus, *In Platonis Timaeum* ii, p. 177, 3–7 (Diehl).

[e] *Cf.* 1022 A *infra* (ἀφαιρουμένου δὲ τούτου [*scil.* διτόνου]
περίεστι τοῦ ὅλου . . .) and Proclus, *In Platonis Timaeum* ii,
p. 177, 10-13 (Diehl).

[f] So it was by Theon Smyrnaeus (pp. 67, 21–68, 12 and
86, 15–87, 3 [Hiller], with which *cf.* Porphyry, *In Ptolemaei
Harmonica*, p. 130, 9-16 [Düring]), by Chalcidius (*Platonis
Timaeus*, pp. 116, 12–118, 3 [Wrobel]=pp. 98, 3–99, 9
[Waszink]), and by Aristides Quintilianus (*De Musica* iii, 1
[p. 96, 25-28, Winnington-Ingram]). Plutarch's argument
for 192 (see 1021 F—1022 A *infra*, and *cf.* Theon Smyrnaeus,
p. 69, 3-6 [Hiller]) is invalid, however, first because Plato
speaks only of ratios (*cf.* Theon Smyrnaeus, p. 69, 7-9
[Hiller], and see note d on 1018 E *supra*) and furthermore
because 192 would not serve the purpose of clearing fractions
after the first fourth but in the second would give 288, 324,
364½ (*cf.* Proclus, *In Platonis Timaeum* ii, p. 177, 8-30
[Diehl]), as Chalcidius himself duly records without recognizing the implication of it (*loc. cit.*, pp. 117, 18–118, 3
[Wrobel]=p. 99, 6-9 [Waszink]).

(1020) τὰ σνϛʹ τῶν¹ δὲ τπδʹ τὰ φιβʹ. καὶ οὐκ ἄλογος ἡ
ἐπὶ τοῦτον ἀναγωγὴ τὸν ἀριθμὸν² ἀλλὰ καὶ τοῖς
περὶ τὸν Κράντορα παρασχοῦσα τὸ³ εὔλογον· τὰ
γὰρ ξδʹ καὶ κύβος ἐστὶν ἀπὸ πρώτου τετραγώνου
καὶ τετράγωνος ἀπὸ πρώτου κύβου γενόμενος δʹ
ἐπὶ τὸν γʹ,⁴ πρῶτον ὄντα περιττὸν⁵ καὶ πρῶτον τρίγωνον καὶ πρῶτον τέλειον ὄντα καὶ ἡμιόλιον, ρϙβʹ
Ε πεποίηκεν, ἔχοντα καὶ αὐτὸν ἐπόγδοον, ὡς δεί-
ξομεν.

17. Πρότερον δὲ τί τὸ λεῖμμά ἐστι καὶ τίς ἡ
διάνοια τοῦ Πλάτωνος μᾶλλον κατόψεσθε τῶν εἰω-
θότων ἐν ταῖς Πυθαγορικαῖς σχολαῖς λέγεσθαι
βραχέως ὑπομνησθέντες. ἔστι γὰρ διάστημα ἐν
μελῳδίᾳ πᾶν τὸ περιεχόμενον ὑπὸ δυεῖν φθόγγων
ἀνομοίων τῇ τάσει· τῶν δὲ διαστημάτων ἓν ὁ κα-

---

¹ E, B, f, m, r ; τὰ -e, u, Escor. 72, Aldine.

² τούτων ἀναγωγία τῶν ἀριθμῶν -r ; τούτ͚ων ἀναγωγ͚ὴ τῶν
ἀριθμ͚ῶν -f, m.　　³ τὸν -f¹.　　⁴ τὸν τρία -E, B.

⁵ περιττὸν καὶ πρῶτον . . . τέλειον ὄντα -omitted by r.

ᵃ i.e. 192 (not Crantor's 384). Plutarch contends in what
follows that the use of 64 as multiplier, by which 192 is
originally reached, is what made Crantor's procedure appear
to be reasonable. In the procedure as given by Proclus
(In Platonis Timaeum ii, p. 177, 3-26 [Diehl]) 64 is first
taken (lines 3-4 ; cf. Theon Smyrnaeus, pp. 67, 21-68, 1
[Hiller]) and is then multiplied by three to give 192 (line 8 ;
cf. Plutarch infra and Theon Smyrnaeus, p. 68, 3-4 [Hiller]),
and finally 192 is doubled to give 384 (lines 22-26).

ᵇ i.e. 64=4³=8². Cf. Philo Jud., De Opificio Mundi 93
and 106 (i, p. 32, 1-4 and p. 38, 2-6 [Cohn]) ; Anatolius,
p. 35, 14-16 (Heiberg)=Iamblichus, Theolog. Arith., p. 54,
13-15 (De Falco). For eight as the first cubic number see
note a on page 281 supra.

ᶜ See note e on page 279 supra.

256 but of 384 to 512. Raising it to this number [a] is not unreasonable either but even for Crantor and his followers is the source of what is reasonable in their procedure, for 64 is both a cubic number from the first square number and a square number from the first cubic number [b] and, multiplied by three, which is the first odd [c] and first triangular number [d] and the first perfect [e] and first sesquialteran number,[f] makes 192, which itself has a sesquioctavan also, as we shall show. [g]

17. What the " leimma " is and what is Plato's meaning you will perceive more clearly, however, after having first been reminded briefly of the customary statements in the Pythagorean treatises. For an interval in music is all that is encompassed by two sounds dissimilar in pitch [h] ; and of the intervals

[d] See note c on *Plat. Quaest.* 1003 F *supra.*

[e] *Cf. Quaest. Romanae* 288 D, *De Iside* 374 A, *Fabius Maximus* iv, 7 (176 D), and *Quaest. Conviv.* 738 F and 744 B for the different senses in which three and six is each the " first perfect number " ; *cf.* also Anatolius, p. 31, 7-9 (Heiberg)=Iamblichus, *Theolog. Arith.*, p. 17, 4-5 (De Falco) and for six see note c on 1018 c *supra.*

[f] *Cf.* Nicomachus, *Arithmetica Introductio* i, xix, 2-3 (p. 49, 10-19 [Hoche]) ; Theon Smyrnaeus, p. 81, 1-2 (Hiller) ; Macrobius, *In Somnium Scipionis* i, vi, 43 ("primus hemiolius tria . . .").

[g] See 1021 F *infra.*

[h] This is not the same as the definition given in 1026 A *supra* (page 253, note a) and is not the " Pythagorean " definition but is that of Aristoxenus (*Elementa Harmonica* i, 15, 25-32) and his followers, as Porphyry says (*In Ptolemaei Harmonica*, p. 91, 1-3 ; p. 93, 19-28 ; p. 125, 16-24 ; p. 128, 5-6 [Düring]). *Cf.* Cleonides and Gaudentius in *Musici Scriptores Graeci*, p. 179, 11-12 and pp. 329, 23-330, 4 (Jan) ; and Aristides Quintilianus, *De Musica* i, 7 (p. 10, 18-19 [Winnington-Ingram]).

(1020) λούμενος τόνος, ᾧ τὸ διὰ πέντε μεῖζόν ἐστι τοῦ διὰ
τεσσάρων. τοῦτον οἱ μὲν ἁρμονικοὶ δίχα τεμνό-
μενον οἴονται δύο διαστήματα ποιεῖν, ὧν ἑκάτερον
ἡμιτόνιον καλοῦσιν· οἱ δὲ Πυθαγορικοὶ τὴν μὲν εἰς
ἴσα τομὴν ἀπέγνωσαν αὐτοῦ τῶν δὲ τμημάτων ἀν-
F ίσων ὄντων λεῖμμα τὸ ἔλαττον ὀνομάζουσιν, ὅτι τοῦ
ἡμίσεος¹ ἀπολείπει. διὸ καὶ τῶν συμφωνιῶν τὴν
διὰ τεσσάρων οἱ μὲν δυεῖν τόνων καὶ ἡμιτονίου
ποιοῦσιν οἱ δὲ δυεῖν καὶ λείμματος. μαρτυρεῖν δὲ
δοκεῖ τοῖς μὲν ἁρμονικοῖς ἡ αἴσθησις τοῖς δὲ μαθηματικοῖς ἡ ἀπόδειξις, ἧς τοιοῦτος ὁ τρόπος ἐστίν·

¹ ἡμίσεως -e, u, m¹ (corrected), Escor. 72¹ (corrected).

ᵃ This definition also is not " Pythagorean " but is that of
Aristoxenus (Elementa Harmonica i, 21, 20-24 and ii, 46, 1-2),
sharply criticized by Ptolemy (Harmonica, pp. 20, 13-21,
20 [Düring] ; cf. Porphyry, In Ptolemaei Harmonica, p. 126,
7-19 [Düring]) ; cf. Bacchius and Gaudentius (Musici
Scriptores Graeci, p. 293, 6-7 and p. 338, 11-12 [Jan]) and
Theon Smyrnaeus, p. 53, 5-8 (Hiller).

ᵇ Aristoxenus, Elementa Harmonica ii, 46, 3 and 57,
11-12 ; cf. Theon Smyrnaeus, p. 53, 8-10 (Hiller) and
Boethius, De Institutione Musica iii, i (p. 268, 21-25 [Fried-
lein]). By οἱ ἁρμονικοί here Plutarch means neither theorists
earlier than Aristoxenus (Elementa Harmonica i, 2, 8-11 and
ii, 40, 25-26) nor " dilettanti " (Maria Timpanaro Cardini,
Pitagorici : Testimonianze e Frammenti, Fasc. ii [Firenze,
1962], p. 213 note) but Aristoxenus and his followers, as is
confirmed by οἱ μὲν δυεῖν τόνων καὶ ἡμιτονίου ποιοῦσιν infra.

ᶜ See 1017 F supra (. . . τὴν εἰς ἴσα τοῦ τόνου διανομὴν
ἀπογιγνώσκοντες) and cf. Porphyry, In Ptolemaei Harmonica,
p. 67, 3-8 (Düring) ; Euclid, Sectio Canonis 16 ; Theon
Smyrnaeus, p. 53, 13-15 (Hiller) ; Boethius, De Institutione
Musica iii, i and xi (pp. 269, 32–270, 1 and pp. 285, 9–286,
4 [Friedlein])=Archytas, frag. A 19 [D.-K.]).

ᵈ See 1018 E supra (page 285, note e).

ᵉ Aristoxenus, Elementa Harmonica i, 24, 9-11 and ii,
46, 2 and 56, 14–58, 5. Cf. Ptolemy, Harmonica, p. 21,
21-22 and Theon Smyrnaeus, p. 67, 10-12 (Hiller).

one is what is called the tone, that by which the fifth
is greater than the fourth.[a] The harmonists think
that this, when divided in two, makes two intervals,
each of which they call a semitone[b] ; but the
Pythagoreans denied that it is divisible into equal
parts[c] and, as the segments are unequal, name the
lesser of them " leimma " because it falls short of the
half.[d] This is also why among the consonances the
fourth is by the former made to consist of two tones
and a semitone[e] and by the latter of two and a
" leimma." [f] Sense-perception seems to testify in
favour of the harmonists but in favour of the mathematicians[g] demonstration,[h] the manner of which is

[f] Cf. Philolaus, frag. B 6 (i, p. 410, 3-8 [D.-K.] with
note e on 1019 A supra) ; Ptolemy, Harmonica, pp. 22,
17-23, 3 (Düring) ; Proclus, In Platonis Timaeum ii, p. 183,
20-21 and 23-25 (Diehl).

[g] i.e. the Pythagoreans just mentioned ; see 1021 D infra
(ὀρθῶς ὑπὸ τῶν μαθηματικῶν λεῖμμα προσηγόρευται) and note d
on 1019 A supra.

[h] Cf. Ptolemy, Harmonica, pp. 21, 25-22, 1 (Düring);
and Theon Smyrnaeus, pp. 69, 17-70, 1 (Hiller), where οἱ
μὴ λόγῳ ἀλλὰ τῇ ἀκοῇ ταῦτα κρίνοντες is the conventional
characterization of the Aristoxenians (cf. Proclus, In Platonis
Timaeum ii, p. 170, 7-10 [Diehl] ; Boethius, De Institutione
Musica ii, xxxi and iii, i=p. 267, 4-5 and p. 268, 21-22
[Friedlein]) in contrast to the Pythagoreans, who made
reason, i.e. mathematical demonstration, the criterion of
musical science (cf. [Plutarch], De Musica, 1144 F ; Aristides
Quintilianus, De Musica iii, 2=p. 97, 3-7 [Winnington-
Ingram] ; Ptolemy, Harmonica, p. 6, 1-13 [Düring] ;
Ptolemais of Cyrene in Porphyry, In Ptolemaei Harmonica,
pp. 25, 9-26, 4 [Düring]). For the attitude of Aristoxenus
himself cf. his Elementa Harmonica ii, 32, 10-33, 2. Theophrastus spoke of τῶν ἁρμονικῶν καὶ αἰσθήσει κρινόντων in contrast to those who made numerical ratio the criterion (Porphyry, In Ptolemaei Harmonica, p. 62, 2-3 [Düring]=Theo-
phrastus, frag. 89, 2 [Wimmer]).

PLUTARCH'S MORALIA

(1020) ἐλήφθη διὰ τῶν ὀργάνων θεωρηθὲν¹ ὅτι τὸ μὲν διὰ
πασῶν τὸν διπλάσιον λόγον ἔχει τὸ δὲ διὰ πέντε τὸν
ἡμιόλιον τὸ δὲ διὰ τεσσάρων τὸν ἐπίτριτον ὁ δὲ
1021 τόνος τὸν ἐπόγδοον. ἔξεστι² δὲ καὶ νῦν βασανίσαι
τἀληθὲς ἢ³ βάρη δυεῖν ἄνισα χορδῶν ἐξαρτήσαντας
ἢ δυεῖν ἰσοκοίλων αὐλῶν τὸν ἕτερον μήκει διπλάσιον τοῦ⁴ ἑτέρου ποιήσαντας· τῶν μὲν γὰρ αὐλῶν ὁ
μείζων βαρύτερον φθέγξεται⁵ ὡς ὑπάτη πρὸς
νήτην,⁶ τῶν δὲ χορδῶν ἡ τῷ διπλασίῳ κατατεινο-
μένη βάρει⁷ τῆς ἑτέρας ὀξύτερον ὡς νήτη πρὸς
ὑπάτην. τοῦτο δ᾽ ἐστὶ διὰ πασῶν.⁸ ὁμοίως δὲ
καὶ τρία πρὸς δύο ληφθέντα μήκη καὶ βάρη τὸ διὰ
πέντε ποιήσει καὶ τέσσαρα πρὸς τρία τὸ διὰ τεσσάρων, ὧν τοῦτο μὲν ἐπίτριτον ἔχει λόγον ἐκεῖνο δὲ
ἡμιόλιον. ἐὰν δὲ ὡς ἐννέα πρὸς ὀκτὼ γένηται⁹ τῶν

---

¹ ληφθὲν -r¹ (corrected in margin).
² ἔστι -f, m, Escor. 72 ; ἔσται -r¹ (ι superscript over αι -r²).
³ εἰ -r.   ⁴ τοῦ -omitted by r.
⁵ φθέγγεται -B.   ⁶ νήτην -omitted by r.
⁷ βάρη -e, u, Escor. 72¹ (corrected).
⁸ ἐστὶ ⟨τὸ⟩ διὰ πασῶν -Hubert ; but cf. 1018 ᴅ supra (πρὸς δὲ τὰ ϛ´ διὰ πασῶν ὡς νήτη πρὸς ὑπάτην).
⁹ E, B ; γίνεται -e, u, Escor. 72, Aldine ; γίνηται -f, m, r.

ᵃ The following two experiments are ascribed to " various Pythagoreans " by Porphyry (*In Ptolemaei Harmonica*, pp. 119, 13–120, 7 [Düring]) and to Pythagoras himself by Censorinus (*De Die Natali* x, 8-12=pp. 17, 19–19, 2 [Hultsch]). Introduced by the story of the blacksmith's hammers, they are among those ascribed to Pythagoras by Nicomachus (*Harmonices Man.* 6= *Musici Scriptores Graeci*, pp. 246, 5–248, 26 [Jan]), whose account was copied by Iamblichus (*Vita Pyth.* 115-119). Versions similar to this are given by Gaudentius (*Musici Scriptores Graeci*, pp. 340, 4—341, 25 [Jan]), Macrobius (*In Somnium Scipionis* ɪɪ, i, 9-14), and Boethius (*De Institutione Musica* ɪ, x-xi). The

306

as follows. It has been found by observation with instruments that the octave has the duple ratio and the fifth the sesquialteran and the fourth the sesquitertian and the tone the sesquioctavan. It is possible even now to test the truth of this [a] either by suspending unequal weights from two strings or by making one of two pipes with equal cavities double the length of the other, for of the two pipes the larger will sound lower as hypatê to nêtê and of the strings the one stretched by the double weight will sound higher than the other as nêtê to hypatê. This is an octave.[b] Similarly too, when lengths and weights of three to two are taken, they will produce the fifth and of four to three the fourth, the latter of which has sesquitertian ratio and the former sesquialteran. If the inequality of the weights or the

longest account of such experiments but without the story of the hammers is given—in part from Adrastus—by Theon Smyrnaeus (pp. 57, 1–61, 11 ; pp. 65, 10–66, 11 ; p. 66, 20–23 [Hiller]), whereas of them all Chalcidius (*Platonis Timaeus*, p. 112, 16–19 [Wrobel]=p. 94, 14–16 [Waszink]) mentions—and ascribes to Pythagoras—only that with the suspended weights (*cf.* Aristides Quintilianus, *De Musica* iii, 1=pp. 94, 11–95, 7 [Winnington-Ingram]). The experiments were dismissed as " inexact " by Ptolemy (*Harmonica*, pp. 16, 32–17, 20 [Düring]) but without mention and presumably without knowledge of the physical laws that make their professed results erroneous (*cf.* Burkert, *Weisheit und Wissenschaft*, pp. 354-357).

[b] The double weight would not produce an octave, for the frequency of vibration and hence the pitch varies with the square root of the weight stretching the string. For the opposite effect of increasing the length of the pipe and the weight suspended from the string *cf.* Nicomachus, *Harmonices Man.* 4 (*Musici Scriptores Graeci*, pp. 243, 10–244, 9 [Jan]) and Censorinus, *De Die Natali* x, 12 (pp. 18, 24–19, 2 [Hultsch]).

(1021)

B βαρῶν ἢ τῶν μηκῶν ἡ ἀνισότης, ποιήσει διάστημα
τονιαῖον οὐ σύμφωνον ἀλλ' ἐμμελές, ὡς εἰπεῖν ἔμ-
βραχυ, τῷ[1] τοὺς φθόγγους, ἂν ἀνὰ μέρος κρου-
σθῶσι, παρέχειν ἡδὺ φωνοῦντας καὶ προσηνές, ἂν
δὲ ὁμοῦ, τραχὺ[2] καὶ λυπηρόν· ἐν δὲ ταῖς συμφω-
νίαις, κἂν ὁμοῦ κρούωνται κἂν ἐναλλάξ, ἡδέως προσ-
ίεται τὴν συνήχησιν[3] ἡ αἴσθησις. οὐ μὴν ἀλλὰ
καὶ[4] διὰ λόγου τοῦτο δεικνύουσιν. ἐν μὲν γὰρ ἁρμονίᾳ τὸ διὰ πασῶν ἔκ τε τοῦ διὰ πέντε σύγκειται
καὶ τοῦ διὰ τεσσάρων, ἐν δ' ἀριθμοῖς τὸ διπλάσιον
ἔκ τε τοῦ ἡμιολίου καὶ τοῦ ἐπιτρίτου· τὰ γὰρ ιβ'
τῶν μὲν θ' ἐστὶν ἐπίτριτα τῶν δ' η' ἡμιόλια τῶν
C δὲ ϛ' διπλάσια. σύνθετος οὖν ὁ τοῦ διπλασίου[5]
λόγος ἐστὶν ἐκ τοῦ ἡμιολίου καὶ τοῦ ἐπιτρίτου
καθάπερ ὁ τοῦ διὰ πασῶν ἐκ[6] τοῦ διὰ πέντε καὶ
τοῦ διὰ τεσσάρων, ἀλλὰ κἀκεῖ τὸ διὰ πέντε τοῦ
διὰ τεσσάρων τόνῳ κἀνταῦθα τὸ ἡμιόλιον τοῦ ἐπιτρίτου τῷ ἐπογδόῳ μεῖζόν ἐστι. φαίνεται τοίνυν
ὅτι τὸ διὰ πασῶν τὸν διπλάσιον λόγον ἔχει καὶ τὸ
διὰ πέντε τὸν ἡμιόλιον καὶ τὸ διὰ τεσσάρων τὸν
ἐπίτριτον καὶ ὁ τόνος τὸν ἐπόγδοον.

18. Ἀποδεδειγμένου δὲ τούτου, σκοπῶμεν εἰ
δίχα τέμνεσθαι πέφυκε τὸ ἐπόγδοον[7]· εἰ γὰρ μὴ

---

[1] τὸ -e, u, r, Escor. 72, Aldine.

[2] παχὺ -f, m, r, Aldine.

[3] συνήθειαν -B ; σύγχυσιν -r.

[4] καὶ -omitted by u.

[5] διπλάσιον -u.

[6] εἰς -e, u, Escor. 72[1] (corrected in margin).

[7] ἀποδεδειγμένου . . . τὸ ἐπόγδοον -omitted by f.

---

[a] Cf. Nicomachus, Harmonices Man. 6 (Musici Scriptores
Graeci, p. 246, 11-14 [Jan]) ; Ptolemy, Harmonica, p. 15, 10-
17 and p. 16, 14-16 and 25-28 (Düring) ; Theon Smyrnaeus,
p. 49, 4-5 and p. 75, 15-17 (Hiller).

lengths be made as nine to eight, however, it will
produce an interval, that of the tone, not concordant
but tuneful [a] because, to put it briefly, the notes it
gives, if they are struck successively, sound sweet and
agreeable but, if struck together, harsh and painful,
whereas in the case of consonances, whether they be
struck together or alternately, the sense accepts with
pleasure the combination of sound.[b] What is more,
they give a rational demonstration of this too.[c] The
reason is that in a musical scale the octave is composed of the fifth and the fourth and arithmetically
the duple is composed of the sesquialter and the
sesquiterce, for twelve is four thirds of nine and half
again as much as eight and twice as much as six.
Therefore the ratio of the duple is composite of the
sesquialter and the sesquiterce just as that of the
octave is of the fifth and the fourth, but in that case
the fifth is greater than the fourth by a tone and in
this the sesquialter greater than the sesquiterce by a
sesquioctave.[d] It is apparent, then, that the octave
has the duple ratio and the fifth the sesquialteran and
the fourth the sesquitertian and the tone the sesquioctavan.

18. Now that this has been demonstrated, let us
see whether the sesquioctave is susceptible of being

[b] Cf. Adrastus in Theon Smyrnaeus, pp. 50, 22–51, 4
(Hiller) and Porphyry, *In Ptolemaei Harmonica*, p. 96, 1-6
(Düring); Nicomachus, *Harmonices Man.* 12 (*Musici Scriptores Graeci*, p. 262, 1-5 [Jan]).
[c] Cf. Adrastus in Theon Smyrnaeus, p. 61, 20-23 and
with the following demonstration Theon Smyrnaeus, pp. 62,
1–63, 2 (Hiller); Chalcidius, *Platonis Timaeus*, p. 113, 1-20
(Wrobel)=p. 95, 1-15 (Waszink); Ptolemy, *Harmonica*,
pp. 11, 24–12, 1 (Düring).
[d] Cf. Euclid, *Sectio Canonis* 13.

(1021) πέφυκεν, οὐδὲ ὁ τόνος. ἐπειδὴ[1] πρῶτοι[2] τὸν ἐπόγ-
D δοον λόγον ὁ θ' καὶ ὁ η' ποιοῦντες οὐδὲν διάστημα
μέσον ἔχουσι διπλασιασθέντων δ' ἀμφοτέρων ὁ
παρεμπίπτων μεταξὺ δύο ποιεῖ διαστήματα, δῆλον
ὅτι τούτων μὲν ἴσων ὄντων δίχα τέμνεται τὸ ἐπόγδοον. ἀλλὰ μὴν διπλάσια γίγνεται τῶν μὲν θ'
τὰ ιη' τῶν δ' η' τὰ ις', δέχονται δὲ οὗτοι μεταξὺ
τὰ ιζ' καὶ γίγνεται τῶν διαστημάτων τὸ μὲν μεῖζον
τὸ δ' ἔλαττον· ἔστι γὰρ τὸ μὲν πρότερον ἐφεπτα-
καιδέκατον τὸ δὲ δεύτερον ἐφεξκαιδέκατον. εἰς
ἄνισα τοίνυν τέμνεται τὸ ἐπόγδοον· εἰ δὲ τοῦτο, καὶ
ὁ τόνος. οὐδέτερον ἄρα γίγνεται διαιρεθέντος
αὐτοῦ τῶν τμημάτων ἡμιτόνιον, ἀλλ' ὀρθῶς ὑπὸ
E τῶν μαθηματικῶν λεῖμμα[3] προσηγόρευται. καὶ
τοῦτ' ἐστὶν ὅ φησιν ὁ Πλάτων τὰ ἐπίτριτα[4] τοῖς
ἐπογδόοις συμπληροῦντα τὸν θεὸν λείπειν ἑκάστου
μόριον αὐτῶν, οὗ λόγος ἐστὶν ὃν ἔχει τὰ ς' καὶ ν'
καὶ σ' πρὸς τὰ γ' καὶ μ' καὶ σ'. εἰλήφθω γὰρ τὸ
διὰ τεσσάρων ἐν ἀριθμοῖς δυσὶ τὸν ἐπίτριτον λόγον

---

[1] ἐπεὶ δὲ -Stephanus.
[2] πρῶτον -r, Aldine.
[3] λεῖμμα ⟨τὸ ἔλαττον⟩ -Maurommates.
[4] f, m, r ; τὰ τρίτα -E, B, e, u, Escor. 72, Aldine.

---

[a] With the following demonstration cf. Anon. in Platonis
Theaetetum (Pap. Berl. 9782), cols. 34, 47-35, 12 (p. 23
[Diels-Schubart]) ; Aristides Quintilianus, De Musica iii, 1
(pp. 95, 19-96, 4 [Winnington-Ingram]) ; Boethius, De
Institutione Musica iii, i (p. 270, 4-18 [Friedlein]) ; and
Proclus, In Platonis Timaeum ii, p. 179, 18-25 (Diehl).
[b] This is inconsistent with the statement that between
nine and eight there is no interval. The authors cited in the
last preceding note speak of numbers and ratios rather than
intervals, whereas Theon Smyrnaeus (p. 70, 1-3 and 15-16
[Hiller]) asserts that the sesquioctave is indivisible because
the interval of nine to eight, i.e. the unit, is indivisible.

divided in half, for, if it is not, neither is the tone.[a]
Since nine and eight, the first numbers producing the
sesquioctavan ratio, have no intermediate interval
but between them when both are doubled the inter-
vening number produces two intervals,[b] it is clear
that, if these intervals are equal, the sesquioctave is
divided in half. But now twice nine is eighteen and
twice eight sixteen; and between them these
numbers contain seventeen, and one of the intervals
turns out to be larger and the other smaller, for the
former is eighteen seventeenths and the second is
seventeen sixteenths. It is into unequal parts, then,
that the sesquioctave is divided; and, if this is, the
tone is also. Neither of its segments, therefore,
when it is divided, turns out to be a semitone; but
it [c] has rightly been called by the mathematicians
" leimma." [d] This is just what Plato says [e] god in
filling in the sesquiterces with the sesquioctaves
leaves a fraction of each of them, the ratio of which
is 256 to 243. For [f] let the fourth be taken as expressed by two numbers comprising the sesquitertian

----

[c] *i.e.* what is commonly called the semitone, for λέγεται
κοινῶς μὲν ἡμιτόνιον ἰδίως δὲ λεῖμμα (Gaudentius in *Musici
Scriptores Graeci*, p. 342, 7-11 [Jan] ; *cf. ibid.*, p. 344, 5-6
and Theon Smyrnaeus, p. 53, 8-13 [Hiller] with Porphyry,
In Ptolemaei Harmonica, p. 67, 5-8 [Düring]).

[d] See *supra* 1020 E-F and 1019 A, notes *d* and *e*.

[e] This sentence is a paraphrase of *Timaeus* 36 B 1-5,
quoted *supra* 1027 c and 1020 B.

[f] With what follows in the rest of this chapter *cf.* especially
Nicomachus, *Excerpta* 2 (*Musici Scriptores Graeci*, pp. 267,
2-268, 2 [Jan]). *Cf.* also Chalcidius, *Platonis Timaeus*,
pp. 117, 1-11 and 118, 4-16 (Wrobel)=pp. 98, 11-99, 1 and
99, 10-19 (Waszink) ; Boethius, *De Institutione Musica*
iii, ii (pp. 272, 11-273, 14 [Friedlein]) ; and most succinctly
Proclus, *In Platonis Timaeum* ii, p. 177, 8-13 (Diehl).

(1021) περιέχουσι, τοῖς σνϛ' καὶ τοῖς ρϞβ', ὧν ὁ μὲν
ἐλάττων, τὰ ρϞβ', κείσθω κατὰ τὸν βαρύτατον[1]
τοῦ τετραχόρδου φθόγγον[2] ὁ δὲ μείζων, τὰ σνϛ',
κατὰ τὸν ὀξύτατον. ἀποδεικτέον ὅτι, τούτου συμ-
πληρουμένου δυσὶν ἐπογδόοις, λείπεται διάστημα
τηλικοῦτον ἡλίκον ὡς ἐν ἀριθμοῖς τὰ ϛ' καὶ ν' καὶ
σ' πρὸς τὰ γ' καὶ μ' καὶ σ'.[3] τοῦ γὰρ βαρυτέρου
F τόνον[4] ἐπιταθέντος,[5] ὅπερ ἐστὶν ἐπόγδοον, γίγνεται
σιϛ'.[6] τούτου πάλιν τόνον ἄλλον[7] ἐπιταθέντος, γίγνεται σμγ'. ταῦτα μὲν γὰρ ὑπερέχει τῶν σιϛ' τοῖς
κζ' τὰ δὲ σιϛ'[8] τῶν ρϞβ' τοῖς κδ', ὧν τὰ μὲν κζ'
τῶν σιϛ' ὄγδοα[9] ἐστι τὰ δὲ κδ' τῶν ρϞβ'. διὸ
γίγνεται τῶν τριῶν τούτων ἀριθμῶν ὅ τε μέγιστος
ἐπόγδοος τοῦ μέσου καὶ ὁ μέσος τοῦ ἐλαχίστου· τὸ
δ' ἀπὸ τοῦ ἐλαχίστου[10] διάστημα μέχρι τοῦ μεγίστου, τουτέστι τὸ ἀπὸ τῶν ρϞβ' μέχρι τῶν σμγ',[11]
1022 δίτονον[12] ἐκ δυεῖν συμπληρούμενον[13] ἐπογδόων. ἀφαιρουμένου δὲ τούτου, περίεστι τοῦ ὅλου διάστημα λοιπὸν τὸ μεταξὺ τῶν σμγ' καὶ τῶν σνϛ', τὰ
ιγ'· διὸ καὶ λεῖμμα τοῦτον τὸν ἀριθμὸν ὠνόμαζον.

---

[1] τὸν βαρύτατον -f ; τὸ βαρύτατον -m, r ; τὸν βαρύτερον -E,
B, e, u ; τὸν βαρύτονον -Escor. 72, Aldine.

[2] φθόγγου -u.

[3] πρὸς τὰ γ' καὶ μ' καὶ σ' -f, m, r (ἔχει πρὸς . . . σ' -Turne-
bus) ; omitted by E, B, e, u, Escor. 72, Aldine.

[4] τόνον -Benseler (De Hiatu, p. 528) ; τόνῳ -MSS.

[5] ἐπιθέντος -f.

[6] σιϛ' -E, B, e, Escor. 72 ; σιβ' -u ; τὰ σιϛ' -f, m, r.

[7] E, B, e, Escor. 72 ; τόνῳ ἄλλῳ -f, m, r ; τόνον ἄλλως -u,
Aldine.

[8] E, B, f, m, r ; τὰ δὲ ιϛ' -e, Escor. 72, Aldine ; τὰ δὲ ιβ'
-u.

[9] Xylander ; ἐπόγδοα -MSS.

[10] τὸ δὲ ἐλαχίστου τὸ -u.

312

ratio, 256 and 192 ; and of these let the smaller, 192, be placed at the lowest note of the tetrachord and the larger, 256, at the highest.[a] It is to be proved that, when this is filled in with two sesquioctaves, there is left an interval of the size that numerically expressed is 256 to 243. This is so, for, when the lower note has been raised a tone, which is a ses- quioctave, it amounts to 216 ; and, when this has been raised again another tone, it amounts to 243, for the latter exceeds 216 by 27 and 216 exceeds 192 by 24, and of these 27 is an eighth of 216 and 24 an eighth of 192. Consequently, of these three numbers the largest turns out to be sesquioctavan of the intermediate and the intermediate sesquioctavan of the smallest ; and the interval from the smallest to the largest, *i.e.* that from 192 to 243, amounts to an interval of two tones filled in with two sesquioctaves. When this is subtracted, however, there remains of the whole as an interval left over what is between 243 and 256, that is thirteen ; and this is the very reason why they named this number " leimma."[b]

---

[a] For the assignment of the larger numbers to the higher notes see 1018 D *supra* with note *c* there, and especially [Plutarch], *De Musica* 1138 E-F, 1139 c, 1140 A and Nico- machus, *Harmonices Man.* 6 and *Excerpta* 7 (*Musici Scriptores Graeci*, p. 248, 18-23 and p. 279, 12-14 [Jan]). For advocacy of the opposite procedure *cf.* Adrastus in Theon Smyrnaeus, pp. 65, 10-66, 11 (Hiller). On the two procedures *cf.* Burkert, *Weisheit und Wissenschaft*, p. 359, n. 54.

[b] See 1018 E *supra* with notes *d* and *e* there.

---

[11] τουτέστι . . . μέχρι τῶν σμγ' -deleted as a scholium by Papabasileios (*Athena*, x [1898], p. 226).

[12] διάτονον -Γ.

[13] Maurommates ; συμπληροῦμεν -MSS.

(1022) ἐγὼ μὲν οὖν εὐσημότατα δηλοῦσθαι τὴν Πλάτωνος
οἶμαι γνώμην ἐν τούτοις τοῖς ἀριθμοῖς.

19. Ἕτεροι δὲ τοῦ[1] διὰ τεσσάρων ὅρους θέμενοι
τὸν μὲν ὀξὺν ἐν ⟨τοῖς⟩[2] σπη' τὸν δὲ βαρὺν ἐν τοῖς
σις' ἀναλόγως ἤδη[3] τοὺς[4] ἑξῆς περαίνουσιν, πλὴν
ὅτι τὸ λεῖμμα τῶν δυεῖν τόνων[5] μεταξὺ λαμβάνουσι.
τοῦ γὰρ βαρυτέρου τόνον[6] ἐπιταθέντος γίγνεται
σμγ', τοῦ δ' ὀξυτέρου τόνον[7] ἀνεθέντος[8] γίγνεται
σνς'· ἔστι γὰρ ἐπόγδοα τὰ μὲν σμγ' τῶν σις' τὰ δὲ
B σπη' τῶν σνς' ὥστε τονιαῖον εἶναι τῶν διαστημάτων ἑκάτερον λείπεσθαι δὲ τὸ[9] μεταξὺ τῶν
σμγ' καὶ τῶν σνς', ὅπερ οὐκ ἔστιν ἡμιτόνιον ἀλλ'
ἔλαττον· τὰ μὲν γὰρ σπη' τῶν σνς' ὑπερέχει τοῖς
λβ' τὰ δὲ σμγ' τῶν σις' ὑπερέχει[10] τοῖς κζ' τὰ δὲ
σνς' τῶν σμγ' ὑπερέχει τοῖς ιγ'· ταῦτα δ' ἀμφοτέρων[11] τῶν ὑπεροχῶν ἐλάττω[12] ἢ ἡμίσεά ἐστι. διὸ
δυεῖν τόνων καὶ λείμματος, οὐ δυεῖν καὶ ἡμίσεος,
εὕρηται τὸ διὰ τεσσάρων. καὶ ταῦτα μὲν ἔχει τοιαύτην ἀπόδειξιν. ἐκεῖνο δ' οὐ πάνυ χαλεπὸν ἐκ

---

[1] τοῦ -Maurommates (p. 42 in note *ad* p. 29, 20), B. Müller
(1873) : τοὺς -mss.   [2] ⟨τοῖς⟩ -added by Stephanus.

[3] ἤδη -E, B, e, u, Escor. 72 ; τοίνυν -f, m, r, Aldine.

[4] τοὺς -H. C. (*scil.* ὅρους) ; τοῖς -mss. ; τὰ -B. Müller
(1873), *cf.* " reliqua " in the versions of Turnebus and
Xylander.

[5] Maurommates after the version of Xylander ; τὸ
λεῖμμα τῶν δυοῖν τῶν -Stephanus ; τῶν λειμμάτων δυεῖν (or
δυοῖν) τῶν -mss. (with cross in margin -E ; τὸ . . . ? . . . in
margin -e) ; τὸ λεῖμμα δυοῖν τόνοιν -f[1], and m[1] in margin ;
τὸ λεῖμμα δυοῖν -r[1] in margin.

[6] τόνον -Benseler (*De Hiatu*, p. 528) ; τόνῳ -mss.

[7] τόνον -e, u, f, m, Escor. 72, Aldine ; τόνου -r (with
three dots above ου) ; τόνῳ -E, B.

[8] Stephanus ; ἀναταθέντος -E (τος superscript over θεν
erased and replaced by τος on the line), B, u (ἀνα over

314

So I, for my part, think that Plato's intention is most clearly explained by these numbers.[a]

19. As terms of the fourth, however, others [b] put the high note at 288 and the low at 216 and then determine proportionally those that come next, except that they take the " leimma " to be between the two tones. For, when the lower note has been raised a tone, the result is 243 and, when the higher has been lowered a tone, it is 256, for 243 is nine eighths of 216 and 288 nine eighths of 256, so that each of the two intervals is that of a tone and there is left what is between 243 and 256 ; and this is not a semitone but is less, for 288 exceeds 256 by 32 and 243 exceeds 216 by 27 but 256 exceeds 243 by thirteen, which is less than half of both the excesses 32 and 27.[c] Consequently it turns out that the fourth consists of two tones and a " leimma," not of two tones and a half. Such, then, is the demonstration of this point. As to the following point, from what has been said

[a] See 1020 c-d *supra* with note f on page 301.

[b] The alternative procedure described in the following lines is given by Nicomachus, *Excerpta 2 (Musici Scriptores Graeci*, pp. 269, 8–270, 6 [Jan]).

[c] This is not proof that the leimma is less than half of the tone, but the same mistake of substituting for the ratios the differences between their terms is committed by Nicomachus in *Excerpta 2 (Musici Scriptores Graeci*, p. 270, 4-6 and 6-12 [Jan] ; *cf.* also *ibid.*, pp. 267, 15–268, 2).

---

erasure), f, m, Escor. 72 ; ἀναθέντος -e[1] (τα superscript between a and θ -e[2]) ; ἀνατεθέντος -r.

[9] Maurommates ; τὸ -E ; τῶν -B, u ; τὸν -all other mss., Aldine.

[10] τοῖς λβ′ . . . τῶν σις′ ὑπερέχει -omitted by f, m, r.

[11] Turnebus ; ἀμφότερα -e, u, f, m, r, Escor. 72, Aldine ; ἀμφότερα after ὑπεροχῶν -E, B.

[12] ἐλάττων -f, r (with three dots above ω).

315

(1022) τῶν προειρημένων συνιδεῖν,[1] τί δήποτε φήσας ὁ
Πλάτων ἡμιολίους καὶ ἐπιτρίτους καὶ ἐπογδόους
C γίγνεσθαι διαστάσεις ἐν τῷ συμπληροῦσθαι τὰς
ἐπιτρίτους[2] ταῖς ἐπογδόοις οὐκ ἐμνήσθη τῶν ἡμιολίων ἀλλὰ παρέλιπε. τὸ γὰρ ἡμιόλιον τοῦ
ἐπιτρίτου τῷ ἐπογδόῳ ⟨μεῖζόν ἐστι, ὥστε τοῦ
ἐπογδόου⟩[3] τῷ ἐπιτρίτῳ προστιθεμένου[4] συμπληροῦσθαι καὶ τὸ ἡμιόλιον.

20. Ὑποδεδειγμένων δὲ τούτων, τὸ μὲν συμ-
πληροῦν τὰ διαστήματα καὶ παρεντάττειν τὰς
μεσότητας, εἰ καὶ μηδεὶς ἐτύγχανε πεποιηκὼς πρότερον, ὑμῖν[5] ἂν αὐτοῖς ἕνεκα[6] γυμνασίας παρῆκα·
νῦν δὲ πολλοῖς κἀγαθοῖς ἀνδράσιν ἐξειργασμένου
τούτου μάλιστα δὲ Κράντορι καὶ Κλεάρχῳ καὶ
Θεοδώρῳ τοῖς[7] Σολεῦσι, μικρὰ περὶ τῆς τούτων
διαφορᾶς εἰπεῖν οὐκ ἄχρηστόν ἐστιν. ὁ γὰρ Θεό-
D δωρος, οὐχ ὡς ἐκεῖνοι δύο στίχους[8] ποιῶν ἀλλ' ἐπὶ
μιᾶς εὐθείας ἐφεξῆς τούς τε διπλασίους ἐκτάττων
καὶ τοὺς τριπλασίους, πρῶτον μὲν ἰσχυρίζεται τῇ

---

[1] συνειδεῖν -u, f, m[1].
[2] τὰς διαστάσεις -r.
[3] ⟨. . .⟩ -added by Leonicus ; τῷ ἐπογδόῳ τῷ -E, e, u, f,
m, r, Escor. 72 ; τῷ ἐπογδόῳ καὶ τῷ -B.
[4] προστιθεμένῳ -f, m, r.
[5] E, B ; ἡμῖν -all other mss., Aldine.
[6] αὐτοῖς ἕνεκἂν -B.
[7] τοῖς -omitted by f.
[8] στοίχους -f, m, r (cf. 1027 d supra [chap. 29 ad finem] :
ἐν δυσὶ στίχοις).

---

[a] i.e. in Timaeus 36 a 6–b 1 (see 1020 b supra), where in
b 1 Plato says τῷ τοῦ ἐπογδόου διαστήματι τὰ ἐπίτριτα πάντα
συνεπληροῦτο. In paraphrasing this Nicomachus explicitly
included the ἡμιόλια (Harmonices Man. 8= Musici Scriptores
Graeci, p. 250, 10-11 [Jan]), and the filling in of the ἡμιόλια
also was taken for granted by Proclus (In Platonis Timaeum

before it is not very difficult either to see why, after
Plato had said that there came to be intervals of
three to two and of four to three and of nine to eight,
when saying that those of four to three are filled in
with those of nine to eight he did not mention those
of three to two but omitted them.[a] The reason is
that the sesquialter ⟨is greater than⟩ the sesquiterce
by the sesquioctave ⟨so that with the sesquioctave's⟩
addition to the sesquiterce the sesquialter is filled in
as well.[b]

20. After the exposition of these matters the task
of filling in the intervals and inserting the means [c] I
should still have left to you for an exercise to do your-
selves though no one at all had happened to have
done it before ; but now that this has been worked
out by many excellent men and especially by Crantor
and Clearchus and Theodorus, all of Soli,[d] it is not
unprofitable to say a few words about the way in
which they disagree. For Theodorus unlike those
others does not make two rows but sets out the
double and the triple numbers one after another in a
single straight line,[e] relying for this in the first place

ii, p. 170, 25-26 and p. 175, 3-5 with p. 179, 3-6 and p. 185,
5-6 and 13-16 [Diehl]) ; *cf.* B. Kytzler, *Hermes*, lxxxvii
(1959), pp. 401-402.

[b] *Cf.* Chalcidius, *Platonis Timaeus*, p. 115, 11-15 (Wrobel)
=p. 97, 7-10 (Waszink).

[c] See 1020 A *supra* with note *b* there.

[d] Crantor, frag. 6 (Kayser)=frag. 6 (Mullach, *Frag.
Philos. Graec.* iii, pp. 143-145) and Clearchus, frag. 4
(Wehrli) ; see 1027 D *supra* (chap. 29 *sub finem*) with notes
d and *e* there.

[e] So later Severus, Porphyry, and Proclus himself
(Proclus, *In Platonis Timaeum* ii, p. 171, 4-9 ; p. 175, 17-
21 ; and p. 192, 24-27 [Diehl]), who does not mention the
priority of Theodorus of Soli.

317

(1022) λεγομένη κατὰ μῆκος σχίσει¹ τῆς οὐσίας δύο ποι-
ούσῃ² μοίρας ὡς ἐκ μιᾶς, οὐ τέσσαρας ἐκ δυεῖν,
ἔπειτά φησι τὰς τῶν μεσοτήτων παρεντάξεις οὕτω
λαμβάνειν προσήκειν³ χώραν· εἰ δὲ μή, ταραχὴν
καὶ σύγχυσιν ἔσεσθαι καὶ μεταστάσεις εἰς⁴ τὸ πρῶτον εὐθὺς τριπλάσιον ἐκ τοῦ πρώτου διπλασίου τῶν
συμπληροῦν⁵ ἑκάτερον ὀφειλόντων. τοῖς δὲ περὶ
τὸν Κράντορα βοηθοῦσιν αἵ τε θέσεις τῶν ἀριθμῶν,
ἐπιπέδων ἐπιπέδοις καὶ τετραγώνων τετραγώνοις
E καὶ κύβων κύβοις ἀντιθέτως συζυγούντων, τῇ τε
μὴ κατὰ τάξιν αὐτῶν λήψει ἀλλ᾽ ἐναλλὰξ ἀρτίων
1027 F καὶ⁶ (30 b.) περιττῶν⁷ ⟨αὐτὸς ὁ Πλάτων⟩.⁸ τὴν γὰρ

¹ σχίσει -m (ῑ over original έ), Turnebus ; σχέσει -all other
mss., Aldine.

² ποιοῦσι -u ; ποιήσῃ -Aldine.

³ f, m, r ; προσήκει -E, B, e, u, Escor. 72.

⁴ Emperius (*Op. Philol.*, p. 340), *cf.* " traiectiones "
-Xylander ; μεταστὰς εἰς -mss.

⁵ E, B ; συμπληροῦντων -all other mss., Aldine.

⁶ ἀρτίων καὶ π . . . vac. 4-1/2 lines -E ; vac. 2-1/2 lines
-B . . . κατὰ τὰ αὐτὰ (1022 e *supra* [chap. 21 *init.*]) -E, B ;
ἀρτίων καὶ ἐπὶ . . . vac. 14 -f ; vac. 13 -m, r . . . κατὰ τὰ αὐτὰ
-f, m, r ; ἀρτίων καὶ ἐπὶ κατὰ (κατὰ -Escor. 72 ; ἐπϊκατὰ -u)
τὰ αὐτὰ -e, u, Escor. 72 ; see 1022 e *supra* (chap. 21 *init.*),
apparatus criticus, note 2 on page 212.

⁷ See 1017 c *supra* (chap. 30, page 268), *apparatus criticus*,
note 9 : δευτέρα περιττῶν -E, B ; δευτέρα (δευτέρα δὲ -f)
τῶν περιττῶν -f, m, r, Aldine ; δευτεριττῶν -e, u, Escor. 72
(ρατῶνπε -Escor. 72 in margin with three dots after δευτε).

⁸ ⟨αὐτὸς ὁ Πλάτων⟩ -added by Pohlenz ; ⟨Πλάτων⟩ -B.
Müller (*Hermes*, iv [1870], pp. 399-403 and v [1871], p.
154).

ᵃ *Timaeus* 36 b 6-7 (ταύτην οὖν τὴν σύστασιν πᾶσαν διπλῆν
κατὰ μῆκος σχίσας . . .) ; *cf.* Proclus (*In Platonis Timaeum*
ii, p. 237, 15-27 [Diehl] and *In Platonis Rem Publicam* ii,

318

upon what is stated to be the cleavage of the substance lengthwise that makes two parts presumably out of one,[a] not four out of two, and in the second place saying that it is suitable for the insertions of the means to be arranged in this sequence, as otherwise there will be disorder and confusion and transpositions to the very first triple from the first double of the terms that ought to fill in each of the two.[b] Crantor and his followers,[c] however, are supported by the position of the numbers, paired off with plane numbers over against plane and square over against square and cubic over against cubic numbers,[d] and in their being taken not in order but alternately even and (30 b.) odd by ⟨Plato himself⟩.[e] For after

p. 143, 20-21 [Kroll]), who also takes this to show that the numbers were meant to be arranged in a single row.

[b] The harmonic and arithmetical means of the first triple ($\frac{3}{2}$ and 2) are already given by the first double and its means (1, $\frac{4}{3}$, $\frac{3}{2}$, 2) ; cf. the objection to the *lambda* of Adrastus made by Proclus, *In Platonis Timaeum* ii, pp. 187, 28–188, 1 and p. 192, 27-29 (Diehl).

[c] Among them Clearchus, who was mentioned with Crantor just above, and Plutarch himself. The arrangement in the form of a *lambda* is assumed later by Theon Smyrnaeus (pp. 94, 11–96, 5 [Hiller]) and Macrobius (*In Somnium Scipionis* i, vi, 46) ; of those who adopted it earlier Proclus names only Adrastus, who elaborated a triple form of it (Proclus, *In Platonis Timaeum* ii, pp. 170, 26–171, 4 ; p. 187, 17-26 ; and p. 192, 24-26 [Diehl]), which is represented by the three successive diagrams of Chalcidius (*Platonis Timaeus*, pp. 98, 13–118, 3 [Wrobel]=pp. 82, 20–99, 9 [Waszink]).

[d] See 1017 D-E *supra* (chap. 11), pages 271, note d–273, note a.

[e] In *Timaeus* 35 B 4–c 2 the order is 2, 3, 4, 9, 8, 27, *i.e.* alternately even and odd (*cf.* Macrobius, *In Somnium Scipionis* ii, ii, 17), whereas the natural order (. . . 4, 8, 9, 27) would be . . . even, even, odd, odd.

(1027) μονάδα κοινὴν οὖσαν ἀμφοῖν προτάξας λαμβάνει
τὰ η' καὶ ἐφεξῆς τὰ κζ', μονονουχὶ¹ δεικνύων ἡμῖν
1028 ἦν ἑκατέρῳ γένει χώραν ἀποδίδωσι. ταῦτα μὲν
οὖν ἑτέροις προσήκει μᾶλλον ἐξακριβοῦν, τὸ δ'
ἀπολειπόμενον οἰκεῖόν ἐστι τῆς ὑποκειμένης ἡμῖν
πραγματείας.

31. Οὐ γὰρ ἐπίδειξιν ὁ Πλάτων θεωρίας μαθη-
ματικῆς ποιούμενος εἰς φυσικὴν ὑπόθεσιν μὴ δεο-
μένην μεσότητας ἀριθμητικὰς καὶ ἁρμονικὰς παρ-
εισήγαγεν ἀλλὰ ὡς μάλιστα δὴ τῇ συστάσει τῆς
ψυχῆς τοῦ λόγου τούτου² προσήκοντος. καίτοι
τινὲς μὲν ἐν τοῖς τάχεσι τῶν πλανωμένων σφαιρῶν τινὲς δὲ μᾶλλον ἐν τοῖς ἀποστήμασιν ἔνιοι δ' ἐν
τοῖς μεγέθεσι τῶν ἀστέρων οἱ δ' ἄγαν ἀκριβοῦν δο-
B κοῦντες ἐν ταῖς τῶν ἐπικύκλων διαμέτροις ζητοῦσι
τὰς εἰρημένας ἀναλογίας, ὡς τὴν ψυχὴν ἕνεκα τούτων τοῦ δημιουργοῦ τοῖς οὐρανίοις ἐναρμόσαντος³

¹ Ε, Β : μονονουχὶ οὖν -all other mss., Aldine.
² τοῦ λόγου τοῦ -u.   ³ οὐρανοῖς ἐναρμώσαντες -u.

ᵃ See 1027 ε *supra* with note a on page 269.
ᵇ Plutarch may have in mind here not only the order ·
9, 8, 27 to which he has just referred but also the omission
of 16, the next power of two between 8 and 27 (*cf.* B. Kytzler,
Hermes, lxxxvii [1959], pp. 404-405).
ᶜ See 1017 ε *supra* (chap. 11) with note f on page 271.
ᵈ With all that follows in this sentence *cf.* Proclus, *In
Platonis Timaeum* ii, pp. 212, 12–213, 7 (Diehl).
ᵉ Plato in *Timaeus* 36 ᴅ 5-7 says that of the seven circles
three move τάχει . . . ὁμοίως and four ἀλλήλοις καὶ τοῖς τρισὶν
ἀνομοίως ἐν λόγῳ δέ and in *Timaeus* 39 ᴅ 4-5 speaks of
ἁπασῶν τῶν ὀκτὼ περιόδων τὰ πρὸς ἄλληλα . . . τάχη (*cf. Republic* 617 ᴀ 7–ʙ 3). For the introduction of " spheres "
into the astronomy of the *Timaeus* see *supra* Plat. *Quaest.*
1007 ᴀ with note d there.
ᶠ Cf. Chalcidius, *Platonis Timaeus*, p. 167, 8-17 (Wrobel)
320

putting at the head the unit, which is common to both,[a] he takes eight and next thereafter twenty-seven,[b] all but showing us[c] the position that he assigns to each of the two kinds. Now, to treat this with greater precision is a task that belongs to others ; but what remains is a proper part of our present disquisition.

31. It is so because Plato did not as a display of mathematical learning drag arithmetical and harmonic means into a discourse on natural philosophy where they are not wanted but introduced them on the assumption that this calculation is especially appropriate to the composition of the soul. Yet certain people [d] look for the prescribed proportions in the velocities of the planetary spheres,[e] certain others rather in their distances,[f] some in the magnitudes of the stars,[g] and those with a reputation for exceedingly exact investigation in the diameters of the epicycles,[h] assuming these to be the ends for which the artificer fitted to the heavenly bodies the

=p. 148, 12-19 (Waszink) ; Macrobius, *In Somnium Scipionis* ii, iii, 14-15 (=*Porphyrii in Platonis Timaeum . . . Fragmenta*, p. 63, 5-21 [Sodano]) ; Hippolytus, *Refutatio* iv, 10, 1-11, 5 (pp. 42, 17-44, 22 [Wendland]). These are all attempts to interpret *Timaeus* 36 D 2-4, for which *cf.* Proclus, *In Platonis Timaeum* ii, p. 265, 8-29 (Diehl).

[g] Perhaps by interpretation of *Republic* 616 E 3-8 : *cf.* Proclus, *In Platonis Rem Publicam* ii, p. 218, 2-28 ; p. 219, 23-29 ; and pp. 221, 28-222, 2 (Kroll) with Theon Smyrnaeus, p. 143, 14-18 (Hiller) and Taylor, *Commentary on Plato's Timaeus*, p. 161, n. 2.

[h] Against the attempt to introduce epicycles into Plato's astronomy (*e.g.* Theon Smyrnaeus, pp. 188, 25-189, 6 [Hiller] ; Chalcidius, *Platonis Timaeus*, p. 176, 6-13 [Wrobel] =p. 156, 19-24 [Waszink]) *cf.* Proclus, *In Platonis Timaeum* ii, p. 264, 19-25 and iii, p. 96, 13-32 and p. 146, 14-28 (Diehl).

(1028) εἰς ἑπτὰ μοίρας νενεμημένην. πολλοὶ δὲ καὶ τὰ
Πυθαγορικὰ δεῦρο μεταφέρουσιν, ἀπὸ τοῦ μέσου
τὰς τῶν σωμάτων ἀποστάσεις¹ τριπλασιάζοντες.
γίγνεται δὲ τοῦτο κατὰ μὲν τὸ πῦρ μονάδος τιθεμένης κατὰ δ' ἀντίχθονα τριῶν κατὰ δὲ γῆν ἐννέα
καὶ κατὰ σελήνην εἰκοσιεπτὰ καὶ κατὰ τὸν Ἑρμοῦ²
μιᾶς καὶ ὀγδοήκοντα κατὰ δὲ Φωσφόρον τριῶν καὶ
μ' καὶ σ' κατ' αὐτὸν δὲ τὸν ἥλιον θ' καὶ κ' καὶ ψ',
ὅς γε³ ἅμα τετράγωνός τε καὶ κύβος ἐστί· διὸ καὶ
τὸν ἥλιον ἔστιν ὅτε τετράγωνον καὶ κύβον προσ-
C αγορεύουσιν. οὕτως δὲ καὶ τοὺς ἄλλους ἐπανάγουσι

¹ ἀποστάσει -B.
² ἑρμῆν -m, r, Escor. 72ᶜᵒʳʳ· (ἦν superscript over οῦ),
Aldine.
³ ὅς γ' -Hubert ; ὅτι -E, B, e, u, Aldine ; ὅτε -f, m, r,
Escor. 72 ; ὅστις -Stephanus (" qui numerus " -Turnebus).

ᵃ Cf. Plutarch, Numa xi, 1-2 (67 ᴅ) : . . . τοῦ σύμπαντος
κόσμου, οὗ μέσον οἱ Πυθαγορικοὶ τὸ πῦρ ἱδρῦσθαι νομίζουσι καὶ
τοῦθ' Ἑστίαν καλοῦσι καὶ μονάδα. . . .
ᵇ Central fire and counter-earth identify this as the
Pythagorean system referred to by Aristotle (De Caelo 293
a 20-27 and Metaphysics 986 a 10-13) and elsewhere ascribed
to Philolaus (frags. A 16 and 17 [D.-K.]) ; but in that
system the orbit of the sun was located immediately above
that of the moon (Philolaus, frag. A 16 [D.-K.] ; Alexander,
Metaph., pp. 38, 20-39, 3 and p. 40, 3-6) as it was by Plato
and Aristotle too (cf. Proclus, In Platonis Timaeum iii,
pp. 60, 31-61, 2 and p. 62, 3-6 [Diehl] and In Platonis Rem
Publicam ii, p. 220, 1-21 [Kroll]). The Pythagoreanizing
interpretation of the Timaeus reported by Plutarch in the
present passage is a contamination of the Philolaic system
and the planetary order widely though not universally
adopted later (cf. Heath, Aristarchus of Samos, pp. 106-107 ;
Burkert, Weisheit und Wissenschaft, pp. 297-299, especially

soul that had been distributed into seven parts. Many carry over into this context Pythagorean notions too, multiplying by three the distances of the bodies from the middle. This is brought about by placing the unit at the central fire,[a] three at the counter-earth, nine at the earth and 27 at the moon and 81 at Mercury, 243 at Venus and at the sun itself 729,[b] which is at the same time a square and a cubic number [c] ; and this is the reason why they sometimes call the sun too a square and a cube.[d] In this way these people increase the other numbers

notes 121, 122, and 129, to which add Plutarch, *De Facie* 925 A), an order which, if the purpose of it was to make the sun midmost of the planets (*cf.* Theon Smyrnaeus, p. 138, 16-18 [Hiller] ; Chalcidius, *Platonis Timaeus*, p. 140, 8-9 [Wrobel]=p. 119, 16-18 [Waszink] ; Philo Jud., *Quis Rerum Div. Heres* 222-224=iii, p. 50, 9-19 [Wendland] ; Proclus, *In Platonis Timaeum* iii, p. 62, 7-9 and 18-22 [Diehl]), is incompatible with a system in which the earth and the counter-earth are planets.

[c] $729 = 27^2 = 9^3$. See the next note *infra*.

[d] Not the Pythagoreans to whom the original Philolaic system is ascribed (see the note next but one *supra*). They are said to have assigned the number seven to the sun as being the seventh of the moving bodies counted inwards from the fixed stars (Alexander, *Metaph.*, pp. 38, 20-39, 3 ; Asclepius, *Metaph.*, p. 36, 5-11 ; A. Delatte, *Études sur la littérature pythagoricienne*, p. 169 [*Anecdota Arith.* A 1, lines 20-22]) ; and, had they applied the triplication from the central fire as the unit that Plutarch here reports, they would have had to associate the number 81 with the sun. The later order with Mercury and Venus located between the moon and the sun, however, makes the sun seventh from the central fire ; and in such triplication or multiplication by any given ratio the seventh number is always both a square and a cube (Philo Jud., *De Opificio Mundi* 92-94=i, pp. 31, 22-32, 12 [Cohn] ; Anatolius, p. 35, 14-21 [Heiberg] and partially in Iamblichus, *Theolog. Arith.*, pp. 54, 13-55, 1 [De Falco] ; *cf.* Theon Smyrnaeus, pp. 34, 16-35, 17 [Hiller]).

(1028) τοῖς τριπλασιασμοῖς,[1] πολὺ τοῦ κατὰ λόγον οὗτοί
γε παραπαίοντες, εἴ τι[2] τῶν γεωμετρικῶν ὄφελός
ἐστιν ἀποδείξεων, καὶ μακρῷ πιθανωτέρους παραβαλεῖν[3] αὑτοῖς ἀποδεικνύοντες τοὺς ὁρμωμένους
ἐκεῖθεν, οὐδ᾽ αὐτοὺς παντάπασιν ἐξακριβοῦντας[4]
ἀλλὰ ὡς ἔγγιστα λέγοντας[5] ὅτι τῆς μὲν ἡλίου διαμέτρου πρὸς τὴν διάμετρον τῆς γῆς λόγος ἐστὶ
δωδεκαπλάσιος τῆς δὲ γῆς αὖ[6] πάλιν διαμέτρου
πρὸς τὴν σελήνης διάμετρον τριπλάσιος ὁ δὲ φαι-
νόμενος ἐλάχιστος τῶν ἀπλανῶν ἀστέρων οὐκ ἐλάτ-
τονα τῆς διαμέτρου τῆς γῆς ἢ τριτημόριον ἔχει
D τὴν διάμετρον τῇ δὲ ὅλῃ σφαίρᾳ τῆς γῆς πρὸς τὴν
ὅλην σφαῖραν τῆς σελήνης ὡς ἑπτὰ καὶ εἴκοσι πρὸς
⟨ἕν⟩ ἐστι,[7] Φωσφόρου δὲ καὶ γῆς αἱ μὲν διάμετροι
τὸν διπλάσιον αἱ δὲ σφαῖραι τὸν ὀκταπλάσιον[8]

[1] τριπλασμοῖς -e, u, Escor. 72, Aldine.
[2] εἴ τε -e, u, f, m, r, Escor. 72, Aldine.
[3] E, B, e, u² (παραβάλλειν -u¹), m, Escor. 72 ; παραλαβεῖν
-f, r ; παραλαβεῖν αὐτοὶ -Wyttenbach ; ⟨ὡς⟩ παραβαλεῖν
-B. Müller (1873) ; but cf. Lucian, Demosthenis Encomium
32 (iii, p. 376, 23-24 [Jacobitz]) : . . . παιδιὰ παραβάλλειν τῷ
τούτου κρότῳ. . . .
[4] f, m, r ; ἐξακριβοῦντες -E, B, e, u, Escor. 72, Aldine.
[5] ε superscript over α -E¹ ; λέγοντας -all other mss.
[6] E, B ; τῆς γῆς δ᾽ αὖ -all other mss., Aldine.
[7] ⟨ἕν⟩ -added by Wyttenbach ; πρόσεστι -mss. ; πρὸς ⟨ἕν
λόγος⟩ ἐστί -B. Müller (1873).
[8] αἱ δὲ σφαῖραι τὸν ὀκταπλάσιον -omitted by r.

---

[a] They would be Mars : 2187, Jupiter : 6561, Saturn :
19,683, fixed stars : 59,049.
[b] These are approximately the figures of Hipparchus (the
diameters of earth, moon, and sun are as $1 : \frac{1}{3} : 12\frac{1}{3}$) ; cf.
Heath, Aristarchus of Samos, pp. 342 and 350.
[c] That is to say not less than the diameter assigned to the
moon by Hipparchus (cf. Boll, R.-E. vi [1909], col. 2411,
6-11). Contrary to the contention that all the fixed stars are

also by triplications,[a] going far astray of what is
reasonable, if there is any use in geometrical demonstrations, and proving that in comparison with themselves those who proceed from such demonstrations
are far more credible, though these are themselves
speaking not with absolute precision either but in
close approximations when they say that the ratio of
the sun's diameter to the diameter of the earth is
twelve to one and of the earth's diameter on the
other hand to the moon's diameter is three to one [b]
and that what appears to be the smallest of the
fixed stars has a diameter not less than a third part
of the diameter of the earth [c] and that for the whole
sphere of the earth to the whole sphere of the moon
the ratio is as twenty-seven to ⟨one⟩ [d] and that the
diameters of Venus and of the earth have the ratio
of two to one [e] and their spheres the ratio of eight to

larger than the earth (*e.g.* Cleomedes, *De Motu Circulari* I,
xi, 58 and II, iii, 97 = pp. 106, 2-8 and 176, 11-24 [Ziegler] ;
Proclus, *In Platonis Rem Publicam* ii, p. 218, 5-13 [Kroll])
Philoponus (*Meteor.*, p. 15, 18-23) in support of Aristotle
(*Meteorology* 339 b 7-9 ; *cf.* Areius Didymus, *Epitomes
Frag. Phys.* 8 [*Dox. Graeci*, p. 450, 10-11]) cites unnamed
astronomers (possibly from Arrian, *cf. ibid.*, p. 15, 13) to
the effect that the earth is not smaller than all the fixed stars.

   [d] *i.e.* 3^3 : 1^3 (*cf.* Euclid, *Elements* xii, Prop. 18). So
Hipparchus as reported by Theon Smyrnaeus, p. 197, 9-12
(Hiller) and Chalcidius, *Platonis Timaeus*, p. 161, 18-22
(Wrobel) = p. 143, 5-8 (Waszink).

   [e] According to Cleomedes, *De Motu Circulari* II, iii, 96
(p. 174, 25-27 [Ziegler]) the diameter of Venus is one-sixth
that of the sun ; it would then be to the earth's diameter as
two to one if, as Plutarch has just said (1028 c *supra*), the
sun's diameter is to the earth's as twelve to one. According
to Ptolemy Hipparchus said that the apparent diameter of
Venus is about a tenth that of the sun (B. R. Goldstein, " The
Arabic Version of Ptolemy's *Planetary Hypotheses*," *Trans-*

(1028) ἔχουσι λόγον, τὸ δὲ διάστημα τῆς ἐκλειπτικῆς
σκιᾶς τῆς[1] διαμέτρου τῆς σελήνης τριπλάσιον, ὃ δ᾽
ἐκτρέπεται πλάτος ἡ σελήνη τοῦ διὰ μέσου[2] τῶν
ζῳδίων[3] ἐφ᾽ ἑκάτερα δωδεκάμοιρον.[4] αἱ δὲ πρὸς
ἥλιον[5] σχέσεις αὐτῆς ἐν τριγώνοις καὶ τετραγώνοις
ἀποστήμασι διχοτόμους καὶ ἀμφικύρτους σχημα-
τισμοὺς λαμβάνουσιν· ἐξ δὲ ζῴδια διελθοῦσα τὴν[6]
πανσέληνον ὥσπερ τινὰ συμφωνίαν ἐν ἑξατόνῳ[7]
E διὰ πασῶν ἀποδίδωσι. τοῦ δὲ ἡλίου περὶ τὰς
τροπὰς ἐλάχιστα καὶ μέγιστα περὶ τὴν ἰσημερίαν[8]
ἔχοντος κινήματα, δι᾽ ὧν ἀφαιρεῖ τῆς ἡμέρας καὶ

---

[1] τοῦ -f.

[2] τοῦ διὰ μέσου (or διὰ μέσων) -Turnebus ; τῆς διαμέτρου
-E, B ; τοῦ διαμέτρου -all other mss., Aldine.

[3] ζῳδίων -E, B, e, u ; ζῴων -f, m, r, Escor. 72, Aldine.

[4] E, B ; δωδεκατημόριον -all other mss., Aldine.

[5] ἥλιον -B ; ἡλίου (with ον superscript over ου and acute
accent superscript over ἡ) -E ; ἡλίου -all other mss., Aldine.

[6] τὸν -u.

[7] E, m, r ; ἑξατόνῳ -B, f ; ἀξατόνῳ -e, u, Escor. 72 (with
ἐ superscript over ἀ).

[8] E, B ; περὶ τῆς ἰσημερίας -all other mss., Aldine.

---

actions of the American Philos. Soc., N.S. lvii, 4 [1967],
p. 8, col. 1 sub finem).

[a] i.e. $2^3 : 1^3$.

[b] Cf. Plutarch, De Facie 923 b and my note ad loc.
(L.C.L. xii, p. 57, note d).

[c] Cf. Theon Smyrnaeus, p. 194, 8-13 and p. 135, 14-15
(Hiller) with Chalcidius, Platonis Timaeus, p. 137, 14-15
(Wrobel)=p. 117, 8-9 (Waszink) ; Geminus, Elementa
Astronomiae xii, 21 with v, 53 (pp. 142, 25–144, 1 and p. 62,
8-9 [Manitius]) ; Martianus Capella, viii, 867. The deviation to either side of the ecliptic is given as five degrees by
Ptolemy, Syntaxis v, 12 (i, p. 407, 10-15 [Heiberg]) and as
five and a half degrees by Proclus, Hypotyposis iv, 2 (pp. 86,
24–88, 1 [Manitius]). For ὁ διὰ μέσου (instead of the more

GENERATION OF THE SOUL, 1028

one *a* and that the extent of the shadow eclipsing the
moon is triple her diameter *b* but that the breadth of
the moon's deviation to one side or the other of the
circle through the middle of the zodiacal signs is
twelve degrees of latitude.*c* Her positions relative
to the sun in trine and quartile aspects assume the
configurations of half and gibbous *d* ; and, when she
has traversed six signs of the zodiac,*e* she exhibits the
plenilune as it were a consonance consisting of the
six tones of an octave.*f* As the sun has his minimal
movement at the solstices and his maximal movement at the equinox,*g* of these movements by which

common ὁ διὰ μέσων) τῶν ζῳδίων *cf.* Theon Smyrnaeus, p.
133, 21 and p. 135, 18 (Hiller) and Simplicius, *De Caelo*,
p. 494, 27-28.

d Cf. Pliny, *N.H.* ii, 80 (" itaque in quadrato solis dividua
est, in triquetro seminani ambitur orbe, inpletur autem in
adverso . . .") and Proclus, *In Platonis Rem Publicam* ii,
p. 44, 18-22 (Kroll). For the terminology *cf.* Geminus,
Elementa Astronomiae ii, 1-19 (pp. 18, 16–26, 2 [Manitius]) ;
Ptolemy, *Tetrabiblos* I, xiv, 1 (pp. 35, 20–36, 4 [Boll-Boer]) ;
and A. Bouché-Leclercq, *L'astrologie grecque* (Paris, 1899),
pp. 165-172.

e i.e. when she is in opposition, ὅταν κατὰ διάμετρον γένηται
τῷ ἡλίῳ . . . (Geminus, *op. cit.*, ix, 9 = p. 126, 24-26 [Mani-
tius]).

f Cf. Censorinus, *De Die Natali* xiii, 5 (p. 24, 2-4
[Hultsch]) : ". . . tonos esse sex, in quibus sit dia pason
symphonia," where the six tones are not as here, however,
the six signs of the zodiac through which the moon passes
from conjunction to opposition. For this correlation of the
plenilune with the octave *cf.* rather Ptolemy, *Harmonica*,
p. 108, 13-18 and p. 109, 4-6 (Düring) and A. Boeckh,
Gesammelte Kleine Schriften iii (Leipzig, 1866), p. 173, n. 3.

g Cf. Cleomedes, *De Motu Circulari* I, vi, 28 and 31-32
(p. 52, 13-20 ; pp. 56, 27–58, 1 ; and p. 58, 13-15 [Ziegler]).
On this and the other errors in this sentence of Plutarch's
cf. O. Neugebauer, *A.J.P.*, lxiii (1942), pp. 458-459.

PLUTARCH'S MORALIA

(1028) τῇ νυκτὶ προστίθησιν ἢ τοὐναντίον, οὗτος ὁ λόγος
ἐστίν· ἐν ταῖς[1] πρώταις ἡμέραις λ' μετὰ τὰς[2] χει-
μερινὰς τροπὰς τῇ ἡμέρᾳ προστίθησι τὸ ἕκτον τῆς
ὑπεροχῆς ἣν ἡ μεγίστη νὺξ πρὸς τὴν βραχυτάτην
ἡμέραν[3] ἐποίει[4] ταῖς[5] δ' ἐφεξῆς λ' τὸ τρίτον τὸ δὲ
ἥμισυ ταῖς λοιπαῖς ἄχρι τῆς ἰσημερίας, ἐν ἑξαπλα-
σίοις καὶ τριπλασίοις διαστήμασι τοῦ χρόνου τὴν
ἀνωμαλίαν ἐπανισῶν.[6] Χαλδαῖοι δὲ λέγουσι τὸ ἔαρ
F ἐν τῷ διὰ τεσσάρων γίγνεσθαι πρὸς τὸ μετόπωρον
ἐν δὲ τῷ διὰ πέντε πρὸς τὸν χειμῶνα πρὸς δὲ τὸ
θέρος ἐν τῷ διὰ πασῶν. εἰ δ' ὀρθῶς ὁ Εὐριπίδης
διορίζεται θέρους τέσσαρας μῆνας καὶ χειμῶνος
ἴσους

> φίλης τ' ὀπώρας διπτύχους ἦρός τ' ἴσους

[1] ἐν ⟨γὰρ⟩ ταῖς -Wyttenbach.
[2] τὰς -Stephanus ; γὰρ -mss.   [3] ἡμέραν -omitted by B.
[4] ἐμποιεῖ -B.   [5] ταῖς -f, m, r ; τὰς -all other mss., Aldine.
[6] B. Müller (1873) ; ἐπανισοῦντος -mss.

---

[a] A sixth, a third, and a half of the excess of the longest
night over the shortest day if added to the shortest day =
the longest day, *i.e.* the day at the summer solstice and not
that at the equinox. Plutarch's fractions should have been
a twelfth, a sixth, and a fourth as in Cleomedes, *De Motu
Circulari* i, vi, 27-28 (pp. 50, 15-52, 2 [Ziegler]) and
Martianus Capella, viii, 878.
[b] *i.e.* the total increment of the second thirty days ($\frac{1}{6} + \frac{1}{3}$)
is threefold and the total increment of the third ($\frac{1}{6} + \frac{1}{3} + \frac{1}{2}$) is
sixfold the first ($\frac{1}{6}$). For the expression compare τὴν τῆς
τύχης ἀνωμαλίαν ἐπανισοῦν (*De Fraterno Amore* 484 D).
[c] So also Aristides Quintilianus, *De Musica* iii, 19, who
says (p. 119, 15-18 [Winnington-Ingram]), however, that
these ratios of the seasons were ascribed to Pythagoras and
that (*ibid.*, p. 119, 10-15) they follow from assignment of
the numbers eight (that of air) to spring, four (that of fire) to
summer, six (that of earth) to autumn, and twelve (that of
water) to winter. The correlation of these numbers with the

he subtracts from the day and adds to the night or contrariwise this is the ratio : in the first thirty days after the winter solstice he adds to the day a sixth of the difference by which the longest night exceeded the shortest day and in the next thirty a third and in the rest until the equinox a half,[a] thus equalizing the disparity of the time in sixfold and threefold intervals.[b] The Chaldaeans assert that spring turns out to be related to autumn in the ratio of the fourth and to winter in that of the fifth and to summer in that of the octave.[c] If Euripides is right, however, in distinguishing four months of summer and an equal number of winter

> And of dear autumn twain and twain of spring,[d]

seasons, however, depends upon the correlation in the *Timaeus* of the four regular solids with air, fire, earth, and water (*ibid.*, pp. 118, 29–119, 9) ; and it results, moreover, in making three to two, the fifth, the ratio of winter to spring rather than that of spring to winter as professed and required. According to O. Neugebauer (*A.J.P.*, lxiii [1942], pp. 455-458) the ratios were derived from twelve, nine, eight, and six, taken to be the number of days by which spring, summer, winter, and autumn respectively exceed a common measure (really eleven, nine, seven, and six respectively according to Callippus in the *Eudoxi Ars Astronomica*, col. xxiii=p. 25 [Blass]), so that originally the ratios of these increments or deviations were : spring to autumn (not to summer) as twelve to six (the octave), to summer as twelve to nine (the fourth), and to winter as twelve to eight (the fifth). This is rejected by Burkert (*Weisheit und Wissenschaft*, p. 333, n. 110), who seems to think that the parallel passage in Aristides Quintilianus makes it wrong to seek the origin of the ratios in any astronomical calculations and that the speculation was obviously meant to show in the numbers the opposition of summer and winter, though in fact neither the ratios nor the numbers in Aristides Quintilianus do this.

[d] Euripides, frag. 990 (Nauck, *Trag. Graec. Frag.²*, p. 679).

(1028) ἐν τῷ διὰ πασῶν αἱ ὧραι μεταβάλλουσιν. ἔνιοι δὲ γῇ μὲν τὴν¹ τοῦ προσλαμβανομένου² χώραν ἀποδιδόντες σελήνῃ³ δὲ τὴν ὑπάτην Στίλβωνα δὲ καὶ
1029 Φωσφόρον ἐν διατόνοις⁴ ⟨παρυπάταις⟩⁵ καὶ λιχανοῖς κινοῦντες αὐτὸν τὸν ἥλιον ὡς μέσην συνέχειν τὸ διὰ πασῶν ἀξιοῦσιν ἀπέχοντα τῆς μὲν γῆς τὸ διὰ πέντε τῆς δὲ τῶν ἀπλανῶν τὸ διὰ τεσσάρων.

32. Ἀλλ᾽ οὔτε τούτων τὸ κομψὸν ἅπτεταί τινος ἀληθείας οὔτ᾽ ἐκεῖνοι παντάπασι τοῦ ἀκριβοῦς

¹ γῇ μὲν ἐν τῇ -E (three dots superscript over ἐν and 'ν superscript over τῇ -E¹), e, u, f, m, r, Escor. 72 ; γῆν μὲν τὴν -B.
² From λαμβανομένου (f. 226 recto) to the end of the essay a new hand in e.
³ σελήνην -r.
⁴ ἐν τοῖς διατόνοις (διαγόνοις -r) -f, m, r.
⁵ ⟨παρυπάταις⟩ -B. Müller (1873) after Maurommates, who wished to substitute it either for λιχανοῖς or for διατόνοις.

---

[a] With what follows cf. especially Excerpta Neapolitana 24 (Musici Scriptores Graeci, pp. 418, 14–419, 7 [Jan])= Inscriptio Canobi (Ptolemaei Opera ii, p. 154, 1-10 [Heiberg]) but with the better alignment of Halma, Hypothèses et Époques des Planètes de C. Ptolémée . . . (Paris, 1820), pp. 61-62 ; also Alexander of Ephesus in Theon Smyrnaeus, pp. 140, 5–141, 4 (Hiller) and Censorinus, De Die Natali xiii, 3-5 (pp. 23, 12–24, 6 [Hultsch]) with W. Burkert, Philologus, cv (1961), pp. 32-43 and B. L. van der Waerden, R.-E. Supplement x (1965), cols. 857, 65–859, 35.
[b] The note added to the scale below the hypatê (the topmost string that gives the lowest tone : see supra note e on Plat. Quaest. 1007 E), as Plutarch himself says in 1029 B infra (see page 335, note b).
[c] For the variation in the oblique cases of Στίλβων as of Φαίνων (1029 B infra) see De Facie 925 A and 941 C with my note ad loc. (L.C.L. xii, p. 184, note a).
[d] Cf. [Plutarch], De Musica 1134 F (. . . τὴν διάτονον παρυπάτην . . . τὴν διάτονον λιχανόν) and the note of Einarson and De Lacy ad loc. (L.C.L. xiv, p. 375, n. d). W. Burkert

it is in the ratio of an octave that the seasons change. Some people,[a] moreover, assigning to earth the position of the proslambanomenos [b] and to the moon the hypatê and having Mercury [c] and Venus move in the positions of the diatonic ⟨parhypatê⟩ and lichanos [d] maintain that the sun himself as mesê holds the octave together,[e] being at the remove of a fifth from the earth and of a fourth from the sphere of the fixed stars.[f]

32. But the cleverness of these people is not concerned with any truth, and those others do not aim at accuracy at all.[g] To those, however, who think

(*Philologus*, cv [1961], p. 33, n. 2) thinks that the illogical ἐν διατόνοις καὶ λιχανοῖς was in Plutarch's source. The expression used for Mercury and Venus may be a reference to the fact that the parhypatê and the lichanos are " movable " notes : contrast τοὺς ἑστῶτας (1029 B *infra*) and *cf.* Cleonides, *Introductio* 6 and Gaudentius, *Harmonica Introductio* 17 (*Musici Scriptores Graeci*, pp. 189, 20–190, 5 and p. 345, 4-12 [Jan]) ; Aristides Quintilianus, *De Musica* i, 6 (p. 9, 25-26 [Winnington-Ingram]).

[e] For the sun as midmost of the seven planets—and so the paradigm of the musical mesê (Nicomachus, *Harmonices Man.* 3= *Musici Scriptores Graeci*, p. 242, 2-7 [Jan])—συνάγοντα καὶ συνδέοντα τὰς ἐφ' ἑκάτερα αὐτοῦ τριάδας *cf.* Proclus, *In Platonis Timaeum* iii, p. 62, 7-9 (Diehl) ; and for the mesê itself as σύνδεσμος *cf.* [Aristotle], *Problemata* 919 a 25-26.

[f] *Cf.* Censorinus, *De Die Natali* xiii, 4-5 (p. 23, 18-20 and pp. 23, 27–24, 2 [Hultsch]) and Alexander of Ephesus in Theon Smyrnaeus, p. 140, 8 and 15 with Theon's criticism *ibid.*, p. 141, 16-19 (Hiller).

[g] *Cf.* οὐδ' αὐτοὺς παντάπασιν ἐξακριβοῦντας (1028 c *supra*), which applies *a fortiori* to the preceding πολλοί who " carry over into this context Pythagorean notions . . . going far astray of what is reasonable . . ." (1028 B–c). It is to these that the ἐκεῖνοι here refers and not, as Hubert supposes, to the " Chaldaeans " of 1028 E-F *supra*.

PLUTARCH'S MORALIA

(1029) ἔχονται. οἷς δ' οὖν οὐ δοκεῖ ταῦτα τῆς τοῦ Πλάτωνος ἀπηρτῆσθαι διανοίας ἐκεῖνα κομιδῇ φανεῖται
τῶν μουσικῶν λόγων ἔχεσθαι, τὸ πέντε τετραχόρ-
δων¹ ὄντων² τῶν ὑπάτων³ καὶ μέσων καὶ συνημ-
μένων καὶ διεζευγμένων⁴ καὶ ὑπερβολαίων ἐν πέντε
διαστήμασι τετάχθαι τοὺς πλάνητας, ὧν τὸ μέν
B ἐστι τὸ ἀπὸ σελήνης ἐφ' ἥλιον καὶ τοὺς ὁμοδρόμους
ἡλίῳ, Στίλβωνα καὶ Φωσφόρον, ἕτερον τὸ ἀπὸ τούτων ἐπὶ τὸν Ἄρεος⁵ Πυρόεντα, τρίτον δὲ τὸ μεταξὺ
τούτου⁶ καὶ Φαέθοντος, εἶθ' ἑξῆς τὸ ἐπὶ Φαίνωνα,
καὶ πέμπτον ἤδη τὸ ἀπὸ τούτου πρὸς τὴν ἀπλανῆ
σφαῖραν· ὥστε τοὺς ὁρίζοντας φθόγγους τὰ τετρά-
χορδα τὸν τῶν πλανωμένων λόγον ἔχειν ἀστέρων.

¹ E, B, f, m, r. Escor. 72 (three dots over χο), Aldine ;
τετραθ . . . vac. 1 . . . ρχ (θ and χ erased) -e ; τετρα . . . vac. 2
. . . ρ . . . vac. 2 . . . -u.
² ὄντας -B.
³ τῶν ὑπάτων -Basil. ; τοῦ ὑπατῶν -E (ὑπάτων -E¹), B ;
τοῦ ὑπόστων -e, Escor. 72 (with ὧν superscript over οὖ) ;
τοῦ ὑπόστον -u ; τῶν ὑπόστων -f, m, r, Aldine.
⁴ διαζευγμένων -r ; διεξαγμένων -e, u.
⁵ B, f, m, r ; ἀέρος -E, e, u, Escor. 72, Aldine.
⁶ τούτων -r.

ᵃ Cf. De Defectu Orac. 430 A ; Nicomachus, Harmonices
Man. 11, 5-6 and Cleonides, Introductio 10 (Musici Scriptores Graeci, pp. 259, 13–260, 4 and p. 201, 8-13 [Jan]).
ᵇ In De Defectu Orac. 430 A it is not the intervals of the
planets that are said to be five but their " periods " (cf.
[Plutarch], De Placitis 892 B= Dox. Graeci, p. 363 A 9-15).
ᶜ So in De Defectu Orac. 430 A (. . . Ἡλίου καὶ Φωσφόρου
καὶ Στίλβωνος ὁμοδρομούντων). In [Plato], Epinomis 987 B 4-5
Mercury is said to be ὁμόδρομος with the sun and Venus ;
and " Timaeus Locrus " uses διὰ τὸ ὁμοδρομῆν ἁλίῳ of Venus
(97 A) just after (96 E) having called Mercury and Venus
ἰσόδρομοι ἀελίῳ (cf. [Plutarch], De Placitis 889 c and 892 B=
Dox. Graeci, p. 346 A 4-6 and p. 363 A 11-13 ; [Aristotle],

these notions not remote from Plato's meaning the following will appear to be closely connected with the musical ratios, that, there being five tetrachords —those of the lowest and middle and conjunct and disjunct and highest—,[a] the planets have been arranged in five intervals,[b] of which one is that from moon to sun and those that keep pace with the sun, Mercury and Venus,[c] second that from these to the fiery planet of Mars,[d] and third that between this and Jupiter, and then next that extending to Saturn,[e] and finally fifth that from this to the sphere of fixed stars,[f] so that the sounds bounding the tetrachords correspond to the planets.[g] Further-

---

De Mundo 399 a 8-9 ; Theon Smyrnaeus, p. 136, 20-21 [Hiller]). Plato himself, however, in *Timaeus* 38 D 2-3 says that the revolution of Venus and of Mercury is τάχει ἰσόδρομον ἡλίῳ (*cf.* 36 D 5 : τάχει τρεῖς μὲν ὁμοίως) ; *cf.* ἰσοταχεῖς in Philo Jud., *De Cherubim* 22 (i, p. 175, 11-13 [Cohn]) and Philoponus, *De Aeternitate Mundi* vi, 24 (p. 199, 10-15 [Rabe]). For the form Στίλβωνα page 330, note *c supra*.

[d] *Cf.* Plutarch, frag. ix, 5 (p. 46, 3 [Bernardakis])=frag. 157, 80 (Sandbach) ; [Plutarch], *De Placitis*, 889 B=*Dox. Graeci*, pp. 344 A 20-345 A 1 ; Theon Smyrnaeus, p. 130, 24 (Hiller).

[e] For the form Φαίνωνα see page 330, note *c supra*.

[f] This reduction of the planetary intervals to five involves not only the mistake of making the orbits of the sun, Mercury, and Venus one and the same but also the inconsistency of counting the interval from Saturn to the fixed stars while at the same time omitting the interval from earth to moon (*cf.* Helmer, *De An. Proc.*, p. 59).

[g] The five tetrachords, not being all consecutive, are bounded by seven different notes (*cf.* Boethius, *De Institutione Musica* iv, xii=pp. 334, 23-335, 6 [Friedlein]) ; but in the preceding scheme the five consecutive intervals must be bounded by six terms, one of which, since three of the seven planets constitute a single boundary, cannot be a planet and is in fact the sphere of the fixed stars.

333

(1029) ἔτι τοίνυν τοὺς παλαιοὺς ἴσμεν ὑπάτας[1] μὲν δύο
τρεῖς δὲ νήτας μίαν[2] δὲ μέσην καὶ μίαν παραμέσην
τιθεμένους, ὥστε[3] τοῖς πλάνησιν ἰσαρίθμους εἶναι
τοὺς ἑστῶτας. οἱ δὲ νεώτεροι τὸν προσλαμβανό-
μενον, τόνῳ διαφέροντα[4] τῆς ὑπάτης,[5] ἐπὶ τὸ βαρὺ
C τάξαντες τὸ μὲν ὅλον σύστημα δὶς διὰ πασῶν ἐ-
ποίησαν τῶν δὲ συμφωνιῶν τὴν κατὰ φύσιν οὐκ
ἐτήρησαν τάξιν· τὸ γὰρ διὰ πέντε πρότερον γίγνεται τοῦ διὰ τεσσάρων, ἐπὶ τὸ βαρὺ τῇ ὑπάτῃ[6]
τόνου[7] προσληφθέντος. ὁ δὲ Πλάτων δῆλός ἐστιν
ἐπὶ τὸ ὀξὺ προσλαμβάνων· λέγει γὰρ ἐν τῇ Πολιτείᾳ τῶν ὀκτὼ σφαιρῶν ἑκάστην περιφέρειν [εἶτ’][8]
ἐπ’ αὐτῇ Σειρῆνα[9] βεβηκυῖαν, ᾄδειν δὲ πάσας ἕνα

---

[1] ὑπάτους -r.
[2] νήτεις καὶ μίαν -r.
[3] ἐν δὲ -u.
[4] διαφέροντος -u.
[5] τῆς ⟨ὑπάτων⟩ ὑπάτης -H. Weil et Th. Reinach, *Plu-tarque : De la musique* (Paris, 1900), p. lxix, n. 4.
[6] E, B, f, m, r ; ἀπάτη -e, u, Escor. 72, Aldine.
[7] E (τόνω -E¹ with ω remade to ου), B, e, u, Escor. 72 ; τοῦ τόνου -f, m, r, Aldine.
[8] Deleted by Hubert ; τὴν -Stephanus.
[9] E, B ; σειρῆναι -e, u, Escor. 72, Aldine ; σειρῆναν -f, m ; σειρῆνας -r.

---

[a] *i.e.*, apart from the proslambanomenos, the seven fixed notes that bound the five tetrachords : *cf.* Boethius, *De Institutione Musica* iv, xiii (pp. 335, 8–337, 18 [Friedlein]) ; Cleonides, *Introductio* 4 and Gaudentius, *Harmonica Intro-*

GENERATION OF THE SOUL, 1029

more, we know that the ancients reckon two notes called hypatê and three nêtê but one mesê and one paramesê, so that the stable notes [a] are equal in number with the planets. The moderns, however, by placing an additional note, the proslambanomenos, lower in the scale than the hypatê,[b] from which it differs by a tone, made the whole scale a double octave [c] but did not preserve the natural order of the consonances, for the fifth turns out to be prior to the fourth when to the hypatê a tone has been added lower in the scale.[d] It is obvious, however, that Plato makes the addition to the higher end of the scale, for in the *Republic* he says [e] that each of the eight spheres [f] carries around in its revolution a Siren standing on it and they all sing emitting a single

ductio 17 (*Musici Scriptores Graeci*, p. 185, 16-25 and p. 345, 1-4 [Jan]).

[b] That is the hypatê of the lowest tetrachord, as would be made explicit by the supplement of Weil-Reinach, τῆς ⟨ὑπάτων⟩ ὑπάτης ; but τῇ ὑπάτῃ τόνου προσληφθέντος at the end of the sentence shows that Plutarch wrote simply τῆς ὑπάτης here just as Nicomachus wrote τὴν ὑπάτην for τὴν ὑπάτων ὑπάτην (cf. *Musici Scriptores Graeci*, p. 258, 2-3 [Jan]).

[c] Cf. Nicomachus, *Harmonices Man.* 11, 4 (*Musici Scriptores Graeci*, p. 258, 2-11 [Jan]) and Boethius, *De Institutione Musica* i, xx (pp. 211, 21–212, 7 [Friedlein]).

[d] *i.e.*, the scale ought to begin with a tetrachord not increased to a fifth by the tone of the proslambanomenos, for the fourth is " naturally prior " to the fifth : cf. Nicomachus, *Harmonices Man.* 7, 9, and 12 (*Musici Scriptores Graeci*, p. 249, 2-19 ; p. 252, 4-15 ; and p. 262, 7-11 [Jan]) and *Arithmetica Introductio* ii, xxvi, 1 (p. 134, 5-15 [Hoche]) ; Theon Smyrnaeus, p. 66, 12-14 (Hiller).

[e] *Republic* 617 B 4-7.

[f] Plato said not " spheres " but ἐπὶ δὲ τῶν κύκλων . . . ἐφ' ἑκάστου. See *supra* 1028 A with note e and *Plat. Quaest.* 1007 A with note d there.

335

(1029) τόνον[1] ἱείσας[2] ἐκ δὲ πασῶν κεράννυσθαι μίαν ἁρμονίαν. αὗται δ᾽ ἀνιέμεναι τὰ θεῖα εἴρουσι καὶ
καταδοῦσι[3] τῆς ἱερᾶς περιόδου[4] καὶ χορείας[5] ὀκτάχορδον[6] ἐμμέλειαν· ὀκτὼ γὰρ ἦσαν καὶ οἱ πρῶτοι
D τῶν διπλασίων καὶ τριπλασίων ὅροι λόγων, ἑκατέρᾳ προσαριθμουμένης μερίδι τῆς μονάδος. οἱ δὲ
πρεσβύτεροι Μούσας παρέδωκαν καὶ ἡμῖν[7] ἐννέα,

[1] ἕνα ⟨ἑκάστην⟩ τόνον -Hubert.
[2] Ε; ἴσας -Β; ἱείσας -all other mss., Aldine.
[3] Stephanus; εἴρουσαι καὶ καταδοῦσαι -mss.
[4] Ε, Β; προόδου -all other mss., Aldine.
[5] Ε, Β; χωρίας -e, u, Escor. 72, Aldine; χορίαις -f, m, r.
[6] τὴν ὀκτάχορδον -f, m, r.
[7] mss. (μούσαν -u); καὶ Μούσας παρέδωκαν ἡμῖν -Pohlenz.

---

[a] Each emits one tone (*Republic* 617 B 6); but even
Proclus, who elsewhere states this clearly (*In Platonis Rem
Publicam* ii, pp. 236, 29–237, 1 and p. 238, 15 [Kroll]), says
κινεῖ δὲ τὰς Σειρῆνας ᾄδειν μίαν φωνὴν ἱείσας ἕνα τόνον . . .
(*ibid.*, i, p. 69, 10-12 [Kroll]). Hubert's supplement, therefore, would be a case of improving rather than restoring
what Plutarch wrote.

[b] Plutarch must assume that the Siren of the moon emits
hypatê of the lowest tetrachord and that of Saturn nêtê of
the highest so that the additional eighth, that of the fixed
stars, would be a tone higher in pitch than the latter. Plato
does not say, however, what tone is emitted by which Siren
and nothing that he does say would prevent the eighth tone
from being understood as an addition to the lower end of the
scale, whether the tone highest in pitch or lowest is associated with the moon, for which two opposed theories *cf.*
Nicomachus, *Harmonices Man.* 3 and *Excerpta* 3 (*Musici
Scriptores Graeci*, pp. 241, 18–242, 11 and pp. 271, 18–273,
24 [Jan]).

[c] *i.e.* " relaxed " in the musical sense, referring to the
gentle sound of the harmony (*cf. De Genio Socratis* 590 c-d :
. . . τὴν πραότητα τῆς φωνῆς ἐκείνης ἐκ πασῶν συνηρμοσμένης)
and so differentiating the tones of these Sirens from the shrill
song, λιγυρὴ ἀοιδή of Homer's (*Odyssey* xii, 44 and 183 ; *cf.*

336

tone *a* and all are blended into a single concord.*b*
These Sirens free from strain *c* entwining things
divine *d* chant a harmony of eight notes over the
sacred circuit of the dance,*e* for eight was also the
number of the primary terms of the double and
triple ratios, the unit being counted along with each
of the two classes.*f* And we too have got from our
elders the tradition that there are nine Muses,*g*

Apollonius Rhodius, iv, 892-893 and 914), λιγυρή being
ὀξεῖα and σύντονος, the opposite of ἀνιεμένη (cf. [Aristotle],
De Audibilibus 804 a 21-29). Proclus is at pains to distinguish
these two groups of Sirens and in fact maintains that according to Plato there are three different kinds (In Platonis
Rem Publicam ii, pp. 238, 21-239, 8 [Kroll] and In Platonis
Cratylum, p. 88, 14-26 [Pasquali]).

d Etymologizing Σειρήν, as is shown by Quaest. Conviv.
745 F (. . . Σειρῆνας ὀνομάζειν, εἰρούσας τὰ θεῖα καὶ λεγούσας ἐν
῞Αιδου . . .), apparently as if from σεῖα (Laconian for θεῖα)
εἴρειν. Etym. Magnum 710, 19-20 (Gaisford) has παρὰ τὸ
εἴρω, τὸ λέγω, εἰρήν· καὶ πλεονασμῷ τοῦ σ, σειρήν. ἢ παρὰ τὸ
εἴρω τὸ συμπλέκω, the latter from Herodian Technicus, Reli-
quiae ii, 1, p. 579, 13-14 (Lenz).

e Cf. Philo Jud., De Mutatione Nominum 72 (iii, p. 169,
27-28 [Wendland]) and De Specialibus Legibus ii, 151 (v,
p. 122, 13-15 [Cohn]); [Plato], Epinomis 982 E 4-6 from
Plato, Timaeus 40 c 3-4.

f For the unit as common to both even numbers and odd
being counted twice and so giving eight terms (1, 2, 4, 8
and 1, 3, 9, 27) see supra 1018 F—1019 A with note *b* there,
but for the same reason being taken only once and so giving
seven terms (1, 2, 4, 8, 3, 9, 27) see 1027 E supra. With
οἱ πρῶτοι τῶν . . . ὅροι λόγων here cf. τῶν ὑποκειμένων ἀριθμῶν
. . . ἐδέησε μείζονας ὅρους λαβεῖν ἐν τοῖς αὐτοῖς λόγοις (1019 B
supra with note *d* there).

g " We too . . .," for this was not the universal belief:
cf. Quaest. Conviv. 744 c—745 B (where at the end Plutarch
identifies the three Fates of Republic 617 c with the three
Delphian Muses) and 746 E; M. Mayer, R.-E. xvi/1 (1933),
cols. 687, 50-691, 66.

(1029) τὰς μὲν ὀκτὼ καθάπερ ὁ Πλάτων περὶ τὰ οὐράνια
τὴν δ' ἐνάτην τὰ περίγεια κηλεῖν¹ ἀνακαλουμένην
καὶ καθιστᾶσαν ἐκ πλάνης καὶ διαφορᾶς ἀνωμαλίαν
καὶ ταραχὴν ἐχούσας.²

33. Σκοπεῖτε³ δὲ μὴ τὸν μὲν οὐρανὸν ἄγει καὶ
τὰ οὐράνια ταῖς περὶ αὐτὴν⁴ ἐμμελείαις καὶ κινήσεσιν ἡ ψυχὴ φρονιμωτάτη καὶ δικαιοτάτη γεγο-
νυῖα, γέγονε δὲ τοιαύτη τοῖς καθ' ἁρμονίαν λόγοις,
ὧν εἰκόνες μὲν ὑπάρχουσιν εἰς τὰ σώματα⁵ ἐν τοῖς
E ὁρατοῖς καὶ ὁρωμένοις μέρεσι τοῦ κόσμου καὶ σώ-
μασιν ἡ δὲ πρώτη καὶ κυριωτάτη δύναμις ἀοράτως⁶
ἐγκέκραται τῇ ψυχῇ καὶ παρέχει σύμφωνον αὐτὴν⁷

¹ καλεῖν -r.
² e, u, f, m, r, Escor. 72, Aldine ; ἐχούσης -E, B.
³ E, B, r ; σκοπεῖται -e, u, f, m, Escor. 72.
⁴ Bernardakis ; αὐτὴν -mss.   ⁵ mss. ; ἀσώματα -Stephanus.
⁶ ἀοράτως -r, f (in margin), m (in margin) ; ὁρατοὺς -u¹
(ου remade to ω) ; ὁρατῶς -all other mss.
⁷ Stephanus ; ἑαυτὴν -mss. ; ἑαυτῇ -Hubert ; ⟨αὐτῇ⟩
αὐτὴν -A. E. Taylor (Commentary on Plato's Timaeus,
p. 157, n. 1).

ᵃ This tacit identification of the Sirens of Republic 617
B 4-7 with the Muses Ammonius in Quaest. Conviv. 745 F
is made to assert explicitly after Plutarch in his own person
had denied it (ibid. 745 c). It is later denied by Proclus too
(In Platonis Rem Publicam ii, p. 237, 16-25 with ii, p. 68,
5-16 [Kroll]), who ascribes it to οἱ παλαιοί (In Platonis
Timaeum ii, p. 208, 9-14 and p. 210, 25-28 [Diehl]). It is
explicit in Macrobius, In Somnium Scipionis ii, iii, 1-2
(=Porphyrii in Platonis Timaeum . . . Fragmenta, pp. 59,
11-60, 10 [Sodano]) and implicit in Porphyry, Περὶ ἀγαλμάτων, frag. 8 (J. Bidez, Vie de Porphyre, p. 12*, 14-15)
=Eusebius, Praep. Evang. iii, 11, 24 (i, p. 139, 19-20
[Mras]) and Vita Pythagorae 31 (pp. 33, 19-34, 2 [Nauck])
and in the citation of Amelius by Joannes Lydus, De
Mensibus iv, 85 (p. 135, 3-7 [Wünsch]). The Muses are
not mentioned in the two interpretations of the Sirens given

eight of them, just as Plato says, being occupied with
things celestial*a* and the ninth with those about the
earth *b* to cast a spell upon them recalling them from
vagrancy and discord and settling their capriciousness and confusion.

33. Consider, however, whether the heavens and
the heavenly bodies are not guided by the soul with
her own harmonious motions *c* when she has become
most provident and most just and whether she has
not become such by reason of the concordant ratios,*d*
semblances of which are incorporated in the parts of
the universe that are visible and seen, that is in
bodies, but the primary and fundamental property of
which has been invisibly blended in the soul *e* and

by Theon Smyrnaeus, pp. 146, 9–147, 6 (Hiller) or in that
given by Chalcidius, *Platonis Timaeus*, p. 167, 1-7 (Wrobel)
=p. 148, 6-11 (Waszink).

b So Ammonius in *Quaest. Conviv.* 746 A (μία δὲ τὸν μεταξὺ
γῆς καὶ σελήνης τόπον ἐπισκοποῦσα καὶ περιπολοῦσα . . .) ; *cf.*
ἥ τε ὑποσελήνιος σφαῖρα in Porphyry, Περὶ ἀγαλμάτων, frag. 8
(cited in the last note *supra*). Others resolved the difficulty
of identifying the nine Muses with Plato's eight Sirens by
making the ninth the concord produced by the other eight
(Macrobius, *In Somnium Scipionis* II, iii, 1-2).

c *Cf.* Porphyry in Proclus, *In Platonis Timaeum* ii, p. 214,
11 (= *Porphyrii in Platonis Timaeum . . . Fragmenta*, p. 60,
18-19 [Sodano]) and Proclus himself, *ibid.* ii, p. 268, 7-8 and
p. 279, 10-12 (Diehl) ; and Simplicius, *De Anima*, p. 40,
37-38. With the reasons given by Plutarch here for rejecting
the astronomical interpretations considered in chaps. 31-32
supra cf. especially Proclus, *ibid.* ii, p. 212, 28-31 (Diehl).

d See *Plat. Quaest.* 1003 A : ἐπεὶ δὲ ἡ ψυχὴ νοῦ μετέλαβε καὶ
ἁρμονίας καὶ γενομένη διὰ συμφωνίας ἔμφρων. . . .

e See 1024 c *supra* (διαδιδοῦσαν ἐνταῦθα τὰς ἐκεῖθεν εἰκόνας);
cf. Porphyry in Proclus, *In Platonis Timaeum* ii, p. 214, 15-16
and pp. 214, 31–215, 3 (= *Porphyrii in Platonis Timaeum
. . . Fragmenta*, p. 60, 22-23 and p. 61, 13-15 [Sodano])
and Proclus himself, *ibid.*, p. 295, 2-9 (Diehl).

(1029) καὶ πειθήνιον, ἀεὶ τῷ κρατίστῳ καὶ θειοτάτῳ
μέρει τῶν ἄλλων ἁπάντων ὁμονοούντων. παραλαβὼν γὰρ ὁ δημιουργὸς ἀταξίαν¹ καὶ πλημμέλειαν
ἐν ταῖς κινήσεσι τῆς ἀναρμόστου καὶ ἀνοήτου ψυχῆς διαφερομένης πρὸς ἑαυτὴν τὰ μὲν διώρισε καὶ
διέστησε τὰ δὲ συνήγαγε πρὸς ἄλληλα καὶ συνέταξεν ἁρμονίαις καὶ ἀριθμοῖς χρησάμενος, οἷς καὶ
τὰ κωφότατα² σώματα, λίθοι καὶ ξύλα καὶ φλοιοὶ³
φυτῶν καὶ θηρίων ὀστᾶ⁴ καὶ πιτύαι,⁵ συγκεραν-
F νύμενα καὶ συναρμοττόμενα θαυμαστὰς μὲν ἀγαλμάτων ὄψεις θαυμαστὰς δὲ παρέχει φαρμάκων καὶ
ὀργάνων δυνάμεις. ᾗ καὶ Ζήνων ὁ Κιτιεὺς ἐπὶ
θέαν αὐλητῶν παρεκάλει τὰ μειράκια καταμανθάνειν οἷαν⁶ κέρατα καὶ ξύλα καὶ κάλαμοι καὶ ὀστᾶ,⁷
λόγου μετέχοντα καὶ συμφωνίας, φωνὴν ἀφίησι.
τὸ⁸ μὲν γὰρ ἀριθμῷ πάντα ἐπεοικέναι⁹ κατὰ τὴν
Πυθαγορικὴν ἀπόφανσιν¹⁰ λόγου δεῖται· τὸ δὲ πᾶσιν,
1030 οἷς¹¹ ἐκ διαφορᾶς καὶ ἀνομοιότητος ἐγγέγονε κοινωνία τις πρὸς ἄλληλα καὶ συμφωνία, ταύτης
αἰτίαν εἶναι μετριότητα καὶ τάξιν, ἀριθμοῦ καὶ

---

¹ Xylander ; κατ' ἀταξίαν -E, B, e, u ; κατ' ἀξίαν (ἀξίαν
corrected to ἀταξίαν in margin -f¹, m¹) -f, m, r, Escor. 72,
Aldine.
² Wyttenbach ; κουφότατα -MSS.
³ φοιοὶ -f, m, r.
⁴ Emperius (Op. Philol., p. 340) ; εἰσὶ (εἰσὶν -e, u) -MSS.
⁵ πιτύαι -E, B, u¹.
⁶ οἷα -B.
⁷ ὀσὰ (?) -e ; ὅσα -u, Aldine.
⁸ τὸ -E, B ; τῷ -all other MSS., Aldine.
⁹ ἐπιοικέναι -e, u², Escor. 72.
¹⁰ E, B, f, m ; ἀπόφασιν -e, u, r, Escor. 72, Aldine.
¹¹ Xylander ; πᾶσι θεοῖς -MSS.

ᵃ Cf. De Genio Socratis 592 B-C.

renders her concordant and docile,[a] all her other
parts always agreeing with the part that is best and
most divine.[b] For the artificer, having taken over [c]
a jangling disorder in the motions of the discordant
and stupid soul which was at odds with herself,[d]
distinguished and separated some parts and brought
others together with one another and organized
them, using concords and numbers [e] by which when
blended and fitted together even the most senseless
bodies, stones and logs and the bark of plants and
bones and beestings of animals, provide statuary of
wonderful appearance and medicines and instruments of wonderful potency. Wherefore it was that
Zeno of Citium [f] summoned the lads to a performance
of pipers to observe what a sound is produced by bits
of horn and wood and reed and bone when they partake of ratio and consonance. For, while it requires
reasoned argument to maintain with the Pythagorean
assertion that all things are like unto number,[g] the
fact that for all things in which out of difference and
dissimilitude there has come to be some union and
consonance with one another the cause is regularity
and order consequent upon their participation in

[b] Cf. Plato, Republic 442 c 10–D 1 and 432 A 6-9.

[c] See note f on 1014 c supra.

[d] See supra 1014 B (page 183, note c) and 1016 c with note f
and the references there.

[e] See supra page 175 note c and 1015 E with note i.

[f] Cf. De Virtute Morali 443 A = S.V.F. i, frag. 299.

[g] Cf. Sextus, Adv. Math. iv, 2 and vii, 94 and 109 ;
Theon Smyrnaeus, p. 99, 16 (Hiller) ; Themistius, De Anima, p. 11, 27 (Xenocrates, frag. 39 [Heinze]); A. Nauck,
Iamblichi De Vita Pythagorica Liber, pp. 234-235, to
which add Anatolius in [Hero Alexandrinus], Def. 138, 9
(iv, p. 166, 16-18 [Heiberg]) ; Burkert, Weisheit und Wissenschaft, pp. 64-65.

(1030) ἁρμονίας μετασχοῦσιν, οὐδὲ τοὺς ποιητὰς λέληθεν
ἄρθμια μὲν τὰ φίλα καὶ προσηνῆ καλοῦντας ἀναρ-
σίους¹ δὲ τοὺς ἐχθροὺς καὶ τοὺς πολεμίους,² ὡς
ἀναρμοστίαν τὴν διαφορὰν οὖσαν. ὁ δὲ τῷ Πιν-
δάρῳ ποιήσας τὸ ἐπικήδειον

ἄρμενος ἦν ξείνοισιν ἀνὴρ ὅδε καὶ φίλος ἀστοῖς
εὐαρμοστίαν δῆλός ἐστι τὴν ἀρετὴν³ ἡγούμενος, ὥς
που καὶ αὐτὸς ὁ Πίνδαρος τοῦ θεοῦ φησιν ἐπα-
κοῦσαι⁴ μουσικὰν ὀρθὰν⁵ ἐπιδεικνυμένου⁶ τὸν Κάδ-
μον. οἵ τε πάλαι θεολόγοι, πρεσβύτατοι φιλοσόφων
B ὄντες, ὄργανα μουσικὰ θεῶν ἐνεχείριζον ἀγάλμα-
σιν, οὐχ ὡς λύραν που ⟨κρούουσι⟩⁷ καὶ αὐλοῦσιν
ἀλλ'⁸ οὐδὲν ἔργον οἰόμενοι θεῶν οἷον ἁρμονίαν

¹ Xylander; ἀναρείους -E, e, u, Escor. 72 ; ἐναρείους -B ;
ἀνάρθμια -f, m ; ἀνάρμιθμια -r.
² τὰ ἐχθρὰ καὶ τὰ πολέμα -f, m, r.
³ ἁρμονίαν -r.
⁴ B. Müller (1873); ἐπακούοντος -mss.; ἐπακούοντα J. G.
Schneider ; ἐπακούειν -Wyttenbach.
⁵ μουσικὰν ὀρθὰν -Heyne (Pindari Carmina iii, pars i
[Göttingen, 1798], pp. 51-52) ; οδουκανορέαν -E ; οὐκανορέαν
(οὐκ ἀνορέαν -u, f, m, r) -all other mss.
⁶ Heyne (loc. cit.) ; ἐπιδεικνύμενοι -E, B, e, u, Escor. 72 ;
ἐπιδεικνύμενος -f, m, r, Aldine.
⁷ ⟨κρούουσι⟩ -supplied by Maurommates ; που . . . vac. 7
. . . καὶ -E, B ; που καὶ (without lacuna) -all other mss.,
Aldine ; λυρίζουσιν καὶ -Wyttenbach.
⁸ αὐλὸν σιν . . . vac. 2 -f, m ; vac. 4 -r . . . ἀλλὰ -f, m, r ;
αὐλὸν ἀλλὰ -Aldine.

ᵃ Cf. Stobaeus, Ecl. i, Prooem., 2 (p. 16, 1-13 [Wachs-
muth]) and Syrianus, Metaph., pp. 103, 29-104, 2.
ᵇ Anth. Pal. vii, 35 ; cf. A. S. F. Gow and D. L. Page, The
Greek Anthology : Hellenistic Epigrams ii (Cambridge, 1965),
p. 395.

number and concord, this has not gone unnoticed even by the poets who call friendly and agreeable things befitting and enemies and foes unbefitting on the assumption that dissension is unfittingness.[a] He who composed the elegy for Pindar

> This was a man who was fitted for guests and friendly to townsmen [b]

is clearly of the belief that virtue is fittingness, as Pindar too says somewhere himself that Cadmus hearkened to the god displaying music fit.[c] The theologians of ancient times, who were the oldest of philosophers,[d] put musical instruments into the hands of the statues of the gods, with the thought, I presume, not that they ⟨do play⟩ the lyre and the pipe but that no work is so like that of gods as concord

---

[c] Pindar, frag. 32 (Bergk, Schroeder, Snell)=22 (Turyn) =13 (Bowra) ; cf. De Pythiae Oraculis 397 A and Aelius Aristides, ii, p. 296, 4-5 (Jebb)=ii, p. 383 (Dindorf). The quotation is relevant to the present context only if Plutarch identified the ὀρθ- of ὀρθάν with the ἀρθ- of ἄρθμιον, which he could the more easily do since in Aeolic and his own Boeotian ορ and ρο often correspond to the αρ and ρα of common Greek (cf. R. Meister, Die griechischen Dialekte . . . i [Göttingen, 1882], p. 34, n. 2 ; pp. 48-49 ; p. 216 and F. Bechtel, Die griechischen Dialekte i [Berlin, 1921], p. 25 ; p. 147 ; pp. 242-243) ; and I have therefore translated ὀρθάν by " fit " (cf. English " fit "=" a strain of music," cognate with " fit "=" juncture ").

[d] Cf. De Iside 360 D, where Plato, Pythagoras, Xenocrates, and Chrysippus are said to have followed τοῖς πάλαι θεολόγοις for their notion of δαίμονες, and 369 B, where a παμπάλαιος δόξα is said to have come down to poets and philosophers ἐκ θεολόγων καὶ νομοθετῶν ; in De Defectu Orac. 436 D οἱ σφόδρα παλαιοὶ θεολόγοι καὶ ποιηταί are contrasted to οἱ νεώτεροι . . . καὶ φυσικοὶ προσαγορευόμενοι, and to the former is ascribed a line of Orpheus, frag. B 6 (D.-K.), for which see De Comm. Not. 1074 E infra with note a there.

(1030) εἶναι καὶ συμφωνίαν. ὥσπερ οὖν ὁ τοὺς ἐπιτρίτους
καὶ ἡμιολίους καὶ διπλασίους λόγους ζητῶν ἐν τῷ
ζυγῷ τῆς λύρας καὶ τῇ χελώνῃ καὶ τοῖς κολλάβοις
γελοῖός ἐστι (δεῖ μὲν γὰρ ἀμέλει καὶ ταῦτα συμ-
μέτρως γεγονέναι πρὸς ἄλληλα μήκεσι καὶ πάχεσι
τὴν δὲ ἁρμονίαν ἐκείνην ἐπὶ τῶν φθόγγων θεωρεῖν)
οὕτως εἰκὸς μέν ἐστι καὶ τὰ σώματα τῶν ἀστέρων
καὶ τὰ διαστήματα τῶν κύκλων καὶ τὰ τάχη τῶν
C περιφορῶν ὥσπερ ὄργανα ἐν τεταγμένοις ⟨λόγοις⟩[1]
ἔχειν ἐμμέτρως πρὸς ἄλληλα καὶ πρὸς τὸ ὅλον, εἰ
καὶ τὸ ποσὸν ἡμᾶς τοῦ μέτρου[2] διαπέφευγε, τῶν
μέντοι λόγων ἐκείνων οἷς ὁ δημιουργὸς ἐχρήσατο
καὶ τῶν ἀριθμῶν ἔργον ἡγεῖσθαι τὴν αὐτῆς τῆς
ψυχῆς ἐμμέλειαν[3] καὶ ἁρμονίαν πρὸς αὑτήν,[4] ὑφ'
ἧς[5] καὶ τὸν οὐρανὸν ἐγγενομένη μυρίων ἀγαθῶν ἐμ-
πέπληκε καὶ τὰ περὶ γῆν ὥραις καὶ μεταβολαῖς
μέτρον ἐχούσαις ἄριστα καὶ κάλλιστα[6] πρός τε
γένεσιν καὶ σωτηρίαν τῶν γιγνομένων διακεκό-
σμηκεν.

[1] ⟨λόγοις⟩ -added by Wyttenbach.
[2] f, m, r ; μετρίου -all other mss.
[3] ἐπιμέλειαν -f[1], m[1], r, Aldine.
[4] E, B, f, m ; αὑτήν -e, u, r, Escor. 72, Aldine.
[5] E, B ; ἐφ' οἷς -all other mss., Aldine.
[6] μάλιστα -u.

---

[a] Cf. Cornutus, xiv and xxxii (p. 17, 11-16 and pp. 67,
17-68, 5 [Lang]) and Sallustius, De Diis et Mundo vi (p. 12,
8-12 [Nock]). Other such symbolic interpretations of the
statues of gods and their attributes are given by Plutarch
in De Iside 381 D-F, De Pythiae Oraculis 400 c and 402 A-B,
An Seni Respublica Gerenda Sit 797 F ; cf. Porphyry,

and consonance.[a] Just as one is ridiculous, then, who looks for the sesquitertian and sesquialteran and duple ratios in the yoke and the shell and the pegs of the lyre (for, while of course these too must have been made proportionate to one another in length and thickness, yet it is in the sounds that that concord is to be observed), so is it reasonable to believe that, while the bodies of the stars and the intervals of the circles and the velocities of the revolutions are like instruments commensurate in fixed ⟨ratios⟩ with one another and with the whole though the quantity of the measurement has eluded us,[b] nevertheless the product of those ratios and numbers used by the artificer [c] is the soul's own harmony and concord with herself,[d] whereby she has filled the heaven, into which she has come, with countless goods and has arrayed the terrestrial regions with seasons and measured changes in the best and fairest way for the generation and preservation of things that come to be.

Περὶ ἀγαλμάτων, frags. 3, 7, and 8 (J. Bidez, *Vie de Porphyre*, pp. 6*, 4–7*, 4 ; p. 9*, 10-21 ; p. 12*, 5-11 ; and p. 17*, 10-18) and Macrobius, *Sat.* i, xvii, 13 and xix, 2 and 8 with R. Pfeiffer, *Journal of the Warburg and Courtauld Institutes*, XV (1952), pp. 20-32 on Callimachus, frag. 114 (Pfeiffer).

[b] So much and only so much, then, is conceded to those referred to in 1028 A-B *supra*, καίτοι τινὲς μὲν ἐν τοῖς τάχεσι . . . τινὲς δὲ μᾶλλον ἐν τοῖς ἀποστήμασιν ἔνιοι δ' ἐν τοῖς μεγέθεσι. . . .

[c] See page 341, note *e* and the references there.

[d] See 1028 A *supra* : . . . ὡς μάλιστα δὴ τῇ συστάσει τῆς ψυχῆς τοῦ λόγου τούτου προσήκοντος.

EPITOME OF THE TREATISE, "ON THE GENERATION OF THE SOUL IN THE TIMAEUS"

(COMPENDIUM LIBRI DE ANIMAE PROCREATIONE IN TIMAEO)

INTRODUCTION

This *Epitome* or "Compendium," which is No. 42 in the Planudean corpus, is not listed in the *Catalogue of Lamprias*. It is rather an excerpt than an epitome or compendium in the proper sense, for it is merely a copy of chaps. 22-25 (1023 b—1025 b) of the treatise with two short paragraphs by way of introduction. In these the "epitomizer" refers to the author of the treatise in the third person, though not by name, and in summarizing his doctrine ineptly ascribes to him a theory of evil that is vehemently rejected in the treatise. The excerpt itself shows in several places that the "epitomizer" did not clearly understand what he was transcribing; and, though he made one intelligent substitution in his text, he also introduced a supplement that reveals his misunderstanding of a Greek verbal form.

It is practically certain that the ms. of the treatise from which the excerpt was taken was not one from which any of the extant mss. of the treatise was copied, for in five cases words absent from all the latter are present in all mss. of the *Epitome*.[a] The text here printed is based upon α, A, β, γ, E, B, and

---

[a] 1031 c (ἕκαστα), 1031 d (πάλιν), 1031 e (καὶ), 1032 d (πλανήτων), 1032 e (τὴν). See besides these the correct forms in all the mss. of the *Epitome*: ἀεικίνητος (1031 a), ἄκρα τὸ (1032 e), τοῦ ταὐτοῦ (1032 f).

n, all of which have been collated from photostats. Their readings are fully reported in the *apparatus*; and so are those of Laurent. Conv. Soppr. 180, which was collated as a sample of the other mss. containing the *Epitome* (*cf.* Hubert-Drexler, *Moralia* vi/1, pp. xvii-xviii). For the few readings cited of Vat. Reg. 80 I have depended upon the *Variae Lectiones* of Cruser-Xylander and the reports of Hubert-Drexler and upon the latter for those of Marc. Append. IV, 1 and Urb. 100(t). There are few decisive indications in this work of the relation among the mss. collated ; but in several cases B and n are in agreement against all the others, and it is quite clear that the scribe of B did not copy the *Epitome* from E.[a]

[a] See 1030 E (ἀναλογίας καὶ; ἀναλογικὰς -B, n), 1031 A (περιλαμβάνων; παραλαμβάνων -B, n), 1031 E (νοερὸν ἡ φύσις; νοερὸν ὥσπερ ἡ φύσις -B, n), 1032 A (πως omitted by B, n). In all these cases the Aldine is in disagreement with B and n.

ΕΠΙΤΟΜΗ ΤΟΥ ΠΕΡΙ[1] ΤΗΣ ΕΝ ΤΩΙ
ΤΙΜΑΙΩΙ ΨΥΧΟΓΟΝΙΑΣ

1. Ὁ περὶ τῆς ἐν τῷ Τιμαίῳ ψυχογονίας ἐπι-
γεγραμμένος λόγος ὅσα Πλάτωνι καὶ τοῖς Πλατω-
E νικοῖς πεφιλοτίμηται ἀπαγγέλλει εἰσάγει δὲ καὶ
γεωμετρικάς τινας ἀναλογίας καὶ ὁμοιότητας[2] πρὸς
τὴν τῆς ψυχῆς, ὡς οἴεται, θεωρίαν συντεινούσας
αὐτῷ καὶ δὴ καὶ μουσικὰ καὶ ἀριθμητικὰ θεωρή-
ματα.

2. Λέγει δὲ τὴν ὕλην διαμορφωθῆναι ὑπὸ τῆς
ψυχῆς καὶ δίδωσι μὲν τῷ παντὶ ψυχὴν δίδωσι δὲ
καὶ ἑκάστῳ ζώῳ τὴν διοικοῦσαν αὐτό,[3] καὶ πῆ μὲν
ἀγένητον[4] εἰσάγει ταύτην πῆ δὲ γενέσει δουλεύου-
σαν ἀίδιον δὲ τὴν ὕλην καὶ ὑπὸ τοῦ θείου διὰ τῆς
ψυχῆς μορφωθῆναι καὶ τὴν κακίαν δὲ βλάστημα
τῆς ὕλης γεγονέναι, ἵνα μή, φησί, τὸ θεῖον αἴτιον
F τῶν κακῶν νομισθείη.

3. Ὅτι οἱ περὶ τὸν Ποσειδώνιον οὐ μακρὰν τῆς

---

[1] τοῦ περὶ -omitted by β.
[2] ἀναλογικὰς ὁμοιότητας -B, n.
[3] αὐτῷ -γ, Laurent. C. S. 180.
[4] α; ἀγέννητον -all other mss., Aldine.

---

[a] The epitomizer passes without notice from the treatise
to its author.
[b] See *supra* 1016 c and 1017 A-B.
[c] See *supra* 1014 B and in the final chapter 1029 D-E and
1030 c, with which *cf. Plat. Quaest.* 1003 A.

EPITOME OF THE TREATISE,
"ON THE GENERATION OF THE SOUL IN THE TIMAEUS"

1. The treatise entitled *On the Generation of the Soul in the Timaeus* reports what all the contentions of Plato and the Platonists have been and also introduces certain geometrical proportions and similarities pertaining, as he thinks,[a] to his theory of the soul and particularly musical and arithmetical speculations.

2. He asserts, moreover, that matter was shaped by soul and ascribes a soul to the universe but ascribes to each living being also the one that manages it ; and he represents this as being in one way ungenerated and in another subject to generation[b] but matter as everlasting and given shape by the divinity through the agency of the soul[c] and evil as being in origin an excrescence of matter,[d] in order, he says, that the divinity might not be thought responsible for evil things.

3. He says that Posidonius and his followers[e] did

[d] As B. Müller observed (*Hermes*, iv [1870], p. 396, n. 1) this is the very opposite to Plutarch's contention in the treatise (see 1015 c-e *supra*).

[e] = F 141 b (Edelstein-Kidd). Save for the differences indicated in the notes the rest of the *Epitome* is an exact copy of *De An. Proc. in Timaeo* 1023 b—1025 b *supra*.

PLUTARCH'S MORALIA

(1030) ὕλης ἀπέστησαν τὴν ψυχὴν¹ ἀλλὰ δεξάμενοι τὴν
τῶν περάτων οὐσίαν περὶ τὰ σώματα λέγεσθαι
μεριστὴν καὶ ταῦτα τῷ νοητῷ μίξαντες ἀπεφήναντο τὴν ψυχὴν ἰδέαν εἶναι τοῦ πάντη διαστατοῦ
1031 κατ' ἀριθμὸν συνεστῶσαν ἁρμονίαν περιέχοντα· τά
τε γὰρ μαθηματικὰ² τῶν πρώτων νοητῶν μεταξὺ
καὶ τῶν αἰσθητῶν τετάχθαι, τῆς τε ψυχῆς, τῷ
νοητῷ³ τὸ ἀίδιον καὶ τῷ αἰσθητικῷ⁴ τὸ παθητικὸν
ἐχούσης, προσῆκον ἐν μέσῳ τὴν οὐσίαν ὑπάρχειν.
ἔλαθε γὰρ καὶ τούτους ὁ θεὸς τοῖς τῶν σωμάτων
πέρασιν ὕστερον, ἀπειργασμένης ἤδη τῆς ψυχῆς,
χρώμενος ἐπὶ τὴν τῆς ὕλης διαμόρφωσιν, τὸ σκεδαστὸν αὐτῆς καὶ ἀσύνδετον ὁρίζων καὶ περιλαμ-
βάνων⁵ ταῖς ἐκ τῶν τριγώνων συναρμοττομένων
ἐπιφανείαις. ἀτοπώτερον δὲ⁶ τὸ τὴν ψυχὴν ἰδέαν
ποιεῖν· ἡ μὲν γὰρ ἀεικίνητος ἡ δ' ἀκίνητος, καὶ ἡ
μὲν ἀμιγὴς πρὸς τὸ αἰσθητὸν ἡ δὲ τῷ σώματι συν-
B ειργμένη.⁷ πρὸς δὲ τούτοις ὁ θεὸς τῆς μὲν ἰδέας
ὡς παραδείγματος γέγονε μιμητὴς τῆς δὲ ψυχῆς
ὥσπερ ἀποτελέσματος δημιουργός. ὅτι δ' οὐδ'

¹ mss. ; τὴν ψυχὴν -omitted 1023 в supra.
² μαθητικὰ -α, A (with μα superscript over ητ), Aldine.
³ mss. ; τῶν νοητῶν -1023 в supra.
⁴ mss. ; τῶν αἰσθητῶν -1023 в-c supra (E, B ; τῶν αἰσθητικῶν -all other mss.).
⁵ παραλαμβάνων -B, n.
⁶ διὰ -Laurent. C. S. 180.
⁷ συνειργομένη -B, n, Laurent. C. S. 180 ; συνηργμένη -Vat.
Reg. 80.

ᵃ The epitomizer misunderstood the second aorist ἀπέστησαν (1023 в supra) and, supposing it to be transitive, added
the object, τὴν ψυχήν, that he thought was to be " supplied."
The original was correctly translated by Turnebus and
Amyot ; but Xylander misunderstood it just as the epitomizer had done, and his mistake has been repeated by

352

not remove the soul[a] far from matter but, having taken divisible in the case of bodies to mean the being of the limits and having mixed these with the intelligible, they declared the soul to be the idea of what is everyway extended, herself constituted according to number that embraces concord, for (they said) the mathematicals have been ranked between the primary intelligibles and the perceptibles and it is an appropriate thing for the soul likewise, possessing as she does everlastingness with the intelligible and passivity with the perceptive,[b] to have her being in the middle. In fact these people too failed to notice that only later, after the soul has already been produced, does god use the limits of the bodies for the shaping of matter by bounding and circumscribing its dispersiveness and incoherence with the surfaces made of the triangles fitted together. What is more absurd, however, is to make the soul an idea, for the former is perpetually in motion but the latter is immobile and the latter cannot mix with the perceptible but the former has been coupled with body ; and, besides, god's relation to the idea is that of imitator to pattern but his relation to the soul is that of artificer to finished product. As to number, however, it has been stated

Helmer (*De An. Proc.*, p. 16, n. 21), Thévenaz (*L'Âme du Monde*, p. 26), Merlan (*Platonism to Neoplatonism*, p. 35), and Marie Laffranque (*Poseidonios d'Apamée* [Paris, 1964], p. 431).

  [b] τῷ νοητῷ . . . τῷ αἰσθητικῷ is a mistake whether of the epitomizer's own or of his original for τῶν νοητῶν . . . τῶν αἰσθητῶν (1023 в *supra*, where, however, all mss. except E and B have αἰσθητικῶν). It is uncertain what the epitomizer thought the text as he wrote it could mean—if indeed he thought about it at all.

(1031) ἀριθμὸν ὁ Πλάτων τὴν οὐσίαν τίθεται τῆς ψυχῆς
ἀλλὰ ταττομένην ὑπ᾽ ἀριθμοῦ, προείρηται.

4. Πρὸς δ᾽ ἀμφοτέροις τούτοις[1] κοινόν ἐστι τὸ
μήτε τοῖς πέρασι μήτε τοῖς ἀριθμοῖς μηδὲν ἴχνος
ἐνυπάρχειν ἐκείνης τῆς δυνάμεως ᾗ τὸ αἰσθητὸν ἡ
ψυχὴ πέφυκε κρίνειν. νοῦν μὲν γὰρ αὐτῇ καὶ
νοητὸν[2] ἡ τῆς νοητῆς μέθεξις ἀρχῆς ἐμπεποίηκε·
δόξας δὲ καὶ πίστεις καὶ τὸ φανταστικὸν καὶ τὸ
παθητικὸν[3] ὑπὸ τῶν περὶ τὸ σῶμα ποιοτήτων [ὃ][4]
οὐκ ἄν τις ἐκ μονάδων οὐδὲ γραμμῶν[5] οὐδ᾽ ἐπι-
C φανειῶν ἁπλῶς νοήσειεν ἐγγινόμενον. καὶ μὴν οὐ
μόνον αἱ τῶν θνητῶν ψυχαὶ γνωστικὴν τοῦ αἰσθητοῦ δύναμιν ἔχουσιν, ἀλλὰ καὶ τὴν τοῦ κύκλου[6]
φησὶν ἀνακυκλουμένην αὐτὴν πρὸς ἑαυτήν, ὅταν
οὐσίαν σκεδαστὴν ἔχοντός τινος[7] ἐφάπτηται καὶ
ὅταν ἀμέριστον, λέγῃ[8] κινουμένην διὰ πάσης[9] ἑαυτῆς, ὅτῳ ἄν[10] τι[11] ταὐτὸν ᾖ καὶ ὅτου[12] ἂν ἕτερον,

---

[1] mss. ; ἀμφοτέρους τούτους -1023 d supra.

[2] mss. here and 1023 d supra ; see the note there on καὶ
⟨τὸ⟩ νοητόν.

[3] παθητὸν -a, B, n.

[4] [ὃ] -omitted by t (Urb. 100) and deleted by Dübner ;
see 1023 d supra : ποιοτήτων, τοῦτ᾽.

[5] οὐδ᾽ ἐκ γραμμῶν -B.

[6] τοῦ κόσμου -Leonicus from 1023 d supra.

[7] τινὰ -γ.

[8] λέγῃ -mss. (η over erasure in a) ; λέγει -Aldine ; λέγειν
-Dübner from 1023 e supra (where E, B, f, m, r also have
λέγῃ).

[9] δὲ ἀπάσης -Laurent. C. S. 180[1].

above [a] that Plato regards the substance of soul not as number either but as being ordered by number.

4. Besides both of these, moreover, there is equally [b] the argument that neither in limits nor in numbers is there any trace of that faculty with which the soul naturally forms judgments of what is perceptible. Intelligence and intelligibility have been produced in her by participation in the intelligible principle ; but opinions and beliefs, that is to say what is imaginative and impressionable by the qualities in body, one could not conceive [. . .] as arising in her simply from units or from lines or surfaces. Now, not only do the souls of mortal beings have a faculty that is cognizant of the perceptible ; but he says [c] that the soul of the circle [d] also as she is revolving upon herself, whenever she touches anything that has being either dispersed or indivisible, is moved throughout herself and states [e] of anything's being the same and different with

---

[a] Thoughtlessly copied from 1023 D, for neither the passage to which it refers (1013 C-D) nor its content has been mentioned in this " epitome."

[b] Plutarch's κοινόν was made meaningless when the epitomizer mistook ἀμφοτέρους τούτους for ἀμφοτέροις τούτοις (see 1023 D *supra* : ". . . against both of these in common . . . ").

[c] Plato, *Timaeus* 37 A 5–B 3.

[d] This is the epitomizer's mistake for " the soul of the universe " (1023 D *supra*).

[e] I translate as if the correct λέγειν stood here (see 1023 E *supra*), for with λέγῃ, which the epitomizer certainly wrote, it is impossible to construe the sentence at all.

---

[10] MSS. ; ὅτῳ τ' ἄν -1023 E *supra*.

[11] τι -B$^{corr.}$; τις -all other MSS., Aldine.

[12] ᾗ καὶ ὅτου -B$^{corr.}$; ἢ καὶ ὅτῳ -all other MSS. (ω over erasure in α), Aldine.

(1031) πρὸς ὅ τι τε μάλιστα καὶ ὅπῃ καὶ ὅπως συμβαίνει καὶ[1] τὰ γιγνόμενα πρὸς ἕκαστον ἕκαστα εἶναι καὶ πάσχειν. ἐν τούτοις ἅμα καὶ τῶν δέκα κατηγοριῶν ποιούμενος ὑπογραφὴν ἔτι μᾶλλον τοῖς ἐφεξῆς διασαφεῖ. " λόγος " γάρ φησιν " ἀληθὴς ὅταν μὲν

D περὶ τὸ αἰσθητὸν γένηται[2] καὶ ὁ τοῦ θατέρου κύκλος ὀρθὸς[3] ἰὼν εἰς πᾶσαν αὐτοῦ τὴν ψυχὴν διαγγείλῃ, δόξαι καὶ πίστεις γίγνονται βέβαιοι καὶ ἀληθεῖς· ὅταν δ' αὖ πάλιν περὶ[4] τὸ λογιστικὸν ᾖ καὶ ὁ τοῦ ταὐτοῦ κύκλος εὔτροχος ὢν αὐτὰ μηνύσῃ, ἐπιστήμη ἐξ ἀνάγκης ἀποτελεῖται· τούτῳ δ' ἐν ᾧ τῶν ὄντων ἐγγίγνεσθον, ἐάν ποτέ τις αὐτὸ ἄλλο πλὴν ψυχὴν προσείπῃ, πᾶν μᾶλλον ἢ τὸ ἀληθὲς ἐρεῖ." πόθεν οὖν ἔσχεν[5] ἡ ψυχὴ τὴν ἀντιληπτικὴν τοῦ αἰσθητοῦ καὶ δοξαστικὴν ταύτην κίνησιν, ἑτέραν τῆς νοητῆς[6] ἐκείνης καὶ τελευτώσης εἰς ἐπιστήμην, ἔργον εἰπεῖν μὴ θεμένους βεβαίως ὅτι νῦν οὐχ ἁπλῶς ψυχὴν ἀλλὰ κόσμου ψυχὴν συνίστησιν

---

[1] καὶ -MSS.; κατὰ -B^{corr.} in margin; see 1023 E supra: κατὰ τὰ γιγνόμενα (καταγινόμενα -MSS.).

[2] γένοιτο -t (Urb. 100), Laurent. 80, 5; γίγνηται -1023 E supra.

[3] ὀρθῶς -a¹ ? (ὃς over erasure), Vat. Reg. 80; see r^{corr.} in 1023 E supra.

[4] MSS., Aldine; δ' αὖ περὶ (without πάλιν) -1023 F supra and Timaeus 37 C 1.

[5] ἔσχεν -omitted by Laurent. C. S. 180, Marc. Append. IV, 1 (cf. Hubert-Drexler, Moralia vi/1, p. xviii).

[6] MSS., Aldine; νοητικῆς -Wyttenbach from 1023 F supra.

---

[a] From this point on the construction of the original is radically altered by the erroneous καὶ τὰ γιγνόμενα which

regard to whatever it is so precisely the respect and context and manner in which[a] even the things that come to be happen to be or to have as attribute either of these in relation to each. As in these words he is simultaneously giving an outline of the ten categories too, in those that follow he states the case more clearly still, for he says[b] : " Whenever true discourse is concerning itself about the perceptible and the circle of difference running aright conveys the message through all its soul, there arise opinions and beliefs steadfast and true ; but, whenever on the other hand again it is concerned about the rational and the circle of sameness running smoothly gives the information, knowledge is of necessity produced ; and, if anyone ever calls by another name than soul that one of existing things in which these two come to be, he will be speaking anything but the truth." Whence, then, did the soul get this motion that can apprehend what is perceptible and form opinions of it, a motion different from that which is intelligible[c] and issues in knowledge ? It is difficult to say without steadfastly maintaining that in the present passage[d] he is constructing not soul in the absolute sense but the soul

the epitomizer wrote instead of κατὰ τὰ γιγνόμενα (see 1023 E *supra*). On the other hand, the ms. that he excerpted must have contained the correct ἕκαστα (*cf. Timaeus* 37 B 2) that is lacking in all our mss. of the treatise.

[b] *Timaeus* 37 B 3–c 5.

[c] The treatise here has " intellective " (1023 F *supra* : νοητικῆς), but the epitomizer probably wrote νοητῆς.

[d] This refers to neither of the two passages just mentioned but to *Timaeus* 35 A 1–B 4, which is quoted at the beginning of the treatise (1012 B-c *supra*) but has not been mentioned in the *Epitome* at all.

(1031)
E ἐξ ὑποκειμένης[1] τῆς τε κρείττονος οὐσίας καὶ ἀμερίστου καὶ τῆς χείρονος, ἣν περὶ[2] τὰ σώματα
μεριστὴν κέκληκεν, οὐχ ἑτέραν οὖσαν ἢ τὴν δοξαστικὴν καὶ φανταστικὴν καὶ συμπαθῆ[3] τῶν αἰσθητῶν[4] κίνησιν, οὐ γενομένην ἀλλὰ ὑφεστῶσαν ἀίδιον
ὥσπερ ἡ ἑτέρα. τὸ γὰρ νοερὸν ἡ φύσις[5] ἔχουσα
καὶ τὸ δοξαστικὸν εἶχεν ἀλλ' ἐκεῖνο μὲν ἀκίνητον
καὶ ἀπαθὲς καὶ περὶ τὴν ἀεὶ μένουσαν ἱδρυμένον
οὐσίαν τοῦτο δὲ μεριστὸν καὶ πλανητόν, ἅτε δὴ
φερομένης καὶ σκεδαννυμένης ἐφαπτόμενον ὕλης.
οὔτε γὰρ τὸ αἰσθητὸν εἰλήχει τάξεως ἀλλ' ἦν ἄμορφον καὶ ἀόριστον, ἥ τε περὶ τοῦτο τεταγμένη δύνα-
F μις οὔτε δόξας ἐνάρθρους οὔτε κινήσεις ἁπάσας
ἔχουσα[6] τεταγμένας ἀλλὰ τὰς πολλὰς ἐνυπνιώδεις
καὶ παραφόρους καὶ ταραττούσας τὸ σωματοειδές,
ὅσα μὴ κατὰ τύχην τῷ βελτίονι περιέπιπτεν· ἐν
μέσῳ γὰρ ἦν ἀμφοῖν καὶ πρὸς ἀμφότερα συμπαθῆ
1032 καὶ συγγενῆ φύσιν εἶχε, τῷ μὲν αἰσθητικῷ[7] τῆς
ὕλης ἀντεχομένη τῷ δὲ κριτικῷ τῶν νοητῶν.
  5. Οὕτω δέ πως[8] καὶ Πλάτων[9] διασαφεῖ τοῖς
ὀνόμασιν· " οὗτος " γάρ φησι " παρὰ τῆς ἐμῆς ψή-

---

[1] mss., Aldine ; ὑποκειμένων -1024 A supra.
[2] παρὰ -E.   [3] συμπλοκὴ -Vat. Reg. 80.
[4] mss., Aldine ; τῷ αἰσθητῷ -1024 A supra.
[5] νοερὸν ὥσπερ ἡ φύσις -B, n.
[6] mss., Aldine ; εἶχε -Wyttenbach from 1024 B supra (B,
E [in margin]).
[7] αἰσθητῷ -B.
[8] πως -omitted by B.
[9] mss. ; αὐτὸς -1024 B supra.

---

[a] Misled by τῆς . . . οὐσίας, which follows immediately,
the epitomizer may have misread an abbreviation of the final
syllable of ὑποκειμένων in the original (1024 A supra).   Both
entities, of course, were already available to the artificer.

358

of the universe out of being that is already available,[a] the superior, that is to say indivisible, and the inferior, which he has called divisible in the case of bodies, this latter being none other than the opinionative and imaginative motion sensitive of the perceptibles,[b] not brought into being but having subsisted everlastingly just like the former. For nature possessing intellectuality possessed the opinionative faculty also, the former, however, immobile and impassive and settled about the being that always remains fixed but the latter divisible and erratic inasmuch as it was in contact with matter which was in motion and dispersion. The fact is that the perceptible had not got any portion of order but was amorphous and indefinite ; and the faculty stationed about this was one having[c] neither articulate opinions nor motions that were all orderly, but most of them were dreamlike and deranged and were disturbing corporeality save in so far as it would by chance encounter that which is the better, for it was intermediate between the two and had a nature sensitive and akin to both, with its perceptivity laying hold on matter and with its discernment on the intelligibles.

5. In terms that go something like this Plato[d] too states the case clearly, for he says[e] : " Let this be

[b] This is the epitomizer's error for " sensitive to what is perceptible " in the original.

[c] I attempt in this way to render ἔχουσα, a mistake for εἶχε that was probably in the epitomizer's original, for it is common to all the mss. here and most of those of the treatise (see 1024 B *supra*).

[d] Here the epitomizer not unintelligently substituted the name of Plato for " he . . . himself " of his original.

[e] *Timaeus* 52 D 2-4.

PLUTARCH'S MORALIA

(1032) φου λογισθεὶς ἐν κεφαλαίῳ δεδόσθω λόγος, ὅν τε[1]
καὶ χώραν καὶ γένεσιν εἶναι τρία τριχῇ καὶ πρὶν
οὐρανὸν γενέσθαι." καὶ[2] χώραν τε γὰρ καλεῖ τὴν
ὕλην ὥσπερ ἕδραν ἔστιν ὅτε καὶ ὑποδοχήν,[3] ὃν δὲ τὸ
νοητόν, γένεσιν δὲ τοῦ κόσμου μήπω γεγονότος
οὐδεμίαν ἄλλην ἢ τὴν ἐν μεταβολαῖς καὶ κινήσεσιν
οὐσίαν, τοῦ τυποῦντος καὶ τοῦ τυπουμένου μεταξὺ
τεταγμένην, διαδιδοῦσαν[4] ἐνταῦθα τὰς ἐκεῖθεν εἰκόνας. διά τε δὴ ταῦτα μεριστὴ προσηγορεύθη καὶ
B ὅτι τῷ αἰσθητῷ τὸ αἰσθανόμενον καὶ τῷ φανταστῷ
τὸ φανταζόμενον ἀνάγκη συνδιανέμεσθαι καὶ συμ-
παρήκειν· ἡ γὰρ αἰσθητικὴ[5] κίνησις, ἰδίᾳ ψυχῆς
οὖσα, κινεῖται πρὸς τὸ αἰσθητὸν ἐκτός· ὁ δὲ νοῦς
αὐτὸς μὲν ἐφ' ἑαυτοῦ[6] μόνιμος ἦν καὶ ἀκίνητος,
ἐγγενόμενος δὲ τῇ ψυχῇ καὶ κρατήσας εἰς ἑαυτὸν
ἐπιστρέφει καὶ συμπεραίνει τὴν ἐγκύκλιον φορὰν
περὶ τὸ μέν⟨ον⟩[7] ἀεὶ μάλιστα[8] ψαύουσαν τοῦ ὄντος.
διὸ καὶ δυσανάκρατος ἡ κοινωνία γέγονεν αὐτῶν,
τῶν ἀμερίστων[9] τὸ μεριστὸν καὶ τῶν μηδαμῇ κινη-

---

[1] ὅν τε -E[1] in margin, Basiliensis ; ὄντος -all other mss.
(two dots under τος -B), Aldine.
[2] καὶ -mss., Aldine ; omitted by Basiliensis and lacking in
1024 c *supra*.
[3] ὑποδοχεῖν -γ.
[4] διαδοῦσαν -γ (so also r in 1024 c *supra*).
[5] αἰσθητὴ -B.
[6] ἀφ' ἑαυτοῦ -Laurent. C. S. 180, Marc. Append. IV, 1 (*cf.*
Hubert-Drexler, *Moralia* vi/1, p. xviii [so also f, m, r, Escor.
72 in 1024 c *supra*]).
360

the account rendered in summation as reckoned from my calculation, that real existence and space and becoming were three and distinct even before heaven came to be." Now, it is matter that he also calls space, as he sometimes calls it abode and receptacle, and the intelligible that he calls real existence ; and what he calls becoming, the universe not yet having come to be, is nothing other than that being involved in changes and motions which, ranged between what makes impressions and what receives them, disperses in this world the semblances from that world yonder. For this very reason it was called divisible and also because it is necessary for that which is perceiving and that which is forming mental images to be divided in correspondence with what is perceptible and with what is imaginable and to be coextensive with them, for the motion of sense-perception, which is the soul's own, moves towards what is perceptible without but the intelligence, while it was abiding and immobile all by itself, upon having got into the soul and taken control makes her turn around to him and with her accomplishes about that which always remains fixed[a] the circular motion most closely in contact with real existence. This is also why the union of them proved to be a difficult fusion, mixing the divisibility of the indivisibles and the

[a] It is probable that the epitomizer faithfully copied τὸ μὲν ἀεὶ from his original ; but, if so, he could not have construed the phrase at all.

---

[7] Wyttenbach from 1024 D *supra* ; τὸ μὲν -MSS. (so u in 1024 D *supra*, where f omits μένον altogether).

[8] μάλιστα -omitted by B.

[9] MSS. ; τῷ ἀμερίστῳ -Stephanus from 1024 D *supra*.

PLUTARCH'S MORALIA

(1032) τῶν¹ τὸ πάντη φορητὸν μιγνύουσα καὶ καταβια-
ζομένη² θάτερον εἰς ταὐτὸν³ συνελθεῖν. ἦν δὲ τὸ
C θάτερον οὐ κίνησις, ὥσπερ οὐδὲ ταὐτὸν στάσις,
ἀλλ' ἀρχὴ διαφορᾶς καὶ ἀνομοιότητος. ἑκάτερον
γὰρ ἀπὸ τῆς ἑτέρας ἀρχῆς κάτεισι, τὸ μὲν ταὐτὸν
ἀπὸ τοῦ ἑνὸς τὸ δὲ θάτερον ἀπὸ τῆς δυάδος· καὶ
μέμικται πρῶτον ἐνταῦθα περὶ τὴν ψυχήν, ἀριθμοῖς καὶ λόγοις συνδεθέντα καὶ μεσότησιν ἐναρμο-
νίοις, καὶ ποιεῖ θάτερον μὲν ἐγγενόμενον τῷ ταὐτῷ⁴
διαφορὰν τὸ δὲ ταὐτὸν ἐν τῷ ἑτέρῳ τάξιν, ὡς δῆλόν
ἐστιν ἐν ταῖς πρώταις τῆς ψυχῆς δυνάμεσιν· εἰσὶ
δὲ αὗται τὸ κριτικὸν καὶ τὸ κινητικόν. ἡ μὲν οὖν
κίνησις εὐθὺς ἐπιδείκνυται περὶ τὸν οὐρανὸν ἐν μὲν
τῇ ταυτότητι τὴν ἑτερότητα τῇ περιφορᾷ τῶν ἀ-
D πλανῶν ἐν δὲ τῇ ἑτερότητι τὴν ταυτότητα τῇ τάξει
τῶν πλανήτων⁵· ἐπικρατεῖ² γὰρ ἐν ἐκείνοις τὸ ταὐτὸν ἐν δὲ τοῖς περὶ γῆν τοὐναντίον. ἡ δὲ κρίσις
ἀρχὰς μὲν ἔχει δύο, τόν τε νοῦν ἀπὸ τοῦ ταὐτοῦ
πρὸς τὰ καθόλου καὶ τὴν αἴσθησιν ἀπὸ τοῦ ἑτέρου
πρὸς τὰ καθ' ἕκαστα. μέμικται δὲ λόγος ἐξ ἀμφοῖν, νόησις ἐν τοῖς νοητοῖς καὶ δόξα γινόμενος ἐν
τοῖς αἰσθητοῖς ὀργάνοις τε μεταξὺ φαντασίαις τε
καὶ μνήμαις χρώμενος, ὧν τὰ μὲν ἐν τῷ ταὐτῷ⁶
τὸ ἕτερον τὰ δ' ἐν τῷ ἑτέρῳ ποιεῖ τὸ ταὐτόν. ἔστι
γὰρ ἡ μὲν νόησις κίνησις τοῦ κινοῦντος⁷ περὶ τὸ

---

¹ mss. (τὸ . . . κινητὸν -t [Urb. 100], Laurent. 80, 5) ; τῷ
μηδαμῆ κινητῷ -Stephanus from 1024 D *supra* (where r has
κινητὸν).   ² καταβιαζομένου -a (?).

³ ταυτὸ -B, Laurent. C. S. 180.

⁴ E ; τῷ αὐτῷ -all other mss.

⁵ πλανων (with ἥτ superscript over νω) -a¹ ; πλανήτων -all
other mss.

⁶ E¹ superscript over αὐτῷ ; αὐτὸ -Vat. Reg. 80 ; αὐτῷ
-all other mss.

362

thorough transience of the utterly immobile [a] and constraining difference to unite with sameness. Difference is not motion, however, as sameness is not rest either, but the principle of differentiation and dissimilitude. In fact, each of the two derives from another of two principles, sameness from the one and difference from the dyad ; and it is first here in the soul that they have been commingled, bound together by numbers and ratios and harmonious means, and that difference come to be in sameness produces differentiation but sameness in difference order, as is clear in the case of the soul's primary faculties. These are the faculties of discernment and motivity. Now, directly in the heaven motion exhibits diversity in identity by the revolution of the fixed stars and identity in diversity by the order of the planets, for in the former sameness predominates but its opposite in the things about the earth. Discernment, however, has two principles, intelligence proceeding from sameness to universals and sense-perception from difference to particulars ; and reason is a blend of both, becoming intellection in the case of the intelligibles and opinion in the case of the perceptibles and employing between them mental images and memories as instruments, of which the former are produced by difference in sameness and the latter by sameness in difference. For intellection is motion of the mover [b] about what remains fixed,

[a] The nonsense of this clause is the result of the epitomizer's reading as genitive plurals the dative singulars of 1024 D *supra*, a mistake that he made in 1031 E *supra* also.

[b] This is the epitomizer's own mistake for " motion of what is cognizing " (1024 F *supra*).

---

7 κινοῦντος -MSS. ; νοοῦντος -Leonicus from 1024 F *supra*.

(1032) μένον, ἡ δὲ δόξα μονὴ τοῦ αἰσθανομένου περὶ τὸ
κινούμενον· φαντασίαν δὲ συμπλοκὴν δόξης πρὸς
E αἴσθησιν οὖσαν ἵστησιν ἐν μνήμῃ τὸ ταὐτὸν τὸ δὲ
θάτερον κινεῖ πάλιν ἐν διαφορᾷ τοῦ πρόσθεν καὶ
νῦν, ἑτερότητος ἅμα καὶ ταὐτότητος ἐφαπτόμενον.[a]
    6. Δεῖ δὲ τὴν περὶ τὸ σῶμα τοῦ κόσμου γενο-
μένην σύνταξιν[1] εἰκόνα λαβεῖν τῆς ἀναλογίας ἐν ᾗ
διηρμόσατο τὴν[2] ψυχήν. ἐκεῖ μὲν γὰρ ἦν ἄκρα τὸ
πῦρ καὶ ἡ γῆ, χαλεπὴν πρὸς ἄλληλα κραθῆναι
φύσιν ἔχοντα μᾶλλον δὲ ὅλως ἄκρατον καὶ ἀσύ-
στατον· ὅθεν ἐν μέσῳ θέμενος αὐτῶν τὸν μὲν ἀέρα
πρὸ τοῦ πυρὸς τὸ δὲ ὕδωρ πρὸ τῆς γῆς, ταῦτα
πρῶτον ἀλλήλοις ἐκέρασεν εἶτα διὰ τούτων ἐκεῖνα
πρός τε ταῦτα καὶ ἄλληλα[3] συνέμιξε καὶ συνήρμο-
F σεν. ἐνταῦθα δὲ πάλιν τὸ ταὐτὸν καὶ τὸ θάτερον,
ἐναντίας δυνάμεις καὶ ἀκρότητας ἀντιπάλους, συν-
ήγαγεν οὐ διὰ αὐτῶν,[4] ἀλλ' οὐσίας ἑτέρας μεταξύ,
τὴν μὲν ἀμέριστον πρὸ[5] τοῦ ταὐτοῦ πρὸ[6] δὲ τοῦ
θατέρου τὴν μεριστήν, ἔστιν ᾗ προσήκουσαν ἑκατέραν ἑκατέρᾳ τάξας εἶτα μιχθείσαις ἐκείναις ἐπ-
εγκεραννύμενος, οὕτως τὸ πᾶν συνύφηνε τῆς ψυχῆς
εἶδος, ὡς ἦν ἀνυστόν, ἐκ διαφόρων ὅμοιον ἔκ τε
πολλῶν ἓν[7] ἀπεργασάμενος.[8]

---

[1] mss.; σύντηξιν -Bernardakis from 1025 A *supra*.
[2] τὴν -mss.; omitted in 1025 A *supra*.
[3] mss.; καὶ πρὸς ἄλληλα -1025 A-B *supra*.
[4] αὐτῶν -a, Laurent. C. S. 180, Aldine.
[5] πρὸς -Vat. Reg. 80.
[6] πρὸς -Vat. Reg. 80.
[7] ἐν -n; ἕνα -Laurent. C. S. 180; omitted by Aldine.
[8] mss.; ἀπειργασμένος -1025 B *supra* (ἀπειργασάμενος -f).

[a] The erroneous ἐφαπτόμενον (in 1025 A *supra* emended
to ἐφαπτομένην), which without doubt was in the ms. excerpted by the epitomizer as it is in all the extant mss. of the

and opinion fixity of what is perceiving about what is in motion ; but mental imagining, which is a combination of opinion with sense-perception, is brought to a stop in memory by sameness and by difference again set moving in the distinction of past and present, being in contact with[a] diversity and identity at once.

6. The construction[b] that was carried out in the case of the body of the universe must be taken as a likeness of the proportion with which he regulated the soul. In the former case, because there were extremes, fire and earth, of a nature difficult to blend together or rather utterly immiscible and incohesive, he accordingly put between them air in front of the fire and water in front of the earth and blended these with each other first and then by means of these commingled and conjoined those extremes with them and each other. And in the latter case again he united sameness and difference, contrary forces and antagonistic extremes, not just by themselves ; but by first interposing other beings, the indivisible in front of sameness and in front of difference the divisible, as each of the one pair is in a way akin to one of the other, and by then making an additional blend with those between after they had been commingled he thus fabricated the whole structure of the soul, from what were various making it as nearly uniform and from what were many as nearly single as was feasible.

treatise, could agree only with τὸ θάτερον (" difference ") and taken with this produces nonsense.

[b] This mistake for " fusion " (σύντηξιν), which occurs in one MS. of the treatise also, may have been in the MS. excerpted by the epitomizer.

Printed in Great Britain by R. & R. CLARK, LIMITED, *Edinburgh*

THE LOEB CLASSICAL
LIBRARY

VOLUMES ALREADY PUBLISHED

LATIN AUTHORS

AMMIANUS MARCELLINUS. J. C. Rolfe. 3 Vols.

APULEIUS : THE GOLDEN ASS (METAMORPHOSES). W. Adlington (1566). Revised by S. Gaselee.

ST. AUGUSTINE : CITY OF GOD. 7 Vols. Vol. I. G. E. McCracken. Vol. II. W. M. Green. Vol. III. D. Wiesen. Vol. IV. P. Levine. Vol. V. E. M. Sanford and W. M. Green. Vol. VI. W. C. Greene. Vol. VII. W. M. Green.

ST. AUGUSTINE, CONFESSIONS OF. W. Watts (1631). 2 Vols.

ST. AUGUSTINE : SELECT LETTERS. J. H. Baxter.

AUSONIUS. H. G. Evelyn White. 2 Vols.

BEDE. J. E. King. 2 Vols.

BOETHIUS : TRACTS AND DE CONSOLATIONE PHILOSOPHIAE. Rev. H. F. Stewart and E. K. Rand. Revised by S. J. Tester.

CAESAR : ALEXANDRIAN, AFRICAN AND SPANISH WARS. A. G. Way.

CAESAR : CIVIL WARS. A. G. Peskett.

CAESAR : GALLIC WAR. H. J. Edwards.

CATO AND VARRO : DE RE RUSTICA. H. B. Ash and W. D. Hooper.

CATULLUS. F. W. Cornish ; TIBULLUS. J. B. Postgate ; and PERVIGILIUM VENERIS. J. W. Mackail.

CELSUS : DE MEDICINA. W. G. Spencer. 3 Vols.

CICERO : BRUTUS AND ORATOR. G. L. Hendrickson and H. M. Hubbell.

CICERO : DE FINIBUS. H. Rackham.

CICERO : DE INVENTIONE, etc. H. M. Hubbell.

CICERO : DE NATURA DEORUM AND ACADEMICA. H. Rackham.

CICERO : DE OFFICIIS. Walter Miller.

CICERO : DE ORATORE, etc. 2 Vols. Vol. I : DE ORATORE, Books I and II. E. W. Sutton and H. Rackham. Vol. II : DE ORATORE, Book III ; DE FATO ; PARADOXA STOICORUM ; DE PARTITIONE ORATORIA. H. Rackham.

CICERO : DE REPUBLICA, DE LEGIBUS, SOMNIUM SCIPIONIS. Clinton W. Keyes.

THE LOEB CLASSICAL LIBRARY

CICERO: DE SENECTUTE, DE AMICITIA, DE DIVINATIONE.
W. A. Falconer.

CICERO: IN CATILINAM, PRO MURENA, PRO SULLA, PRO
FLACCO. New version by C. Macdonald.

CICERO: LETTERS TO ATTICUS. E. O. Winstedt. 3 Vols.

CICERO: LETTERS TO HIS FRIENDS. W. Glynn Williams,
M. Cary, M. Henderson. 4 Vols.

CICERO: PHILIPPICS. W. C. A. Ker.

CICERO: PRO ARCHIA, POST REDITUM, DE DOMO, DE HA-
RUSPICUM RESPONSIS, PRO PLANCIO. N. H. Watts.

CICERO: PRO CAECINA, PRO LEGE MANILIA, PRO CLUENTIO,
PRO RABIRIO. H. Grose Hodge.

CICERO: PRO CAELIO, DE PROVINCIIS CONSULARIBUS, PRO
BALBO. R. Gardner.

CICERO: PRO MILONE, IN PISONEM, PRO SCAURO, PRO
FONTEIO, PRO RABIRIO POSTUMO, PRO MARCELLO, PRO
LIGARIO, PRO REGE DEIOTARO. N. H. Watts.

CICERO: PRO QUINCTIO, PRO ROSCIO AMERINO, PRO ROSCIO
COMOEDO, CONTRA RULLUM. J. H. Freese.

CICERO: PRO SESTIO, IN VATINIUM. R. Gardner.

[CICERO]: RHETORICA AD HERENNIUM. H. Caplan.

CICERO: TUSCULAN DISPUTATIONS. J. E. King.

CICERO: VERRINE ORATIONS. L. H. G. Greenwood. 2 Vols.

CLAUDIAN. M. Platnauer. 2 Vols.

COLUMELLA: DE RE RUSTICA, DE ARBORIBUS. H. B. Ash,
E. S. Forster, E. Heffner. 3 Vols.

CURTIUS, Q.: HISTORY OF ALEXANDER. J. C. Rolfe. 2 Vols.

FLORUS. E. S. Forster; and CORNELIUS NEPOS. J. C. Rolfe.

FRONTINUS: STRATAGEMS AND AQUEDUCTS. C. E. Bennett
and M. B. McElwain.

FRONTO: CORRESPONDENCE. C. R. Haines. 2 Vols.

GELLIUS. J. C. Rolfe. 3 Vols.

HORACE: ODES AND EPODES. C. E. Bennett.

HORACE: SATIRES, EPISTLES, ARS POETICA. H. R. Fairclough.

JEROME: SELECT LETTERS. F. A. Wright.

JUVENAL AND PERSIUS. G. G. Ramsay.

LIVY. B. O. Foster, F. G. Moore, Evan T. Sage, A. C.
Schlesinger and R. M. Geer (General Index). 14 Vols.

LUCAN. J. D. Duff.

LUCRETIUS. W. H. D. Rouse. Revised by M. F. Smith.

MARTIAL. W. C. A. Ker. 2 Vols.

MINOR LATIN POETS: from PUBLILIUS SYRUS to RUTILIUS
NAMATIANUS, including GRATTIUS, CALPURNIUS SICULUS,
NEMESIANUS, AVIANUS, with "Aetna," "Phoenix" and
other poems. J. Wight Duff and Arnold M. Duff.

THE LOEB CLASSICAL LIBRARY

OVID : THE ART OF LOVE AND OTHER POEMS. J. H. Mozley.
OVID : FASTI. Sir James G. Frazer.
OVID : HEROIDES AND AMORES. Grant Showerman.
OVID : METAMORPHOSES. F. J. Miller. 2 Vols.
OVID : TRISTIA AND EX PONTO. A. L. Wheeler.
PETRONIUS. M. Heseltine ; SENECA : APOCOLOCYNTOSIS.
W. H. D. Rouse.
PHAEDRUS AND BABRIUS (Greek). B. E. Perry.
PLAUTUS. Paul Nixon. 5 Vols.
PLINY : LETTERS, PANEGYRICUS. B. Radice. 2 Vols.
PLINY : NATURAL HISTORY. 10 Vols. Vols. I-V. H. Rack-
ham. Vols. VI-VIII. W. H. S. Jones. Vol. IX. H. Rack-
ham. Vol. X. D. E. Eichholz.
PROPERTIUS. H. E. Butler.
PRUDENTIUS. H. J. Thomson. 2 Vols.
QUINTILIAN. H. E. Butler. 4 Vols.
REMAINS OF OLD LATIN. E. H. Warmington. 4 Vols.
Vol. I (Ennius and Caecilius). Vol. II (Livius, Naevius,
Pacuvius, Accius). Vol. III (Lucilius, Laws of the XII
Tables). Vol. IV (Archaic Inscriptions).
SALLUST. J. C. Rolfe.
SCRIPTORES HISTORIAE AUGUSTAE. D. Magie. 3 Vols.
SENECA : APOCOLOCYNTOSIS. Cf. PETRONIUS.
SENECA : EPISTULAE MORALES. R. M. Gummere. 3 Vols.
SENECA : MORAL ESSAYS. J. W. Basore. 3 Vols.
SENECA : NATURALES QUAESTIONES. T. H. Corcoran. 2 Vols.
SENECA : TRAGEDIES. F. J. Miller. 2 Vols.
SENECA THE ELDER : CONTROVERSIAE SUASORIAE. M.
Winterbottom. 2 Vols.
SIDONIUS : POEMS AND LETTERS. W. B. Anderson. 2 Vols.
SILIUS ITALICUS. J. D. Duff. 2 Vols.
STATIUS. J. H. Mozley. 2 Vols.
SUETONIUS. J. C. Rolfe. 2 Vols.
TACITUS : AGRICOLA AND GERMANIA. M. Hutton ; DIALOGUS.
Sir Wm. Peterson. Revised by R. M. Ogilvie, E. H.
Warmington, M. Winterbottom.
TACITUS : HISTORIES AND ANNALS. C. H. Moore and J.
Jackson. 4 Vols.
TERENCE. John Sargeaunt. 2 Vols.
TERTULLIAN : APOLOGIA AND DE SPECTACULIS. T. R. Glover ;
MINUCIUS FELIX. G. H. Rendall.
VALERIUS FLACCUS. J. H. Mozley.
VARRO : DE LINGUA LATINA. R. G. Kent. 2 Vols.
VELLEIUS PATERCULUS AND RES GESTAE DIVI AUGUSTI.
F. W. Shipley.

THE LOEB CLASSICAL LIBRARY

Virgil. H. R. Fairclough. 2 Vols.
Vitruvius : De Architectura. F. Granger. 2 Vols.

GREEK AUTHORS

Achilles Tatius. S. Gaselee.
Aelian : On the Nature of Animals. A. F. Scholfield. 3 Vols.
Aeneas Tacticus, Asclepiodotus and Onasander. The Illinois Greek Club.
Aeschines. C. D. Adams.
Aeschylus. H. Weir Smyth. 2 Vols.
Aliciphron, Aelian and Philostratus : Letters. A. R. Benner and F. H. Fobes.
Apollodorus. Sir James G. Frazer. 2 Vols.
Apollonius Rhodius. R. C. Seaton.
The Apostolic Fathers. Kirsopp Lake. 2 Vols.
Appian's Roman History. Horace White. 4 Vols.
Aratus. Cf. Callimachus : Hymns and Epigrams.
Aristides. C. A. Behr. 4 Vols. Vol. I.
Aristophanes. Benjamin Bickley Rogers. 3 Vols. Verse trans.
Aristotle : Art of Rhetoric. J. H. Freese.
Aristotle : Athenian Constitution, Eudemian Ethics, Virtues and Vices. H. Rackham.
Aristotle : The Categories. On Interpretation. H. P. Cooke ; Prior Analytics. H. Tredennick.
Aristotle : Generation of Animals. A. L. Peck.
Aristotle : Historia Animalium. A. L. Peck. 3 Vols. Vols. I and II.
Aristotle : Metaphysics. H. Tredennick. 2 Vols.
Aristotle : Meteorologica. H. D. P. Lee.
Aristotle : Minor Works. W. S. Hett. "On Colours," "On Things Heard," "Physiognomics," "On Plants," "On Marvellous Things Heard," "Mechanical Problems," "On Invisible Lines," "Situations and Names of Winds," "On Melissus, Xenophanes, and Gorgias."
Aristotle : Nicomachean Ethics. H. Rackham.
Aristotle : Oeconomica and Magna Moralia. G. C. Armstrong. (With Metaphysics, Vol. II.)
Aristotle : On the Heavens. W. K. C. Guthrie.
Aristotle : On the Soul, Parva Naturalia, On Breath. W. S. Hett.

4

THE LOEB CLASSICAL LIBRARY

ARISTOTLE: PARTS OF ANIMALS. A. L. Peck; MOVEMENT
AND PROGRESSION OF ANIMALS. E. S. Forster.

ARISTOTLE: PHYSICS. Rev. P. Wicksteed and F. M. Cornford. 2 Vols.

ARISTOTLE: POETICS; LONGINUS ON THE SUBLIME. W. Ham-
ilton Fyfe; DEMETRIUS ON STYLE. W. Rhys Roberts.

ARISTOTLE: POLITICS. H. Rackham.

ARISTOTLE: POSTERIOR ANALYTICS. H. Tredennick; TOPICS.
E. S. Forster.

ARISTOTLE: PROBLEMS. W. S. Hett. 2 Vols.

ARISTOTLE: RHETORICA AD ALEXANDRUM. H. Rackham.
(With PROBLEMS, Vol. II.)

ARISTOTLE: SOPHISTICAL REFUTATIONS. COMING-TO-BE AND
PASSING-AWAY. E. S. Forster; ON THE COSMOS. D. J.
Furley.

ARRIAN: HISTORY OF ALEXANDER AND INDICA. Rev. E.
Iliffe Robson. 2 Vols.

ATHENAEUS: DEIPNOSOPHISTAE. C. B. Gulick. 7 Vols.

BABRIUS AND PHAEDRUS (Latin). B. E. Perry.

ST. BASIL: LETTERS. R. J. Deferrari. 4 Vols.

CALLIMACHUS: FRAGMENTS. C. A. Trypanis; MUSAEUS:
HERO AND LEANDER. T. Gelzer and C. Whitman.

CALLIMACHUS: HYMNS AND EPIGRAMS, AND LYCOPHRON.
A. W. Mair; ARATUS. G. R. Mair.

CLEMENT OF ALEXANDRIA. Rev. G. W. Butterworth.

COLLUTHUS. *Cf.* OPPIAN.

DAPHNIS AND CHLOE. *Cf.* LONGUS.

DEMOSTHENES I: OLYNTHIACS, PHILIPPICS AND MINOR
ORATIONS: I-XVII AND XX. J. H. Vince.

DEMOSTHENES II: DE CORONA AND DE FALSA LEGATIONE.
C. A. Vince and J. H. Vince.

DEMOSTHENES III: MEIDIAS, ANDROTION, ARISTOCRATES,
TIMOCRATES, ARISTOGEITON. J. H. Vince.

DEMOSTHENES IV-VI: PRIVATE ORATIONS AND IN NEAERAM.
A. T. Murray.

DEMOSTHENES VII: FUNERAL SPEECH, EROTIC ESSAY, EX-
ORDIA AND LETTERS. N. W. and N. J. DeWitt.

DIO CASSIUS: ROMAN HISTORY. E. Cary. 9 Vols.

DIO CHRYSOSTOM. 5 Vols. Vols. I and II. J. W. Cohoon.
Vol. III. J. W. Cohoon and H. Lamar Crosby. Vols. IV
and V. H. Lamar Crosby.

DIODORUS SICULUS. 12 Vols. Vols. I-VI. C. H. Oldfather.
Vol. VII. C. L. Sherman. Vol. VIII. C. B. Welles. Vols.
IX and X. Russel M. Geer. Vols. XI and XII. F. R.
Walton. General Index. Russel M. Geer.

THE LOEB CLASSICAL LIBRARY

DIOGENES LAERTIUS. R. D. Hicks. 2 Vols. New Introduction by H. S. Long.

DIONYSIUS OF HALICARNASSUS: CRITICAL ESSAYS. S. Usher. 2 Vols.

DIONYSIUS OF HALICARNASSUS: ROMAN ANTIQUITIES. Spelman's translation revised by E. Cary. 7 Vols.

EPICTETUS. W. A. Oldfather. 2 Vols.

EURIPIDES. A. S. Way. 4 Vols. Verse trans.

EUSEBIUS: ECCLESIASTICAL HISTORY. Kirsopp Lake and J. E. L. Oulton. 2 Vols.

GALEN: ON THE NATURAL FACULTIES. A. J. Brock.

THE GREEK ANTHOLOGY. W. R. Paton. 5 Vols.

THE GREEK BUCOLIC POETS (THEOCRITUS, BION, MOSCHUS). J. M. Edmonds.

GREEK ELEGY AND IAMBUS WITH THE ANACREONTEA. J. M. Edmonds. 2 Vols.

GREEK MATHEMATICAL WORKS. Ivor Thomas. 2 Vols.

HERODES. Cf. THEOPHRASTUS: CHARACTERS.

HERODIAN. C. R. Whittaker. 2 Vols.

HERODOTUS. A. D. Godley. 4 Vols.

HESIOD AND THE HOMERIC HYMNS. H. G. Evelyn White.

HIPPOCRATES AND THE FRAGMENTS OF HERACLEITUS. W. H. S. Jones and E. T. Withington. 4 Vols.

HOMER: ILIAD. A. T. Murray. 2 Vols.

HOMER: ODYSSEY. A. T. Murray. 2 Vols.

ISAEUS. E. S. Forster.

ISOCRATES. George Norlin and LaRue Van Hook. 3 Vols.

[ST. JOHN DAMASCENE]: BARLAAM AND IOASAPH. Rev. G. R. Woodward, Harold Mattingly and D. M. Lang.

JOSEPHUS. 9 Vols. Vols. I-IV. H. St. J. Thackeray. Vol. V. H. St. J. Thackeray and Ralph Marcus. Vols. VI and VII. Ralph Marcus. Vol. VIII. Ralph Marcus and Allen Wikgren. Vol. IX. L. H. Feldman.

JULIAN. Wilmer Cave Wright. 3 Vols.

LIBANIUS: SELECTED WORKS. A. F. Norman. 3 Vols. Vol. I.

LONGUS: DAPHNIS AND CHLOE. Thornley's translation revised by J. M. Edmonds; and PARTHENIUS. S. Gaselee.

LUCIAN. 8 Vols. Vols. I-V. A. M. Harmon. Vol. VI. K. Kilburn. Vols. VII and VIII. M. D. Macleod.

LYCOPHRON. Cf. CALLIMACHUS: HYMNS AND EPIGRAMS.

LYRA GRAECA. J. M. Edmonds. 3 Vols.

LYSIAS. W. R. M. Lamb.

MANETHO. W. G. Waddell; PTOLEMY: TETRABIBLOS. F. E. Robbins.

THE LOEB CLASSICAL LIBRARY

MARCUS AURELIUS. C. R. Haines.

MENANDER. F. G. Allinson.

MINOR ATTIC ORATORS. 2 Vols.. K. J. Maidment and
J. O. Burtt.

MUSAEUS: HERO AND LEANDER. *Cf.* CALLIMACHUS: FRAG-
MENTS.

NONNOS: DIONYSIACA. W. H. D. Rouse. 3 Vols.

OPPIAN, COLLUTHUS, TRYPHIODORUS. A. W. Mair.

PAPYRI. NON-LITERARY SELECTIONS. A. S. Hunt and C. C.
Edgar. 2 Vols. LITERARY SELECTIONS (Poetry). D. L.
Page.

PARTHENIUS. *Cf.* LONGUS.

PAUSANIAS: DESCRIPTION OF GREECE. W. H. S. Jones. 4
Vols. and Companion Vol. arranged by R. E. Wycherley.

PHILO. 10 Vols. Vols. I-V. F. H. Colson and Rev. G. H.
Whitaker. Vols. VI-X. F. H. Colson. General Index.
Rev. J. W. Earp.
Two Supplementary Vols. Translation only from an
Armenian Text. Ralph Marcus.

PHILOSTRATUS: THE LIFE OF APOLLONIUS OF TYANA. F. C.
Conybeare. 2 Vols.

PHILOSTRATUS: IMAGINES; CALLISTRATUS: DESCRIPTIONS.
A. Fairbanks.

PHILOSTRATUS AND EUNAPIUS: LIVES OF THE SOPHISTS.
Wilmer Cave Wright.

PINDAR. Sir J. E. Sandys.

PLATO: CHARMIDES, ALCIBIADES, HIPPARCHUS, THE LOVERS,
THEAGES, MINOS AND EPINOMIS. W. R. M. Lamb.

PLATO: CRATYLUS, PARMENIDES, GREATER HIPPIAS, LESSER
HIPPIAS. H. N. Fowler.

PLATO: EUTHYPHRO, APOLOGY, CRITO, PHAEDO, PHAEDRUS.
H. N. Fowler.

PLATO: LACHES, PROTAGORAS, MENO, EUTHYDEMUS.
W. R. M. Lamb.

PLATO: LAWS. Rev. R. G. Bury. 2 Vols.

PLATO: LYSIS, SYMPOSIUM, GORGIAS. W. R. M. Lamb.

PLATO: REPUBLIC. Paul Shorey. 2 Vols.

PLATO: STATESMAN, PHILEBUS. H. N. Fowler; ION.
W. R. M. Lamb.

PLATO: THEAETETUS AND SOPHIST. H. N. Fowler.

PLATO: TIMAEUS, CRITIAS, CLITOPHO, MENEXENUS, EPISTU-
LAE. Rev. R. G. Bury.

PLOTINUS. A. H. Armstrong. 6 Vols. Vols. I-III.

PLUTARCH: MORALIA. 17 Vols. Vols. I-V. F. C. Babbitt.
Vol. VI. W. C. Helmbold. Vol. VII. P. H. De Lacy and

THE LOEB CLASSICAL LIBRARY

B. Einarson. Vol. VIII. P. A. Clement, H. B. Hoffleit.
Vol. IX. E. L. Minar, Jr., F. H. Sandbach, W. C.
Helmbold. Vol. X. H. N. Fowler. Vol. XI. L. Pearson,
F. H. Sandbach. Vol. XII. H. Cherniss, W. C. Helmbold.
Vol. XIII, Parts 1 and 2. H. Cherniss. Vol. XIV. P. H.
De Lacy and B. Einarson. Vol. XV. F. H. Sandbach.

PLUTARCH : THE PARALLEL LIVES. B. Perrin. 11 Vols.

POLYBIUS. W. R. Paton. 6 Vols.

PROCOPIUS : HISTORY OF THE WARS. H. B. Dewing. 7 Vols.

PTOLEMY : TETRABIBLOS. *Cf.* MANETHO.

QUINTUS SMYRNAEUS. A. S. Way. Verse trans.

SEXTUS EMPIRICUS. Rev. R. G. Bury. 4 Vols.

SOPHOCLES. F. Storr. 2 Vols. Verse trans.

STRABO : GEOGRAPHY. Horace L. Jones. 8 Vols.

THEOPHRASTUS : CHARACTERS. J. M. Edmonds ; HERODES,
etc. A. D. Knox.

THEOPHRASTUS : DE CAUSIS PLANTARUM. G. K. K. Link and
B. Einarson. 3 Vols. Vol. 1,

THEOPHRASTUS : ENQUIRY INTO PLANTS. Sir Arthur Hort.
2 Vols.

THUCYDIDES. C. F. Smith. 4 Vols.

TRYPHIODORUS. *Cf.* OPPIAN.

XENOPHON : ANABASIS. C. L. Brownson.

XENOPHON : CYROPAEDIA. Walter Miller. 2 Vols.

XENOPHON : HELLENICA. C. L. Brownson.

XENOPHON : MEMORABILIA AND OECONOMICUS. E. C. Marchant ; SYMPOSIUM AND APOLOGY. O. J. Todd.

XENOPHON : SCRIPTA MINORA. E. C. Marchant and G. W.
Bowersock.

VOLUMES IN PREPARATION

GREEK AUTHORS

ARRIAN I. New version by P. Brunt.
LIBANIUS II. A. F. Norman.

LATIN AUTHORS

MANILIUS. G. P. Goold.

DESCRIPTIVE PROSPECTUS ON APPLICATION

CAMBRIDGE, MASS.   LONDON
HARVARD UNIV. PRESS   WILLIAM HEINEMANN LTD